Friedrich Max
Mu

ller

A Sanskrit Grammar for Beginners in Devanagari and Roman Letters Throughout by Max Muller

Friedrich Max
Mu
..
ller

A Sanskrit Grammar for Beginners in Devanagari and Roman Letters Throughout by Max Muller

ISBN/EAN: 9783337815264

Printed in Europe, USA, Canada, Australia, Japan

Cover: Foto ©ninafisch / pixelio.de

More available books at **www.hansebooks.com**

A

SANSKRIT GRAMMAR

FOR BEGINNERS,

IN

DEVANÂGARÎ AND ROMAN LETTERS THROUGHOUT,

BY

MAX MÜLLER.

PREFACE.

THE present grammar, which is chiefly intended for beginners, is believed to contain all the information that a student of Sanskrit is likely to want during the first two or three years of his reading. Rules referring to the language of the Vedas have been entirely excluded, for it is not desirable that the difficulties of that ancient dialect should be approached by any one who has not fully mastered the grammar of the ordinary Sanskrit such as it was fixed by Pâṇini and his successors. All allusions to cognate forms in Greek, Latin, or Gothic, have likewise been suppressed, because, however interesting and useful to the advanced student, they are apt to deprive the beginner of that clear and firm grasp of the grammatical system peculiar to the language of ancient India, which alone can form a solid foundation for the study both of Sanskrit and of Comparative Philology.

The two principal objects which I have kept in view while composing this grammar, have been clearness and correctness. With regard to clearness, my chief model has been the grammar of Bopp; with regard to correctness, the grammar of Colebrooke. If I may hope, without presumption, to have simplified a few of the intricacies of Sanskrit grammar which were but partially cleared up by Bopp, Benfey, Flecchia, and others, I can hardly flatter myself to have reached, with regard to correctness, the high standard of Colebrooke's great, though unfinished work. I can only say in self-defence, that it is far more difficult to be correct on every minute point, if one endeavours to re-arrange, as I have done, the materials collected by Pâṇini, and to adapt them to the grammatical system current in Europe, than if one follows so closely as Colebrooke, the system of native grammarians, and adopts nearly the whole of their technical terminology. The grammatical system elaborated by native grammarians is, in itself, most perfect; and those who have tested Pâṇini's work, will readily admit that there is no grammar in any language that could vie with the wonderful mechanism of his eight books of grammatical rules. But unrivalled as that system is, it is not suited to the wants of English students, least of all to the wants of beginners. While availing myself therefore of the materials collected in the grammar of Pâṇini and in later works, such as the Prakriyâ-Kaumudî, the Siddhânta-Kaumudî, the Sârasvatî Prakriyâ, and the Mâdhavîya-dhâtu-vṛitti, I have abstained, as much as possible, from introducing any more of the peculiar system and of the terminology of Indian grammarians* than has already found admittance into our Sanskrit grammars; nay, I have frequently rejected the grammatical observations supplied ready to hand in their works, in order not to overwhelm the memory of the student with too many rules and too many exceptions. Whether I have always been successful in drawing a line between what is essential in Sanskrit grammar and what is not, I must leave to the judgment of those who enjoy the good fortune of being engaged in the practical teaching of a language the students of which may be counted no longer by tens, but by hundreds†.

* The few alterations that I have made in the usual terminology have been made solely with a view of facilitating the work of the learner. Thus instead of numbering the ten classes of verbs, I have called each by its first verb. This relieves the memory of much unnecessary trouble, as the very name indicates the character of each class; and though the names may at first sound somewhat uncouth, they are after all the only names recognized by native grammarians. Knowing from my experience as an examiner, how difficult it is to remember the merely numerical distinction between the first, second, or third preterites, or the first and second futures, I have kept as much as possible to the terminology with which classical scholars are familiar, calling the tense corresponding to the Greek Imperfect, Imperfect; that corresponding to the Perfect, Reduplicated Perfect; that corresponding to the Aorist, Aorist; and the mood corresponding to the Optative, Optative. The names of Periphrastic Perfect and Periphrastic Future tell their own story; and if I have retained the merely numerical distinction between the First and Second Aorists, it was because this distinction seemed to be more intelligible to a classical scholar than the six or seven forms of the so-called multiform Preterite.

† In the University of Leipzig alone, as many as twenty-five pupils attend the classes of Professor Brockhaus in order to acquire a knowledge of the elements of Sanskrit, previous to the study of Comparative Philology.

I only wish it to be understood that where I have left out rules or exceptions, contained in other grammars, whether native or European, I have done so after mature consideration, deliberately preferring the less complete to the more complete, but, at the same time, more bewildering statement of the anomalies of the Sanskrit language. Thus, to mention one or two cases, when giving the rules on the employment of the suffixes *vat* and *mat* (§ 187), I have left out the rule that bases ending in *m*, though the *m* be preceded by other vowels than *a*, always take *vat* instead of *mat*. I did so partly because there are very few bases ending in *m*, partly because, if a word like *kim-vân* should occur, it would be easy to discover the reason why here too *v* was preferred to *m*, viz. in order to avoid the clashing of two *m*'s. Again, when giving the rules on the formation of denominatives (§ 495), I passed over, for very much the same reason, the prohibition given in Pâṇ. III. 1, 8, 3, viz. that bases ending in *m* are not allowed to form denominatives. It is true, no doubt, that the omission of such rules or exceptions may be said to involve an actual misrepresentation, and that a pupil might be misled to form such words as *kim-mân* and *kim-yati*. But this cannot be avoided in an elementary grammar; and the student who is likely to come in contact with such recondite forms, will no doubt be sufficiently advanced to be able to consult for himself the rules of Pâṇini and the explanations of his commentators.

My own fear is that, in writing an elementary grammar, I have erred rather in giving too much than in giving too little. I have therefore in the table of contents marked with an asterisk all such rules as may be safely left out in a first course of Sanskrit grammar, and I have in different places informed the reader whether certain portions might be passed over quickly, or should be carefully committed to memory. Here and there, as for instance in § 103, a few extracts are introduced from Pâṇini, simply in order to give to the student a foretaste of what he may expect in the elaborate works of native grammarians, while lists of verbs like those contained in § 332 or § 462 are given, as everybody will see, for the sake of reference only. The somewhat elaborate treatment of the nominal bases in *t* and *n*, from § 220 to § 226, became necessary, partly because in no grammar had the different paradigms of this class been correctly given, partly because it was impossible to bring out clearly the principle on which the peculiarities and apparent irregularities of these nouns are based without entering fully into the systematic arrangement of native grammarians. Of portions like this I will not say indeed, *μωμήσεταί τις μᾶλλον ἢ μιμήσεται*, but I feel that I may say, यत्ने कृते यदि न सिध्यति कोऽत्र दोषः; and I know that those who will take the trouble to examine the same mass of evidence which I have weighed and examined, will be the most lenient in their judgment, if hereafter they should succeed better than I have done, in unravelling the intricate argumentations of native scholars *.

But while acknowledging my obligations to the great grammarians of India, it would be ungrateful were I not to acknowledge as fully the assistance which I have derived from the works of European scholars. My first acquaintance with the elements of Sanskrit was gained from Bopp's grammar. Those only who know the works of his predecessors, of Colebrooke, Carey, Wilkins, and Forster, can appreciate the advance made by Bopp in explaining the difficulties, and in lighting up, if I may say so, the dark lanes and alleys of the Sanskrit language. I doubt whether Sanskrit scholarship would have flourished as it has, if students had been obliged to learn their grammar from Forster or Colebrooke, and I believe that to Bopp's little grammar is due a great portion of that success which has attended the study of Sanskrit literature in Germany. Colebrooke, Carey, Wilkins, and Forster worked independently of each other. Each derived his information from native teachers and from native grammars. Among these four scholars, Wilkins seems to have been the first to compose a Sanskrit grammar, for he informs us that the first

* To those who have the same faith in the accurate and never swerving argumentations of Sanskrit commentators, it may be a saving of time to be informed that in the new and very useful edition of the Siddhânta-Kaumudî by Srî Târânâtha-tarkavâchaspati there are two misprints which hopelessly disturb the order of the rules on the proper declension of nouns in ई and ऊ. On page 136, l. 7, read धीवत् instead of स्त्रीवत्; this is corrected in the Corrigenda, and the right reading is found in the old edition. On the same page, l. 13, insert न after विभा, or join विभास्त्रीबोधकत्वं.

printed sheet of his work was destroyed by fire in 1795. The whole grammar, however, was not published till 1808. In the mean time Forster had finished his grammar, and had actually delivered his MS. to the Council of the College of Fort William in 1804. But it was not published till 1810. The first part of Colebrooke's grammar was published in 1805, and therefore stands first in point of time of publication. Unfortunately it was not finished, because the grammars of Forster and Carey were then in course of publication, and would, as Colebrooke imagined, supply the deficient part of his own. Carey's grammar was published in 1806. Among these four publications, which as first attempts at making the ancient language of India accessible to European scholars, deserve the highest credit, Colebrooke's grammar is *facile princeps.* It is derived at first hand from the best native grammars, and evinces a familiarity with the most intricate problems of Hindu grammarians such as few scholars have acquired after him. No one can understand and appreciate the merits of this grammar who has not previously acquired a knowledge of the grammatical system of Pâṇini, and it is a great loss to Sanskrit scholarship that so valuable a work should have remained unfinished.

I owe most, indeed, to Colebrooke and Bopp, but I have derived many useful hints from other grammars also. There are some portions of Wilson's grammar which show that he consulted native grammarians, and the fact that he possessed the remaining portion of Colebrooke's* MS., gives to his list of verbs, with the exception of the Bhû class, which was published by Colebrooke, a peculiar interest. Professor Benfey in his large grammar performed a most useful task in working up independently the materials supplied by Pâṇini and Bhaṭṭojidîkshita; and his smaller grammars too, published both in German and in English, have rendered good service to the cause of sound scholarship. There are besides, the grammars of Boller in German, of Oppert in French, of Westergaard in Danish, of Flecchia in Italian, each supplying something that could not be found elsewhere, and containing suggestions, many of which have proved useful to the writer of the present grammar.

* See Wilson's Sanscrit and English Dictionary, first edition, preface, p. xlv.

But while thus rendering full justice to the honest labours of my predecessors, I am bound to say, at the same time, that with regard to doubtful or difficult forms, of which there are many in the grammar of the Sanskrit language, not one of them can be appealed to as an ultimate authority. Every grammar contains, as is well known, a number of forms which occur but rarely, if ever, in the literary language. It is necessary, however, for the sake of systematic completeness, to give these forms; and if they are to be given at all, they must be given on competent authority. Now it might be supposed that a mere reference to any of the numerous grammars already published would be sufficient for this purpose, and that the lists of irregular or unusual forms might safely be copied from their pages. But this is by no means the case. Even with regard to regular forms, whoever should trust implicitly in the correctness of any of the grammars, hitherto published, would never be certain of having the right form. I do not say this lightly, or without being able to produce proofs. When I began to revise my manuscript grammar which I had composed for my own use many years ago, and when on points on which I felt doubtful, I consulted other grammars, I soon discovered either that, with a strange kind of sequacity, they all repeated the same mistake, or that they varied widely from each other, without assigning any reason or authority. I need not say that the grammars which we possess differ very much in the degree of their trustworthiness; but with the exception of the first volume of Colebrooke and of Professor Benfey's larger Sanskrit grammar, it would be impossible to appeal to any of my predecessors as an authority on doubtful points. Forster and Carey, who evidently depend almost entirely on materials supplied to them by native assistants, give frequently the most difficult forms with perfect accuracy, while they go wildly wrong immediately after, without, it would seem, any power of controlling their authorities. The frequent inaccuracies in the grammars of Wilkins and Wilson have been pointed out by others; and however useful these works may have been for practical purposes, they were never intended as authorities on contested points of Sanskrit grammar.

Nothing remained in fact, in order to arrive at any satisfactory result, but to collate the whole of my grammar, with regard not only to the irregular but likewise to the regular forms, with Pâṇini and other native grammarians, and to supply for each doubtful case, and for rules that might seem to differ from those of any of my predecessors, a reference to Pâṇini or to other native authorities. This I have done, and in so doing I had to re-write nearly the whole of my grammar; but though the time and trouble expended on this work have been considerable, I believe that they have not been bestowed in vain. I only regret that I did not give these authoritative references throughout the whole of my work, because, even where there cannot be any difference of opinion, some of my readers might thus have been saved the time and trouble of looking through Pâṇini to find the Sûtras that bear on every form of the Sanskrit language.

By this process which I have adopted, I believe that on many points a more settled and authoritative character has been imparted to the grammar of Sanskrit than it possessed before; but I do by no means pretend to have arrived on all points at a clear and definite view of the meaning of Pâṇini and his successors. The grammatical system of Hindu grammarians is so peculiar, that rules which we should group together, are scattered about in different parts of their manuals. We may have the general rule in the last, and the exceptions in the first book, and even then we are by no means certain that exceptions to these exceptions may not occur somewhere else. I shall give but one instance. There is a root जागृ *jâgṛi*, which forms its Aorist by adding इषं *isham*, ईः *îḥ*, ईत् *ît*. Here the simplest rule would be that final ऋ *ṛi* before इषं *isham* becomes र् *r* (Pâṇ. VI. 1, 77). This, however, is prevented by another rule which requires that final ऋ *ṛi* should take Guṇa before इषं *isham* (Pâṇ. VII. 3, 84). This would give us अजागरिषं *ajâgar-isham*. But now comes another general rule (Pâṇ. VII. 2, 1) which prescribes Vṛiddhi of final vowels before इषं *isham*, i. e. अजागारिषं *ajâgârisham*. Against this change, however, a new rule is cited (Pâṇ. VII. 3, 85), and this secures for जागृ *jâgṛi* a special exception from Vṛiddhi, and leaves its base again as जागर् *jâgar*. As soon as the base has been changed to जागर् *jâgar*, it falls under a new rule (Pâṇ. VII. 2, 3), and is forced to take Vṛiddhi, until this rule is again nullified by Pâṇ. VII.

2, 4, which does not allow Vṛiddhi in an Aorist that takes intermediate इ *i*, like अजागरिषं *ajâgarisham*. There is an exception, however, to this rule also, for bases with short अ *a*, beginning and ending with a consonant, may optionally take Vṛiddhi (Pâṇ. VII. 2, 7). This option is afterwards restricted, and roots with short अ *a*, beginning with a consonant and ending in र् *r*, like जागर् *jâgar*, have no option left, but are restricted afresh to Vṛiddhi (Pâṇ. VII. 2, 2). However, even this is not yet the final result. Our base जागर् *jâgar* is after all not to take Vṛiddhi, and hence a new special rule (Pâṇ. VII. 2, 5) settles the point by granting to जागृ *jâgṛi* a special exception from Vṛiddhi, and thereby establishing its Guṇa. No wonder that these manifold changes and chances in the formation of the First Aorist of जागृ *jâgṛi* should have inspired a grammarian, who celebrates them in the following couplet:

गुणो वृद्धिर्गुणो वृद्धिः प्रतिषेधो विकल्पनं ।
पुनर्वृद्धिर्निषेधोऽतो यण्पूर्वाः प्राप्तयो नव ॥

"Guṇa, Vṛiddhi, Guṇa, Vṛiddhi, prohibition, option, again Vṛiddhi and then exception, these, with the change of *ṛi* into a semivowel in the first instance, are the nine results."

Another difficulty consists in the want of critical accuracy in the editions which we possess of Pâṇini, the Siddhânta-Kaumudî, the Laghu-Kaumudî, the Sârasvatî, and Vopadeva. Far be it from me to wish to detract from the merits of native editors, like Dharaṇîdhara, Kâśînâtha, Târânâtha, still less from those of Professor Boehtlingk, who published his text and notes nearly thirty years ago, when few of us were able to read a single line of Pâṇini. But during those thirty years considerable progress has been made in unravelling the mysteries of the grammatical literature of India. The commentary of Sâyaṇa to the Rig-veda has shown us how practically to apply the rules of Pâṇini; and the translation of the Laghu-Kaumudî by the late Dr. Ballantyne has enabled even beginners to find their way through the labyrinth of native grammar. The time has come, I believe, for new and critical editions of Pâṇini and his commentators. A few instances may suffice to show the insecurity of our ordinary editions. The commentary to Pâṇ. VII. 2, 42, as well as the Sârasvatî II. 25, 1, gives the Benedictive Âtmanepada वर्षिषीष्ट *varshishṭa* and वरिषीष्ट

starîshṭshṭa; yet a reference to Pâṇ. VII. 2, 39 and 40, shows that these forms are impossible. Again, if Pâṇini (VIII. 3, 92) is right in using अग्रगामिनि *agragâmini* with a dental *n* in the last syllable, it is clear that he extends the prohibition given in VIII. 4, 34, with regard to Upasargas, to other compounds. It is useless to inquire whether in doing so he was right or wrong, for it is an article of faith with every Hindu grammarian that whatever word is used by Pâṇini in his Sûtras, is *eo ipso* correct. Otherwise, the rules affecting compounds with Upasargas are by no means identical with those that affect ordinary compounds; and though it may be right to argue *a fortiori* from प्रगामिनि *pragâmini* to अग्रगामिनि *agragâmini*, it would not be right to argue from अग्रयान *agrayâna* to प्रयान *prayâna*, this being necessarily प्रयाण *prayâṇa*. But assuming अग्रगामिनि *agragâmini* to be correct, it is quite clear that the compounds स्वर्गकामिणौ *svargakâmiṇau*, वृषगामिणौ *vrishagâmiṇau*, हरिकामाणि *harikâmâṇi*, and हरिकामेण *harikâmeṇa*, given in the commentary to VIII. 4, 13, are all wrong, though most of them occur not only in the printed editions of Pâṇini and the Siddhânta-Kaumudî, but may be traced back to the MSS. of the Prakriyâ-Kaumudî, the source, though by no means the model, of the Siddhânta-Kaumudî. I was glad to learn from my friend Professor Goldstücker, who is preparing an edition of the Kâśikâ-Vṛitti, and whom I consulted on these forms, that the MSS. of Vâmana which he possesses, carefully avoid these faulty examples to Pâṇ. VIII. 4, 13.

After these explanations I need hardly add that I am not so sanguine as to suppose that I could have escaped scot free where so many men of superior knowledge and talent have failed to do so. All I can say is, that I shall be truly thankful to any scholar who will take the trouble to point out any mistakes into which I may have fallen; and I hope that I shall never so far forget the regard due to truth as to attempt to represent simple corrections, touching the declension of nouns or the conjugation of verbs, as matters of opinion, or so far lower the character of true scholarship as to appeal from the verdict of the few to the opinion of the many.

Hearing from my friend Professor Bühler that he had finished a Sanskrit Syntax, based on the works of Pâṇini and other native grammarians, which will soon be published, I gladly omitted that portion of my grammar. The rules on the derivation of nouns, by means of Kṛit, Uṇâdi, and Taddhita suffixes, do not properly belong to the sphere of an elementary grammar. If time and health permit, I hope to publish hereafter, as a separate treatise, the chapter of the Prakriyâ-Kaumudî bearing on this subject.

In the list of verbs which I have given as an Appendix, pp. 245–299, I have chiefly followed the Prakriyâ-Kaumudî and the Sârasvatî. These grammars do not conjugate every verb that occurs in the Dhâtupâṭha, but those only that serve to illustrate certain grammatical rules. Nor do they adopt, like the Siddhânta-Kaumudî, the order of the verbs as given in Pâṇini's Dhâtupâṭha, but they group the verbs of each class according to their voices, treating together those that take the terminations of the Parasmaipada, those that take the terminations of the Âtmanepada, and, lastly, those that admit of both voices. In each of these subdivisions, again, the single verbs are so arranged as best to illustrate certain grammatical rules. In making a new selection among the verbs selected by Râmachandra and Anubhûtisvarûpâchârya, I have given a preference to those which occur more frequently in Sanskrit literature, and to those which illustrate some points of grammar of peculiar interest to the student. In this manner I hope that the Appendix will serve two purposes: it will not only help the student, when doubtful as to the exact forms of certain verbs, but it will likewise serve as a useful practical exercise to those who, taking each verb in turn, will try to account for the exact forms of its persons, moods, and tenses by a reference to the rules of this grammar. In some cases references have been added to guide the student, in others he has to find by himself the proper warranty for each particular form.

My kind friends Professor Cowell and Professor Kielhorn have revised some of the proof-sheets of my grammar, for which I beg to express to them my sincere thanks.

MAX MÜLLER.

PARIS,
5th April, 1866.

TABLE OF CONTENTS.

CHAPTER III.—Declension.

CHAPTER IV.—Adjectives.

CHAPTER V.—Numerals.

CHAPTER VI.—Pronouns.

CHAPTER VII.—Conjugation.

CHAPTER VIII.—The Ten Classes.

CHAPTER XVII.—Verbal Adjectives.

CHAPTER XVIII.—Causative Verbs.

CHAPTER XIX.—Desiderative Verbs.

APPENDIX.

SANSKRIT GRAMMAR.

CHAPTER I.

THE ALPHABET.

§ 1. SANSKRIT is properly written with the Devanâgarî alphabet; but the Bengali, Telugu, and other modern Indian alphabets are commonly employed for writing Sanskrit in their respective provinces.

Note—*Devanâgarî* means the *Nâgarî* of the gods, or, possibly, of the Brâhmans. A more current style of writing, used by Hindus in all common transactions where Hindi is the language employed, is called simply *Nâgarî*. Why the alphabet should have been called *Nâgarî*, is unknown. If derived from *nagara*, city, it might mean the art of writing as first practised in cities. (Pân. IV. 2, 128.) No authority has yet been adduced from any ancient author for the employment of the word *Devanâgarî*. In the *Lalita-vistara* (a life of Buddha, translated from Sanskrit into Chinese 76 A.D.), where a list of alphabets is given, the *Devanâgarî* is not mentioned, unless it be intended by the *Deva* alphabet. (See History of Ancient Sanskrit Literature, p. 518.) Albiruni, in the 11th century, speaks of the *Nagara* alphabet as current in Malva. (Reinaud, Mémoire sur l'Inde, p. 298.)

No inscriptions have been met with in India anterior to the rise of Buddhism. The earliest authentic specimens of writing are the inscriptions of king *Priyadarśi* or *Aśoka*, about 250 B.C. These are written in two different alphabets. The alphabet which is found in the inscription of Kapurdigiri, and which in the main is the same as that of the Arianian coins, is written from right to left. It is clearly of Semitic origin, and most closely connected with the Aramaic branch of the old Semitic or Phenician alphabet. The Aramaic letters, however, which we know from Egyptian and Palmyrenian inscriptions, have experienced further changes since they served as the model for the alphabet of Kapurdigiri, and we must have recourse to the more primitive types of the ancient Hebrew coins and of the Phenician inscriptions in order to explain some of the letters of the Kapurdigiri alphabet.

But while the transition of the Semitic types into this ancient Indian alphabet can be proved with scientific precision, the second Indian alphabet, that which is found in the inscription of Girnar, and which is the real source of all other Indian alphabets, as well as of those of Tibet and Burmah, has not as yet been traced back in a satisfactory manner to any Semitic prototype. (Prinsep's Indian Antiquities by Thomas, vol. II. p. 42.) To admit, however, the independent invention of a native Indian alphabet is impossible. Alphabets were never invented, in the usual sense of that word. They were formed gradually, and purely phonetic alphabets always point back to earlier, syllabic or ideographic, stages. There are no such traces of the growth of an alphabet on Indian soil; and it is to be hoped that new discoveries may still bring to light the intermediate links by which the alphabet of Girnar, and through it the modern Devanâgarî, may be connected with one of the leading Semitic alphabets.

§ 2. Sanskrit is written from left to right.

Note—*Saṁskṛita* (संस्कृत) means what is rendered fit or perfect. But *Sanskrit* is not called so because the Brâhmans, or still less, because the first Europeans who became acquainted with it, considered it the most perfect of all languages. *Saṁskṛita* meant what is rendered fit for sacred purposes; hence purified, sacred. A vessel that is purified, a sacrificial victim that is properly dressed, a man who has passed through all the initiatory rites or *saṁskâras*; all these are called *saṁskṛita*. Hence the language which alone was fit for sacred acts, the ancient idiom of the Vedas, was called *Saṁskṛita*, or the sacred language. The local spoken dialects received the general name of *prâkṛita*. This did not mean originally vulgar, but derived, secondary, second-rate, literally 'what has a source or type,' this source or type (*prakṛiti*) being the Saṁskṛita or sacred language. (See Vararuchi's Prâkṛita-Prakâśa, ed. Cowell, p. xvii.)

§ 3. In writing the Devanâgarî alphabet, the distinctive portion of each letter is written first, then the perpendicular, and lastly the horizontal line. Ex. [illegible], [illegible], क *k*; [illegible], [illegible], ख *kh*; [illegible], [illegible], ग *g*; [illegible], [illegible], घ *gh*; [illegible], ङ *ṅ*, &c.

Beginners will find it useful to trace the letters on transparent paper, till they know them well, and can write them fluently and correctly.

§ 4. The following are the sounds which are represented in the Devanâgarî alphabet:

	Hard. (tenues.)	Hard and aspirated. (tenues aspiratae.)	Soft. (mediae.)	Soft and aspirated. (mediae aspiratae.)	Nasals.	Liquids.	Sibilants.	Vowels. Short,	Long.	Diphthongs.
1. Gutturals,	क *k*	ख *kh*	ग *g*	घ *gh*	ङ *ṅ*	ह *h*[2]	≍[4] (χ)	अ *a*	आ *â*	ए *e* ऐ *âi*
2. Palatals,	च *ch*	छ *chh*	ज *j*	झ *jh*	ञ *ñ*	य *y*	श *ś*	इ *i*	ई *î*	
3. Linguals,	ट *ṭ*	ठ *ṭh*	ड *ḍ*[1]	ढ *ḍh*[1]	ण *ṇ*	र *r*	ष *sh*	ऋ *ṛi*	ॠ *ṛî*	ओ *o* औ *âu*
4. Dentals,	त *t*	थ *th*	द *d*	ध *dh*	न *n*	ल *l*	स *s*	ऌ *ḷi*	(ॡ *ḷî*)	
5. Labials,	प *p*	फ *ph*	ब *b*	भ *bh*	म *m*	व *v*[3]	≍[4] (φ)	उ *u*	ऊ *û*	

Unmodified Nasal or Anusvâra, ं *ṁ* or ँ *m̐*.

Unmodified Sibilant or Visarga, ः *ḥ*.

Students should be cautioned against using the Roman letters instead of the Devanâgarî when beginning to learn Sanskrit. The paradigms should

[1] In the Veda ड *ḍ* and ढ *ḍh*, if between two vowels, are in certain schools written ळ *ḷ* and ळ्ह *ḷh*.

[2] ह *h* is not properly a liquid, but a soft breathing.

[3] व *v* is sometimes called Dento-labial.

[4] The signs for the guttural and labial sibilants have become obsolete, and are replaced by the two dots ः *ḥ*.

be impressed on the memory in their real and native form, otherwise their first impressions will become unsettled and indistinct. After some progress has been made in mastering the grammar and in reading Sanskrit, the Roman alphabet may be used safely and with advantage.

§ 5. There are fifty letters in the Devanâgarî alphabet, thirty-seven consonants and thirteen vowels, representing every sound of the Sanskrit language.

§ 6. One letter, the long ॡ *ḹ*, is merely a grammatical invention; it never occurs in the spoken language.

§ 7. Two sounds, the guttural and labial sibilants, are now without distinctive representatives in the Devanâgarî alphabet. They are called *Jihvâmûlîya*, the tongue-root sibilant, formed near the base of the tongue; and *Upadhmânîya*, i. e. afflandus, the labial sibilant. They are said to have been represented by the signs X (called *Vajrâkṛiti*, having the shape of the thunderbolt) and ≍ (called *Gajakumbhâkṛiti*, having the shape of an elephant's two frontal bones). [See Vopadeva's Sanskrit Grammar, I. 18; History of Ancient Sanskrit Literature, p. 508.] Sometimes the sign ᳲ, called *Ardhavisarga*, half-Visarga, is used for both. But in common writing these two signs are now replaced by the two dots, the *Dvivindu*, :, (*dvi*, two, *vindu*, dot,) properly the sign of the unmodified Visarga.

§ 8. There are five distinct letters for the five nasals, ङ् *ṅ*, ञ् *ñ*, ण् *ṇ*, न् *n*, म् *m*, as there were originally five distinct signs for the five sibilants. When, in the middle of words, these nasals are followed by consonants of their own class, (*ṅ* by *k*, *kh*, *g*, *gh*; *ñ* by *ch*, *chh*, *j*, *jh*; *ṇ* by *ṭ*, *ṭh*, *ḍ*, *ḍh*; *n* by *t*, *th*, *d*, *dh*; *m* by *p*, *ph*, *b*, *bh*,) they are often, for the sake of more expeditious writing, replaced by the dot, which is properly the sign of the unmodified nasal or Anusvâra. Thus we find

अंकिता instead of अङ्किता *aikitá*.
अंचिता instead of अञ्चिता *añchitá*.
कुंडिता instead of कुण्डिता *kuṇḍitá*.
नंदिता instead of नन्दिता *nanditá*.
कंपिता instead of कम्पिता *kampitá*.

The pronunciation remains unaffected by this style of writing. अंकिता must be pronounced as if it were written अङ्किता *aṅkitá*, &c.

The same applies to final म् *m* at the end of a sentence. This too, though frequently written and printed with the dot above the line, is to be pronounced as *m*. अहं, I, is to be pronounced like अहम् *aham*. (See Preface to Hitopadeśa, in M. M.'s Handbooks for the Study of Sanskrit, p. viii.)

Note.—According to the Kaumâras final म् m *in pausâ* may be pronounced as Anusvâra;

cf. Sarasvatî-Prakriyâ, ed. Bombay, 1829 *, pp. 12 and 13. कौमारास्तु यवलपरे स्वानुनासिकमिच्छन्ति । यवलपरे वा । यवलपरे मकारस्यानुस्वारो भवति वा । देवं । देवम् ॥ The Kaumâras are the followers of Kumâra, the reputed author of the Kâtantra or Kalâpa grammar. (See Colebrooke, Sanskrit Grammar, Preface; and page 315, note.) S'arvavarman is sometimes quoted by mistake as the author of this grammar, and an unnecessary distinction is made between the Kaumâras and the followers of the Kalâpa grammar.

§ 9. Besides the five nasal letters, expressing the nasal sound as modified by guttural, palatal, lingual, dental, and labial pronunciation, there are still three nasalized letters, the य्ँ, ल्ँ, व्ँ, or यँ, लँ, वँ, ỹ, l̃, ṽ, which are used to represent a final म् *m*, if followed by an initial य् *y*, ल् *l*, व् *v*, and modified by the pronunciation of these three semivowels.

Thus instead of तं याति *taṁ yâti* we may write तय्ँयाति *taỹ yâti*;

instead of तं लभते *taṁ labhate* we may write तल्ँलभते *tal̃ labhate*;

instead of तं वहति *taṁ vahati* we may write तव्ँवहति *taṽ vahati*.

Or in composition,

संयानं *saṁyânam* or सय्ँयानं *saỹ yânam*;

संलब्धं *saṁlabdham* or सल्ँलब्धं *sal̃ labdham*;

संवहति *saṁvahati* or सव्ँवहति *saṽ vahati*.

§ 10. The only consonants which have no corresponding nasals are र् *r*, श् *ś*, ष् *sh*, स् *s*, ह् *h*. A final म् *m*, therefore, before any of these letters at the beginning of words, can only be represented by the neutral or unmodified nasal, the Anusvâra.

तं रक्षति *taṁ rakshati*. Or in composition, संरक्षति *saṁrakshati*.

तं शृणोति *taṁ śriṇoti*. संशृणोति *saṁśriṇoti*.

तं षकारं *taṁ shakâram*. संष्ठीवति *saṁshṭhîvati*.

तं सरति *taṁ sarati*. संसरति *saṁsarati*.

तं हरति *taṁ harati*. संहरति *saṁharati*.

§ 11. In the body of a word the only letters which can be preceded by Anusvâra are श् *ś*, ष् *sh*, स् *s*, ह् *h*. Thus अंशः *aṁśaḥ*, धनूंषि *dhanûṁshi*, यशांसि *yaśâṁsi*, सिंहः *siṁhaḥ*. Before the semivowels य् *y*, र् *r*, ल् *l*, व् *v*, the म् *m*, in the body of a word, is never changed into Anusvâra. Thus गम्यते *gamyate*, नम्रः *namraḥ*, अम्लः *amlaḥ*. As to म् *m* before semivowels in the middle of compounds, see § 9.

§ 12. With the exception of *Jihvâmûlîya* ✕ χ (tongue-root letter), *Upadhmânîya* ✕ φ (to be breathed upon), *Anusvâra* ं *ṁ* (after-sound), *Visarga* : *ḥ* (emission, see Taitt.-Brâhm. III. p. 23 a), and *Repha r* (burring), all letters

---

* This edition, which has lately been reprinted, contains the text—ascribed either to Vâṇî herself, i. e. Sarasvatî, the goddess of speech (MS. Bodl. 386), or to Anubhûti-svarûpa-âchârya, whoever that may be—and a commentary. The commentary printed in the Bombay editions is called महीधरी, or in MS. Bodl. 382. मैदासी, i. e. महीदासी. In MS. Bodl. 382. Mahîdhara or Mahîdâsabhaṭṭa is said to have written the Sârasvata in order that his children might read it, and to please Îśa, the Lord. The date given is 1634, the place Benares, (Sivarâjadhanî.)

are named in Sanskrit by adding *kâra* (making) to their sounds. Thus अ *a* is called अकारः *akâraḥ*; क *ka*, ककारः *kakâraḥ*.

§ 13. The vowels, if initial, are written,

अ, आ, इ, ई, ऋ, ॠ, ऌ, (ॡ), उ, ऊ, ए, ऐ, ओ, औ;
a, â, i, î, ṛi, ṛî, ḷi, (ḷî), u, û, e, ai, o, au;

if they follow a consonant, they are written with the following signs—

—, ा, ि, ी, ृ, ॄ, ॢ, (ॣ), ु, ू, े, ै, ो, ौ.
a, â, i, î, ṛi, ṛî, ḷi, (ḷî), u, û, e, ai, o, au.

There is one exception. If the vowel ऋ *ṛi* follows the consonant र् *r*, it retains its initial form, and the *r* is written over it. Ex. निर्ऋतिः *nirṛitiḥ*.

In certain words which tolerate an hiatus in the body of the word, the second vowel is written in its initial form. Ex. गोअग्र *goagra*, adj. preceded by cows, instead of गोऽग्र *go'gra* or गवाग्र *gavâgra*; गोअश्वं *goaśvam*, cows and horses; प्रउग *praüga*, yoke; तितउ *titaü*, sieve.

§ 14. Every consonant, if written by itself, is supposed to be followed by a short *a*. Thus क is not pronounced *k*, but *ka*; य not *y*, but *ya*. But क *k* or any other consonant, if followed by any vowel except *a*, is pronounced without the inherent *a*. Thus

का *kâ*, कि *ki*, की *kî*, कृ *kṛi*, कॄ *kṛî*, कॢ *kḷi*, (कॣ *kḷî*), कु *ku*, कू *kû*, के *ke*, कै *kai*, को *ko*, कौ *kau*.

The only peculiarity is that short ि *i* is apparently written before the consonant after which it is sounded. This arose from the fact that in the earliest forms of the Indian alphabet the long and short *i*'s were both written over the consonant, the short *i* inclining to the left, the long *i* inclining to the right. Afterwards these top-marks were, for the sake of distinctness, drawn across the top-line, so as to become कि and की, instead of कि and की. (See Prinsep's Indian Antiquities by Thomas, vol. II. p. 40.)

§ 15. If a consonant is to be pronounced without any vowel after it, the consonant is said to be followed by *Virâma*, i. e. stoppage, which is marked by ्. Thus *ak* must be written अक्; *kar*, कर्; *ik*, इक्.

§ 16. If a consonant is followed immediately by another consonant, the two or three or four or five or more consonants are written in one group (*saṁyoga*). Thus *atka* is written अत्क; *alpa* is written अल्प; *kârtsnya* is written कार्त्स्न्य. These groups or compound consonants must be learnt by practice. It is easy, however, to discover some general laws in their formation. Thus the perpendicular and horizontal lines are generally dropt in one of the letters: क्+क=क्क *kka*; ङ्+द=ङ्द *ṅda*; त्+व=त्व *tva*; ष्+ख=ष्ख *ṣkha*; च्+य=च्य *chya*; प्+त=प्त *pta*; क्+त=क्त *kta*; क्+त्+व=क्त्व *ktva*; क्+त्+य=क्त्य *ktya*.

§ 17. The र् *r* following a consonant is written by a short transverse stroke at the foot of the letter; as क् + र = क्र or क्र *kra*; ग् + र = ग्र *gra*; त् + र = त्र or त्र *tra*; द् + र = द्र *dra*; ष् + ट् + र = ष्ट्र *shṭra*.

The र् *r* preceding a consonant is written by ॅ placed at the top of the consonant before which it is to be sounded. Thus अर् + क = अर्क *arka*; वर् + ष् + म = वर्ष्म *varshma*. This sign for र् *r* is placed to the right of any other marks at the top of the same letter. Ex. अर्कं *arkam*; अर्केण *arkeṇa*; अर्केन्दु *arkendu*.

क् *k* followed by ष *sh* is written क्ष *ksha*.

ज् *j* followed by ञ *ñ* is written ज्ञ *jña*.

र् *r* followed by उ *u* and ऊ *ú* is written रु *ru*, रू *rú*.

द् *d* followed by उ *u* and ऊ *ú* is written दु *du*, दू *dú*.

श् *ś*, particularly in combination with other letters, is frequently written श्.
Ex. शु *śu*; शू *śú*; श्र *śra*.

§ 18. The sign of *Viráma* ् (stoppage), which if placed at the foot of a consonant, shows that its inherent short *a* is stopped, is sometimes, when it is difficult to write (or to print) two or three consonants in one group, placed after one of the consonants: thus युङ्क्ते instead of युङ्क्ते *yuṅkte*.

§ 19. The proper use of the Virâma, however, is at the end of a sentence, or portion of a sentence, the last word of which ends in a consonant.

At the end of a sentence, or of a half-verse, the sign । is used; at the end of a verse, or of a longer sentence, the sign ॥.

§ 20. The sign ऽ (*Avagraha* or *Arddhákára*) is used in many editions to mark the elision of an initial अ *a*, after a final ओ *o* or ए *e*. Ex. सोऽपि *so'pi* for सो अपि *so api*, i. e. सस् अपि *sas api*; तेऽपि *te'pi* for ते अपि *te api*.

List of Compound Consonants.

क्क *k-ka*, क्ख *k-kha*, क्च *k-cha*, क्त *k-ta*, क्त्य *k-t-ya*, क्त्र *k-t-ra*, क्त्र्य *k-t-r-ya*, क्त्व *k-t-va*, क्न *k-na*, क्न्य *k-n-ya*, क्म *k-ma*, क्य *k-ya*, क्र or क्र *k-ra*, क्र्य or क्र्य *k-r-ya*, क्ल *k-la*, क्व *k-va*, क्व्य *k-v-ya*, क्ष *k-sha*, क्ष्म *k-sh-ma*, क्ष्य *k-sh-ya*, क्ष्व *k-sh-va*;— ख्य *kh-ya*, ख्र *kh-ra*;— ग्य *g-ya*, ग्र *g-ra*, ग्र्य *g-r-ya*;— घ्न *gh-na*, घ्न्य *gh-n-ya*, घ्म *gh-ma*, घ्य *gh-ya*, घ्र *gh-ra*;— ङ्क *ṅ-ka*, ङ्क्त *ṅ-k-ta*, ङ्क्त्य *ṅ-k-t-ya*, ङ्क्य *ṅ-k-ya*, ङ्क्ष *ṅ-k-sha*, ङ्क्ष्व *ṅ-k-sh-va*, ङ्ख *ṅ-kha*, ङ्ख्य *ṅ-kh-ya*, ङ्ग *ṅ-ga*, ङ्ग्य *ṅ-g-ya*, ङ्घ *ṅ-gha*, ङ्घ्य *ṅ-gh-ya*, ङ्घ्र *ṅ-gh-ra*, ङ्ङ *ṅ-ṅa*, ङ्म *ṅ-ma*, ङ्य *ṅ-ya*.

च्च *ch-cha*, च्छ *ch-chha*, च्छ्र *ch-chh-ra*, च्ञ *ch-ña*, च्म *ch-ma*, च्य *ch-ya*;— छ्य *chh-ya*, छ्र *chh-ra*;— ज्ज *j-ja*, ज्झ *j-jha*, ज्ञ *j-ña*, ज्ञ्य *j-ñ-ya*, ज्म *j-ma*, ज्य *j-ya*, ज्र *j-ra*, ज्व *j-va*;— ञ्च *ñ-cha*, ञ्च्म *ñ-ch-ma*, ञ्च्य *ñ-ch-ya*, ञ्छ *ñ-chha*, ञ्ज *ñ-ja*, ञ्ञ *ñ-ña*, ञ्य *ñ-ya*.

ट्ट *ṭ-ṭa*, ट्य *ṭ-ya*;— ठ्य *ṭh-ya*, ठ्र *ṭh-ra*;— ड्ग *ḍ-ga*, ड्ग्य *ḍ-g-ya*, ड्घ *ḍ-gha*, ड्घ्र *ḍ-gh-ra*, ड्म *ḍ-ma*, ड्य *ḍ-ya*;— ढ्य *ḍh-ya*, ढ्र *ḍh-ra*;— ण्ट *ṇ-ṭa*, ण्ठ *ṇ-ṭha*,

ण्ड *ṇ-ḍa*, ण्ड्य *ṇ-ḍ-ya*, ण्ड्र *ṇ-ḍ-ra*, ण्ड्र्य *ṇ-ḍ-r-ya*, ण्ढ *ṇ-ḍha*, ण्ण *ṇ-ṇa*, ण्म *ṇ-ma*, ण्य *ṇ-ya*, ण्व *ṇ-va*.

त्क *t-ka*, त्क्र *t-k-ra*, त्त *t-ta*, त्त्य *t-t-ya*, त्त्र *t-t-ra*, त्त्व *t-t-va*, त्थ *t-tha*, त्न *t-na*, त्न्य *t-n-ya*, त्प *t-pa*, त्प्र *t-p-ra*, त्म *t-ma*, त्म्य *t-m-ya*, त्य *t-ya*, त्र or त्र *t-ra*, त्र्य *t-r-ya*, त्व *t-va*, त्स *t-sa*, त्स्न *t-s-na*, त्स्न्य *t-s-n-ya*, त्स्य *t-s-ya*;—थ्य *th-ya*;— द्ग *d-ga*, द्घ *d-gha*, द्घ्र *d-gh-ra*, द्द *d-da*, द्द्य *d-d-ya*, द्ध *d-dha*, द्ध्य *d-dh-ya*, द्न *d-na*, द्ब *d-ba*, द्भ *d-bha*, द्भ्य *d-bh-ya*, द्म *d-ma*, द्य *d-ya*, द्र *d-ra*, द्र्य *d-r-ya*, द्व *d-va*, द्व्य *d-v-ya*;—ध्न *dh-na*, ध्न्य *dh-n-ya*, ध्म *dh-ma*, ध्य *dh-ya*, ध्र *dh-ra*, ध्र्य *dh-r-ya*, ध्व *dh-va*;—न्त *n-ta*, न्त्य *n-t-ya*, न्त्र *n-t-ra*, न्द *n-da*, न्द्र *n-d-ra*, न्ध *n-dha*, न्ध्र *n-dh-ra*, न्न *n-na*, न्प *n-pa*, न्प्र *n-p-ra*, न्म *n-ma*, न्य *n-ya*, न्र *n-ra*, न्स *n-sa*.

प्त *p-ta*, प्त्य *p-t-ya*, प्न *p-na*, प्प *p-pa*, प्म *p-ma*, प्य *p-ya*, प्र *p-ra*, प्ल *p-la*, प्व *p-va*, प्स *p-sa*, प्स्व *p-s-va*;—ब्घ *b-gha*, ब्ज *b-ja*, ब्द *b-da*, ब्ध *b-dha*, ब्न *b-na*, ब्ब *b-ba*, ब्भ *b-bha*, ब्भ्य *b-bh-ya*, ब्य *b-ya*, ब्र *b-ra*, ब्व *b-va*;—भ्न *bh-na*, भ्य *bh-ya*, भ्र *bh-ra*, भ्व *bh-va*;—म्न *m-na*, म्प *m-pa*, म्प्र *m-p-ra*, म्ब *m-ba*, म्भ *m-bha*, म्म *m-ma*, म्य *m-ya*, म्र *m-ra*, म्ल *m-la*, म्व *m-va*.

य्य *y-ya*, य्व *y-va*;—ल्क *l-ka*, ल्प *l-pa*, ल्म *l-ma*, ल्य *l-ya*, ल्ल *l-la*, ल्व *l-va*;— व्न *v-na*, व्य *v-ya*, व्र *v-ra*, व्व *v-va*.

श्च *ś-cha*, श्च्य *ś-ch-ya*, श्न *ś-na*, श्य *ś-ya*, श्र *ś-ra*, श्र्य *ś-r-ya*, श्ल *ś-la*, श्व *ś-va*, श्व्य *ś-v-ya*, श्श *ś-śa*;—ष्ट *sh-ṭa*, ष्ट्य *sh-ṭ-ya*, ष्ट्र *sh-ṭ-ra*, ष्ट्र्य *sh-ṭ-r-ya*, ष्ट्व *sh-ṭ-va*, ष्ठ *sh-ṭha*, ष्ण *sh-ṇa*, ष्ण्य *sh-ṇ-ya*, ष्प *sh-pa*, ष्प्र *sh-p-ra*, ष्म *sh-ma*, ष्य *sh-ya*, ष्व *sh-va*;—स्क *s-ka*, स्ख *s-kha*, स्त *s-ta*, स्त्य *s-t-ya*, स्त्र *s-t-ra*, स्त्व *s-t-va*, स्थ *s-tha*, स्न *s-na*, स्न्य *s-n-ya*, स्प *s-pa*, स्फ *s-pha*, स्म *s-ma*, स्म्य *s-m-ya*, स्य *s-ya*, स्र *s-ra*, स्व *s-va*, स्स *s-sa*.

ह्ण *h-ṇa*, ह्न *h-na*, ह्म *h-ma*, ह्य *h-ya*, ह्र *h-ra*, ह्ल *h-la*, ह्व *h-va*.

Numerical Figures.

§ 21. The numerical figures in Sanskrit are

१	२	३	४	५	६	७	८	९	०
1	2	3	4	5	6	7	8	9	0

These figures were originally abbreviations of the initial letters of the Sanskrit numerals. The Arabs, who adopted them from the Hindus, called them Indian figures; in Europe, where they were introduced by the Arabs, they were called Arabic figures.

Thus १ stands for ए *e* of एकः *ekaḥ*, one.
२ stands for द्व *dv* of द्वौ *dvau*, two.
३ stands for त्र *tr* of त्रयः *trayaḥ*, three.
४ stands for च *ch* of चत्वारः *chatvâraḥ*, four.
५ stands for प *p* of पंच *pañcha*, five.

The similarity becomes more evident by comparing the letters and numerals as used in ancient inscriptions. See Woepcke, 'Mémoire sur la Propagation des Chiffres Indiens,' in Journal Asiatique, vi série, tome 1; Prinsep's Indian Antiquities by Thomas, vol. ii. p. 70.

Pronunciation.

§ 22. The Sanskrit letters should be pronounced in accordance with the transcription given page 2. The following rules, however, are to be observed:

1. The vowels should be pronounced like the vowels in Italian. The short अ *a*, however, has rather the sound of the English *a* in 'America.'
2. The aspiration of the consonants should be heard distinctly. Thus ख *kh* is said, by English scholars who learnt Sanskrit in India, to sound almost like *kh* in 'inkhorn;' थ *th* like *th* in 'pothouse;' फ *ph* like *ph* in 'topheavy;' घ *gh* like *gh* in 'loghouse;' ध *dh* like *dh* in 'madhouse;' भ *bh* like *bh* in 'Hobhouse.' This, no doubt, is a somewhat exaggerated description, but it is well in learning Sanskrit to distinguish from the first the aspirated from the unaspirated letters by pronouncing the former with an unmistakable emphasis.
3. The guttural ङ *ṅ* has the sound of *ng* in 'king.'
4. The palatal letters च *ch* and ज *j* have the sound of *ch* in 'church' and of *j* in 'join.'
5. The lingual letters are said to be pronounced by bringing the lower surface of the tongue against the roof of the palate. As a matter of fact the ordinary pronunciation of *t*, *d*, *n* in English is what Hindus would call lingual, and it is essential to distinguish the Sanskrit dentals by bringing the tip of the tongue against the very edge of the upper front-teeth. In transcribing English words the natives naturally represent the English dentals by their linguals, not by their own dentals; e. g. डिरेक्टर *Ḍirekṭar*, गवर्नमेंट् *Gavarṇmaṇṭ*, &c. *
6. The Visarga, *Jihvâmûlîya* and *Upadhmânîya* are not now articulated audibly.
7. The dental स *s* sounds like *s* in 'sin,' the lingual ष *sh* like *sh* in 'shun,' the palatal श *ś* like *ss* in 'session.'

The real Anusvâra is sounded as a very slight nasal, like *n* in French 'bon.' If the dot is used as a graphic sign in place of the other five nasals it must, of course, be pronounced like the nasal which it represents †.

---

* Bühler, Madras Literary Journal, February, 1864. Rajendralal Mitra, 'On the Origin of the Hindvî Language,' Journal of the Asiatic Society, Bengal, 1864, p. 509.

† According to Sanskrit grammarians the Anusvâra is pronounced in the nose only, the five nasals by their respective organs and the nose. Siddh.-Kaum. to Pâṇ. 1. 1, 9. ञमङ-णनानां नासिका च (चकारेण स्वस्ववर्गीयस्थानानुकूलं स्थानादि समुच्चीयते) ॥ नासिकानुस्वारस्य ॥

CHAPTER II.

RULES OF SANDHI OR THE COMBINATION OF LETTERS.

§ 23. In Sanskrit every sentence is considered as one unbroken chain of syllables. Except where there is a stop, which we should mark by interpunction, the final letters of each word are made to coalesce with the initial letters of the following word. This coalescence of final and initial letters, (of vowels with vowels, of consonants with consonants, and of consonants with vowels,) is called *Sandhi*.

As certain letters in Sanskrit are incompatible with each other, i. e. cannot be pronounced one immediately after the other, they have to be modified or assimilated in order to facilitate their pronunciation. The rules, according to which either one or both letters are thus modified, are called *the rules of Sandhi*.

As according to a general rule the words in a sentence must thus be glued together, the mere absence of Sandhi is in many cases sufficient to mark the stops which we have to mark in English by interpunction. Ex. अस्त्वग्निमाहात्म्यं इंद्रस्तु देवानां महत्तमः *astvagnimâhâtmyam, indrastu devânâm mahattamaḥ*, Let there be the greatness of Agni; nevertheless Indra is the greatest of the gods.

Distinction between External and Internal Sandhi.

§ 24. It is essential, in order to avoid confusion, to distinguish between the rules of Sandhi which determine the changes of final and initial letters of words (*padas*), and between those other rules of Sandhi which apply to the final letters of verbal roots (*dhâtu*) and nominal bases (*prâtipadika*) when followed by certain terminations or suffixes. Though both are based on the same phonetic principles and are sometimes identical, their application is different. For shortness' sake it will be best to apply the name of *External Sandhi* to the changes which take place at the meeting of final and initial letters of words, and that of *Internal Sandhi* to the changes produced by the meeting of radical and formative elements.

The rules which apply to final and initial letters of words (*padas*) apply, with few exceptions, to the final and initial letters of the component parts of compounds, and likewise to the final letters of nominal bases (*prâtipadika*) when followed by the so-called *Pada*-terminations (भ्यां *bhyâm*, भिः *bhiḥ*, भ्यः *bhyaḥ*, सु *su*), or by secondary (*taddhita*) suffixes beginning with any consonants except *y*.

The changes produced by the contact of incompatible letters in the body of a word should properly be treated under the heads of declension, conjugation, and derivation. In many cases it is far easier to remember the words ready-made from the dictionary, or the grammatical paradigms from the grammar, than to acquire the complicated rules with their numerous exceptions which are generally detailed in Sanskrit grammars under the head of Sandhi. It is easier to learn that the participle passive of लिह् *lih*, to lick, is लीढः *lîḍhaḥ*, than to remember the rules according to which इ + ह् *h* + *t* are changed into इ + ढ् *ḍh* + *t*, इ + ड् *ḍ* + *dh*, and इ + ड् *ḍ* + *ḍh*; ड् *ḍ* is dropt and the vowel lengthened: while in परिवृह् + तः *parivṛih* + *taḥ*, the vowel, under the same circumstances, remains short; *parivṛih* + *taḥ* = *parivṛiḍh* + *taḥ*, *parivṛiḍ* + *dhaḥ* = *parivṛiḍ* + *ḍhaḥ* = *parivṛiḍhaḥ*. In Greek and Latin no rules are given with regard to changes of this kind. If they are to be given at all in Sanskrit grammars, they should, to avoid confusion, be kept perfectly distinct from the rules affecting the final and initial letters of words as brought together in one and the same sentence.

Classification of Vowels.

§ 25. Vowels are divided into short (*hrasva*), long (*dîrgha*), and protracted (*pluta*) vowels. Short vowels have one measure (*mâtrâ*), long vowels two, protracted vowels three. A consonant is said to last half the time of a short vowel.

1. Short vowels: अ *a*, इ *i*, उ *u*, ऋ *ṛi*, ऌ *ḷi*.
2. Long vowels: आ *â*, ई *î*, ऊ *û*, ॠ *ṛî*, ए *e*, ऐ *ai*, ओ *o*, औ *au*.
3. Protracted vowels are indicated by the figure ३ 3; अ३ *a* 3, आ३ *â* 3, इ३ *i* 3, ई३ *î* 3, ए३ *e* 3, औ३ *au* 3. Sometimes we find अ३इ, *a* 3 *i*, instead of ए३, *e* 3; or आ३उ, *â* 3 *u*, instead of औ३, *au* 3.

§ 26. Vowels are likewise divided into

1. Monophthongs (*samânâkshara*): अ *a*, आ *â*, इ *i*, ई *î*, उ *u*, ऊ *û*, ऋ *ṛi*, ॠ *ṛî*, ऌ *ḷi*.
2. Diphthongs (*sandhyakshara*): ए *e*, ऐ *ai*, ओ *o*, औ *au*.

§ 27. All vowels are liable to be nasalized, or to become *anunâsika*: अँ *ã*, आँ *ẫ*.

§ 28. Vowels are again divided into light (*laghu*) and heavy (*guru*). This division is important for metrical purposes.

1. Light vowels are अ *a*, इ *i*, उ *u*, ऋ *ṛi*, ऌ *ḷi*, if not followed by a double consonant.
2. Heavy vowels are ए *e*, ऐ *ai*, ओ *o*, औ *au*, and any short vowel, if followed by more than one consonant.

§ 29. Vowels are, lastly, divided according to accent, into *acute* (udâtta), *grave* (anudâtta), and *circumflexed* (svarita). The acute vowels are pronounced with a raised tone, the grave vowels with a low, the circumflexed with an even tone. Accents are marked in Vedic literature only.

Guṇa and Vṛiddhi.

§ 30. Guṇa is the strengthening of इ *i*, ई *î*, उ *u*, ऊ *û*, ऋ *ṛi*, ॠ *ṛî*, ऌ *ḷi*, by means of a preceding अ *a*, which raises इ *i* and ई *î* to ए *e*, उ *u* and ऊ *û* to ओ *o*, ऋ *ṛi* and ॠ *ṛî* to अर् *ar*, ऌ *ḷi* to अल् *al*.

By a repetition of the same process the Vṛiddhi (increase) vowels are formed, viz. ऐ *ai* instead of ए *e*, औ *au* instead of ओ *o*, आर् *âr* instead of अर् *ar*, and आल् *âl* instead of अल् *al*.

Vowels are thus divided again into

1. Simple vowels: अ *a*, आ *â*, इ *i*, ई *î*, उ *u*, ऊ *û*, ऋ *ṛi*, ॠ *ṛî*, ऌ *ḷi*.
2. Guṇa vowels: —— ए *e* (*a* + *i*), ओ *o* (*a* + *u*), अर् *ar*, अल् *al*.
3. Vṛiddhi vowels: आ *â* ऐ *ai*(*a*+*a*+*i*), औ *au*(*a*+*a*+*u*), आर् *âr*, आल् *âl*.

§ 31. अ *a* and आ *â* do not take Guṇa, or, as other grammarians say, remain unchanged after taking Guṇa. Thus in the first person sing. of the reduplicated perfect, which requires Guṇa or Vṛiddhi, हन् *han* forms with Guṇa जघन *jaghana*, or with Vṛiddhi जघान *jaghâna*, I have killed.

Combination of Vowels at the end and beginning of words.

§ 32. As a general rule, Sanskrit allows of no hiatus (*vivṛitti*) in a sentence. If a word ends in a vowel, and the next word begins with a vowel, certain modifications take place in order to remove this hiatus.

§ 33. If any simple vowel, long or short, follows the same simple vowel, long or short, the two coalesce into their corresponding long vowel. Thus

अ or आ + अ or आ = आ *ă* + *ă* = *â*.
इ or ई + इ or ई = ई *ĭ* + *ĭ* = *î*.
उ or ऊ + उ or ऊ = ऊ *ŭ* + *ŭ* = *û*.
ऋ or ॠ + ऋ or ॠ = ॠ *ṛĭ* + *ṛĭ* = *ṛî*.*

Ex. उक्त्वा अपगच्छति = उक्त्वापगच्छति *uktvâ* + *apagachchhati* = *uktvâpagachchhati*, having spoken he goes away.
नदी ईदृशी = नदीदृशी *nadî* + *îdṛiśî* = *nadîdṛiśî*, such a river.
कर्तृ ऋजु = कर्तॄजु *kartṛi* + *ṛiju* = *kartṛîju*, doing (neuter) right.
किंतु उदेति = किंतूदेति *kintu* + *udeti* = *kintûdeti*, but he rises.

Or in compounds, मही + ईशः = महीशः *mahî* + *îśaḥ* = *mahîśaḥ*, lord of the earth.

§ 34. If final अ, आ *ă* are followed by any other vowel (except diphthongs), the two vowels coalesce into the corresponding Guṇa-vowel. Thus

अ or आ + इ or ई = ए *ă* + *ĭ* = *e* (*ăi*).
अ or आ + उ or ऊ = ओ *ă* + *ŭ* = *o* (*ău*).
अ or आ + ऋ or ॠ = अर् *ă* + *ṛĭ* = *ar*.

Ex. तव इन्द्रः = तवेन्द्रः *tava* + *indraḥ* = *tavendraḥ*, thine is Indra.
सा उक्त्वा = सोक्त्वा *sâ* + *uktvâ* = *soktvâ*, she having spoken.

---

* The letter ॡ *ḷî* is left out, because it is of no practical utility. It is treated like ॠ *ṛî*, only substituting ल् *l* for र् *r* in Guṇa and Vṛiddhi. Thus ॡ + अनुबन्धः *ḷî*+*anubandhaḥ* becomes लनुबन्धः *lanubandhaḥ*, i. e. having *ḷî* as indicatory letter.

* सा ऋद्धिः = सर्द्धिः *sá + ṛiddhiḥ = sarddhiḥ*, this wealth.

तव ऌकारः = तवल्कारः *tava + ḷikâraḥ = tavalkâraḥ*, thy letter *ḷi*.

Or in compounds, काम्य + इष्टिः = काम्येष्टिः *kâmya + ishṭiḥ = kâmyeshṭiḥ*, an offering for a certain boon.

हित + उपदेशः = हितोपदेशः *hita + upadeśaḥ = hitopadeśaḥ*, good advice.

§ 35. If final अ, आ *â* are followed by a diphthong, whether Guṇa or Vṛiddhi, the two vowels coalesce into the corresponding Vṛiddhi-vowel. Thus

अ or आ + ए = ऐ *â + e = âi.*
अ or आ + ऐ = ऐ *â + âi = âi.*
अ or आ + ओ = औ *â + o = âu.*
अ or आ + औ = औ *â + âu = âu.*

Ex. तव एव = तवैव *tava + eva = tavaiva*, of thee only.

सा ऐक्षिष्ट = सैक्षिष्ट *sá + aikshishṭa = saikshishṭa*, she saw.

तव ओष्ठः = तवौष्ठः *tava + oshṭhaḥ = tavaushṭhaḥ*, thy lip.

सा औत्सुक्यवती = सौत्सुक्यवती *sá + autsukyavatí = sautsukyavatí*, she desirous.

Or in compounds, राम + ऐश्वर्यं = रामैश्वर्यं *râma + aiśvaryam = râmaiśvaryam*, the lordship of Râma.

सीता + औपम्यं = सीतौपम्यं *sítá + aupamyam = sítaupamyam*, similarity with Sítâ, the wife of Râma.

§ 36. If a simple vowel (except *â*) is followed by a dissimilar vowel (simple or diphthong), the former is changed into its corresponding semivowel. Thus

इ or ई	अ or आ = य or या	*í*	*â = yâ.*
	ऋ or ॠ = यृ or यॄ		*ṛí = yṛí.*
	उ or ऊ = यु or यू		*ú = yú.*
	ए or ऐ = ये or यै		*e, ai = ye, yai.*
	ओ or औ = यो or यौ		*o, au = yo, yau.*
ऋ or ॠ	अ or आ = र or रा	*ṛí*	*â = râ.*
	इ or ई = रि or री		*í = rí.*
	उ or ऊ = रु or रू		*ú = rú.*
	ए or ऐ = रे or रै		*e, ai = re, rai.*
	ओ or औ = रो or रौ		*o, au = ro, rau.*
उ or ऊ	अ or आ = व or वा	*ú*	*â = vâ.*
	इ or ई = वि or वी		*í = ví.*
	ऋ or ॠ = वृ or वॄ		*ṛí = vṛí.*
	ए or ऐ = वे or वै		*e, ai = ve, vai.*
	ओ or औ = वो or वौ		*o, au = vo, vau.*

* Some grammarians consider the Sandhi of *â* with *ṛi* optional, but they require the shortening of the long *â*. Ex. ब्रह्मा + ऋषिः *brahmâ + ṛishiḥ* = ब्रह्मर्षिः *brahmarshiḥ* or ब्रह्म ऋषिः *brahma ṛishiḥ*, Brahmâ, a Ṛishi.

Ex. दधि अत्र = दध्यत्र *dadhi + atra = dadhyatra*, milk here.
कर्तृ उत = कर्त्रुत *kartṛi + uta = kartruta*, doing moreover.
मधु इव = मध्विव *madhu + iva = madhviva*, like honey.
नदी ऐडस्य = नद्यैडस्य *nadí + aiḍasya = nadyaiḍasya*, the river of Aiḍa.

In compounds, नदी + अर्थं = नद्यर्थं *nadí + artham = nadyartham*, for the sake of a river.

Note—Some native grammarians allow, except in compounds, the omission of this Sandhi, but they require in that case that a long final vowel be shortened. Ex. चक्री अत्र *chakrí atra* may be चक्र्यत्र *chakryatra* or चक्रि अत्र *chakri atra*.

§ 37. If the Guṇa-vowels ए *e* and ओ *o* are followed by any vowel, simple or diphthong (except *ă*), their last element is changed into the semivowel. Thus

ए (*e*) + any vowel (except *ă*) = अय् (*ay*).
ओ (*o*) + any vowel (except *ă*) = अव् (*av*).

Ex. सखे आगच्छ = सखयागच्छ *sakhe ágachchha = sakhayágachchha*, Friend, come!
सखे इह = सखयिह *sakhe iha = sakhayiha*, Friend, here!
प्रभो एहि = प्रभवेहि *prabho ehi = prabhavehi*, Lord, come near!
प्रभो औषधं = प्रभवौषधं *prabho aushadham = prabhavaushadham*, Lord, medicine.

In compounds, गो + ईशः = गवीशः *go + íśaḥ = gavíśaḥ*. There are various exceptions in compounds where गो *go* is treated as गव *gava*. (§ 41.)

§ 38. If the Vṛiddhi-vowels ऐ *ai* and औ *au* are followed by any vowel, simple or diphthong, their last element is changed into the semivowel. Thus

ऐ (*ai*) + any vowel = आय् (*áy*).
औ (*au*) + any vowel = आव् (*áv*).

Ex. श्रियै अर्थः = श्रियायर्थः *śriyai arthaḥ = śriyáyarthaḥ*.
श्रियै ऋते = श्रियायृते *śriyai ṛite = śriyáyṛite*.
रवौ अस्तमिते = रवावस्तमिते *ravau astamite = ravávastamite*, after sunset.
तौ इति = ताविति *tau iti = táviti*.

In composition, नौ + अर्थं = नावर्थं *nau + artham = návartham*, for the sake of ships.

§ 39. These two rules, however, are liable to certain modifications:

1. The final य् *y* and व् *v* of अय् *ay*, अव् *av*, which stand according to rule for ए *e*, ओ *o*, may be dropt before all vowels, except *ă*; not, however, in composition. Thus most MSS. and printed editions change

सखे आगच्छ *sakhe ágachchha*, not into सखयागच्छ *sakhayágachchha*, but into सख आगच्छ *sakha ágachchha*.
सखे इह *sakhe iha*, not into सखयिह *sakhayiha*, but into सख इह *sakha iha*.
प्रभो एहि *prabho ehi*, not into प्रभवेहि *prabhavehi*, but into प्रभ एहि *prabha ehi*.
प्रभो औषधं *prabho aushadham*, not into प्रभवौषधं *prabhavaushadham*, but into प्रभ औषधं *prabha aushadham*.

2. The final य् *y* of आय् *ây*, which stands for ऐ *âi*, may be dropt before all vowels, and it is usual to drop it in our editions. Thus

श्रियै अर्थः *śriyai arthaḥ* is more usually written श्रिया अर्थः *śriyâ arthaḥ* instead of श्रियायर्थः *śriyâyarthaḥ*.

3. The final व् *v* of आव् *âv*, for औ *âu*, may be dropt before all vowels, but is more usually retained in our editions. Thus

तौ इति *tau iti* is more usually written ताविति *tâviti*, and not ता इति *tâ iti*.

Note—Before the particle उ *u* the dropping of the final य् *y* and व् *v* is obligatory.

§ 40. In all these cases the hiatus, occasioned by the dropping of य् *y* and व् *v*, remains, and the rules of Sandhi are not to be applied again.

§ 41. ए *e* and ओ *o*, before short अ *a*, remain unchanged, and the initial अ *a* is elided.

Ex. शिवे अत्र = शिवेऽत्र *śive atra* = *śive 'tra*, in Śiva there.

प्रभो अनुगृहाण = प्रभोऽनुगृहाण *prabho anugṛihâṇa* = *prabho 'nugṛihâṇa*, Lord, please.

In composition this elision is optional.

Ex. गो + अश्वाः = गोऽश्वाः or गोअश्वाः *go* + *aśvâḥ* = *go 'śvâḥ* or *go aśvâḥ*, cows and horses.

In some compounds गव *gava* must or may be substituted for गो *go*, if a vowel follows; गवाक्षः *gavâkshaḥ*, a window, lit. a bull's eye; गवेन्द्रः *gavendraḥ*, lord of kine, (a name of Kṛishṇa); गवाजिनं or गोऽजिनं *gavâjinam* or *go 'jinam*, a bull's hide.

Unchangeable Vowels (Pragṛihya).

§ 42. There are certain terminations the final vowels of which are not liable to any Sandhi rules. They are called *pragṛihya* vowels by Sanskrit grammarians. They are,

1. The terminations of the dual in ई *î*, ऊ *û*, and ए *e*, whether of nouns or verbs.

Ex. कवी इमौ *kavî imau*, these two poets.

गिरी एतौ *girî etau*, these two hills.

साधू इमौ *sâdhû imau*, these two merchants.

बन्धू आनय *bandhû ânaya*, bring the two friends.

लते एते *late ete*, these two creepers.

विद्ये इमे *vidye ime*, these two sciences.

शयेते अर्भकौ *śayete arbhakau*, the two children lie down.

शयावहे आवां *śayâvahe âvâm*, we two lie down.

याचेते अर्थं *yâchete artham*, they two ask for money.

Note—Exceptions occur, as मणीव *maṇîva*, i. e. मणी इव *maṇî iva*, like two jewels; दंपतीव *dampatîva*, i. e. दंपती इव *dampatî iva*, like husband and wife.

2. The terminations of अमी *amî* and अमू *amû*, the nom. plur. masc. and the nom. *dual* of the pronoun अदस् *adas*.

Ex. अमी अश्वाः *amî aśvâḥ*, these horses.
अमी इषवः *amî ishavaḥ*, these arrows.
अमू अर्भकौ *amû arbhakau*, these two children. (This follows from rule 1.)

Irregular Sandhi.

§ 43. The following are a few cases of irregular Sandhi which require to be stated. When a preposition ending in अ or आ *â* is followed by a verb beginning with ए *e* or ओ *o*, the result of the coalescence of the vowels is ए *e* or ओ *o*, not ऐ *ai* or औ *au*.

Ex. प्र + एजते = प्रेजते *pra + ejate = prejate.*
उप + एषते = उपेषते *upa + eshate = upeshate.*
प्र + एषयति = प्रेषयति *pra + eshayati = preshayati* *.
परा + एखति = परेखति *parâ + ekhati = parekhati.*
उप + ओषति = उपोषति *upa + oshati = uposhati.*
परा + ओहति = परोहति *parâ + ohati = parohati.*

This is not the case before the two verbs एध् *edh*, to grow, and इ *i*, to go, if raised by Guṇa to ए *e*.

Ex. उप + एधते = उपैधते *upa + edhate = upaidhate.*
अव + एति = अवैति *ava + eti = avaiti.*

In verbs derived from nouns, and beginning with ए or ओ *e* or *o*, the elision of the final अ or आ *â* of the preposition is optional.

§ 44. If a root beginning with ऋ *ṛi* is preceded by a preposition ending in अ *a* or आ *â*, the two vowels coalesce into आर् *âr* instead of अर् *ar*.

Ex. अप + ऋच्छति = अपार्च्छति *apa + ṛichchhati = apârchchhati.*
अव + ऋणाति = अवार्णाति *ava + ṛiṇâti = avârṇâti.*
प्र + ऋजते = प्रार्जते *pra + ṛijate = prârjate.*
परा + ऋषति = परार्षति *parâ + ṛishati = parârshati.*

In verbs derived from nouns and beginning with ऋ *ṛi*, this lengthening of the अ *a* of the preposition is optional.

In certain compounds ऋणं *ṛiṇam*, debt, and ऋतः *ṛitaḥ*, affected, take Vṛiddhi instead of Guṇa if preceded by अ *a*; प्र + ऋणं = प्रार्णं *pra + ṛiṇam = prârṇam*, principal debt; ऋण + ऋणं = ऋणार्णं *ṛiṇa + ṛiṇam = ṛiṇârṇam*, debt contracted to liquidate another debt; शोक + ऋतः = शोकार्तः *śoka + ṛitaḥ = śokârtaḥ*, affected by sorrow. Likewise ऊह् *ûh*, the substitute for वाह् *vâh*, carrying, forms Vṛiddhi with a preceding अ *a* in a compound. Thus विश्व + ऊहः *viśva + ûhaḥ*, the acc. plur. of विश्ववाह् *viśvavâh*, is विश्वौहः *viśvauhaḥ*.

---

* In nouns derived from प्रेष् *presh*, the rule is optional. Ex. प्रेष्य or प्रैष्य *preshya* or *praishya*, a messenger. प्रेष *presha*, a gleaner, is derived from प्र *pra* and ईष् *îsh*.

§ 45. If the initial ओ *o* in ओष्ठः *oshṭhaḥ*, lip, and ओतुः *otuḥ*, cat, is preceded in a compound by अ or आ *â*, the two vowels may coalesce into औ *au* or ओ *o*.

Ex. अधर + ओष्ठः = अधरौष्ठः or अधरोष्ठः *adhara + oshṭhaḥ = adharaushṭhaḥ* or *adharoshṭhaḥ*, the lower lip.

स्थूल + ओतुः = स्थूलौतुः or स्थूलोतुः *sthûla + otuḥ = sthûlautuḥ* or *sthûlotuḥ*, a big cat.

If ओष्ठ *oshṭha* and ओतु *otu* are preceded by अ or आ *â* in the middle of a sentence, they follow the general rule.

Ex. मम + ओष्ठः = ममौष्ठः *mama + oshṭhaḥ = mamaushṭhaḥ*, my lip.

§ 46. As irregular compounds the following are mentioned by native grammarians:

स्वैरं *svairam*, wilfulness, and स्वैरिन् *svairin*, self-willed, from स्व + ईर *sva + îra*.

अक्षौहिणी *akshauhiṇî*, a complete army, from अक्ष + ऊहिनी *aksha + ûhinî*.

प्रौढः *prauḍhaḥ*, from प्र + ऊढः *pra + ûḍhaḥ*, full-grown.

प्रौहः *prauhaḥ*, investigation, from प्र + ऊहः *pra + ûhaḥ*.

प्रैषः *praishaḥ*, a certain prayer, from प्र + एषः *pra + eshaḥ*. (See § 43.)

प्रैष्यः *praishyaḥ*, a messenger.

§ 47. The final ओ *o* of indeclinable words is not liable to the rules of Sandhi.

Ex. अहो अपेहि *aho apehi*, Halloo, go away!

§ 48. Indeclinables consisting of a single vowel, with the exception of आ *â* (§ 49), are not liable to the rules of Sandhi.

Ex. इ इन्द्र *i indra*, Oh Indra! उ उमेश *u umeśa*, Oh lord of Umâ!

आ एवं *â evam*, Is it so indeed?

§ 49. If आ *â* (which is written by Indian grammarians आङ् *âṅ*) is used as a preposition before verbs, or before nouns in the sense of 'so far as' (inclusively or exclusively) or 'a little,' it is liable to the rules of Sandhi.

Ex. आ अध्ययनात् = आध्ययनात् *â adhyayanât = âdhyayanât*, until the reading begins.

आ एकदेशात् = ऐकदेशात् *â ekadeśât = aikadeśât*, to a certain place.

आ आलोचितं = आलोचितं *â âlochitam = âlochitam*, regarded a little.

आ उष्णं = ओष्णं *â ushṇam = oshṇam*, a little warm.

आ इहि = एहि *â ihi = ehi*, come here.

If आ *â* is used as an interjection, it is not liable to Sandhi, according to § 48.

Ex. आ एवं किल तत् *â, evam kila tat*, Ah,—now I recollect,—it is just so.

§ 50. Certain particles remain unaffected by Sandhi.

Ex. हे इन्द्र *he indra*, O Indra.

§ 51. A protracted vowel remains unaffected by Sandhi.

Ex. देवदत्ता३ एहि *devadattâ 3 ehi*, Devadatta, come here!

§ 52. *Table showing the Combination of Final with Initial Vowels.*

FINAL.	WITH INITIAL. अ *a*	आ *á*	इ *i*	ई *í*	उ *u*	ऊ *ú*	ऋ *ṛi*	ॠ *ṛí*	ऌ *ḷi*	ए *e*	ऐ *ai*	ओ *o*	औ *au*
अ *a* आ *á*	आ *á*		ए *e*		ओ *o*		अर् *ar*		अल् *al*	ऐ *ai*		औ *au*	
इ *i* ई *í*	य *ya*	या *yá*	ई *í*		यु *yu*	यू *yú*	यृ *yṛi*	यॄ *yṛí*	यॢ *yḷi*	ये *ye*	यै *yai*	यो *yo*	यौ *yau*
उ *u* ऊ *ú*	व *va*	वा *vá*	वि *vi*	वी *ví*	ऊ *ú*		वृ *vṛi*	वॄ *vṛí*	वॢ *vḷi*	वे *ve*	वै *vai*	वो *vo*	वौ *vau*
ऋ *ṛi* ॠ *ṛí*	र *ra*	रा *rá*	रि *ri*	री *rí*	रु *ru*	रू *rú*	ॠ *ṛí*		र्ऌ *rḷi*	रे *re*	रै *rai*	रो *ro*	रौ *rau*
ऌ *ḷi*	ल *la*	ला *lá*	लि *li*	ली *lí*	लु *lu*	लू *lú*	लृ *lṛi*	लॄ *lṛí*	ॡ *ḷí*	ले *le*	लै *lai*	लो *lo*	लौ *lau*
ए *e*	एऽ *e'*	(अया *ayá* अ आ *a á*	अयि *ayi* अ इ *a i*	अयी *ayí* अ ई *a í*	अयु *ayu* अ उ *a u*	अयू *ayú* अ ऊ *a ú*	अयृ *ayṛi* अ ऋ *a ṛi*	अयॄ *ayṛí* अ ॠ *a ṛí*	अयॢ *ayḷi* अ ऌ *a ḷi*	अये *aye* अ ए *a e*	अयै *ayai* अ ऐ *a ai*	अयो *ayo* अ ओ *a o*	अयौ *ayau*) अ औ *a au*
ऐ *ai*	(आय *áya* आ अ *á a*	आया *áyá* आ आ *á á*	आयि *áyi* आ इ *á i*	आयी *áyí* आ ई *á í*	आयु *áyu* आ उ *á u*	आयू *áyú* आ ऊ *á ú*	आयृ *áyṛi* आ ऋ *á ṛi*	आयॄ *áyṛí* आ ॠ *á ṛí*	आयॢ *áyḷi* आ ऌ *á ḷi*	आये *áye* आ ए *á e*	आयै *áyai* आ ऐ *á ai*	आयो *áyo* आ ओ *á o*	आयौ *áyau*) आ औ *á au*
ओ *o*	ओऽ *o'*	अवा *avá* (अ आ *a á*	अवि *avi* अ इ *a i*	अवी *aví* अ ई *a í*	अवु *avu* अ उ *a u*	अवू *avú* अ ऊ *a ú*	अवृ *avṛi* अ ऋ *a ṛi*	अवॄ *avṛí* अ ॠ *a ṛí*	अवॢ *avḷi* अ ऌ *a ḷi*	अवे *ave* अ ए *a e*	अवै *avai* अ ऐ *a ai*	अवो *avo* अ ओ *a o*	अवौ *avau* अ औ *a au*)
औ *au*	आव *áva* (आ अ *á a*	आवा *ává* आ आ *á á*	आवि *ávi* आ इ *á i*	आवी *áví* आ ई *á í*	आवु *ávu* आ उ *á u*	आवू *ávú* आ ऊ *á ú*	आवृ *ávṛi* आ ऋ *á ṛi*	आवॄ *ávṛí* आ ॠ *á ṛí*	आवॢ *ávḷi* आ ऌ *á ḷi*	आवे *áve* आ ए *á e*	आवै *ávai* आ ऐ *á ai*	आवो *ávo* आ ओ *á o*	आवौ *ávau* आ औ *á au*)

Combination of Final and Initial Consonants.

§ 53. Here, as in the case of vowels, the rules which apply to the final consonants of words following each other in a sentence are equally applicable to the final consonants of words following each other in a compound. The final consonants of nominal bases too, before the so-called *Pada*-terminations (भ्याम् *bhyám*, भिः *bhiḥ*, भ्यः *bhyaḥ*, सु *su*) and before secondary (*taddhita*) suffixes beginning with any consonant but य् *y*, are treated according to the same rules. But the derivatives formed by means of these and other suffixes are best learnt from the dictionary in their ready-made state; while the changes of nominal and verbal bases ending in consonants, before the terminations of declension and conjugation and other suffixes, are regulated by different laws, and are best acquired in learning by heart the principal paradigms of nouns and verbs.

§ 54. In order to simplify the rules concerning the changes of final consonants, it is important to state at the outset that *eleven* only out of the thirty-five consonants can ever stand in Sanskrit at the end of a word; viz.

क् *k*, ङ् *ṅ*, ट् *ṭ*, ण् *ṇ*, त् *t*, न् *n*, प् *p*, म् *m*, ल् *l*, : *ḥ*, ं *ṁ*.

1. There are five classes of consonants, consisting of five letters each; thus giving twenty-five. In every one of these five classes the aspirates, if final, are replaced by their corresponding unaspirated letters: ख् *kh* by क् *k*; घ् *gh* by ग् *g*; छ् *chh*, however, not by च् *ch*, but by ट् *ṭ*. Ex. चित्रलिख् *chitralikh*, painter; voc. चित्रलिक् *chitralik*. This reduces the twenty-five letters to fifteen.

2. In every class the sonant (§ 58) letters, if final, are replaced by their corresponding surd letters; ग् *g* by क् *k*; ड् *d* by त् *t*, &c. Ex. हृद् *hṛid*, heart; nom. हृत् *hṛit*. This reduces the fifteen to ten*.

3. The palatal च् *ch* can never be final, but is replaced by the corresponding guttural क् *k*†. Ex. वाच् *vâch*, speech; voc. वाक् *vâk*. Final ञ् *ñ* does not occur. This reduces the ten to eight. In a few roots the final ज् *j* is replaced by a lingual instead of a guttural.

4. Of the semivowels, (य् *y*, र् *r*, ल् *l*, व् *v*,) ल् *l* is the only one that is found at the end of words. This raises the eight to nine letters.

5. ह् *h* cannot be final, but is changed into ट् *ṭ*; sometimes into क् *k* or त् *t*.

6. Of the sibilants, the only one that is found at the end of words is Visarga. For radical ष् *sh* cannot be final, but is replaced by ट् *ṭ*. Thus द्विष् *dvish*

* Some grammarians allow the soft or sonant letters as final, but the MSS. and editions generally change them into the corresponding hard letters.

† The only exceptions are technical terms such as अच् *ach*, a vowel; अजन्तः *ajantaḥ*, ending in a vowel, instead of अगन्तः *agantaḥ*.

becomes द्विट् *dviṭ*. In a few words final ष् *sh* is changed into क् *k* or Visarga.

Radical श् *ś* cannot be final, but is replaced by ट् *ṭ*. Thus विश् *viś* becomes विट् *viṭ*. In some words final श् *ś* is changed into क् *k*.

Final radical स् *s* is treated as Visarga.

The Visarga, therefore, raises the nine to ten; and the Anusvâra, to eleven letters, the only ones that can ever stand at the end of real words.

Hence the rules of Sandhi affecting final consonants are really reduced to *eleven* heads.

§ 55. It is important to observe that no word in Sanskrit ever ends in more than one consonant, the only exception being when an र् *r* precedes a final radical tenuis क् *k*, ट् *ṭ*, त् *t*, प् *p*. Thus

अबिभर् + त् = अबिभर् *abibhar* + *t* = *abibhar*, 3. p. sing. impf. of भृ *bhṛi*, to carry.

अबिभर् + स् = अबिभर् *abibhar* + *s* = *abibhar*, 2. p. sing. impf. of भृ *bhṛi*, to carry.

सुवल्ग् + स् = सुवल् *suvalg* + *s* = *suval*, nom. sing. well jumping.

But ऊर्क् *ûrk*, strength, nom. sing. of ऊर्ज् *ûrj*.

अवरीवर्त् *avarîvart*, 3. p. sing. impf. intens. of वृत् *vṛit* or वृध् *vṛidh*.

अमार्ट् *amârṭ*, from मृज् *mṛij*. (Pâṇ. VIII. 2, 24.)

The nom. sing. of चिकीर्ष् *chikîrsh* is चिकीः *chikîḥ*, because here the *r* is not followed by a tenuis.

Classification of Consonants.

§ 56. Before we can examine the changes of final and initial consonants, according to the rules of external Sandhi, we have to explain what is meant by the place and the quality of consonants.

1. The throat, the palate, the roof of the palate, the teeth, the lips, and the nose are called the places or organs of the letters. See § 4.
2. By contact between the tongue and the four places,—throat, palate, roof, teeth,—the guttural, palatal, lingual, and dental consonants are formed. Labial consonants are formed by contact between the lips.
3. In forming the nasals of the five classes the veil which separates the nose from the pharynx is withdrawn *. Hence these letters are called *Anunâsika*, i. e. co-nasal or nasalized.
4. The real Anusvâra is formed in the nose only, and is called *Nâsikya*, i.e. nasal.
5. The Visarga is said to be pronounced in the chest (*urasya*); the three or five sibilants in their respective places.
6. The semivowels, too, are referred to these five places, and three of them,

* Lectures on the Science of Language, Second Series, p. 145.

य *y*, ल *l*, व *v*, can be nasalized, and are then called *anunâsika*. (यँ, लँ, वँ, or यं, लं, वं, *ỹ*, *l̃*, *ṽ*.) र *r* cannot be nasalized in Sanskrit.

§ 57. According to their quality (*prayatna* *, effort) letters are divided into,

1. Letters formed by complete contact (*spṛishṭa*) of the organs: क *k*, ख *kh*, ग *g*, घ *gh*, ङ *ṅ*; च *ch*, छ *chh*, ज *j*, झ *jh*, ञ *ñ*; ट *ṭ*, ठ *ṭh*, ड *ḍ*, ढ *ḍh*, ण *ṇ*; त *t*, थ *th*, द *d*, ध *dh*, न *n*; प *p*, फ *ph*, ब *b*, भ *bh*, म *m*. These are called *Sparśa* in Sanskrit, and, if they did not comprehend the nasals, would correspond to the classical *mutes*.
2. Letters formed by slight contact (*ishat spṛishṭa*): य *y*, र *r*, ल *l*, व *v* (not ह *h*). These are called *Antaḥsthâ* (fem.), i. e. intermediate between Sparśas and Ûshmans, which has been freely translated by *semivowel* or *liquid*.
3. Letters formed by slight opening (*ishad vivṛita*): × *χ*, श *ś*, ष *sh*, स *s*, × *φ*, ह *h*. These are called *Ûshman* (flatus) in Sanskrit, which may be rendered by *sibilant* or *flatus*.
4. Vowels are said to be formed by complete opening (*vivṛita*) †.

§ 58. A second division, according to quality, is,

1. Surd letters: क *k*, ख *kh*, च *ch*, छ *chh*, ट *ṭ*, ठ *ṭh*, त *t*, थ *th*, प *p*, फ *ph*; × *χ*, श *ś*, ष *sh*, स *s*, × *φ*, and Visarga : *ḥ*. In their formation the glottis is open. They are called *Aghosha*, non-sonant.
2. Sonant letters: ग *g*, घ *gh*, ज *j*, झ *jh*, ड *ḍ*, ढ *ḍh*, द *d*, ध *dh*, ब *b*, भ *bh*, ङ *ṅ*, ञ *ñ*, ण *ṇ*, न *n*, म *m*; ह *h*, य *y*, र *r*, ल *l*, व *v*, the Anusvâra ं *ṁ*, and all vowels. In their formation the glottis is closed. They are called *Ghoshavat*.

§ 59. Lastly, consonants are divided, according to quality, into,

1. Aspirated (*mahâprâṇa*): ख *kh*, घ *gh*, छ *chh*, झ *jh*, ठ *ṭh*, ढ *ḍh*, थ *th*, ध *dh*, फ *ph*, भ *bh*; × *χ*, श *ś*, ष *sh*, स *s*, × *φ*; ह *h*; the Visarga : *ḥ* and Anusvâra ं *ṁ*.
2. Unaspirated (*alpaprâṇa*): all the rest.

It will be seen, therefore, that the change of च् *ch* into क् *k* is a change of place, and that the change of च् *ch* into ज् *j* is a change of quality; while in the

* Sanskrit grammarians call this आभ्यंतरः प्रयत्नः *âbhyantaraḥ prayatnaḥ*, mode of articulation preparatory to the utterance of the sound, and distinguish it from बाह्यः प्रयत्नः *vâhyaḥ prayatnaḥ*, mode of articulation at the close of the utterance of the sound, which produces the qualities of surd, sonant, aspirated, and unaspirated, as explained in § 58, 59.

† Some grammarians differ in their description of the degrees of closing or opening of the organs. Some ascribe to the semivowels *duḥspṛishṭa*, imperfect contact, or *ishadaspṛishṭa*, slight non-contact, or *ishadvivṛita*, slight opening; to the sibilants *nemaspṛishṭa*, half-contact, i. e. greater opening than is required for the semivowels, or *vivṛita*, complete opening; while they require for the vowels either *vivṛita*, complete opening, or *aspṛishṭa*, non-contact. Siddh.-Kaum. p. 10. Rig-veda-prâtiś. XIII. 3. In the Atharva-veda-prâtiśâkhya I. 33. we ought to read एकेऽस्पृष्टं *eke 'spṛishṭam* instead of एके स्पृष्टं *eke spṛishṭam*.

transition of च् *ch* into ग् *g*, or of ट् *ṭ* into न् *n*, we should have a change both of place and of quality.

§ 60. The changes which take place by the combination of the eleven final letters with initial vowels or consonants may be divided therefore into two classes.

Final letters are changed, 1. with regard to their places or organs, 2. with regard to their quality.

1. *Changes of Place.*

§ 61. The only final consonants which are liable to change of place are the Dentals, the Anusvâra, and Visarga. The Dentals, being incompatible with Palatals and Linguals, become palatal and lingual before these letters. Anusvâra and Visarga adapt themselves as much as possible to the place of the letter by which they are followed. All other changes of consonants are merely changes of quality; these in the case of Dentals, Anusvâra, and Visarga, being superadded to the changes of place.

§ 62. Final त् *t* before palatals (च् *ch*, छ् *chh*, ज् *j*, झ् *jh*, ञ् *ñ*, श् *ś*) is changed into a palatal.

Ex. तत् + च = तच्च *tat + cha = tachcha*, and this.

तत् + छिनत्ति = तच्छिनत्ति *tat + chhinatti = tachchhinatti*, he cuts this.

तत् + शृणोति = तच्शृणोति *tat + śriṇoti = tachśriṇoti*, he hears this *.

तत् + जायते = तज्जायते *tat + jâyate = tajjâyate*, this is born. The final त् *t* is changed into च् *ch* and then into ज् *j* according to § 66.

In composition, जगत् + जेता = जगज्जेता *jagat + jetâ = jagajjetâ*, conqueror of the world.

The same change would take place before an initial झ् *jh*; and before an initial ञ् *ñ*, त् *t* might become either ज् *j* or ञ् *ñ*. § 68.

§ 63. Final न् *n* before ज् *j*, झ् *jh*, ञ् *ñ*, and श् *ś* is changed to palatal ञ् *ñ*.

Ex. तान् + जयति = ताञ्जयति *tân + jayati = tâñjayati*, he conquers them.

Note—Rules on the changes of final न् *n* before च् *ch*, छ् *chh*, and श् *ś* will be given hereafter. See § 73, 74.

§ 64. Final त् *t* before ट् *ṭ*, ठ् *ṭh*, ड् *ḍ*, ढ् *ḍh*, ण् *ṇ* (not ष् *sh*, Pâṇ. VIII. 4, 43) is changed into a lingual.

Ex. तत् + डयते = तड्डयते *tat + ḍayate = taḍḍayate*. The final त् *t* is changed into ट् *ṭ* and then into ड् *ḍ* according to § 66.

In composition, तत् + टीका = तट्टीका *tat + ṭîkâ = taṭṭîkâ*, a gloss on this.

एतत् + ठक्कुरः = एतट्ठक्कुरः *etat + ṭhakkuraḥ = etaṭṭhakkuraḥ*, the idol of him.

The same change would take place before an initial ढ् *ḍh*; and before an initial ण् *ṇ*, त् *t* might become either ड् *ḍ* or ण् *ṇ*. § 68.

---

* श् *ś*, according to § 92, is generally changed to छ् *chh*: तच्छृणोति *tachchhriṇoti*.

§ 65. Final न् *n* before ड् *ḍ*, ढ् *ḍh*, ण् *ṇ* (not ष् *sh*, Pâṇ. VIII. 4, 43) is changed to ण् *ṇ*.

Ex. महान् + डामरः = महाण्डामरः *mahân + ḍâmaraḥ = mahâṇḍâmaraḥ*, a great uproar.

Note—Rules on the changes of न् *n* before ट् *ṭ* and ठ् *ṭh* (not ष् *sh*) will be given hereafter (§ 74). The changes of place with regard to final Anusvâra (*ṁ*) and Visarga (*ḥ*) will be explained together with the changes of quality to which these letters are liable.

2. *Changes of Quality.*

§ 66. Sonant initials require sonant finals.
Surd initials require surd finals.

As all final letters (except nasals and ल् *l*) are surd, they remain surd before surds. They are changed into their corresponding sonant letters before sonants.

As the nasals have no corresponding surd letters, they remain unchanged in quality, though followed by surd letters.

Examples: 1. क् *k* before sonants, changed into ग् *g*:

सम्यक् + उक्तं = सम्यगुक्तं *samyak + uktam = samyaguktam*, Well said!

धिक् + धनगर्वितं = धिग्धनगर्वितं *dhik + dhanagarvitam = dhigdhanagarvitam*, Fie on the purse-proud man!

In composition, दिक् + गजः = दिग्गजः *dik + gajaḥ = diggajaḥ*, an elephant supporting the globe at one of the eight points of the compass.

Before Pada-terminations: दिक् + भिः = दिग्भिः *dik + bhiḥ = digbhiḥ*, instrum. plur.

Before secondary suffixes beginning with consonants, except य् *y*: वाक् + मिन् = वाग्मिन् *vâk + min = vâgmin*, eloquent.

2. ट् *ṭ* before sonants, changed into ड् *ḍ*:

परिव्राट् + अयं = परिव्राडयं *parivrâṭ + ayam = parivrâḍayam*, he is a mendicant.

परिव्राट् + हसति = परिव्राड्हसति *parivrâṭ + hasati = parivrâḍ hasati*, the mendicant laughs; (also परिव्राड् ढसति *parivrâḍ ḍhasati*. § 70.)

In composition, परिव्राट् + मित्रं = परिव्राड्मित्रं *parivrâṭ + mitram = parivrâḍmitram*, a beggar's friend.

Before Pada-terminations: परिव्राट् + भिः = परिव्राड्भिः *parivrâṭ + bhiḥ = parivrâḍbhiḥ*.

3. प् *p* before sonants, changed into ब् *b*:

ककुप् + अत्र = ककुबत्र *kakup + atra = kakubatra*, a region there, (inflectional base ककुभ् *kakubh*.)

अप् + घटः = अब्घटः *ap + ghaṭaḥ = abghaṭaḥ*, a water-jar.

अप् + जयः = अब्जयः *ap + jayaḥ = abjayaḥ*, obtaining water.

अप् + मयः = अम्मयः *ap + mayaḥ = ammayaḥ*, watery. § 69.

ककुप् + भिः = ककुब्भिः *kakup + bhiḥ = kakubbhiḥ*, instrum. plur.

4. त् *t* before sonants, changed into द् *d*, except before sonant palatals and linguals, when (according to § 62) it is changed into ज् *j* and ड् *ḍ*:

सरित् + अत्र = सरिदत्र *sarit + atra = saridatra*, the river there.

जगत् + ईशः = जगदीशः *jagat + îśaḥ = jagadîśaḥ*, lord of the world.

महत् + धनुः = महद्धनुः *mahat + dhanuḥ = mahaddhanuḥ*, a large bow.

महत् + भिः = महद्भिः *mahat + bhiḥ = mahadbhiḥ*, instrum. plur.

त् *t* before sonant palatals, changed into ज् *j*: see § 62:

सरित् + जलं = सरिज्जलं *sarit + jalam = sarijjalam*, water of the river.

त् *t* before sonant linguals, changed into ड् *ḍ*: see § 62:

एतत् + डामरः = एतड्डामरः *etat + ḍâmaraḥ = etaḍḍâmaraḥ*, the uproar of them.

Note—There are exceptions to this rule, but they are confined to Taddhita derivatives which are found in dictionaries. Thus final त् *t* before the possessive suffixes मत् *mat*, वत् *vat*, विन् *vin*, वल *vala* is not changed. Ex. विद्युत् + वत् = विद्युत्वत् *vidyut + vat = vidyutvat*, possessed of lightning. Final स् *s* too, which represents Visarga, remains unchanged before the same Taddhitas. Thus तेजस् + विन् = तेजस्विन् *tejas + vin = tejasvin*, instead of तेजोविन् *tejovin*; see § 84. 3. ज्योतिस् + मत् = ज्योतिष्मत् *jyotis + mat = jyotishmat*, instead of ज्योतिर्मत् *jyotirmat*. § 84.

§ 67. त् *t* before ल् *l* is not changed into द् *d*, but into ल् *l*.

Ex. तत् + लब्धं = तल्लब्धं *tat + labdham = tallabdham*, this is taken.

बृहत् + ललाटं = बृहल्ललाटं *bṛihat + lalâṭam = bṛihallalâṭam*, a large forehead.

§ 68. Additional changes take place if the final surds क् *k*, ट् *ṭ*, त् *t*, प् *p* are followed by nasals, chiefly न् *n* and म् *m*. The nasals being sonant, they require the change of क् *k*, ट् *ṭ*, त् *t*, and प् *p* into ग् *g*, ड् *ḍ*, द् *d*, and ब् *b*; but these final sonants may be further infected by the nasal character of the initial nasals, and may be written ङ् *ṅ*, ण् *ṇ*, न् *n*, म् *m*.

Ex. दिक् + नागः = दिग्नागः or दिङ्नागः *dik + nâgaḥ = dignâgaḥ* or *diṅnâgaḥ*, a world-elephant.

मधुलिट् + नर्दति = मधुलिड्नर्दति or मधुलिण्णर्दति *madhuliṭ + nardati = madhuliḍnardati* or *madhuliṇnardati*, the bee hums.

जगत् + नाथः = जगद्नाथः or जगन्नाथः *jagat + nâthaḥ = jagadnâthaḥ* or *jagannâthaḥ*, lord of the world.

अप् + नदी = अब्नदी or अम्नदी *ap + nadî = abnadî* or *amnadî*, water-river.

प्राक् + मुखः = प्राग्मुखः or प्राङ्मुखः *prâk + mukhaḥ = prâgmukhaḥ* or *prâṅmukhaḥ*, facing the east.

भवत् + मतं = भवद्मतं or भवन्मतं *bhavat + matam = bhavadmatam* or *bhavanmatam*, your opinion.

Note—If a word should begin with a palatal or lingual *n* (ञ् *ñ* or ण् *ṇ*) then a final त् *t* would change its place or organ at the same time that it became a nasal. It would become ञ् *ñ* or ण् *ṇ*. There are, however, no words in common use beginning with ञ *ñ* or ण *ṇ*.

§ 69. Before the suffix मय *maya* and before मात्र *mâtra* the change into the nasal is not optional, but obligatory.

Ex. वाक् + मयं = वाङ्मयं *vâk + mayam = vâṅmayam*, consisting of speech.
मधुलिट् + मात्रं = मधुलिण्मात्रं *madhuliṭ + mâtram = madhuliṇmâtram*, merely a bee.
तत् + मात्रं = तन्मात्रं *tat + mâtram = tanmâtram*, element.

Note—Ninety-six is always षण्णवति *shaṇṇavati*, never षड्नवति *shaḍnavati*.

§ 70. The initial ह् *h*, if brought into immediate contact with a final क् *k* (ग् *g*), ट् *ṭ* (ड् *ḍ*), त् *t* (द् *d*), प् *p* (ब् *b*), is commonly, not necessarily, changed into the sonant aspirate of the class of the final letter; घ *gh*, ढ *ḍh*, ध *dh*, भ *bh*.

Ex. धिक् + हस्तिनः = धिग्हस्तिनः or धिग्घस्तिनः *dhik + hastinaḥ = dhighastinaḥ* or *dhigghastinaḥ*, Fie on the elephants!
परिव्राट् + हतः = परिव्राड्हतः or परिव्राड्ढतः *parivrâṭ + hataḥ = parivrâḍhataḥ* or *parivrâḍḍhataḥ*, the mendicant is killed.
तत् + हुतं = तद्हुतं or तद्धुतं *tat + hutam = tadhutam* or *taddhutam*, this is sacrificed.
अप् + हरणं = अब्हरणं or अब्भरणं *ap + haraṇam = abharaṇam* or *abbharaṇam*, water-fetching.

§ 71. Final ङ् *ṅ*, ण् *ṇ*, and न् *n*, preceded by a short vowel and followed by any vowel, are doubled.

Ex. धावन् + अश्वः = धावन्नश्वः *dhâvan + aśvaḥ = dhâvannaśvaḥ*, a running horse.
प्रत्यङ् + आस्ते = प्रत्यङ्ङास्ते *pratyaṅ + âste = pratyaṅṅâste*, he sits turned toward the west.
सुगण् + आस्ते = सुगण्णास्ते *sugaṇ + âste = sugaṇṇâste*, he sits counting well*.

If ङ् *ṅ*, ण् *ṇ*, and न् *n* are preceded by a long vowel and followed by any vowel, no change takes place.

Ex. कवीन् + आह्वयस्व *kavîn âhvayasva*, call the poets.

§ 72. Final ङ् *ṅ* and ण् *ṇ* may be followed by initial श् *ś*, ष् *sh*, स् *s* without causing any change; but it is optional to add a क् *k* after the ङ् *ṅ* and a ट् *ṭ* after the ण् *ṇ*. Thus ङ्श *ṅśa* becomes ङ्क्श *ṅkśa* (or ङ्क्छ *ṅkchha*, § 92); ङ्ष *ṅsha* becomes ङ्क्ष *ṅksha*; ङ्स *ṅsa* becomes ङ्क्स *ṅksa*; ण्श *ṇśa* becomes ण्ट्श *ṇṭśa* (or ण्ट्छ *ṇṭchha*); ण्ष *ṇsha* becomes ण्ट्ष *ṇṭsha*; ण्स *ṇsa* becomes ण्ट्स *ṇṭsa*.

Ex. प्राङ् + शेते = प्राङ्शेते or प्राङ्क्शेते (or प्राङ्क्छेते) *prâṅ + śete = prâṅśete* or *prâṅkśete* (or *prâṅkchhete*).

---

* Technical terms like उणादि *uṇâdi*, a list of suffixes beginning with उण्, or तिङन्त *tiṅanta*, words ending in *tiṅ*, are exempt from this rule. See also Wilkins, Sanskrita Grammar, § 30.

सुगण् + सरति = सुगण्सरति or सुगण्ट्सरति *sugaṇ + sarati = sugaṇsarati* or *sugaṇṭsarati.*

§ 73. The same rule applies to final न् *n* before श् *ś* and स् *s*, but not before ष् *sh*, where it remains unchanged. Before श् *ś* it is first changed into palatal ञ् *ñ** (§ 63); and ञ्श् *ñś* may again be changed to ञ्च्श् *ñchś*, ञ्च्छ् *ñchchh* (§ 72, 92), or ञ्छ् *ñchh*. Before स् *s*, न् *n* may remain unchanged, or न्स् *ns* may be changed into न्त्स् *nts*.

Ex. तान् + षट् = तान्षट् *tân + shaṭ = tânshaṭ*, those six.

तान् + शार्दूलान् = ताञ्शार्दूलान् or ताञ्च्शार्दूलान् or ताञ्च्छार्दूलान् or ताञ्छार्दूलान् *tân + śârdûlân = tâñśârdûlân* or *tâñchśârdûlân* or *tâñchchhârdûlân* or *tâñchhârdûlân*, those tigers.

तान् + सहते = तान्सहते or तान्त्सहते *tân + sahate = tânsahate* or *tântsahate*, he bears them.

हिन् (हिंस्) + सु = हिन्सु or हिन्त्सु *hin (hiṁs) + su = hinsu* or *hintsu*, among enemies. (The base हिंस् *hiṁs*, before the सु *su* of the loc. plur., is treated as a Pada.) See § 53, 55.

§ 74. Final न् *n* before initial क् *k*, ख् *kh*, and प् *p*, फ् *ph*, remains unchanged.
Final न् *n* before च् *ch*, छ् *chh*, requires the intercession of श् *ś*.
Final न् *n* before ट् *ṭ*, ठ् *ṭh*, requires the intercession of ष् *sh*.
Final न् *n* before त् *t*, थ् *th*, requires the intercession of स् *s*.

Before these inserted sibilants the original न् *n* is changed to Anusvâra.

Ex. हसन् + चकार = हसंश्चकार *hasan + chakâra = hasaṁśchakâra*, he did it laughing.

धावन् + छागः = धावंश्छागः *dhâvan + chhâgaḥ = dhâvaṁśchhâgaḥ*, a running goat.

चलन् + टिट्टिभः = चलंष्टिट्टिभः *chalan + ṭiṭṭibhaḥ = chalaṁshṭiṭṭibhaḥ*, a moving ṭiṭṭibha-bird.

महान् + ठक्कुरः = महांष्ठक्कुरः *mahân + ṭhakkuraḥ = mahâṁshṭhakkuraḥ*, a great idol.

पतन् + तरुः = पतंस्तरुः *patan + taruḥ = pataṁstaruḥ*, a falling tree.

Note—प्रशान् *praśân*, quiet, forms the nom. प्रशान् *praśân;* but this final न् *n* is treated before च् *ch*, छ् *chh*, ट् *ṭ*, ठ् *ṭh*, त् *t*, थ् *th*, like a final म् *m*. Ex. प्रशान् + चिनोति = प्रशांचिनोति, i.e. प्रशाञ्चिनोति *praśân + chinoti = praśâñchinoti;* not प्रशांश्चिनोति *praśâṁśchinoti*. (Pâṇ. VIII. 3, 7.)

§ 75. Final न् *n* before ल् *l* is changed into ल् *l*. This ल् *l* is pronounced through the nose, and is written with the Anusvâra dot over it. It is usual in this case to write the Anusvâra as a half-moon, called *Arddha-chandra.*

Ex. महान् + लाभः = महाँल्लाभः *mahân + lâbhaḥ = mahâl̐ lâbhaḥ*, large gain.

* To allow न् *n* to remain unchanged before श् *ś* is a misprint which occurred in Benfey's large grammar, but has long been corrected by that scholar.

§ 76. A final ट् *ṭ* before स् *s* may remain unchanged, or त् *t* may be inserted.

Ex. षट् + सरितः = षट्सरितः or षट्त्सरितः *shaṭ* + *saritaḥ* = *shaṭsaritaḥ* or *shaṭtsaritaḥ*, six rivers.

Anusvâra and Final म् m.

§ 77. म् *m* at the end of words remains unchanged if followed by any initial vowel.

Ex. किम् + अत्र *kim* + *atra* = किमत्र *kimatra*, What is there?

Before consonants it may, without exception, be changed to Anusvâra.

This is the general rule. The exceptions are simply optional, viz.

Before क् *k*, ख् *kh*, ग् *g*, घ् *gh*, ङ् *ṅ*, the final म् *m* or Anusvâra may be changed into ङ् *ṅ*.
Before च् *ch*, छ् *chh*, ज् *j*, झ् *jh*, ञ् *ñ*, to ञ् *ñ*.
Before ट् *ṭ*, ठ् *ṭh*, ड् *ḍ*, ढ् *ḍh*, ण् *ṇ*, to ण् *ṇ*.
Before त् *t*, थ् *th*, द् *d*, ध् *dh*, न् *n*, to न् *n*.
Before प् *p*, फ् *ph*, ब् *b*, भ् *bh*, म् *m*, to म् *m*.
Before य् *y*, ल् *l*, व् *v*, to यँ *ỹ*, लँ *l̃*, वँ *ṽ*. See § 56. 6.

Hence it follows that final म् m *may* be changed into Anusvâra before all consonants, and *must* be so changed only before श् *ś*, ष् *sh*, स् *s*, ह् *h*, and र् *r*, the five consonants which have no corresponding nasal class-letter.

It would be most desirable if scholars would never avail themselves of the optional change of final Anusvâra into ङ् *ṅ*, ञ् *ñ*, ण् *ṇ*, न् *n*, म् *m*. We should then be spared a number of compound letters which are troublesome both in writing and printing; and we should avoid the ambiguity as to the original nature of these class-nasals when followed by initial sonant palatals, linguals, and dentals. Thus if तां जयति *tâṁ jayati*, he conquers her, is written ताञ्जयति *tâñ jayati*, it may be taken for तान् जयति *tân jayati*, he conquers them, which, according to § 63, must be changed into ताञ्जयति *tâñ jayati*. In the same manner तान्दमयति *tân damayati* may be either तान् दमयति *tân damayati*, he tames them, or ताम् दमयति *tâm damayati*, he tames her. All this uncertainty is at once removed if final म् *m* is always changed into Anusvâra, whatever be the initial consonant of the following word.

§ 78. म् *m* at the end of a word *in pausâ*, i. e. at the end of a sentence, remains unchanged. Some grammarians (§ 8, note) allow its being changed into Anusvâra, and it is written so throughout in this grammar. Ex. एवं *evaṁ*, thus, (or एवम् *evam*.)

Ex. किम् + करोषि = किं करोषि (or किङ्करोषि) *kim* + *karoshi* = *kiṁ karoshi* (or *kiṅ karoshi*), What doest thou?

शत्रुम् + जहि = शत्रुं जहि (or शत्रुञ्जहि) *śatrum* + *jahi* = *śatruṁ jahi* (or *śatruñ jahi*), kill the enemy.

नदीम् + तरति = नदीं तरति (or नदीन्तरति) *nadím + tarati = nadíṁ tarati* (or *nadín tarati*), he crosses the river.

गुरुम् + नमति = गुरुं नमति (or गुरुन्नमति) *gurum + namati = guruṁ namati* (or *gurun namati*), he salutes the teacher.

किम् + फलं = किं फलं (or किम्फलं) *kim + phalam = kiṁ phalam* (or *kim phalam*), What is the use?

शास्त्रम् + मीमांसते = शास्त्रं मीमांसते (or शास्त्रम्मीमांसते) *śástram + mímáṁsate = śástraṁ mímáṁsate* (or *śástram mímáṁsate*), he studies the book.

Before य् *y*, ल् *l*, व् *v*:

सत्वरम् + याति = सत्वरं याति (or सत्वरय्ँयाति) *satvaram + yáti = satvaraṁ yáti* (or *satvaray̐ yáti*), he walks quickly.

विद्याम् + लभते = विद्यां लभते (or विद्याल्ँलभते) *vidyám + labhate = vidyáṁ labhate* (or *vidyál̐ labhate*), he acquires wisdom.

तम् + वेद = तं वेद (or तव्ँवेद) *tam + veda = taṁ veda* (or *tav̐ veda*), I know him.

Before र् *r*, श् *ś*, ष् *sh*, स् *s*, ह् *h*:

करुणम् + रोदिति = करुणं रोदिति *karuṇam + roditi = karuṇaṁ roditi*, he cries piteously.

शय्यायाम् + शेते = शय्यायां शेते *śayyáyám + śete = śayyáyáṁ śete*, he lies on the couch.

मोक्षम् + सेवेत = मोक्षं सेवेत *moksham + seveta = mokshaṁ seveta*, let a man cultivate spiritual freedom.

मधुरम् + हसति = मधुरं हसति *madhuram + hasati = madhuraṁ hasati*, he laughs sweetly.

§ 79. Final म् *m* before ह् *h*, if ह् *h* be immediately followed by न् *n*, म् *m*, य् *y*, ल् *l*, व् *v*, may be treated as if it were immediately followed by these letters. See, however, § 77.

Ex. किम् + ह्नुते = किं ह्नुते or किन्ह्नुते *kim + hnute = kiṁ hnute* or *kin hnute*, What does he hide?

किम् + ह्यः = किं ह्यः or किय्ँ ह्यः *kim + hyaḥ = kiṁ hyaḥ* or *kiy̐ hyaḥ*, What about yesterday?

किम् + ह्मलयति = किं ह्मलयति or किम्ह्मलयति *kim + hmalayati = kiṁ hmalayati* or *kimhmalayati*, What does he move?

§ 80. If कृ *kṛi* is preceded by the preposition सम् *sam*, an स् *s* is inserted, and म् *m* changed to Anusvâra.

Ex. सम् + कृतः = संस्कृतः *sam + kṛitaḥ = saṁskṛitaḥ*, hallowed.

§ 81. In सम्राज् *samráj*, nom. सम्राट् *samráṭ*, king, म् *m* is never changed.

Visarga and Final स् *s and* र् *r.*

§ 82. The phonetic changes of final sibilants, which are considered the most difficult, may be reduced to a few very simple rules. It should only be borne in mind:

1. That there are really five sibilants, and not three; that the signs for the guttural and labial sibilants became obsolete, and were replaced by the two dots (:) which properly belong to the Visarga only, i. e. to the unmodified sibilant.
2. That all sibilants and Visarga are surd, and that their proper corresponding sonant is the र् *r*.

§ 83. The only sibilant which can be final *in pausâ* is the Visarga. If Visarga is followed by a surd letter, it is changed into the sibilant of that class to which the following surd letter belongs.

It should be observed, however, that the guttural and labial sibilants are now written by : *ḥ*, and that the same sign may also be used instead of any sibilant, if followed by a sibilant.

Ex. ततः + कामः = ततः कामः (originally ततχ कामः) *tataḥ* + *kâmaḥ* = *tataḥ kâmaḥ* (originally *tataχ kâmaḥ*), hence love.

पूर्णः + चंद्रः = पूर्णश्चंद्रः *pûrṇaḥ* + *chandraḥ* = *pûrṇaś chandraḥ*, the full moon.

तरोः + छाया = तरोश्छाया *taroḥ* + *chhâyâ* = *taroś chhâyâ*, the shade of the tree.

भीतः + टलति = भीतष्टलति *bhîtaḥ* + *ṭalati* = *bhîtashṭalati*, the frightened man is disturbed.

भग्नः + ठक्कुरः = भग्नष्ठक्कुरः *bhagnaḥ* + *ṭhakkuraḥ* = *bhagnashṭhakkuraḥ*, the broken idol.

नद्याः + तीरं = नद्यास्तीरं *nadyâḥ* + *tîram* = *nadyâstîram*, the border of the river.

नद्याः + पारं = नद्याः पारं (originally नद्याɸ पारं) *nadyâḥ* + *pâram* = *nadyâḥ pâram* (originally *nadyâ ɸ pâram*), the opposite shore of a river.

Visarga before sibilants:

सुप्तः + शिशुः = सुप्तश्शिशुः or सुप्तः शिशुः *suptaḥ* + *śiśuḥ* = *suptaś śiśuḥ* or *suptaḥ śiśuḥ*, the child sleeps.

भागः + षोडशः = भागष्षोडशः or भागः षोडशः *bhâgaḥ* + *shoḍaśaḥ* = *bhâgash shoḍaśaḥ* or *bhâgaḥ shoḍaśaḥ*, a sixteenth part.

प्रथमः + सर्गः = प्रथमस्सर्गः or प्रथमः सर्गः *prathamaḥ* + *sargaḥ* = *prathamas-sargaḥ* or *prathamaḥ sargaḥ*, the first section.

Note 1—If Visarga is followed by an initial त्स् *ts*, it is not necessarily changed into dental स् *s*, but may remain Visarga, as if followed by स् *s*.

Ex. शठः + त्सरति = शठः त्सरति *śaṭhaḥ + tsarati = śaṭhaḥ tsarati*, a wicked man cheats.

कः + त्सरुः = कः त्सरुः *kaḥ + tsaruḥ = kaḥ tsaruḥ*, Which is the handle of the sword?

Note 2—If, on the contrary, Visarga is followed by a sibilant with a surd letter, the Visarga is frequently dropt in MSS. (Pâṇ. VIII. 3, 36, v.)

Ex. देवाः + स्थ = देवाः स्थ or देवा स्थ *devâḥ + stha = devâḥ stha* or *devâ stha*, you are gods; (also देवास्स्थ *devâs stha*.)

हरिः + स्फुरति = हरिः स्फुरति or हरि स्फुरति *hariḥ + sphurati = hariḥ sphurati* or *hari sphurati*, Hari appears.

Note 3—If nouns ending in इस् *is* or उस् *us*, like हविः *haviḥ* or धनुः *dhanuḥ*, are followed by words beginning with क् *k*, ख् *kh*, प् *p*, फ् *ph*, and are governed by these words, ष् *sh* may be substituted for final Visarga. सर्पिष्पिबति or सर्पिः पिबति *sarpishpibati* or *sarpiḥ pibati*, he drinks ghee; but तिष्ठतु सर्पिः पिब त्वमुदकं *tishṭhatu sarpiḥ, piba tvam udakam*, let the ghee stand, drink thou water.

§ 84. If final Visarga is followed by a sonant letter, consonant or vowel, the *general* rule is that it be changed into र् *r*. (See, however, § 86.) This rule admits, however, of the following exceptions:

1. If the Visarga is preceded by आ *â*, and followed by a sonant letter (vowel or consonant), the Visarga is dropt.
2. If the Visarga is preceded by अ *a*, and followed by any vowel except अ *a*, the Visarga is dropt.
3. If the Visarga is preceded by अ *a*, and followed by a sonant consonant, the Visarga is dropt, and the अ *a* changed to ओ *o*.
4. If the Visarga is preceded by अ *a*, and followed by अ *a*, the Visarga is dropt, अ *a* changed into ओ *o*, and the initial अ *a* elided. The sign of the elision is ऽ, called *Avagraha*.

Examples of the general rule:

कविः + अयं = कविरयं *kaviḥ + ayam = kavirayam*, this poet.

रविः + उदेति = रविरुदेति *raviḥ + udeti = ravir udeti*, the sun rises.

गौः + गच्छति = गौर्गच्छति *gauḥ + gachchhati = gaur gachchhati*, the ox walks.

विष्णुः + जयति = विष्णुर्जयति *vishṇuḥ + jayati = vishṇur jayati*, Vishṇu is victorious.

पशोः + बंधः = पशोर्बंधः *paśoḥ + bandhaḥ = paśorbandhaḥ*, the binding of the cattle.

मुहुः + मुहुः = मुहुर्मुहुः *muhuḥ + muhuḥ = muhurmuhuḥ*, gradually.

वायुः + वाति = वायुर्वाति *vâyuḥ + vâti = vâyur vâti*, the wind blows.

शिशुः + हसति = शिशुर्हसति *śiśuḥ + hasati = śiśur hasati*, the child laughs.

निः + धनः = निर्धनः *niḥ + dhanaḥ = nirdhanaḥ*, without wealth.

दुः + नीतिः = दुर्नीतिः *duḥ + nîtiḥ = durṇîtiḥ*, of bad manners.

ज्योतिः + भिः = ज्योतिर्भिः *jyotiḥ + bhiḥ = jyotirbhiḥ*, instrum. plur.

Examples of the first exception:

अश्वाः + अमी = अश्वा अमी *aśvâḥ + amî = aśvâ amî*, these horses.

आगताः + ऋषयः = आगता ऋषयः *âgatâḥ + ṛishayaḥ = âgatâ ṛishayaḥ*, the poets have arrived.

हताः + गजाः = हता गजाः *hatâḥ + gajâḥ = hatâ gajâḥ*, the elephants are killed.

उन्नताः + नगाः = उन्नता नगाः *unnatâḥ + nagâḥ = unnatâ nagâḥ*, the high mountains.

छात्राः + यतन्ते = छात्रा यतन्ते *chhâtrâḥ + yatante = chhâtrâ yatante*, the pupils strive.

माः + भिः = माभिः *mâḥ + bhiḥ = mâbhiḥ*, instrum. plur. of मास् *mâs*, moon.

Examples of the second exception:

कुतः + आगतः = कुत आगतः *kutaḥ + âgataḥ = kuta âgataḥ*, Whence come?

कः + एषः = क एषः *kaḥ + eshaḥ = ka eshaḥ*, Who is he?

कः + ऋषिः = क ऋषिः *kaḥ + ṛishiḥ = ka ṛishiḥ*, Who is the poet?

मनः + आदि = मन आदि *manaḥ + âdi = mana âdi*, beginning with mind.

Examples of the third exception:

शोभनः + गन्धः = शोभनो गन्धः *śobhanaḥ + gandhaḥ = śobhano gandhaḥ*, a sweet scent.

नूतनः + घटः = नूतनो घटः *nûtanaḥ + ghaṭaḥ = nûtano ghaṭaḥ*, a new jar.

मूर्धन्यः + णकारः = मूर्धन्यो णकारः *mûrdhanyaḥ + ṇakâraḥ = mûrdhanyo ṇakâraḥ*, the lingual ṇ.

निर्वाणः + दीपः = निर्वाणो दीपः *nirvâṇaḥ + dîpaḥ = nirvâṇo dîpaḥ*, the lamp is blown out.

अतीतः + मासः = अतीतो मासः *atîtaḥ + mâsaḥ = atîto mâsaḥ*, the past month.

कृतः + यत्नः = कृतो यत्नः *kṛitaḥ + yatnaḥ = kṛito yatnaḥ*, effort is made.

मनः + रमः = मनोरमः *manaḥ + ramaḥ = manoramaḥ*, (a compound), pleasing to the mind, delightful.

मनः + भिः = मनोभिः *manaḥ + bhiḥ = manobhiḥ*, instrum. plur.

Examples of the fourth exception:

नरः + अयं = नरोऽयं *naraḥ + ayam = naro 'yam*, this man.

वेदः + अधीतः = वेदोऽधीतः *vedaḥ + adhîtaḥ = vedo 'dhîtaḥ*, the Veda has been read.

अयः + अस्त्रं = अयोऽस्त्रं *ayaḥ + astram = ayo 'stram*, an iron-weapon.

§ 85. There are a few words in which the final letter is etymologically र् *r**.

---

* It is called रजातो विसर्गः *rajâto visargaḥ*, the Visarga produced from *r*. It occurs, preceded by अ *a*, in पुनः *punaḥ*, again; प्रातः *prâtaḥ*, early; अन्तः *antaḥ*, within; स्वः *svaḥ*, heaven; in the voc. sing. of nouns in ऋ *ṛi*, ex. पितः *pitaḥ*, father, from पितृ *pitṛi*, &c.; and in verbal forms such as अजागर् *ajâgar*, 2. 3. sing. impf. of जागृ *jâgṛi*.

This र् *r*, as a final, is changed into Visarga, according to § 82, and it follows all the rules affecting the Visarga except the exceptional rules § 84. 2, 3, 4; i.e. if preceded by अ *a*, and followed by any sonant letter, vowel or consonant, the र् *r* is retained.

Ex. पुनः + अपि = पुनरपि *punaḥ + api = punarapi*, even again.
प्रातः + एव = प्रातरेव *prâtaḥ + eva = prâtareva*, very early.
भ्रातः + देहि = भ्रातर्देहि *bhrâtaḥ + dehi = bhrâtar dehi*, Brother, give!

§ 86. No र् *r* can ever be followed by another र् *r*. Hence final Visarga, whether etymologically स् *s* or र् *r*, if followed by initial र् *r*, and therefore by § 84 changed to र् *r*, is dropt, and its preceding vowel lengthened.

Ex. विधुः + राजते = विधू राजते *vidhuḥ + râjate = vidhû râjate*, the moon shines.
भ्रातः + रक्ष = भ्राता रक्ष *bhrâtaḥ + raksha = bhrâtâ raksha*, Brother, protect!
पुनः + रोगी = पुना रोगी *punaḥ + rogî = punâ rogî*, ill again.

These are the general rules on the Sandhi of final Visarga, स् *s* and र् *r*. The following rules refer to a few exceptional cases.

§ 87. The two pronouns सः *saḥ* and एषः *eshaḥ*, this, become स *sa* and एष *esha* before consonants and vowels, except before short अ *a* and at the end of a sentence.

Ex. सः + ददाति = स ददाति *saḥ + dadâti = sa dadâti*, he gives.
सः इंद्रः = स इंद्रः *saḥ indraḥ = sa indraḥ*, this Indra. The two vowels are not liable to Sandhi.

But सः + अभवत् = सोऽभवत् *saḥ + abhavat = so 'bhavat*, he was.
मृतः सः *mṛitaḥ saḥ*, he is dead.

Sometimes Sandhi takes place, particularly for the sake of the metre. Thus स एष *sa esha* becomes occasionally सैष *saisha*, he, this person. स इंद्रः *sa indraḥ* appears as सेंद्रः *sendraḥ*. (Pâṇ. VI. 1, 134.)

The pronoun स्यः *syaḥ*, he, follows the same rule optionally in poetry. (Pâṇ. VI. 1, 133.)

§ 88. भोः *bhoḥ*, an irregular vocative of भवत् *bhavat*, thou, drops its Visarga before all vowels and all sonant consonants.

Ex. भोः + ईशान = भो ईशान *bhoḥ + îśâna = bho îśâna*, Oh lord!
भोः + देवाः = भो देवाः *bhoḥ + devâḥ = bho devâḥ*, Oh gods!

The same applies to the interjections भगोः *bhagoḥ* and अघोः *aghoḥ*, really irregular vocatives of भगवत् *bhagavat*, God, and अघवत् *aghavat*, sinner.

§ 89. Numerous exceptions, which are best learnt from the dictionary, occur in compound and derivative words. A few of the more important may here be mentioned.

I. *Nouns in* अस् as, इस् is, उस् us, *forming the first part of a Compound.*

1. Before derivatives of कृ *kṛi*, to do (e. g. कर *kara*, कार *kâra*), before derivatives of कम् *kam*, to desire (e. g. कांत *kânta*, काम *kâma*), before कंस *kaṁsa*, goblet, कुंभ *kumbha*, jar, पात्र *pâtra*, vessel, कुशा *kuśâ*, counter, कर्णी *karṇî*, ear, the final Visarga of bases in अस् *as* is changed to स् *s*. (Pâṇ. VIII. 3, 46.)

Ex. श्रेयः + करः = श्रेयस्करः *śreyaḥ + karaḥ = śreyaskaraḥ*, making happy.
अहः + करः = अहस्करः *ahaḥ + karaḥ = ahaskaraḥ*, sun.
अयः + कुंभः = अयस्कुंभः *ayaḥ + kumbhaḥ = ayaskumbhaḥ*, iron-pot.

There are several words of the same kind—which are best learnt from the dictionary—in which the Visarga is changed into dental sibilant. (Pâṇ. VIII. 3, 47.)

Ex. अधः + पदं = अधस्पदं *adhaḥ + padam = adhaspadam*.
दिवः + पतिः = दिवस्पतिः *divaḥ + patiḥ = divaspatiḥ*, lord of heaven.
वाचः + पतिः = वाचस्पतिः *vâchaḥ + patiḥ = vâchaspatiḥ*, lord of speech.
भाः + करः = भास्करः *bhâḥ + karaḥ = bhâskaraḥ*, sun, &c.

2. Nouns in इस् *is* and उस् *us*, such as हविः *haviḥ*, धनुः *dhanuḥ*, &c., before words beginning with क् *k*, ख् *kh*, प् *p*, and फ् *ph*, always take ष् *sh*. (Pâṇ. VIII. 3, 45.)

Ex. सर्पिः + पानं = सर्पिष्पानं *sarpiḥ + pânam = sarpishpânam*, ghee-drinking.
आयुः + कामः = आयुष्कामः *âyuḥ + kâmaḥ = âyushkâmaḥ*, fond of life.

Note—भ्रातुष्पुत्रः *bhrâtushputraḥ*, nephew, is used instead of भ्रातुः पुत्रः *bhrâtuḥ putraḥ*, the son of the brother.

II. *Words in* अस् as, इस् is, उस् us, *treated as Prepositions.*

1. The words नमः *namaḥ*, पुरः *puraḥ*, तिरः *tiraḥ*, if compounded prepositionally with कृ *kṛi*, change Visarga into स् *s*. (Pâṇ. VIII. 3, 40.)

Ex. नमः + कारः = नमस्कारः *namaḥ + kâraḥ = namaskâraḥ*, adoration; (but नमः कृत्वा *namaḥ kṛitvâ*, having performed adoration.)
पुरः + कृत्य = पुरस्कृत्य *puraḥ + kṛitya = puraskṛitya*, having preferred.
तिरः + कारी = तिरस्कारी *tiraḥ + kârî = tiraskârî*, despising. In तिरः *tiraḥ* the change is considered optional. (Pâṇ. VIII. 3, 42.)

2. The words निः *niḥ*, दुः *duḥ*, बहिः *vahiḥ*, आविः *âviḥ*, प्रादुः *prâduḥ*, चतुः *chatuḥ*, if compounded with words beginning with क् *k*, ख् *kh*, प् *p* or फ् *ph*, take ष् *sh* instead of final Visarga. (Pâṇ. VIII. 3, 41.)

Ex. निः + कामः = निष्कामः *niḥ + kâmaḥ = nishkâmaḥ*, loveless.
निः + फलः = निष्फलः *niḥ + phalaḥ = nishphalaḥ*, fruitless.
आविः + कृतं = आविष्कृतं *âviḥ + kṛitam = âvishkṛitam*, made manifest.
दुः + कृतं = दुष्कृतं *duḥ + kṛitam = dushkṛitam*, badly done, criminal.
चतुः + कोणं = चतुष्कोणं *chatuḥ + koṇam = chatushkoṇam*, square.

III. *Nouns in* अस् as, इस् is, उस् us, *before certain Taddhita Suffixes.*

1. Before the Taddhita suffixes मत् *mat*, वत् *vat*, विन् *vin*, and वल *vala*, the final स् *s* appears as स् *s* or ष् *sh* (§ 100).

Ex. तेजः + विन् = तेजस्विन् *tejaḥ + vin = tejasvin*, with splendour.
ज्योतिः + मत् = ज्योतिष्मत् *jyotiḥ + mat = jyotishmat*, with light.
रजः + वल = रजस्वल *rajaḥ + vala = rajasvala*, a buffalo.

2. Before Taddhita suffixes beginning with त् *t*, the स् *s*, preceded by इ *i* or उ *u*, is changed into ष् *sh*, after which the त् *t* becomes ट् *ṭ*.

Ex. अर्चिः + त्वं = अर्चिष्ट्वं *archiḥ + tvam = archishṭvam*, brightness.
चतुः + तयं = चतुष्टयं *chatuḥ + tayam = chatushṭayam*, the aggregate of four.

3. Before the Taddhita suffixes पाश *pâśa*, कल्प *kalpa*, क *ka*, and in composition with the verb काम्यति *kâmyati*, nouns in अस् *as* retain their final स् *s*, while nouns in इस् *is* and उस् *us* change it into ष् *sh* (§ 100).

Ex. पयः + पाशं = पयस्पाशं *payaḥ + pâśam = payaspâśam*, bad milk.
पयः + कल्पं = पयस्कल्पं *payaḥ + kalpam = payaskalpam*, a little milk.
यशः + कः = यशस्कः *yaśaḥ + kaḥ = yaśaskaḥ*, glorious.
यशः + काम्यति = यशस्काम्यति *yaśaḥ + kâmyati = yaśaskâmyati*, he is ambitious.
सर्पिः + पाशं = सर्पिष्पाशं *sarpiḥ + pâśam = sarpishpâśam*, bad ghee.
सर्पिः + कल्पं = सर्पिष्कल्पं *sarpiḥ + kalpam = sarpishkalpam*, a little ghee.
धनुः + कः = धनुष्कः *dhanuḥ + kaḥ = dhanushkaḥ*, belonging to the bow.
धनुः + काम्यति = धनुष्काम्यति *dhanuḥ + kâmyati = dhanushkâmyati*, he desires a bow.

§ 90. Nouns ending in radical र् *r* (§ 85) retain the र् *r* before the सु *su* of the loc. plur., and in composition before nouns even though beginning with surds.

Ex. वार् + सु = वार्षु *vâr + su = vârshu*, in the waters.
गिर् + पतिः = गीर्पतिः *gir + patiḥ = gîrpatiḥ*, lord of speech.

In compounds, however, like गीर्पतिः *gîrpatiḥ*, the optional use of Visarga is sanctioned (Pâṇ. VIII. 2, 70, v.), and we meet with गीःपतिः *gîḥpatiḥ*, धूःपतिः *dhûḥpatiḥ*, and धूर्पतिः *dhûrpatiḥ*; स्वःपतिः *svaḥpatiḥ* and स्वर्पतिः *svarpatiḥ*, lord of heaven; अहःपतिः *ahaḥpatiḥ* and अहर्पतिः *aharpatiḥ*, lord of the day.

अहर् *ahar*, the Pada base of अहन् *ahan*, day, is further irregular, because its final र् *r* is treated like स् *s* before the Pada-terminations, and in composition before words beginning with र् *r*: hence अहः + भिः = अहोभिः *ahaḥ + bhiḥ = ahobhiḥ*; अहः + सु = अहःसु *ahaḥ + su = ahaḥsu*; अहः + रात्रः = अहोरात्रः *ahaḥ + râtraḥ = ahorâtraḥ*, day and night. (Pâṇ. VIII. 2, 68, v.)

§ 91. छ *chh* at the beginning of a word, after a final short vowel, and after the particles आ *á* and मा *má*, is changed to च्छ *chchh*.

Ex. तव + छाया = तव च्छाया *tava + chháyá = tava chchháyá*, thy shade.
मा + छिदत् = मा च्छिदत् *má + chhidat = má chchhidat*, let him not cut.
आ + छादयति = आच्छादयति *á + chhádayati = áchchhádayati*, he covers.

After any other long vowels, this change is optional.
बदरीछाया or बदरीच्छाया *badaríchháyá* or *badaríchchháyá*, shade of Badarís.

In the body of a word, the change of छ *chh* into च्छ *chchh* is necessary both after long and short vowels.

Ex. इच्छति *ichchhati*, he wishes. म्लेच्छः *mlechchhaḥ*, a barbarian. (Pâṇ. VI. 1, 73–76.)

§ 92. Initial श *ś*, not followed by a hard consonant, may be changed into छ *chh*, if the final letter of the preceding word is a hard consonant or ञ् *ñ* (for न् *n*).

Ex. वाक् + शतं = वाक्शतं or वाक्छतं *vák + śatam = vákśatam* or *vákchhatam*, a hundred speeches.
परिव्राट् + शेते = परिव्राट् शेते or परिव्राट्छेते *parivráṭ + śete = parivráṭ śete* or *parivráṭ chhete*, the beggar lies down.
महत् + शकटं = महच्शकटं or महच्छकटं *mahat + śakaṭam = mahach śakaṭam* or *mahach chhakaṭam*, a great car.
धावन् + शशः = धावञ्शशः or धावञ्छशः *dhávan + śaśaḥ = dhávañ śaśaḥ* or *dhávañ chhaśaḥ*, a running hare.
अप् + शब्दः = अप्शब्दः or अप्छब्दः *ap + śabdaḥ = ap śabdaḥ* or *apchhabdaḥ*, the sound of water.

§ 93. If ह् *h*, घ् *gh*, ढ् *ḍh*, ध् *dh*, or भ् *bh* stand at the end of a syllable which begins with ग् *g*, ड् *ḍ*, द् *d*, or ब् *b*, and lose their aspiration as final or otherwise, the initial consonants ग् *g*, ड् *ḍ*, द् *d*, or ब् *b* are changed into घ् *gh*, ढ् *ḍh*, ध् *dh*, भ् *bh*.

Ex. दुह् *duh*, a milker, becomes धुक् *dhuk*.
विश्वगुध् *viśvagudh*, all attracting, becomes विश्वघुत् *viśvaghut*.
बुध् *budh*, wise, becomes भुत् *bhut*.

§ 94. Table showing the Combination of Final with Initial Consonants.

	FINAL.	1 IN PAUSÂ.	2 A Á &c.	3 K	4 KH	5 G	6 GH	7 Ṅ	8 CH	9 CHH	10 J	11 JH	12 Ñ	13 Ṭ	14 ṬH	15 Ḍ	16 ḌH	17 Ṇ
I.	K	k (g)	ga gá	..	..	gg	ggh	gṅ ṅṅ	..	..	gj	gjh	gñ ññ	..	..	gḍ	gḍh	gṇ ṅṇ
II.	Ṅ	..	˘ṅṅa ¯ṅá	..	..	..	..	..	..	..	..	..	..	..	..	..	..	..
III.	Ṭ	ṭ (ḍ)	ḍa ḍá	..	..	ḍg	ḍgh	ḍṅ ṇṅ	..	..	ḍj	ḍjh	ḍñ ṇñ	..	..	ḍḍ	ḍḍh	ḍṇ ṇṇ
IV.	Ṇ	..	˘ṇṇa ¯ṇá	..	..	..	..	..	..	..	..	..	..	..	..	..	..	..
V.	T	t (d)	da dá	..	..	dg	dgh	dṅ nṅ	chch	chchh	jj	jjh	jñ ññ	ṭṭ	ṭṭh	ḍḍ	ḍḍh	ḍṇ ṇṇ
VI.	N	..	˘nna ¯ná	..	..	..	..	..	ṁśch	ṁśchh	ñj	ñjh	ññ	ṁshṭ	ṁshṭh	ṇḍ	ṇḍh	ṇṇ
VII.	P	p (b)	ba bá	..	..	bg	bgh	bṅ mṅ	..	..	bj	bjh	bñ mñ	..	..	bḍ	bḍh	bṇ mṇ
VIII.	M	m (ṁ)	.. ..	ṁk (ṅk)	ṁkh (ṅkh)	ṁg (ṅg)	ṁgh (ṅgh)	ṁṅ (ṅṅ)	ṁch (ñch)	ṁchh (ñchh)	ṁj (ñj)	ṁjh (ñjh)	ṁñ (ññ)	ṁṭ (ṇṭ)	ṁṭh (ṇṭh)	ṁḍ (ṇḍ)	ṁḍh (ṇḍh)	ṁṇ (ṇṇ)
IX a.	Ḥ and R exc. ÂḤ and ÁḤ	ḥ	ra rá	χk ḥk	χkh ḥkh	rg	rgh	rṅ	śch	śchh	rj	rjh	rñ	shṭ	shṭh	rḍ	rḍh	rṇ
IX b.	ÂḤ ÁḤ (not ÂR)	id. id.	áa áá o' aá	id. id.	id. id.	ág og	ágh ogh	áṅ oṅ	id. id.	id. id.	áj oj	ájh ojh	áñ oñ	id. id.	id. id.	áḍ oḍ	áḍh oḍh	áṇ oṇ

	FINAL.	18 T	19 TH	20 D	21 DH	22 N	23 P	24 PH	25 B	26 BH	27 M	28 Y	29 R	30 L	31 V	32 Ś	33 SH	34 S	35 H
I.	K	..	..	gd	gdh	gn ṅn	..	..	gb	gbh	gm ṅm	gy	gr	gl	gv	kś kchh	..	..	g-h ggh
II.	Ṅ	..	..	..	..	..	..	..	..	..	..	..	..	..	..	ṅś ṅkś ṅkchh	ṅsh ṅksh	ṅs ṅks	..
III.	Ṭ	..	..	ḍd	ḍdh	ḍn ṇn	..	..	ḍb	ḍbh	ḍm ṇm	ḍy	ḍr	ḍl	ḍv	ṭś ṭchh	..	ṭs ṭts	ḍ-h ḍḍh
IV.	Ṇ	..	..	..	..	..	..	..	..	..	..	..	..	..	..	ṇś ṇṭś ṇṭchh	ṇsh ṇṭsh	ṇs ṇṭs	..
V.	T	..	..	dd	ddh	dn nn	..	..	db	dbh	dm nm	dy	dr	ll	dv	(chś) chchh	..	..	d-h ddh
VI.	N	ṁst	ṁsth	..	..	..	..	..	..	..	..	..	..	l̃l	..	ñś ñchś ñchchh ñchh	..	ns nts	..
VII.	P	..	..	bd	bdh	bn mn	..	..	bb	bbh	bm mm	by	br	bl	bv	pś pchh	..	..	b-h bbh
VIII.	M	ṁt (nt)	ṁth (nth)	ṁd (nd)	ṁdh (ndh)	ṁn (nn)	ṁp (mp)	ṁph (mph)	ṁb (mb)	ṁbh (mbh)	ṁm (mm)	ṁy ỹy	ṁr	ṁl l̃l	ṁv ṽv	ṁś	ṁsh	ṁs	ṁh
IX a.	Ḥ and R exc. ÂḤ and ÁḤ	st	sth	rd	rdh	rn	φp ḥp	φph ḥph	rb	rbh	rm	ry	◦r	rl	rv	śś ḥś	shsh ḥsh	ss ḥs	rh
IX b.	ÂḤ ÁḤ (not ÂR)	id. id.	id. id.	ád od	ádh odh	án on	id. id.	id. id.	áb ob	ábh obh	ám om	áy oy	ár or	ál ol	áv ov	id. id.	id. id.	id. id.	áh oh

Note—I. The sign .. means that no change takes place in the initial or final letter. II. The sign ˘, before a letter, indicates that it is preceded by a short: the sign ¯, that it is preceded by a long vowel: the sign ◦, that the letter is to be elided. III. In col. IX b, id. means that the form is the same as in col. IX a. IV. The sign ˜ is used to distinguish the real and necessary from the optional Anusvára.

Table showing the Combination of Final with Initial Consonants.

FINAL.		1 IN PAUSÂ.	2 अ आ &c.	3 क	4 ख	5 ग	6 घ	7 ङ	8 च	9 छ	10 ज	11 झ	12 ञ	13 ट	14 ठ	15 ड	16 ढ	17 ण
I.	क्	क् (ग्)	ग गा	...	...	ग्ग	ग्घ	ग्ङ ङ्ङ	...	...	ग्ज	ग्झ	ग्ञ ङ्ञ	...	...	ग्ड	ग्ढ	ग्ण ङ्ण
II.	ङ्	...	˘ङ्ङ ^ङा	...	...	...	...	...	...	...	...	...	...	...	...	...	...	...
III.	ट्	ट् (ड्)	ड डा	...	...	ड्ग	ड्घ	ड्ङ ण्ङ	...	...	ड्ज	ड्झ	ड्ञ ण्ञ	...	...	ड्ड	ड्ढ	ड्ण ण्ण
IV.	ण्	...	˘ण्ण ^णा	...	...	...	...	...	...	...	...	...	...	...	...	...	...	...
V.	त्	त् (द्)	द दा	...	...	द्ग	द्घ	द्ङ न्ङ	च्च	च्छ	ज्ज	ज्झ	ज्ञ ञ्ञ	ट्ट	ट्ठ	ड्ड	ड्ढ	ड्ण ण्ण
VI.	न्	...	˘न्न ^ना	...	...	...	...	...	˘ंश्च	˘ंश्छ	ञ्ज	ञ्झ	ञ्ञ	˘ंष्ट	˘ंष्ठ	ण्ड	ण्ढ	ण्ण
VII.	प्	प् (ब्)	ब बा	...	...	ब्ग	ब्घ	ब्ङ म्ङ	...	...	ब्ज	ब्झ	ब्ञ म्ञ	...	...	ब्ड	ब्ढ	ब्ण म्ण
VIII.	म्	म् (ं)	... ...	ंक (ङ्क)	ंख (ङ्ख)	ंग (ङ्ग)	ंघ (ङ्घ)	ंङ (ङ्ङ)	ंच (ञ्च)	ंछ (ञ्छ)	ंज (ञ्ज)	ंझ (ञ्झ)	ंञ (ञ्ञ)	ंट (ण्ट)	ंठ (ण्ठ)	ंड (ण्ड)	ंढ (ण्ढ)	ंण (ण्ण)
IX *a*.	: and र् exc. अः and आः	:	र रा	+ क : क	+ ख : ख	र्ग	र्घ	र्ङ	श्च	श्छ	र्ज	र्झ	र्ञ	ष्ट	ष्ठ	र्ड	र्ढ	र्ण
IX *b*.	आः अः (not अर्)	id. id.	आ अ आ आ ओ ऽ अ आ	id. id.	id. id.	आ ग ओ ग	आ घ ओ घ	आ ङ ओ ङ	id. id.	id. id.	आ ज ओ ज	आ झ ओ झ	आ ञ ओ ञ	id. id.	id. id.	आ ड ओ ड	आ ढ ओ ढ	आ ण ओ ण

Note—I. The sign ... means that no change takes place in the initial or final letter. II. The sign ˘, before a letter, indicates that it is preceded by a short; the sign ^, that it is preceded by a long vowel; the sign o, that the letter is to be elided. III. In col. IX *b*, *id.* means that the form is the same as in col. IX *a*. IV. The sign ं is used to distinguish the real and necessary from the optional Anusvâra.

	FINAL.	18 त	19 थ	20 द	21 ध	22 न	23 प	24 फ	25 ब	26 भ	27 म	28 य	29 र	30 ल	31 व	32 श	33 ष	34 स	35 ह
I.	क्	...	...	ग्द	ग्ध	ग्न ङ्न	...	...	ग्ब	ग्भ	ग्म ङ्म	ग्य	ग्र	ग्ल	ग्व	क्श क्छ	...	...	ग्घ ग्ह
II.	ङ्	...	...	...	...	...	...	...	...	...	...	...	...	...	...	ङ्श ङ्क्श ङ्छ	ङ्ष ङ्क्ष	ङ्स ङ्क्स	...
III.	ट्	...	...	ड्द	ड्ध	ड्न ण्ण	...	...	ड्ब	ड्भ	ड्म ण्म	ड्य	ड्र	ड्ल	ड्व	ट्श ट्छ	...	ट्स ट्त्स	ड्ढ ड्ह
IV.	ण्	...	...	...	...	...	...	...	...	...	...	...	...	...	...	ण्श ण्ट्श ण्छ	ण्ष ण्ट्ष	ण्स ण्ट्स	...
V.	त्	...	...	द्द	द्ध	द्न न्न	...	...	द्ब	द्भ	द्म न्म	द्य	द्र	ल्ल	द्व	(च्श) च्छ	...	...	द्ध द्ह
VI.	न्	ंस्त	ंस्थ	...	...	...	...	...	...	...	...	...	...	ँल्ल	...	ञ्श ञ्च्श ञ्छ ञ्च्छ	...	न्स न्त्स	...
VII.	प्	...	...	ब्द	ब्ध	ब्न म्न	...	...	ब्ब	ब्भ	ब्म म्म	ब्य	ब्र	ब्ल	ब्व	प्श प्छ	...	...	ब्भ ब्ह
VIII.	म्	ंत (न्त)	ंथ (न्थ)	ंद (न्द)	ंध (न्ध)	ंन (न्न)	ंप (म्प)	ंफ (म्फ)	ंब (म्ब)	ंभ (म्भ)	ंम (म्म)	ंय य्ँय	ंर	ंल ल्ँल	ंव व्ँव	ंश	ंष	ंस	ंह
IXa.	: and र् exc. अः and आः	स्त	स्थ	र्द	र्ध	र्न	ᳵप :प	ᳵफ :फ	र्ब	र्भ	र्म	र्य	ˆ०र	र्ल	र्व	श्श :श	ष्ष :ष	स्स :स	र्ह
IXb.	आः अः (not अर्)	id. id.	id. id.	आ द ओ द	आ ध ओ ध	आ न ओ न	id. id.	id. id.	आ ब ओ ब	आ भ ओ भ	आ म ओ म	आ य ओ य	आ र ओ र	आ ल ओ ल	आ व ओ व	id. id.	id. id.	id. id.	आ ह ओ ह

NATI, or Change of Dental न् n *and* स् s *into Lingual* ण् ṇ *and* ष् sh.

§ 95. In addition to the rules which require the modification of certain letters at the beginning and end of words, there are some other rules to be remembered which regulate the transition of dental न् *n* and स् *s* into lingual ण् *ṇ* and ष् *sh* in the body of words. Beginners should try to impress on their memory these rules as far as they concern the change of the dental nasal and sibilant into the lingual nasal and sibilant *in simple words*: with regard to compound nouns and verbs, the rules are very complicated and capricious, and can only be learnt by long practice.

Change of न् n *into* ण् ṇ.

§ 96. The dental न् *n*, followed by a vowel, or by न् *n*, म् *m*, य् *y*, and व् *v*, is, in the middle of a word, changed into the lingual ण् *ṇ* if it is preceded by the linguals ऋ *ri*, ॠ *rî*, र् *r*, or ष् *sh*. The influence of these letters on a following न् *n* is not stopt by any vowel, by any guttural (क *k*, ख *kh*, ग *g*, घ *gh*, ङ *ṅ*, ह *h*, ं *ṁ*), or by any labial (प *p*, फ *ph*, ब *b*, भ *bh*, म *m*, व *v*), or by य् *y*, intervening between the linguals and the न् *n*.

Ex. नृ + नां = नृणां *nri* + *nâm* = *nriṇâm*, gen. plur. of नृ *nri*, man.
कर्णः *karṇaḥ*, ear.
दूषणं *dûshaṇam*, abuse.
बृंहणं *vriṁhaṇam*, nourishing, (ह् *h* is guttural and preceded by Anusvâra.)
अर्केण *arkeṇa*, by the sun, (क् *k* is guttural.)
गृह्णाति *grihṇâti*, he takes, (ह् *h* is guttural.)
क्षिप्णुः *kshipṇuḥ*, throwing, (प् *p* is labial.)
प्रेम्णा *premṇâ*, by love, (म् *m* is labial.)
ब्रह्मण्यः *brahmaṇyaḥ*, (ह् *h* is guttural, म् *m* is labial, and न् *n* followed by य् *y*.)
निषण्णः *nishaṇṇaḥ*, (न् *n* is followed by न् *n*, which is itself afterwards changed to ण् *ṇ*.)
अक्षण्वत् *akshaṇvat*, (ण् *ṇ* is followed by व् *v*.)
प्रायेण *prâyeṇa*, generally, (य् *y* does not prevent the change.)
But अर्चन *archana*, worship, (च् *ch* is palatal.)
अर्णवेन *arṇavena*, by the ocean, (ण् *ṇ* is lingual.)
दर्शनं *darśanam*, a system of philosophy, (श् *ś* is palatal.)
अर्धेन *ardhena*, by half, (ध् *dh* is dental.)
कुर्वन्ति *kurvanti*, they do, (न् *n* is followed by त् *t*.)
रामान् *râmân*, the Râmas, (न् *n* is final.)

Note—रुग्णः *rugṇaḥ*, like वृक्णः *vrikṇaḥ* (Pâṇ. VI. 1, 16), should be written with ण् *ṇ*. The ग् *g* is no protection for the न् *n*. Thus अग्नि *agni* has to be especially mentioned as an exception for not changing its न् *n* into ण् *ṇ* in compounds, such as शराग्निः *śarâgniḥ*. (Pâṇ. *Gaṇa kshubhnâdi*.)

§ 97. The न् *n* of नु *nu*, the sign of the Su conjugation, and the न् *n* of ना *nâ*, the sign of the Krî conjugation, are not changed into ण् *ṇ* in the two verbs तृप् *trip* and क्षुभ् *kshubh* (Pâṇ. VIII. 4, 39). Hence

तृप्नोति *tripnoti*, he pleases*. क्षुभ्नाति *kshubhnâti*, he shakes.
But शृणोति *śriṇoti*, he hears. पुष्णाति *pushṇâti*, he nourishes.
क्षुभाण *kshubhâṇa*, imper. shake.

Table showing the Changes of न् n *into* ण् ṇ.

ऋ *ri*,	in spite of intervening Vowels,	change	if there follow Vowels, or
ॠ *rî*,	Gutturals (including ह् *h* and Anusvâra),	न् *n*	न् *n*,
र् *r*,	Labials (including व् *v*),	into	म् *m*,
			य् *y*,
ष् *sh*,	and य् *y*,	ण् *ṇ*	व् *v*.

§ 98. The changes here explained of न् *n* in the middle of simple words, (whether it belongs to a suffix or a termination,) are the most important to remember. But न् *n* is likewise liable to be changed into ण् *ṇ* when it occurs in the second part of a compound the first part of which contains one of the letters ऋ *ri*, ॠ *rî*, र् *r*, or ष् *sh*, and particularly after certain prepositions. Here, however, the rules are much more uncertain, and we must depend on the dictionary rather than on the grammar for the right employment of the dental or lingual nasals. The following rules are the most important:

1. The change of न् *n* into ण् *ṇ* does not take place unless the two members of the compound are combined so as to express a single conception. Hence वार्ध्री *bârdhrî*, a leathern thong, + नस *nasa*, nose, gives वार्ध्रीणसः *bârdhrîṇasa*, if it is the name of a certain animal; according to Wilson, of a goat with long ears; according to others, of a rhinoceros, or a bird. (Uṇâdi-Sûtras, ed. Aufrecht, s. v. Pâṇ. VIII. 4, 3.) But चर्मन् *charman*, leather, + नासिका *nâsikâ*, nose, gives चर्मनासिकः *charmanâsikaḥ*, if it means having a leathern nose. An important exception is सर्वनामन् *sarvanâman*, a technical term for pronouns, (सर्व *sarva* being the first in their list,) which Pâṇini himself employs with the dental न् *n* only. (Pâṇ. I. 1, 27.) Other proper names not following the general rule, are त्रिनयनः *trinayanaḥ*, three-eyed, name of Śiva; रघुनंदनः *raghunandanaḥ*, name of Râma; स्वर्भानुः *svarbhânuḥ*, name of Rahu, &c.

* In the Veda we find तृप्णुहि *tripṇuhi*, Rv. II. 16, 6; तृप्णवः *tripṇavaḥ*, Rv. III. 42, 2.

Words to be remembered:

अग्रणीः *agraṇîḥ*, first, principal, from अग्र *agra*, front, and नी *nî*, to lead.

ग्रामणीः *grâmaṇîḥ*, head borough, from ग्राम *grâma*, multitude, and नी *nî*, to lead.

वृत्रघ्नः *vṛitraghnaḥ*, Indra, killer of Vṛitra; but वृत्रहणं *vṛitrahaṇam*, acc. of वृत्रहन् *vṛitrahan*. (Pâṇ. VIII. 4, 12; 22.)

गिरिनदी or गिरिणदी *girinadî* or *giriṇadî*, mountain-stream.

पराह्णं *parâhṇam*, afternoon, from परा *parâ*, over, and अहन् *ahan*, day; but सर्वाह्णः *sarvâhṇaḥ*, the whole day, from सर्व *sarva*, all, and अहन् *ahan*, day; and the same whenever the first word ends in अ *a*. (Pâṇ. VIII. 4, 7.)

There are minute distinctions, according to which, for instance, क्षीरपानं *kshîrapânam* if it means the drinking of milk, or a vessel for drinking milk, कंसः क्षीरपानः *kaṁsaḥ kshîrapânaḥ*, may be pronounced with dental or lingual *n* (न् *n* or ण् *ṇ*); but if it is the name of a tribe who live on milk, it must be pronounced क्षीरपाणाः *kshîrapâṇâḥ*, milk-drinking. (Pâṇ. VIII. 4, 9 and 10.) In the same manner दर्भवाहणं *darbhavâhaṇam*, a hay-cart, is spelt with lingual ण् *ṇ*; while in ordinary compounds, such as इंद्रवाहनं *indravâhanam*, a vehicle belonging to Indra, the dental न् *n* remains unchanged. (Pâṇ. VIII. 4, 8.)

2. In a compound consisting of more than two words the न् *n* of any one word can only be affected by the word immediately preceding. Hence माषवापेण *mâsha-vâpeṇa*, by sowing beans; but माषकुंभवापेन *mâsha-kumbha-vâpena*, by sowing from a bean-jar. (Pâṇ. VIII. 4, 38.)

3. In a compound the change of न् *n* into ण् *ṇ* does not take place if the first word ends in ग् *g*.

Ex. ऋक् + अयनं = ऋगयनं *ṛik + ayanam = ṛigayanam*.

Some grammarians restrict this to proper names. (Pâṇ. VIII. 4, 3, 5.)

Or if it ends in ष् *sh*, and the next is formed by a primary suffix with न् *n*.

Ex. निः + पानं = निष्पानं *niḥ + pânam = nishpânam*.

यजुः + पावनं = यजुष्पावनं *yajuḥ + pâvanam = yajushpâvanam*. (Pâṇ. VIII. 4, 35.)

4. In compounds the न् *n* of nouns ending in न् *n*, and the न् *n* of case-terminations, if followed by a vowel, are always liable to change.

व्रीहिवापिन् *vrîhivâpin*, rice-sowing, may form the genitive व्रीहिवापिणः *vrîhivâpiṇaḥ*; but also व्रीहिवापिनः *vrîhivâpinaḥ*.

व्रीहिवापाणि or व्रीहिवापानि *vrîhivâpâṇi* or *vrîhivâpâni*, nom. plur. neut.

व्रीहिवापेण or व्रीहिवापेन *vrîhivâpeṇa* or *vrîhivâpena*, instrum. sing.

Likewise feminines such as व्रीहिवापिणी or व्रीहिवापिनी *vrîhivâpiṇî* or *vrîhivâpinî*. (Kâś.-Vṛitti VIII. 4, 11.)

Note—The न् n of secondary suffixes, attached to the end of compounds, is, under the general conditions, always changed to ण् ṇ. Thus खरपः *kharapaḥ* (i. e. donkey-keeper) becomes खारपायणः *khârapâyaṇaḥ*, the descendant of Kharapa. मातृभोगीणः *mâtṛibhogîṇaḥ*, fit to be possessed by a mother, from मातृ *mâtṛi*, mother, and भोगः *bhogaḥ*, enjoyment, with the adjectival suffix ईन *îna* (*samâsânta*), is always spelt with ण् ṇ. (See also § 98. 6.) Again, while गर्गभगिनी *gargabhaginî*, the sister of Garga, always retains its dental न् n, being an ordinary compound, गर्गभागिणी *gargabhâgiṇî* would have the lingual ण् ṇ, if it was derived from गर्गभागः *gargabhâgaḥ*, the share of Garga, with the adjectival suffix इन् *in*, fem. इनी *inî*, enjoying the share of Garga. Words which after they have been compounded take a new suffix are treated in fact like single words (*samâsapada*), and therefore follow the general rule of § 96. (Pâṇ. VIII. 4, 3. Kâś.-Vṛitti VIII. 4, 11, v.)

5. If the second part of the compound is monosyllabic, then the change of a final न् n followed by a terminational vowel, or of a terminational न् n, is obligatory. (Pâṇ. VIII. 4, 12.)

Ex. वृत्रहन् *vṛitrahan*, Vṛitra-killer; gen. वृत्रहणः *vṛitrahaṇaḥ*.
सुरापः *surâpaḥ*, drinking surâ; nom. plur. neut. सुरापाणि *surâpâṇi*.
क्षीरपः *kshîrapaḥ*, drinking milk; instrum. sing. क्षीरपेण *kshîrapeṇa*.

6. If the second part of a compound contains a guttural, the change is obligatory, even though the second part be not monosyllabic. (Pâṇ. VIII. 4, 13.)

Ex. हरिकामः *harikâmaḥ*, loving Hari; instrum. sing. हरिकामेण *harikâmeṇa*.
शुष्कगोमयेण *śushkagomayeṇa*, instrum. sing. of शुष्कगोमय *śushkagomaya*; (शुष्क *śushka*, dry, गोमय *gomaya*, dung.)

7. Likewise after prepositions which contain an र् r, the न् n of primary affixes, such as अन *ana*, अनि *ani*, अनीय *anîya*, इन् *in*, न *na* (if preceded by a vowel), and मान *mâna*, is changed to ण् ṇ, but under certain restrictions. (Pâṇ. VIII. 4, 29.)

Ex. प्रवपणं *pravapaṇam*; प्रमाणं *pramâṇam*; प्राप्यमाणं *prâpyamâṇam*.

While in these cases the change is pronounced obligatory, it is said to be optional after causative verbs (Pâṇ. VIII. 4, 30), and after verbs beginning and ending in consonants with any vowel but अ *a* (Pâṇ. VIII. 4, 31); hence प्रयापणं and °नं *prayâpaṇam* and *prayâpanam*; प्रकोपणं or °नं *prakopaṇam* or *prakopanam*. Again, after verbs beginning in a vowel (not अ *a*) and strengthening their bases by nasalization, the change is necessary; it is forbidden in other verbs, not beginning with vowels, though they require nasalization: hence प्र + इंगनं = प्रेंगणं *pra* + *iṅganam* = *preṅgaṇam*; but प्र + कंपनं = प्रकंपनं *pra* + *kampanam* = *prakampanam*. Lastly, there are several roots which defy all these rules, viz. भा *bhâ*, भू *bhû*, पू *pû*, कम् *kam*, गम् *gam*, प्याय् *pyây*, वेप् *vep*: hence प्रभानं *prabhânam* &c., never प्रभाणं *prabhâṇam*; प्रवेपनं *pravepanam*, never प्रवेपणं *pravepaṇam*.

8. After prepositions containing an र् r, such as अंतर् *antar*, निर् *nir*, परा *parâ*,

परि *pari*, and प्र *pra*, and after दुर् *dur*, the change of न् *n* into ण् *ṇ* takes place:

1. In most roots beginning with न् *n*. (Pâṇ. VIII. 4, 14.)
   प्र + नमति = प्रणमति *pra* + *namati* = *praṇamati*, he bows.
   परा + नुदति = पराणुदति *parâ* + *nudati* = *parâṇudati*, he pushes away.
   अंतः + नयति = अंतर्णयति *antaḥ* + *nayati* = *antarṇayati*, he leads in.
   प्र + नायकः = प्रणायकः *pra* + *nâyakaḥ* = *praṇâyakaḥ*, a leader.

The roots which are liable to this change of their initial न् *n* are entered in the Dhâtupâṭha, the list of roots of native grammarians, as beginning with ण् *ṇ*. Thus we should find the root नम् *nam* entered as णम् *ṇam*, simply in order thus to indicate its liability to change.

2. In a few roots this change is optional if they are followed by Kṛit affixes, viz. (Pâṇ. VIII. 4, 33.)

निंस् *nis*, to kiss; प्रणिंसितव्यं or प्रनिंसितव्यं *praṇiṁsitavyam* or *praniṁsitavyam*.
निक्ष् *niksh*, to kiss; प्रणिक्षणं or प्रनिक्षणं *praṇikshaṇam* or *pranikshaṇam*.
निंद् *nid*, to blame; प्रणिंदनं or प्रनिंदनं *praṇindanam* or *pranindanam*.

3. In a few roots the initial न् *n* resists all change, and these roots are entered in the Dhâtupâṭha as beginning with न् *n*, viz. (Pâṇ. VI. 1, 65, v.)

नृत् *nṛit*, to dance.	नाट् *nâṭ*, to fall down, (Chur.) *
नंद् *nand*, to rejoice.	नाथ् *nâth*, to ask.
नर्द् *nard*, to howl.	नाध् *nâdh*, to beg.
नक्क् *nakk*, to destroy.	नी *nî*, to lead.

Ex. परिनर्तनं *parinartanam*; परिनंदनं *parinandanam*.

4. The root नश् *naś*, to destroy, changes न् *n* into ण् *ṇ* only when its श् *ś* is not changed to ष् *sh*. प्र + नश्यते = प्रणश्यते *pra* + *naśyate* = *praṇaśyate*; but प्र + नष्टः = प्रनष्टः *pra* + *nashṭaḥ* = *pranashṭaḥ*, destroyed. (Pâṇ. VIII. 4, 36.)
5. In the root अन् *an*, to breathe, the न् *n* is changed to ण् *ṇ* if the र् *r* is not separated from the न् *n* by more than one letter. Thus प्र + अनिति = प्राणिति *pra* + *aniti* = *prâṇiti*, he breathes; but परि + अनिति = पर्यनिति *pari* + *aniti* = *paryaniti*. The reduplicated aorist forms प्राणिणत् *prâṇiṇat*; the desiderative with परा *parâ* is पराणिणिषति *parâṇiṇishati*. (Pâṇ. VIII. 4, 19, 21.)
6. In the root हन् *han*, to kill, the न् *n* is changed except where ह् *h* has to be changed to घ् *gh*. (Pâṇ. VIII. 4, 22.) Thus प्र + हन्यते = प्रहण्यते *pra* + *hanyate* = *prahaṇyate*, he is struck down; अंतर्हण्यते *antarhaṇyate* (Pâṇ. VIII. 4, 24); but प्र + घ्नंति = प्रघ्नंति *pra* + *ghnanti* = *praghnanti*, they kill. Also प्रहणनं *prahaṇanam*, killing.

---

* It is not नट् *naṭ*, to dance, but नट् *naṭ* of the Chur class, and hence written with a long *â*. Siddh.-Kaum. II. p. 41, note.

The change is optional again where न् *n* is followed by म् *m* or व् *v*. (Pâṇ. VIII. 4, 23.) Thus प्रहन्मि or प्रहण्मि *prahanmi* or *prahaṇmi*; प्रहन्वः or प्रहण्वः *prahanvaḥ* or *prahaṇvaḥ*.

7. The न् *n* of नु *nu* of the Su and of ना *nâ* of the Krî conjugation is changed to ण् *ṇ* in the verbs हि *hi*, to send, and मी *mî*, to destroy. (Pâṇ. VIII. 4, 15.)

Ex. प्रहिण्वन्ति *prahiṇvanti*; प्रमीणन्ति *pramîṇanti*.

8. The न् *n* of the termination आनि *âni* in the imperative is changeable. (Pâṇ. VIII. 4, 16.) Thus प्र + भवानि = प्रभवाणि *pra* + *bhavâni* = *prabhavâṇi*.

9. The न् *n* of the preposition नि *ni*, if preceded by प्र *pra*, परि *pari*, &c., is changed into ण् *ṇ* before the verbs (Pâṇ. VIII. 4, 17) गद् *gad*, to speak, नद् *nad*, to be happy, पत् *pat*, to fall, पद् *pad*, to go, the verbs called घु *ghu*, माङ्* *mâ*, to measure, मेङ् *me*, to change, षो *so*, to destroy, हन् *han*, to kill, या *yâ*, to go, वा *vâ*, to blow, द्रा *drâ*, to flee, प्सा *psâ*, to eat, वप् *vap*, to weave, वह् *vah*, to bear, शम् *śam*, to be tranquil (*div*), चि *chi*, to collect, दिह् *dih*, to anoint.

The same change takes place even when the augment intervenes. (Pâṇ. VIII. 4, 17, v.)

प्रण्यगदत् *praṇyagadat*; प्रण्यनदत् *praṇyanadat*.

§ 99. In all other verbs except those which follow गद् *gad*, the change of नि *ni* after प्र *pra*, परि *pari*, &c., is optional.

प्रनिपचति or प्रणिपचति *pranipachati* or *praṇipachati*.

Except again in verbs beginning with क *ka* or ख *kha*, or ending in ष् *sh* (Pâṇ. VIII. 4, 18), in which the न् *n* of नि *ni* remains unchanged.

प्रनिकरोति *pranikaroti*; प्रनिखादति *pranikhâdati*; प्रनिपिनष्टि *pranipinashṭi*.

Change of स् s *into* ष् sh.

§ 100. A dental स् *s* (chiefly of suffixes and terminations), if preceded by any vowel except अ, आ *â*, or by क् *k*, र् *r*, ल् *l*, is always changed into the lingual ष् *sh*, provided it be followed by a vowel, or by त् *t*, थ् *th*, न् *n*, म् *m*, य् *y*, or व् *v*; likewise by certain Taddhita suffixes, क *ka*, कल्प *kalpa*, पाश *pâśa*, &c.

* Where it seemed likely to be useful, the Sanskrit roots have been given with their diacritical letters (*anubandhas*), but only in their Devanâgarî form. Pâṇini in enumerating the roots which change नि *ni* after प्र *pra*, प्रति *prati*, &c., into णि *ṇi*, mentions मा *mâ*, but this, according to the commentaries, includes two roots, the root माङ् *mâ*(*ṅ*), which forms मिमीते *mimîte*, he measures, and the root मेङ् *me*(*ṅ*), which forms मयते *mayate*, he changes. Where in this grammar the transcribed form of a root differs from its Devanâgarî original, the additional letters may always be looked upon as diacritical marks employed by native grammarians. Sometimes the class to which certain verbs belong has been indicated by adding the first verb of that class in brackets. Thus *śam* (*div*) means *śâmyati*, or *śam* conjugated like *div*, and not *śâmayate*.

If Anusvâra* or Visarga or ष् sh intervenes between the vowel and the स् s, the change into ष् sh takes place nevertheless.

Ex. सर्पिस् *sarpis*, inflectional base; सर्पिः *sarpiḥ*, nom. sing. neut. clarified butter; instrum. सर्पिषा *sarpishâ;* nom. plur. सर्पींषि *sarpîṁshi* (here the Anusvâra intervenes); loc. plur. सर्पिःषु *sarpiḥshu* (here the Visarga intervenes), or सर्पिष्षु *sarpishshu* (here the ष् *sh* intervenes).

वाक्षु *vâkshu*, loc. plur. of वाच् *vâch*, speech.

सर्वशक् + सु = सर्वशक्षु *sarvaśak + su = sarvaśakshu*, omnipotent.

चित्रलिख् (क्) + सु = चित्रलिक्षु *chitralikh (k) + su = chitralikshu*, painter.

गीर्षु *gîrshu*, loc. plur. of गिर् *gir*, speech.

कमल् + सु = कमल्षु *kamal + su = kamalshu*, naming the goddess Lakshmî.

धोक्ष्यति *dhokshyati*, fut. of द्रुह् *druh*, to hate; (here ह् *h* is changed to क् *k*, and the aspiration thrown on the initial द् *d*.)

पोक्ष्यति *pokshyati*, fut. of पुष् *push*, to nourish; (here ष् *sh* is changed into क् *k*.)

सर्पिः + कः = सर्पिष्कः *sarpiḥ + kaḥ = sarpishkaḥ;* adj. formed by क *ka*, having clarified butter.

सर्पिः + तरः = सर्पिष्टरः *sarpiḥ + taraḥ = sarpishṭaraḥ;* (here the त् *t* of तरः *taraḥ* is changed into ट् *ṭ*, as in § 89, III. 2.) If the penultimate vowel be long, no change takes place; गीस्तरा *gîstarâ*. (Pâṇ. VIII. 3, 101.)

सर्पिः + मत् = सर्पिष्मत् *sarpiḥ + mat = sarpishmat*, having clarified butter.

Table showing the Changes of स् s *into* ष् sh.

Any Vowel except अ, आ â, (in spite of intervening Anusvâra or Visarga or sibilant,) and क् *k*, र् *r*, ल् *l* if immediately preceding,	change स् *s* into ष् *sh*	if there follow Vowels, or त् *t*, थ् *th*, न् *n*, म् *m*, य् *y*, व् *v*.

§ 101. The same rule produces the change of स् *s* into ष् *sh* in roots beginning with स् *s*, if reduplicated, provided the vowel of the reduplicated syllable is not अ, आ *â:* Ex. स्वप् *svap*, to sleep; Redupl. Perf. सुष्वाप *sushvâpa*,

* The Anusvâra must not represent a radical nasal; hence पुंसु *puṁsu*, not पुंषु *puṁshu*, loc. plur. of पुंस् *puṁs*, man; Pada base पुम् *pum*. (Pâṇ. VIII. 3, 58.) The Sârasvatî prescribes पुंक्षु *puṅkshu*. The स् *s* must not be a radical स् *s;* hence सुपिसौ *supisau*, because the स् *s* belongs to the root पिस् *pis*. (Pâṇ. VIII. 3, 59.) Yet आशिषः *âśishaḥ*, from root शास् *śâs*. The rules do not apply to final स् *s;* hence अग्निस्तत्र *agnis tatra*. (Pâṇ. VIII. 3, 55.)

I have slept. सिध् *sidh*, Des. सिषित्सति *sishitsati*. This rule is liable to exceptions.

§ 102. Again, many roots beginning with स् *s* change it into ष् *sh* after prepositions requiring such a change, viz. अति *ati*, over, अनु *anu*, after, अपि *api*, upon, अभि *abhi*, towards, नि *ni*, in, निर् *nir*, out, परि *pari*, round, प्रति *prati*, towards, वि *vi*, away: Ex. अभि + स्तौति = अभिष्टौति *abhi* + *stauti* = *abhishṭauti*, he praises. The same change takes place even after the augment has been added, in which case the स् *s* is really preceded by an अ *a*: Ex. अभ्यष्टौत् *abhyashṭaut*, he praised. Some verbs, after these prepositions, keep the ष् *sh* in the reduplicated perfect: Ex. सिच् *sich*, to sprinkle; अभिषिञ्चति *abhishiñchati*, he sprinkles; अभिषिषेच *abhishishecha*, he has sprinkled. In the intensive सिच् *sich* does not follow this rule; hence अभिसेसिच्यते *abhisesichyate* (Pâṇ. VIII. 3, 112); but in the desiderative स् *s* is changed, अभिषिषिक्षति *abhishishikshati*. Many other cases must be learnt from the dictionary or from Pâṇini.

§ 103. In order to give an idea of the minuteness of the rules as collected by native grammarians, and of the complicated manner in which these rules are laid down, the following extracts from Pâṇini have been subjoined, though they by no means exhaust the subject according to the views of native grammarians. It need hardly be added that beginners should not attempt to burden their memory with these rules, though a glance at them may be useful by giving them an idea of the intricacies of Sanskrit grammar.

Native grammarians enumerate all monosyllabic verbs beginning with स् *s*, and followed by a vowel or by a dental consonant, (likewise स्मि *smi*, स्विद् *svid*, स्वद् *svad*, स्वञ्ज् *svañj*, स्वप् *svap*,) as if beginning with ष् *sh*. Thus they write षिध् *shidh*, ष्ठा *shṭhâ*, ष्मि *shmi*. (Pâṇ. VI. 1, 64.)

This is not done with सृप् *sṛip*, सृज् *sṛij*, स्तॄ *stṝ*, स्तृ *stṛi*, स्त्यै *styai*, सेक् *sek*, सृ *sṛi*, in order to show that their initial स् *s* is not liable to be changed into ष् *sh* under any circumstances.

They then give the general rule that this initial ष् *sh* is to be changed into स् *s*, in all these verbs, except ष्ठिव् *shṭhiv* and ष्वष्क् *shvashk*, (and according to some in ष्ट्यै *shṭyai*, Sâr.,) unless where ष् *sh* is enjoined a second time.

Now ष् *sh* for स् *s* in these verbs is enjoined a second time:

1. When a preposition, or what else precedes it, requires such permutation, according to general rules. वि + स्तौति = विष्टौति *vi* + *stauti* = *vishṭauti*. सेव् *sev* forms सिषेव *sisheva* in the reduplicated perfect.
2. In desideratives, when the reduplicative syllable contains इ or उ, *i* or *u*. सिध् *sidh*, Des. सिषित्सति *sishitsati*.

But if the स् *s* of the desiderative element must itself be changed to ष् *sh*, the initial स् *s* remains unchanged. सिध् *sidh*, सिसेधिषति *sisedhishati*. (Pâṇ. VIII. 3, 61.)

Except in स्तु *stu*, and in derivative verbs in अय *aya*, where स् *s* is changed to ष् *sh*. स्तु *stu*, Des. तुष्टूषति *tushṭûshati*. सिध् *sidh*, Caus. सेधयति *sedhayati*, Des. सिषेधयिषति *sishedhayishati;* but सुसूषति *susûshati*. (VIII. 3, 61.)

Except again, in certain causatives, in अय *aya* (VIII. 3, 62), where स् *s* is not changed into ष् *sh*. स्विद् *svid*, सिस्वेदयिषति *sisvedayishati*. स्वद् *svad*, सिस्वादयिषति *sisvâdayishati*. सह् *sah*, सिसाहयिषति *sisâhayishati*.

3. In certain verbs, after prepositions which require such a change, even when they are separated from the verb by the augment, viz. सु *su* (*su*), सू *sû* (*tud*), सो *so* (*div*), स्तु *stu* (*ad*), स्तुभ् *stubh* (*bhû*); or even if separated by reduplication, in the verbs स्था *sthâ*, सेनय *senaya*, सिध् *sidh*, सिच् *sich*, संज् *sañj*, स्वंज् *svañj*, सद् *sad*, स्तंभ् *stambh*, स्वन् *svan*, सेव् *sev*, (the last only after परि *pari*, नि *ni*, वि *vi*: VIII. 3, 65.)

After prepositions: अभिषुणोति *abhishuṇoti*. अभिषुवति *abhishuvati*. अभिष्यति *abhishyati*. परिष्टौति *parishṭauti*. परिष्टोभते *parishṭobhate*. अभिष्ठास्यति *abhishṭhâsyati*. अभिषेणयति *abhisheṇayati*. परिषेधति *parishedhati*. अभिषिंचति *abhishiñchati*. परिषजति *parishajati*. परिष्वजते *parishvajate* (VIII. 3, 65). निषीदति *nishîdati*, but प्रतिसीदति *pratisîdati* (VIII. 3, 66). अभिष्टभ्नाति *abhishṭabhnâti* (VIII. 3, 67 and 114). Also अवष्टभ्य *avashṭabhya* (VIII. 3, 68, in certain senses). वि and अवष्वणति *vi* and *avashvaṇati* (VIII. 3, 69, in the sense of eating). परिषेवते *parishevate*.

After prepositions and augment: अभ्यषुणोत् *abhyashuṇot*. पर्यषुवत् *paryashuvat*. अभ्यष्यत् *abhyashyat*. पर्यष्टौत् *paryashṭaut*. अभ्यष्टोभत *abhyashṭobhata*. अभ्यष्ठात् *abhyashṭhât*. अभ्यषेणयत् *abhyasheṇayat*. पर्यषेधत् *paryashedhat*. अभ्यषिंचत् *abhyashiñchat*. पर्यषजत *paryashajata*. अभ्यष्वजत *abhyashvajata*. अभ्यषीदत् *abhyashîdat*. अभ्यष्टभ्नात् *abhyashṭabhnât*. व्यष्वणत् *vyashvaṇat* and अवाष्वणत् *avâshvaṇat*. पर्यषेवत *paryashevata*.

After prepositions and reduplication (VIII. 3, 64): अभितष्ठौ *abhitashṭhau*. अभिषिषेणयिषति *abhishisheṇayishati*. अभिषिषेधयिषति *abhishishedhayishati*. अभिषिषिक्षति *abhishishikshati*. अभिषिषंक्षति *abhishishaṅkshati* and अभ्यषिषंक्षत् *abhyashishaṅkshat*. परिषिष्वंक्षते *parishishvaṅkshate*. निषिषत्सति *nishishatsati* (VIII. 3, 118). अभितष्टंभ *abhitashṭambha*. अवषष्वाण *avashashvâṇa*. परिषिषेव *parishisheva*, (the last only after परि *pari*, नि *ni*, वि *vi*.)

4. Only after the prepositions परि *pari*, नि *ni*, वि *vi*, the following words (VIII. 3, 70): the part. सितः *sitaḥ*, the subst. सयः *sayaḥ*, सिव् *siv*, सह् *sah*; कृ *kṛi* (if with initial स् *s*, स्कृ *skṛi*) and similar verbs; स्तु *stu*.

The words mentioned in 4. and स्वंज् *svañj* may optionally retain स् *s*, if the augment intervenes. (VIII. 3, 71.)

5. After the prepositions अनु *anu*, वि *vi*, परि *pari*, अभि *abhi*, नि *ni*, स्यन्द् *syand* may take ष् *sh*, except when applied to living beings. (VIII. 3, 72.)
6. After the prep. वि *vi*, स्कन्द् *skand* may take ष् *sh*, though not in the past participle in त *ta* (VIII. 3, 73), but after the prep. परि *pari*, throughout, even in the past participle (VIII. 3, 74). परिष्कन्नः or परिस्कन्नः *parishkannaḥ* or *pariskannaḥ*.
7. After the prep. निर् *nir*, नि *ni*, वि *vi*, the verbs स्फुर् *sphur* and स्फुल् *sphul* may take ष् *sh*. (VIII. 3, 76.)
8. After the prep. वि *vi*, स्कम्भ् *skambh* must always take ष् *sh*. (VIII. 3, 77.)
9. The verb अस् *as*, after dropping its initial vowel, takes ष् *sh* after prepositions which cause such a change, and after प्रादुर् *prâdur*, if the ष् *sh* is followed by य् *y* or a vowel (VIII. 3, 87). अभिष्यात् *abhishyât*. प्रादुःष्यात् *prâduḥshyât*. प्रादुःषन्ति *prâduḥshanti*.
10. The verb स्वप् *svap*, when changed to सुप् *sup*, takes ष् *sh*, after सु *su*, वि *vi*, निर् *nir*, दुर् *dur* (VIII. 3, 88). सुषुप्तः *sushuptaḥ*. दुःषुप्तः *duḥshuptaḥ*.

Exceptional cases, where स् *s* is used, and not ष् *sh*:

11. The verb सिच् *sich*, followed by the intensive affix (VIII. 3, 112). अभिसेसिच्यते *abhisesichyate*.
12. The verb सिध् *sidh*, signifying to go (VIII. 3, 113). परिसेधति *parisedhati*.
13. The verb सह् *sah*, if changed to सोढ् *soḍh* (VIII. 3, 115). परिसोढुं *parisoḍhum*.
14. The verbs स्तम्भ् *stambh*, सिव् *siv*, सह् *sah*, in the reduplicated aorist (VIII. 3, 116). पर्यसीषहत् *paryasîshahat*.
15. The verb सु *su*, followed by the affixes of the 1st future, the conditional, or the desiderative (VIII. 3, 117). अभिसोष्यति *abhisoshyati*. अभिसुसूः *abhisusûḥ*.
16. The verbs सद् *sad*, स्वञ्ज् *svañj*, in the reduplicated perfect (VIII. 3, 118). अभिषसाद *abhishasâda*. अभिषस्वजे *abhishasvaje*.
17. The verb सद् *sad*, optionally, if preceded by the augment (VIII. 3, 119). न्यषीदत् or न्यसीदत् *nyashîdat* or *nyasîdat*.

§ 104. There are many compounds in which the initial स् *s* of the second word is changed to ष् *sh*, if the first word ends in a vowel (except *â*). Ex. युधिष्ठिर *yudhishṭhira*, from युधि *yudhi*, in battle, and स्थिर *sthira*, firm; सुष्ठु *sushṭhu*, well; दुष्ठु *dushṭhu*, ill; सुषमः *sushamaḥ*, beautiful, विषमः *vishamaḥ*, difficult, from समः *samaḥ*, even; त्रिष्टुभ् *trishṭubh*, a metre; अग्नीषोमौ *agnishomau*, Agni and Soma; मातृष्वसृ *mâtṛishvasṛi*, mother's sister; पितृष्वसृ *pitṛishvasṛi*, father's sister; गोष्ठः *goshṭhaḥ*, cow-stable; अग्निष्टोमः *agnishṭomaḥ*, a sacrifice; ज्योतिष्टोमः *jyotishṭomaḥ*, a sacrifice, (here the final स् *s* of ज्योतिस् *jyotis* is dropt.) In तुरासाह् *turâsâh*, a name of Indra, and similar compounds,

स् *s* is changed to ष् *sh* whenever ह् *h* becomes ट् *ṭ*; nom. तुराषाट् *turâshâṭ*; acc. तुरासाहं *turâsâham*. (Pâṇ. VIII. 3, 56.)

Change of Dental ध् dh *into Lingual* ढ् ḍh.

§ 105. The ध् *dh* of the second pers. plur. Âtm. is changed to ढ् *ḍh* in the reduplicated perfect, the aorist, and in षीध्वं *shîdhvam* of the benedictive, provided the ध् *dh*, or the षी *shî* of षीध्वं *shîdhvam*, follows immediately an inflective root ending in any vowel but अ, आ *a*, *â*. (Pâṇ. VIII. 3, 78.)

Ex. कृ *kṛi*; Perf. चकृढ्वे *chakṛiḍhve*.
च्यु *chyu*; Aor. अच्योढ्वं *achyoḍhvam*.
प्लु *plu*; Bened. प्लोषीढ्वं *ploshîḍhvam*.
But क्षिप् *kship*; Aor. अक्षिब्ध्वं *akshibdhvam*.
यज् *yaj*; Bened. यक्षीध्वं *yakshîdhvam*.

If the same terminations are preceded by the intermediate इ *i*, and the इ *i* be preceded by य् *y*, र् *r*, ल् *l*, व् *v*, ह् *h*, the change is optional.

Ex. लु *lu*; Perf. लुलुविध्वे *luluvidhve* or लुलुविढ्वे *luluviḍhve*.
लु *lu*; Aor. अलविध्वं *alavidhvam* or अलविढ्वं *alaviḍhvam*.
लु *lu*; Bened. लविषीध्वं *lavishîdhvam* or लविषीढ्वं *lavishîḍhvam*.
But बुध् *budh*; Aor. अबोधिध्वं *abodhidhvam*.

Rules of Internal Sandhi.

§ 106. The phonetic rules contained in the preceding paragraphs (§ 32–94) apply, as has been stated, to the final and initial letters of words (*padas*), when brought into immediate contact with each other in a sentence, to the final and initial letters of words formed into compounds, and to the final letters of nominal bases before the Pada-terminations, and before certain secondary or Taddhita suffixes, beginning with any consonant except य् *y*.

There is another class of phonetic rules applicable to the final letters of nominal (*prâtipadika*) and verbal bases (*dhâtu*) before the other terminations of declension and conjugation, before primary or Kṛit suffixes, and before secondary or Taddhita suffixes, beginning with a vowel or य् *y*. Some of these rules are general, and deserve to be remembered. But in many cases they either agree with the rules of External Sandhi, or are themselves liable to such numerous exceptions, that it is far easier to learn the words or grammatical forms themselves, as we do in Greek and Latin, than to try to master the rules according to which they are formed or supposed to be formed.

The following are a few of the phonetic rules of what may be called *Internal Sandhi*. The student will find it useful to glance at them, without endeavouring, however, to impress them on his memory. After he has learnt that द्विष् *dvish*, to hate, forms द्वेष्मि *dveshmi*, I hate, द्वेक्षि *dvekshi*, thou hatest, द्वेष्टि *dveshṭi*, he hates, अद्वेट् *adveṭ*, he hated, द्विड्ढि *dviḍḍhi*, Hate! द्विट् *dviṭ*, a hater, द्विषः *dvishaḥ*, of a hater, द्विट्सु *dviṭsu*, among haters,—he will refer back with advantage to the rules, more or less general, which regulate the change of final ष् *sh* into क् *k*, ट् *ṭ*, ड् *ḍ*, &c.; but he will never learn his declensions and conjugations properly, if, instead of acquiring first the paradigms as they are, he endeavours to construct each form by itself, according to the phonetic rules laid down in the following paragraphs.

1. *Final Vowels.*

§ 107. No hiatus is tolerated in the middle of Sanskrit words. Words such as प्रउग *praüga*, fore-yoke, तितउ *titaü*, sieve, are isolated exceptions. The hiatus in compounds, such as पुरएता *pura-etâ*, going in front, नमउक्तिः *nama-uktiḥ*, saying of praise, which is produced by the elision of a final स् *s* before certain vowels, has been treated of under the head of External Sandhi. (§ 84. 2.)

§ 108. Final अ *a* and आ *â* coalesce with following vowels according to the general rules of Sandhi.

तुद + अमि *tuda* + *ami* = तुदामि *tudâmi*, I beat.
तुद + इ *tuda* + *i* = तुदे *tude*, I beat, Âtm.
दान + इ *dâna* + *i* = दाने *dâne*, in the gift.
दान + ई *dâna* + *î* = दाने *dâne*, the two gifts.

If we admit the same set of terminations after bases ending in consonants and in short अ *a*, it becomes necessary to lay down some rules requiring final अ *a* to be dropt before certain vowels. Thus if अम् *am* is put down as the general termination of the acc. sing., as in वाचं *vâch-am*, it is necessary to enjoin the omission of final अ *a* of शिव *śiva* before the अं *am* of the acc. sing., in order to arrive at शिवं *śivam*. In the same manner, if अं *am* is put down as the termination of the 1. p. sing. impf. Par., and ए *e* as that of the 1. p. sing. pres. Âtm., we can form regularly अद्वेषं *advesh-am* and द्विषे *dvishe*; but we have to lay down a new rule, according to which the final अ *a* of तुद *tuda* is dropt, in order to arrive at the correct forms अतुदं *atud*(*a*)-*am* and तुदे *tud*(*a*)*e*. By following the system adopted in this grammar of giving two sets of terminations, and thus enabling the student to arrive at the actual forms of declension and conjugation by a merely mechanical combination of base and termination, it is possible to dispense with a number of these phonetic rules.

Again, in the declension of bases ending in radical आ *â*, certain phonetic rules had to be laid down, according to which the final आ *â* had to be elided before certain terminations beginning with vowels. Thus the dative शंखध्मा + ए *śaṅkhadhmâ + e* was said to form शंखध्मे *śaṅkhadhme*, (to the shell-blower,) by dropping the final आ *â*, and not शंखध्मै *śaṅkhadhmai*. Here, too, the same result is obtained by admitting two bases for this as for many other nouns, and assigning the weak base, in which the आ *â* is dropt, to all the so-called Bha cases, the cases which Bopp calls the weakest cases (Pâṇ. VI. 4, 140). Each of these systems has its advantages and defects, and the most practical plan is, no doubt, to learn the paradigms by heart without asking any questions as to the manner in which the base and the terminations were originally combined or glued together.

§ 109. With regard to verbal bases ending in long आ *â*, many special rules have to be observed, according to which final आ *â* is either elided, or changed to ई *î* or to ए *e*. These rules will be given in the chapter on Conjugation. Thus

पुना + अंति *punâ + anti* = पुनंति *punanti*, they cleanse.
पुना + मः *punâ + maḥ* = पुनीमः *punîmaḥ*, we cleanse.
दा + हि *dâ + hi* = देहि *dehi*, Give!

§ 110. Final इ *i*, ई *î*, उ *u*, ऊ *û*, ऋ *ṛi*, if followed by vowels or diphthongs, are generally changed to य् *y*, व् *v*, र् *r*.

Ex. मति + ऐ = मत्यै *mati + ai* = *matyai*, to the mind.
जिगि + उः = जिग्युः *jigi + uḥ* = *jigyuḥ*, they have conquered.
भानु + ओः = भान्वोः *bhânu + oḥ* = *bhânvoḥ*, of the two splendours.
पितृ + आ = पित्रा *pitṛi + â* = *pitrâ*, by the father.
बिभी + अति = बिभ्यति *bibhî + ati* = *bibhyati*, they fear.

In some cases इ *i* and ई *î* are changed to इय् *iy*; उ *u* and ऊ *û* to उव् *uv*; ऋ *ṛi* to रि *ri*; ॠ *ṛî* to इर् *ir* and, after labials, to उर् *ur*.

Ex. वी + अंति = वियंति *vî + anti* = *viyanti*, they go.
भी + इ = भियि *bhî + i* = *bhiyi*, in fear.
सुषू + ए = सुषुवे *sushû + e* = *sushuve*, I have brought forth.
भू + इ = भुवि *bhû + i* = *bhuvi*, on earth.
गॄ + अति = गिरति *gṛî + ati* = *girati*, he swallows.
पपॄ + इ = पपुरि *papṛî + i* = *papuri*, liberal.
यु + अंति = युवंति *yu + anti* = *yuvanti*, they join.
युयु + उः = युयुवुः *yuyu + uḥ* = *yuyuvuḥ*, they have joined.

When either the one or the other takes place must be learnt from paradigms and from special rules given under the heads of Declension and Conjugation.

§ 111. Final ॠ *ṛî*, if followed by terminational consonants, is changed to ईर् *îr*; and after labials to ऊर् *ûr*.

गॄ gṝ, to shout; Passive गीर्यते gîr-yate; Part. गीर्णः gîrṇaḥ.
पॄ pṝ, to fill; Passive पूर्यते pûr-yate; Part. पूर्णः pûrṇaḥ.

§ 112. ए e, ऐ ai, ओ o, औ au, before vowels and diphthongs, are generally changed into अय् ay, आय् ây, अव् av, आव् âv.

दे + अते = दयते de + ate = dayate, he protects.
रै + ए = राये rai + e = râye, to wealth.
गो + ए = गवे go + e = gave, to the cow.
नौ + अः = नावः nau + aḥ = nâvaḥ, the ships.

Roots terminated by a radical diphthong (except व्ये vye in redupl. perf., Pâṇ. vi. 1, 46) change it into आ â before any affix except those of the so-called special tenses. (Pâṇ. vi. 1, 45.)

दे + ता = दाता de + tâ = dâtâ, he will protect.
दे + सीय = दासीय de + sîya = dâsîya, May I protect!
म्लै + ता = म्लाता mlai + tâ = mlâtâ, he will wither.
शो + ता = शाता śo + tâ = śâtâ, he will pare.

But in the Present ग्लै + अति = ग्लायति glai + ati = glâyati, he is weary.

2. *Final Consonants.*

§ 113. The rules according to which the consonants which can occur at the end of a word are restricted to क् k, ङ् ṅ, ट् ṭ, ण् ṇ, त् t, न् n, प् p, म् m, ल् l, : ḥ, ∸ ṁ, must likewise be observed where the last letter of a nominal or verbal base becomes final, i. e. where it is not followed by any derivative letter or syllable.

Thus the nominal base युध् yudh, battle, would in the vocative singular be युध् yudh. Here, however, the ध् dh must be changed into द् d, because no aspirate is tolerated as a final (§ 54. 1); and द् d is changed into त् t, because no word can end in a soft consonant (§ 54. 2). वाच् vâch, speech, in the voc. sing. would change its च् ch into क् k, because palatals can never be final (§ 54. 3).

In अधोक् adhok, the aspiration of the final is thrown back on the initial द् d (§ 118). The final ह् h or घ् gh, after losing its aspiration, becomes ग् g, which is further changed to क् k.

§ 114. Nominal or verbal bases ending in consonants and followed by terminations consisting of a single consonant, drop the termination altogether, two consonants not being tolerated at the end of a word (§ 55). The final consonants of the base are then treated like other final consonants.

वाच् + स् = वाक् vâch + s = vâk, speech; nom. sing.
प्राञ्च् + स् = प्राङ् prâñch + s = prâṅ, eastern; nom. sing. masc. Here प्राङ्क् prâṅk, which remains after the dropping of स् s, is, according to the

same rule, reduced again to प्राङ् *prâṅ*, the final nasal remaining guttural, as it would have been guttural if the final क् *k* had remained.

सुवल्ग् + स् = सुवल् *suvalg* + *s* = *suval*, well jumping. Here, after the dropping of स् *s*, there would remain सुवल्क् *suvalk;* but as no word can end in two consonants, this is reduced to सुवल् *suval*. Before the Pada-terminations सुवल्ग् *suvalg* assumes its Pada form सुवल् *suval* (§ 53); hence instrum. plur. सुवल्भिः *suvalbhiḥ*.

अहन् + स् = अहन् *ahan* + *s* = *ahan*, thou killedst; 2. p. sing. impf. Par.

अद्वेष् + त् = अद्वेट् *advesh* + *t* = *adveṭ*, he hated; 3. p. sing. impf. Par.

अदोह् + त् = अधोक् *adoh* + *t* = *adhok*, he milked; 3. p. sing. impf. Par.

Exceptions will be seen under the heads of Declension and Conjugation.

§ 115. With regard to the changes of the final consonants of nominal and verbal bases, before terminations, the general rule is,

1. Terminations beginning with sonant letters, require a sonant letter at the end of the nominal or verbal base.
2. Terminations beginning with surd letters, require a surd letter at the end of the nominal or verbal base.
3. In this general rule the terminations beginning with *vowels*, *semivowels*, or *nasals* are excluded, i. e. they produce no change in the final consonant of the base.

1. वच् + धि = वग्धि *vach* + *dhi* = *vagdhi*, Speak! 2. p. sing. imp. Par.
   पृच् + ध्वे = पृग्ध्वे *pṛich* + *dhve* = *pṛigdhve*, you mix; 2. p. plur. pres. Âtm.
2. अद् + सि = अत्सि *ad* + *si* = *atsi*, 2. p. sing. pres. thou eatest.
   अद् + ति = अत्ति *ad* + *ti* = *atti*, 3. p. sing. pres. he eats.
3. मरुत् + इ = मरुति *marut* + *i* = *maruti*, loc. sing. in the wind.
   वच् + मि = वच्मि *vach* + *mi* = *vachmi*, I speak.
   ग्रथ् + यते = ग्रथ्यते *grath* + *yate* = *grathyate*, it is arranged.

Exceptions such as भिद् + नः = भिन्नः *bhid* + *naḥ* = *bhinnaḥ*, divided, भञ्ज् + नः = भग्नः *bhañj* + *naḥ* = *bhagnaḥ*, broken, must be learnt by practice rather than by rule.

§ 116. Aspirates, if followed by terminations beginning with any letter (except vowels and semivowels and nasals), lose their aspiration. (§ 54. 1.)

Ex. मामथ् + ति = मामत्ति *mâmath* + *ti* = *mâmatti*, 3. p. sing. pres. Par. of the intensive मामथ् *mâmath*, he shakes much.

रुन्ध् + ध्वे = रुन्द्ध्वे *rundh* + *dhve* = *runddhve*, 2. p. plur. pres. Âtm. of रुध् *rudh*, you impede.

लभ् + स्ये = लप्स्ये *labh* + *sye* = *lapsye*, I shall take.

But युध् + इ = युधि *yudh* + *i* = *yudhi*, loc. sing. in battle.

लुभ् + यः = लुभ्यः *lubh + yaḥ = lubhyaḥ*, to be desired.

क्षुभ् + नाति = क्षुभ्नाति *kshubh + nâti = kshubhnâti*, he agitates.

It is a general rule that two aspirates can never meet in ordinary Sanskrit.

§ 117. If final घ् *gh*, ढ् *ḍh*, ध् *dh*, भ् *bh* are followed by त् *t* or थ् *th*, they are changed to the corresponding soft letters, ग् *g*, ड् *ḍ*, द् *d*, ब् *b*, but the त् *t* and थ् *th* are likewise softened, and the द् *d* receives the aspiration. See also § 128.

Ex. रुणध् + ति = रुणद्धि *ruṇadh + ti = ruṇaddhi*, he obstructs.

लभ् + तः = लब्धः *labh + taḥ = labdhaḥ*, taken.

रुंध् + थः = रुंद्धः *rundh + thaḥ = runddhaḥ* (also spelt रुंधः *rundhaḥ*), you two obstruct.

रुंध् + तः = रुंद्धः *rundh + taḥ = runddhaḥ*, they two obstruct.

अबांध् + तं = अबांद्धं *abândh + tam = abânddham*, 2. p. dual aor. 1. Par. you two bound.

अबंध् + थाः = अबंद्धाः *abandh + thâḥ = abanddhâḥ*, 2. p. sing. aor. 1. Âtm. thou boundest.

In अबांद्धं *abânddham*, 2. p. dual aor. 1. Par., the aspiration of final ध् *dh* is not thrown back upon the initial ब् *b*, because it is supposed to be absorbed by the तं *tam* of the termination, changed into द्धं *dham*. The same applies to अबंद्धाः *abanddhâḥ*, though here the termination थाः *thâḥ* was aspirated in itself.

§ 118. If घ् *gh*, ढ् *ḍh*, ध् *dh*, भ् *bh*, ह् *h*, at the end of a syllable, lose their aspiration either as final or as being followed by ध्व् *dhv*, भ् *bh*, स् *s*, they throw their aspiration back upon the initial letters, provided these letters be no other than ग् *g*, ड् *ḍ*, द् *d*, ब् *b*. See § 93.

Ex. Inflective base बुध् *budh*, to know; nom. sing. भुत् *bhut*, knowing.

Instrum. plur. भुद्भिः *bhudbhiḥ*.

Loc. plur. भुत्सु *bhutsu*.

Second pers. plur. aor. Âtm. अभुद्ध्वं *abhuddhvam*.

Second pers. sing. pres. Intens. बोबोध् + सि = बोभोत्सि *bobodh + si = bobhotsi*.

Desiderative of दभ् *dabh*, धिप्सति *dhipsati*, he wishes to hurt.

First pers. sing. fut. of बंध् + स्यामि = भंत्स्यामि *bandh + syâmi = bhantsyâmi*, I shall bind.

दह् *dah*, to burn; धक् *dhak*, nom. sing. a burner.

दुह् *duh*, to milk; अधुग्ध्वं *adhugdhvam*, 2. p. plur. impf. Âtm.: but 2. p. sing. imp. Par. दुग्धि *dugdhi*.

Note—दध् *dadh*, the reduplicated base of धा *dhâ*, दधामि *dadhâmi*, I place, throws the lost aspiration of the final ध् *dh* back on the initial द् *d*, not only before ध्व् *dhv*, स् *s*, but likewise before त् *t* and थ् *th*, where we might have expected the application of § 117. दध् + तः = धत्तः

dadh + *taḥ* = *dhattaḥ*: दध् + तः = धत्तः *dadh* + *thaḥ* = *dhatthaḥ*; दध् + से = धत्से *dadh* + *se* = *dhatse*; दध् + ध्वं = धद्ध्वं *dadh* + *dhvam* = *dhaddhvam*.

§ 119. If च् *ch*, ज् *j*, झ् *jh* are final, or followed by a termination beginning with any letter, except vowels, semivowels, or nasals, they are changed to क् *k* or ग् *g*.

Ex. Nominal base वाच् *vâch*; voc. वाक् *vâk*, speech.
Verbal base वच् *vach*; 3. p. sing. pres. वच् + ति = वक्ति *vach* + *ti* = *vakti*.
युञ्ज् + धि = युङ्ग्धि *yuñj* + *dhi* = *yuṅgdhi*, 2. p. sing. imp. Join!
But loc. sing. वाच् + इ = वाचि *vâch* + *i* = *vâchi*.
वाच् + य = वाच्य *vâch* + *ya* = *vâchya*, to be spoken.
वच् + मः = वच्मः *vach* + *maḥ* = *vachmaḥ*, we speak.
वच् + वः = वच्वः *vach* + *vaḥ* = *vachvaḥ*, we two speak. (See also § 124.)

§ 120. ष् *sh* at the end of nominal and verbal bases, if it becomes the final of a word, is changed into ट् *ṭ*.

Ex. Nominal base द्विष् *dvish*; nom. sing. द्विट् *dviṭ*, a hater.
Verbal base द्विष् *dvish*; 3. p. sing. impf. Par. अद्वेट् *adveṭ*, he hated.

§ 121. Before verbal terminations beginning with स् *s*, it is treated like क् *k*.

Ex. द्वेष् + सि = द्वेक्षि *dvesh* + *si* = *dvekshi*, thou hatest; aor. अद्विक्षत् *advikshat*, he hated.
पोक्ष्यति *pokshyati* (*push* + *syati*), he will nourish.

§ 122. Before त् *t* or थ् *th* it remains unchanged itself, but changes त् *t* and थ् *th* into ट् *ṭ* and ठ् *ṭh*.

Ex. द्विष् + तः = द्विष्टः *dvish* + *taḥ* = *dvishṭaḥ*, they (two) hate.

This rule admits of a more general application, namely, that every dental त् *t*, थ् *th*, द् *d*, ध् *dh*, न् *n*, and स् *s*, is changed into the corresponding lingual, if preceded by ट् *ṭ*, ठ् *ṭh*, ड् *ḍ*, ढ् *ḍh*, ण् *ṇ*, and ष् *sh*.

Ex. द्विड् + धि = द्विड्ढि *dviḍ* + *dhi* = *dviḍḍhi*, hate thou.
मृड् + नाति = मृड्णाति *mṛiḍ* + *nâti* = *mṛiḍṇâti*.
ईड् + ते = ईट्टे *îḍ* + *te* = *îṭṭe*, he praises.

§ 123. Before other consonantal terminations ष् *sh* is treated like ड् *ḍ*.

Ex. द्विष् + ध्वं = द्विड्ढ्वं *dvish* + *dhvam* = *dviḍḍhvam*, 2. p. plur. impf. Âtm. Hate ye!
द्विष् + सु = द्विट्सु *dvish* + *su* = *dviṭsu*, loc. plur. among haters.

Exceptions to this rule, such as धृष् *dhṛish*, nom. धृक् *dhṛik*, and to other rules will be seen under the heads of Declension and Conjugation.

§ 124. In the roots भ्राज् *bhrâj*, to shine, मृज् *mṛij*, to wipe, यज् *yaj*, to sacrifice, राज् *râj*, to shine, सृज् *sṛij*, to let forth, and भ्रज् *bhraj*, to roast (भ्रज्ज

bhrañja, Pâṇ. VIII. 2, 36), the final ज् *j* is replaced by ष् *sh*, which, in the case enumerated above, is liable to the same changes as an original ष् *sh*. Thus

मृज् + थ = मृष्ट *mṛij* + *tha* = *mṛishṭha*, you wipe.
राज् + सु = राट्सु *râj* + *su* = *râṭsu*, &c.

§ 125. Most verbal and nominal bases ending in श् *ś*, छ् *chh*, क्ष् *ksh*, श्च् *śch* (some in ज् *j*, § 124) are treated exactly like those ending in simple ष् *sh*.

Ex. Nominal base विश् *viś*; nom. विट् *viṭ*, a man of the third caste.
Fut. वेश् + स्यामि = वेक्ष्यामि *veś* + *syâmi* = *vekshyâmi*, I shall enter.
Fut. periphr. वेश् + ता = वेष्टा *veś* + *tâ* = *veshṭâ*, I shall enter.
विश् + ध्वं = विड्ढ्वं *viś* + *dhvam* = *viḍḍhvam*, enter you.
Loc. plur. विश् + सु = विट्सु *viś* + *su* = *viṭsu*, among men.
Nominal base प्राछ् *prâchh*; nom. प्राट् *prâṭ*, an asker.
Verbal base प्रछ् *prachh*; प्रछ् + स्यामि = प्रक्ष्यामि *prachh* + *syâmi* = *prakshyâmi*, I shall ask.
प्रछ् + ता = प्रष्टा *prachh* + *tâ* = *prashṭâ*, I shall ask.
प्राछ् + सु = प्राट्सु *prâchh* + *su* = *prâṭsu*, among askers.
Nominal base तक्ष् *taksh*; तक्ष् + सु = तट्सु *taksh* + *su* = *taṭsu*, among carpenters.
Nominal base रक्ष् *raksh*; गोरक्ष् + सु = गोरट्सु *goraksh* + *su* = *goraṭsu*, among cowherds.
Verbal base चक्ष् *chaksh*; चक्ष् + से = चक्षे *chaksh* + *se* = *chakshe*, thou seest.
चक्ष् + ध्वे = चड्ढ्वे *chaksh* + *dhve* = *chaḍḍhve*, you see.
व्रश्च् *vraśch*, to cut; nom. sing. व्रट् *vraṭ*.
व्रश्च् + स्यामि = व्रक्ष्यामि *vraśch* + *syâmi* = *vrakshyâmi*, I shall cut.
व्रश्च् + ता = व्रष्टा *vraśch* + *tâ* = *vrashṭâ*, he will cut.

§ 126. The श् *ś* of दिश् *diś*, to show, दृश् *dṛiś*, to see, मृश् *mṛiś*, to stroke, स्पृश् *spṛiś*, to touch, if final, or followed by Pada-terminations, is changed into क् *k*.

Ex. Nominal base दिश् *diś*; nom. sing. दिक् *dik*; instrum. plur. दिग्भिः *digbhiḥ*; loc. plur. दिक्षु *dikshu*.
दृश् *dṛiś*; nom. sing. दृक् *dṛik*; instrum. plur. दृग्भिः *dṛigbhiḥ*.

In the root नश् *naś*, the change of श् *ś* into क् *k* or ट् *ṭ* is optional (Pâṇ. VIII. 2, 63). For further particulars see Declension and Conjugation.

§ 127. ह् *h* at the end of verbal bases, if followed by a termination beginning with स् *s*, is treated like घ् *gh*, i.e. like a guttural with an inherent aspiration, which aspiration may be thrown forward on the initial letter.

Ex. लेह् + स्यामि = लेक्ष्यामि *leh* + *syâmi* = *lekshyâmi*, I shall lick.
दोह् + स्यामि = धोक्ष्यामि *doh* + *syâmi* = *dhokshyâmi*, I shall milk.

§ 128. In all other cases, whether at the end of a word or followed by terminations, ह् *h* is treated either (1) like घ् *gh* in most words beginning with द् *d* (Pâṇ. VIII. 2, 32), and in उष्णिह् *ushṇih;* or (2) like ढ् *ḍh* in all other words.

Ex. (1) दुह् *duh;* nom. धुक् *dhuk;* instrum. plur. धुग्भिः *dhugbhiḥ;* loc. plur. धुक्षु *dhukshu;* part. pass. दुग्धः *dugdhaḥ.*

दृह् + तः = दृढः *dṛih* + *taḥ* = *dṛiḍhaḥ*, fast, is an exception.

Ex. (2) लिह् *lih;* nom. लिट् *liṭ;* instrum. plur. लिड्भिः *liḍbhiḥ;* loc. plur. लिट्सु *liṭsu* (वाह् *vâh*, वाट्सु *vâṭsu*).

लिह् + तः = लीढः *lih* + *taḥ* = *lîḍhaḥ.*

रुह् + तः = रूढः *ruh* + *taḥ* = *rûḍhaḥ.*

In लीढः *lîḍhaḥ* and रूढः *rûḍhaḥ*, ह् + त् *ḍh* + *t* are changed (§ 117) to ड् *ḍ* + ढ् *ḍh;* then the first ड् *ḍ* is dropt and the vowel lengthened. The only vowel which is not lengthened is ऋ *ṛi;* e.g. वृह् + त = वृढ् + त = वृड्ढ = वृढ *vṛih* + *ta* = *vṛiḍh* + *ta* = *vṛiḍ-ḍha* = *vṛiḍha.*

§ 129. The final ह् of certain roots (द्रुह् *druh*, मुह् *muh*, स्नुह् *snuh*, स्निह् *snih*) is treated either as घ् *gh* or ढ् *ḍh*. From द्रुह् *druh*, to hate, we have in compounds the nom. sing. ध्रुक् *dhruk* and ध्रुट् *dhruṭ* (Pâṇ. VIII. 2, 33); past participle द्रुग्धः *drugdhaḥ* or द्रूढः *drûḍhaḥ.*

§ 130. The final ह् *h* of नह् *nah*, to bind, is treated as ध् *dh*.

Ex. उपानह् *upânah*, slipper; nom. sing. उपानत् *upânat;* instrum. plur. उपानद्भिः *upânadbhiḥ.*

Past part. pass. नह् + तः = नद्धः *nah* + *taḥ* = *naddhaḥ*, bound.

As to अनडुह् *anaḍuh*, ox, &c., see Declension.

§ 131. Nominal bases ending in radical स् *s*, change it to त् *t*, if final, and before the Pada-terminations. (Pâṇ. VIII. 2, 72.)

ध्वस् *dhvas*, to fall; nom. sing. ध्वत् *dhvat*, nom. plur. ध्वसः *dhvasaḥ*, instrum. plur. ध्वद्भिः *dhvadbhiḥ.*

§ 132. Verbal bases ending in स् *s*, change it to त् *t*, before terminations of the general tenses beginning with स् *s*. (Pâṇ. VII. 4, 49.)

वस् *vas*, to dwell; fut. वस् + स्यामि = वत्स्यामि *vas* + *syâmi* = *vatsyâmi.*

Before other terminations beginning with स् *s*, final स् *s* remains unchanged.

वस् + से = वस्से *vas* + *se* = *vasse*, thou dwellest.

सस् + सि = सस्सि *sas* + *si* = *sassi*, thou sleepest.

निंस् + से = निंस्से *niṁs* + *se* = *niṁsse*, thou kissest.

पेपेस् + सि = पेपेक्षि *pepes* + *si* = *pepeshshi*, thou hurtest. (§ 100.)

In certain verbs final स् *s* is dropt before धि *dhi* of the imp.

शास् + धि = शाधि *śâs* + *dhi* = *śâdhi.* (Pâṇ. VI. 4, 35.)

चकास् + धि = चकाधि *chakâs* + *dhi* = *chakâdhi.*

In the same verbs final स् *s*, if immediately followed by the termination of the second person, स् *s*, may be changed to त् *t* or remain स् *s*.

अशास् + स् = अशात् or अशाः *aśâs* + *s* = *aśât* or *aśâḥ*.

Before the त् *t* of the third person, it always becomes त् *t*.

अशास् + त् = अशात् *aśâs* + *t* = *aśât*. (Pâṇ. VIII. 2, 73, 74.)

§ 133. न् *n* and म् *m* at the end of a nominal or verbal base, before sibilants (but not before the सु *su* of the loc. plur.), are changed to Anusvâra

Ex. जिघांसति *jighâṁsati*, he wishes to kill, from हन् *han*.

क्रंस्यते *kraṁsyate*, he will step, from क्रम् *kram*.

§ 134. न् *n* remains unchanged before semivowels.

Ex. हन्यः *hanyaḥ*, to be killed, from हन् *han*.

तन्वन् *tanvan*, extending, from तन् *tan*.

प्रेन्वनं *prenvanam**, propelling, from इन्व् *inv*.

§ 135. म् *m* remains unchanged before the semivowels य् *y*, र् *r*, ल् *l*.

Ex. काम्यः *kâm-yaḥ*, to be loved, from कम् *kam*.

ताम्रं *tâmram*, copper, from तम् *tam* and suffix र *ra*.

अम्लः *amlaḥ*, sour, from अम् *am* and suffix ल *la*.

§ 136. म् *m* at the end of a nominal or verbal base, if no suffix follows, or if followed by a Pada-termination, or by personal terminations beginning with म् *m* or व् *v*, is changed into न् *n*. (Pâṇ. VIII. 2, 65.)

Ex. प्रशान् *praśân*, nom. sing., and प्रशान्भिः *praśânbhiḥ*, instrum. plur., प्रशान्सु *praśânsu*, loc. plur., from प्रशाम् *praśâm*, quieting. (Pâṇ. VIII. 2, 64.)

अगन्म *aganma*, we went, and अगन्व *aganva*, we two went, from गम् + म *gam* + *ma*, गम् + व *gam* + *va*.

But nom. plur. प्रशामः *praśâmaḥ*.

§ 137. With regard to nasals, the general rule is that in the body of a word the firsts, the seconds, the thirds, and the fourths of each class can only be preceded by their own fifths, though in writing the dot may be used as a general substitute. (§ 8.)

Ex. आशङ्कते or आशंकते *âśaṅkate* or *âśaṁkate*, he fears.

आलिङ्गति or आलिंगति *âliṅgati* or *âliṁgati*, he embraces.

वञ्चयति or वंचयति *vañchayati* or *vaṁchayati*, he cheats.

उत्कण्ठते or उत्कंठते *utkaṇṭhate* or *utkaṁṭhate*, he longs.

गन्तुं or गंतुं *gantum* or *gaṁtum*, to go.

कम्पते or कंपते *kampate* or *kaṁpate*, he trembles.

In compounds, such as सम् + कल्पः *sam* + *kalpaḥ*, it is optional to change

* If the न् *n* before व् *v* were treated as Anusvâra, the second न् *n* would have to be changed into a lingual (§ 96). Pâṇ. VIII. 4, 2, v.

final म् *m*, standing at the end of a Pada, into the fifth or into real Anusvâra; संकल्पः or सङ्कल्पः *saṁkalpaḥ* or *saṅkalpaḥ*. (See § 77.)

§ 138. In the body of a word, Anusvâra is the only nasal that can stand before the sibilants श् *ś*, ष् *sh*, स् *s*, and ह् *h*.

Ex. दंशनं *daṁśanam*, biting. यजूंषि *yajûṁshi*, the prayers.
हंसः *haṁsaḥ*, goose. रंहते *raṁhate*, he goes.

§ 139. न् *n* following immediately after च् *ch* or ज् *j* is changed to ञ् *ñ*.

Ex. याच्ञा *yâchñâ*, prayer. राज्ञी *râjñî*, queen. जज्ञे *jajñe*, he was born.

§ 140. छ *chh* in the middle of a word between vowels or diphthongs must be changed to च्छ *chchh*. (See § 91.)

Ex. ऋछ् *ṛichh*, to go; ऋच्छति *ṛichchhati*, he goes.
म्लेच्छः *mlechchhaḥ*, a barbarian.

§ 141. छ् *chh* before a suffix beginning with न् *n* or म् *m* is changed to श् *ś*.

Ex. प्रछ् + न = प्रश्न *prachh* + *na* = *praśna*, question.
पाप्रछ् + मि = पाप्रश्मि *pâprachh* + *mi* = *pâpraśmi*, I ask frequently.

Before व् *v* this change is optional.

§ 142. Roots ending in य् *y* and व् *v* throw off their final letters before terminations beginning with consonants, except य् *y*.

Ex. पूय् + तः = पूतः *pûy* + *taḥ* = *pûtaḥ*, decaying.
तुर्व् + नः = तूर्णः *turv* + *naḥ* = *tûrṇaḥ*, killed.

§ 143. Roots ending in व् *v* and र् *r*, if preceded by इ *i* or उ *u*, lengthen their इ *i* and उ *u*, if व् *v* or र् *r* is followed immediately by a terminational consonant. (Pâṇ. VIII. 2, 77.)

Ex. दिव् *div*, to play, दीव्यति *dîvyati*, he plays. Bened. दीव्यासं *dîv-yâsam*.
गुर् *gur*, to exert, गूर्णः *gûrṇaḥ*.
जॄ *jṝ* (i. e. जिर् *jir*), to grow old, जीर्यति *jîryati*.
गिर् *gir*, voice; instrum. plur. गीर्भिः *gîrbhiḥ*, loc. plur. गीर्षु *gîrshu*.

There are exceptions. (Pâṇ. VIII. 2, 79.)

कुर् *kur*, to sound. Bened. कुर्यासं *kuryâsam*.

On a similar principle उ *u* is lengthened in तुर्व् + आवः = तूर्वावः *turv* + *âvaḥ* = *tûrvâvaḥ*. (Pâṇ. VIII. 2, 78.)

§ 144. Nominal and verbal bases ending in इर् *ir* and उर् *ur* lengthen इ *i* and उ *u*, when र् *r* becomes final after the loss of another final consonant. (Pâṇ. VIII. 2, 76.)

Ex. गिर् + स् = गीर् or गीः *gir* + *s* = *gîr* or *gîḥ*, nom. sing. voice.

§ 145. Nominal bases ending in इस् *is* or उस् *us* (the इस् *is* or उस् *us* being radical) lengthen इ *i* and उ *u* when final, and before terminations beginning with भ् *bh* or स् *s*. Likewise सजुस् *sajus*.

Loc. plur. सुपिस् + सु = सुपीःषु *supis + su = supîḥshu*; nom. sing. masc. and neut. सुपीः *supîḥ*.

Nom. sing. masc. सजुस् + स् = सजूः *sajus + s = sajûḥ*; nom. sing. neut. सजूः *sajûḥ*.

Doubling of Consonants.

According to some grammarians any consonant except र् *r* and ह् *h*, followed by another consonant and preceded by a vowel, may be doubled; likewise any consonant preceded by र् *r* or ह् *h*, these letters being themselves preceded by a vowel. As no practical object is obtained by this practice, it is best, with Śâkalya, to discontinue it throughout.

In our editions doubling takes place most frequently where any consonant, except the sibilants and ह् *h*, is preceded by र् *r* or ह् *h*, these being again preceded by a vowel. Thus

अर्क *arka*, sun, is frequently written अर्क्क *arkka*.

ब्रह्मन् *brahman* may be written ब्रह्म्मन् *brahmman*.

§ 146. If an aspirated consonant has to be doubled, the first loses its aspiration. Thus वर्धन or वर्द्धन *vardhana* or *varddhana*, increase.

§ 147. A sibilant after र् *r* must not be doubled, unless it is followed by a consonant. Thus it is always, वर्षाः *varshâḥ*, rainy season; आदर्शः *âdarśaḥ*, mirror. But we may write either दर्श्यते or दर्श्श्यते *darśyate* or *darśśyate*, it is shown.

Explanation of some Grammatical Terms used by Native Grammarians.

§ 148. Some of the technical terms used by native grammarians have proved so useful that they have found ready admittance into our own grammatical terminology. *Guṇa* and *Vṛiddhi* are terms adopted by comparative grammarians in the absence of any classical words to mark the exact changes of vowels comprehended under these words by Pâṇini and others. Most Sanskrit grammars have besides sanctioned the use of such terms as *Parasmaipada*, *Âtmanepada*, *Tatpurusha*, *Bahuvrîhi*, *Karmadhâraya*, *Kṛit*, *Taddhita*, *Uṇâdi*, and many more. Nothing can be more perfect than the grammatical terminology of Pâṇini; but as it was contrived for his own peculiar system of grammar, it is difficult to adopt part of it without at the same time adopting the whole of his system. A few remarks, however, on some of Pâṇini's grammatical terms may be useful.

All words without exception, or according to some grammarians with very few exceptions, are derived from roots or *dhâtus*. These roots have been collected in what are called *Dhâtupâṭhas*, root-recitals, the most important of which is ascribed by tradition to Pâṇini *.

* Siddhânta-Kaumudî, ed. Târânâtha, vol. II. p. 1.

From these *dhâtus* or roots are derived by means of *pratyayas* or suffixes, not only all kinds of verbs, but all substantives and adjectives, and according to some, even all pronouns and particles. Thus from the root मन् *man*, to think, we have not only मनुते *man-u-te*, he thinks, but likewise मनस् *man-as*, mind, मानस *mânas-a*, mental, &c. Words thus formed, but without as yet any case-terminations attached to them, are called *Prâtipadika*, nominal bases. Thus from the root जन् *jan*, to beget, we have the *prâtipadika* or nominal base जन *jan-a*, man, and this by the addition of the sign of the nom. sing. becomes जनः *jan-a-ḥ*, a man.

Suffixes for the formation of nouns are of two kinds:

1. Those by which nouns are derived direct from roots; Primary Suffixes.
2. Those by which nouns are derived from other nouns; Secondary Suffixes.

The former are called *Kṛit*, the latter *Taddhita*. Thus जन *jana*, man, is derived from the root जन् *jan* by the Kṛit suffix अ *a*; but जनीन *janîna*, appropriate for man, is derived from जन *jana* by the Taddhita suffix ईन *îna*. The name *prâtipadika* would apply both to जन *jana* and जनीन *janîna*, as nominal bases, ready to receive the terminations of declension.

The Kṛit suffixes are subdivided into three classes:

1. *Kṛit*, properly so called, i.e. suffixes by which nouns can be regularly formed from roots with certain more or less definite meanings. Thus by means of the suffix अथु *athu*, Sanskrit grammarians form

   वेपथु *vepathu*, trembling, from वेप् *vep*, to tremble.
   श्वयथु *śvayathu*, swelling, from श्वि *śvi*, to swell.
   क्षवथु *kshavathu*, sneezing, from क्षु *kshu*, to sneeze.
   दवथु *davathu*, vexation, from दु *du*, to vex, to burn.

2. *Kṛitya*, certain suffixes, such as तव्य *tavya*, अनीय *anîya*, य *ya*, एलिम *elima*, which may be treated as declinable verbal terminations. Thus from कर् *kar*, to do, is formed कर्तव्य *kartavya*, करणीय *karaṇîya*, कार्य *kârya*, what is to be done, *faciendum*.

3. *Uṇâdi*, suffixes used in the formation of nouns which to native grammarians seemed more or less irregular, either in form or meaning. Thus from वस् *vas*, to dwell, both वस्तु *vastu*, a thing, and वास्तु *vâstu*, a house.

The *Taddhita* suffixes are no further subdivided, but the feminine suffixes (*strîpratyaya*) are sometimes treated as a separate class.

A root, followed by a suffix (*pratyaya*), whether *Kṛit* or *Taddhita*, is raised to the dignity of a base (*prâtipadika*), and finally becomes a real word (*pada*) when it is finished by receiving a case-termination (*vibhakti*).

Every base, with regard to the suffix which is attached to it, is called *Aṅga*, body. For technical purposes, however, new distinctions have been introduced by Sanskrit grammarians, according to which, in certain declensions, a base is only called *Aṅga* before the terminations of the nom. and acc. sing., nom. and acc. dual, and nom. plur. of masc. and fem. nouns; besides the nom. and acc. plur. of neuters. The vocative generally follows the nominative. These *Aṅga* cases together are called the *Sarvanâmasthâna*. Bopp calls them the *Strong Cases*.

Before terminations beginning with consonants (likewise before *Taddhitas* beginning with any consonant except य् *y*) the base is called *Pada*, the same term which, as we saw before, was used to signify a noun, with a case-termination attached to it. The rules of Sandhi before these terminations are the same as at the end of words.

Before the remaining terminations which begin with vowels (likewise before *Taddhitas* beginning with vowels and य् *y*) the base is called *Bha*. Bopp calls the Pada and Bha cases together the *Weak Cases*; and when it is necessary to distinguish, he calls the Pada the *Middle* and the Bha the *Weakest Cases*.

Nouns, whether substantives, adjectives, or pronouns, are declined through three numbers with seven or, if we include the vocative, eight cases. A case-termination is called सुप् *sup* or विभक्ति *vibhakti*, lit. division.

Verbs are conjugated througb the active and passive voices, and some through a middle voice also, in ten moods and tenses, with three persons and three numbers. A personal termination is called तिङ् *tiṅ* or विभक्ति *vibhakti*.

A declined noun as well as a conjugated verb, ending in a *vibhakti*, is called *Pada*.

Particles are comprebended under the name of *Nipâta*, literally what falls into a sentence, what takes its place before or after other words.

All particles are indeclinable (*avyaya*).

Particles are,

1. Those beginning with च *cha*, and, i. e. a list of words consisting of conjunctions, adverbs, interjections, collected by native grammarians.
2. Those beginning with प्र *pra*, before, i. e. a list of prepositions collected in tbe same manner by native grammarians.

When the prepositions beginning with प्र *pra* govern a substantive, they are called *Karmapravachanîya*. When tbey are joined to a root, they are called *Upasarga* or *Gati*. The name of *Gati* is also given to a class of adverbs which enter into close combination with verbs. Ex. उरी *ûrî* in उरीकृत्य *ûrîkṛitya*, assenting; खाट् *khâṭ* in खाट्कृत्य *khâṭkṛitya*, having made *khâṭ*, i. e. the sound produced by clearing the throat.

CHAPTER III.

DECLENSION.

§ 149. Sanskrit nouns have three genders, Masculine, Feminine, and Neuter; three numbers, Singular, Dual, and Plural; and eight cases, Nominative, Accusative, Instrumental, Dative, Ablative, Genitive, Locative, and Vocative.

Note—There are a few nouns which are indeclinable in Sanskrit: स्वर् *svar*, heaven; अयास् *ayâs*, fire; संवत् *samvat*, year, (of Vikramâditya's era); स्वयं *svayam*, self; सामि *sâmi*, half; भूर् *bhûr*, atmosphere; सुदि *sudi*, light fortnight; बदि *badi*, dark fortnight, &c.

Some nouns are *pluralia tantum*, used in the plural only; दाराः *dârâḥ*, plur. masc. wife; आपः *âpaḥ*, plur. fem. water; वर्षाः *varshâḥ*, plur. fem. the rainy season, i.e. the rains; सिकताः *sikatâḥ*, plur. fem. sand.

§ 150. Sanskrit nouns may be divided into two classes:

1. Those that have bases ending in consonants.
2. Those that have bases ending in vowels.

1. *Bases ending in Consonants.*

§ 151. Nominal bases may end in all consonants except ङ् *ṅ*, ञ् *ñ*, य् *y*. The final letters of the inflective bases of nouns, being either final or brought in contact with the initial letters of the terminations, are subject to some of the phonetic rules explained above.

§ 152. Bases ending in consonants receive the following terminations:

Terminations for Masculines and Feminines.

	Singular.	Dual.	Plural.
Nom.	स् *s* (which is always dropt)	} औ *au*	} अः *aḥ*
Acc.	अं *am*		
Instr.	आ *â*	} भ्यां *bhyâm*	भिः *bhiḥ*
Dat.	ए *e*		} भ्यः *bhyaḥ*
Abl.	अः *aḥ*		
Gen.	अः *aḥ*	} ओः *oḥ*	आं *âm*
Loc.	इ *i*		सु *su*
Voc.	like Nom., except bases in न् *n* and स् *s*	औ *au*	अः *aḥ*

Neuters have no termination in the Nom., Acc., and Voc. singular (Pada cases).

They take ई *î* in the Nom., Acc., and Voc. dual (Bha cases).

They take इ *i* in the Nom., Acc., and Voc. plural, and insert a nasal before the final consonant of the inflective base (Aṅga cases). This nasal is determined by the consonant which follows it; hence ङ् *ṅ* before gutturals, ञ् *ñ* before palatals, ण् *ṇ* before linguals, न् *n* before dentals, म् *m* before labials, Anusvâra before sibilants and ह् *h*. Neuters ending in a nasal or a semivowel do not insert the nasal in the plural. (See Sârasv. I. 8, 5; Colebrooke, p. 83.)

§ 153. Bases ending in consonants are divided again into two classes:

1. Unchangeable bases.
2. Changeable bases.

Nouns of the first class have the same base before all terminations, this base being liable to such changes only as are required by the rules of Sandhi. Nouns of the second class have two or three bases, according as they are followed by certain terminations.

Thus from प्रत्यच् *pratyach*, Nom. Dual प्रत्यञ्चौ *pratyañch-au*; base प्रत्यञ्च् *pratyañch*. (Aṅga.)

Instrum. Plur. प्रत्यग्भिः *pratyag-bhiḥ*; base प्रत्यच् *pratyach*. (Pada.)

Gen. Dual प्रतीचोः *pratîch-oḥ*; base प्रतीच् *pratîch*. (Bha.)

1. Unchangeable Bases.

Paradigm of a regular Noun with unchangeable Base.

§ 154. Bases ending in ण् *ṇ* and ल् *l* are not liable to any phonetic changes before the terminations, except that in the Nom. Sing. the स् *s* of the termination is dropt (see §§ 114; 55); and that in the Loc. Plur. a ट् *ṭ* *may* be inserted after the final ण् *ṇ*.

Base सुगण् *sugaṇ*, a ready reckoner, masc. fem. neut. (from सु *su*, well, and root गण् *gaṇ*, to count.)

	Singular. Masc. Fem.	Dual. Masc. Fem.	Plural. Masc. Fem.
N.	सुगण् *sugaṇ*	सुगणौ *sugaṇ-au* (N. A.)	सुगणः *sugaṇ-aḥ* (N. A.)
A.	सुगणं *sugaṇ-am*		
I.	सुगणा *sugaṇ-â*	सुगण्भ्यां *sugaṇ-bhyâm* (I. D. Ab.)	सुगण्भिः *sugaṇ-bhiḥ*
D.	सुगणे *sugaṇ-e*		सुगण्भ्यः *sugaṇ-bhyaḥ* (D. Ab.)
Ab.	सुगणः *sugaṇ-aḥ* (Ab. G.)		
G.		सुगणोः *sugaṇ-oḥ* (G. L.)	सुगणां *sugaṇ-âm*
L.	सुगणि *sugaṇ-i*		सुगण्सु *sugaṇ-su**
V.	सुगण् *sugaṇ*	सुगणौ *sugaṇ-au*	सुगणः *sugaṇ-aḥ*

Neuter.

	Singular.	Dual.	Plural.
N. A. V.	सुगण् *sugaṇ*	सुगणी *sugaṇ-î*	सुगणि *sugaṇ-i*

* Or सुगण्ट्सु *sugaṇṭ-su*, § 72.

§ 155. Bases ending in gutturals, क् *k*, ख् *kh*, ग् *g*, घ् *gh*.

These bases require no special rules.

Base सर्वशक् *sarvaśak*, omnipotent, masc. fem. neut. (from सर्व *sarva*, all, and root शक् *śak*, to be able.)

	SINGULAR. MASC. FEM.	DUAL. MASC. FEM.	PLURAL. MASC. FEM.
N.V.	सर्वशक् *sarvaśak*	सर्वशकौ *sarvaśakau* (N.V.A.)	सर्वशकः *sarvaśakaḥ* (N.V.A.)
A.	सर्वशकम् *sarvaśakam*		
I.	सर्वशका *sarvaśakâ*	सर्वशग्भ्याम् *sarvaśagbhyâm* (I.D.Ab.)	सर्वशग्भिः *sarvaśagbhiḥ*
D.	सर्वशके *sarvaśake*		सर्वशग्भ्यः *sarvaśagbhyaḥ* (D.Ab.)
Ab.	सर्वशकः *sarvaśakaḥ* (Ab.G.)		
G.		सर्वशकोः *sarvaśakoḥ* (G.L.)	सर्वशकाम् *sarvaśakâm*
L.	सर्वशकि *sarvaśaki*		सर्वशक्षु *sarvaśakshu* *

NEUTER.

	SINGULAR.	DUAL.	PLURAL.
N.A.V.	सर्वशक् *sarvaśak*	सर्वशकी *sarvaśakî*	सर्वशंकि *sarvaśaṅki*

All regular nouns ending in क् *k*, ख् *kh*, ग् *g*, घ् *gh*, ट् *ṭ*, ठ् *ṭh*, ड् *ḍ*, ढ् *ḍh*, त् *t*, थ् *th*, द् *d*, ध् *dh*, प् *p*, फ् *ph*, ब् *b*, भ् *bh*, may be declined after the model of सर्वशक् *sarvaśak*.

§ 156. Base ending in ख् *kh*. चित्रलिख् *chitralikh*, painter, (from चित्र *chitra*, picture, and root लिख् *likh*, to paint.)

	SINGULAR. MASC. FEM.	DUAL. MASC. FEM.	PLURAL. MASC. FEM.
N. V.	चित्रलिक् *chitralik* †	चित्रलिखौ *chitralikhau* (N.V.A.)	चित्रलिखः *chitralikhaḥ* (N.V.A.)
A.	चित्रलिखम् *chitralikham*		
I.	चित्रलिखा *chitralikhâ*	चित्रलिग्भ्याम् *chitraligbhâm* (I.D.Ab.)	चित्रलिग्भिः *chitraligbhiḥ*
D.	चित्रलिखे *chitralikhe*		चित्रलिग्भ्यः *chitraligbhyaḥ* (D.Ab.)
Ab.	चित्रलिखः *chitralikhaḥ* (Ab.G.)		
G.		चित्रलिखोः *chitralikhoḥ* (G.L.)	चित्रलिखाम् *chatralikhâm*
L.	चित्रलिखि *chitralikhi*		चित्रलिक्षु *chitralikshu* *

NEUTER.

	SINGULAR.	DUAL.	PLURAL.
N. A. V.	चित्रलिक् *chitralik* †	चित्रलिखी *chitralikhî*	चित्रलिंखि *chitraliṅkhi*

Note—In the paradigms of regular nouns with unchangeable consonantal bases it will be sufficient to remember the Nom. Sing., Nom. Plur., Instr. Plur., Loc. Plur., and Nom.

* On the change of सु *su* after क् *k*, see § 100.

† क् *k* instead of ख् *kh*, see §§ 113; 54. 1.

Plur. Neut. The Acc. Instr. Dat. Abl. Gen. Loc. Sing., Nom. Acc. Voc. Gen. Loc. Dual, Acc. Gen. Plur., follow the Nom. Plur. The Instr. Dat. Abl. Dual, Dat. Abl. Plur., follow the Instr. Plur. The Vocative is the same as the Nominative.

§ 157. Regular nouns to be declined like सर्वशक् *sarvaśak*.

BASE.	NOM. S.	NOM. PL. M. F.	INSTR. PL.	LOC. PL.	NOM. PL. NEUT.
हरित् *harit*, green	हरित्	हरितः	हरिद्भिः	हरित्सु	हरिंति
m. f. n.	*harit*	*haritaḥ*	*haridbhiḥ*	*haritsu*	*harinti*
अग्निमथ् *agnimath*, fire-kindling	अग्निमत्	अग्निमथः	अग्निमद्भिः	अग्निमत्सु	अग्निमंथि
m. f. n.	*agnimat* *	*agnimathaḥ*	*agnimadbhiḥ* †	*agnimatsu* ‡	*agnimanthi*
सुहृद् *suhṛid*, friendly	सुहृत्	सुहृदः	सुहृद्भिः	सुहृत्सु	सुहृंदि
m. f. n.	*suhṛit*	*suhṛidaḥ*	*suhṛidbhiḥ*	*suhṛitsu*	*suhṛindi*
बुध् *budh*, knowing	भुत्	बुधः	भुद्भिः	भुत्सु	बुंधि
m. f. n.	*bhut* ‖	*budhaḥ*	*bhudbhiḥ*	*bhutsu*	*bundhi*
गुप् *gup*, guardian	गुप्	गुपः	गुब्भिः	गुप्सु	गुंपि
m. f. n.	*gup*	*gupaḥ*	*gubbhiḥ*	*gupsu*	*gumpi*
ककुभ् *kakubh*, region	ककुप्	ककुभः	ककुब्भिः	ककुप्सु	°ककुंभि
f.	*kakup*	*kakubhaḥ*	*kakubbhiḥ*	*kakupsu*	-*kakumbhi*

§ 158. Bases ending in palatals, च् *ch*, छ् *chh*, ज् *j*, झ् *jh*.

Bases ending in च् *ch* change च् *ch* into क् *k*, or ग् *g*, except when followed by a termination beginning with a vowel.

Base जलमुच् *jalamuch*, masc. cloud (water-dropping).

	SINGULAR. MASC. FEM.	DUAL. MASC. FEM.	PLURAL. MASC. FEM.
N.V.	जलमुक् *jalamuk*	} जलमुचौ *jalamuchau* (N.V. A.)	} जलमुचः *jalamuchaḥ* (N.V. A.)
A.	जलमुचं *jalamucham*		
I.	जलमुचा *jalamuchâ*	} जलमुग्भ्यां *jalamugbhyâm* (I. D. Ab.)	जलमुग्भिः *jalamugbhiḥ*
D.	जलमुचे *jalamuche*		} जलमुग्भ्यः *jalamugbhyaḥ* (D. Ab.)
Ab.	} जलमुचः *jalamuchaḥ* (Ab. G.)		
G.		} जलमुचोः *jalamuchoḥ* (G. L.)	जलमुचां *jalamuchâm*
L.	जलमुचि *jalamuchi*		जलमुक्षु *jalamukshu*

NEUTER.

	SINGULAR.	DUAL.	PLURAL.
N. A. V.	जलमुक् *jalamuk*	जलमुची *jalamuchî*	जलमुंचि *jalamuñchi*

Decline like जलमुच् *jalamuch*,—वाच् *vâch*, fem. speech; त्वच् *tvach*, fem. skin; रुच् *ruch*, fem. light; स्रुच् *sruch*, fem. ladle.

---

* थ् *th* final changed into त् *t*. See §§ 113; 54. 1. Final स् *s* dropt, § 55.

† See § 66. ‡ See § 54. 1. ‖ See § 118.

§ 159. Special bases in च् *ch*.

BASE.	NOM. SING.	INSTR. PLUR.	LOC. PLUR.	NOM. PLUR.
क्रुञ्च् *kruñch**, moving crookedly, a curlew	क्रुङ् *kruṅ*	क्रुङ्भिः *kruṅbhiḥ*	क्रुङ्क्षु *kruṅkshu*	क्रुञ्चः *kruñchaḥ*
प्राञ्च् *prâñch*, if it means worshipping	प्राङ् *prâṅ*	प्राङ्भिः *prâṅbhiḥ*	प्राङ्क्षु *prâṅkshu*	प्राञ्चः *prâñchaḥ* (Acc. the same)
वृश्च् *vṛiśch* †, cutting	वृट् *vṛiṭ* ‡	वृड्भिः *vṛiḍbhiḥ*	वृट्सु *vṛiṭsu*	वृश्चः *vṛiśchaḥ*

§ 160. Bases ending in छ् *chh* change छ् *chh* into ट् *ṭ* when final, and before consonants. (See § 125.)

BASE.	NOM. SING.	NOM. PL.	INSTR. PL.	LOC. PL.	NOM. PL. NEUT.
प्राछ् *prâchh* ‖, an asker	प्राट् *prâṭ*	प्राछः *prâchhaḥ*	प्राड्भिः *prâḍbhiḥ*	प्राट्सु *prâṭsu*	प्रांछि *prâñchhi*

§ 161. Bases ending in ज् *j*, if regular, follow the example of nouns in च् *ch*, except that they preserve ज् *j* before vowels.

BASE.	NOM. SING.	NOM. PL.	INSTR. PL.	LOC. PL.	NOM. PL. NEUT.
रुज् *ruj*, disease	रुक् *ruk*	रुजः *rujaḥ*	रुग्भिः *rugbhiḥ*	रुक्षु *rukshu*	रुंजि *ruñji*
ऊर्ज् *ûrj* ¶, strength	ऊर्क् *ûrk*	ऊर्जः *ûrjaḥ*	ऊर्ग्भिः *ûrgbhiḥ*	ऊर्क्षु *ûrkshu*	ऊंर्जि *ûṁrji*

Other regular nouns in ज् *j*,—वणिज् *vaṇij*, m. merchant; भिषज् *bhishaj*, m. physician; ऋत्विज् *ṛitvij*, m. priest; स्रज् *sraj*, f. garland; असृज् *asṛij*, n. blood. (On the optional forms of असृज् *asṛij*, see further on.) मज्ज् *majj*, Nom. Sing. मक् *mak*, diving.

§ 162. Bases ending in ज् *j* changeable to ड् *ḍ*.

Some bases ending in ज् *j* change ज् *j* into ट् *ṭ* or ड् *ḍ* when final, and before terminations beginning with consonants.

---

* Derived from the root क्रुञ्च् *kruñch*. The Nom. Sing. would have been क्रुङ्क् + स् *kruṅk* + *s*; स् *s* and क् *k* are dropt, see § 114.

† Derived from the root व्रश्च् *vraśch*, (in the Dhâtupâṭha, ओव्रश्चू), to cut. According to Sanskrit grammarians, the penultimate स् *s* or श् *ś* is dropt, and च् *ch* before consonants or if final changed into ट् *ṭ*. (See § 114.)

‡ The form वृट् *vṛiṭ* (not व्रट् *vraṭ*) is confirmed by Siddhânta-Kaumudî (1863), I. p. 182.

‖ Some authorities admit प्राशः *prâśaḥ*, in the Nom. Plur., and the same base प्राश् *prâś* in all other cases beginning with a vowel.

¶ On the two final consonants, see § 55. The Nom. Plur. Neut. would be ऊंर्जि *ûṁrji* or ऊर्जि *ûrji* in compounds; बहूंर्जि *bahûṁrji* or बहूर्जि *bahûrji* (Siddh.-Kaum. I. p. 194).

Base सम्राज् *samráj*, masc. sovereign.

	SINGULAR. MASC. FEM.	DUAL. MASC. FEM.	PLURAL. MASC. FEM.
N.V.	सम्राट् *samráṭ*	सम्राजौ *samrájau*	सम्राजः *samrájaḥ*
A.	सम्राजम् *samrájam*	(N.V.A.)	(N.V.A.)
I.	सम्राजा *samrájá*	सम्राड्भ्याम् *samráḍbhyám*	सम्राड्भिः *samráḍbhiḥ*
D.	सम्राजे *samráje*	(I.D.Ab.)	सम्राड्भ्यः *samráḍbhyaḥ*
Ab.	सम्राजः *samrájaḥ*	(I.D.Ab.)	(D.Ab.)
G.	(Ab.G.)	सम्राजोः *samrájoḥ*	सम्राजाम् *samrájám*
L.	सम्राजि *samráji*	(G.L.)	सम्राट्सु *samráṭsu* or सम्राट्त्सु *samráṭtsu**

The words which follow this declension are mostly nouns derived, without any suffix, from the roots भ्राज् *bhráj* (टुभ्राजृ, not भ्राजृ), to shine; मृज् *mṛij*, to clean; यज् *yaj* (except ऋत्विज् *ṛitvij*), to sacrifice; राज् *ráj*, to shine, to rule; सृज् *sṛij*, to dismiss, to create, (स्रज् *sraj*, wreath, and असृज् *asṛij*, blood, are not derived from सृज् *sṛij*); भ्रज्ज् *bhrajj*, to roast (भ्रस्जो). Also परिव्राज् *parivráj*, a mendicant.

BASE.	NOM. SING.	NOM. PLUR.	INSTR. PLUR.	LOC. PLUR.
विभ्राज् *vibhráj*, resplendent	विभ्राट् *vibhráṭ*†	विभ्राजः *vibhrájaḥ*	विभ्राड्भिः *vibhráḍbhiḥ*	विभ्राट्सु *vibhráṭsu*
देवेज् *devej*‡, worshipper of the gods	देवेट् *deveṭ*	देवेजः *devejaḥ*	देवेड्भिः *deveḍbhiḥ*	देवेट्सु *deveṭsu*
विश्वसृज् *viśvasṛij*, creator of the universe	विश्वसृट् *viśvasṛiṭ*	विश्वसृजः *viśvasṛijaḥ*	विश्वसृड्भिः *viśvasṛiḍbhiḥ*	विश्वसृट्सु *viśvasṛiṭsu*
परिव्राज् *parivráj*, a mendicant	परिव्राट् *parivráṭ*	परिव्राजः *parivrájaḥ*	परिव्राड्भिः *parivráḍbhiḥ*	परिव्राट्सु *parivráṭsu*
विश्वराज् *viśvaráj*‖, an universal monarch	विश्वाराट् *viśváráṭ*	विश्वराजः *viśvarájaḥ*	विश्वाराड्भिः *viśváráḍbhiḥ*	विश्वाराट्सु *viśváráṭsu*
भृज्ज् *bhṛijj*, roasting	भृट् *bhṛiṭ*	भृज्जः *bhṛijjaḥ*	भृड्भिः *bhṛiḍbhiḥ*	भृट्सु *bhṛiṭsu*

§ 163. Irregular bases in ज् *j*.

BASE.	NOM. SING.	NOM. PLUR.	INSTR. PLUR.	LOC. PLUR.
1. खञ्ज् *khañj*¶, lame	खन् *khan*	खञ्जः *khañjaḥ*	खन्भिः *khanbhiḥ*	खन्सु *khansu*

* Cf. § 76.

† From another root, विभ्राज् *vibhráḍ*, विभ्राड्भिः *vibhráḍbhiḥ* &c. may be formed. (Siddh.-Kaum. I. p. 165.)

‡ From देव *deva*, god, and यज् *yaj*, to sacrifice, contracted into इज् *ij*.

‖ The lengthening of the अ *a* in विश्व *viśva* takes place whenever ज् *j* is changed into a lingual. (Pâṇ. VI. 3, 128.)

¶ See Siddh.-Kaum. ed. Târânâtha, vol. I. p. 165.

2. अवयाज् *avayáj*, name of a Vedic priest, has two bases. The Nom. Sing. is अवयाः *avayáḥ*, and all the cases beginning with consonants (Pada cases) are formed from the same base, अवयस् *avayas*. The Voc. Sing., too, is irregular, being, against the rule of these bases, identical with the Nom. Sing. Some grammarians, however, allow हे अवयः *he avayaḥ*.

Base अवयस् *avayas* and अवयाज् *avayáj*.

	SINGULAR. MASC. FEM.	DUAL. MASC. FEM.	PLURAL. MASC. FEM.
N.	अवयाः *avayáḥ*	अवयाजौ *avayájau* (N. A.)	अवयाजः *avayájaḥ* (N. A.)
A.	अवयाजम् *avayájam*		
I.	अवयाजा *avayájá*	अवयोभ्याम् *avayobhyám* (I. D. Ab.)	अवयोभिः *avayobhiḥ*
D.	अवयाजे *avayáje*		अवयोभ्यः *avayobhyaḥ* (D. Ab.)
Ab.	अवयाजः *avayájaḥ* (Ab. G.)		
G.		अवयाजोः *avayájoḥ* (G. L.)	अवयाजाम् *avayájám*
L.	अवयाजि *avayáji*		अवयःसु *avayaḥsu*
V.	अवयाः *avayáḥ* or अवयः *avayaḥ*	like Nom.	like Nom.

§ 164. Bases ending in र् *r*.

Bases ending in र् *r* are regular, only इ *i* and उ *u*, preceding the र् *r*, are lengthened, if the र् *r* is final or followed by a consonant (§ 144). In the Loc. Plur. the final र् *r* remains unchanged though followed by ष् *sh*. (§ 90.)

Base गिर् *gir*, fem. voice.

	SINGULAR. MASC. FEM.	DUAL. MASC. FEM.	PLURAL. MASC. FEM.
N.V.	गीः *gíḥ*	गिरौ *girau* (N.V. A.)	गिरः *giraḥ* (N.V. A.)
A.	गिरम् *giram*		
I.	गिरा *girá*	गीर्भ्याम् *gírbhyám* (I. D. Ab.)	गीर्भिः *gírbhiḥ*
D.	गिरे *gire*		गीर्भ्यः *gírbhyaḥ* (D. Ab.)
Ab.	गिरः *giraḥ* (Ab. G.)		
G.		गिरोः *giroḥ* (G. L.)	गिराम् *girám*
L.	गिरि *giri*		गीर्षु *gírshu*

Base वार् *vár*, neut. water.

NEUTER.

	SINGULAR.	DUAL.	PLURAL.
N.A.V.	वाः *váḥ*	वारी *várí*	वारि *vári*
I.	वारा *várá*	वार्भ्याम् *várbhyám*	वार्भिः *várbhiḥ*, &c.

BASE.	NOM. SING.	NOM. PLUR.	INSTR. PLUR.	LOC. PLUR.
पुर् *pur*, f. town	पूः *púḥ*	पुरः *puraḥ*	पूर्भिः *púrbhiḥ*	पूर्षु *púrshu*
द्वार् *dvár*, f. door	द्वाः *dváḥ*	द्वारः *dváraḥ*	द्वार्भिः *dvárbhiḥ*	द्वार्षु *dvárshu*
किर् *kir*, m. f. n. scattering	कीः *kíḥ*	किरः *kiraḥ*	कीर्भिः *kírbhiḥ*	कीर्षु *kírshu* *

* Siddh.-Kaum. I. p. 125.

§ 165. Bases in स् *s*.

(A.) Bases formed by the suffixes अस् *as*, इस् *is*, उस् *us*.

Bases ending in स् *s* change the स् *s* according to the general euphonic rules explained above. Thus

अस् *as*, if final, becomes अः *aḥ*. (§ 83.)

अस् *as* followed by terminations beginning with vowels remains unchanged.

इस् and उस् *is* and *us* followed by terminations beginning with vowels are changed to इष् and उष् *ish* and *ush*. (See § 100.)

अस् *as* before भ् *bh* becomes ओ *o* (§ 84. 3); इस् *is* and उस् *us* before भ् *bh* become इर् *ir* and उर् *ur*. (§ 82.)

अस् *as* before सु *su* becomes अस् *as* or अः *aḥ*; इस् *is* and उस् *us* before सु *su* become इष् *ish* or इः *iḥ*, उष् *ush* or उः *uḥ*.

Besides these general rules, the following special rules should be observed:

1. Nouns formed by the suffix अस् *as* lengthen their अ *a* in the Nom. Sing. masc. and fem., but not in the Vocative. Thus Nom. Sing. m. f. सुमनाः *sumanâḥ*, well-minded (εὐμενής); Voc. सुमनः *sumanaḥ*.
2. Nouns formed by the suffixes इस् or उस् *is* or *us* do not lengthen their vowel in the Nom. Sing. masc. and fem. Hence Nom. Sing. m. f. सुज्योतिः *sujyotiḥ*, having good light, from सु *su*, good, and ज्योतिः *jyotiḥ*, n. light; सुचक्षुः *suchakshuḥ*, having good eyes, from सु *su*, good, and चक्षुः *chakshuḥ*, n. eye. (Pâṇ. v. 4, 133, com.)
3. Neuter nouns in अस् *as*, इस् *is*, उस् *us*, lengthen their vowel and nasalize it in the Nom. Acc. Voc. Plur. From मनः *manaḥ*, मनांसि *manâṁsi*; from ज्योतिः *jyotiḥ*, ज्योतींषि *jyotîṁshi*; from चक्षुः *chakshuḥ*, चक्षूंषि *chakshûṁshi*.

Base सुमनस् *sumanas*, well-minded, masc. fem. neut. (from सु *su* and मनस् *manas*, neut. mind.)

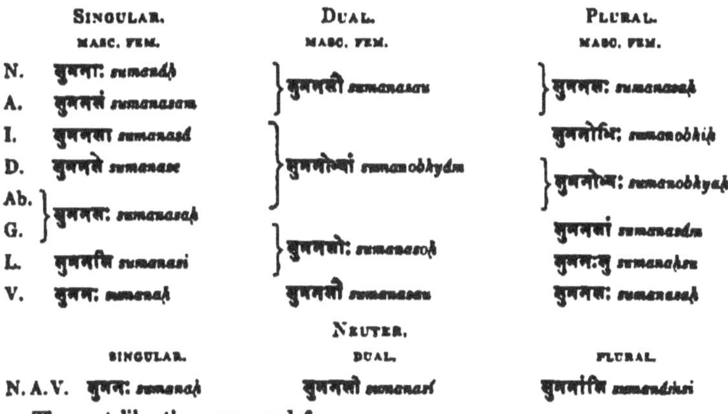

	SINGULAR. MASC. FEM.	DUAL. MASC. FEM.	PLURAL. MASC. FEM.
N.	सुमनाः *sumanâḥ*	सुमनसौ *sumanasau* (N. A.)	सुमनसः *sumanasaḥ* (N. A.)
A.	सुमनसं *sumanasam*		
I.	सुमनसा *sumanasâ*	सुमनोभ्यां *sumanobhyâm* (I. D. Ab.)	सुमनोभिः *sumanobhiḥ*
D.	सुमनसे *sumanase*		सुमनोभ्यः *sumanobhyaḥ* (D. Ab.)
Ab.	सुमनसः *sumanasaḥ* (Ab. G.)		
G.		सुमनसोः *sumanasoḥ* (G. L.)	सुमनसां *sumanasâm*
L.	सुमनसि *sumanasi*		सुमनःसु *sumanaḥsu*
V.	सुमनः *sumanaḥ*	सुमनसौ *sumanasau*	सुमनसः *sumanasaḥ*

NEUTER.

	SINGULAR.	DUAL.	PLURAL.
N. A. V.	सुमनः *sumanaḥ*	सुमनसी *sumanasî*	सुमनांसि *sumanâṁsi*

The rest like the masc. and fem.

Base सुज्योतिस् *sujyotis*, well-lighted, masc. fem. neut. (from सु *su* and ज्योतिस् *jyotis*, neut. light.)

	SINGULAR. MASC. FEM.	DUAL. MASC. FEM.	PLURAL. MASC. FEM.
N.V.	सुज्योतिः *sujyotiḥ*	सुज्योतिषौ *sujyotishau*	सुज्योतिषः *sujyotishaḥ*
A.	सुज्योतिषं *sujyotisham*		
I.	सुज्योतिषा *sujyotishâ*	सुज्योतिर्भ्यां *sujyotirbhyâm*	सुज्योतिर्भिः *sujyotirbhiḥ*
D.	सुज्योतिषे *sujyotishe*		सुज्योतिर्भ्यः *sujyotirbhyaḥ*
Ab.	सुज्योतिषः *sujyotishaḥ*		
G.		सुज्योतिषोः *sujyotishoḥ*	सुज्योतिषां *sujyotishâm*
L.	सुज्योतिषि *sujyotishi*		सुज्योतिःषु *sujyotiḥshu*

NEUTER.

	SINGULAR.	DUAL.	PLURAL.
N.A.V.	सुज्योतिः *sujyotiḥ*	सुज्योतिषी *sujyotishî*	सुज्योतींषि *sujyotîṁshi*

The rest like the masc. and fem.

Decline after the model of सुमनस् *sumanas* and सुज्योतिस् *sujyotis* the following bases:

वेधस् *vedhas*, Nom. sing. वेधाः *vedhâḥ*, m. wise. चंद्रमस् *chandramas*, N. s. चंद्रमाः *chandramâḥ*, m. moon. प्रचेतस् *prachetas*, N. s. प्रचेताः *prachetâḥ*, m., Nom. prop. of a lawgiver. दिवौकस् *divaukas*, N. s. दिवौकाः *divaukâḥ*, m. a deity. विहायस् *vihâyas*, N. s. विहायाः *vihâyâḥ*, m. bird. अप्सरस् *apsaras*, N. s. अप्सराः *apsarâḥ*, f. a nymph. महौजस् *mahaujas*, N. s. महौजाः *mahaujâḥ*, m. f. n. very mighty. पयस् *payas*, N. s. पयः *payaḥ*, n. milk. अयस् *ayas*, N. s. अयः *ayaḥ*, n. iron. यशस् *yaśas*, N. s. यशः *yaśaḥ*, n. praise. हविस् *havis*, N. s. हविः *haviḥ*, n. oblation. अर्चिस् *archis*, N. s. अर्चिः *archiḥ*, n. splendour. आयुस् *âyus*, N. s. आयुः *âyuḥ*, n. life, age. वपुस् *vapus*, N. s. वपुः *vapuḥ*, n. body *.

§ 166. जरा *jarâ*, old age, may be declined throughout regularly as a feminine. (See further on, Bases ending in Vowels, Feminines in आ *â*.) There is, however, another base जरस् *jaras*, equally feminine †, and equally regular, except that it is defective in all cases the terminations of which begin with consonants.

---

* Any of these neuter nouns may assume masc. and fem. terminations at the end of a compound; नष्टहविः *nashṭahaviḥ*, Nom. sing. masc. one whose oblation is destroyed.

† Boehtlingk (Declination im Sanskrit, p. 125) gave जरस् *jaras*, rightly as feminine; in the dictionary, though oxytone, it is by mistake put down as neuter.

Base जरा *jarā.*	Base जरस् *jaras.*
SINGULAR.	SINGULAR.
N. जरा *jarā**	deest; term. स् *s*
A. जरां *jarām*	जरसं *jaras-am*
I. जरया *jarayā*	जरसा *jaras-ā*
D. जरायै *jarāyai*	जरसे *jaras-e*
Ab. जरायाः *jarāyāḥ*	जरसः *jaras-aḥ*
G. जरायाः *jarāyāḥ*	जरसः *jaras-aḥ*
L. जरायां *jarāyām*	जरसि *jaras-i*
V. जरे *jare*	deest
DUAL.	DUAL.
N. A. V. जरे *jare*	जरसौ *jaras-au*
I. D. Ab. जराभ्यां *jarābhyām*	deest; term. भ्यां *bhyām*
G. L. जरयोः *jarayoḥ*	जरसोः *jaras-oḥ*
PLURAL.	PLURAL.
N. V. जराः *jarāḥ*	जरसः *jaras-aḥ*
A. जराः *jarāḥ*	जरसः *jaras-aḥ*
I. जराभिः *jarābhiḥ*	deest; term. भिः *bhiḥ*
D. Ab. जराभ्यः *jarābhyaḥ*	deest; term. भ्यः *bhyaḥ*
G. जराणां *jarāṇām*	जरसां *jaras-ām*
L. जरासु *jarāsu*	deest; term. सु *su*

§ 167. In compositions, besides the regular forms from जरा *jarā*, viz. निर्जरः *nirjaraḥ*, निर्जरा *nirjarā*, निर्जरं *nirjaram*, (ageless,) grammarians allow the base in स् *s* to be used before all terminations beginning with vowels†.

	SINGULAR. MASC.	SINGULAR. MASC. FEM.
N.	निर्जरः *nirjaraḥ*‡	deest
A.	निर्जरं *nirjaram* or	निर्जरसं *nirjarasam*
I.	निर्जरेण *nirjareṇa* or	निर्जरसा *nirjarasā* (निर्जरसिन *nirjarasina*, masc.)

---

* The declension of जरा *jarā*, as a regular fem. in आ *ā*, is given here by anticipation for the sake of comparison with the defective जरस् *jaras*.

† By a pedantic adherence to the Sûtras of Pâṇini some monstrous forms (included in brackets) have been deduced by certain native grammarians, but deservedly reprobated by others. (Siddh.-Kaum. I. pp. 103, 141.)

‡ The declension of निर्जरः *nirjaraḥ*, as a regular masc. in अ *a*, is given by anticipation for the sake of comparison with the defective निर्जरस् *nirjaras*.

D.	निर्जराय *nirjarâya* or	निर्जरसे *nirjarase*
Ab.	निर्जरात् *nirjarât* or	निर्जरसः *nirjarasaḥ* (निर्जरसात् *nirjarasât*, masc.)
G.	निर्जरस्य *nirjarasya* or	निर्जरसः *nirjarasaḥ* (निर्जरसस्य *nirjarasasya*, masc.)
L.	निर्जरे *nirjare* or	निर्जरसि *nirjarasi*
V.	निर्जर *nirjara*	deest
	Dual.	**Dual.**
N.A.V.	निर्जरौ *nirjarau* or	निर्जरसौ *nirjarasau*
I.D.Ab.	निर्जराभ्यां *nirjarâbhyâm*	deest
G.L.	निर्जरयोः *nirjarayoḥ* or	निर्जरसोः *nirjarasoḥ*
	Plural.	**Plural.**
N.V.	निर्जराः *nirjarâḥ* or	निर्जरसः *nirjarasaḥ*
A.	निर्जरान् *nirjarân* or	निर्जरसः *nirjarasaḥ*
I.	निर्जरैः *nirjaraiḥ*	deest (निर्जरसैः *nirjarasaiḥ*, masc.)
D.Ab.	निर्जरेभ्यः *nirjarebhyaḥ*	deest
G.	निर्जराणां *nirjarâṇâm* or	निर्जरसां *nirjarasâm*
L.	निर्जरेषु *nirjareshu*	deest

Fem. निर्जरा *nirjarâ*, like कांता *kântâ*.
Neut. निर्जरं *nirjaram*, like कांतं *kântam*.

Neut. Sing. deest (निर्जरसं *nirjarasam*); Dual निर्जरसी *nirjarasî*; Plur. निर्जरांसि *nirjarâṁsi*.

§ 168. अनेहस् *anehas*, m. time, पुरुदंशस् *purudaṁśas*, m. name of Indra, form the Nom. Sing. अनेहा *anehâ*, पुरुदंशा *purudaṁśâ*, without final Visarga. The other cases are regular, like सुमनस् *sumanas*, m. Voc. हे अनेहः *he anehaḥ*.

§ 169. उशनस् *uśanas*, m. proper name, forms the Nom. Sing. उशना *uśanâ* and the Voc. Sing. उशनन् *uśanan* or उशनः *uśanaḥ* or उशन *uśana*. (Sâr. I, 9, 73.)

§ 170. (B.) Bases ending in radical स् *s*.

1. From पिंड *piṇḍa*, a lump, and ग्रस् *gras*, to swallow, a compound is formed, पिंडग्रस् *piṇḍagras*, a lump-eater.

   From पिस् *pis*, to walk, and सु *su*, well, a compound is formed, सुपिस् *supis*, well-walking.

   From तुस् *tus*, to sound, and सु *su*, well, a compound is formed, सुतुस् *sutus*, well-sounding.

2. In forming the Nom. Sing. m. f. (and neuter), the rules laid down before with regard to nouns in which अस् *as*, इस् *is*, उस् *us*, belong to a suffix, are simply inverted. Nouns in इस् *is* and उस् *us* lengthen the vowel, nouns in अस् *as* leave it short.

   Ex. Nom. Sing. m. f. n. पिंडग्रः *piṇḍagraḥ*, सुपीः *supîḥ*, सुतूः *sutûḥ*.

3. In the Nom. Acc. Voc. Plur. of neuters, nouns in अस् *as*, इस् *is*, उस् *us*, nasalize their vowels, but do not lengthen them.

Ex. Nom. Acc. Voc. Plur. neut. पिंडग्रंसि *piṇḍagraṁsi*, सुपिंसि *supiṁsi*, सुतुंसि *sutuṁsi*.

4. Nouns in इस् *is* and उस् *us* lengthen their vowels before all terminations beginning with consonants.

Ex. Instr. Plur. सुपीर्भिः *supîrbhiḥ*, सुतूर्भिः *sutûrbhiḥ*, सुतूःषु *sutûḥshu*.

5. The radical स् *s* of nouns ending in इस् *is* and उस् *us*, though followed by vowels, is not liable to be changed into ष् *sh*. (See § 100, note.)

Base पिंडग्रस् *piṇḍagras*, eating a mouthful, masc. fem. neut.

	SINGULAR. MASC. FEM.	DUAL. MASC. FEM.	PLURAL. MASC. FEM.
N.V.	पिंडग्रः *piṇḍagraḥ*	पिंडग्रसौ *piṇḍagrasau*	पिंडग्रसः *piṇḍagrasaḥ*
A.	पिंडग्रसं *piṇḍagrasam*		
I.	पिंडग्रसा *piṇḍagrasâ*	पिंडग्रोभ्यां *piṇḍagrobhyâm*	पिंडग्रोभिः *piṇḍagrobhiḥ*
D.	पिंडग्रसे *piṇḍagrase*		पिंडग्रोभ्यः *piṇḍagrobhyaḥ*
Ab.	पिंडग्रसः *piṇḍagrasaḥ*		
G.		पिंडग्रसोः *piṇḍagrasoḥ*	पिंडग्रसां *piṇḍagrasâm*
L.	पिंडग्रसि *piṇḍagrasi*		पिंडग्रःसु *piṇḍagraḥsu*

NEUTER.

	SINGULAR.	DUAL.	PLURAL.
N.A.V.	पिंडग्रः *piṇḍagraḥ*	पिंडग्रसी *piṇḍagrasî*	पिंडग्रंसि *piṇḍagraṁsi*

Base सुतुस् *sutus*, well-sounding, masc. fem. neut.

	SINGULAR. MASC. FEM.	DUAL. MASC. FEM.	PLURAL. MASC. FEM.
N.V.	सुतूः *sutûḥ*	सुतुसौ *sutusau*	सुतुसः *sutusaḥ*
A.	सुतुसं *sutusam*		
I.	सुतुसा *sutusâ*	सुतूर्भ्यां *sutûrbhyâm*	सुतूर्भिः *sutûrbhiḥ*
D.	सुतुसे *sutuse*		सुतूर्भ्यः *sutûrbhyaḥ*
Ab.	सुतुसः *sutusaḥ*		
G.		सुतुसोः *sutusoḥ*	सुतुसां *sutusâm*
L.	सुतुसि *sutusi*		सुतूःषु *sutûḥshu* or सुतूष्षु *sutûshshu**

NEUTER.

	SINGULAR.	DUAL.	PLURAL.
N.A.V.	सुतूः *sutûḥ*	सुतुसी *sutusî*	सुतुंसि *sutuṁsi*

§ 171. Nouns derived from desiderative verbs change स् *s* into ष् *sh* when necessary.

* Siddh.-Kaum. I. p. 187. § 83.

Base पिपठिस् *pipaṭhis*, wishing to read, masc. fem. neut.

	Singular. masc. fem.	Dual. masc. fem.	Plural. masc. fem.
N.	पिपठीः *pipaṭhīḥ*	पिपठिषौ *pipaṭhishau* (N. A.)	पिपठिषः *pipaṭhishaḥ* (N. A.)
A.	पिपठिषं *pipaṭhisham*		
I.	पिपठिषा *pipaṭhishā*	पिपठीर्भ्याम् *pipaṭhīrbhyām* (I. D. Ab.)	पिपठीर्भिः *pipaṭhīrbhiḥ*
D.	पिपठिषे *pipaṭhishe*		पिपठीर्भ्यः *pipaṭhīrbhyaḥ* (D. Ab.)
Ab.	पिपठिषः *pipaṭhishaḥ* (Ab. G.)		
G.		पिपठिषोः *pipaṭhishoḥ* (G. L.)	पिपठिषाम् *pipaṭhishām*
L.	पिपठिषि *pipaṭhishi*		पिपठीःषु *pipaṭhīḥshu*

Neuter.

	Singular.	Dual.	Plural.
N. A. V.	पिपठीः *pipaṭhīḥ*	पिपठिषी *pipaṭhishī*	पिपठिषि *pipaṭhishi* (see § 172)

§ 172. The nouns आशिस् *āśis*, fem. blessing, and सजुस् *sajus*, masc. a companion, are declined like पिपठिस् *pipaṭhis*, except in the Nom. and Acc. Plur., if they should be used as neuters at the end of compounds.

List of different Bases in स् *s*.

Base.	Nom. Sing. masc. fem.	Nom. Sing. neut.	Nom. Pl. masc. fem.	Nom. Pl. neut.	Instr. Pl.	Loc. Pl.
सुमनस् *sumanas*, kind, m. f. n.	सुमनाः *sumanāḥ*[1]	सुमनः *sumanaḥ*	सुमनसः *sumanasaḥ*	सुमनांसि *sumanāṃsi*	सुमनोभिः *sumanobhiḥ*	सुमनस्सु *sumanassu*[2]
सुज्योतिस् *sujyotis*, well-lighted, m. f. n.	सुज्योतिः *sujyotiḥ*	id.	सुज्योतिषः *sujyotishaḥ*	सुज्योतींषि *sujyotīṃshi*	सुज्योतिर्भिः *sujyotirbhiḥ*	सुज्योतिष्षु *sujyotishshu*[3]
पिंडग्रस् *piṇḍagras*, lump-eating, m. f. n.	पिंडग्रः *piṇḍagraḥ*	id.	पिंडग्रसः *piṇḍagrasaḥ*	पिंडग्रंसि *piṇḍagraṃsi*	पिंडग्रोभिः *piṇḍagrobhiḥ*	पिंडग्रस्सु *piṇḍagrassu*[4]
चकास् *chakās*, splendid, m. f. n.	चकाः *chakāḥ*	id.	चकासः *chakāsaḥ*	चकांसि *chakāṃsi*	चकाभिः *chakābhiḥ*	चकास्सु *chakāssu*[5]
दोस् *dos*[6], arm, m. (n.)	दोः *doḥ*	id.	दोषः *doshaḥ*	दोंषि *doṃshi*	दोर्भिः *dorbhiḥ*	दोष्षु *doshshu*[7]
सुपिस् *supis*, well-going, m. f. n.	सुपीः *supīḥ*	id.[8]	सुपिसः *supisaḥ*[9]	सुपिंसि *supiṃsi*	सुपीर्भिः *supīrbhiḥ*	सुपीष्षु *supīshshu*[10]

[1] The Vocative is सुमनः *sumanaḥ*. In the other paradigms it is the same as the Nominative.

[2] Or सुमनःसु *sumanaḥsu*.

[3] Or सुज्योतिःषु *sujyotiḥshu*.

[4] Or पिंडग्रःसु *piṇḍagraḥsu*.

[5] Or चकाःसु *chakāḥsu*.

[6] दोस् *dos* may be declined regularly throughout as a masculine. But it is likewise declined as a neuter. On its irregular or optional forms, see § 214.

[7] Or दोःषु *doḥshu*.

[8] Siddh.-Kaum. I. p. 197.

[9] स् *s* not changed into ष् *sh*; see § 100, note.

[10] Or सुपीःषु *supīḥshu*.

सुतुस् *sutus*, well-sounding, m. f. n.	सुतूः *sutūḥ*	id.	सुतुषः *sutushaḥ*	सुतूंषि *sutūṁshi*	सुतूर्भिः *sutūrbhiḥ*	सुतूष्षु *sutūshshu*[1]
पिपठिस् *pipaṭhis*, desirous of reading, m. f. n.	पिपठीः *pipaṭhīḥ*	id.[2]	पिपठिषः *pipaṭhishaḥ*	पिपठिषि *pipaṭhishi*[2]	पिपठीर्भिः *pipaṭhīrbhiḥ*	पिपठीष्षु *pipaṭhīshshu*[3]
चिकीर्ष् *chikīrs*, desirous of acting, m. f. n.	चिकीः *chikīḥ*	id.	चिकीर्षः *chikīrshaḥ*	चिकीर्षि *chikīrshi*[4]	चिकीर्भिः *chikīrbhiḥ*	चिकीर्षु *chikīrshu*
आशिस् *āśis*, blessing, f.	आशीः *āśīḥ* (Voc. id.)	id.	आशिषः *āśishaḥ*	आशींषि *āśīṁshi*	आशीर्भिः *āśīrbhiḥ*	आशीष्षु *āśīshshu*[5]
सजुस् *sajus*, companion, m.	सजूः *sajūḥ* (Voc. id.)	id.	सजुषः *sajushaḥ*	सजूंषि *sajūṁshi*	सजूर्भिः *sajūrbhiḥ*	सजूष्षु *sajūshshu*[6]
सुहिंस् *suhiṁs*, one who strikes well, m. f. n.	सुहिन् *suhin*	id.	सुहिंसः *suhiṁsaḥ*	सुहिंसि *suhiṁsi*	सुहिन्भिः *suhinbhiḥ*	सुहिन्सु *suhinsu*[7]

§ 173. ध्वस् *dhvas* (from ध्वंस् *dhvaṁs*, to fall) and स्रस् *sras* (from स्रंस् *sraṁs*, to fall) and भ्रस् *bhras* (from भ्रंस् *bhraṁs*, to fall), when used at the end of compounds, change their स् *s* into त् *t*, in the Nom. and Voc. Sing., and before terminations beginning with consonants. § 131 ought to be restricted to these bases and to participial bases in वस् *vas*, § 204.

N.V. पर्णध्वत् *parṇadhvat*	N.A.V. पर्णध्वसौ *parṇadhvasau*	N.A. पर्णध्वसः *parṇadhvasaḥ*
A. पर्णध्वसम् *parṇadhvasam*	I.Ab.D. पर्णध्वद्भ्याम् *parṇadhvadbhyām*	I. पर्णध्वद्भिः *parṇadhvadbhiḥ*
I. पर्णध्वसा *parṇadhvasā*	G.L. पर्णध्वसोः *parṇadhvasoḥ*	L. पर्णध्वत्सु *parṇadhvatsu*

§ 174. Bases ending in श् *ś*, ष् *sh*, छ् *chh*, क्ष् *ksh*, ह् *h*.

Bases ending in these consonants retain them unchanged before all terminations beginning with vowels. Before all other terminations and when final, their final consonants are treated either like ट् *ṭ* or like क् *k*.

1. Bases derived from दिश् *diś*, to show, दृश् *dṛiś*, to see, मृश् *mṛiś*, to stroke, स्पृश् *spṛiś*, to touch, change श् *ś* into क् *k*.

BASE.	NOM. SING.	NOM. PLUR.	NOM. PLUR. NEUT.	INSTR. PLUR.	LOC. PLUR.
दिश् *diś*, f. country	दिक् *dik*	दिशः *diśaḥ*	दिंशि *diṁśi*	दिग्भिः *digbhiḥ*	दिक्षु *dikshu*

2. Bases derived from नश् *naś*, to destroy, change श् *ś* into ट् *ṭ* or क् *k*.

BASE.	NOM. SING.	N. PL.	N. PL. NEUT.	INSTR. PL.	LOC. PL.
जीवनश् *jīvanaś*, m.f.n. life destroying	जीवनट् or °नक् *jīvanaṭ* or *-nak*	°नशः *-naśaḥ*	°नंशि *-naṁśi*	°नड्भिः or °नग्भिः *-naḍbhiḥ* or *-nagbhiḥ*	°नट्सु or °नक्षु *-naṭsu* or *-nakshu*

3. All other bases in श् *ś* change their final into ट् *ṭ*.

BASE.	NOM. SING.	NOM. PL.	NOM. PL. NEUT.	INSTR. PL.	LOC. PL.
विश् *viś*, m. f. n. one who enters	विट् *viṭ*	विशः *viśaḥ*	विंशि *viṁśi*	विड्भिः *viḍbhiḥ*	विट्सु *viṭsu*

---

[1] Or सुतूःषु *sutūḥshu*. [2] Siddh.-Kaum. I. p. 197. [3] Or पिपठीःषु *pipaṭhīḥshu*.
[4] Siddh.-Kaum. I. p. 194. [5] Or आशीःषु *āśīḥshu*. [6] Or सजूःषु *sajūḥshu*.
[7] See § 73.

4. Bases derived from धृष् *dhṛish*, to dare, change ष् *sh* into क् *k*.

BASE.	NOM. SING.	NOM. PL.	NOM. PL. NEUT.	INSTR. PL.	LOC. PL.
दधृष् *dadhṛish*, m.f.n. bold	दधृक् *dadhṛik*	दधृषः *dadhṛishaḥ*	दधृंषि *dadhṛiṁshi*	दधृग्भिः *dadhṛigbhiḥ*	दधृक्षु *dadhṛikshu*

5. All other bases derived from verbs with final ष् *sh* change ष् *sh* into ट् *ṭ*.

BASE.	NOM. SING.	NOM. PL.	NOM. PL. NEUT.	INSTR. PL.	LOC. PL.
द्विष् *dvish*, m.f.n. hating	द्विट् *dviṭ*	द्विषः *dvishaḥ*	द्विंषि *dviṁshi*	द्विड्भिः *dviḍbhiḥ*	द्विट्सु *dviṭsu*

6. Bases ending in छ् *chh* change छ् *chh* into ट् *ṭ*.

BASE.	NOM. SING.	NOM. PL.	NOM. PL. NEUT.	INSTR. PL.	LOC. PL.
प्राछ् *prâchh*, m.f.n. asking	प्राट् *prâṭ*	प्राछः *prâchhaḥ*	प्रांछि *prâṁchhi*	प्राड्भिः *prâḍbhiḥ*	प्राट्सु *prâṭsu*

Some grammarians allow प्राशः *prâśaḥ* in the Nom. Plur. and other cases beginning with vowels.

7. Bases ending in क्ष् *ksh* change क्ष् *ksh* into ट् *ṭ*.

BASE.	NOM. SING.	NOM. PL.	NOM. PL. NEUT.	INSTR. PL.	LOC. PL.
तक्ष् *taksh*, m.f.n. paring	तट् *taṭ**	तक्षः *takshaḥ*	तंक्षि *taṁkshi*	तड्भिः *taḍbhiḥ*	तट्सु *taṭsu*

8. Most bases ending in ह् *h* change ह् *h* into ट् *ṭ*.

BASE.	NOM. SING.	NOM. PL.	NOM. PL. NEUT.	INSTR. PL.	LOC. PL.
लिह् *lih*, m.f.n. licking	लिट् *liṭ*	लिहः *lihaḥ*	लिंहि *liṁhi*	लिड्भिः *liḍbhiḥ*	लिट्सु *liṭsu*
गुह् *guh*, m.f.n. covering	घुट् *ghuṭ*	गुहः *guhaḥ*	गुंहि *guṁhi*	घुड्भिः *ghuḍbhiḥ*	घुट्सु *ghuṭsu*

On the change of initial ग् *g* into घ् *gh*, see § 93.

9. Bases derived from roots ending in ह् *h*, and beginning with द् *d*, change ह् *h* into क् *k*. Likewise उष्णिह् *ushṇih*, a metre.

BASE.	NOM. SING.	NOM. PL.	NOM. PL. NEUT.	INSTR. PL.	LOC. PL.
दुह् *duh*, m.f.n. milking	धुक् *dhuk*	दुहः *duhaḥ*	दुंहि *duṁhi*	धुग्भिः *dhugbhiḥ*	धुक्षु *dhukshu*

10. Bases derived from the roots द्रुह् *druh*, to hate, मुह् *muh*, to confound, स्निह् *snih*, to love, स्नुह् *snuh*, to spue, may change the final ह् *h* into ट् *ṭ* or क् *k*.

BASE.	NOM. SING.	NOM. PL.	N. PL. NEUT.	INSTR. PL.	LOC. PL.
द्रुह् *druh*, m.f.n. hating	ध्रुट् or ध्रुक् *dhruṭ* or *dhruk*	द्रुहः *druhaḥ*	द्रुंहि *druṁhi*	ध्रुड्भिः or ध्रुग्भिः *dhruḍbhiḥ* or *dhrugbhiḥ*	ध्रुट्सु or ध्रुक्षु *dhruṭsu* or *dhrukshu*

11. Bases derived from नह् *nah*, to bind, change ह् *h* into त् *t*.

BASE.	NOM. SING.	NOM. PL.	INSTR. PL.	LOC. PL.
उपानह् *upânah*, f. a shoe	उपानत् *upânat*	उपानहः *upânahaḥ*	उपानद्भिः *upânadbhiḥ*	उपानत्सु *upânatsu*

---

* If differently derived तक्ष् *taksh* may form its Nom. Sing. तक् *tak*. गोरक्ष् *goraksh*, cow-herd, which regularly forms its Nom. Sing. गोरट् *goraṭ*, may, according to a different derivation, form गोरक् *gorak*. (See Colebrooke, p. 90, note.) So पिपक्ष् *pipak*, Nom. Dual पिपक्षौ *pipakshau*, desirous of maturing; विवक्ष् *vivak*, Nom. Dual विवक्षौ *vivakshau*, desirous of saying; दिधक्ष् *didhak*, Nom. Dual दिधक्षौ *didhakshau*, desirous of burning.

Decline विपाश् *vipâś*, f. the Beyah river in the Punjab. विष् *vish*, f. ordure. रुष् *rush*, f. anger. विप्रुष् *viprush*, f. drop of water. विविक्ष् *viviksh*, wishing to enter. स्निह् *snih*, loving. गोदुह् *goduh*, cow-milker. मधुलिह् *madhulih*, bee. त्विष् *tvish*, f. splendour. बहुत्विष् *bahutvish*, m. f. n. very splendid. रत्नमुष् *ratnamush*, a stealer of gems. ईदृश् *îdṛiś*, m. f. n. such. कीदृश् *kîdṛiś*, m. f. n. Which? मर्मस्पृश् *marmaspṛiś*, giving pain.

§ 175. तुरासाह् *turâsâh*, m. name of Indra, changes स् *s* into ष् *sh* whenever ह् *h* is changed into ड् *ḍ* or ट् *ṭ*.

Nom. Sing. तुराषाट् *turâshâṭ*. Nom. Dual तुरासाहौ *turâsâhau*. Instr. Plur. तुराषाड्भिः *turâshâḍbhiḥ*.

§ 176. पुरोडाश् *puroḍâś*, m. an offering, or a priest, is irregular. The Nom. Sing. is पुरोडाः *puroḍâḥ*, and all the cases beginning with consonants (Pada cases) are formed from a base पुरोडस् *puroḍas*. The Voc. Singular, too, is irregular, being identical with the Nom. Sing. (§ 152), though some grammarians allow हे पुरोडः *he puroḍaḥ*.

	Singular.	Dual.	Plural.
N.	पुरोडाः *puroḍâḥ*	पुरोडाशौ *puroḍâśau*	पुरोडाशः *puroḍâśaḥ*
A.	पुरोडाशं *puroḍâśam*	पुरोडाशौ *puroḍâśau*	पुरोडाशः *puroḍâśaḥ*
I.	पुरोडाशा *puroḍâśâ*	पुरोडोभ्यां *puroḍobhyâm*	पुरोडोभिः *puroḍobhiḥ*
D.	पुरोडाशे *puroḍâśe*	पुरोडोभ्यां *puroḍobhyâm*	पुरोडोभ्यः *puroḍobhyaḥ*
Ab.	पुरोडाशः *puroḍâśaḥ*	पुरोडोभ्यां *puroḍobhyâm*	पुरोडोभ्यः *puroḍobhyaḥ*
G.	पुरोडाशः *puroḍâśaḥ*	पुरोडाशोः *puroḍâśoḥ*	पुरोडाशां *puroḍâśâm*
L.	पुरोडाशि *puroḍâśi*	पुरोडाशोः *puroḍâśoḥ*	पुरोडःसु *puroḍaḥsu*
V.	पुरोडाः or °डः *puroḍâḥ* or *-ḍaḥ*	पुरोडाशौ *puroḍâśau*	पुरोडाशः *puroḍâśaḥ*

§ 177. Another word, उक्थशाः *ukthaśâḥ*, a reciter of hymns, is declined like पुरोडाश् *puroḍâś*.

Nom. उक्थशाः *ukthaśâḥ*. Acc. Sing. उक्थशासं *ukthaśâsam*. Instr. Plur. उक्थशोभिः *ukthaśobhiḥ*. Voc. Sing. उक्थशाः or उक्थशः *ukthaśâḥ* or *ukthaśaḥ*.

§ 178. Bases in म् *m*.

Bases ending in म् *m* retain म् *m* before all terminations beginning with vowels. Before all other terminations and when final, the म् *m* is changed into न् *n*.

Base प्रशाम् *praśâm*, mild.

	Singular. masc. fem.	Dual. masc. fem.	Plural. masc. fem.
Nom. Voc.	प्रशान् *praśân*	प्रशामौ *praśâmau*	प्रशामः *praśâmaḥ*
Acc.	प्रशामं *praśâmam*	प्रशामौ *praśâmau*	प्रशामः *praśâmaḥ*
Instr.	प्रशामा *praśâmâ*	प्रशान्भ्यां *praśânbhyâm*	प्रशान्भिः *praśânbhiḥ*
Loc.	प्रशामि *praśâmi*	प्रशामोः *praśâmoḥ*	प्रशान्सु *praśânsu*

2. Nouns with changeable Bases.

A. *Nouns with two Bases.*

§ 179. Many nouns in Sanskrit have more than one base, or rather they modify their base according to rule before certain terminations.

Nouns with two bases, have one base for the

Nom. Voc. and Acc. Sing.
Nom. Voc. and Acc. Dual } of masc. nouns*;
Nom. Voc. (not Acc.) Plural
Nom. Voc. and Acc. Plural of neuter nouns;

and a second base for all other cases.

The former base will be called the *Aṅga* base. Bopp calls it the strong base, and the terminations the weak terminations.

The second base will be called the *Pada and Bha* base. Bopp calls it the weak base, and the terminations the strong terminations.

The general rule is that the simple base, which appears in the Pada and Bha cases, is strengthened in the Aṅga cases. Thus the Pada and Bha base प्राच् *prâch* becomes in the Aṅga cases प्राञ्च् *prâñch*. The Pada base of the present participle अदत् *adat*, eating, becomes अदन्त् *adant* in the Aṅga cases. This gives us the following system of terminations for words with two bases:

	Singular. masc.	Dual. masc.	Plural. masc.
Nom. Voc.	स् *s* (which is always dropt)	औ *au*	अः *aḥ* †
Acc.	अं *am*	औ *au*	अः *aḥ*
Instr.	आ *á*	भ्यां *bhyám*	भिः *bhiḥ*
Dat.	ए *e*	भ्यां *bhyám*	भ्यः *bhyaḥ*
Abl.	अः *aḥ*	भ्यां *bhyám*	भ्यः *bhyaḥ*
Gen.	अः *aḥ*	ओः *oḥ*	आं *ám*
Loc.	इ *i*	ओः *oḥ*	सु *su*

Neuter.

	singular.	dual.	plural.
Nom. Acc.	——	ई *í*	इ i †

§ 180. Certain words derived from अञ्च् *añch*, to move, have two, others three bases.

प्राच् *prâch*, forward, eastern, has two bases, प्राञ्च् *prâñch* for its Aṅga, प्राच् *prâch* for its Pada and Bha base, and is declined accordingly.

---

* Most nouns with changeable bases form their feminines in ई *í*. A few, however, such as दामन् *dâman*, are said to be feminine without taking the ई *í*, and some of them occur as feminine at the end of compounds.

† Aṅga base, or, according to Bopp, strong base with weak terminations.

	SINGULAR. MASC.	DUAL. MASC.	PLURAL. MASC.
N. V.	प्राङ् *prâṅ* *	प्राञ्चौ *prâñchau*	प्राञ्चः *prâñchaḥ*
A.	प्राञ्चं *prâñcham*	प्राञ्चौ *prâñchau*	प्राचः *prâchaḥ*
I.	प्राचा *prâchâ*	प्राग्भ्यां *prâgbhyâm* (I. D. Ab.)	प्राग्भिः *prâgbhiḥ*
D.	प्राचे *prâche*		प्राग्भ्यः *prâgbhyaḥ* (D. Ab.)
Ab.	प्राचः *prâchaḥ* (Ab. G.)		
G.		प्राचोः *prâchoḥ* (G. L.)	प्राचां *prâchâm*
L.	प्राचि *prâchi*		प्राक्षु *prâkshu*

NEUTER.

	SINGULAR.	DUAL.	PLURAL.
N.A.V.	प्राक् *prâk*	प्राची *prâchî*	प्राञ्चि *prâñchi*
I.	प्राचा *prâchâ*	same as masc.	

The feminine of प्राच् *prâch* is प्राची *prâchî*, declined like fem. in ई *î*.
Decline अवाच् *avâch*, downward, south. Strong base अवाञ्च् *avâñch*.

B. *Nouns with three Bases.*

Nouns with three bases have their *Aṅga* or strong base in the same cases as the nouns with two bases. In the other cases, however, they have one base, the Pada base, before all terminations beginning with consonants; and another base, the Bha base, before all terminations beginning with vowels.

In these nouns with three cases, Bopp calls Aṅga base the strong base;
the Pada base the middle base;
the Bha base the weakest base.

This gives us the following system of terminations for words with three bases:

	SINGULAR. MASC.	DUAL. MASC.	PLURAL. MASC.
Nom. Voc.	स् *s* (always dropt)	औ *au*	अः *aḥ*
Acc.	अं *am*	औ *au*	अः *aḥ*
Instr.	आ *â*	भ्यां *bhyâm*	भिः *bhiḥ*
Dat.	ए *e*	भ्यां *bhyâm*	भ्यः *bhyaḥ*
Abl.	अः *aḥ*	भ्यां *bhyâm*	भ्यः *bhyaḥ*
Gen.	अः *aḥ*	ओः *oḥ*	आं *âm*
Loc.	इ *i*	ओः *oḥ*	सु *su*

* प्राङ् *prâṅ* stands for प्राङ्क् *prâṅk*; this for प्राञ्च् *prâñch* + स् *s*.

NEUTER.

	SINGULAR.	DUAL.	PLURAL.
Nom. Acc.	—	ई î	इ i

Terminations included in two lines require Aṅga or strong base.
Terminations included in one line require Pada or middle base.
Terminations not included in lines require Bha or weakest base.

181. Words derived from अञ्च् *añch*, to move, with three bases.

प्रत्यच् *pratyach*, behind, has for its Aṅga or strongest base प्रत्यञ्च् *pratyañch*; for its Bha or weakest प्रतीच् *pratîch*. The Pada or middle base is प्रत्यच् *pratyach*. Hence प्रत्यङ् *pratyaṅ*, Nom. Sing. masc.; प्रत्यक् *pratyak*, Nom. Sing. neut.; प्रतीची *pratîchî*, Nom. Sing. fem.

	SINGULAR. MASC.	DUAL. MASC.	PLURAL. MASC.
N. V.	प्रत्यङ् *pratyaṅ*	प्रत्यञ्चौ *pratyañchau*	प्रत्यञ्चः *pratyañchaḥ*
A.	प्रत्यञ्चम् *pratyañcham*	प्रत्यञ्चौ *pratyañchau*	प्रतीचः *pratîchaḥ*
I.	प्रतीचा *pratîchâ*	प्रत्यग्भ्याम् *pratyagbhyâm*	प्रत्यग्भिः *pratyagbhiḥ*
D.	प्रतीचे *pratîche*	प्रत्यग्भ्याम् *pratyagbhyâm*	प्रत्यग्भ्यः *pratyagbhyaḥ*
Ab.	प्रतीचः *pratîchaḥ*	प्रत्यग्भ्याम् *pratyagbhyâm*	प्रत्यग्भ्यः *pratyagbhyaḥ*
G.	प्रतीचः *pratîchaḥ*	प्रतीचोः *pratîchoḥ*	प्रतीचाम् *pratîchâm*
L.	प्रतीचि *pratîchi*	प्रतीचोः *pratîchoḥ*	प्रत्यक्षु *pratyakshu*

NEUTER.

	SINGULAR.	DUAL.	PLURAL.
N. A.	प्रत्यक् *pratyak*	प्रतीची *pratîchî*	प्रत्यञ्चि *pratyañchi*

FEM.

	SINGULAR.
N.	प्रतीची *pratîchî*

The following words, derived from अञ्च् *añch*, to move, have three bases:

Aṅga or strong base.	Pada or middle base.	Bha or weak base.
प्रत्यञ्च् *pratyañch*, behind	प्रत्यच् *pratyach*	प्रतीच् *pratîch*
सम्यञ्च् *samyañch*, right	सम्यच् *samyach*	समीच् *samîch*
न्यञ्च् *nyañch*, low	न्यच् *nyach*	नीच् *nîch*
सध्र्यञ्च् *sadhryañch*, accompanying	सध्र्यच् *sadhryach*	सध्रीच् *sadhrîch*
अन्वञ्च् *anvañch*, following	अन्वच् *anvach*	अनूच् *anûch*
विष्वञ्च् *vishvañch*, all-pervading	विष्वच् *vishvach*	विषूच् *vishûch*
उदञ्च् *udañch*, upward	उदच् *udach*	उदीच् *udîch*
तिर्यञ्च् *tiryañch*, tortuous	तिर्यच् *tiryach*	तिरश्च् *tiraśch*

Bases in अत् *at* and अंत् *ant*.

1. *Participles Present.*

§ 182. Participles of the present have two bases, the Pada and Bha base in अत् *at*, the Aṅga base in अंत् *ant*.

	SINGULAR. MASC.	DUAL. MASC.	PLURAL. MASC.
N.V.	अदन् *adan*	अदंतौ *adantau*	अदंतः *adantaḥ*
A.	अदंतं *adantam*	अदंतौ *adantau*	अदतः *adataḥ*
I.	अदता *adatâ*	अदद्भ्यां *adadbhyâm*	अदद्भिः *adadbhiḥ*
D.	अदते *adate*		अदद्भ्यः *adadbhyaḥ*
Ab.	अदतः *adataḥ*		
G.		अदतोः *adatoḥ*	अदतां *adatâm*
L.	अदति *adati*		अदत्सु *adatsu*

NEUTER.

	SINGULAR.	DUAL.	PLURAL.
N.A.	अदत् *adat*	अदती *adatî*	अदंति *adanti*

FEM.
SINGULAR.

N. अदती *adatî*, &c., like नदी *nadî*.

§ 183. There is a very difficult rule according to which certain participles keep the न् *n* in the Nom. and Acc. Dual of neuters, and before the ई *î* of the feminine. This rule can only be fully understood by those who are acquainted with the ten classes of conjugations. It is this,

I. Participles of verbs following the Bhû, Div, and Chur classes *must* preserve the न् *n*.

II. Participles of verbs following the Tud class *may* or *may not* preserve the न् *n*. The same applies to all participles of the future in स्यत् *syat*, and to the participles of verbs of the Ad class in आ *â*.

III. Participles of all other verbs *must* reject the न् *n*.

		Nom. and Acc. Dual Neut.
I.	भवत् *bhavat*.	भवंती *bhavantî*.
	दीव्यत् *dîvyat*.	दीव्यंती *dîvyantî*.
	चोरयत् *chorayat*.	चोरयंती *chorayantî*.
II.	तुदत् *tudat*.	तुदंती *tudantî* or तुदती *tudatî*.
	भविष्यत् *bhavishyat* (fut.).	भविष्यंती *bhavishyantî* or भविष्यती *bhavishyatî*.
	यात् *yât*.	यांती *yântî* or याती *yâtî*.

III.	अदत् *adat.*	Nom. and Acc. Dual Neut.	अदती *adatí.*
	जुह्वत् *juhvat.*		जुह्वती *juhvatí.*
	सुन्वत् *sunvat.*		सुन्वती *sunvatí.*
	रुन्धत् *rundhat.*		रुन्धती *rundhatí.*
	तन्वत् *tanvat.*		तन्वती *tanvatí.*
	क्रीणत् *krîṇat.*		क्रीणती *krîṇatí.*

The feminine base is throughout identical in form with the Nom. Dual Neut. Hence भवन्ती *bhavantí*, being, fem.; तुदन्ती *tudantí* or तुदती *tudatí*, striking, fem.; अदती *adatí*, eating, fem. The feminine base is declined regularly as a base in ई *í*.

§ 184. Another rule, which ought not to be mixed up with the preceding rule, prohibits the strengthening of the Aṅga base throughout in the participles present of reduplicated verbs, except in the Nom. Acc. Voc. Plur. Neut., where the insertion of न् *n* is optional. With this exception, these participles are therefore really declined like nouns in त् *t* with unchangeable bases.

Base ददत् *dadat*, giving, from दा *dá*, to give, ददामि *dadámi*, I give.

	SINGULAR. MASC.	SINGULAR. NEUT.	DUAL. MASC.	DUAL. NEUT.	PLURAL. MASC.	PLURAL. NEUT.
N.V.	ददत् *dadat*	ददत् *dadat*	ददतौ *dadatau*	ददती *dadatí*	ददतः *dadataḥ*	ददति *dadati**
A.	ददतम् *dadatam*	ददत् *dadat*	ददतौ *dadatau*	ददती *dadatí*	ददतः *dadataḥ*	ददति *dadati**
I.	ददता *dadatá*		ददद्भ्याम् *dadadbhyám*		ददद्भिः *dadadbhiḥ*	
D.	ददते *dadate*		ददद्भ्याम् *dadadbhyám*		ददद्भ्यः *dadadbhyaḥ*	
Ab.	ददतः *dadataḥ*		ददद्भ्याम् *dadadbhyám*		ददद्भ्यः *dadadbhyaḥ*	
G.	ददतः *dadataḥ*		ददतोः *dadatoḥ*		ददताम् *dadatám*	
L.	ददति *dadati*		ददतोः *dadatoḥ*		ददत्सु *dadatsu*	

The same rule applies to the participles जक्षत् *jakshat*, eating; जाग्रत् *jágrat*, waking; दरिद्रत् *daridrat*, being poor; शासत् *śásat*, commanding; चकासत् *chakásat*, shining. But जगत् *jagat*, neut. the world, forms Nom. Plur. जगन्ति *jaganti*, only.

§ 185. बृहत् *brihat*, great, पृषत् *prishat*, m. a deer, n. a drop of water, are declined like participles of verbs of the Ad class.

	SINGULAR. MASC.	DUAL. MASC.	PLURAL. MASC.
N. V.	बृहन् *brihan*	बृहन्तौ *brihantau*	बृहन्तः *brihantaḥ*
A.	बृहन्तम् *brihantam*	बृहन्तौ *brihantau*	बृहतः *brihataḥ*

* Or ददन्ति *dadanti*.

NEUTER.

	SINGULAR.	DUAL.	PLURAL.
N. A.	बृहत् *bṛihat*	बृहती *bṛihatî*	बृहंति *bṛihanti*

FEM.

	SINGULAR.
N.	बृहती *bṛihatî*

§ 186. महत् *mahat*, great, likewise originally a participle of the Ad class, forms its Aṅga or strong base in आंत् *ânt*.

	SINGULAR. MASC.	DUAL. MASC.	PLURAL. MASC.
N.	महान् *mahân*	महांतौ *mahântau*	महांतः *mahântaḥ*
A.	महांतं *mahântam*	महांतौ *mahântau*	महतः *mahataḥ*
I.	महता *mahatâ*	महद्भ्यां *mahadbhyâm*	महद्भिः *mahadbhiḥ*
D.	महते *mahate*	महद्भ्यां *mahadbhyâm*	महद्भ्यः *mahadbhyaḥ*
Ab.	महतः *mahataḥ*	महद्भ्यां *mahadbhyâm*	महद्भ्यः *mahadbhyaḥ*
G.	महतः *mahataḥ*	महतोः *mahatoḥ*	महतां *mahatâm*
L.	महति *mahati*	महतोः *mahatoḥ*	महत्सु *mahatsu*
V.	महन् *mahan*		

NEUTER.

	SINGULAR.	DUAL.	PLURAL.
N. A. V.	महत् *mahat*	महती *mahatî*	महांति *mahânti*

The rest like the masculine.

FEM.

	SINGULAR.
N.	महती *mahatî*

Bases ending in the Suffixes मत् mat *and* वत् vat, *forming their Aṅga Bases in* मंत् mant *and* वंत् vant.

§ 187. The possessive suffixes मत् *mat* and वत् *vat* form their Aṅga or strong base in मंत् *mant* and वंत् *vant*. They lengthen their vowel in the Nom. Sing. Masc. These suffixes are of very frequent occurrence.

अग्निमत् *agnimat*, having fire.

	SINGULAR. MASC.	DUAL. MASC.	PLURAL. MASC.
N.	अग्निमान् *agnimân*	अग्निमंतौ *agnimantau*	अग्निमंतः *agnimantaḥ*
A.	अग्निमंतं *agnimantam*	अग्निमंतौ *agnimantau*	अग्निमतः *agnimataḥ*
V.	अग्निमन् *agniman*		

NEUTER.

	SINGULAR.	DUAL.	PLURAL.
N.V.	अग्निमत् *agnimat*	अग्निमती *agnimatî*	अग्निमंति *agnimanti*

FEM.

	SINGULAR.
N.	अग्निमती *agnimatî*

वत् *vat* is used 1. after bases in अ *a* and आ *â*.

Ex. ज्ञानवत् *jñânavat*, having knowledge. विद्यावत् *vidyâvat*, having knowledge.

But अग्निमत् *agnimat*, having fire. हनुमत् *hanumat*, having jaws.

2. After bases ending in nasals, semivowels, or sibilants, if preceded by अ *a* or आ *â*.

Ex. पयस्वत् *payasvat*, having milk. उदन्वत् *udanvat*, having water.

But ज्योतिष्मत् *jyotishmat*, having light. गीर्वत् *gîrvat*, having a voice.

3. After bases ending in any other consonants, by whatever vowel they may be preceded.

Ex. विद्युत्वत् *vidyutvat*, having lightning.

There are exceptions to these rules. (Pâṇ. VIII. 2, 9–16.)

§ 188. भवत् *bhavat*, Your Honour, which is frequently used in place of the pronoun of the second person, is declined like a noun derived by वत् *vat*. Native grammarians derive it from भा *bhâ*, with the suffix वत् *vat*, and keep it distinct from भवत् *bhavat*, being, the participle present of भू *bhû*, to be.

भवत् *bhavat*, Your Honour.

	SINGULAR. MASC.	DUAL. MASC.	PLURAL. MASC.
N.	भवान् *bhavân*	भवंतौ *bhavantau*	भवंतः *bhavantaḥ*
A.	भवंतं *bhavantam*	भवंतौ *bhavantau*	भवतः *bhavataḥ*
V.	भवन् *bhavan* or भोः *bhoḥ*		

NEUTER.

	SINGULAR.	DUAL.	PLURAL.
N.A.V.	भवत् *bhavat*	भवती *bhavatî*	भवंति *bhavanti*

FEM.

	SINGULAR.
N.	भवती *bhavatî*

भवत् *bhavat*, being, part. present.

	SINGULAR. MASC.	DUAL. MASC.	PLURAL. MASC.
N.	भवन् *bhavan*	भवंतौ *bhavantau*	भवंतः *bhavantaḥ*
A.	भवंतं *bhavantam*	भवंतौ *bhavantau*	भवतः *bhavataḥ*
V.	भवन् *bhavan*		

NEUTER.

	SINGULAR.	DUAL.	PLURAL.
N.A.V.	भवत् *bhavat*	भवन्ती *bhavantî*	भवन्ति *bhavanti*

FEM.

	SINGULAR.
N.	भवन्ती *bhavantî*

§ 189. अर्वत् *arvat*, masc. horse, is declined regularly like nouns in वत् *vat*, except in the Nom. Sing., where it has अर्वा *arvâ*. अर्वन् *arvan* in अनर्वन् *anarvan*, without a foe, is a totally different word, and declined like a noun in अन् *an*; Nom. Sing. अनर्वा *anarvâ*; Nom. Dual अनर्वाणौ *anarvâṇau*; Acc. Sing. अनर्वाणं *anarvâṇam*; Instr. Sing. अनर्वणा *anarvaṇâ*; Instr. Plur. अनर्वभिः *anarvabhiḥ*. The feminine of अर्वत् *arvat* is अर्वती *arvatî*.

§ 190. कियत् *kiyat*, How much? इयत् *iyat*, so much, are declined like bases in मत् *mat*. Their feminines are कियती *kiyatî*, इयती *iyatî*.

	SINGULAR. MASC.	DUAL. MASC.	PLURAL. MASC.
N.	कियान् *kiyân*	कियन्तौ *kiyantau*	कियन्तः *kiyantaḥ*
A.	कियन्तं *kiyantam*	कियन्तौ *kiyantau*	कियतः *kiyataḥ*
I.	कियता *kiyatâ*	कियद्भ्यां *kiyadbhyâm*	कियद्भिः *kiyadbhiḥ*
V.	कियन् *kiyan*		

NEUTER.

	SINGULAR.	DUAL.	PLURAL.
N.A.V.	कियत् *kiyat*	कियती *kiyatî*	कियन्ति *kiyanti*

Bases in अन् an (अन् an, मन् man, वन् van).

§ 191. Words in अन् *an* have three bases: their Aṅga or strong base is आन् *ân*; their Bha or weakest base न् *n*; and their Pada or middle base अ *a*.

Mark besides,

1. That the Nom. Sing. masc. has आ *â*, not आन् *ân(s)*.
2. That the Nom. Sing. neut. has अ *a*, not अन् *an*.
3. That the Voc. Sing. neut. may be either identical with the Nominative, or take न् *n*.
4. That words ending in मन् *man* and वन् *van* keep मन् *man* and वन् *van* as their Bha bases, without dropping the अ *a*, when there is a consonant immediately before the मन् *man* and वन् *van*. This is to avoid the concurrence of three consonants, such as पर्व्न् *parvn* from पर्वन् *parvan*, or आत्म्न् *âtmn* from आत्मन् *âtman*. This rule applies only to words ending in मन् *man* and वन् *van*, not to words ending in simple

अन् *an.* Thus तक्षन् *takshan* forms तक्ष्णा *takshṇá;* मूर्धन् *múrdhan,* मूर्ध्ना *múrdhná,* &c.

5. That in all other words the loss of the अ *a* is optional in the Loc. Sing., and in the Nom. Acc. Voc. Dual of neuters. The feminine, however, drops the अ *a;* thus राज्ञी *rájñí.*

राजन् *rájan,* m. king. Aṅga, राजान् *rájân;* Pada, राज *rája;* Bha, राज्ञ् *rájñ.*

MASCULINE.

	SINGULAR.	DUAL.	PLURAL.
N.	राजा *rájá*	राजानौ *rájánau*	राजानः *rájánaḥ*
A.	राजानं *rájánam*	राजानौ *rájánau*	राज्ञः *rájñaḥ*
V.	राजन् *rájan*		
I.	राज्ञा *rájñá*	राजभ्यां *rájabhyám*	राजभिः *rájabhiḥ*
D.	राज्ञे *rájñe*	राजभ्यां *rájabhyám*	राजभ्यः *rájabhyaḥ*
Ab.	राज्ञः *rájñaḥ*	राजभ्यां *rájabhyám*	राजभ्यः *rájabhyaḥ*
G.	राज्ञः *rájñaḥ*	राज्ञोः *rájñoḥ*	राज्ञां *rájñám*
L.	राज्ञि *rájñi* or राजनि *rájani*	राज्ञोः *rájñoḥ*	राजसु *rájasu*

नामन् *náman,* n. name. Aṅga, नामान् *námán;* Pada, नाम *náma;* Bha, नाम्न् *námn.*

NEUTER.

	SINGULAR.	DUAL.	PLURAL.
N. A.	नाम *náma*	नाम्नी *námní* or नामनी *námaní*	नामानि *námáni*
V.	नाम *náma* or नामन् *náman*		
I.	नाम्ना *námná*	नामभ्यां *námabhyám*	नामभिः *námabhiḥ*
D.	नाम्ने *námne*	नामभ्यां *námabhyám*	नामभ्यः *námabhyaḥ*
Ab.	नाम्नः *námnaḥ*	नामभ्यां *námabhyám*	नामभ्यः *námabhyaḥ*
G.	नाम्नः *námnaḥ*	नाम्नोः *námnoḥ*	नाम्नां *námnám*
L.	नाम्नि *námni* or नामनि *námani*	नाम्नोः *námnoḥ*	नामसु *námasu*

§ 192. Nouns in which the suffixes मन् *man* and वन् *van* are preceded by a consonant, such as ब्रह्मन् *brahman,* m. n. the creator, यज्वन् *yajvan,* m. sacrificer, पर्वन् *parvan,* n. joint, form their Bha base in मन् *man* and वन् *van.*

ब्रह्मन् *brahman,* m. creator. Aṅga, ब्रह्मान् *brahmân;* Pada, ब्रह्म *brahma;* Bha, ब्रह्मन् *brahman.*

MASCULINE.

	SINGULAR.	DUAL.	PLURAL.
N.	ब्रह्मा *brahmâ*	ब्रह्माणौ *brahmâṇau*	ब्रह्माणः *brahmâṇaḥ*
A.	ब्रह्माणं *brahmâṇam*	ब्रह्माणौ *brahmâṇau*	ब्रह्मणः *brahmaṇaḥ*
V.	ब्रह्मन् *brahman*		
I.	ब्रह्मणा *brahmaṇâ*	ब्रह्मभ्यां *brahmabhyâm*	ब्रह्मभिः *brahmabhiḥ*
D.	ब्रह्मणे *brahmaṇe*	ब्रह्मभ्यां *brahmabhyâm*	ब्रह्मभ्यः *brahmabhyaḥ*
Ab.	ब्रह्मणः *brahmaṇaḥ*	ब्रह्मभ्यां *brahmabhyâm*	ब्रह्मभ्यः *brahmabhyaḥ*
G.	ब्रह्मणः *brahmaṇaḥ*	ब्रह्मणोः *brahmaṇoḥ*	ब्रह्मणां *brahmaṇâm*
L.	ब्रह्मणि *brahmaṇi*	ब्रह्मणोः *brahmaṇoḥ*	ब्रह्मसु *brahmasu*

NEUTER.

	SINGULAR.	DUAL.	PLURAL.
N.A.	ब्रह्म *brahma*	ब्रह्मणी *brahmaṇî*	ब्रह्माणि *brahmâṇi*
V.	ब्रह्म *brahma* or ब्रह्मन् *brahman*		

Decline यज्वन् *yajvan*, sacrificer; आत्मन् *âtman*, self; सुधर्मन् *sudharman*, virtuous.

प्रतिदिवन् *pratidivan*, one who sports, from दिव् दीव्यति *div dîvyati*, lengthens the दि *di* to दी *dî*, whenever the व् *v* is immediatcly followed by न् *n*. Nom. Sing. प्रतिदिवा *pratidivâ*; Nom. Plur. प्रतिदिवानः *pratidivânaḥ*; Acc. Plur. प्रतिदीव्नः *pratidîvnaḥ* (§ 143).

§ 193. Words in अन् *an*, like राजन् *râjan*, king, form their feminine in ई *î*, dropping the अ *a* before the न् *n*; राज्ञी *râjñî*, queen.

Words in वन् *van*, like धीवन् *dhîvan*, fisherman, form their feminine in वरी *varî*; धीवरी *dhîvarî*, wife of a fisherman. See, however, Pâṇ. IV. 1, 7, v.

Words in मन् *man*, if feminine, are declined like masculines. दामन् *dâman*, fem. rope; Nom. Sing. दामा *dâmâ*, Acc. दामानं *dâmânam*; but there is an optional base दामा *dâmâ*, Acc. Sing. दामां *dâmâm*. (Pâṇ. IV. 1, 11; 13.)

§ 194. Nouns in अन् *an*, मन् *man*, वन् *van*, at the end of adjectival compounds, may either use their masculine forms as feminines, or form feminines in आ *â*. Those in अन् *an*, if in the Bha base they can drop the अ *a* before the न् *n*, may also take ई *î* (Pâṇ. IV. 1, 28). Thus, Nom. Sing. masc. and fem. सुचर्मा *sucharmâ*, having good leather, Nom. Dual सुचर्माणौ *sucharmâṇau*; सुपर्वा *suparvâ*, सुपर्वाणौ *suparvâṇau*: or, Nom. Sing. fem. सुचर्मा *sucharmâ*, Nom. Dual सुचर्मे *sucharme*, Plur. सुचर्माः *sucharmâḥ*; सुपर्वा *suparvâ*, सुपर्वे *suparve*, सुपर्वाः *suparvâḥ*. Of बहुराजन् *bahurâjan*, having many kings, the feminine may be,

1. बहुराजा *bahurâjâ*, Dual बहुराजानौ *bahurâjânau*.
2. बहुराजा *bahurâjâ*, Dual बहुराजे *bahurâje*.
3. बहुराज्ञी *bahurâjñî*, Dual बहुराज्ञ्यौ *bahurâjñyau*.

द्विदाम्नी *dvidâmnî* (Pâṇ. IV. 1, 27), having two ropes, is an exception.

Adjectives in वन् *van*, which form their fem. in वरी *varî*, धीवन् *dhîvan*, a fisherman, धीवरी *dhîvarî*, पीवन् *pîvan*, पीवरी *pîvarî*, fat, may do the same at the end of compounds, or take वा *vâ*. बहुधीवरी *bahudhîvarî* or बहुधीवा *bahudhîvâ*, Nom. Dual बहुधीवे *bahudhîve*, having many fishermen. (Siddh.-Kaum. I. p. 209.)

§ 195. पथिन् *pathin*, m. path, has
for its Aṅga base पंथान् *panthân* (like राजान् *râjân*);
for its Bha base पथ् *path*;
for its Pada base पथि *pathi*.

It is irregular in the Nom. and Voc. Sing., where it is पंथाः *panthâḥ*.

	Singular.	Dual.		Plural.
N.V.	पंथाः *panthâḥ*	पंथानौ *panthânau*	N.	पंथानः *panthânaḥ*
A.	पंथानं *panthânam*	पंथानौ *panthânau*	A.	पथः *pathaḥ*
I.	पथा *pathâ*	पथिभ्यां *pathibhyâm*	I.	पथिभिः *pathibhiḥ*

ऋभुक्षिन् *ṛibhukshin*, m. a name of Indra, and मथिन् *mathin*, m. a churning-stick, are declined in the same manner. The three bases are,

ऋभुक्षान् *ṛibhukshân*, मंथान् *manthân* } Aṅga;
ऋभुक्ष् *ṛibhuksh*, मथ् *math* } Bha;
ऋभुक्षि *ṛibhukshi*, मथि *mathi* } Pada.

The Nom. and Voc. Sing. are ऋभुक्षाः *ṛibhukshâḥ* and मंथाः *manthâḥ*.

पथिन् *pathin*, ऋभुक्षिन् *ṛibhukshin*, and मथिन् *mathin* form their feminines पथी *pathî*, ऋभुक्षी *ṛibhukshî*, मथी *mathî*.

§ 196. A word of very frequent occurrence is अहन् *ahan*, n. day, which takes अहस् *ahas* as its Pada base. Otherwise it is declined like नामन् *nâman*.

	Singular.			Dual.			Plural.	
P.	N.A.V.	अहः *ahaḥ*	Bh.	N.A.V.	अह्नी *ahnî**	Aṅ.	N.A.V.	अहानि *ahâni*
Bh.	I.	अह्ना *ahnâ*	P.	I.D.Ab.	अहोभ्यां *ahobhyâm*	P.	I.	अहोभिः *ahobhiḥ*
Bh.	D.	अह्ने *ahne*	Bh.	G.L.	अह्नोः *ahnoḥ*	P.	D.Ab.	अहोभ्यः *ahobhyaḥ*
Bh.	Ab.G.	अह्नः *ahnaḥ*				Bh.	G.	अह्नां *ahnâm*
Bh.	L.	अह्नि *ahni* †				P.	L.	अहस्सु *ahassu* ‡

The Visarga in the Nominative Singular is treated like an original र् *r* (§ 85). Hence अहरहः *ahar-ahaḥ*, day by day. In composition, too, the same rule

* Or अहनी *ahanî*. † Or अहनि *ahani*. ‡ Or अहःसु *ahaḥsu*.

applies; अहर्गणः *ahargaṇaḥ*, a month (Pâṇ. VIII. 2, 69): though not always, अहोरात्रः *ahorâtraḥ*, day and night. (See § 90.)

§ 197. At the end of a compound, too, अहन् *ahan* is irregular. Thus दीर्घाहन् *dîrghâhan*, having long days, is declined:

Singular.	Dual.	Plural.
N. दीर्घाहाः *dîrghâhâḥ**	N.A.V. दीर्घाहाणौ *dîrghâhâṇau*	N.V. दीर्घाहाणः *dîrghâhâṇaḥ*
V. दीर्घाहः *dîrghâhaḥ*		A. दीर्घाह्नः *dîrghâhnaḥ*
A. दीर्घाहाणं *dîrghâhâṇam*		I. दीर्घाहोभिः *dîrghâhobhiḥ*, &c.

Feminine, दीर्घाह्नी *dîrghâhnî* (Pâṇ. VIII. 4, 7).

§ 198. In derivative compounds with numerals, and with वि *vi* and साय *sâya*, अह्न *ahna* is substituted for अहन् *ahan*: but in the Loc. Sing. both forms are admitted; e.g. द्व्यह्नः *dvyahnaḥ*, produced in two days; Loc. Sing. द्व्यह्ने *dvyahne* or द्व्यह्नि *dvyahni* or द्व्यहनि *dvyahani*. (Pâṇ. VI. 3, 110.)

§ 199. श्वन् *śvan*, m. dog, युवन् *yuvan*, m. young, take शुन् *śun*, यून् *yûn* as their Bha bases. For the rest, they are declined regularly, like ब्रह्मन् *brahman*, m.

Singular.	Dual.	Plural.
N. श्वा *śvâ*	N.A.V. श्वानौ *śvânau*	N. श्वानः *śvânaḥ*
A. श्वानं *śvânam*		A. शुनः *śunaḥ*
V. श्वन् *śvan*		I. श्वभिः *śvabhiḥ*

The feminine of श्वन् *śvan* is शुनी *śunî*; of युवन् *yuvan*, युवतिः *yuvatiḥ*; according to some grammarians, यूनी *yûnî*.

§ 200. मघवन् *maghavan*, the Mighty, a name of Indra, takes मघोन् *maghon* as its Bha base.

Singular.	Dual.	Plural.
N. मघवा *maghavâ*	N.A.V. मघवानौ *maghavânau*	N. मघवानः *maghavânaḥ*
A. मघवानं *maghavânam*		A. मघोनः *maghonaḥ*
V. मघवन् *maghavan*		I. मघवभिः *maghavabhiḥ* †

The same word may likewise be declined like a masculine with the suffix वत् *vat* or मत् *mat*; (see अग्निमत् *agnimat*.)

Singular.	Dual.	Plural.
N. मघवान् *maghavân*	N.A.V. मघवन्तौ *maghavantau*	N. मघवन्तः *maghavantaḥ*
A. मघवन्तं *maghavantam*		A. मघवतः *maghavataḥ*
V. मघवन् *maghavan*		I. मघवद्भिः *maghavadbhiḥ*

The feminine is accordingly either मघोनी *maghonî* or मघवती *maghavatî*.

---

* Pâṇ. VIII. 2, 69, 1; Siddh.-Kaum. I. p. 194; but Colebrooke, p. 83, has दीर्घाहा *dîrghâhâ* as Nom. Sing.

† Colebrooke, Sanskrit Grammar, p. 81.

§ 201. पूषन् *púshan* and अर्यमन् *aryaman*, two names of Vedic deities, do not lengthen their vowel except in the Nom. Sing. and the Nom. Acc. Voc. Plur. neut.; (in this they follow the bases in इन् *in;* § 203.) For the rest, they are declined like nouns in अन् *an;* (see राजन् *rájan.*)

BASE.	NOM. SING.	NOM. PL.	ACC. PL.	INSTR. PL.	NOM. PL. NEUT.
पूषन्, पूष, पूष्ण् *púshan, púsha, púshṇ*	पूषा *púshá*	पूषणः *púshaṇaḥ*	पूष्णः *púshṇaḥ*	पूषभिः *púshabhiḥ*	पूषाणि *púsháṇi*
अर्यमन्, अर्यमण, अर्यम्ण् *aryaman, aryamaṇa, aryamṇ*	अर्यमा *aryamá*	अर्यमणः *aryamaṇaḥ*	अर्यम्णः *aryamṇaḥ*	अर्यमभिः *aryamabhiḥ*	अर्यमाणि *aryamáṇi*

Loc. Sing. पूष्णि *púshṇi* or पूषणि *púshaṇi;* or, according to some, पूषि *púshi.* (Sâr. 1. 9, 31.)

§ 202. The root हन् *han*, to kill, if used as a noun, follows the same rule; only that when the vowel between ह् *h* and न् *n* is dropt, ह् *h* becomes घ् *gh.*

BASE.	NOM. SING.	NOM. PL.	ACC. PL.	INSTR. PL.	NOM. PL. NEUT.
हन् *han*, ह *ha*, घ्न् *ghn*	हा *há*	हनः *hanaḥ*	घ्नः *ghnaḥ*	हभिः *habhiḥ*	हाणि *háṇi*
ब्रह्महन्, ह, घ्न् *brahmahan, ha, ghn*	ब्रह्महा *brahmahá*	ब्रह्महणः *brahmahaṇaḥ*	ब्रह्मघ्नः *brahmaghnaḥ*	ब्रह्महभिः *brahmahabhiḥ*	ब्रह्महाणि *brahmaháṇi*

Loc. Sing. ब्रह्मघ्नि *brahmaghni* or ब्रह्महणि *brahmahaṇi.*

Bases in इन् in.

§ 203. Words in इन् *in* are almost regular; it is to be observed that

1. They drop the न् *n* at the end of the Pada base.
2. They form the Nom. Sing. masc. in ई *í;* the Nom. Acc. Sing. neut. in इ *i;* and the Nom. Acc. Plur. neut. in ईनि *íni.*

MASCULINE.

	SINGULAR.	DUAL.	PLURAL.
N.	धनी *dhaní*	धनिनौ *dhaninau*	धनिनः *dhaninaḥ*
A.	धनिनं *dhaninam*	धनिनौ *dhaninau*	धनिनः *dhaninaḥ*
I.	धनिना *dhaniná*	धनिभ्यां *dhanibhyám*	धनिभिः *dhanibhiḥ*
D.	धनिने *dhanine*	धनिभ्यां *dhanibhyám*	धनिभ्यः *dhanibhyaḥ*
Ab.	धनिनः *dhaninaḥ*	धनिभ्यां *dhanibhyám*	धनिभ्यः *dhanibhyaḥ*
G.	धनिनः *dhaninaḥ*	धनिनोः *dhaninoḥ*	धनिनां *dhaninám*
L.	धनिनि *dhanini*	धनिनोः *dhaninoḥ*	धनिषु *dhanishu*
V.	धनिन् *dhanin*	धनिनौ *dhaninau*	धनिनः *dhaninaḥ*

NEUTER.

	SINGULAR.	DUAL.	PLURAL.
N. A.	धनि *dhani*	धनिनी *dhaniní*	धनीनि *dhaníni*
V.	धनि *dhani* or धनिन् *dhanin*		

FEM.

	SINGULAR.
N.	धनिनी *dhaniní*

Decline मेधाविन् *medhávin*, wise; यशस्विन् *yaśasvin*, glorious; वाग्मिन् *vágmin*, loquacious; कारिन् *kárin*, doing.

Note—These nouns in इन् *in*, (etymologically a shortened form of अन् *an*,) follow the analogy of nouns in अन् *an* (like राजन् *rájan*, नामन् *náman*) in the Nom. Sing. masc. and neut., and in the Voc. Sing. and in the Nom. Acc. Plur. neut. They might be ranged, in fact, with the nouns having unchangeable bases; for the lengthening of the vowel in the Nom. and Acc. Plur. neut. is but a compensation for the absence of the nasal which is inserted in these cases in all bases except those ending in nasals and semivowels.

Participles in वस् vas.

§ 204. Participles of the reduplicated perfect in वस् *vas* have three bases; वांस् *váṁs* as the Aṅga, उष् *ush* as the Bha, and वस् *vas* as the Pada base. They change the स् *s* of वस् *vas* into त् *t*, if the स् *s* is final, or if it is followed by terminations beginning with भ् *bh* and स् *s*. (See §§ 173, 131.)

Aṅga, रुरुद्वांस् *rurudváṁs*; Pada, रुरुद्वस् *rurudvas*; Bha, रुरुदुष् *rurudush*.

MASCULINE.

	SINGULAR.	DUAL.	PLURAL.
N.	रुरुद्वान् *rurudván*	रुरुद्वांसौ *rurudváṁsau*	रुरुद्वांसः *rurudváṁsaḥ*
A.	रुरुद्वांसम् *rurudváṁsam*	रुरुद्वांसौ *rurudváṁsau*	रुरुदुषः *rurudushaḥ*
V.	रुरुद्वन् *rurudvan*		
I.	रुरुदुषा *rurudushá*	रुरुद्वद्भ्याम् *rurudvadbhyám*	रुरुद्वद्भिः *rurudvadbhiḥ*
D.	रुरुदुषे *rurudushe*	रुरुद्वद्भ्याम् *rurudvadbhyám*	रुरुद्वद्भ्यः *rurudvadbhyaḥ*
Ab.	रुरुदुषः *rurudushaḥ*	रुरुद्वद्भ्याम् *rurudvadbhyám*	रुरुद्वद्भ्यः *rurudvadbhyaḥ*
G.	रुरुदुषः *rurudushaḥ*	रुरुदुषोः *rurudushoḥ*	रुरुदुषाम् *rurudushám*
L.	रुरुदुषि *rurudushi*	रुरुदुषोः *rurudushoḥ*	रुरुद्वत्सु *rurudvatsu*

NEUTER.

	SINGULAR.	DUAL.	PLURAL.
N.	रुरुद्वत् *rurudvat*	रुरुदुषी *rurudushí*	रुरुद्वांसि *rurudváṁsi*

FEM.

	SINGULAR.
N.	रुरुदुषी *rurudushí*

§ 205. Participles in वस् *vas* which insert an इ *i* between the reduplicated root and the termination, drop the इ *i* whenever the termination वस् *vas* is changed into उष् *ush*. Thus

तस्थिवान् *tasthiván*, from स्था *sthá*, to stand, forms the fem. तस्थुषी *tasthushí*.
पेचिवान् *pechiván*, from पच् *pach*, to cook, forms the fem. पेचुषी *pechushí*.

A very common word following this declension is विद्वान् *vidvān*, wise, (for विविद्वान् *vividvān*); fem. विदुषी *vidushī*.

If the root ends in इ *i* or ई *ī*, this radical vowel is never dropt before उष् *ush*, the contracted form of वस् *vas*. Hence from नी *nī*, निनीवान् *ninīvān*; Instr. निन्युषा *ninyushā*; fem. निन्युषी *ninyushī*.

Decline the following participles:

PADA BASE.	NOM. SING.	NOM. PLUR.	ACC. PLUR.	INSTR. PLUR.
शुश्रुवस् *śuśruvas*	शुश्रुवान् *śuśruvān*	शुश्रुवांसः *śuśruvāṃsaḥ*	शुश्रुवुषः *śuśruvushaḥ*	शुश्रुवद्भिः *śuśruvadbhiḥ*
पेचिवस् *pechivas*	पेचिवान् *pechivān*	पेचिवांसः *pechivāṃsaḥ*	पेचुषः *pechushaḥ*	पेचिवद्भिः *pechivadbhiḥ*
जग्मिवस् *jagmivas*	जग्मिवान् *jagmivān*	जग्मिवांसः *jagmivāṃsaḥ*	जग्मुषः *jagmushaḥ*	जग्मिवद्भिः *jagmivadbhiḥ*
जगन्वस्* *jaganvas*	जगन्वान् *jaganvān*	जगन्वांसः *jaganvāṃsaḥ*	जग्मुषः *jagmushaḥ*	जगन्वद्भिः *jaganvadbhiḥ*
जघ्निवस् *jaghnivas*	जघ्निवान् *jaghnivān*	जघ्निवांसः *jaghnivāṃsaḥ*	जघ्नुषः *jaghnushaḥ*	जघ्निवद्भिः *jaghnivadbhiḥ*
जघन्वस् *jaghanvas*	जघन्वान् *jaghanvān*	जघन्वांसः *jaghanvāṃsaḥ*	जघ्नुषः *jaghnushaḥ*	जघन्वद्भिः *jaghanvadbhiḥ*

Bases in ईयस् īyas.

§ 206. Bases in ईयस् *īyas* (termination of the comparative) form their Aṅga base in ईयांस् *īyāṃs*.

Pada and Bha base गरीयस् *garīyas*, heavier; Aṅga base गरीयांस् *garīyāṃs*.

MASCULINE.

	SINGULAR.	DUAL.	PLURAL.
N.	गरीयान् *garīyān*	गरीयांसौ *garīyāṃsau*	गरीयांसः *garīyāṃsaḥ*
A.	गरीयांसं *garīyāṃsam*	गरीयांसौ *garīyāṃsau*	गरीयसः *garīyasaḥ*
V.	गरीयन् *garīyan*		
I.	गरीयसा *garīyasā*	गरीयोभ्यां *garīyobhyām*	गरीयोभिः *garīyobhiḥ*, &c.

NEUTER.

	SINGULAR.	DUAL.	PLURAL.
N.	गरीयः *garīyaḥ*	गरीयसी *garīyasī*	गरीयांसि *garīyāṃsi*

FEM.

	SINGULAR.
N.	गरीयसी *garīyasī*

Miscellaneous Nouns with changeable Consonantal Bases.

§ 207. Words ending in पाद् *pād*, foot, retain पाद् *pād* as Aṅga and Pada base, but shorten it to पद् *pad* as Bha base.

* म् *m* changed into न् *n* according to § 136.

	SINGULAR.	DUAL.	PLURAL.	
N.V.	सुपाद् supâd	सुपादौ supâdau	सुपादः supâdaḥ	(Aṅga)
A.	सुपादम् supâdam	सुपादौ supâdau	सुपदः supadaḥ	(Bha)
			I. सुपाद्भिः supâdbhiḥ	(Pada)

The feminine is either सुपाद् *supâd* or सुपदी *supadî* (Pâṇ. IV. 1, 8); but a metre consisting of two feet is called द्विपदा *dvipadâ*.

§ 208. Words ending in वाह् *vâh*, carrying, retain वाह् *vâh* as Aṅga and Pada base, but shorten it to ऊह् *ûh* as Bha base. The fem. is ऊही *ûhî*.

Final ह् *h* is interchangeable with ढ् *ḍh*, ड् *ḍ*, ट् *ṭ*. (See §§ 128; 174, 8.)

The ऊ *û* of ऊह् *ûh* forms Vṛiddhi with a preceding अ *a* (§ 46). Thus विश्ववाह् *viśvavâh*, upholder of the universe.

	SINGULAR.	DUAL.	PLURAL.
N.V.	विश्ववाट् viśvavâṭ	विश्ववाहौ viśvavâhau	विश्ववाहः viśvavâhaḥ
A.	विश्ववाहम् viśvavâham	विश्ववाहौ viśvavâhau	विश्वौहः viśvauhaḥ
			I. विश्ववाड्भिः viśvavâḍbhiḥ

§ 209. श्वेतवाह् *śvetavâh* is further irregular, forming its Pada base in वस् *vas*, and retaining it in the Nom. and Voc. Sing.; e. g. Nom. Voc. श्वेतवाः *śvetavâḥ*; Acc. श्वेतवाहम् *śvetavâham*; Instr. श्वेतौहा *śvetauhâ*; Instr. Plur. श्वेतवोभिः *śvetavobhiḥ*, &c.; Loc. Plur. श्वेतवःसु *śvetavaḥsu*.

Some grammarians allow श्वेतवाह् *śvetavâh*, instead of श्वेतौह् *śvetauh*, in all the Bha cases (Sâr. I. 9, 14), and likewise श्वेतव: *śvetavaḥ* in Voc. Sing.

§ 210. A more important compound with वाह् *vâh* is अनडुह् *anaḍuh*, an ox, (i. e. a cart-drawer.) It has three bases:

1. The Aṅga base अनड्वाह् *anaḍvâh*.
2. The Pada base अनडुद् *anaḍud*.
3. The Bha base अनडुह् *anaḍuh*.

It is irregular besides in the Nom. and Voc. Sing.

SINGULAR.	DUAL.	PLURAL.
N. अनड्वान् anaḍvân	N. A. V. अनड्वाहौ anaḍvâhau	N. अनड्वाहः anaḍvâhaḥ
V. अनड्वन् anaḍvan	I. D. Ab. अनडुद्भ्याम् anaḍudbhyâm	A. अनडुहः anaḍuhaḥ
A. अनड्वाहम् anaḍvâham	G. L. अनडुहोः anaḍuhoḥ	I. अनडुद्भिः anaḍudbhiḥ
I. अनडुहा anaḍuhâ		L. अनडुत्सु anaḍutsu

If used as a neuter, at the end of a compound, it forms

	SINGULAR.	DUAL.	PLURAL.
N. A. V.	अनडुद् anaḍud	अनडुही anaḍuhî	अनड्वांहि anaḍvâṁhi

The rest like the masculine.

The feminine is अनडुही *anaḍuhî* or अनड्वाही *anaḍvâhî* (Siddh.-Kaum. I. p. 228).

§ 211. अप् *ap*, water, is invariably plural, and makes its अ *a* long in the Aṅga base, and substitutes त् *t* for प् *p* before an affix beginning with भ् *bh*.

PLURAL.

Nom.	आपः *âpaḥ*
Acc.	अपः *ăpaḥ*
Instr.	अद्भिः *adbhiḥ*
Loc.	अप्सु *apsu*

In composition अप् *ap* is said to form स्वाप् *svâp*, Nom. Sing. masc. and fem., having good water; Acc. स्वापं *svâpam*; Instr. स्वपा *svapâ*, &c. Nom. Plur. स्वापः *svâpaḥ*; Acc. स्वपः *svapaḥ*; Instr. स्वद्भिः *svadbhiḥ*, &c. The neuter forms the Nom. Sing. स्वप् *svap*; Nom. Plur. स्वंपि *svampi* or स्वांपि *svâmpi*, according to different interpretations of Pâṇini. (Colebrooke, p. 101, note.) The Sârasvatî (1. 9, 62) gives स्वांपि तडागानि *svâmpi taḍâgâni*, tanks with good water.

§ 212. पुंस् *puṁs*, man, has three bases:

1. The Aṅga base पुमांस् *pumâṁs*.
2. The Pada base पुम् *pum*.
3. The Bha base पुंस् *puṁs*.

SINGULAR.	DUAL.	PLURAL.
N. पुमान् *pumân*	N.A.V. पुमांसौ *pumâṁsau*	N. पुमांसः *pumâṁsaḥ*
V. पुमन् *puman*	I.D.Ab. पुंभ्यां *pumbhyâm*	A. पुंसः *puṁsaḥ*
A. पुमांसं *pumâṁsam*	G.L. पुंसोः *puṁsoḥ*	I. पुंभिः *pumbhiḥ*
I. पुंसा *puṁsâ*		

The Loc. Plur. is पुंसु *punsu*, not पुंषु *puṁshu* (§ 136). The Sârasvatî gives पुंक्षु *puṅkshu* (1. 9, 70).

In composition it is declined in the same manner if used in the masc. or fem. gender. As a neuter it is, Nom. Sing. सुपुम् *supum*, Nom. Dual सुपुंसी *supuṁsî*, Nom. Plur. सुपुमांसि *supumâṁsi*.

§ 213. दिव् *div* or द्यु *dyu*, f. sky, is declined as follows:

Base दिव् *div*, द्यु *dyu*.

SINGULAR.	DUAL.	PLURAL.
N.V. द्यौः *dyauḥ*	N.A.V. दिवौ *divau*	N. दिवः *divaḥ*
A. दिवं *divam*	I.D.Ab. द्युभ्यां *dyubhyâm*	A. दिवः *divaḥ*
I. दिवा *divâ*	G.L. दिवोः *divoḥ*	I. द्युभिः *dyubhiḥ*
D. दिवे *dive*		D.Ab. द्युभ्यः *dyubhyaḥ*
Ab.G. दिवः *divaḥ*		G. दिवां *divâm*
L. दिवि *divi*		L. द्युषु *dyushu*

Another base द्यो *dyo* is declined as a base ending in a vowel, and follows the paradigm of गो *go*, § 219. (See Siddh.-Kaum. 1. p. 138.)

Compounds like सुदिव् *sudiv*, having a good sky, are declined in the masc. and fem. like दिव् *div*. Hence सुद्यौः *sudyauḥ*, सुदिवं *sudivam*, &c.

In the neuter they form Nom. Acc. Voc. Sing. सुद्यु *sudyu*, having a good sky; Dual सुदिवी *sudivî*; Plur. सुदीवि *sudîvi*.

§ 214. A number of words in Sanskrit are what Greek grammarians would call *Metaplasta*, i. e. they exist under two forms, each following a different declension, but one being deficient in Nom. Sing. Dual and Plural, and in the Acc. Sing. and Dual. (Pâṇ. VI. 1, 63.) Thus

1. असन् *asan*, n. blood, is defective;	असृज् *asṛij*, n. is declined throughout.			
2. आसन् *âsan*, n. face,	—	आस्य *âsya*, n.	—	—
3. उदन् *udan*, n. water,	—	उदक *udaka*, n.	—	—
4. दत् *dat*, m. tooth,	—	दंत *danta*, m.	—	—
5. दोषन् *doshan*, (m.) n. arm,	—	दोस् *dos*, m. n.	—	—
6. नस् *nas*, f. nose,	—	नासिका *nâsikâ*, f.	—	—
7. निश् *niś*, f. night,	—	निशा *niśâ*, f.	—	—
8. पद् *pad*, m. foot,	—	पाद *pâda*, m.	—	—
9. पृत् *pṛit*, f. army*,	—	पृतना *pṛitanâ*, f.	—	—
10. मांस् *mâṁs*, n. meat†,	—	मांस *mâṁsa*, n.	—	—
11. मास् *mâs*, m. month‡,	—	मास *mâsa*, m.	—	—
12. यकन् *yakan*, n. liver‖,	—	यकृत् *yakṛit*, n.	—	—
13. यूषन् *yûshan*, m. pea-soup,	—	यूष *yûsha*, m.	—	—
14. शकन् *śakan*, n. ordure,	—	शकृत् *śakṛit*, n.	—	—
15. स्नु *snu*, n. ridge,	—	सानु *sânu*, n.	—	—
16. हृद् *hṛid*, n. (m.)	—	हृदय *hṛidaya*, n.	—	—

Hence in

No. 1.	N. V. A. Sing. is असृक् *asṛik* only;	A. Plur. असृंजि *asṛiñji* or असानि *asâni*.
	N. V. A. Dual is असृजी *asṛijî* only;	but I. Sing. असृजा *asṛijâ* or अस्ना *asnâ*.
	N. V. Plur. is असृंजि *asṛiñji* only;	I. Du. असृग्भ्यां *asṛigbhyâm* or असभ्यां *asabhyâm*.
No. 4.	N. A. V. Sing. is दंतः, °तं, °त *dantaḥ, am, a*, only;	A. Plur. दंतान् *dantân* or दतः *dataḥ*.
	N. V. A. Dual is दंतौ *dantau* only;	but I. Sing. दंतेन *dantena* or दता *datâ*.
	N. V. Plur. is दंताः *dantâḥ* only;	I. Dual दंताभ्यां *dantâbhyâm* or दद्भ्यां *dadbhyâm*.
No. 11.	N. A. V. Sing. is मासः, °सं, °स *mâsaḥ, am, a*, only;	A. Plur. मासान् *mâsân* or मासः *mâsaḥ*.
	N. V. A. Dual is मासौ *mâsau* only;	but I. Sing. मासेन *mâsena* or मासा *mâsâ*.
	N. V. Plur. is मासाः *mâsâḥ* only;	I. Dual मासाभ्यां *mâsâbhyâm* or माभ्यां *mâbhyâm*.
No. 13.	N. A. V. Sing. is यूषः, °षं, °ष *yûshaḥ, am, a*, only;	A. Plur. यूषान् *yûshân* or यूष्णः *yûshṇaḥ*.
	N. A. V. Dual is यूषौ *yûshau* only;	but I. Sing. यूषेण *yûsheṇa* or यूष्णा *yûshṇâ*.
	N. V. Plur. is यूषाः *yûshâḥ* only;	I. Du. यूषाभ्यां *yûshâbhyâm* or °षभ्यां *-shabhyâm*.
		L. Sing. यूषे *yûshe* or °षणि *-shaṇi* or °ष्णि *-shṇi*.

* Siddh.-Kaum. I. p. 131. † Siddh.-Kaum. I. p. 141.

‡ The Sârasvatî gives all cases of मास् *mâs* (I. 6, 35). ‖ Pâṇ. VI. 1, 63.

Grammarians differ on the exact meaning of Pâṇini's rule; and forms such as दोषणी *doshaṇî*, Nom. Dual Neut., would seem to show that in the Nom. Acc. Voc. Dual the base दोषन् *doshan* may be used. (See Siddh.-Kaum. I. pp. 107, 131, 141, 144.) By some the rule is restricted to the Veda.

2. *Bases ending in Vowels.*

§ 215. Bases ending in vowels may be subdivided into two classes:

1. Bases ending in any vowels, except अ *a* and आ *â*.
2. Bases ending in अ *a* and आ *â*.

1. *Bases ending in any Vowels, except* अ a *and* आ â.

§ 216. Instead of attempting to learn, either according to the system followed by native grammarians, or according to the more correct views of comparative philologists, how the terminations appended to consonantal bases are changed when appended to bases ending in vowels, it will be far easier to learn by heart the paradigms such as they are, without entering at all into the question whether there was originally but one set of terminations for all nouns, or whether, from the beginning, different terminations were used after bases ending in consonants and after bases ending in vowels.

Bases in ऐ ai *and* औ au.

§ 217. These bases are, with few exceptions, declined like bases ending in consonants. The principal rules to be observed are that before consonants ऐ *ai* becomes आ *â*, while औ *au* remains unchanged; and that before vowels both ऐ *ai* and औ *au* become आय् *ây* and आव् *âv*.

Base रै *rai*, राय् *rây*, m. wealth. नौ *nau*, नाव् *nâv*, f. ship.

	Singular.		Dual.		Plural.	
N.V.	राः *râ-ḥ*	नौः *nau-ḥ*	रायौ *rây-au*	नावौ *nâv-au*	रायः *rây-aḥ*	नावः *nâv-aḥ*
A.	रायं *rây-am*	नावं *nâv-am*				
I.	राया *rây-â*	नावा *nâv-â*	राभ्यां *râ-bhyâm*	नौभ्यां *nau-bhyâm*	राभिः *râ-bhiḥ*	नौभिः *nau-bhiḥ*
D.	राये *rây-e*	नावे *nâv-e*			राभ्यः *râ-bhyaḥ*	नौभ्यः *nau-bhyaḥ*
Ab. G.	रायः *rây-aḥ*	नावः *nâv-aḥ*				
G.			रायोः *rây-oḥ*	नावोः *nâv-oḥ*	रायां *rây-âm*	नावां *nâv-âm*
L.	रायि *rây-i*	नावि *nâv-i*			रासु *râ-su*	नौषु *nau-shu*

Decline ग्लौः *glauḥ*, m. the moon.

Bases in ओ o.

§ 218. The only noun of importance is गो *go*, a bull or cow. It is slightly irregular in Nom. Acc. Abl. and Gen. Sing. and in the Acc. Plur.

	SINGULAR.	DUAL.	PLURAL.
N.V.	गौः *gau-ḥ*	गावौ *gâv-au*	गावः *gâv-aḥ*
A.	गां *gâ-m*		गाः *gâ-ḥ*
I.	गवा *gav-â*	गोभ्यां *go-bhyâm*	गोभिः *go-bhiḥ*
D.	गवे *gav-e*		गोभ्यः *go-bhyaḥ*
Ab.	गोः *go-ḥ*		
G.		गवोः *gav-oḥ*	गवां *gav-âm*
L.	गवि *gav-i*		गोषु *go-shu*

If bases in ऐ *ai*, ओ *o*, औ *au* are to be declined as neuters at the end of compounds, they shorten ऐ *ai* to इ *i*, and ओ *o* and औ *au* to उ *u*, and are then declined like neuters in इ *i* and उ *u*. The masculine forms, however, are equally allowed (if the base is masculine) in all cases except the Nom. Acc. Voc. Sing. Dual and Plural. Hence Instr. Sing. neut. सुरिणा *suriṇâ* or सुराया *surâyâ*; but only सुनुना *sununâ*.

§ 219. द्यो *dyo*, fem. heaven, is declined like गो *go*. It coincides in the Nom. and Voc. Sing. with दिव् *div*, sky, but differs from it in all other cases.

	SINGULAR.	DUAL.	PLURAL.
N.V.	द्यौः *dyauḥ*	द्यावौ *dyâvau*	द्यावः *dyâvaḥ*
A.	द्यां *dyâm* *		द्याः *dyâḥ* *
I.	द्यवा *dyavâ*	द्योभ्यां *dyobhyâm*	द्योभिः *dyobhiḥ*
D.	द्यवे *dyave*		द्योभ्यः *dyobhyaḥ*
Ab.	द्योः *dyoḥ*		
G.		द्यवोः *dyavoḥ*	द्यवां *dyavâm*
L.	द्यवि *dyavi*		द्योषु *dyoshu*

Being used at the end of a compound द्यो *dyo* forms its neuter base as द्यु *dyu*; e.g. प्रद्यु *pradyu*, eminently celestial, Dual प्रद्युनी *pradyunî*, Plur. प्रद्यूनि *pradyûni* (Siddh.-Kaum. I. pp. 144, 145); while from दिव् *div* the neuter adjective was, as we saw, सुद्यु *sudyu*, having a good sky, Dual सुदिवी *sudivî*, Plur. सुदीवि *sudîvi* (Colebr. pp. 67, 73). प्रद्यु *pradyu*, as a neuter, cannot take the optional masculine cases (Siddh.-Kaum. I. p. 145).

Note—There are no real nouns ending in ए *e*, though grammarians imagine such words as एः *eḥ*, the sun, उद्यदेः *udyadeḥ*, the rising sun; Nom. Dual उद्यदयौ *udyadayau*, Nom. Plur. उद्यदयः *udyadayaḥ*.

Bases in ई *î* and ऊ *û*.

1. *Monosyllabic Bases in* ई î *and* ऊ û, *being both Masculine and Feminine.*

(A.) By themselves.

§ 220. Monosyllabic bases, derived from verbs without any suffix, like धी *dhî*, thinking, क्री *krî*, buying, लू *lû*, cutting, take the same terminations

* Kâśikâ vi. 1, 93.

as consonantal bases. They remain unchanged before terminations beginning with consonants, but change final ई *î* and ऊ *û* into इय् *iy* and उव् *uv*, before vowels. (Pâṇ. VI. 4, 82, 83.) Their Vocative is the same as their Nominative.

(B.) At the end of compounds.

§ 221. These monosyllabic bases rarely occur except at the end of compounds. Here they may either change ई *î* and ऊ *û* into इय् *iy* and उव् *uv*, or into य् *y* and व् *v*. They change it

1. Into इय् *iy* and उव् *uv:*

a. If the first member of the compound forms the predicate of the second, and the second maintains its nominal character. Thus परमनीः *paramanîḥ*, the best leader, Acc. Sing. परमनियं *paramaniyam*. Here नीः *nîḥ* is treated as a noun, and seems to have lost its verbal character. शुद्धधीः *śuddhadhîḥ*, a pure thinker, a man of pure thought, Acc. Sing. शुद्धधियं *śuddhadhiyam;* कुधीः *kudhîḥ*, a man of bad thought, Acc. Sing. कुधियं *kudhiyam*. (Sâr.)

b. If ई *î* and ऊ *û* are preceded by two radical initial consonants. जलक्रीः *jalakrîḥ*, a buyer of water, makes Acc. Sing. जलक्रियं *jalakriyam*. सुश्रीः *suśrîḥ*, well faring, Acc. Sing. सुश्रियं *suśriyam*. (Siddh.-Kaum. I. p. 119.) This is a merely phonetic change, intended to facilitate pronunciation. (Pâṇ. VI. 4, 82.)

2. Into य् *y* and व् *v*, under all other circumstances, i. e. wherever the monosyllabic bases retain their verbal character. ग्रामणीः *grâmaṇîḥ*, leader of a village, Acc. Sing. ग्रामण्यं *grâmaṇyam;* here ग्राम *grâma* is not the predicate of नीः *nîḥ*, but is governed by नीः *nîḥ*, which retains so far its verbal character. प्रधीः *pradhîḥ*, thinking in a high degree, Acc. Sing. प्रध्यं *pradhyam;* here प्र *pra* is a preposition belonging to धी *dhî*, which retains its verbal nature. उन्नीः *unnîḥ*, leading out, Acc. Sing. उन्न्यं *unnyam;* here उद् *ud* is a preposition belonging to नी *nî*. Though ई *î* is preceded by two consonants, one only belongs to the root. शुद्धधीः *śuddhadhîḥ* (if a Tatpurusha compound), thinking pure things, would form the Acc. Sing. शुद्धध्यं *śuddhadhyam*, and thus be distinguished from शुद्धधीः *śuddhadhîḥ* (as a Karmadhâraya compound), a pure thinker, or as a Bahuvrîhi compound, a man possessed of pure thoughts (Siddh.-Kaum. I. p. 119), which both have शुद्धधियं *śuddhadhiyam* for their accusative. The general idea which suggested the distinction between bases changing their final ई *î* and ऊ *û* either into इय् *iy* and उव् *uv*, or into य् *y* and व् *v*, seems to have been that the

former were treated as real monosyllabic nouns that might be used by themselves (धीः *dhîḥ*, a thinker), or in such compounds as a noun admits of (सुधीः *sudhîḥ**, a good thinker; शुद्धधीः *śuddhadhîḥ*, a pure thinker or pure thoughted); while the latter always retained somewhat of their verbal character, and could therefore not be used by themselves, but only at the end of compounds, preceded either by a preposition (प्रधीः *pradhîḥ*, providens) or by a noun which was governed by them. The nouns in which ई *î* and ऊ *û* stand after two radical consonants form an exception to this general rule, which exception admits, however, of a phonetic explanation, so that the only real exception would be in the case of certain compounds ending in भू *bhû*. This भू *bhû* becomes भुव् *bhuv* before vowels, whether it be verbal or nominal. (Pâṇ. VI. 4, 85.) Ex. स्वयंभूः *svayambhûḥ*, self-existing, Acc. Sing. स्वयंभुवं *svayambhuvam*. (Sâr. I. 6, 61. Siddh.-Kaum. I. p. 119.) Not, however, in वर्षाभूः *varshâbhûḥ*, frog, Acc. Sing. वर्षाभ्वं *varshâbhvam* (Pâṇ. VI. 4, 84), and in some other compounds, such as करभूः *karabhûḥ* or कारभूः *kârabhûḥ*, nail, पुनर्भूः *punarbhûḥ*, re-born, दृन्भूः *drinbhûḥ*, thunderbolt. (Pâṇ. VI. 4, 84, v.)

2. *Polysyllabic Bases in* ई î *and* ऊ û.

§ 222. Polysyllabic bases in ई *î* and ऊ *û* being both masculine and feminine, such as पपीः *papîḥ*, protector, the sun, ययीः *yayîḥ*, road, and नृतूः *nritûḥ*, dancer, are declined like the verbal compounds प्रधीः *pradhîḥ* and वृक्षलूः *vrikshalûḥ*, except

1. they form the Acc. Sing. in ईम् *îm* and ऊम् *ûm*;
2. they form the Acc. Plur. in ईन् *în* and ऊन् *ûn*.

Remember also, that those in ई *î* form the Loc. Sing. in ई *î*, not in यि *yi*.

वातप्रमीः *vâtapramîḥ*, antelope, may be declined like पपीः *papîḥ*; but if derived by क्विप् *kvip*, it may entirely follow the verbal प्रधीः *pradhîḥ* (Siddh.-Kaum. I. p. 116). The same applies to nouns like सुतीः *sutîḥ*, wishing for a son; सुखीः *sukhîḥ*, wishing for pleasure. They follow the verbal प्रधीः *pradhîḥ* throughout, but they have their Gen. and Abl. Sing. in उः *uḥ*; सुत्युः *sutyuḥ* (Siddh.-Kaum. I. p. 120). If the final long ई *î* is preceded by two consonants, it is changed before vowels into इय् *iy*. Ex. शुष्कीः *śushkîḥ*, शुष्कियौ *śushkiyau*, &c.

---

* सुधीः *sudhîḥ* is never to be treated as a verbal compound, but always forms Acc. Sing. सुधियं *sudhiyam*, &c., as if it were a Karmadhâraya compound. (Pâṇ. VI. 4, 85.)

	Monosyllabic, masc. and fem.	The same, at the end of compounds, used as a noun, masc. and fem.	The same, at the end of compounds, with initial double consonants, masc. and fem.	The same, in composition with prepositions, masc. and fem.	The same, in composition with a governed noun, masc. and fem.	Polysyllabic, masc. and fem.
	thinking.	a pure thinker.	water-buyer.	high-thinking.	village-leader.	sun.
	SINGULAR.	SINGULAR.	SINGULAR.	SINGULAR.	SINGULAR.	SINGULAR.
N.	धीः *dhíḥ*	शुद्धधीः *śuddhadhíḥ*	जलक्रीः *jalakríḥ*	प्रधीः *pradhíḥ*	ग्रामणीः *grámaṇíḥ*	पपीः *papíḥ*
A.	धियं *dhiyam*	शुद्धधियं *śuddhadhiyam*	जलक्रियं *jalakriyam*	प्रध्यं *pradhyam*	ग्रामण्यं *grámaṇyam*	पपीं *papím*
I.	धिया *dhiyá*	शुद्धधिया *śuddhadhiyá*	जलक्रिया *jalakriyá*	प्रध्या *pradhyá*	ग्रामण्या *grámaṇyá*	पप्या *papyá*
D.	धिये *dhiye*	शुद्धधिये *śuddhadhiye*	जलक्रिये *jalakriye*	प्रध्ये *pradhye*	ग्रामण्ये *grámaṇye*	पप्ये *papye*
Ab. G.	धियः *dhiyaḥ*	शुद्धधियः *śuddhadhiyaḥ*	जलक्रियः *jalakriyaḥ*	प्रध्यः *pradhyaḥ*	ग्रामण्यः *grámaṇyaḥ*	पप्यः *papyaḥ*
L.	धियि *dhiyi*	शुद्धधियि *śuddhadhiyi*	जलक्रियि *jalakriyi*	प्रध्यि *pradhyi*	ग्रामण्यां *grámaṇyám* *	पपी *papí*
V.	धीः *dhíḥ*	शुद्धधीः *śuddhadhíḥ*	जलक्रीः *jalakríḥ*	प्रधीः *pradhíḥ*	ग्रामणीः *grámaṇíḥ*	पपीः *papíḥ*
	DUAL.	DUAL.	DUAL.	DUAL.	DUAL.	DUAL.
N. A. V.	धियौ *dhiyau*	शुद्धधियौ *śuddhadhiyau*	जलक्रियौ *jalakriyau*	प्रध्यौ *pradhyau*	ग्रामण्यौ *grámaṇyau*	पप्यौ *papyau*
I. D. Ab.	धीभ्यां *dhíbhyám*	शुद्धधीभ्यां *śuddhadhíbhyám*	जलक्रीभ्यां *jalakríbhyám*	प्रधीभ्यां *pradhíbhyám*	ग्रामणीभ्यां *grámaṇíbhyám*	पपीभ्यां *papíbhyám*
G. L.	धियोः *dhiyoḥ*	शुद्धधियोः *śuddhadhiyoḥ*	जलक्रियोः *jalakriyoḥ*	प्रध्योः *pradhyoḥ*	ग्रामण्योः *grámaṇyoḥ*	पप्योः *papyoḥ*
	PLURAL.	PLURAL.	PLURAL.	PLURAL.	PLURAL.	PLURAL.
N.	धियः *dhiyaḥ*	शुद्धधियः *śuddhadhiyaḥ*	जलक्रियः *jalakriyaḥ*	प्रध्यः *pradhyaḥ*	ग्रामण्यः *grámaṇyaḥ*	पप्यः *papyaḥ*
A.	धियः *dhiyaḥ*	शुद्धधियः *śuddhadhiyaḥ*	जलक्रियः *jalakriyaḥ*	प्रध्यः *pradhyaḥ*	ग्रामण्यः *grámaṇyaḥ*	पपीन् *papín* ‡
I.	धीभिः *dhíbhiḥ*	शुद्धधीभिः *śuddhadhíbhiḥ*	जलक्रीभिः *jalakríbhiḥ*	प्रधीभिः *pradhíbhiḥ*	ग्रामणीभिः *grámaṇíbhiḥ*	पपीभिः *papíbhiḥ*
D. Ab.	धीभ्यः *dhíbhyaḥ*	शुद्धधीभ्यः *śuddhadhíbhyaḥ*	जलक्रीभ्यः *jalakríbhyaḥ*	प्रधीभ्यः *pradhíbhyaḥ*	ग्रामणीभ्यः *grámaṇíbhyaḥ*	पपीभ्यः *papíbhyaḥ*
G.	धियां *dhiyám*	शुद्धधियां *śuddhadhiyám*	जलक्रियां *jalakriyám*	प्रध्यां *pradhyám*	ग्रामण्यां *grámaṇyám* †	पप्यां *papyám* ‖
L.	धीषु *dhíshu*	शुद्धधीषु *śuddhadhíshu*	जलक्रीषु *jalakríshu*	प्रधीषु *pradhíshu*	ग्रामणीषु *grámaṇíshu*	पपीषु *papíshu*

* Words ending in नी *ní*, leader, form their Loc. Sing. in आं *ám*. (Sâr.) † Or ग्रामणीनां *grámaṇínám*. Words of the Senání class take आं *ám* or नां *nám*. (Sâr. 1. 6, 62.) ‡ पपीः *papíḥ*, at the end of a fem. comp.; Rûpâvali, p. 9 b. ‖ It does not take नां *nám*. (Siddh.-Kaum. I. p. 116.)

	Monosyllabic, masc. and fem.	The same, at the end of compounds, used as a noun, masc. and fem.	The same, at the end of compounds, with initial double consonants, masc. and fem.	The same, in composition with prepositions, masc. and fem.	The same, in composition with a governed noun, masc. and fem.	Polysyllabic, masc. and fem.
	cutter.	best cutter.	dice-player.	cutting asunder.	corn-cutter.	dancer.
	SINGULAR.	SINGULAR.	SINGULAR.	SINGULAR.	SINGULAR.	SINGULAR.
N.	लूः *lúḥ*	परमलूः *paramalúḥ*	कटप्रूः *kaṭaprúḥ*	विलूः *vilúḥ*	यवलूः *yavalúḥ*	नृतूः *nṛitúḥ*
A.	लुवं *luvam*	परमलुवं *paramaluvam*	कटप्रुवं *kaṭapruvam*	विल्वं *vilvam*	यवल्वं *yavalvam*	नृतूं *nṛitúm*
I.	लुवा *luvá*	परमलुवा *paramaluvá*	कटप्रुवा *kaṭapruvá*	विल्वा *vilvá*	यवल्वा *yavalvá*	नृत्वा *nṛitvá*
D.	लुवे *luve*	परमलुवे *paramaluve*	कटप्रुवे *kaṭapruve*	विल्वे *vilve*	यवल्वे *yavalve*	नृत्वे *nṛitve*
Ab. G.	लुवः *luvaḥ*	परमलुवः *paramaluvaḥ*	कटप्रुवः *kaṭapruvaḥ*	विल्वः *vilvaḥ*	यवल्वः *yavalvaḥ*	नृत्वः *nṛitvaḥ*
L.	लुवि *luvi*	परमलुवि *paramaluvi*	कटप्रुवि *kaṭapruvi*	विल्वि *vilvi*	यवल्वि *yavalvi*	नृत्वि *nṛitvi*
V.	लूः *lúḥ*	परमलूः *paramalúḥ*	कटप्रूः *kaṭaprúḥ*	विलूः *vilúḥ*	यवलूः *yavalúḥ*	नृतूः *nṛitúḥ*
	DUAL.	DUAL.	DUAL.	DUAL.	DUAL.	DUAL.
N. A. V.	लुवौ *luvau*	परमलुवौ *paramaluvau*	कटप्रुवौ *kaṭapruvau*	विल्वौ *vilvau*	यवल्वौ *yavalvau*	नृत्वौ *nṛitvau*
I. D. Ab.	लूभ्यां *lúbhyám*	परमलूभ्यां *paramalúbhyám*	कटप्रूभ्यां *kaṭaprúbhyám*	विलूभ्यां *vilúbhyám*	यवलूभ्यां *yavalúbhyám*	नृतूभ्यां *nṛitúbhyám*
G. L.	लुवोः *luvoḥ*	परमलुवोः *paramaluvoḥ*	कटप्रुवोः *kaṭapruvoḥ*	विल्वोः *vilvoḥ*	यवल्वोः *yavalvoḥ*	नृत्वोः *nṛitvoḥ*
	PLURAL.	PLURAL.	PLURAL.	PLURAL.	PLURAL.	PLURAL.
N.	लुवः *luvaḥ*	परमलुवः *paramaluvaḥ*	कटप्रुवः *kaṭapruvaḥ*	विल्वः *vilvaḥ*	यवल्वः *yavalvaḥ*	नृत्वः *nṛitvaḥ*
A.	लुवः *luvaḥ*	परमलुवः *paramaluvaḥ*	कटप्रुवः *kaṭapruvaḥ*	विल्वः *vilvaḥ*	यवल्वः *yavalvaḥ*	नृतून् *nṛitún* †
I.	लूभिः *lúbhiḥ*	परमलूभिः *paramalúbhiḥ*	कटप्रूभिः *kaṭaprúbhiḥ*	विलूभिः *vilúbhiḥ*	यवलूभिः *yavalúbhiḥ*	नृतूभिः *nṛitúbhiḥ*
D. Ab.	लूभ्यः *lúbhyaḥ*	परमलूभ्यः *paramalúbhyaḥ*	कटप्रूभ्यः *kaṭaprúbhyaḥ*	विलूभ्यः *vilúbhyaḥ*	यवलूभ्यः *yavalúbhyaḥ*	नृतूभ्यः *nṛitúbhyaḥ*
G.	लुवां *luvám*	परमलुवां *paramaluvám*	कटप्रुवां *kaṭapruvám*	विल्वां *vilvám*	यवल्वां *yavalvám* *	नृत्वां *nṛitvám*
L.	लूषु *lúshu*	परमलूषु *paramalúshu*	कटप्रूषु *kaṭaprúshu*	विलूषु *vilúshu*	यवलूषु *yavalúshu*	नृतूषु *nṛitúshu*

* The Sár. gives also यवलूनां *yavalúnám*.

† नृतूः *nṛitúḥ*, at the end of a fem. comp.

§ 223. All these compounds may be used without any change, whether they refer to nouns in the masculine or in the feminine gender. If the head-borough or the sweeper should be of the female sex, the Dat. Sing. would still be ग्रामण्ये स्त्रियै *grâmaṇye striyai*, खलप्वे स्त्रियै *khalapve striyai* (Kâśikâ 1. 4, 3). Sometimes, however, if the meaning of a compound is such that it may by itself be applied to a woman as well as to a man, e. g. प्रधीः *pradhîḥ*, thinking, some grammarians allow such compounds to be declined in the feminine, like लक्ष्मीः *lakshmîḥ*, except in the Acc. Sing. and Plur., where they take अं *am* and अः *aḥ*; प्रध्यं *pradhyam*, प्रध्यः *pradhyaḥ*, not प्रधीं *pradhîm* or प्रधीः *pradhîḥ* (Siddh.-Kaum. 1. p. 136). A similar argument is applied to पुनर्भूः *punarbhûḥ*, if it means a woman married a second time. It may then form its Vocative हे पुनर्भु *he punarbhu* (Siddh.-Kaum. 1. p. 138), and take the *five fuller feminine terminations* (§ 224).

	Masc. and Fem.	Fem. only.
	SINGULAR.	SINGULAR.
N.	प्रधीः *pradhîḥ*	प्रधीः *pradhîḥ*
A.	प्रध्यं *pradhyam*	प्रध्यं *pradhyam*
I.	प्रध्या *pradhyâ*	प्रध्या *pradhyâ*
D.	प्रध्ये *pradhye*	or प्रध्यै *pradhyai*
Ab.	प्रध्यः *pradhyaḥ*	or प्रध्याः *pradhyâḥ*
G.	प्रध्यः *pradhyaḥ*	or प्रध्याः *pradhyâḥ*
L.	प्रध्यि *pradhyi*	or प्रध्यां *pradhyâm*
V.	प्रधीः *pradhîḥ*	or प्रधि *pradhi*
	DUAL.	DUAL.
N. A. V.	प्रध्यौ *pradhyau*	प्रध्यौ *pradhyau*
I. D. Ab.	प्रधीभ्यां *pradhîbhyâm*	प्रधीभ्यां *pradhîbhyâm*
G. L.	प्रध्योः *pradhyoḥ*	प्रध्योः *pradhyoḥ*
	PLURAL.	PLURAL.
N.	प्रध्यः *pradhyaḥ*	प्रध्यः *pradhyaḥ*
A.	प्रध्यः *pradhyaḥ*	प्रध्यः *pradhyaḥ*
I.	प्रधीभिः *pradhîbhiḥ*	प्रधीभिः *pradhîbhiḥ*
D. Ab.	प्रधीभ्यः *pradhîbhyaḥ*	प्रधीभ्यः *pradhîbhyaḥ*
G.	प्रध्यां *pradhyâm*	or प्रधीनां *pradhînâm*
L.	प्रधीषु *pradhîshu*	प्रधीषु *pradhîshu*

1. *Monosyllabic Bases in* ई î *and* ऊ û, *being Feminine only.*

§ 224. Bases like धी *dhî*, intellect, श्री *śrî*, happiness, ह्री *hrî*, shame, भी *bhî*, fear, and भ्रू *bhrû*, brow, may be declined throughout exactly like the monosyllabic bases in ई *î* and ऊ *û*, such as लू *lû*, a cutter. Their only peculiarity consists in their admitting a number of optional forms in the Dat. Abl. Gen. and Loc. Sing. and Gen. Plur. These may be called the *five fuller feminine terminations* in ऐ *ai*, आः *âḥ*, आः *âḥ*, आं *âm*, and नां *nâm*.

Monosyllabic, fem. only.	Optional fuller forms.	Monosyllabic, fem. only.	Optional fuller forms.
thought.		earth.	
SINGULAR.		SINGULAR.	
N. धीः *dhîḥ*		भूः *bhûḥ*	
A. धियं *dhiyam*		भुवं *bhuvam*	
I. धिया *dhiyâ*		भुवा *bhuvâ*	
D. धिये *dhiye*	धियै *dhiyai*	भुवे *bhuve*	भुवै *bhuvai*
Ab. धियः *dhiyaḥ*	धियाः *dhiyâḥ*	भुवः *bhuvaḥ*	भुवाः *bhuvâḥ*
G. धियः *dhiyaḥ*	धियाः *dhiyâḥ*	भुवः *bhuvaḥ*	भुवाः *bhuvâḥ*
L. धियि *dhiyi*	धियां *dhiyâm*	भुवि *bhuvi*	भुवां *bhuvâm*
V. धीः *dhîḥ*		भूः *bhûḥ*	
DUAL.		DUAL.	
N.A.V. धियौ *dhiyau*		भुवौ *bhuvau*	
I.D.Ab. धीभ्यां *dhîbhyâm*		भूभ्यां *bhûbhyâm*	
G.L. धियोः *dhiyoḥ*		भुवोः *bhuvoḥ*	
PLURAL.		PLURAL.	
N. धियः *dhiyaḥ*		भुवः *bhuvaḥ*	
A. धियः *dhiyaḥ*		भुवः *bhuvaḥ*	
I. धीभिः *dhîbhiḥ*		भूभिः *bhûbhiḥ*	
D. Ab. धीभ्यः *dhîbhyaḥ*		भूभ्यः *bhûbhyaḥ*	
G. धियां *dhiyâm*	धीनां *dhînâm*	भुवां *bhuvâm*	भूनां *bhûnâm*
L. धीषु *dhîshu*		भूषु *bhûshu*	

2. *Polysyllabic Bases in* ई î *and* ऊ û, *being Feminine only.*

§ 225. (1) These bases always take the full feminine terminations.

(2) They change their final ई *î* and ऊ *û* into य् *y* and व् *v* before terminations beginning with vowels.

(3) They take म् *m* and स् *s* as the terminations of the Acc. Sing. and Plural.

(4) They shorten their final ई *î* and ऊ *û* in the Vocative Singular.

(5) Remember that most nouns in ई *î* have no स् *s* in the Nom. Sing., while those in ऊ *û* have it.

Note—Some nouns in ई *î* take स् *s* in the Nom. Sing.: अवीः *avîḥ*, not desiring (applied to women); लक्ष्मीः *lakshmîḥ*, goddess of prosperity; तरीः *tarîḥ*, boat; तंत्रीः *tantrîḥ*, lute.

Versus memorialis: अवीलक्ष्मीतरीतंत्रीधीह्रीश्रीणामुदाहृतः सप्तानामेव शब्दानां सिलोपो न कदाचन ॥ (Sâr. p. 18 a.)

Base नदी *nadî* and नद्य् *nady*.

SINGULAR.

FEM.

N. नदी *nadî*

A. नदीं *nadî-m*

I. नद्या *nady-â*

Base वधू *vadhû* and वध्व् *vadhv*.

SINGULAR.

FEM.

N. वधूः *vadhû-ḥ*

A. वधूं *vadhû-m*

I. वध्वा *vadhv-â*

D.	नद्यै *nady-ai*	D.	वध्वै *vadhv-ai*
Ab.	नद्याः *nady-âḥ*	Ab.	वध्वाः *vadhv-âḥ*
G.	नद्याः *nady-âḥ*	G.	वध्वाः *vadhv-âḥ*
L.	नद्याम् *nady-âm*	L.	वध्वाम् *vadhv-âm*
V.	नदि *nadi*	V.	वधु *vadhu*
	DUAL.		DUAL.
N. A. V.	नद्यौ *nady-au*	N. A. V.	वध्वौ *vadhv-au*
I. D. Ab.	नदीभ्याम् *nadî-bhyâm*	I. D. Ab.	वधूभ्याम् *vadhû-bhyâm*
G. L.	नद्योः *nady-oḥ*	G. L.	वध्वोः *vadhv-oḥ*
	PLURAL.		PLURAL.
N. V.	नद्यः *nady-aḥ*	N. V.	वध्वः *vadhv-aḥ*
A.	नदीः *nadî-ḥ*	A.	वधूः *vadhû-ḥ*
I.	नदीभिः *nadî-bhiḥ*	I.	वधूभिः *vadhû-bhiḥ*
D.	नदीभ्यः *nadî-bhyaḥ*	D.	वधूभ्यः *vadhû-bhyaḥ*
Ab.	नदीभ्यः *nadî-bhyaḥ*	Ab.	वधूभ्यः *vadhû-bhyaḥ*
G.	नदीनाम् *nadî-nâm*	G.	वधूनाम् *vadhû-nâm*
L.	नदीषु *nadî-shu*	L.	वधूषु *vadhû-shu*

Compounds ending in Monosyllabic Feminine Bases in ई î *and* ऊ û.

§ 226. Compounds the last member of which is a monosyllabic feminine base in ई *î* or ऊ *û*, are declined alike in the masculine and feminine. Thus सुधीः *sudhîḥ*, masc. and fem.* if it means a good mind, or having a good mind, is declined exactly like धीः *dhîḥ*. सुभ्रूः *subhrûḥ*, masc. and fem. having a good brow, is declined exactly like भ्रूः *bhrûḥ* †, without excluding the fuller

* The following rule is taken from the Siddh.-Kaum. I. p. 136. If धीः *dhîḥ*, intellect, stands at the end of the Karmadhâraya compound like प्रधीः *pradhîḥ*, eminent intellect, or if it is used as a Bahuvrîhi compound in the feminine, such as प्रधीः *pradhîḥ*, possessed of eminent intellect, it is in both cases declined like लक्ष्मीः *lakshmîḥ*. It would thus become identical with प्रधीः *pradhîḥ*, thinking eminently, when it takes exceptionally the feminine terminations (§ 223). The Acc. Sing. and Plur., however, take अम् *am* and अः *aḥ*. The difference, therefore, would be the substitution of य् *y* for इय् *iy* before vowels, the obligation of using the fuller fem. terminations only, and the Vocative in ई î, for these are the only points of difference between the declension of लक्ष्मीः *lakshmîḥ* and धीः *dhîḥ*, fem. The Siddhânta-Kaumudî, while giving these rules for प्रधीः *pradhîḥ*, agrees with the rules given above with regard to सुधीः *sudhîḥ*, &c.

† The Voc. Sing. सुभ्रु *subhru* is used by Bhaṭṭi, in a passage where Râma in great grief exclaims, हा पितः क्वासि हे सुभ्रु *hâ pitaḥ kvâsi he subhru*, Oh father, where art thou, Oh thou fine-browed (wife)! Some grammarians admit this Vocative as correct; others call it a mistake of Bhaṭṭi; others, again, while admitting that it is a mistake, consider that Bhaṭṭi made Râma intentionally commit it as a token of his distracted mind. (Siddh.-Kaum. I. p. 137.)

terminations (ऐ *ai*, आः *âḥ*, आं *âm*, नां *nâm*)* for the masculine, or the simple terminations (ए *e*, अः *aḥ*, अः *aḥ*, इ *i*, आं *âm*) for the feminine. The same applies to the compound सुधीः *sudhîḥ*, when used as a substantive, good intellect.

If the same compounds are used as neuters, they shorten the final ई *î* or ऊ *û* of their base, and are declined like वारि *vâri* and मृदु *mṛidu*, with this difference, however, that in the Inst. Dat. Abl. Gen. Loc. Sing. Dual and Plural they may optionally take the masculine forms.

Masc. and Fem.	Optional fuller forms.	Optional forms for neuters, except Nom. Acc. Voc.
good-thoughted.		
SINGULAR.	SINGULAR.	SINGULAR.
N. सुधीः *sudhîḥ*		सुधि *sudhi*
A. सुधियं *sudhiyam*		सुधि *sudhi*
I. सुधिया *sudhiyâ*		or सुधिना *sudhinâ*
D. सुधिये *sudhiye*	सुधियै *sudhiyai*	or सुधिने *sudhine*
Ab. सुधियः *sudhiyaḥ*	सुधियाः *sudhiyâḥ*	or सुधिनः *sudhinaḥ*
G. सुधियः *sudhiyaḥ*	सुधियाः *sudhiyâḥ*	or सुधिनः *sudhinaḥ*
L. सुधियि *sudhiyi*	सुधियां *sudhiyâm*	or सुधिनि *sudhini*
V. सुधीः *sudhîḥ*		सुधि *sudhi* or सुधे *sudhe*
DUAL.	DUAL.	DUAL.
N. A. V. सुधियौ *sudhiyau*		सुधिनी *sudhinî*
I. D. Ab. सुधीभ्यां *sudhîbhyâm*		or सुधिभ्यां *sudhibhyâm*
G. L. सुधियोः *sudhiyoḥ*		or सुधिनोः *sudhinoḥ*
PLURAL.	PLURAL.	PLURAL.
N. V. सुधियः *sudhiyaḥ*		सुधीनि *sudhîni*
A. सुधियः *sudhiyaḥ*		सुधीनि *sudhîni*
I. सुधीभिः *sudhîbhiḥ*		or सुधिभिः *sudhibhiḥ*
D. सुधीभ्यः *sudhîbhyaḥ*		or सुधिभ्यः *sudhibhyaḥ*
Ab. सुधीभ्यः *sudhîbhyaḥ*		or सुधिभ्यः *sudhibhyaḥ*
G. सुधियां *sudhiyâm*	सुधीनां *sudhînâm*	or सुधीनां *sudhînâm*
L. सुधीषु *sudhîshu*		or सुधिषु *sudhishu*

* I can find no authority by which these fuller terminations are excluded. In बहुश्रेयसी *bahuśreyasî*, the feminine श्रेयसी *śreyasî* retains its feminine character (*nadîtva*) throughout (Siddh.-Kaum. I. p. 116); and the same is distinctly maintained for the compound प्रधीः *pradhîḥ*, possessed of distinguished intellect, if used as a masculine (Siddh.-Kaum. I. p. 119).

Masc. and Fem.	Optional fuller forms.	Optional forms for neuters, except Nom. Acc. Voc.
with beautiful brows.		
SINGULAR.	SINGULAR.	SINGULAR.
N. सुभ्रूः *subhrûḥ*		सुभ्रु *subhru*
A. सुभ्रुवं *subhruvam*		सुभ्रु *subhru*
I. सुभ्रुवा *subhruvâ*		or सुभ्रुणा *subhruṇâ*
D. सुभ्रुवे *subhruve*	सुभ्रुवै *subhruvai*	or सुभ्रुणे *subhruṇe*
Ab. सुभ्रुवः *subhruvaḥ*	सुभ्रुवाः *subhruvâḥ*	or सुभ्रुणः *subhruṇaḥ*
G. सुभ्रुवः *subhruvaḥ*	सुभ्रुवाः *subhruvâḥ*	or सुभ्रुणः *subhruṇaḥ*
L. सुभ्रुवि *subhruvi*	सुभ्रुवां *subhruvâm*	or सुभ्रुणि *subhruṇi*
V. सुभ्रूः *subhrûḥ*		सुभ्रु *subhru* or °भ्रो *-bhro*
DUAL.	DUAL.	DUAL.
N. A. V. सुभ्रुवौ *subhruvau*		सुभ्रुणी *subhruṇî*
I. D. Ab. सुभ्रूभ्यां *subhrûbhyâm*		or सुभ्रुभ्यां *subhrubhyâm*
G. L. सुभ्रुवोः *subhruvoḥ*		or सुभ्रुणोः *subhruṇoḥ*
PLURAL.	PLURAL.	PLURAL.
N. V. सुभ्रुवः *subhruvaḥ*		सुभ्रूणि *subhrûṇi*
A. सुभ्रुवः *subhruvaḥ*		सुभ्रूणि *subhrûṇi*
I. सुभ्रूभिः *subhrûbhiḥ*		or सुभ्रुभिः *subhrubhiḥ*
D. सुभ्रूभ्यः *subhrûbhyaḥ*		or सुभ्रुभ्यः *subhrubhyaḥ*
Ab. सुभ्रूभ्यः *subhrûbhyaḥ*		or सुभ्रुभ्यः *subhrubhyaḥ*
G. सुभ्रुवां *subhruvâm*	सुभ्रूणां *subhrûṇâm*	or सुभ्रूणां *subhrûṇâm*
L. सुभ्रूषु *subhrûshu*		or सुभ्रुषु *subhrushu*

Compounds ending in Polysyllabic Feminine Bases in ई î and ऊ û.

§ 227. Feminine nouns like नदी *nadî* and चमू *chamû* may form the last portion of compounds which are used in the masculine gender. Thus बहुश्रेयसी *bahuśreyasî*, a man who has many auspicious qualities (Siddh.-Kaum. I. pp. 116, 117), and अतिचमू *atichamû*, one who is better than an army (Siddh.-Kaum. I. p. 123), are declined in the masculine and feminine:

	SINGULAR.	DUAL.	PLURAL.
N.	बहुश्रेयसी *bahuśreyasî**	बहुश्रेयस्यौ *bahuśreyasyau*	बहुश्रेयस्यः *bahuśreyasyaḥ*
A.	बहुश्रेयसीं *bahuśreyasîm*	बहुश्रेयस्यौ *bahuśreyasyau*	बहुश्रेयसीन् *bahuśreyasîn*
I.	बहुश्रेयस्या *bahuśreyasyâ*	बहुश्रेयसीभ्यां *bahuśreyasîbhyâm*	बहुश्रेयसीभिः *bahuśreyasîbhiḥ*
D.	बहुश्रेयस्यै *bahuśreyasyai*	बहुश्रेयसीभ्यां *bahuśreyasîbhyâm*	बहुश्रेयसीभ्यः *bahuśreyasîbhyaḥ*
Ab.	बहुश्रेयस्याः *bahuśreyasyâḥ*	बहुश्रेयसीभ्यां *bahuśreyasîbhyâm*	बहुश्रेयसीभ्यः *bahuśreyasîbhyaḥ*
G.	बहुश्रेयस्याः *bahuśreyasyâḥ*	बहुश्रेयस्योः *bahuśreyasyoḥ*	बहुश्रेयसीनां *bahuśreyasînâm*
L.	बहुश्रेयस्यां *bahuśreyasyâm*	बहुश्रेयस्योः *bahuśreyasyoḥ*	बहुश्रेयसीषु *bahuśreyasîshu*
V.	बहुश्रेयसि *bahuśreyasi*	बहुश्रेयस्यौ *bahuśreyasyau*	बहुश्रेयस्यः *bahuśreyasyaḥ*

* From लक्ष्मीः *lakshmîḥ*, the Nom. Sing. would be अतिलक्ष्मीः *atilakshmîḥ*.

	SINGULAR.	DUAL.	PLURAL.
N.	अतिचमूः *atichamúḥ*	अतिचम्वौ *atichamvau*	अतिचम्वः *atichamvaḥ*
A.	अतिचमूम् *atichamúm*	अतिचम्वौ *atichamvau*	अतिचमून् *atichamún*
I.	अतिचम्वा *atichamvá*	अतिचमूभ्यां *atichamúbhyám*	अतिचमूभिः *atichamúbhiḥ*
D.	अतिचम्वै *atichamvai*	अतिचमूभ्यां *atichamúbhyám*	अतिचमूभ्यः *atichamúbhyaḥ*
Ab.	अतिचम्वाः *atichamváḥ*	अतिचमूभ्यां *atichamúbhyám*	अतिचमूभ्यः *atichamúbhyaḥ*
G.	अतिचम्वाः *atichamváḥ*	अतिचम्वोः *atichamvoḥ*	अतिचमूनां *atichamúnám*
L.	अतिचम्वां *atichamvám*	अतिचम्वोः *atichamvoḥ*	अतिचमूषु *atichamúshu*
V.	अतिचमु *atichamu*	अतिचम्वौ *atichamvau*	अतिचम्वः *atichamvaḥ* *

Nouns like कुमारी *kumárí*, a man who behaves like a girl, are declined like बहुश्रेयसी *bahuśreyasí*, except in the Acc. Sing. and Plur., where they form कुमार्यं *kumáryam* and कुमार्यः *kumáryaḥ*. (Siddh.-Kaum. I. pp. 118, 119.)

§ 228. स्त्री *strí*, woman, is declined like नदी *nadí*, only that the accumulation of three consonants is avoided by the regular insertion of an इ *i*, e.g. स्त्रिया *striyá*, and not स्त्र्या *stryá*. Remember also two optional forms in the Acc. Sing. and Plur.

Base स्त्री *strí* and स्त्रिय् *striy*.

SINGULAR.	DUAL.	PLURAL.
N. स्त्री *strí*	N.A.V. स्त्रियौ *striyau*	N. स्त्रियः *striyaḥ*
A. स्त्रीं *strím* or स्त्रियं *striyam*	I.D.Ab. स्त्रीभ्यां *stríbhyám*	A. स्त्रीः *stríḥ* or स्त्रियः *striyaḥ*
I. स्त्रिया *striyá*	G.L. स्त्रियोः *striyoḥ*	I. स्त्रीभिः *stríbhiḥ*
D. स्त्रियै *striyai*		D.Ab. स्त्रीभ्यः *stríbhyaḥ*
Ab.G. स्त्रियाः *striyáḥ*		G. स्त्रीणां *stríṇám* (Páṇ. I. 4, 5)
L. स्त्रियां *striyám*		L. स्त्रीषु *stríshu*
V. स्त्रि *stri* (Páṇ. I. 4, 4)		

§ 229. When स्त्री *strí* forms the last portion of a compound, and has to be treated as a masculine, feminine, and neuter, the following forms occur:

SINGULAR.

	MASC.	FEM.	NEUT.
N.	अतिस्त्रिः *atistriḥ*	अतिस्त्रिः *atistriḥ*	अतिस्त्रि *atistri*
A.	अतिस्त्रिं *atistrim* or अतिस्त्रियं *atistriyam*	अतिस्त्रिं *atistrim* or अतिस्त्रियं *atistriyam*	अतिस्त्रि *atistri*
I.	अतिस्त्रिणा *atistriṇá*	अतिस्त्रिया *atistriyá*	अतिस्त्रिणा *atistriṇá*
D.	अतिस्त्रये *atistraye*	अतिस्त्रियै *atistriyai* or अतिस्त्रये *atistraye*	अतिस्त्रिणे *atistriṇe* or अतिस्त्रये *atistraye*
Ab. G.	अतिस्त्रेः *atistreḥ*	अतिस्त्रियाः *atistriyáḥ* or अतिस्त्रेः *atistreḥ*	अतिस्त्रिणः *atistriṇaḥ* or अतिस्त्रेः *atistreḥ*
L.	अतिस्त्रौ *atistrau*	अतिस्त्रियां *atistriyám* or अतिस्त्रौ *atistrau*	अतिस्त्रिणि *atistriṇi* or अतिस्त्रौ *atistrau*
V.	अतिस्त्रे *atistre*	अतिस्त्रे *atistre*	अतिस्त्रे *atistre*

* The neuter is said to be N.A.V. Sing. बहुश्रेयसि *bahuśreyasi*, N.A.V. Dual बहुश्रेयसिनी *bahuśreyasiní*, N.A.V. Plur. बहुश्रेयसीनि *bahuśreyasíni*, Dat. Sing. बहुश्रेयस्यै, °स्ये, or °सिने, *bahuśreyasyai*, *-sye*, or *-sine*, &c.

DUAL.

	MASC.	FEM.	NEUT.
N.A.V.	अतिस्त्रियौ *atistriyau*	अतिस्त्रियौ *atistriyau*	अतिस्त्रिणी *atistriṇî*
I.D.Ab.	अतिस्त्रिभ्याम् *atistribhyâm*	अतिस्त्रिभ्याम् *atistribhyâm*	अतिस्त्रिभ्याम् *atistribhyâm*
G.L.	अतिस्त्रियोः *atistriyoḥ*	अतिस्त्रियोः *atistriyoḥ*	अतिस्त्रिणोः *atistriṇoḥ*

PLURAL.

	MASC.	FEM.	NEUT.
N.V.	अतिस्त्रयः *atistrayaḥ*	अतिस्त्रयः *atistrayaḥ*	अतिस्त्रीणि *atistrîṇi*
A.	अतिस्त्रीन् *atistrîn* or अतिस्त्रियः *atistriyaḥ*	अतिस्त्रीः *atistrîḥ* or अतिस्त्रियः *atistriyaḥ*	अतिस्त्रीणि *atistrîṇi*
I.	अतिस्त्रिभिः *atistribhiḥ*	अतिस्त्रिभिः *atistribhiḥ*	अतिस्त्रिभिः *atistribhiḥ*
D.Ab.	अतिस्त्रिभ्यः *atistribhyaḥ*	अतिस्त्रिभ्यः *atistribhyaḥ*	अतिस्त्रिभ्यः *atistribhyaḥ*
G.	अतिस्त्रीणाम् *atistrîṇâm*	अतिस्त्रीणाम् *atistrîṇâm*	अतिस्त्रीणाम् *atistrîṇâm*
L.	अतिस्त्रिषु *atistrishu*	अतिस्त्रिषु *atistrishu*	अतिस्त्रिषु *atistrishu*

In the masculine final ई *î* is shortened to इ *i*, and the compound declined like कविः *kaviḥ*, except in the Nom. Acc. Voc. and Gen. Loc. Dual. In the Acc. Sing. and Plur. optional forms are admitted. (Siddh.-Kaum. I. p. 134.)

The feminine may be the same as the masculine, except in the Instr. Sing. and Acc. Plur., but it may likewise be declined like स्त्री *strî* in the Dat. Abl. Gen. Loc. Sing.

The neuter has the usual optional forms.

Bases in इ i *and* उ u, *Masculine, Feminine, Neuter.*

§ 230. There are masculine, feminine, and neuter bases in इ *i* and उ *u*. They are of frequent occurrence and should be carefully committed to memory.

Adjectives in इ *i* are declined like substantives, only that the masculine may optionally be substituted for the neuter in all cases except the Nom. and Acc. Sing.; Nom. Acc. and Voc. Dual and Plur. Ex. शुचिः *śuchiḥ*, masc. bright; शुचिः *śuchiḥ*, fem.; शुचि *śuchi*, neut.

The same applies to adjectives in उ *u*, except that they may form their feminine either without any change, or by adding ई *î*. Thus लघुः *laghuḥ*, light, is in the fem. either लघुः *laghuḥ*, to be declined as a feminine, or लघ्वी *laghvî*, to be declined like नदी *nadî*.

If the final उ *u* is preceded by more than one consonant, the fem. does not take ई *î*. Thus पाण्डु *pâṇḍu*, pale; fem. पाण्डुः *pâṇḍuḥ*.

Some adjectives in उ *u* lengthen their vowel in the fem., and are then declined like वधूः *vadhûḥ*. Thus पङ्गुः *paṅguḥ*, lame; fem. पङ्गूः *paṅgûḥ*. Likewise कुरुः *kuruḥ*, a Kuru; fem. कुरूः *kurûḥ*: some compounds ending in ऊरुः *ûruḥ*, thigh, such as वामोरुः *vâmoruḥ*, with handsome thighs, fem. वामोरूः *vâmorûḥ*.

Bases in इ *i*. Bases in उ *u*.

SINGULAR.

	MASC.	FEM.	NEUT.	MASC.	FEM.	NEUT.
Base	कवि *kavi*, poet	मति *mati*, thought	वारि *vâri*, water	मृदु *mṛidu*, soft	मृदु *mṛidu*, soft	मृदु *mṛidu*, soft
N.	कविः *kavi-ḥ*	मतिः *mati-ḥ*	वारि *vâri*	मृदुः *mṛidu-ḥ*	मृदुः *mṛidu-ḥ*	मृदु *mṛidu*
A.	कविं *kavi-m*	मतिं *mati-m*	वारि *vâri*	मृदुं *mṛidu-m*	मृदुं *mṛidu-m*	मृदु *mṛidu*
I.	कविना *kavi-nâ*	मत्या *maty-â*	वारिणा *vâri-ṇâ*	मृदुना *mṛidu-nâ*	मृद्वा *mṛidv-â*	मृदुना *mṛidu-nâ*
D.	कवये *kavay-e*	मतये *matay-e* or मत्यै *maty-ai*	वारिणे *vâri-ṇe*	मृदवे *mṛidav-e*	मृदवे *mṛidav-e* or मृद्वै *mṛidv-ai*	मृदुने *mṛidu-ne* or मृदवे *mṛidav-e*
Ab. G.	कवेः *kave-ḥ*	मतेः *mate-ḥ* or मत्याः *maty-âḥ*	वारिणः *vâri-ṇaḥ*	मृदोः *mṛido-ḥ*	मृदोः *mṛido-ḥ* or मृद्वाः *mṛidv-âḥ*	मृदुनः *mṛidu-naḥ* or मृदोः *mṛido-ḥ*
L.	कवौ *kavau*	मतौ *matau* or मत्यां *maty-âm*	वारिणि *vâri-ṇi*	मृदौ *mṛidau*	मृदौ *mṛidau* or मृद्वां *mṛidv-âm*	मृदुनि *mṛidu-ni* or मृदौ *mṛidau*
V.	कवे *kave*	मते *mate*	वारि *vâri* or वारे *vâre**	मृदो *mṛido*	मृदो *mṛido*	मृदु *mṛidu* or मृदो *mṛido**

DUAL.

	MASC.	FEM.	NEUT.	MASC.	FEM.	NEUT.
N. A. V.	कवी *kavî*	मती *matî*	वारिणी *vâri-ṇî*	मृदू *mṛidû*	मृदू *mṛidû*	मृदुनी *mṛidu-nî*
I. D. Ab.	कविभ्यां *kavi-bhyâm*	मतिभ्यां *mati-bhyâm*	वारिभ्यां *vâri-bhyâm*	मृदुभ्यां *mṛidu-bhyâm*	मृदुभ्यां *mṛidu-bhyâm*	मृदुभ्यां *mṛidu-bhyâm*
G. L.	कव्योः *kavy-oḥ*	मत्योः *maty-oḥ*	वारिणोः *vâri-ṇoḥ*	मृद्वोः *mṛidv-oḥ*	मृद्वोः *mṛidv-oḥ*	मृदुनोः *mṛidu-noḥ* or मृद्वोः *mṛidv-oḥ*

PLURAL.

	MASC.	FEM.	NEUT.	MASC.	FEM.	NEUT.
N. V.	कवयः *kavay-aḥ*	मतयः *matay-aḥ*	वारीणि *vârî-ṇi*	मृदवः *mṛidav-aḥ*	मृदवः *mṛidav-aḥ*	मृदूनि *mṛidû-ni*
A.	कवीन् *kavî-n*	मतीः *matî-ḥ*	वारीणि *vârî-ṇi*	मृदून् *mṛidû-n*	मृदूः *mṛidû-ḥ*	मृदूनि *mṛidû-ni*
I.	कविभिः *kavi-bhiḥ*	मतिभिः *mati-bhiḥ*	वारिभिः *vâri-bhiḥ*	मृदुभिः *mṛidu-bhiḥ*	मृदुभिः *mṛidu-bhiḥ*	मृदुभिः *mṛidu-bhiḥ*
D. Ab.	कविभ्यः *kavi-bhyaḥ*	मतिभ्यः *mati-bhyaḥ*	वारिभ्यः *vâri-bhyaḥ*	मृदुभ्यः *mṛidu-bhyaḥ*	मृदुभ्यः *mṛidu-bhyaḥ*	मृदुभ्यः *mṛidu-bhyaḥ*
G.	कवीनां *kavî-nâm*	मतीनां *matî-nâm*	वारीणां *vârî-ṇâm*	मृदूनां *mṛidû-nâm*	मृदूनां *mṛidû-nâm*	मृदूनां *mṛidû-nâm*
L.	कविषु *kavi-shu*	मतिषु *mati-shu*	वारिषु *vâri-shu*	मृदुषु *mṛidu-shu*	मृदुषु *mṛidu-shu*	मृदुषु † *mṛidu-shu*

* The Guṇa in the Voc. Sing. of neuters in इ *i*, उ *u*, ऋ *ṛi*, is approved by Mâdhyandini Vyâghrapâd, as may be seen from the following verse: संबोधने तूशनसस्त्रिरूपं सान्तं तथा नान्तमथाप्यदन्तं । माध्यंदिनिर्वष्टि गुणं त्विगन्ते नपुंसके व्याघ्रपदां वरिष्ठः ॥

† The lines of separation placed in the transcribed paradigms are not intended to divide the real terminations from the real base, but only to facilitate the learning by heart of these

§ 231. कति *kati*, how many, यति *yati*, as many (relat.), and तति *tati*, so many, are used in the Plural only, and take no terminations in the Nom. and Acc. Plural. For the rest, they are declined like कवि *kavi*, and without distinction of gender.

Nom. Voc.	कति *kati*
Acc.	कति *kati*
Instr.	कतिभिः *katibhiḥ*
Dat.	कतिभ्यः *katibhyaḥ*
Abl.	कतिभ्यः *katibhyaḥ*
Gen.	कतीनां *katînâm*
Loc.	कतिषु *katishu*

§ 232. सखि *sakhi*, friend, has two bases:

सखाय् *sakhây* for the Aṅga, i. e. the strong base.

सखि *sakhi* for the Pada and Bha base.

It is irregular in some of its cases.

	Singular.	Dual.	Plural.
N.	सखा *sakhâ*	सखायौ *sakhâyau*	सखायः *sakhâyaḥ*
A.	सखायं *sakhâyam*	सखायौ *sakhâyau*	सखीन् *sakhîn*
I.	सख्या *sakhyâ*	सखिभ्यां *sakhibhyâm*	सखिभिः *sakhibhiḥ*
D.	सख्ये *sakhye*	सखिभ्यां *sakhibhyâm*	सखिभ्यः *sakhibhyaḥ*
Ab.	सख्युः *sakhyuḥ*	सखिभ्यां *sakhibhyâm*	सखिभ्यः *sakhibhyaḥ*
G.	सख्युः *sakhyuḥ*	सख्योः *sakhyoḥ*	सखीनां *sakhînâm*
L.	सख्यौ *sakhyau*	सख्योः *sakhyoḥ*	सखिषु *sakhishu*
V.	सखे *sakhe*	like Nom.	like Nom.

The feminine सखी *sakhî* is regular, like नदी *nadî*.

At the end of compounds, we find सखि *sakhi*, masc. declined as follows:

Base सुसखि *susakhi*, a good friend, masc.

	Singular.	Dual.	Plural.
N.	सुसखा *susakhâ*	सुसखायौ *susakhâyau*	सुसखायः *susakhâyaḥ* *
A.	सुसखायं *susakhâyam*	सुसखायौ *susakhâyau*	सुसखीन् *susakhîn*
I.	सुसखिना *susakhinâ*	सुसखिभ्यां *susakhibhyâm*	सुसखिभिः *susakhibhiḥ*
D.	सुसखये *susakhaye*	सुसखिभ्यां *susakhibhyâm*	सुसखिभ्यः *susakhibhyaḥ*
Ab.	सुसखेः *susakheḥ*	सुसखिभ्यां *susakhibhyâm*	सुसखिभ्यः *susakhibhyaḥ*
G.	सुसखेः *susakheḥ*	सुसख्योः *susakhyoḥ*	सुसखीनां *susakhînâm*
L.	सुसखौ *susakhau*	सुसख्योः *susakhyoḥ*	सुसखिषु *susakhishu*
V.	सुसखे *susakhe*	सुसखायौ *susakhâyau*	सुसखायः *susakhâyaḥ*

At the end of a neuter compound सखि *sakhi* is declined like वारि *vâri* (§ 230).

---

nouns. Masculine nouns in short उ *u* are भानु *bhânu*, sun, वायु *vâyu*, wind, विष्णु *vishṇu*, nom. prop. पीलु *pîlu*, as masc., is the name of a tree; as neuter, the name of its fruit (Sâr. 1. 8, 17). Feminine nouns in short उ *u* are धेनुः *dhenuḥ*, cow, रज्जुः *rajjuḥ*, rope, तनुः *tanuḥ*, body.

* Siddh.-Kaum. I. p. 112.

§ 233. पति *pati*, lord, is irregular:

SINGULAR.	DUAL.	PLURAL.
N. पतिः *patiḥ*	N. A. V. पती *patí*	N. पतयः *patayaḥ*
A. पतिम् *patim*	I. D. Ab. पतिभ्याम् *patibhyám*	A. पतीन् *patín*
I. पत्या *patyá*	G. L. पत्योः *patyoḥ*	I. पतिभिः *patibhiḥ*
D. पत्ये *patye*		D. Ab. पतिभ्यः *patibhyaḥ*
Ab. G. पत्युः *patyuḥ*		G. पतीनाम् *patínám*
L. पत्यौ *patyau*		L. पतिषु *patishu*
V. पते *pate*		V. पतयः *patayaḥ*

पति *pati* at the end of compounds, e. g. भूपति *bhúpati*, lord of the earth, प्रजापति *prajápati*, lord of creatures, is regular, like कवि *kavi*. The feminine of पति *pati* is पत्नी *patní*, wife, i. e. legitimate wife, she who takes part in the sacrifices of her husband. (Pâṇ. IV. 1, 33.)

§ 234. The neuter bases अक्षि *akshi*, eye, अस्थि *asthi*, bone, दधि *dadhi*, curds, सक्थि *sakthi*, thigh, are declined regularly like वारि *vári*; but in the Bha cases they substitute the bases अक्ष्न् *akshṇ*, अस्थ्न् *asthn*, दध्न् *dadhn*, सक्थ्न् *sakthn*. In these cases they are declined, in fact, like neuters in अन् *an*, such as नामन् *náman*. (See note to § 203.)

Aṅga and Pada base अक्षि *akshi*, Bha base अक्ष्न् *akshṇ*.

SINGULAR.	DUAL.	PLURAL.
N. A. अक्षि *akshi*	N. A. V. अक्षिणी *akshiṇí*	N. A. V. अक्षीणि *akshíṇi*
I. अक्ष्णा *akshṇá*	I. D. Ab. अक्षिभ्याम् *akshibhyám*	I. अक्षिभिः *akshibhiḥ*
D. अक्ष्णे *akshṇe*	G. L. अक्ष्णोः *akshṇoḥ*	D. Ab. अक्षिभ्यः *akshibhyaḥ*
Ab. G. अक्ष्णः *akshṇaḥ*		G. अक्ष्णाम् *akshṇám*
L. अक्ष्णि *akshṇi* and अक्षणि *akshaṇi*		L. अक्षिषु *akshishu*
V. अक्षे *akshe* (or अक्षि *akshi*)		

Bases in ऋ ṛi, *Masculine, Feminine, Neuter.*

§ 235. These bases are declined after two models:

SINGULAR.

I.	MASC.	FEM.	NEUT.
Base	नप्तृ *naptṛi*, grandson	स्वसृ *svasṛi*, sister	धातृ *dhátṛi*, providence
N.	नप्ता *naptá*	स्वसा *svasá*	धातृ *dhátṛi*
A.	नप्तारम् *naptár-am*	स्वसारम् *svasár-am*	धातृ *dhátṛi*
I.	नप्त्रा *naptr-á*	स्वस्रा *svasr-á*	धातृणा *dhátṛi-ṇá*
D.	नप्त्रे *naptr-e*	स्वस्रे *svasr-e*	धातृणे *dhátṛi-ṇe*
Ab. G.	नप्तुः *naptuḥ*	स्वसुः *svasuḥ*	धातृणः *dhátṛi-ṇaḥ*
L.	नप्तरि *naptar-i*	स्वसरि *svasar-i*	धातृणि *dhátṛi-ṇi*
V.	नप्तः *naptaḥ(r)*	स्वसः *svasaḥ(r)*	धातृ *dhátṛi* or धातः *dhátaḥ(r)*

PLURAL.

N.	नप्तारः *naptâr-aḥ*	स्वसारः *svasâr-aḥ*	धातॄणि *dhâtṛî-ṇi*
A.	नप्तॄन् *naptṛî-n*	स्वसॄः *svasṛî-ḥ*	धातॄणि *dhâtṛî-ṇi*
I.	नप्तृभिः *naptṛi-bhiḥ*	स्वसृभिः *svasṛi-bhiḥ*	धातृभिः *dhâtṛi-bhiḥ*
D.	नप्तृभ्यः *naptṛi-bhyaḥ*	स्वसृभ्यः *svasṛi-bhyaḥ*	धातृभ्यः *dhâtṛi-bhyaḥ*
Ab.	नप्तृभ्यः *naptṛi-bhyaḥ*	स्वसृभ्यः *svasṛi-bhyaḥ*	धातृभ्यः *dhâtṛi-bhyaḥ*
G.	नप्तॄणाम् *naptṛî-ṇâm*	स्वसॄणाम् *svasṛî-ṇâm*	धातॄणाम् *dhâtṛî-ṇâm*
L.	नप्तृषु *naptṛi-shu*	स्वसृषु *svasṛi-shu*	धातृषु *dhâtṛi-shu*

DUAL.

N.A.V.	नप्तारौ *naptâr-au*	स्वसारौ *svasâr-au*	धातृणी *dhâtṛi-ṇî*
I.D.Ab.	नप्तृभ्याम् *naptṛi-bhyâm*	स्वसृभ्याम् *svasṛi-bhyâm*	धातृभ्याम् *dhâtṛi-bhyâm*
G.L.	नप्त्रोः *naptr-oḥ*	स्वस्रोः *svasr-oḥ*	धातृणोः *dhâtṛi-ṇoḥ*

2. The second model differs from the first in the Acc. Sing., Nom. Acc. Voc. Dual, and Nom. Plur., by not lengthening the अ *a* before the र् *r*.

Base पितृ *pitṛi*, मातृ *mâtṛi*.

	SINGULAR.		DUAL.		PLURAL.	
	MASC.	FEM.	MASC.	FEM.	MASC.	FEM.
N.	पिता *pitâ*	माता *mâtâ*	पितरौ *pitar-au*	मातरौ *mâtar-au*	पितरः *pitar-aḥ*	मातरः *mâtar-aḥ*
A.	पितरम् *pitar-am*	मातरम् *mâtar-am*	(like N.)	(like N.)	पितॄन् *pitṛî-n*	मातॄः *mâtṛî-ḥ*
I.	पित्रा *pitr-â*	मात्रा *mâtr-â*	पितृभ्याम् *pitṛi-bhyâm*	मातृभ्याम् *mâtṛi-bhyâm*	पितृभिः *pitṛi-bhiḥ*	मातृभिः *mâtṛi-bhiḥ*
D.	पित्रे *pitr-e*	मात्रे *mâtr-e*	(like I.)	(like I.)	पितृभ्यः *pitṛi-bhyaḥ*	मातृभ्यः *mâtṛi-bhyaḥ*
Ab.	पितुः *pituḥ*	मातुः *mâtuḥ*	(like I.)	(like I.)	(like D.)	(like D.)
G.	पितुः *pituḥ*	मातुः *mâtuḥ*	पित्रोः *pitr-oḥ*	मात्रोः *mâtr-oḥ*	पितॄणाम् *pitṛî-ṇâm*	मातॄणाम् *mâtṛî-ṇâm*
L.	पितरि *pitar-i*	मातरि *mâtar-i*	(like G.)	(like G.)	पितृषु *pitṛi-shu*	मातृषु *mâtṛi-shu*
V.	पितः *pitaḥ(r)*	मातः *mâtaḥ(r)*	like Nom.	like Nom.	like Nom.	like Nom.

After the first model are declined most *nomina actoris* derived from verbs by the suffix तृ *tṛi*: दातृ *dâtṛi*, giver; कर्तृ *kartṛi*, doer; त्वष्टृ *tvashṭṛi*, carpenter; होतृ *hotṛi*, sacrificer; भर्तृ *bhartṛi*, husband.

After the second model are declined masculines, such as भ्रातृ *bhrâtṛi*, brother; जामातृ *jâmâtṛi*, son-in-law; देवृ *devṛi*, husband's brother; सव्येष्ठृ *savyeshṭhṛi*, a charioteer: and feminines, such as दुहितृ *duhitṛi*, daughter; ननान्दृ *nanandṛi*, husband's sister; यातृ *yâtṛi*, husband's brother's wife. Most terms of relationship in ऋ *ṛi* (except स्वसृ *svasṛi*, sister, and नप्तृ *naptṛi*, grandson) do not lengthen their अर् *ar*.

Note—If words in ऋ *ṛi* are used as adjectives, the masculine forms may be used for the neuter also, except in the Nom. and Acc. Sing. and Nom. Acc. Voc. Dual and Plural. The feminine is formed by ई *î*; कर्तृ *kartṛi*, fem. कर्त्री *kartrî*, like नदी *nadî*.

§ 236. क्रोष्टु *kroshṭu*, a jackal, is irregular; but most of its irregularities may be explained by admitting two bases, क्रोष्टु *kroshṭu* (like मृदु *mṛidu*) and क्रोष्टृ *kroshṭṛi* (like नप्तृ *naptṛi*).

Singular.	Dual.	Plural.
N. क्रोष्टा kroshṭâ	N.A.V. क्रोष्टारौ kroshṭârau	N. क्रोष्टारः kroshṭâraḥ
A. क्रोष्टारं kroshṭâram		A. क्रोष्टून् kroshṭûn
I. { क्रोष्टुना kroshṭunâ / क्रोष्ट्रा kroshṭrâ }	I.D.Ab. क्रोष्टुभ्यां kroshṭubhyâm	I. क्रोष्टुभिः kroshṭubhiḥ
D. { क्रोष्टवे kroshṭave / क्रोष्ट्रे kroshṭre }		D.Ab. क्रोष्टुभ्यः kroshṭubhyaḥ
Ab.G. { क्रोष्टोः kroshṭoḥ / क्रोष्टुः kroshṭuḥ }	G.L. { क्रोष्ट्वोः kroshṭvoḥ / क्रोष्ट्रोः kroshṭroḥ }	G. क्रोष्टूनां kroshṭûnâm
L. { क्रोष्टौ kroshṭau / क्रोष्टरि kroshṭari }		L. क्रोष्टुषु kroshṭushu
V. क्रोष्टो kroshṭo		

The base क्रोष्टृ kroshṭṛi is the only one admissible as Aṅga, i.e. in the strong cases, excepting the Vocative. (हे क्रोष्टः he kroshṭaḥ is, I believe, wrongly admitted by Wilson.)

The base क्रोष्टु kroshṭu is the only one admissible as Pada, i.e. before terminations beginning with consonants.

The other cases may be formed from both bases, but the Acc. Plur. is क्रोष्टून् kroshṭûn only. (Pâṇ. VII. 1, 95–97.)

Those who admit क्रोष्टॄन् kroshṭṝn as Acc. Plur. likewise admit क्रोष्टुं kroshṭum as Acc. Sing. (Sâr. I. 6, 70.)

The feminine is क्रोष्ट्री kroshṭrî, declined like नदी nadî.

§ 237. नृ nṛi, man, a word of frequent occurrence, though, for convenience sake, often replaced by नर nara, is declined regularly like पितृ pitṛi, except in the Gen. Plural, where it may be either नृणां nṛiṇâm or नॄणां nṝṇâm. (Pâṇ. VI. 4, 6.)

Singular.	Dual.	Plural.
N. ना nâ	नरौ narau	नरः naraḥ
A. नरं naram	नरौ narau	नॄन् nṝn
I. न्रा nrâ	नृभ्यां nṛibhyâm	नृभिः nṛibhiḥ
D. न्रे nre	नृभ्यां nṛibhyâm	नृभ्यः nṛibhyaḥ
Ab. नुः nuḥ	नृभ्यां nṛibhyâm	नृभ्यः nṛibhyaḥ
G. नुः nuḥ	न्रोः nroḥ	नृणां nṛiṇâm or नॄणां nṝṇâm
L. नरि nari	न्रोः nroḥ	नृषु nṛishu
V. नः naḥ	नरौ narau	नरः naraḥ

The feminine is नारी nârî.

2. *Bases ending in* अ a *and* आ â.

§ 238. This class is the most numerous and most important in Sanskrit, like the corresponding classes of nouns and adjectives in *us*, *a*, *um*, in Latin, and ος, η, ον in Greek. The case-terminations are peculiar, and it is best to learn कांतः *kántaḥ*, कांता *kántá*, कांतं *kántam* by heart in the same manner as we learn *bonus, bona, bonum*, without asking any questions as to the origin of the case-terminations, or their relation to the terminations appended to bases ending in consonants.

SINGULAR.

	MASC.	FEM.	NEUT.
Base	कांत *kánta*	कांता *kántá*	कांत *kánta*
N.	कांतः *kántaḥ*	कांता *kántá*	कांतं *kántam*
A.	कांतं *kántam*	कांतां *kántám*	कांतं *kántam*
I.	कांतेन *kántena*	कांतया *kántayá*	कांतेन *kántena*
D.	कांताय *kántáya*	कांतायै *kántáyai*	कांताय *kántáya*
Ab.	कांतात् *kántát*	कांतायाः *kántáyáḥ*	कांतात् *kántát*
G.	कांतस्य *kántasya*	कांतायाः *kántáyáḥ*	कांतस्य *kántasya*
L.	कांते *kánte*	कांतायां *kántáyám*	कांते *kánte*
V.	कांत *kánta*	कांते *kánte* *	कांत *kánta*

DUAL.

N. A. V.	कांतौ *kántau*	कांते *kánte*	कांते *kánte*
I. D. Ab.	कांताभ्यां *kántábhyám*	कांताभ्यां *kántábhyám*	कांताभ्यां *kántábhyám*
G. L.	कांतयोः *kántayoḥ*	कांतयोः *kántayoḥ*	कांतयोः *kántayoḥ*

PLURAL.

N. V.	कांताः *kántáḥ*	कांताः *kántáḥ*	कांतानि *kántáni*
A.	कांतान् *kántán*	कांताः *kántáḥ*	कांतानि *kántáni*
I.	कांतैः *kántaiḥ*	कांताभिः *kántábhiḥ*	कांतैः *kántaiḥ*
D. Ab.	कांतेभ्यः *kántebhyaḥ*	कांताभ्यः *kántábhyaḥ*	कांतेभ्यः *kántebhyaḥ*
G.	कांतानां *kántánám*	कांतानां *kántánám*	कांतानां *kántánám*
L.	कांतेषु *kánteshu*	कांतासु *kántásu*	कांतेषु *kánteshu*

Note—Certain adjectives in अः *aḥ*, आ *á*, अं *am*, which follow the ancient pronominal declension, will be explained in the chapter on Pronouns (§ 278).

Bases in आ *á, Masculine and Feminine.*

§ 239. These bases are derived immediately from verbs ending in आ *á*, such as पा *pá*, ध्मा *dhmá*. They are declined in the same way in the masculine and feminine gender. In the neuter the final आ *á* is shortened, and the word declined like कांतं *kántam*.

Aṅga and Pada base विश्वपा *viśvapá*, Bha base विश्वप् *viśvap*, all-preserving.

* Bases in आ *á*, meaning mother, form their Vocative in अ *a*; e. g. अक्क *akka*, अंब *amba*, अल्ल *alla!* But अंबाडा *ambáḍá*, अंबाला *ambálá*, and अंबिका *ambiká* form the regular Vocatives अंबाडे *ambáḍe*, अंबाले *ambále*, अंबिके *ambike*.

Masculine and Feminine.

	Singular.	Dual.	Plural.
N. V.	विश्वपाः viśvapá-ḥ	विश्वपौ viśvapau	विश्वपाः viśvapá-ḥ
A.	विश्वपां viśvapá-m	विश्वपौ viśvapau	विश्वपः viśvap-aḥ
I.	विश्वपा viśvap-á	विश्वपाभ्यां viśvapá-bhyám	विश्वपाभिः viśvapá-bhiḥ
D.	विश्वपे viśvap-e	विश्वपाभ्यां viśvapá-bhyám	विश्वपाभ्यः viśvapá-bhyaḥ
Ab.	विश्वपः viśvap-aḥ	विश्वपाभ्यां viśvapá-bhyám	विश्वपाभ्यः viśvapá-bhyaḥ
G.	विश्वपः viśvap-aḥ	विश्वपोः viśvap-oḥ	विश्वपां viśvap-ám
L.	विश्वपि viśvap-i	विश्वपोः viśvap-oḥ	विश्वपासु viśvapá-su

Neuter.

N.	विश्वपं viśvapam	विश्वपे viśvape	विश्वपानि viśvapáni, &c.

Decline सोमपाः somapáḥ, Soma drinker; शंखध्माः śaṅkhadhmáḥ, shell-blower; धनदाः dhanadáḥ, wealth giver.

§ 240. Masculines in आ á, not being derived by a Kṛit suffix from verbal roots, are declined as follows:

Base हाहा háhá.

	Singular.	Dual.	Plural.
N. V.	हाहाः háháḥ	हाहौ háhau	हाहाः háháḥ
A.	हाहां háhám	हाहौ háhau	हाहान् háhán *
I.	हाहा háhá	हाहाभ्यां háhábhyám	हाहाभिः háhábhiḥ
D.	हाहै háhai	हाहाभ्यां háhábhyám	हाहाभ्यः háhábhyaḥ
Ab.	हाहाः háháḥ	हाहाभ्यां háhábhyám	हाहाभ्यः háhábhyaḥ
G.	हाहाः háháḥ	हाहौः háhauḥ	हाहां háhám
L.	हाहे háhe	हाहौः háhauḥ	हाहासु háhásu

CHAPTER IV.

DECLENSION OF ADJECTIVES.

§ 241. As every noun in Sanskrit may, at the end of a compound, form the final portion of an adjective, all the essential rules for the declension of such compound adjectives had to be given in the preceding chapter. Thus in the declension of neuter nouns in अस् as, like मनस् manas, mind, the declension of सुमनस् sumanas, as an adjective masc. fem. and neut., was exhibited at the same time (§ 165). In the declension of nouns ending in consonants, and admitting of no distinction between masculine and feminine terminations, (this applies to all nouns with unchangeable bases,) the special forms of the neuter in Nom. Acc. Voc. Sing. Dual and Plur. had to be exhibited. See § 158, जलमुच् jalamuk, जलमुची jalamuchí, जलमुंचि jalamuñchi. In the declension of nouns with

* The Sár. I. 6, 38, gives the optional form हाहाः háháḥ in the masculine. At the end of a feminine compound the same form is sanctioned in the Rûpávali, p. 9 b.

changeable bases, the more important feminine and neuter forms were separately mentioned; and in the declension of nouns ending in vowels, all necessary rules with regard to the same subject were fully stated.

§ 242. The chief difficulty which remains with regard to the declension of adjectives is the exact formation of the feminine base, and the rules on this subject are often so complicated that they have to be learnt by practice rather than by rule. The feminine bases, however, once given, there can be no doubt as to their declension, as they follow exactly the declension of the corresponding feminine nouns. A few observations on this point must suffice.

§ 243. Adjectives * in अ *a* form their feminines in आ *á*. Ex. प्रिय *priya*, dear, masc. प्रियः *priyaḥ*, fem. प्रिया *priyá*, neut. प्रियं *priyam*, to be declined like कान्त *kánta* (§ 238).

§ 244. Certain adjectives derived by अक *aka* form their feminines in इका *iká*. Ex. पाचक *páchaka*, cooking, masc. पाचकः *páchakaḥ*, fem. पाचिका *páchiká*, neut. पाचकं *páchakam*. Likewise masc. सर्वकः *sarvakaḥ*, fem. सर्विका *sarviká*, every; कारकः *kárakaḥ*, doing, कारिका *káriká*; इहत्यकः *ihatyakaḥ*, present here, इहत्यिका *ihatyiká*. But क्षिपका *kshipaká*, fem. one who sends; कन्यका *kanyaká*, fem. maiden; चटका *chaṭaká*, fem. sparrow; तारका *táraká*, fem. star. Sometimes both forms occur; अजका *ajaká* and अजिका *ajiká*, a she-goat.

§ 245. Bases in ऋ *ṛi* and in न् *n* take ई *í* as the sign of the feminine: कर्तृ *kartṛi*, doer, कर्त्री *kartrí* (§ 235); दण्डिन् *daṇḍin*, a mendicant, दण्डिनी *daṇḍiní* (§ 203). Likewise most bases ending in consonants, if they admit of a separate feminine base: प्राच् *prách*, प्राची *práchí* (§ 181); श्वन् *śvan*, dog, शुनी *śuní* (§ 199); भवत् *bhavat*, भवती *bhavatí* (§ 188). Some adjectives in वन् *van* form their feminine base in वरी *varí*: पीवन् *pívan*, fat, पीवरी *pívarí* (§ 193).

§ 246. Many adjectives in अ *a* form their feminine base in ई *í* (§ 225), instead of आ *á*: तृणमयः *tṛiṇamayaḥ*, made of grass, तृणमयी *tṛiṇamayí*; देवः *devaḥ*, god, divine, देवी *deví*; तरुणः *taruṇaḥ* or तलुनः *talunaḥ*, a youth, तरुणी *taruṇí*; कुमारः *kumáraḥ*, a boy, कुमारी *kumárí*; गोपः *gopaḥ*, cowherd, गोपी *gopí*, his wife, but गोपा *gopá*, a female shepherd; नर्तकः *nartakaḥ*, actor, नर्तकी *nartakí*; मृगः *mṛigaḥ*, a deer, मृगी *mṛigí*, a doe; सूकरः *súkaraḥ*, boar, सूकरी *súkarí*; कुम्भकारः *kumbhakáraḥ*, a potter, कुम्भकारी *kumbhakárí*. It will be observed, however, that many of these words are substantives rather than adjectives. Thus मत्स्यः *matsyaḥ*, fish, forms मत्सी *matsí* (य *ya* being expunged before ई *í*); मनुष्यः *manushyaḥ*, man, मनुषी *manushí*.

§ 247. Certain adjectives in तः *taḥ*, expressive of colour, form their feminine either in ता *tá* or in नी *ní*: श्येतः *śyetaḥ*, white, श्येता *śyetá*, श्येनी *śyení*; एतः *etaḥ*, variegated, एता *etá* or एनी *ení*; रोहितः *rohitaḥ*, red, रोहिता *rohitá* or रोहिणी *rohiṇí*, but श्वेतः *śvetaḥ*, white, श्वेता *śvetá*; असिता *asitá*, white; पलिता *palitá*, grey-haired.

* गुणवचन *guṇavachana*, the name for adjective, occurs in Páṇ. v. 3, 58.

§ 248. The formation of feminine substantives must be learnt from the dictionary. Thus

अजः *ajaḥ*, goat, forms अजा *ajá*. अश्वः *aśvaḥ*, horse, forms अश्वा *aśvá*.

बालः *bálaḥ*, boy, forms बाला *bálá*.

शूद्रः *śúdraḥ*, a Śúdra, forms { शूद्रा *śúdrá*, a woman of the Śúdra caste. / शूद्री *śúdrí*, the wife of a Śúdra. }

मातुलः *mátulaḥ*, maternal uncle, forms मातुली *mátulí* or मातुलानी *mátulání*, an uncle's wife.

आचार्यः *ácháryaḥ*, teacher, forms आचार्यानी *ácháryání**, wife of the teacher; but आचार्या *áchâryá*, a female teacher.

पतिः *patiḥ*, lord, forms पत्नी *patní*, wife, &c.

Degrees of Comparison.

§ 249. The Comparative is formed by तर *tara*, or ईयस् *íyas* (§ 206); the Superlative by तम *tama*, or इष्ठ *ishṭha*. These terminations तर *tara* and तम *tama* are not restricted in Sanskrit to adjectives. Substantives such as नृ *nṛi*, man, form नृतमः *nṛitamaḥ*, a thorough man; स्त्री *strí*, woman, स्त्रीतरा *strítará*†, more of a woman. Even after case-terminations or personal terminations, तर *tara* and तम *tama* may be used. Thus from पूर्वाह्णे *púrváhṇe*, in the forenoon, पूर्वाह्णेतरे *púrváhṇetare*, earlier in the forenoon (Pâṇ. vi. 3, 17). From पचति *pachati*, he cooks, पचतितरां *pachatitarám*, he cooks better (Pâṇ. v. 3, 57), पचतितमां *pachatitamám*, he cooks best (Pâṇ. v. 3, 56).

§ 250. तर *tara* and तम *tama*, if added to changeable bases, require the Pada base. Thus from प्राच् *prách* (§ 180), प्राक्तर *práktara*; from धनिन् *dhanin* (§ 203), धनितर *dhanitara*; from धनवत् *dhanavat* (§ 187), धनवत्तर *dhanavattara*; from विद्वस् *vidvas* (§ 204), विद्वत्तम *vidvattama*; from प्रत्यच् *pratyach* (§ 181), प्रत्यक्तर *pratyaktara*. There are, however, a few exceptions, such as दस्युहन्तमः *dasyuhantamaḥ*, from दस्युहन् *dasyuhan*, demon-killer; सुपथिन्तरः *supathintaraḥ*, from सुपथिन् *supathin*, with good roads.

§ 251. ईयस् *íyas* and इष्ठ *ishṭha* are never added to the secondary suffixes तृ *tṛi*, मत् *mat*, वत् *vat*, वल *vala*, विन् *vin*, इन् *in*. If adjectives ending in these suffixes require ईयः *íyaḥ* and इष्ठ *ishṭha*, the suffixes are dropt, and the ईयः *íyaḥ* and इष्ठ *ishṭha* added to the last consonant of the original base. बलवान् *balaván*, strong, बलीयस् *bal-íyas*, बलिष्ठ *bal-ishṭha*. दोग्धृ *dogdhṛi*, milking, दुहीयस् *duh-íyas*, दुहिष्ठ *duh-ishṭha*. स्रग्विन् *sragvin*, garlanded, स्रजीयस् *sraj-íyas*, more profusely garlanded. मतिमान् *matimán*, wise, मतीयस् *mat-íyas*, मतिष्ठ *mat-ishṭha*.

---

* On the dental न् *n*, see Gaṇa Kshubhnádi in the Káś.-Vṛitti.

† Feminines in ई *í*, derived from masculines, must shorten the ई *í* before तर *tara* and तम *tama*; ब्राह्मणी *bráhmaṇí* forms ब्राह्मणितरा *bráhmaṇitará*. Other feminines in ई *í* or ऊ *ú* may or may not shorten their vowels; स्त्री *strí* forms स्त्रीतरा *strítará* or स्त्रितरा *stritará*. Also श्रेयसीतरा *śreyasítará* or श्रेयसितरा *śreyasitará*; विदुषीतरा *vidushítará* or विदुषितरा *vidushitará* (Pâṇ. vi. 3, 43—45).

§ 252. Other adjectives, too, lose their derivative elements before ईयस् *íyas* and इष्ठ *ishṭha*, or are otherwise irregular by substituting new bases for the Comparative and Superlative. पापः *pápaḥ*, bad; पापीयस् *páp-íyas*, worse; पापिष्ठ *páp-ishṭha*, worst.

	SECOND BASE.	COMPARATIVE.	SUPERLATIVE.
1. अंतिक *antika*, near	नेद् *ned*	नेदीयस् *nedíyas*	नेदिष्ठ *nedishṭha*
2. अल्प *alpa*, small	कन् *kan*	कनीयस् *kaníyas*	कनिष्ठ *kanishṭha*
		or अल्पीयस् *alpíyas*	अल्पिष्ठ *alpishṭha*
3. उरु *uru*, wide	वर् *var*	वरीयस् *varíyas*	वरिष्ठ *varishṭha*
4. ऋजु *ṛiju*, straight	ऋज् *ṛij*	ऋजीयस् *ṛijíyas*	ऋजिष्ठ *ṛijishṭha*
		Vedic रजीयस् *rajíyas*	रजिष्ठ *rajishṭha**
5. कृश *kṛiśa*, lean	क्रश् *kraś*	क्रशीयस् *kraśíyas*	क्रशिष्ठ *kraśishṭha*
6. क्षिप्र *kshipra*, quick	क्षेप् *kshep*	क्षेपीयस् *kshepíyas*	क्षेपिष्ठ *kshepishṭha*
7. क्षुद्र *kshudra*, mean	क्षोद् *kshod*	क्षोदीयस् *kshodíyas*	क्षोदिष्ठ *kshodishṭha*
8. गुरु *guru*, heavy	गर् *gar*	गरीयस् *garíyas*	गरिष्ठ *garishṭha*
9. तृप्र *tṛipra*, satisfied	त्रप् *trap*	त्रपीयस् *trapíyas*	त्रपिष्ठ *trapishṭha*
10. दीर्घ *dírgha*, long	द्राघ् *drágh*	द्राघीयस् *drághíyas*	द्राघिष्ठ *drághishṭha*
11. दूर *dúra*, far	दव् *dav*	दवीयस् *davíyas*	दविष्ठ *davishṭha*
12. दृढ *dṛiḍha*, firm	द्रढ् *draḍh*	द्रढीयस् *draḍhíyas*	द्रढिष्ठ *draḍhishṭha*
13. परिवृढ *parivṛiḍha*, exalted	परिव्रढ् *parivraḍh*	परिव्रढीयस् *parivraḍhíyas*	परिव्रढिष्ठ *parivraḍhishṭha*
14. पृथु *pṛithu*, broad	प्रथ् *prath*	प्रथीयस् *prathíyas*	प्रथिष्ठ *prathishṭha*
15. प्रशस्य *praśasya*, praiseworthy	श्र *śra*	श्रेयस् *śreyas*	श्रेष्ठ *śreshṭha*
	or ज्य *jya*	ज्यायस् *jyáyas*	ज्येष्ठ *jyeshṭha*
16. प्रिय *priya*, dear	प्र *pra*	प्रेयस् *preyas*	प्रेष्ठ *preshṭha*
17. बहु *bahu*, many	भू *bhú*	भूयस् *bhúyas*	भूयिष्ठ *bhúyishṭha*
18. बहुल *bahula*, frequent	बंह् *baṁh*	बंहीयस् *baṁhíyas*	बंहिष्ठ *baṁhishṭha*
19. भृश *bhṛiśa*, excessive	भ्रश् *bhraś*	भ्रशीयस् *bhraśíyas*	भ्रशिष्ठ *bhraśishṭha*
20. मृदु *mṛidu*, soft	म्रद् *mrad*	म्रदीयस् *mradíyas*	म्रदिष्ठ *mradishṭha*
21. युवन् *yuvan*, young	यव् *yav*	यवीयस् *yavíyas*	यविष्ठ *yavishṭha*
	or कन् *kan*	कनीयस् *kaníyas*	कनिष्ठ *kanishṭha*
22. बाढ *váḍha*, firm	साध् *sádh*	साधीयस् *sádhíyas*	साधिष्ठ *sádhishṭha*†
23. वृद्ध *vṛiddha*, old	वर्ष् *varsh*	वर्षीयस् *varshíyas*	वर्षिष्ठ *varshishṭha*
	or ज्य *jya*	ज्यायस् *jyáyas*	ज्येष्ठ *jyeshṭha*
24. वृंदारक *vṛindáraka*, beautiful	वृंद् *vṛind*	वृंदीयस् *vṛindíyas*	वृंदिष्ठ *vṛindishṭha*
25. स्थिर *sthira*, firm	स्थ *stha*	स्थेयस् *stheyas*	स्थेष्ठ *stheshṭha*
26. स्थूल *sthúla*, strong	स्थव् *sthav*	स्थवीयस् *sthavíyas*	स्थविष्ठ *sthavishṭha*
27. स्फिर *sphira*, thick	स्फ *spha*	स्फेयस् *spheyas*	स्फेष्ठ *spheshṭha*
28. ह्रस्व *hrasva*, short	ह्रस् *hras*	ह्रसीयस् *hrasíyas*	ह्रसिष्ठ *hrasishṭha*

* Páṇ. vi. 4, 162.

† Páṇ. v. 3, 63.

CHAPTER V.

NUMERALS.

Cardinals.

1 १ एकः, एका, एकं, *ekaḥ*, *ekâ*, *ekam*, one. (Base एक *eka*.)

2 २ द्वौ, द्वे, द्वे, *dvau*, *dve*, *dve*, two. (Base द्व *dva*; in comp. द्वि *dvi*.)

3 ३ त्रयः, तिस्रः, त्रीणि, *trayaḥ*, *tisraḥ*, *trîṇi*, three. (Base त्रि *tri*.)

4 ४ चत्वारः, चतस्रः, चत्वारि, *chatvâraḥ*, *chatasraḥ*, *chatvâri*, four. (Base चतुर् *chatur*.)

5 ५ पंच *pañcha*, m. f. n. five. (Base पंचन् *pañchan*.)

6 ६ षट् *shaṭ*, m. f. n. six. (Base षष् *shash*.)

7 ७ सप्त *sapta*, m. f. n. seven. (Base सप्तन् *saptan*.)

8 ८ अष्टौ *ashṭau*, m. f. n. eight. (Base अष्टन् *ashṭan*.)

9 ९ नव *nava*, m. f. n. nine. (Base नवन् *navan*.)

10 १० दश *daśa*, m. f. n. ten. (Base दशन् *daśan*.)

11 ११ एकादश *ekâdaśa*, eleven. (Base as in दशन् *daśan*.)

12 १२ द्वादश *dvâdaśa*.

13 १३ त्रयोदश *trayodaśa*.

14 १४ चतुर्दश *chaturdaśa*.

15 १५ पंचदश *pañchadaśa*.

16 १६ षोडश *shoḍaśa*.

17 १७ सप्तदश *saptadaśa*.

18 १८ अष्टादश *ashṭâdaśa*.

19 १९ नवदश *navadaśa* or ऊनविंशतिः *ûnaviṁśatiḥ*.

20 २० विंशतिः *viṁśatiḥ*, fem.

21 २१ एकविंशतिः *ekaviṁśatiḥ*.

22 २२ द्वाविंशतिः *dvâviṁśatiḥ*.

23 २३ त्रयोविंशतिः *trayoviṁśatiḥ*.

24 २४ चतुर्विंशतिः *chaturviṁśatiḥ*.

25 २५ पंचविंशतिः *pañchaviṁśatiḥ*.

26 २६ षड्विंशतिः *shaḍviṁśatiḥ*.

27 २७ सप्तविंशतिः *saptaviṁśatiḥ*.

28 २८ अष्टाविंशतिः *ashṭâviṁśatiḥ*.

29 २९ नवविंशतिः *navaviṁśatiḥ*.

30 ३० त्रिंशत् *triṁśat*, fem.

31 ३१ एकत्रिंशत् *ekatriṁśat*.

32 ३२ द्वात्रिंशत् *dvâtriṁśat*.

33 ३३ त्रयस्त्रिंशत् *trayastriṁśat*.

34 ३४ चतुस्त्रिंशत् *chatustriṁśat*.

35 ३५ पंचत्रिंशत् *pañchatriṁśat*.

36 ३६ षट्त्रिंशत् *shaṭtriṁśat*.

37 ३७ सप्तत्रिंशत् *saptatriṁśat*.

38 ३८ अष्टात्रिंशत् *ashṭâtriṁśat*.

39 ३९ नवत्रिंशत् *navatriṁśat*.

40 ४० चत्वारिंशत् *chatvâriṁśat*, fem.

41 ४१ एकचत्वारिंशत् *ekachatvâriṁśat*.

42 ४२ द्वाचत्वारिंशत् *dvâchatvâriṁśat* or द्विचत्वारिंशत् *dvichatvâriṁśat*.

43 ४३ त्रयश्चत्वारिंशत् *trayaśchatvâriṁśat* or त्रिचत्वारिंशत् *trichatvâriṁśat*.

44 ४४ चतुश्चत्वारिंशत् *chatuśchatvâriṁśat*.

45 ४५ पंचचत्वारिंशत् *pañchachatvâriṁśat*.

46 ४६ षट्चत्वारिंशत् *shaṭchatvâriṁśat*.

47 ४७ सप्तचत्वारिंशत् *saptachatvâriṁśat*.

48 ४८ अष्टाचत्वारिंशत् *ashṭâchatvâriṁśat* or अष्टचत्वारिंशत् *ashṭachatvâriṁśat*.

49 ४९ नवचत्वारिंशत् *navachatvâriṁśat*.

50 ५० पंचाशत् *pañchâśat*, fem.

51 ५१ एकपंचाशत् *ekapañchâśat*.

52 ५२ द्वापंचाशत् *dvâpañchâśat* or द्विपंचाशत् *dvipañchâśat*.

53 ५३ त्रयःपंचाशत् *trayaḥpañchâśat* or
त्रिपंचाशत् *tripañchâśat*.
54 ५४ चतुःपंचाशत् *chatuḥpañchâśat*.
55 ५५ पंचपंचाशत् *pañchapañchâśat*.
56 ५६ षट्पंचाशत् *shaṭpañchâśat*.
57 ५७ सप्तपंचाशत् *saptapañchâśat*.
58 ५८ अष्टापंचाशत् *ashṭápañchâśat* or
अष्टपंचाशत् *ashṭapañchâśat*.
59 ५९ नवपंचाशत् *navapañchâśat*.
60 ६० षष्टिः *shashṭiḥ*, fem.
61 ६१ एकषष्टिः *ekashashṭiḥ*.
62 ६२ द्वाषष्टिः *dváshashṭiḥ* or
द्विषष्टिः *dvishashṭiḥ*.
63 ६३ त्रयःषष्टिः *trayaḥshashṭiḥ* or
त्रिषष्टिः *trishashṭiḥ*.
64 ६४ चतुष्षष्टिः *chatushshashṭiḥ*.
65 ६५ पंचषष्टिः *pañchashashṭiḥ*
66 ६६ षट्षष्टिः *shaṭshashṭiḥ*.
67 ६७ सप्तषष्टिः *saptashashṭiḥ*.
68 ६८ अष्टाषष्टिः *ashṭáshashṭiḥ* or
अष्टषष्टिः *ashṭashashṭiḥ*.
69 ६९ नवषष्टिः *navashashṭiḥ*.
70 ७० सप्ततिः *saptatiḥ*, fem.
71 ७१ एकसप्ततिः *ekasaptatiḥ*.
72 ७२ द्वासप्ततिः *dvásaptatiḥ* or
द्विसप्ततिः *dvisaptatiḥ*.
73 ७३ त्रयःसप्ततिः *trayaḥsaptatiḥ* or
त्रिसप्ततिः *trisaptatiḥ*.
74 ७४ चतुःसप्ततिः *chatuḥsaptatiḥ*.
75 ७५ पंचसप्ततिः *pañchasaptatiḥ*.
76 ७६ षट्सप्ततिः *shaṭsaptatiḥ*.
77 ७७ सप्तसप्ततिः *saptasaptatiḥ*.
78 ७८ अष्टासप्ततिः *ashṭásaptatiḥ* or
अष्टसप्ततिः *ashṭasaptatiḥ*.
79 ७९ नवसप्ततिः *navasaptatiḥ*.
80 ८० अशीतिः *aśítiḥ*.
81 ८१ एकाशीतिः *ekáśítiḥ*.
82 ८२ द्व्यशीतिः *dvyaśítiḥ*.
83 ८३ त्र्यशीतिः *tryaśítiḥ*.
84 ८४ चतुरशीतिः *chaturaśítiḥ*.
85 ८५ पंचाशीतिः *pañcháśítiḥ*.
86 ८६ षडशीतिः *shaḍaśítiḥ*.
87 ८७ सप्ताशीतिः *saptáśítiḥ*.
88 ८८ अष्टाशीतिः *ashṭáśítiḥ*.
89 ८९ नवाशीतिः *naváśítiḥ*.
90 ९० नवतिः *navatiḥ*.
91 ९१ एकनवतिः *ekanavatiḥ*.
92 ९२ द्वानवतिः *dvánavatiḥ* or
द्विनवतिः *dvinavatiḥ*.
93 ९३ त्रयोनवतिः *trayonavatiḥ* or
त्रिनवतिः *trinavatiḥ* (not ण् ṇ).
94 ९४ चतुर्नवतिः *chaturnavatiḥ*.
95 ९५ पंचनवतिः *pañchanavatiḥ*.
96 ९६ षण्णवतिः *shaṇṇavatiḥ*.
97 ९७ सप्तनवतिः *saptanavatiḥ*.
98 ९८ अष्टानवतिः *ashṭánavatiḥ* or
अष्टनवतिः *ashṭanavatiḥ*.
99 ९९ नवनवतिः *navanavatiḥ* or
ऊनशतं *únaśatam*.

100 १०० शतं *śatam*, neut. and masc. (Siddh.-Kaum. II. p. 635.)
101 १०१ एकाधिकं शतं *ekádhikam śatam*, hundred exceeded by one; or as a compound, एकाधिकशतं *ekádhika-śatam*, or एकशतं *ekaśatam*, as before.
102 १०२ द्व्यधिकं शतं *dvyadhikam śatam* or द्विशतं *dviśatam*. (Pâṇ. VI. 3, 49.)
103 १०३ त्र्यधिकं शतं *tryadhikam śatam* or त्रिशतं *triśatam*.
104 १०४ चतुरधिकं शतं *chaturadhikam śatam* or चतुःशतं *chatuḥśatam*.
105 १०५ पंचाधिकं शतं *pañchádhikam śatam* or पंचशतं *pañchaśatam*.
106 १०६ षडधिकं शतं *shaḍadhikam śatam* or षट्शतं *shaṭśatam*.
107 १०७ सप्ताधिकं शतं *saptádhikam śatam* or सप्तशतं *saptaśatam*.
108 १०८ अष्टाधिकं शतं *ashṭádhikam śatam* or अष्टशतं *ashṭaśatam*. (Pâṇ. VI. 3, 49.)

109 १०९ नवाधिकं शतं *navâdhikam śatam* or नवशतं *navaśatam.*

110 ११० दशाधिकं शतं *daśâdhikam śatam* or दशशतं *daśaśatam.*

111 १११ एकादशाधिकं शतं *ekâdaśâdhikam śatam* or एकादशशतं *ekâdaśaśatam* &c. or एकादशं शतं *ekâdaśam śatam*, i. e. a hundred having eleven (in excess). Pâṇ. v. 2, 45.

112 ११२ द्वादशाधिकं शतं *dvâdaśâdhikam śatam* or द्वादशं शतं *dvâdaśam śatam.*

113 ११३ त्रयोदशाधिकं शतं *trayodaśâdhikam śatam* or त्रयोदशं शतं *trayodaśam śatam.*

114 ११४ चतुर्दशाधिकं शतं *chaturdaśâdhikam śatam* or चतुर्दशं शतं *chaturdaśam śatam.*

115 ११५ पंचदशाधिकं शतं *pañchadaśâdhikam śatam* or पंचदशं शतं *pañchadaśam śatam.*

116 ११६ षोडशाधिकं शतं *shoḍaśâdhikam śatam* or षोडशं शतं *shoḍaśam śatam.*

117 ११७ सप्तदशाधिकं शतं *saptadaśâdhikam śatam* or सप्तदशं शतं *saptadaśam śatam.*

118 ११८ अष्टादशाधिकं शतं *ashṭâdaśâdhikam śatam* or अष्टादशं शतं *ashṭâdaśam śatam.*

119 ११९ नवदशाधिकं शतं *navadaśâdhikam śatam* or नवदशं शतं *navadaśam śatam.*

120 १२० विंशत्यधिकं शतं *viṁśatyadhikam śatam* or विंशं शतं *viṁśam śatam**.

121 १२१ एकविंशत्यधिकं शतं *ekaviṁśatyadhikam śatam* or एकविंशं शतं *ekaviṁśam śatam**, &c.)

130 १३० त्रिंशदधिकं शतं *triṁśadadhikam śatam* or त्रिंशं शतं *triṁśam śatam**.

140 १४० चत्वारिंशदधिकं शतं *chatvâriṁśadadhikam śatam* or चत्वारिंशं शतं *chatvâriṁśam śatam**.

150 १५० पंचाशदधिकं शतं *pañchâśadadhikam śatam* or पंचाशं शतं *pañchâśam śatam** or सार्धशतं *sârdhaśatam*, 100 + ½ (hundred).

160 १६० षष्ट्यधिकं शतं *shashṭyadhikam śatam* or षष्टिशतं *shashṭiśatam.*

170 १७० सप्तत्यधिकं शतं *saptatyadhikam śatam* or सप्ततिशतं *saptatiśatam.*

180 १८० अशीत्यधिकं शतं *aśîtyadhikam śatam* or अशीतिशतं *aśîtiśatam.*

190 १९० नवत्यधिकं शतं *navatyadhikam śatam* or नवतिशतं *navatiśatam.*

200 २०० द्वे शते *dve śate* or द्विशतं *dviśatam* or द्विशती *dviśatî.*

300 ३०० त्रीणि शतानि *trîṇi śatâni* or त्रिशतं *triśatam.*

400 ४०० चत्वारि शतानि *chatvâri śatâni* or चतुःशतं *chatuḥśatam.*

500 ५०० पंच शतानि *pañcha śatâni* or पंचशतं *pañchaśatam.*

600 ६०० षट् शतानि *shaṭ śatâni* or षट्शतं *shaṭśatam.*

700 ७०० सप्त शतानि *sapta śatâni* or सप्तशतं *saptaśatam.*

800 ८०० अष्ट शतानि *ashṭa śatâni* or अष्टशतं *ashṭaśatam.*

900 ९०० नव शतानि *nava śatâni* or नवशतं *navaśatam.*

1000 १००० दश शतानि *daśa śatâni* or दशशती *daśaśatî*, fem., or सहस्रं *sahasram*, neut. and masc.†

2000 २००० द्वे सहस्रे *dve sahasre.*

---

* Pâṇ. v. 2, 46. The same rules apply to सहस्रं *sahasram*, 1000, so that 1011 might be rendered by एकादशं सहस्रं *ekâdaśam sahasram*, 1041 by एकचत्वारिंशं सहस्रं *ekachatvâriṁśam sahasram*, &c.

† Siddh.-Kaum. II. p. 635.

3000 ३००० त्रीणि सहस्राणि *trîṇi sahasrâṇi.*

10,000 १०,००० अयुतं *ayutam*, neut. and masc. *

100,000 १००,००० लक्षं *laksham*, neut. or fem. *, or नियुतं *niyutam*, neut. and masc. †

One million, प्रयुतं *prayutam*, neut. or masc. *

Ten millions, कोटि *koṭi*, fem.

A hundred millions, अर्बुद *arbuda*, masc. and neut.

A thousand millions, महार्बुद *mahârbuda*, masc. and neut., or पद्म *padma*, neut., i. e. lotus.

Ten thousand millions, खर्व *kharva*, neut., i. e. minute.

A hundred thousand millions, निखर्व *nikharva*, neut.

A billion, महापद्म *mahâpadma*, neut.

Ten billions, शङ्कु *śaṅku*, masc., i. e. an ant-hill.

A hundred billions, शङ्ख *śaṅkha*, masc. neut., i. e. a conch-shell, or समुद्र *samudra*, masc., i. e. sea.

A thousand billions, महाशङ्ख *mahâśaṅkha*, or अन्त्य *antya*, ultimate.

Ten thousand billions, हाहा *hâhâ*, masc., or मध्य *madhya*, middle.

A hundred thousand billions, महाहाहा *mahâhâhâ*, or परार्ध *parârdha*, i. e. half more.

One million billions, धुन *dhuna*, neut.

Ten million billions, महाधुन *mahâdhuna.*

A hundred million billions, अक्षौहिणी *akshauhiṇî*, fem., i. e. a host.

A thousand million billions, महाक्षौहिणी *mahâkshauhiṇî.*

In the same manner as अधिक *adhika*, exceeding, ऊन *ûna*, diminished, may be used to form numerical compounds. पञ्चोनं शतं *pañchonam śatam* or पञ्चोनशतं *pañchonaśatam*, 100 — 5, i. e. 95. If one is to be deducted, ऊन *ûna*, without एक *eka*, suffices. ऊनविंशतिः *ûnaviṁśatiḥ* or एकोनविंशतिः *ekonaviṁśatiḥ*, 20 — 1, i. e. 19. Another way of expressing nineteen and similar numbers is by prefixing एकान्न *ekânna*, i. e. by one not; एकान्नविंशतिः *ekânnaviṁśatiḥ*, by one not twenty, i. e. 19. (Pâṇ. VI. 3, 76.)

§ 253. *Declension of Cardinals.*

एक *eka*, one.

	SINGULAR.			PLURAL.		
	MASC.	FEM.	NEUT.	MASC.	FEM.	NEUT.
N.	एकः *ekaḥ*	एका *ekâ*	एकं *ekam*	एके *eke*	एकाः *ekâḥ*	एकानि *ekâni*
A.	एकं *ekam*	एकां *ekâm*	एकं *ekam*	एकान् *ekân*	एकाः *ekâḥ*	एकानि *ekâni*
I.	एकेन *ekena*	एकया *ekayâ*	एकेन *ekena*	एकैः *ekaiḥ*	एकाभिः *ekâbhiḥ*	एकैः *ekaiḥ*
D.	एकस्मै *ekasmai*	एकस्यै *ekasyai*	एकस्मै *ekasmai*	एकेभ्यः *ekebhyaḥ*	एकाभ्यः *ekâbhyaḥ*	एकेभ्यः *ekebhyaḥ*
Ab.	एकस्मात् *ekasmât*	एकस्याः *ekasyâḥ*	एकस्मात् *ekasmât*	एकेभ्यः *ekebhyaḥ*	एकाभ्यः *ekâbhyaḥ*	एकेभ्यः *ekebhyaḥ*
G.	एकस्य *ekasya*	एकस्याः *ekasyâḥ*	एकस्य *ekasya*	एकेषां *ekeshâm*	एकासां *ekâsâm*	एकेषां *ekeshâm*
L.	एकस्मिन् *ekasmin*	एकस्यां *ekasyâm*	एकस्मिन् *ekasmin*	एकेषु *ekeshu*	एकासु *ekâsu*	एकेषु *ekeshu*
V.	एक *eka*	एके *eke*	एक *eka*	एके *eke*	एकाः *ekâḥ*	एकानि *ekâni*

* Siddh.-Kaum. II. p. 635. † Amara-Kosha III. 6, 3, 24.

§ 254. द्वि *dvi*, two, base द्व *dva*, like कान्त *kânta* (§ 238).

DUAL.

	MASC.	FEM.	NEUT.
N.A.V.	द्वौ *dvau*	द्वे *dve*	द्वे *dve*
I.D.Ab.	द्वाभ्यां *dvâbhyâm*	द्वाभ्यां *dvâbhyâm*	द्वाभ्यां *dvâbhyâm*
G.L.	द्वयोः *dvayoḥ*	द्वयोः *dvayoḥ*	द्वयोः *dvayoḥ*

§ 255. त्रि *tri*, three, fem. तिसृ *tisṛi*.

N.V.	त्रयः *trayaḥ*	तिस्रः *tisraḥ*	त्रीणि *trîṇi*
A.	त्रीन् *trîn*	तिस्रः *tisraḥ* *	त्रीणि *trîṇi*
I.	त्रिभिः *tribhiḥ*	तिसृभिः *tisṛibhiḥ*	त्रिभिः *tribhiḥ*
D.Ab.	त्रिभ्यः *tribhyaḥ*	तिसृभ्यः *tisṛibhyaḥ*	त्रिभ्यः *tribhyaḥ*
G.	त्रयाणां *trayâṇâm*	तिसृणां *tisṛiṇâm* †	त्रयाणां *trayâṇâm*
L.	त्रिषु *trishu*	तिसृषु *tisṛishu*	त्रिषु *trishu*

§ 256. चतुर् *chatur*, four, fem. चतसृ *chatasṛi*.

N.V.	चत्वारः *chatvâraḥ*	चतस्रः *chatasraḥ*	चत्वारि *chatvâri*
A.	चतुरः *chaturaḥ*	चतस्रः *chatasraḥ* *	चत्वारि *chatvâri*
I.	चतुर्भिः *chaturbhiḥ*	चतसृभिः *chatasṛibhiḥ*	चतुर्भिः *chaturbhiḥ*
D.Ab.	चतुर्भ्यः *chaturbhyaḥ*	चतसृभ्यः *chatasṛibhyaḥ*	चतुर्भ्यः *chaturbhyaḥ*
G.	चतुर्णां *chaturṇâm*	चतसृणां *chatasṛiṇâm* †	चतुर्णां *chaturṇâm*
L.	चतुर्षु *chaturshu*	चतसृषु *chatasṛishu*	चतुर्षु *chaturshu*

§ 257. पंचन् *pañchan*, five. षष् *shash*, six. अष्टन् *ashṭan*, eight.

N.A.V.	पंच *pañcha*	षट् *shaṭ*	अष्टौ *ashṭau* or अष्ट *ashṭa*
I.	पंचभिः *pañchabhiḥ*	षड्भिः *shaḍbhiḥ*	अष्टाभिः *ashṭâbhiḥ* or अष्टभिः *ashṭabhiḥ*
D.Ab.	पंचभ्यः *pañchabhyaḥ*	षड्भ्यः *shaḍbhyaḥ*	अष्टाभ्यः *ashṭâbhyaḥ* or अष्टभ्यः *ashṭabhyaḥ*
G.	पंचानां *pañchânâm* ‡	षण्णां *shaṇṇâm* ‡	अष्टानां *ashṭânâm* ‡
L.	पंचसु *pañchasu*	षट्सु *shaṭsu*	अष्टासु *ashṭâsu* or अष्टसु *ashṭasu*

Cardinals with bases ending in न् *n*, such as सप्तन् *saptan*, नवन् *navan*, दशन् *daśan*, एकादशन् *ekâdaśan*, &c., follow the declension of पंचन् *pañchan*. विंशतिः *viṁśatiḥ* is declined like a feminine in इ *i*; those in त् *t* like feminines in त् *t*; शतं *śatam* like a neut. or masc. in अ *a*.

§ 258. The construction of the cardinals from 1 to 19 requires a few remarks. एक *eka* is naturally used in the singular only, except when it means some; एके वदन्ति *eke vadanti*, some people say. द्वि *dvi* is always used as a dual, all the rest from 3 to 19 as plurals. Ex. त्रिभिः पुरुषैः *tribhiḥ purushaiḥ*, with three men; एकादश पुरुषान् *ekâdaśa purushân*, eleven men, acc. The

* Not तिसृः *tisṛîḥ*, not चतसृः *chatasṛîḥ*.

† Not तिसॄणां *tisṛîṇâm*, not चतसॄणां *chatasṛîṇâm* (Pâṇ. VI. 3, 4), though these forms occur in Epic poetry.

‡ Pâṇ. VII. 1, 55.

cardinals after four do not distinguish the gender; एकादश नार्यः *ekádaśa nárîḥ*, eleven women, acc.

While the numerals from 1 to 19 are treated as adjectives, agreeing with their substantives in gender, if possible, and in number and case, विंशतिः *viṁśatiḥ* and the rest may be treated both as adjectives and as substantives. Hence विंशतिः शत्रूणां *viṁśatiḥ śatrûṇâm*, twenty enemies, or विंशतिः शत्रवः *viṁśatiḥ śatravaḥ*; षष्टिः शिशवः *shashṭiḥ śiśavaḥ*, sixty boys; शतं फलानि *śatam phaláni*, a hundred fruits; त्रिंशता वृद्धैः *triṁśatâ vṛiddhaiḥ*, by thirty elders; शतं दासीनां *śatam dâsînâm* or शतं दास्यः *śatam dâsyaḥ*, a hundred slaves; सहस्रं पितरः *sahasram pitaraḥ*, a thousand ancestors.

Exceptionally these cardinals may take the plural number: पंचाशद्भिर्हयैः *pañchâśadbhir hayaiḥ*, with fifty horses.

§ 259. *Ordinals.*

प्रथमः, °मा, °मं, *prathamaḥ, â, am,*	the first.
अग्रिमः, °मा, °मं, *agrimaḥ, â, am,*	
आदिमः, °मा, °मं, *âdimaḥ, â, am,*	
द्वितीयः, °या, °यं, *dvitîyaḥ, â, am,*	the second.
तृतीयः, °या, °यं, *tṛitîyaḥ, â, am,*	the third.
चतुर्थः, °र्थी, °र्थं, *chaturthaḥ, î, am,*	the fourth.
तुरीयः, °या, °यं, *turîyaḥ, â, am,*	
तुर्यः, °र्या, °र्यं, *turyaḥ, â, am,*	
पंचमः, °मी, °मं, *pañchamaḥ, î, am,*	the fifth.
षष्ठः, °ष्ठी, °ष्ठं, *shashṭhaḥ, î, am,*	the sixth.
सप्तमः, °मी, °मं, *saptamaḥ, î, am,*	the seventh.
अष्टमः, °मी, °मं, *ashṭamaḥ, î, am,*	the eighth.
नवमः, °मी, °मं, *navamaḥ, î, am,*	the ninth.
दशमः, °मी, °मं, *daśamaḥ, î, am,*	the tenth.
एकादशः, °शी, °शं, *ekâdaśaḥ, î, am,*	the eleventh.
नवदशः, °शी, °शं, *navadaśaḥ, î, am,*	the nineteenth.
ऊनविंशः, °शी, °शं, *ûnaviṁśaḥ, î, am,*	
ऊनविंशतितमः, °मी, °मं, *ûnaviṁśatitamaḥ, î, am,*	
विंशः, °शी, °शं, *viṁśaḥ, î, am* (Pâṇ. v. 2, 56),	the twentieth.
विंशतितमः, °मी, °मं, *viṁśatitamaḥ, î, am,*	
त्रिंशः, °शी, °शं, *triṁśaḥ, î, am,*	the thirtieth.
त्रिंशत्तमः, °मी, °मं, *triṁśattamaḥ, î, am,*	
चत्वारिंशः, °शी, °शं, *chatvâriṁśaḥ, î, am,*	the fortieth.
चत्वारिंशत्तमः, °मी, °मं, *chatvâriṁśattamaḥ, î, am,*	
पंचाशः, °शी, °शं, *pañchâśaḥ, î, am,*	the fiftieth.
पंचाशत्तमः, °मी, °मं, *pañchâśattamaḥ, î, am,*	

षष्टितमः *shashṭitamaḥ*, the sixtieth*.

एकषष्टितमः *ekashashṭitamaḥ*,
एकषष्टः *ekashashṭaḥ*, } the sixty-first.

सप्ततितमः *saptatitamaḥ*, the seventieth.

एकसप्ततितमः *ekasaptatitamaḥ*,
एकसप्ततः *ekasaptataḥ*, } the seventy-first.

अशीतितमः *aśîtitamaḥ*, the eightieth.

एकाशीतितमः *ekâśîtitamaḥ*,
एकाशीतः *ekâśîtaḥ*, } the eighty-first.

नवतितमः, °मी, °मं, *navatitamaḥ, î, am*, the ninetieth.

एकनवतितमः *ekanavatitamaḥ*,
एकनवतः *ekanavataḥ*, } the ninety-first.

शततमः, °मी, °मं, *śatatamaḥ, î, am*, the hundredth. (Pâṇ. v. 2, 57.)

एकशततमः *ekaśatatamaḥ*, the hundred and first.

सहस्रतमः *sahasratamaḥ*, the thousandth.

§ 260. *Numerical Adverbs and other Derivatives.*

सकृत् *sakṛit*, once.	एकधा *ekadhâ*, in one way.
द्विः *dviḥ*, twice.	द्विधा *dvidhâ* or द्वेधा *dvedhâ*, in two ways.
त्रिः *triḥ*, thrice.	त्रिधा *tridhâ* or त्रेधा *tredhâ*, in three ways.
चतुः *chatuḥ*, four times.	चतुर्धा *chaturdhâ*, in four ways.
पंचकृत्वः *pañchakṛitvaḥ*, five times.	पंचधा *pañchadhâ*, in five ways.
षट्कृत्वः *shaṭkṛitvaḥ*, six times, &c.	षोढा *shoḍhâ*, in six ways, &c.

एकशः *ekaśaḥ*, one-fold.
द्विशः *dviśaḥ*, two-fold.
त्रिशः *triśaḥ*, three-fold, &c. (Pâṇ. v. 4, 43.)

द्वयं *dvayam* or द्वितयं *dvitayam*, a pair. (Pâṇ. v. 2, 42.)
त्रयं *trayam* or त्रितयं *tritayam* or त्रयी *trayî*, a triad.
चतुष्टयं *chatushṭayam*, a tetrad.
पंचतयं *pañchatayam*, a pentad, &c.

These are also used as adjectives, in the sense of five-fold &c., and may then form their plural as पंचतयाः *pañchatayâḥ* or पंचतये *pañchataye* (§ 283).

पंचत् *pañchat*, a pentad, दशत् *daśat*, a decad (Pâṇ. v. 1, 60), are generally used as feminine; but both words occur likewise as masculine in the commentary to Pâṇ. v. 1, 59, and in the Kâśikâ-Vṛitti.

* The ordinals from sixty admit of one form only, that is तमः *tamaḥ*; but if preceded by another numeral, both forms are allowed (Pâṇ. v. 2, 58). शतं *śatam* forms its ordinal as शततमः *śatatamaḥ* only (Pâṇ. v. 2, 57).

CHAPTER VI.

PRONOUNS AND PRONOMINAL ADJECTIVES.

§ 261. *Personal Pronouns.*

	Base (in composition) मद् *mad* and अस्मद् *asmad.*	Base (in composition) त्वद् *tvad* and युष्मद् *yushmad.*
	Singular.	
N.	अहं *aham*, I	त्वं *tvam*, thou
A.	मां *mâm*, मा *mâ*, me	त्वां *tvâm*, त्वा *tvá*, thee
I.	मया *mayá*, by me	त्वया *tvayá*, by thee
D.	मह्यं *mahyam*, मे *me*, to me	तुभ्यं *tubhyam*, ते *te*, to thee
Ab.	मत् *mat*, from me	त्वत् *tvat*, from thee
G.	मम *mama*, मे *me*, of me	तव *tava*, ते *te*, of thee
L.	मयि *mayi*, in me	त्वयि *tvayi*, in thee
	Dual.	
N.	आवां *ávám*, we two	युवां *yuvám*, you two
A.	आवां *ávâm*, नौ *nau*, us two	युवां *yuvám*, वौ *vau*, you two
I.	आवाभ्यां *ávábhyâm*, by us two	युवाभ्यां *yuvâbhyám*, by you two
D.	आवाभ्यां *âvâbhyám*, नौ *nau*, to us two	युवाभ्यां *yuvábhyâm*, वां *vám*, to you two
Ab.	आवाभ्यां *ávábhyám*, from us two	युवाभ्यां *yuvâbhyám*, from you two
G.	आवयोः *ávayoḥ*, नौ *nau*, of us two	युवयोः *yuvayoḥ*, वां *vám*, of you two
L.	आवयोः *ávayoḥ*, नौ *nau*, in us two	युवयोः *yuvayoḥ*, in you two
	Plural.	
N.	वयं *vayam*, we	यूयं *yûyam*, you
A.	अस्मान् *asmân*, नः *naḥ*, us	युष्मान् *yushmán*, वः *vaḥ*, you
I.	अस्माभिः *asmábhiḥ*, by us	युष्माभिः *yushmábhiḥ*, by you
D.	अस्मभ्यं *asmabhyam*, नः *naḥ*, to us	युष्मभ्यं *yushmabhyam*, वः *vaḥ*, to you
Ab.	अस्मत् *asmat*, from us	युष्मत् *yushmat*, from you
G.	अस्माकं *asmákam*, नः *naḥ*, of us	युष्माकं *yushmákam*, वः *vaḥ*, of you
L.	अस्मासु *asmâsu*, in us	युष्मासु *yushmâsu*, in you

The substitutes in the even cases, मा *mâ*, मे *me*, नौ *nau*, नः *naḥ*, त्वा *tvá*, ते *te*, वां *vám*, वः *vaḥ*, are never used at the beginning of a sentence, nor can they be followed by such particles as च *cha*, and, वा *vá*, or, एव *eva*, indeed, ह *ha*, अह *aha*.

§ 262. Base (in composition) तद् *tad*, he, she, it.

	SINGULAR. MASC.	FEM.	NEUT.	PLURAL. MASC.	FEM.	NEUT.
N.	सः *saḥ*	सा *sâ*	तत् *tat*	ते *te*	ताः *tâḥ*	तानि *tâni*
A.	तं *tam*	तां *tâm*	तत् *tat*	तान् *tân*	ताः *tâḥ*	तानि *tâni*
I.	तेन *tena*	तया *tayâ*	तेन *tena*	तैः *taiḥ*	ताभिः *tâbhiḥ*	तैः *taiḥ*
D.	तस्मै *tasmai*	तस्यै *tasyai*	तस्मै *tasmai*	तेभ्यः *tebhyaḥ*	ताभ्यः *tâbhyaḥ*	तेभ्यः *tebhyaḥ*
Ab.	तस्मात् *tasmât*	तस्याः *tasyâḥ*	तस्मात् *tasmât*	तेभ्यः *tebhyaḥ*	ताभ्यः *tâbhyaḥ*	तेभ्यः *tebhyaḥ*
G.	तस्य *tasya*	तस्याः *tasyâḥ*	तस्य *tasya*	तेषां *teshâm*	तासां *tâsâm*	तेषां *teshâm*
L.	तस्मिन् *tasmin*	तस्यां *tasyâm*	तस्मिन् *tasmin*	तेषु *teshu*	तासु *tâsu*	तेषु *teshu*

DUAL.

	MASC.	FEM.	NEUT.
N. A.	तौ *tau*	ते *te*	ते *te*
I. D. Ab.	ताभ्यां *tâbhyâm*	ताभ्यां *tâbhyâm*	ताभ्यां *tâbhyâm*
G. L.	तयोः *tayoḥ*	तयोः *tayoḥ*	तयोः *tayoḥ*

§ 263. Base (in composition) त्यद् *tyad*.

	SINGULAR. MASC.	FEM.	NEUT.	PLURAL. MASC.	FEM.	NEUT.
N.	स्यः *syaḥ*	स्या *syâ*	त्यत् *tyat*	त्ये *tye*	त्याः *tyâḥ*	त्यानि *tyâni*
A.	त्यं *tyam*	त्यां *tyâm*	त्यत् *tyat*	त्यान् *tyân*	त्याः *tyâḥ*	त्यानि *tyâni*
I.	त्येन *tyena*	त्यया *tyayâ*	त्येन *tyena*	त्यैः *tyaiḥ*	त्याभिः *tyâbhiḥ*	त्यैः *tyaiḥ*
D.	त्यस्मै *tyasmai*	त्यस्यै *tyasyai*	त्यस्मै *tyasmai*	त्येभ्यः *tyebhyaḥ*	त्याभ्यः *tyâbhyaḥ*	त्येभ्यः *tyebhyaḥ*
Ab.	त्यस्मात् *tyasmât*	त्यस्याः *tyasyâḥ*	त्यस्मात् *tyasmât*	त्येभ्यः *tyebhyaḥ*	त्याभ्यः *tyâbhyaḥ*	त्येभ्यः *tyebhyaḥ*
G.	त्यस्य *tyasya*	त्यस्याः *tyasyâḥ*	त्यस्य *tyasya*	त्येषां *tyeshâm*	त्यासां *tyâsâm*	त्येषां *tyeshâm*
L.	त्यस्मिन् *tyasmin*	त्यस्यां *tyasyâm*	त्यस्मिन् *tyasmin*	त्येषु *tyeshu*	त्यासु *tyâsu*	त्येषु *tyeshu*

DUAL.

	MASC.	FEM.	NEUT.
N. A.	त्यौ *tyau*	त्ये *tye*	त्ये *tye*
I. D. Ab.	त्याभ्यां *tyâbhyâm*	त्याभ्यां *tyâbhyâm*	त्याभ्यां *tyâbhyâm*
G. L.	त्ययोः *tyayoḥ*	त्ययोः *tyayoḥ*	त्ययोः *tyayoḥ*

Possessive Pronouns.

§ 264. From the bases of the three personal pronouns, possessive adjectives are formed by means of ईय *îya*.

मदीयः, °या, °यं, *madîyaḥ, yâ, yam*, mine.

त्वदीयः, °या, °यं, *tvadîyaḥ, yâ, yam*, thine.

तदीयः, °या, °यं, *tadîyaḥ, yâ, yam*, his, her, its.

अस्मदीयः, °या, °यं, *asmadîyaḥ, yâ, yam*, our.

युष्मदीयः, °या, °यं, *yushmadîyaḥ, yâ, yam*, your.

तदीयः, °या, °यं, *tadîyaḥ, yâ, yam*, their.

Other derivative possessive pronouns are मामकः* *mâmakaḥ*, mine; तावकः *tâvakaḥ*, thine; आस्माकः *âsmâkaḥ*, our; यौष्माकः *yaushmâkaḥ*, your. Likewise

* Pâṇ. IV. 3, 3; IV. 1, 30; VII. 3, 44.

मामकीनः *mâmakînaḥ*, mine; तावकीनः *tâvakînaḥ*, thine; आस्माकीनः *âsmâkînaḥ*, our; यौष्माकीणः *yaushmâkîṇaḥ*, your.

Reflexive Pronouns.

§ 265. स्वयं *svayam*, self, is indeclinable. स्वयं वृतवान् *svayam vṛitavân*, I chose it myself, thou chosest it thyself, he chose it himself; स्वयं वृतवती *svayam vṛitavatî*, she chose it herself; स्वयं वृतवन्तः *svayam vṛitavantaḥ*, we, you, they chose it by our, your, themselves.

§ 266. आत्मन् *âtman*, self, is declined like ब्रह्मन् *brahman* (§ 192). Ex. आत्मानमात्मना पश्य *âtmânam âtmanâ paśya*, see thyself by thyself, *gnosce te ipsum*; आत्मनो दोषं ज्ञात्वा *âtmano dosham jñâtvâ*, having known his own fault. It is used in the singular even when referring to two or three persons: आत्मनो देशमागम्य मृताः *âtmano deśamâgamya mṛitâḥ*, having returned to their country, they died.

§ 267. स्वः, स्वा, स्वं, *svaḥ*, *svâ*, *svam*, is a reflexive adjective, corresponding to Latin *suus*, *sua*, *suum*. स्वं पुत्रं दृष्ट्वा *svam putram dṛishṭvâ*, having seen his own son. On the declension of स्व *sva*, see § 278.

Demonstrative Pronouns.

§ 268. Base (in composition) एतद् *etad*, this (very near).

	SINGULAR.			PLURAL.		
	MASC.	FEM.	NEUT.	MASC.	FEM.	NEUT.
N.	एषः *eshaḥ*	एषा *eshâ*	एतत् *etat*	एते *ete*	एताः *etâḥ*	एतानि *etâni*
A.	एतं *etam*	एतां *etâm*	एतद् *etat*	एतान् *etân*	एताः *etâḥ*	एतानि *etâni*
I.	एतेन *etena*	एतया *etayâ*	एतेन *etena*	एतैः *etaiḥ*	एताभिः *etâbhiḥ*	एतैः *etaiḥ*
D.	एतस्मै *etasmai*	एतस्यै *etasyai*	एतस्मै *etasmai*	एतेभ्यः *etebhyaḥ*	एताभ्यः *etâbhyaḥ*	एतेभ्यः *etebhyaḥ*
Ab.	एतस्मात् *etasmât*	एतस्याः *etasyâḥ*	एतस्मात् *etasmât*	एतेभ्यः *etebhyaḥ*	एताभ्यः *etâbhyaḥ*	एतेभ्यः *etebhyaḥ*
G.	एतस्य *etasya*	एतस्याः *etasyâḥ*	एतस्य *etasya*	एतेषां *eteshâm*	एतासां *etâsâm*	एतेषां *eteshâm*
L.	एतस्मिन् *etasmin*	एतस्यां *etasyâm*	एतस्मिन् *etasmin*	एतेषु *eteshu*	एतासु *etâsu*	एतेषु *eteshu*

DUAL.

	MASC.	FEM.	NEUT.
N.A.	एतौ *etau*	एते *ete*	एते *ete*
I.D.Ab.	एताभ्यां *etâbhyâm*	एताभ्यां *etâbhyâm*	एताभ्यां *etâbhyâm*
G.L.	एतयोः *etayoḥ*	एतयोः *etayoḥ*	एतयोः *etayoḥ*

§ 269. Base (in composition) इदं *idam*, this (indefinitely).

	SINGULAR.			PLURAL.		
	MASC.	FEM.	NEUT.	MASC.	FEM.	NEUT.
N.	अयं *ayam*	इयं *iyam*	इदं *idam*	इमे *ime*	इमाः *imâḥ*	इमानि *imâni*
A.	इमं *imam*	इमां *imâm*	इदं *idam*	इमान् *imân*	इमाः *imâḥ*	इमानि *imâni*
I.	अनेन *anena*	अनया *anayâ*	अनेन *anena*	एभिः *ebhiḥ*	आभिः *âbhiḥ*	एभिः *ebhiḥ*
D.	अस्मै *asmai*	अस्यै *asyai*	अस्मै *asmai*	एभ्यः *ebhyaḥ*	आभ्यः *âbhyaḥ*	एभ्यः *ebhyaḥ*
Ab.	अस्मात् *asmât*	अस्याः *asyâḥ*	अस्मात् *asmât*	एभ्यः *ebhyaḥ*	आभ्यः *âbhyaḥ*	एभ्यः *ebhyaḥ*
G.	अस्य *asya*	अस्याः *asyâḥ*	अस्य *asya*	एषां *eshâm*	आसां *âsâm*	एषां *eshâm*
L.	अस्मिन् *asmin*	अस्यां *asyâm*	अस्मिन् *asmin*	एषु *eshu*	आसु *âsu*	एषु *eshu*

DUAL.

	MASC.	FEM.	NEUT.
N.A.V.	इमौ *imau*	इमे *ime*	इमे *ime*
I.D.Ab.	आभ्यां *âbhyâm*	आभ्यां *âbhyâm*	आभ्यां *âbhyâm*
G.L.	अनयोः *anayoḥ*	अनयोः *anayoḥ*	अनयोः *anayoḥ*

§ 270. एतद् *etad* and इदं *idam*, when repeated in a second sentence with reference to a preceding एतद् *etad* and इदं *idam*, vary in the following cases, by substituting एन *ena*.

SINGULAR. / PLURAL.

	MASC.	FEM.	NEUT.		MASC.	FEM.	NEUT.
A.	एनं *enam*	एनां *enâm*	एनत् *enat*	A.	एनान् *enân*	एनाः *enâḥ*	एनानि *enâni*
I.	एनेन *enena*	एनया *enayâ*	एनेन *enena*				

DUAL.

	MASC.	FEM.	NEUT.
A.	एनौ *enau*	एने *ene*	एने *ene*
G.L.	एनयोः *enayoḥ*	एनयोः *enayoḥ*	एनयोः *enayoḥ*

Ex. अनेन व्याकरणमधीतं एनं छंदोऽध्यापय *anena vyâkaraṇam adhîtam, enam chhando 'dhyâpaya*, the grammar has been studied by this person, teach him prosody.

अनयोः पवित्रं कुलं एनयोः प्रभूतं स्वं *anayoḥ pavitram kulam, enayoḥ prabhûtam svam*, the family of these two persons is decent, and their wealth vast.

§ 271. Base (in composition) अदस् *adas*, that (mediate).

SINGULAR.

	MASC.	FEM.	NEUT.
N.	असौ *asau*	असौ *asau*	अदः *adaḥ*
A.	अमुं *amum*	अमूं *amûm*	अदः *adaḥ*
I.	अमुना *amunâ*	अमुया *amuyâ*	अमुना *amunâ*
D.	अमुष्मै *amushmai*	अमुष्यै *amushyai*	अमुष्मै *amushmai*
Ab.	अमुष्मात् *amushmât*	अमुष्याः *amushyâḥ*	अमुष्मात् *amushmât*
G.	अमुष्य *amushya*	अमुष्याः *amushyâḥ*	अमुष्य *amushya*
L.	अमुष्मिन् *amushmin*	अमुष्यां *amushyâm*	अमुष्मिन् *amushmin*

PLURAL.

	MASC.	FEM.	NEUT.
N.	अमी *amî*	अमूः *amûḥ*	अमूनि *amûni*
A.	अमून् *amûn*	अमूः *amûḥ*	अमूनि *amûni*
I.	अमीभिः *amîbhiḥ*	अमूभिः *amûbhiḥ*	अमीभिः *amîbhiḥ*
D.Ab.	अमीभ्यः *amîbhyaḥ*	अमूभ्यः *amûbhyaḥ*	अमीभ्यः *amîbhyaḥ*
G.	अमीषां *amîshâm*	अमूषां *amûshâm*	अमीषां *amîshâm*
L.	अमीषु *amîshu*	अमूषु *amûshu*	अमीषु *amîshu*

DUAL.

MASC. FEM. NEUT.

N.A.V. अमू *amû* I.D.Ab. अमूभ्यां *amûbhyâm* G.L. अमुयोः *amuyoḥ*

Relative Pronoun.

§ 272. Base (in composition) यद् *yad*, who or which.

	SINGULAR.			PLURAL.		
	MASC.	FEM.	NEUT.	MASC.	FEM.	NEUT.
N.	यः *yaḥ*	या *yá*	यत् *yat*	ये *ye*	याः *yáḥ*	यानि *yáni*
A.	यं *yam*	यां *yám*	यत् *yat*	यान् *yán*	याः *yáḥ*	यानि *yáni*
I.	येन *yena*	यया *yayá*	येन *yena*	यैः *yaiḥ*	याभिः *yábhiḥ*	यैः *yaiḥ*
D.	यस्मै *yasmai*	यस्यै *yasyai*	यस्मै *yasmai*	येभ्यः *yebhyaḥ*	याभ्यः *yábhyaḥ*	येभ्यः *yebhyaḥ*
Ab.	यस्मात् *yasmát*	यस्याः *yasyáḥ*	यस्मात् *yasmát*	येभ्यः *yebhyaḥ*	याभ्यः *yábhyaḥ*	येभ्यः *yebhyaḥ*
G.	यस्य *yasya*	यस्याः *yasyáḥ*	यस्य *yasya*	येषां *yeshám*	यासां *yásám*	येषां *yeshám*
L.	यस्मिन् *yasmin*	यस्यां *yasyám*	यस्मिन् *yasmin*	येषु *yeshu*	यासु *yásu*	येषु *yeshu*

	DUAL.		
	MASC.	FEM.	NEUT.
N. A. V.	यौ *yau*	ये *ye*	ये *ye*
I. D. Ab.	याभ्यां *yábhyám*	याभ्यां *yábhyám*	याभ्यां *yábhyám*
G. L.	ययोः *yayoḥ*	ययोः *yayoḥ*	ययोः *yayoḥ*

Interrogative Pronouns.

§ 273. Base (in composition) किं *kim*, Who or which?

	SINGULAR.			PLURAL.		
	MASC.	FEM.	NEUT.	MASC.	FEM.	NEUT.
N.	कः *kaḥ*	का *ká*	किं *kim*	के *ke*	काः *káḥ*	कानि *káni*
A.	कं *kam*	कां *kám*	किं *kim*	कान् *kán*	काः *káḥ*	कानि *káni*
I.	केन *kena*	कया *kayá*	केन *kena*	कैः *kaiḥ*	काभिः *kábhiḥ*	कैः *kaiḥ*
D.	कस्मै *kasmai*	कस्यै *kasyai*	कस्मै *kasmai*	केभ्यः *kebhyaḥ*	काभ्यः *kábhyaḥ*	केभ्यः *kebhyaḥ*
Ab.	कस्मात् *kasmát*	कस्याः *kasyáḥ*	कस्मात् *kasmát*	केभ्यः *kebhyaḥ*	काभ्यः *kábhyaḥ*	केभ्यः *kebhyaḥ*
G.	कस्य *kasya*	कस्याः *kasyáḥ*	कस्य *kasya*	केषां *keshám*	कासां *kásám*	केषां *keshám*
L.	कस्मिन् *kasmin*	कस्यां *kasyám*	कस्मिन् *kasmin*	केषु *keshu*	कासु *kásu*	केषु *keshu*

	DUAL.		
	MASC.	FEM.	NEUT.
N. A.	कौ *kau*	के *ke*	के *ke*
I. D. Ab.	काभ्यां *kábhyám*	काभ्यां *kábhyám*	काभ्यां *kábhyám*
G. L.	कयोः *kayoḥ*	कयोः *kayoḥ*	कयोः *kayoḥ*

§ 274. Pronouns admit the interposition of अक् *ak* before their last vowel or syllable, to denote contempt or dubious relation (Pâṇ. v. 3, 71). त्वयका *tvayaká*, By thee! instead of त्वया *tvayá*. युवकयोः *yuvakayoḥ*, Of you two! अस्मकाभिः *asmakábhiḥ*, With us! अयकं *ayakam*. असकौ *asakau*, &c. (See Siddh.-Kaum. I. p. 706.)

Compound Pronouns.

§ 275. By adding दृश् *driś*, दृश *driśa*, or दृक्ष *driksha*, to certain pronominal bases, the following compound pronouns have been formed:

तादृश् *tâdriś*, तादृश *tâdriśa*, तादृक्ष *tâdriksha*, such like.
एतादृश् *etâdriś*, एतादृश *etâdriśa*, एतादृक्ष *etâdriksha*, this like.
यादृश् *yâdriś*, यादृश *yâdriśa*, यादृक्ष *yâdriksha*, what like.
ईदृश् *îdriś*, ईदृश *îdriśa*, ईदृक्ष *îdriksha*, this like.
कीदृश् *kîdriś*, कीदृश *kîdriśa*, कीदृक्ष *kîdriksha*, What like?

These are declined in three genders, forming the feminine in ई *î*. तादृक् *tâdrik*, m. n.; तादृशी *tâdriśî*, f.; or तादृशः, °शी, °शं, *tâdriśaḥ, î, am.* Similarly formed are मादृश *mâdriśa*, त्वादृश *tvâdriśa*, like me, like thee, &c.

§ 276. By adding वत् *vat* and यत् *yat* to certain pronominal bases, the following compound pronouns, implying quantity, have been formed:

तावत् *tâvat*, so much, एतावत् *etâvat*, so much, यावत् *yâvat*, as much,	declined like nouns in वत् *vat* (§ 187).
इयत् *iyat*, so much, कियत् *kiyat*, How much?	इयान् *iyân*, इयती *iyatî*, इयत् *iyat*.

Note—On the declension of कति *kati*, How many? तति *tati*, so many, and यति *yati*, as many, see § 231.

§ 277. By adding चित् *chit*, चन *chana*, or अपि *api*, to the interrogative pronoun किम् *kim*, it is changed into an indefinite pronoun.

कश्चित् *kaśchit*, काचित् *kâchit*, किंचित् *kiṁchit*, some one; also कच्चित् *kachchit*, anything.
कश्चन *kaśchana*, काचन *kâchana*, किंचन *kiṁchana*, some one.
कोऽपि *ko 'pi*, कापि *kâpi*, किमपि *kimapi*, some one.

In the same manner indefinite adverbs are formed: कदा *kadâ*, When? कदाचित् *kadâchit*, कदाचन *kadâchana*, once; क्व *kva*, Where? न क्वापि *na kvâpi*, not anywhere.

Sometimes the relative pronoun is prefixed to the interrogative, to render it indefinite: यः कः *yaḥ kaḥ*, whosoever; यस्य कस्य *yasya kasya*, whosesoever. Likewise यः कश्चित् *yaḥ kaśchit*, whosoever, or यः कश्च *yaḥ kaścha*, or यः कश्चन *yaḥ kaśchana*.

The relative pronoun, if doubled, assumes an indefinite or rather distributive meaning: यो यः, या या, यद्यद्, *yo yaḥ, yâ yâ, yad yad*, whosoever. Occasionally the relative and demonstrative pronouns are combined for the same purpose: यत्तद् *yattad*, whatsoever.

Pronominal Adjectives.

§ 278. Under the name of *Sarvanâman*, which has been freely translated by Pronoun, but which really means a class of words beginning with *sarva*, native grammarians have included, besides the real pronouns mentioned before, the following words which share in common with the real pronouns certain peculiarities of declension. They may be called Pronominal Adjectives, and it is to be remembered that they are affected by these peculiarities of declension only if they are used in certain senses.

1. सर्व *sarva*, all; 2. विश्व *viśva*, all; 3. उभ *ubha*, two; 4. उभय *ubhaya*, both; 5. अन्य *anya*, other; 6. अन्यतर *anyatara*, either; 7. इतर *itara*, other; 8. त्व *tva*, other (some add त्वद् *tvad*, other); 9. words formed by the suffixes तर *tara* and तम *tama*, such as 9. कतर *katara*, Which of two? 10. कतम *katama*, Which of many? 10. सम *sama*, all; 11. सिम *sima*, whole; 12. नेम *nema*, half; 13. एक *eka*, one; 14. पूर्व *pûrva*, east or prior; 15. पर *para*, subsequent; 16. अवर *avara*, west or posterior; 17. दक्षिण *dakshiṇa*, south or right; 18. उत्तर *uttara*, north or subsequent; 19. अपर *apara*, other or inferior; 20. अधर *adhara*, west or inferior; 21. स्व *sva*, own; 22. अन्तर *antara*, outer, (except अन्तरा पूः *antarâ pûḥ*, suburb,) or lower (scil. garment).

If सम *sama* means equal or even, it is not a pronominal adjective; nor दक्षिण *dakshiṇa*, if it means clever; nor स्व *sva*, if it means kinsman or wealth; nor अन्तर *antara*, if it means interval, &c.; nor any of the seven from पूर्व *pûrva* to अवर *avara*, unless they imply a relation in time or space. Hence दक्षिणा गाथकाः *dakshiṇâ gâthakâḥ*, clever minstrels; उत्तराः कुरवः *uttarâḥ kuravaḥ*, the northern Kurus, (a proper name); प्रभूताः स्वाः *prabhûtâḥ svâḥ*, great treasures (Kâś. 1. 1, 35); ग्रामयोरन्तरे वसति *grâmayor antare vasati*, he lives between the two villages.

MASCULINE.

	SINGULAR.	DUAL.	PLURAL.
N.	सर्वः *sarvaḥ*	सर्वौ *sarvau*	सर्वे *sarve*
A.	सर्वं *sarvam*	सर्वौ *sarvau*	सर्वान् *sarvân*
I.	सर्वेण *sarveṇa*	सर्वाभ्यां *sarvâbhyâm*	सर्वैः *sarvaiḥ*
D.	सर्वस्मै *sarvasmai*	सर्वाभ्यां *sarvâbhyâm*	सर्वेभ्यः *sarvebhyaḥ*
Ab.	सर्वस्मात् *sarvasmât*	सर्वाभ्यां *sarvâbhyâm*	सर्वेभ्यः *sarvebhyaḥ*
G.	सर्वस्य *sarvasya*	सर्वयोः *sarvayoḥ*	सर्वेषां *sarveshâm*
L.	सर्वस्मिन् *sarvasmin*	सर्वयोः *sarvayoḥ*	सर्वेषु *sarveshu*
V.	सर्व *sarva*	सर्वौ *sarvau*	सर्वे *sarve*

FEMININE.

	SINGULAR.	DUAL.	PLURAL.
N.	सर्वा *sarvâ*	सर्वे *sarve*	सर्वाः *sarvâḥ*
A.	सर्वां *sarvâm*	सर्वे *sarve*	सर्वाः *sarvâḥ*
I.	सर्वया *sarvayâ*	सर्वाभ्यां *sarvâbhyâm*	सर्वाभिः *sarvâbhiḥ*
D.	सर्वस्यै *sarvasyai*	सर्वाभ्यां *sarvâbhyâm*	सर्वाभ्यः *sarvâbhyaḥ*

Ab.	सर्वस्याः *sarvasyâḥ*	सर्वाभ्यां *sarvâbhyâm*	सर्वाभ्यः *sarvâbhyaḥ*
G.	सर्वस्याः *sarvasyâḥ*	सर्वयोः *sarvayoḥ*	सर्वासां *sarvâsâm*
L.	सर्वस्यां *sarvasyâm*	सर्वयोः *sarvayoḥ*	सर्वासु *sarvâsu*

NEUTER.

	SINGULAR.	DUAL.	PLURAL.
N.A.V.	सर्वं *sarvam*	सर्वे *sarve*	सर्वाणि *sarvâṇi*

The rest like the masculine.

§ 279. अन्य *anya*, अन्यतर *anyatara*, इतर *itara*, कतर *katara*, कतम *katama*, take त् *t* in the Nom. Acc. Voc. Sing. of the neuter:

Nom. Sing. अन्यः *anyaḥ*, masc.; अन्या *anyâ*, fem.; अन्यत् *anyat*, neut.

§ 280. उभ *ubha* is used in the Dual only:

Masc. N. A. V. उभौ *ubhau*, I. D. Ab. उभाभ्यां *ubhâbhyâm*, G. L. उभयोः *ubhayoḥ*; उभे *ubhe*, N. A. V. fem. and neut.

§ 281. उभयः *ubhayaḥ*, °या *-yâ*, °यं *-yam*, is never used in the Dual, but only in the Sing. and Plur. Haradatta admits the Dual.

MASCULINE.

	SINGULAR.		PLURAL.
N.	उभयः *ubhayaḥ*	——	उभये *ubhaye*
A.	उभयं *ubhayam*		उभयान् *ubhayân*
I.	उभयेन *ubhayena*		उभयैः *ubhayaiḥ*
D.	उभयस्मै *ubhayasmai*, &c.		उभयेभ्यः *ubhayebhyaḥ*, &c.

§ 282. The nine words from पूर्व *pûrva* to अंतर *antara* (14 to 22), though used in their pronominal senses, may take in the Nom. Plur. ए *e* or अः *aḥ*; in the Abl. Sing. स्मात् *smât* or आत् *at*; in the Loc. Sing. स्मिन् *smin* or इ *i*.

	SINGULAR.	DUAL.	PLURAL.
N.	पूर्वः *pûrvaḥ*	पूर्वौ *pûrvau*	पूर्वे *pûrve* or पूर्वाः *pûrvâḥ*
A.	पूर्वं *pûrvam*	पूर्वौ *pûrvau*	पूर्वान् *pûrvân*
I.	पूर्वेण *pûrveṇa*	पूर्वाभ्यां *pûrvâbhyâm*	पूर्वैः *pûrvaiḥ*
D.	पूर्वस्मै *pûrvasmai*	पूर्वाभ्यां *pûrvâbhyâm*	पूर्वेभ्यः *pûrvebhyaḥ*
Ab.	पूर्वस्मात् *pûrvasmât* or पूर्वात् *pûrvât*	पूर्वाभ्यां *pûrvâbhyâm*	पूर्वेभ्यः *pûrvebhyaḥ*
G.	पूर्वस्य *pûrvasya*	पूर्वयोः *pûrvayoḥ*	पूर्वेषां *pûrveshâm*
L.	पूर्वस्मिन् *pûrvasmin* or पूर्वे *pûrve*	पूर्वयोः *pûrvayoḥ*	पूर्वेषु *pûrveshu*

§ 283. The following words may likewise take अः *aḥ* or ए *e* in the Nom. Plur. masc. (Pâṇ. I. 1, 33.)

प्रथमः *prathamaḥ*, first, प्रथमौ *prathamau*, प्रथमे *prathame* or प्रथमाः *prathamâḥ*; fem. प्रथमा *prathamâ*.

चरमः *charamaḥ*, last, चरमौ *charamau*, चरमे *charame* or चरमाः *charamâḥ*.

द्वितयः *dvitayaḥ*, two-fold, fem. द्वितयी *dvitayî*, and similar words in तय *taya*; त्रितयः *tritayaḥ*, three-fold; त्रितये *tritaye* or त्रितयाः *tritayâḥ*.

द्वयः *dvayaḥ*, two-fold, fem. द्वयी *dvayî*, and similar words in य *ya*; त्रयः *trayaḥ*.

अल्पः *alpaḥ*, few, अल्पे *alpe* or अल्पाः *alpâḥ*.

अर्धः *ardhaḥ*, half, अर्धे *ardhe* or अर्धाः *ardhâḥ*.

कतिपयः *katipayaḥ*, some, कतिपये *katipaye* or कतिपयाः *katipayâḥ*.

नेमः *nemaḥ*, half, नेमे *neme* or नेमाः *nemâḥ*.

In all other cases these words are regular, like कान्तः *kântaḥ*.

§ 284. द्वितीयः *dvitîyaḥ* and other words in तीय *tîya* are declined like कान्त *kânta*, but in the Dat. Abl. and Loc. Sing. they may follow सर्व *sarva*.

MASCULINE.

	SINGULAR.	DUAL.	PLURAL.
N.	द्वितीयः *dvitîyaḥ*	द्वितीयौ *dvitîyau*	द्वितीयाः *dvitîyâḥ*
A.	द्वितीयं *dvitîyam*	द्वितीयौ *dvitîyau*	द्वितीयान् *dvitîyân*
I.	द्वितीयेन *dvitîyena*	द्वितीयाभ्यां *dvitîyâbhyâm*	द्वितीयैः *dvitîyaiḥ*
D.	द्वितीयाय *dvitîyâya* or द्वितीयस्मै *dvitîyasmai*	द्वितीयाभ्यां *dvitîyâbhyâm*	द्वितीयेभ्यः *dvitîyebhyaḥ*
Ab.	द्वितीयात् *dvitîyât* or द्वितीयस्मात् *dvitîyasmât*	द्वितीयाभ्यां *dvitîyâbhyâm*	द्वितीयेभ्यः *dvitîyebhyaḥ*
G.	द्वितीयस्य *dvitîyasya*	द्वितीययोः *dvitîyayoḥ*	द्वितीयानां *dvitîyânâm*
L.	द्वितीये *dvitîye* or द्वितीयस्मिन् *dvitîyasmin*	द्वितीययोः *dvitîyayoḥ*	द्वितीयेषु *dvitîyeshu*

At the end of Bahuvrihi compounds the Sarvanâman's are treated like ordinary words: Dat. Sing. प्रियोभयाय *priyobhayâya*, to him to whom both are dear (Pâṇ. I. 1, 29). The same at the end of compounds such as मासपूर्वः *mâsapûrvaḥ*, a month earlier; Dat. मासपूर्वाय *mâsapûrvâya* (Pâṇ. I. 1, 30). Likewise in Dvandvas; पूर्वापराणां *pûrvâparâṇâm*, of former and later persons (Pâṇ. I. 1, 31), though in the Nom. Plur. these Dvandvas may take ए *e*; पूर्वापरे *pûrvâpare* or पूर्वापराः *pûrvâparâḥ*. Only in compounds expressive of points of the compass, such as उत्तरपूर्व *uttara-pûrva*, north-east, the last element may throughout take the pronominal terminations (Pâṇ. I. 1, 28).

Adverbial Declension.

§ 285. In addition to the regular case-terminations by which the declension of nouns is effected, the Sanskrit language possesses other suffixes which differ from the ordinary terminations chiefly by being restricted in their use to certain words, and particularly to pronominal bases. The ordinary case-terminations, too, are frequently used in an adverbial sense. Thus

Acc. चिरं *chiram*, a long time.
Instr. चिरेण *chireṇa*, in a long time.
Dat. चिराय *chirâya*, for a long time.
Abl. चिरात् *chirât*, long ago.
Gen. चिरस्य *chirasya*, a long time.
Loc. चिरे *chire*, long.

Other adverbial terminations are,

1. तः *taḥ*, with an ablative meaning, becoming generally local.
2. त्र *tra*, with a locative meaning.
3. दा *dâ*, with a temporal meaning; also raised to दानीं *dânîm*.

4. तात् *tât*, with a locative meaning.

5. था *thâ*, with a meaning of modality; likewise थं *tham* and थ *tha*.

6. सात् *sât*, expressive of effect.

7. आ *â* and आहि *âhi*, local.

8. र्हि *rhi*, temporal and causal.

9. तर् *tar*, local.

10. ह *ha*, local.

See also the terminations for forming numeral adverbs (§ 260).

1. तः *taḥ*, with an ablative meaning.

ततः *tataḥ*, thence. यतः *yataḥ*, whence. इतः *itaḥ*, hence; (cf. इति *iti*, thus, इव *iva*, as.) अतः *ataḥ*, hence. कुतः *kutaḥ*, Whence? अमुतः *amutaḥ*, thence. मत्तः *mattaḥ*, from me. अस्मत्तः *asmattaḥ*, from us. भवत्तः *bhavattaḥ*, from your Honour. पूर्वतः *pûrvataḥ*, before (in a general local or temporal sense). सर्वतः *sarvataḥ*, always. अग्रतः *agrataḥ*, before, like अग्रे *agre*. अभितः *abhitaḥ*, around, near. उभयतः *ubhayataḥ*, on both sides. परितः *paritaḥ*, all round. ग्रामतः *grâmataḥ*, from the village. अज्ञानतः *ajñânataḥ*, from ignorance.

2. त्र *tra*, locative; originally त्रा *trâ*, as in पुरुषत्रा *purushatrâ*, amongst men.

तत्र *tatra*, there. यत्र *yatra*, where. कुत्र *kutra*, Where? अत्र *atra*, here. अमुत्र *amutra*, there, in the next world. एकत्र *ekatra*, at one place, together. सत्रा *satrâ*, with, and सत्रं *satram*, with (see सह *saha*).

3. दा *dâ*, temporal.

तदा *tadâ*, then, and तदानीं *tadânîm*. यदा *yadâ*, when. कदा *kadâ*, When? अन्यदा *anyadâ*, another time. सर्वदा *sarvadâ*, always, at all times. एकदा *ekadâ*, at one time. सदा *sadâ*, always. इदा *idâ*, in the Veda, later इदानीं *idânîm*, now.

4. तात् *tât*, local.

प्राक्तात् *prâktât*, in front.

Frequently after a base in स् *s*:

पुरस्तात् *purastât*, before. अधरस्तात् *adharastât*, below. परस्तात् *parastât*, afterwards. अधस्तात् *adhastât*, below. उपरिष्टात् *uparishṭât*, above.

5. था *thâ*, modal.

तथा *tathâ*, thus. यथा *yathâ*, as. सर्वथा *sarvathâ*, in every way. उभयथा *ubhayathâ*, in both ways. अन्यथा *anyathâ*, in another way. अन्यतरथा *anyatarathâ*, in one of two ways. इतरथा *itarathâ*, in the other way. वृथा *vṛithâ*, vainly (?). Or थं *tham*, in कथं *katham*, How? इत्थं *ittham*, thus. Or थ *tha*, in अथ *atha*, thus.

6. सात् *sât*, effective.

राजसात् *râjasât*, (राज्ञोऽधीनं *râjño 'dhînam*, dependent on the king.) भस्मसात् *bhasmasât*, reduced to ashes. अग्निसात् *agnisât*, reduced to fire.

7. आ *á* and आहि *áhi*, local.

दक्षिणाहि *dakshiṇáhi*, in the South, or दक्षिणा *dakshiṇá*. उत्तराहि *uttaráhi*, in the North, or उत्तरा *uttará*. अंतरा *antará* (or °रं *-ram*, or °रे *-re*, or °रेण *-reṇa*), between. पुरा *purá*, in the East, in front, formerly, (or पुरः *puraḥ* and पुरस्तात् *purastát*, before.) पश्चा *paśchá*, behind, (or पश्चात् *paśchát*.)

Adverbs such as मुधा *mudhá*, in vain, मृषा *mṛishá*, falsely, are instrumental cases of obsolete nouns ending in consonants.

8. र्हि *rhi*, temporal and causal.

एतर्हि *etarhi*, at this time, (Wilson.) कर्हि *karhi*, At what time? यर्हि *yarhi*, wherefore. तर्हि *tarhi*, therefore, at that time, (Wilson.)

9. तर् *tar*, local.

प्रातर् *prátar*, early, in the morning. सनुतर् *sanutar*, in concealment.

10. ह *ha*, locative.

कुह *kuha*, Where? इह *iha*, here. सह *saha*, with.

CHAPTER VII.

CONJUGATION.

§ 286. Sanskrit verbs are conjugated in the Active and the Passive. Ex. बोधति *bodhati*, he knows; बुध्यते *budhyate*, he is known.

§ 287. The Active has two forms:

1. The *Parasmai-pada*, i. e. transitive, (from परस्मै *parasmai*, Dat. Sing. of पर *para*, another, i. e. a verb the action of which refers to another.) Ex. ददाति *dadáti*, he gives.

2. The *Átmane-pada*, i. e. intransitive, (from आत्मने *átmane*, Dat. Sing. of आत्मन् *átman*, self, i. e. a verb the action of which refers to the agent.) Ex. आदत्ते *ádatte*, he takes.

Note—The distinction between the Parasmaipada and Átmanepada is fixed by usage rather than by rule. Certain verbs in Sanskrit are used in the Parasmaipada only, others in the Átmanepada only; others in both voices. Those which are used in the Parasmaipada only, are verbs the action of which was originally conceived as transitive; e. g. भूमिं मंथति *bhúmim manthati*, he shakes the earth; मांसं खादति *mánsam khádati*, he eats meat; ग्राममटति *grámam atati*, he goes to or approaches the village. Those which are used in the Átmanepada only, were originally verbs expressive of states rather than of actions; e. g. एधते *edhate*, he grows; स्पंदते *spandate*, he trembles; मोदते *modate*, he rejoices; शेते *śete*, he lies down.

In the language of the best authors, however, many verbs which we should consider intransitive, are conjugated in the Parasmaipada, while others which govern an accusative, are always conjugated in the Âtmanepada. हसति *hasati*, he laughs, is always Parasmaipadin, whether used as transitive or neuter (Colebr. p. 297): it is so even when reciprocity of action is indicated, in which case verbs in Sanskrit mostly take the Âtmanepada; e.g. व्यतिहसन्ति *vyatihasanti*, they laugh at each other (Pâṇ. 1. 3, 15, 1). But स्मयते *smayate*, he smiles, is restricted by grammarians to the Âtmanepada; and verbs like त्रायते *trâyate*, he protects, are Âtmanepadin (i. e. used in the Âtmanepada), though they govern an accusative; e.g. त्रायस्व मां *trâyasva mâm*, Protect me! These correspond to the Latin deponents.

Verbs which are used both in the Parasmaipada and Âtmanepada, take the one or the other form according as the action of the verb is conceived to be either transitive or reflective; e.g. पचति *pachati*, he cooks; पचते *pachate*, he cooks for himself; यजति *yajati*, he sacrifices; यजते *yajate*, he sacrifices for himself. The same applies to Causals (Pâṇ. 1. 3, 74).

These distinctions, however, rest in many cases, in Sanskrit as well as in Greek, on peculiar conceptions which it is difficult to analyse or to realize; and in Sanskrit as well as in Greek, the right use of the active and middle voices is best learnt by practice. Thus नी *nî*, to lead, is used as Parasmaipada in such expressions as गण्डं विनयति *gaṇḍam vinayati* *, he carries off a swelling; but as Âtmanepada, in क्रोधं विनयते *krodham vinayate*, he turns away or dismisses wrath; a subtle distinction which it is possible to appreciate when stated, but difficult to bring under any general rules.

Again, in Sanskrit as well as in Greek, some verbs are middle in certain tenses only, but active or middle in others; e.g. Âtm. वर्धते *vardhate*, he grows, never वर्धति *vardhati*; but Aor. अवृधत् *avṛidhat*, Par., or अवर्धिष्ट *avardhishṭa*, Âtm. he grew. (Pâṇ. 1. 3, 91.)

Others take the Parasmaipada or Âtmanepada according as they are compounded with certain prepositions; e.g. विशति *viśati*, he enters; but निविशते *ni-viśate*, he enters in. (Pâṇ. 1. 3, 17.)

§ 288. Causal verbs are conjugated both in the Parasmaipada and Âtmanepada. Desideratives generally follow the Pada of the simple root (Pâṇ. 1. 3, 62). Denominatives ending in आय *âya* have both forms (Pâṇ. 1. 3, 90). The intensives have two forms: one in य *ya*, which is always Âtmanepada; the other without य *ya*, which is always Parasmaipada.

§ 289. The passive takes the terminations of the Âtmanepada, and prefixes य *ya* to them in the four special or modified tenses. In the other tenses the forms of the passive are, with a few exceptions, the same as those of the Âtmanepada.

§ 290. There are in Sanskrit thirteen different forms, corresponding to the tenses and moods of Greek and Latin.

I. *Formed from the Special or Modified Base.*

	PARASMAIPADA.	ÂTMANEPADA.
1. The Present (Laṭ)	भवामि *bhavâmi*	भवे *bhave*
2. The Imperfect (Laṅ)	अभवं *abhavam*	अभवे *abhave*
3. The Optative (Liṅ)	भवेयं *bhaveyam*	भवेय *bhaveya*
4. The Imperative (Loṭ)	भवानि *bhavâni*	भवै *bhavai*

* Cf. Siddhânta-Kaumudî, ed. Târânâtha, vol. II. p. 250. Colebrooke, Grammar, p. 337.

II. *Formed from the General or Unmodified Base.*

	Parasmaipada.	Âtmanepada.
5. The Reduplicated Perfect (Liṭ)	बभूव *babhûva*	बभूवे *babhûve*
6. The Periphrastic Perfect (Liṭ)	चोरयां बभूव *chorayâm babhûva*	चोरयां चक्रे *chorayâm chakre*
7. The First Aorist (Luṅ)	अबोधिषं *abodhisham*	अभविषि *abhavishi*
8. The Second Aorist (Luṅ)	अभूवं *abhûvam*	असिचे *asiche*
9. The Future (Lṛiṭ)	भविष्यामि *bhavishyâmi*	भविष्ये *bhavishye*
10. The Conditional (Lṛiṅ)	अभविष्यं *abhavishyam*	अभविष्ये *abhavishye*
11. The Periphrastic Future (Luṭ)	भवितास्मि *bhavitâsmi*	भविताहे *bhavitâhe*
12. The Benedictive (Âśir liṅ)	भूयासं *bhûyâsam*	भविषीय *bhavishîya*

13. The Subjunctive (Leṭ) occurs in the Veda only.

Signification of the Tenses and Moods.

§ 291. 1. 2. The Present and Imperfect require no explanation. The Imperfect takes the Augment (§ 299).

3. The principal senses of the Optative are,

a. Command; e.g. त्वं ग्रामं गच्छेः *tvam grâmam gachchheḥ*, thou mayest go, i.e. go thou to the village.

b. Wish; e.g. भवानिहासीत *bhavân ihâsîta*, Let your honour sit here!

c. Inquiring; e.g. वेदमधीयीय उत तर्कमधीयीय *vedam adhîyîya, uta tarkam adhîyîya*, Shall I study the Veda or shall I study logic?

d. Supposition (*sambhâvana*); e.g. भवेदसौ वेदपारगो ब्राह्मणत्वात् *bhaved asau vedapârago brâhmaṇatvât*, he probably is a student of the Veda, because he is a Brâhman.

e. Condition; e.g. दंडश्चेन्न भवेल्लोके विनश्येयुरिमाः प्रजाः *daṇḍaś chen na bhavel loke vinaśyeyur imâḥ prajâḥ*, if there were not punishment in the world, the people would perish. यः पठेत् स आप्नुयात् *yaḥ paṭhet sa âpnuyât*, he who studies, will obtain. यद्यद्रोचेत विप्रेभ्यस्तत्तद्दद्यादमत्सरः *yad yad rocheta viprebhyas tat tad dadyâd amatsaraḥ*, whatever pleases the Brâhmans let one give that to them not niggardly.

f. It is used in relative dependent sentences; e.g. यच्च त्वमेवं कुर्या न श्रद्दधे *yach cha tvam evam kuryâ na śraddadhe*, I believed not that thou couldst act thus. यत्तादृशाः कृष्णं निन्देरन्नाश्चर्यं *yat tâdṛiśâḥ kṛishṇam ninderann âścharyam*, that such persons should revile Kṛishṇa, is wonderful.

4. The Imperative requires no explanation, as far as the second person is concerned; e.g. तुद *tuda*, Strike! The first and third persons are used in many cases in place of the Optative; e.g. इच्छामि भवान्भुङ्क्तां *ichchhâmi bhavân bhuṅktâm*, I wish your honour may eat.

5. The Reduplicated Perfect denotes something absolutely past.

6. Certain verbs which are not allowed to form the reduplicated perfect, form their perfect periphrastically, i. e. by means of an auxiliary verb.

7. 8. The First and Second Aorists refer generally to time past, and are the common historical tenses in narration. They take the Augment (§ 299).

9. The Future, also called the Indefinite future; e. g. देवश्चेद्वर्षिष्यति धान्यं वप्स्यामः *devaś ched varshishyati dhânyam vapsyâmaḥ*, if it rain, we shall sow rice. यावज्जीवमन्नं दास्यति *yávaj-jívam annam dásyati*, as long as life lasts, he will give food. Under certain circumstances this Future may be used optionally with the Periphrastic Future; e. g. कदा भोक्ता *kadâ bhoktá* or भोक्ष्यते *bhokshyate*, When will he eat?

10. The Conditional is used, instead of the Optative, if things are spoken of that might have, but have not happened (Pâṇ. III. 3, 139); e. g. सुवृष्टिश्चेदभविष्यत्तदा सुभिक्षमभविष्यत् *suvṛishṭiś ched abhavishyat tadá subhiksham abhavishyat*, if there had been abundant rain, there would have been plenty. The Conditional takes the Augment (§ 299).

11. The Periphrastic or Definite Future; e. g. अयोध्यां श्वः प्रयातासि *ayodhyám śvaḥ prayátási*, thou wilt to-morrow proceed to Ayodhyâ.

12. The Benedictive is used for expressing not only a blessing, but also a wish in general; e. g. श्रीमान्भूयात् *śrîmán bhûyát*, May he be happy! चिरं जीव्यात् *chiram jîvyát*, May he live long!

13. The Subjunctive occurs in the Veda only.

§ 292. The Sanskrit verb has in each tense and mood three numbers, Singular, Dual, and Plural, with three persons in each.

CHAPTER VIII.

SPECIAL AND GENERAL TENSES AND THE TEN CLASSES OF VERBS.

§ 293. Sanskrit grammarians have divided all verbs into ten classes, according to certain modifications which their roots undergo before the terminations of the Present, the Imperfect, the Optative, and Imperative. This division is very useful, and will be retained with some slight alterations. One and the same root may belong to different classes. Thus भ्राश् *bhráś*, भ्लाश् *bhláś*, भ्रम् *bhram*, क्रम् *kram*, क्लम् *klam*, त्रस् *tras*, त्रुट् *truṭ*, लष् *lash* belong to the Bhû and Div classes; भ्राशते *bhráśate* or भ्राश्यते *bhrâśyate*, &c. (Pâṇ. III. 1, 70). Again, स्कु *sku*, स्तम्भ् *stambh*, स्तुम्भ् *stumbh*, स्कम्भ् *skambh*, स्कुम्भ् *skumbh* belong to the Su and Krî classes; स्कुनोति *skunoti* or स्कुनाति *skunáti* (Pâṇ. III. 1, 82).

§ 294. The four tenses and moods which require this modification of the root will be called the *Special or Modified Tenses*; the rest the *General or Unmodified Tenses*. Thus the root चि *chi* is changed in the Present, Imperfect, Optative, and Imperative into चिनु *chi-nu*. Hence चिनुमः *chi-nu-maḥ*, we search; अचिनुम *achi-nu-ma*, we searched. But the Past Participle चितः *chitaḥ*, searched, or the Reduplicated Perfect चिच्युः *chichy-uḥ*, they have searched, without the नु *nu*. We call चि *chi*, the root, चिनु *chinu*, the base of the special tenses.

§ 295. Verbal bases are first divided into two divisions:

I. Bases which in the modified tenses end in अ *a*.

II. Bases which in the modified tenses end in any letter but अ *a*.

This second division is subdivided into,

II *a*. Bases which insert नु *nu*, उ *u*, or नी *nî*, between the root and the terminations.

II *b*. Bases which take the terminations without any intermediate element.

I. *First Division.*

§ 296. The first division comprises four classes:

1. The Bhû class (the first with native grammarians, and called by them भ्वादि *bhvâdi*, because the first verb in their lists is भू *bhû*, to be).

a. अ *a* is added to the last letter of the root.

b. The vowel of the root takes Guṇa, where possible (i. e. long or short *i*, *u*, *ṛi*, if final; short *i*, *u*, *ṛi*, *ḷi*, if followed by *one* consonant).

बुध् *budh*, to know; बोधति *bodh-a-ti*, he knows. भू *bhû*, to be; भवति *bhav-a-ti*, he is.

Note—The accent in verbs of the Bhû class was originally (as we know from the ancient Vedic language) on the radical vowel; hence Guṇa of that vowel.

Many derivative verbs,—such as causatives, भावयति *bhâvayati*, he causes to be; desideratives, बुभूषति *bubhûshati*, he wishes to be, from भू *bhû*; intensives in the Âtmanepada, बेभिद्यते *bebhidyate*, he cuts much; and denominatives, लोहितायति *lohitâyati*, he grows red,—follow this class.

2. The Tud class (the sixth with native grammarians, and called by them तुदादि *tudâdi*, because the first root in their lists is तुद् *tud*, to strike).

a. अ *a* is added to the last letter of the root.

b. Before this अ *a*, final इ *i* and ई *î* are changed to इय् *iy*.

उ *u* and ऊ *û*	to उव् *uv*.
ऋ *ṛi*	to रिय् *riy*.
ॠ *ṛî*	to इर् *ir* (§ 110).

तुद् *tud*, to strike; तुदति *tud-a-ti*.

रि *ri*, to go; रियति *riy-a-ti*.

नू *nû*, to praise; नुवति *nuv-a-ti*.

मृ *mṛi*, to die; म्रियते *mriy-a-te*.

कॄ *kṝi*, to scatter; किरति *kir-a-ti*.

Note—The accent in verbs of the Tud class was originally on the intermediate अ *a*; hence never Guṇa of the radical vowel.

3. The Div class (the fourth with native grammarians, and called by them दिवादि *divâdi*, because the first root in their lists is दिव् *div*, to play).

a. य *ya* is added to the last letter of the root.

नह् *nah*, to bind; नह्यति *nah-ya-ti*.

बुध् *budh*, to awake; बुध्यते *budh-ya-te*.

Note—The accent in verbs of the Div class is now on the radical vowel; but there are traces to show that some verbs of this class had the accent originally on य *ya*.

4. The Chur class (the tenth with native grammarians, and called by them चुरादि *churâdi*, because the first root in their lists is चुर् *chur*, to steal).

a. अय *aya* is added to the last letter of the root.

b. If the root ends in a simple consonant, preceded by अ *a*, अ *a* is lengthened to आ *â*.

दल् *dal*, to cut; दालयति *dâl-aya-ti*, (many exceptions.)

c. If the root ends in a simple consonant, preceded by इ *i*, उ *u*, ऋ *ṛi*, ऌ *ḷi*, these vowels take Guṇa, while ॠ *ṝî* becomes ईर् *îr*.

श्लिष् *ślish*, to embrace; श्लेषयति *ślesh-aya-ti*.

चुर् *chur*, to steal; चोरयति *chor-aya-ti*.

मृष् *mṛish*, to endure; मर्षयते *marsh-aya-te*.

कॄत् *kṝit*, to praise; कीर्तयति *kîrt-aya-ti*.

d. Final इ *i*, ई *î*, उ *u*, ऊ *û*, ऋ *ṛi*, and ॠ *ṝî*, take Vṛiddhi.

जि *jri*, to grow old; जाययति *jrây-aya-ti*.

मी *mî*, to walk; माययति *mây-aya-ti*.

धृ *dhṛi*, to hold; धारयति *dhâr-aya-ti*.

पॄ *pṝî*, to fill; पारयति *pâr-aya-ti*.

Note—Many, if not all roots arranged under this class by native grammarians, are secondary roots, and identical in form with causatives, denominatives, &c. This class differs from other classes, inasmuch as verbs belonging to it, keep their modificatory syllable अय *aya* throughout, in the unmodified as well as in the modified tenses, except in the Benedictive Par. The accent was on the first अ *a* of अय *áya*.

II. *Second Division*.

§ 297. The second division comprises all verbs which do not, in the special tenses, end in अ *a* before the terminations.

It is a distinguishing feature of this second division that, before certain terminations, all verbs belonging to it require strengthening of their radical vowel, or if they take नु *nu*, उ *u*, नी *nî*, strengthening of the vowels of these syllables. This strengthening generally takes place by means of Guṇa, but नी *nî* is raised to ना *nâ* in the Krî, and न् *n* to न *na* in the Rudh class.

We shall call the terminations which require strengthening of the inflective base, the weak terminations, and the base before them, the strong base; and *vice versâ*, the terminations which do not require strengthening of the base, the strong terminations, and the base before them, the weak base.

Originally the accent fell on the strong terminations, and on the strong base, thus establishing throughout an equilibrium between base and termination.

II *a.* Bases which take नु *nu*, उ *u*, नी *nî*.

§ 298. This first subdivision comprises three classes:

1. The Su class (the fifth class with native grammarians, and called by them स्वादि *svâdi*, because the first root in their lists is सु *su*).
   a. नु *nu* is added to the last letter of the root, before strong terminations, नो *no* before weak terminations.

Ex. सु *su*, to squeeze out; सुनुमः *su-nu-máḥ*, 1st pers. plur. Pres.
सुनोमि *su-nó-mi*, 1st pers. sing. Pres.

2. The Tan class (the eighth class with native grammarians, and called by them तनादि *tanâdi*, because the first root in their lists is तन् *tan*).
   a. उ *u* is added to the last letter of the root, before strong terminations, ओ *o* before weak terminations.

Ex. तन् *tan*, to stretch; तनुमः *tan-u-máḥ*, 1st pers. plur. Pres.
तनोमि *tan-ó-mi*, 1st pers. sing. Pres.

Note—All verbs belonging to this class end in न् *n*, except one, कृ *kṛi*, करोमि *karomi*, I do.

3. The Krî class (the ninth with native grammarians, and called by them क्र्यादि *kryâdi*, because the first root in their lists is क्री *krî*).
   a. नी *nî* is added to the last letter of the root, before strong terminations, ना *nâ* before weak terminations,
   न *na* before strong terminations beginning with vowels.

Ex. क्री *krî*, to buy; क्रीणीमः *krî-ṇî-máḥ*, 1st pers. plur. Pres.
क्रीणामि *krî-ṇâ-mi*, 1st pers. sing. Pres.
क्रीणन्ति *krî-ṇ-ánti*, 3rd pers. plur. Pres.

II *b.* Bases to which the terminations are joined immediately.

§ 299. The second division comprises three classes:

1. The Ad class (the second class with native grammarians, and called by them अदादि *adâdi*, because the first root in their lists is अद् *ad*, to eat).
   a. The terminations are added immediately to the last letter of the base;

and in the contact of vowels with vowels, vowels with consonants, consonants with vowels, and consonants with consonants, the phonetic rules explained above (§§ 107–145) must be carefully observed.

b. The strong base before the weak terminations takes Guṇa, where possible (§ 296, 1, *b*).

Ex. लिह् *lih*, to lick; लिह्मः *lih-máḥ*, we lick.
लेह्मि *léh-mi*, I lick.
लेक्षि *lek-shi*, thou lickest (§ 127).
लीढ *lîḍha*, you lick (§ 128).
अलेट् *aleṭ*, thou lickedst (§ 128).

The intensive verbs, conjugated in the Parasmaipada, follow this class.

2. The Hu class (the third class with native grammarians, and called by them जुहोत्यादि *juhotyádi*, because the first root in their lists is हु *hu*, जुहोति *juhoti*).

a. The terminations are added as in the Ad class.

b. The strong base before the weak terminations takes Guṇa, where possible.

c. The root takes reduplication. (Rules of Reduplication, § 302.)

Ex. हु *hu*, to sacrifice; जुहुमः *ju-hu-máḥ*, we sacrifice.
जुहोमि *ju-hó-mi*, I sacrifice. (Pâṇ. VI. 1, 192.)

3. The Rudh class (the seventh class with native grammarians, and called by them रुधादि *rudhâdi*, because the first root in their lists is रुध् *rudh*, रुणद्धि *ruṇaddhi*, to obstruct).

a. The terminations are added as in the Ad class.

b. Between the radical vowel and the final consonant न् *n* is inserted, which in the strong base before weak terminations is raised to न *na*.

Ex. युज् *yuj*, to join; युञ्ज्मः *yu-ñ-j-máḥ*, we join.
युनज्मि *yu-ná-j-mi*, I join.

First Division.

Bhû class,	with native grammarians,		Bhvâdi, I class.
Tud class,	—	—	Tudâdi, VI class.
Div class,	—	—	Divâdi, IV class.
Chur class,	—	—	Churâdi, X class.

Second Division.

Su class,	with native grammarians,		Svâdi, V class.
Tan class,	—	—	Tanâdi, VIII class.
Krî class,	—	—	Kryâdi, IX class.
Ad class,	—	—	Adâdi, II class.
Hu class,	—	—	Juhotyâdi, III class.
Rudh class,	—	—	Rudhâdi, VII class.

CHAPTER IX.

AUGMENT, REDUPLICATION, AND TERMINATIONS.

§ 300. Before we can leave the subject which occupies us at present, viz. the preparation of the root previous to its assuming the terminations, we have to consider two processes, the Augment and the Reduplication, modifications of the root with which we are familiar in Greek, and which in Sanskrit as well as in Greek form the distinguishing features of certain tenses (Imperfect, Aorist, Conditional, and Perfect) in every verb.

§ 301. Roots beginning with consonants take short अ *a* as their initial augment. This अ *a* has the accent. Thus from बुध् *budh*, Present बोधामि *bodhâmi*; Imperfect अबोधम् *ábodham*.

Roots beginning with vowels always take Vṛiddhi, the irregular result of the combination of the augment with the initial vowels. (Pâṇ. VI. 1, 90.)

अ *a* with अ *a*, or आ *â*, = आ *â*.
अ *a* with इ *i*, ई *î*, ए *e*, or ऐ *ai*, = ऐ *ai*.
अ *a* with उ *u*, ऊ *û*, ओ *o*, or औ *au*, = औ *au*.
अ *a* with ऋ *ṛi*, or ॠ *ṛî*, = आर् *âr*.

From अर्च् *arch*, अर्चति *archati*, he praises, आर्चत् *ârchat*, he praised.
From ईक्ष् *îksh*, ईक्षते *îkshate*, he sees, ऐक्षत *aikshata*, he saw.
From उन्द् *und*, उनत्ति *unatti*, he wets, औनत् *aunat*, he wetted.
From ऋ *ṛi*, ऋच्छति *ṛichchhati*, he goes आर्च्छत् *ârchchhat*, he went.

In the more ancient Sanskrit, as in the more ancient Greek, the augment is frequently absent. In the later Sanskrit, too, it has to be dropt after the negative particle मा *mâ* (Pâṇ. VI. 4, 74). मा भवान् कार्षीत् *mâ bhavân kârshît*, Let not your Honour do this! or मा स्म करोत् *mâ sma karot*, May he not do it!

Reduplication.

§ 302. Reduplication takes place in Sanskrit not only in the reduplicated perfect, but likewise in all verbs of the Hu class. Most of the rules of reduplication are the same in forming the base of the perfect of all verbs, and in forming the special base of the verbs of the Hu class. These will be stated first; afterwards those that are peculiar either to the reduplication of the perfect or to that of the verbs of the Hu class.

The reduplication in intensive and desiderative verbs and in one form of the aorist will have to be treated separately.

General Rules of Reduplication.

§ 303. The first syllable of a root (i. e. that portion of it which ends with a vowel) is repeated.

बुध् *budh* = बुबुध् *bubudh*. भू *bhû* is exceptional in forming बभू *babhû*. (Pâṇ. VII. 4, 73.)

§ 304. Aspirated letters are represented in reduplication by their corresponding unaspirated letters.

भिद् *bhid*, to cut, = बिभिद् *bibhid*.
धू *dhû*, to shake, = दुधू *dudhû*.

§ 305. Gutturals are represented in reduplication by their corresponding palatals; ह् *h* by ज् *j*. (Pâṇ. VII. 4, 62.)

कुट् *kuṭ*, to sever, = चुकुट् *chukuṭ*.
खन् *khan*, to dig, = चखन् *chakhan*.
गम् *gam*, to go, = जगम् *jagam*.
हस् *has*, to laugh, = जहस् *jahas*.

§ 306. If a root begins with more than one consonant, the first only is reduplicated.

क्रुश् *kruś*, to shout, = चुक्रुश् *chukruś*.
क्षिप् *kship*, to throw, = चिक्षिप् *chikship*.

§ 307. If a root begins with a sibilant followed by a tenuis or aspirated tenuis, the tenuis only is reduplicated.

स्तु *stu*, to praise, = तुष्टु *tushṭu* (§ 103, 1).
स्तन् *stan*, to sound, = तस्तन् *tastan*.
स्पर्ध् *spardh*, to strive, = पस्पर्ध् *paspardh*.
स्था *sthâ*, to stand, = तस्था *tasthâ*.
श्च्युत् *śchyut*, to drop, = चुश्च्युत् *chuśchyut*.
But स्मृ *smṛi*, to pine, = सस्मृ *sasmṛi*.

§ 308. If the radical vowel, whether final or medial, is long, it is shortened in the reduplicative syllable.

गाह् *gâh*, to enter, = जगाह् *jagâh*.
क्री *krî*, to buy, = चिक्री *chikrî*.
सूद् *sûd*, to strike, = सुषूद् *sushûd*.

§ 309. If the radical (not final) vowel is ए *e* or ऐ *ai*, it becomes इ *i*; if it is ओ *o* or औ *au*, it becomes उ *u*.

सेव् *sev*, to worship, = सिषेव् *sishev*.
ढौक् *ḍhauk*, to approach, = डुढौक् *ḍuḍhauk*.

§ 310. Roots with final ए *e*, ऐ *ai*, ओ *o*, are treated like roots ending in आ *â*, taking अ *a* in the reduplicative syllable.

धे *dhe*, to feed, = दधौ *dadhau*.
गै *gai*, to sing, = जगौ *jagau*.
शो *śo*, to sharpen, = शशौ *śaśau*.

§ 311. The following roots are slightly irregular on account of the semivowels which they contain, and which are liable to be changed into vowels. (This change is called *Samprasâraṇa*.) Pâṇ. VI. 1, 17.

Root.	1st Pers. Sing. Redupl. Perf.	Weak Form *.	Weakest Form †.
यज् *yaj*	= इयाज *iyâja*, to sacrifice, (for ययाज *yayâja*.)	ईज् *îj*.	(इज् *ij*.)
वच् *vach*	= उवाच *uvâcha*, to speak.	ऊच् *ûch*.	(उच् *uch*.)
वद् *vad*	= उवाद *uvâda*, to say.	ऊद् *ûd*.	(उद् *ud*.)
वप् *vap*	= उवाप *uvâpa*, to sow.	ऊप् *ûp*.	(उप् *up*.)
वश् *vaś*	= उवाश *uvâśa*, to wish.	ऊश् *ûś*.	(उश् *uś*.)
वस् *vas*	= उवास *uvâsa*, to dwell.	ऊस् *ûs*.	(उस् *us*.)
वह् *vah*	= उवाह *uvâha*, to carry.	ऊह् *ûh*.	(उह् *uh*.)
वय् *vay* ‡	= उवाय *uvâya*, to weave.	ऊय् *ûy* or ऊव् *ûv* ‖.	(उ *u*.)
व्यच् *vyach*	= विव्याच *vivyâcha*, to surround.	विविच् *vivich*.	(विच् *vich*.)
व्यध् *vyadh*	= विव्याध *vivyâdha*, to strike.	विविध् *vividh*.	(विध् *vidh*.)
व्यथ् *vyath*	= विव्यथे *vivyathe* (Pâṇ. VII. 4, 68).	विव्यथ् *vivyath*.	(व्यथ् *vyath*.)
स्वप् *svap*	= सुष्वाप *sushvâpa*, to sleep.	सुषुप् *sushup*.	(सुप् *sup*.)
श्वि *śvi*	= शुशाव *śuśâva*, to swell ¶.	शुशू *śuśû*.	(शू *śû*.)
व्ये *vye*	= विव्याय *vivyâya*, to cover.	विवी *vivî*.	(वी *vî*.)
ज्या *jyâ*	= जिज्यौ *jijyau*, to grow old.	जिजी *jijî*.	(जी *jî*.)
ह्वे *hve*	= जुहाव *juhâva*, to call (Pâṇ. VI. 1, 33).	जुहू *juhû*	(हू *hû*.)
प्याय् *pyây*	= पिप्ये *pipye*, to grow fat (Pâṇ. VI. 1, 29).	पिपी *pipî*.	(पी *pî*.)
ग्रह् *grah*	= जग्राह *jagrâha*, to take.	जगृह् *jagṛih*.	(गृह् *gṛih*.)

§ 312. Roots beginning with short अ *a*, and ending in a single consonant, contract अ *a* + अ *a* into आ *â*.

अद् *ad*, to eat, = आद् *âd*.

§ 313. Roots beginning with short अ *a*, and ending with more than one consonant, prefix आन् *ân*.

अर्च् *arch* = आनर्च् *ânarch*. (Also अश् *aś* (Su), आनशे *ânaśe*.) Pâṇ. VII. 4, 72.

§ 314. Roots beginning with इ *i* or उ *u* (not prosodially long), contract इ + इ *i* + *i* and उ + उ *u* + *u* into ई *î* and ऊ *û*; but if the radical इ *i* or उ *u* take Guṇa or Vṛiddhi, य् *y* and व् *v* are inserted between the reduplicative syllable and the base. (Pâṇ. VI. 4, 78.)

---

* The weak forms appear in all persons of the reduplicated perfect where neither Vṛiddhi nor Guṇa is required.

† The weakest forms of these verbs do not belong to the reduplicated perfect, but have been added as useful hereafter for the formation of the past participle, the benedictive, the passive, &c.

‡ वय् *vay* is a substitute for वे *ve*, in the reduplicated perfect (Pâṇ. II. 4, 41). If that substitution does not take place, then वे *ve* forms ववौ *vavau*, ववुः *vavuḥ* (Pâṇ. VI. 1, 40).

‖ Pâṇ. VI. 1, 38, 39.

¶ Or शिश्वाय *śiśvâya* (Pâṇ. VI. 1, 30).

इष् *ish* = ईषतुः *ísh-atuḥ*, they two have gone.
= इयेष *iy-esh-a* (Guṇa), I have gone.
उख् *ukh* = ऊखतुः *úkh-atuḥ*, they two have withered.
= उवोख *uv-okh-a* (Guṇa), I have withered.

§ 315. The root ऋ *ṛi* forms the base of the reduplicated perfect as आर् *âr*. Other roots beginning with ऋ *ṛi* prefix आन् *ân*. (Pâṇ. VII. 4, 71.)

ऋज् *ṛij*, to obtain, = आनृज् *ân-ṛij*.

As to roots which cannot be reduplicated or are otherwise irregular, see the rules given for the formation of the Reduplicated and Periphrastic Perfect.

Special Rules of Reduplication.

§ 316. So far the process of reduplication would be the same, whether applied to the bases of the Reduplicated Perfect or to those of the Hu class. But there are some points on which these two classes of reduplicated bases differ; viz.

1. In the Reduplicated Perfect, radical ऋ *ṛi*, ॠ *ṛî*, whether final or medial, are represented in reduplication by अ *a*.
2. In the bases of the Hu class, final ऋ *ṛi* and ॠ *ṛî* (they do not occur as medial) are represented in reduplication by इ *i*.

Reduplicated Perfect.	Hu Class. Present, &c.
भृ *bhṛi*, to bear, = बभार *babhâra*.	भृ *bhṛi* = बिभर्ति *bibharti*.
सृ *sṛi*, to go, = ससार *sasâra*.	सृ *sṛi* = सिसर्ति *sisarti*.
हृ *hṛi*, to take, = जहार *jahâra*.	हृ *hṛi* = जिहर्ति *jiharti*.

The root ऋ *ṛi*, to go, forms इयर्ति *iy-arti*; पॄ *pṝi*, to fill, पिपर्ति *piparti*.

§ 317. The three verbs निज् *nij*, विज् *vij*, and विष् *vish* of the Hu class take Guṇa in the reduplicated syllable. (Pâṇ. VII. 4, 75.)

निज् *nij*, to wash, नेनेक्ति *nenekti*, नेनिक्ते *nenikte*; विज् *vij*, to separate, वेवेक्ति *vevekti*; विष् *vish*, to pervade, वेवेष्टि *veveshṭi*.

§ 318. The two verbs मा *mâ*, to measure, and हा *hâ*, to go, of the Hu class take इ *i* in the reduplicative syllable. (Pâṇ. VII. 4, 76.)

मा *mâ*, मिमीते *mimîte*; हा *hâ*, जिहीते *jihîte*.

§ 319. Certain roots change their initial consonant if they are reduplicated.

हन् *han*, to kill, जघान *jaghâna*. Likewise in the desiderative जिघांसति *jighâṁsati*, and the intensive जंघन्यते *jaṅghanyate*. (Pâṇ. VII. 3, 55.)

हि *hi*, to send (Su), जिघाय *jighâya*. Likewise in the desiderative जिघीषति *jighîshati*, and the intensive जेघीयते *jeghîyate*. (Pâṇ. VII. 3, 56.)

जि *ji*, to conquer, जिगाय *jigâya*. Likewise in the desiderative जिगीषति *jigîshati*; but not in the intensive, which is always जेजीयते *jejîyate*. (Pâṇ. VII. 3, 57.)

चि *chi*, to gather, has optionally चिचाय *chichâya* or चिकाय *chikâya*. The same option applies to the desiderative, but in the intensive we have चेचीयते *chechîyate* only. (Pâṇ. VII. 3, 58.)

Terminations.

§ 320. After having explained how the verbal roots are modified in ten different ways before they receive the terminations of the four special tenses, the Present, Imperfect, Optative, and Imperative, we give a table of the terminations for the special or modified tenses and moods.

§ 321. The terminations for the modified tenses, though on the whole the same for all verbs, are subject to certain variations, according as the verbal bases take अ *a* (First Division), or नु *nu*, उ *u*, नी *nî* (Second Division, A.), or nothing (Second Division, B.) between themselves and the terminations. Instead of giving the table of terminations according to the system of native grammarians, or according to that of comparative philologists, and explaining the real or fanciful changes which they are supposed to have undergone in the different classes of verbs, it will be more useful to give them in that form in which they may mechanically be attached to each verbal base. The beginner should commit to memory the actual paradigms rather than the different sets of terminations. Instead of taking आथे *âthe* as the termination of the 2nd pers. dual Âtm., and learning that the आ *â* of आथे *âthe* is changed to इ *i* after bases in अ *a* (Pâṇ. VII. 2, 81), it is simpler to take इथे *ithe* as the termination in the First Division; but still simpler to commit to memory such forms as बोधेथे *bodhethe*, द्विषाथे *dvishâthe*, मिमाथे *mimâthe*, without asking at first any questions as to how they came to be what they are.

First Division.

Bhû, Tud, Div, and Chur Classes.

	Parasmaipada.				Âtmanepada.			
	Present.	Imperf.	Optative.	Imperat.	Present.	Imperfect.	Optative.	Imperative.
1.	आमि *âmi*	म् *m*	इयं *iyam*	आनि *âni*	इ *i*	इ *i*	इय *iya*	ए *e*
2.	सि *si*	ः *ḥ*	इः *iḥ*	—*	से *se*	थाः *thâḥ*	इथाः *ithâḥ*	स्व *sva*
3.	ति *ti*	त् *t*	इत् *it*	तु *tu**	ते *te*	त *ta*	इत *ita*	तां *tâm*
1.	आवः *âvaḥ*	आव *âva*	इव *iva*	आव *âva*	आवहे *âvahe*	आवहि *âvahi*	इवहि *ivahi*	आवहै *âvahai*
2.	थः *thaḥ*	तं *tam*	इतं *itam*	तं *tam*	इथे *ithe*	इथां *ithâm*	इयाथां *iyâthâm*	इथां *ithâm*
3.	तः *taḥ*	तां *tâm*	इतां *itâm*	तां *tâm*	इते *ite*	इतां *itâm*	इयातां *iyâtâm*	इतां *itâm*
1.	आमः *âmaḥ*	आम *âma*	इम *ima*	आम *âma*	आमहे *âmahe*	आमहि *âmahi*	इमहि *imahi*	आमहै *âmahai*
2.	थ *tha*	त *ta*	इत *ita*	त *ta*	ध्वे *dhve*	ध्वं *dhvam*	इध्वं *idhvam*	ध्वं *dhvam*
3.	न्ति *nti*	न् *n*	इयुः *iyuḥ*	न्तु *ntu*	न्ते *nte*	न्त *nta*	इरन् *iran*	न्तां *ntâm*

* In the second and third persons तात् *tât* may be used as termination after all verbs, if the sense is benedictive.

Second Division.

Su, Tan, Krî, Ad, Hu, and Rudh Classes.

	Parasmaipada.				Âtmanepada.			
	Present.	Imperfect.	Optative.	Imperative.	Present.	Imperfect.	Optative.	Imperative.
1.	मि *mi*	अम् *am*	यां *yâm*	आनि *âni*	ए *e*	इ *i*	ईय *îya*	ऐ *ai*
2.	सि *si*	: *ḥ*	याः *yâḥ*	हि *hi* *	से *se*	थाः *thâḥ*	ईथाः *îthâḥ*	स्व *sva*
3.	ति *ti*	त् *t*	यात् *yât*	तु *tu*	ते *te*	त *ta*	ईत *îta*	तां *tâm*
1.	वः *vaḥ*	व *va*	याव *yâva*	आव *âva*	वहे *vahe*	वहि *vahi*	ईवहि *îvahi*	आवहै *âvahai*
2.	थः *thaḥ*	तं *tam*	यातं *yâtam*	तं *tam*	आथे *âthe*	आथां *âthâm*	ईयाथां *îyâthâm*	आथां *âthâm*
3.	तः *taḥ*	तां *tâm*	यातां *yâtâm*	तां *tâm*	आते *âte*	आतां *âtâm*	ईयातां *îyâtâm*	आतां *âtâm*
1.	मः *maḥ*	म *ma*	याम *yâma*	आम *âma*	महे *mahe*	महि *mahi*	ईमहि *îmahi*	आमहै *âmahai*
2.	थ *tha*	त *ta*	यात *yâta*	त *ta*	ध्वे *dhve*	ध्वं *dhvam*	ईध्वं *îdhvam*	ध्वं *dhvam*
3.	अन्ति *anti* †	अन् *an* ‡	युः *yuḥ*	अन्तु *antu* ‖	अते *ate*	अत *ata*	ईरन् *îran*	अतां *atâm*

The terminations enclosed in squares are the weak, i. e. unaccented terminations which require strengthening of the base.

§ 322. By means of these terminations the student is able to form the Present, Imperfect, Optative, and Imperative in the Parasmaipada and Âtmanepada of all regular verbs in Sanskrit; and any one who has clearly understood how the verbal bases are prepared in ten different ways for receiving their terminations, and who will attach to these verbal bases the terminations as given above, according to the rules of Sandhi, will have no difficulty in writing out for himself the paradigms of any Sanskrit verb in four of the most important tenses and moods, both in the Parasmaipada and Âtmanepada. Some verbs, however, are irregular in the formation of their base; these must be learnt from the Dhâtupâṭha.

---

* The Su and Tan classes take no termination, except when उ *u* is preceded by a conjunct consonant.

† Hu class and अभ्यस्त *abhyasta*, i. e. reduplicated bases, take अति *ati*.

‡ Hu class, reduplicated bases, and विद् *vid*, to know, take उः *uḥ*, before which, verbs ending in a vowel, require Guṇa. उः *uḥ* is used optionally after verbs in आ *â*, and after द्विष् *dvish*, to hate. (Pâṇ. III. 4. 109—112.)

‖ Hu class and reduplicated bases take अतु *atu*.

PARASMAIPADA.

Present.

Root.	Verbal Base.									
	First Division.	आमि *ami*	सि *si*	ति *ti*	आवः *avaḥ*	थः *thaḥ*	तः *taḥ*	आमः *amaḥ*	थ *tha*	न्ति *nti*
भू *bhû*	भव *bhava*	भवामि *bhavâmi*	भवसि *bhavasi*	भवति *bhavati*	भवावः *bhavâvaḥ*	भवथः *bhavathaḥ*	भवतः *bhavataḥ*	भवामः *bhavâmaḥ*	भवथ *bhavatha*	भवन्ति *bhavanti*
तुद् *tud*	तुद *tuda*	तुदामि *tudâmi*	तुदसि *tudasi*	तुदति *tudati*	तुदावः *tudâvaḥ*	तुदथः *tudathaḥ*	तुदतः *tudataḥ*	तुदामः *tudâmaḥ*	तुदथ *tudatha*	तुदन्ति *tudanti*
दिव् *div*	दीव्य *dîvya*	दीव्यामि *dîvyâmi*	दीव्यसि *dîvyasi*	दीव्यति *dîvyati*	दीव्यावः *dîvyâvaḥ*	दीव्यथः *dîvyathaḥ*	दीव्यतः *dîvyataḥ*	दीव्यामः *dîvyâmaḥ*	दीव्यथ *dîvyatha*	दीव्यन्ति *dîvyanti*
चुर् *chur*	चोरय *choraya*	चोरयामि *chorayâmi*	चोरयसि *chorayasi*	चोरयति *chorayati*	चोरयावः *chorayâvaḥ*	चोरयथः *chorayathaḥ*	चोरयतः *chorayataḥ*	चोरयामः *chorayâmaḥ*	चोरयथ *chorayatha*	चोरयन्ति *chorayanti*
	Second Division.	मि *mi*	सि *si*	ति *ti*	वः *vaḥ*	थः *thaḥ*	तः *taḥ*	मः *maḥ*	थ *tha*	अन्ति *anti*
सु *su*	सुनु सुनो *sunu suno*	सुनोमि *sunomi*	सुनोषि *sunoshi*	सुनोति *sunoti*	सुनुवः[1] *sunuvaḥ*	सुनुथः *sunuthaḥ*	सुनुतः *sunutaḥ*	सुनुमः[2] *sunumaḥ*	सुनुथ *sunutha*	सुन्वन्ति *sunvanti*
तन् *tan*	तनु तनो *tanu tano*	तनोमि *tanomi*	तनोषि *tanoshi*	तनोति *tanoti*	तनुवः[3] *tanuvaḥ*	तनुथः *tanuthaḥ*	तनुतः *tanutaḥ*	तनुमः[4] *tanumaḥ*	तनुथ *tanutha*	तन्वन्ति *tanvanti*
क्री *krî*	क्रीणी क्रीणा क्रीण् *krîṇî krîṇâ krîṇ*	क्रीणामि *krîṇâmi*	क्रीणासि *krîṇâsi*	क्रीणाति *krîṇâti*	क्रीणीवः *krîṇîvaḥ*	क्रीणीथः *krîṇîthaḥ*	क्रीणीतः *krîṇîtaḥ*	क्रीणीमः *krîṇîmaḥ*	क्रीणीथ *krîṇîtha*	क्रीणन्ति *krîṇanti*
अद् *ad*	अद् अद् *ad ad*	अद्मि *admi*	अत्सि *atsi*	अत्ति *atti*	अद्वः *advaḥ*	अत्थः *atthaḥ*	अत्तः *attaḥ*	अद्मः *admaḥ*	अत्थ *attha*	अदन्ति *adanti*
हु *hu*	जुहु जुहो *juhu juho*	जुहोमि *juhomi*	जुहोषि *juhoshi*	जुहोति *juhoti*	जुहुवः *juhuvaḥ*	जुहुथः *juhuthaḥ*	जुहुतः *juhutaḥ*	जुहुमः *juhumaḥ*	जुहुथ *juhutha*	जुह्वति[5] *juhvati*
रुध् *rudh*	रुन्ध् रुणध् *rundh ruṇadh*	रुणध्मि *ruṇadhmi*	रुणत्सि *ruṇatsi*	रुणद्धि *ruṇatti*	रुन्ध्वः *rundhvaḥ*	रुन्द्धः *runddhaḥ*	रुन्द्धः *runddhaḥ*	रुन्ध्मः *rundhmaḥ*	रुन्द्ध *runddha*	रुन्धन्ति *rundhanti*

[1] Or सुन्वः *sunvaḥ*. [2] Or सुन्मः *sunmaḥ*. [3] Or तन्वः *tanvaḥ*. [4] Or तन्मः *tanmaḥ*. [5] See § 321, note †.

PARASMAIPADA.
Imperfect.

Root.	Verbal Base.									
	First Division.	म् m	: ḥ	त् t	आव âva	तं tam	तां tâm	आम âma	त ta	न् n
भू bhû	भव bhava	अभवं abhavam	अभवः abhavaḥ	अभवत् abhavat	अभवाव abhavâva	अभवतं abhavatam	अभवतां abhavatâm	अभवाम abhavâma	अभवत abhavata	अभवन् abhavan
तुद् tud	तुद tuda	अतुदं atudam	अतुदः atudaḥ	अतुदत् atudat	अतुदाव atudâva	अतुदतं atudatam	अतुदतां atudatâm	अतुदाम atudâma	अतुदत atudata	अतुदन् atudan
दिव् div	दीव्य dîvya	अदीव्यं adîvyam	अदीव्यः adîvyaḥ	अदीव्यत् adîvyat	अदीव्याव adîvyâva	अदीव्यतं adîvyatam	अदीव्यतां adîvyatâm	अदीव्याम adîvyâma	अदीव्यत adîvyata	अदीव्यन् adîvyan
चुर् chur	चोरय choraya	अचोरयं achorayam	अचोरयः achorayaḥ	अचोरयत् achorayat	अचोरयाव achorayâva	अचोरयतं achorayatam	अचोरयतां achorayatâm	अचोरयाम achorayâma	अचोरयत achorayata	अचोरयन् achorayan
	Second Division.	अं am	: ḥ	त् t	व va	तं tam	तां tâm	म ma	त ta	अन् an
सु su	सुनु सुनो sunu suno	असुनवं asunavam	असुनोः asunoḥ	असुनोत् asunot	असुनुव[1] asunuva	असुनुतं asunutam	असुनुतां asunutâm	असुनुम[2] asunuma	असुनुत asunuta	असुन्वन् asunvan
तन् tan	तनु तनो tanu tano	अतनवं atanavam	अतनोः atanoḥ	अतनोत् atanot	अतनुव[3] atanuva	अतनुतं atanutam	अतनुतां atanutâm	अतनुम[4] atanuma	अतनुत atanuta	अतन्वन् atanvan
क्री krî	क्रीणी क्रीणा क्रीण् krîṇî krîṇâ krîṇ	अक्रीणां akrîṇâm	अक्रीणाः akrîṇâḥ	अक्रीणात् akrîṇât	अक्रीणीव akrîṇîva	अक्रीणीतं akrîṇîtam	अक्रीणीतां akrîṇîtâm	अक्रीणीम akrîṇîma	अक्रीणीत akrîṇîta	अक्रीणन् akrîṇan
अद् ad	अद् अद् ad ad	आदं[5] âdam	आदः âdaḥ	आदत् âdat	आद्व âdva	आत्तं âttam	आत्तां âttâm	आद्म âdma	आत्त âtta	आदन् âdan
हु hu	जुहु जुहो juhu juho	अजुहवं ajuhavam	अजुहोः ajuhoḥ	अजुहोत् ajuhot	अजुहुव ajuhuva	अजुहुतं ajuhutam	अजुहुतां ajuhutâm	अजुहुम ajuhuma	अजुहुत ajuhuta	अजुहवुः[6] ajuhavuḥ
रुध् rudh	रुन्ध् रुणध् rundh ruṇadh	अरुणधं aruṇadham	अरुणत्[7] aruṇat	अरुणत् aruṇat	अरुन्ध्व arundhva	अरुन्द्धं arunddham	अरुन्द्धां arunddhâm	अरुन्ध्म arundhma	अरुन्द्ध arunddha	अरुन्धन् arundhan

[1] Or असुन्व asunva. [2] Or असुन्म asunma. [3] Or अतन्व atanva. [4] Or अतन्म atanma. [5] See § 301. [6] See § 321, note ‡. [7] Or अरुणः aruṇaḥ, §§ 114, 132.

Root.	Verbal Base.	PARASMAIPADA. Optative.								
	First Division.	इयं *iyam*	इः *iḥ*	इत् *it*	इव *iva*	इतं *itam*	इतां *itám*	इम *ima*	इत *ita*	इयुः *iyuḥ*
भू *bhú*	भव *bhava*	भवेयं *bhaveyam*	भवेः *bhaveḥ*	भवेत् *bhavet*	भवेव *bhaveva*	भवेतं *bhavetam*	भवेतां *bhavetám*	भवेम *bhavema*	भवेत *bhaveta*	भवेयुः *bhaveyuḥ*
तुद् *tud*	तुद *tuda*	तुदेयं *tudeyam*	तुदेः *tudeḥ*	तुदेत् *tudet*	तुदेव *tudeva*	तुदेतं *tudetam*	तुदेतां *tudetám*	तुदेम *tudema*	तुदेत *tudeta*	तुदेयुः *tudeyuḥ*
दिव् *div*	दीव्य *dívya*	दीव्येयं *dívyeyam*	दीव्येः *dívyeḥ*	दीव्येत् *dívyet*	दीव्येव *dívyeva*	दीव्येतं *dívyetam*	दीव्येतां *dívyetám*	दीव्येम *dívyema*	दीव्येत *dívyeta*	दीव्येयुः *dívyeyuḥ*
चुर् *chur*	चोरय *choraya*	चोरयेयं *chorayeyam*	चोरयेः *chorayeḥ*	चोरयेत् *chorayet*	चोरयेव *chorayeva*	चोरयेतं *chorayetam*	चोरयेतां *chorayetám*	चोरयेम *chorayema*	चोरयेत *chorayeta*	चोरयेयुः *chorayeyuḥ*
	Second Division.	यां *yám*	याः *yáḥ*	यात् *yát*	याव *yáva*	यातं *yátam*	यातां *yátám*	याम *yáma*	यात *yáta*	युः *yuḥ*
सु *su*	सुनु *sunu*	सुनुयां *sunuyám*	सुनुयाः *sunuyáḥ*	सुनुयात् *sunuyát*	सुनुयाव *sunuyáva*	सुनुयातं *sunuyátam*	सुनुयातां *sunuyátám*	सुनुयाम *sunuyáma*	सुनुयात *sunuyáta*	सुनुयुः *sunuyuḥ*
तन् *tan*	तनु *tanu*	तनुयां *tanuyám*	तनुयाः *tanuyáḥ*	तनुयात् *tanuyát*	तनुयाव *tanuyáva*	तनुयातं *tanuyátam*	तनुयातां *tanuyátám*	तनुयाम *tanuyáma*	तनुयात *tanuyáta*	तनुयुः *tanuyuḥ*
क्री *krí*	क्रीणी *kríṇí*	क्रीणीयां *kríṇíyám*	क्रीणीयाः *kríṇíyáḥ*	क्रीणीयात् *kríṇíyát*	क्रीणीयाव *kríṇíyáva*	क्रीणीयातं *kríṇíyátam*	क्रीणीयातां *kríṇíyátám*	क्रीणीयाम *kríṇíyáma*	क्रीणीयात *kríṇíyáta*	क्रीणीयुः *kríṇíyuḥ*
अद् *ad*	अद् *ad*	अद्यां *adyám*	अद्याः *adyáḥ*	अद्यात् *adyát*	अद्याव *adyáva*	अद्यातं *adyátam*	अद्यातां *adyátám*	अद्याम *adyáma*	अद्यात *adyáta*	अद्युः *adyuḥ*
हु *hu*	जुहु *juhu*	जुहुयां *juhuyám*	जुहुयाः *juhuyáḥ*	जुहुयात् *juhuyát*	जुहुयाव *juhuyáva*	जुहुयातं *juhuyátam*	जुहुयातां *juhuyátám*	जुहुयाम *juhuyáma*	जुहुयात *juhuyáta*	जुहुयुः *juhuyuḥ*
रुध् *rudh*	रुन्ध् *rundh*	रुन्ध्यां *rundhyám*	रुन्ध्याः *rundhyáḥ*	रुन्ध्यात् *rundhyát*	रुन्ध्याव *rundhyáva*	रुन्ध्यातं *rundhyátam*	रुन्ध्यातां *rundhyátám*	रुन्ध्याम *rundhyáma*	रुन्ध्यात *rundhyáta*	रुन्ध्युः *rundhyuḥ*

PARASMAIPADA.

Imperative.

Root.	Verbal Base.									
	First Division.	आनि âni	—	तु tu	आव ava	तं tam	तां tâm	आम ama	त ta	न्तु ntu
भू bhû	भव bhava	भवानि bhavâni	भव bhava	भवतु bhavatu	भवाव bhavâva	भवतं bhavatam	भवतां bhavatâm	भवाम bhavâma	भवत bhavata	भवन्तु bhavantu
तुद् tud	तुद tuda	तुदानि tudâni	तुद tuda	तुदतु tudatu	तुदाव tudâva	तुदतं tudatam	तुदतां tudatâm	तुदाम tudâma	तुदत tudata	तुदन्तु tudantu
दिव् div	दीव्य dîvya	दीव्यानि dîvyâni	दीव्य dîvya	दीव्यतु dîvyatu	दीव्याव dîvyâva	दीव्यतं dîvyatam	दीव्यतां dîvyatâm	दीव्याम dîvyâma	दीव्यत dîvyata	दीव्यन्तु dîvyantu
चुर् chur	चोरय choraya	चोरयाणि chorayâṇi	चोरय choraya	चोरयतु chorayatu	चोरयाव chorayâva	चोरयतं chorayatam	चोरयतां chorayatâm	चोरयाम chorayâma	चोरयत chorayata	चोरयन्तु chorayantu
	Second Division.	आनि âni	हि hi	तु tu	आव âva	तं tam	तां tâm	आम âma	त ta	अन्तु antu
सु su	सुनु सुनो sunu suno	सुनवानि sunavâni	सुनु[1] sunu	सुनोतु sunotu	सुनवाव sunavâva	सुनुतं sunutam	सुनुतां sunutâm	सुनवाम sunavâma	सुनुत sunuta	सुन्वन्तु sunvantu
तन् tan	तनु तनो tanu tano	तनवानि tanavâni	तनु tanu	तनोतु tanotu	तनवाव tanavâva	तनुतं tanutam	तनुतां tanutâm	तनवाम tanavâma	तनुत tanuta	तन्वन्तु tanvantu
क्री krî	क्रीणी क्रीणा क्रीण् krîṇî krîṇâ krîṇ	क्रीणानि krîṇâni	क्रीणीहि[2] krîṇîhi	क्रीणातु krîṇâtu	क्रीणाव krîṇâva	क्रीणीतं krîṇîtam	क्रीणीतां krîṇîtâm	क्रीणाम krîṇâma	क्रीणीत krîṇîta	क्रीणन्तु krîṇantu
अद् ad	अद् अद् ad ad	अदानि adâni	अद्धि[3] addhi	अत्तु attu	अदाव adâva	अत्तं attam	अत्तां attâm	अदाम adâma	अत्त atta	अदन्तु adantu
हु hu	जुहु जुहो juhu juho	जुहवानि juhavâni	जुहुधि[4] juhudhi	जुहोतु juhotu	जुहवाव juhavâva	जुहुतं juhutam	जुहुतां juhutâm	जुहवाम juhavâma	जुहुत juhuta	जुह्वतु[5] juhvatu
रुध् rudh	रुंध् रुणध् rundh ruṇadh	रुणधानि ruṇadhâni	रुंद्धि[3] runddhi	रुणद्धु ruṇaddhu	रुणधाव ruṇadhâva	रुंद्धं runddham	रुंद्धां runddhâm	रुणधाम ruṇadhâma	रुंद्ध runddha	रुंधन्तु rundhantu

[1] From आप् âp, आप्नुहि âpnuhi, § 321, note *. [2] Verbs of this class, if ending in a consonant, drop both नी nî and हि hi, and add आन âna to the root. Thus from अश् aś, अशान aśâna, not अश्नीहि aśnîhi; but 3rd pers. sing. अश्नातु aśnâtu. (Pâṇ. III. 1, 83.) [3] Roots of the Ad and Rudh classes ending in consonants, except nasals and semivowels, take धि dhi, instead of हि hi. (Pâṇ. VI. 4, 101.) [4] This is the only verb of the Hu class which takes धि dhi, though ending in a vowel. (Pâṇ. VI. 4, 101.) [5] See § 321, note ‖.

ÂTMANEPADA.

Present.

Root.	Verbal Base.									
	First Division.	इ *i*	से *se*	ते *te*	आवहे *avahe*	इथे *ithe*	इते *ite*	आमहे *amahe*	ध्वे *dhve*	न्ते *nte*
भू *bhû*	भव *bhava*	भवे *bhave*	भवसे *bhavase*	भवते *bhavate*	भवावहे *bhavâvahe*	भवेथे *bhavethe*	भवेते *bhavete*	भवामहे *bhavâmahe*	भवध्वे *bhavadhve*	भवन्ते *bhavante*
तुद् *tud*	तुद *tuda*	तुदे *tude*	तुदसे *tudase*	तुदते *tudate*	तुदावहे *tudâvahe*	तुदेथे *tudethe*	तुदेते *tudete*	तुदामहे *tudâmahe*	तुदध्वे *tudadhve*	तुदन्ते *tudante*
दिव् *div*	दीव्य *dîvya*	दीव्ये *dîvye*	दीव्यसे *dîvyase*	दीव्यते *dîvyate*	दीव्यावहे *dîvyâvahe*	दीव्येथे *dîvyethe*	दीव्येते *dîvyete*	दीव्यामहे *dîvyâmahe*	दीव्यध्वे *dîvyadhve*	दीव्यन्ते *dîvyante*
चुर् *chur*	चोरय *choraya*	चोरये *choraye*	चोरयसे *chorayase*	चोरयते *chorayate*	चोरयावहे *chorayâvahe*	चोरयेथे *chorayethe*	चोरयेते *chorayete*	चोरयामहे *chorayâmahe*	चोरयध्वे *chorayadhve*	चोरयन्ते *chorayante*
	Second Division.	ए *e*	से *se*	ते *te*	वहे *vahe*	आथे *âthe*	आते *âte*	महे *mahe*	ध्वे *dhve*	अते *ate*
सु *su*	सुनु *sunu*	सुन्वे *sunve*	सुनुषे *sunushe*	सुनुते *sunute*	सुनुवहे *sunuvahe*	सुन्वाथे *sunvâthe*	सुन्वाते *sunvâte*	सुनुमहे *sunumahe*	सुनुध्वे *sunudhve*	सुन्वते *sunvate*
तन् *tan*	तनु *tanu*	तन्वे *tanve*	तनुषे *tanushe*	तनुते *tanute*	तनुवहे *tanuvahe*	तन्वाथे *tanvâthe*	तन्वाते *tanvâte*	तनुमहे *tanumahe*	तनुध्वे *tanudhve*	तन्वते *tanvate*
क्री *krî*	क्रीणी क्रीण् *krîṇî krîṇ*	क्रीणे *krîṇe*	क्रीणीषे *krîṇîshe*	क्रीणीते *krîṇîte*	क्रीणीवहे *krîṇîvahe*	क्रीणाथे *krîṇâthe*	क्रीणाते *krîṇâte*	क्रीणीमहे *krîṇîmahe*	क्रीणीध्वे *krîṇîdhve*	क्रीणते *krîṇate*
अद् *ad*	अद् *ad*	अदे *ade*	अत्से *atse*	अत्ते *atte*	अद्वहे *advahe*	अदाथे *adâthe*	अदाते *adâte*	अद्महे *admahe*	अद्ध्वे *addhve*	अदते *adate*
हु *hu*	जुहु *juhu*	जुह्वे *juhve*	जुहुषे *juhushe*	जुहुते *juhute*	जुहुवहे *juhuvahe*	जुह्वाथे *juhvâthe*	जुह्वाते *juhvâte*	जुहुमहे *juhumahe*	जुहुध्वे *juhudhve*	जुह्वते *juhvate*
रुध् *rudh*	रुन्ध् *rundh*	रुन्धे *rundhe*	रुन्त्से *runtse*	रुन्द्धे *runddhe*	रुन्ध्वहे *rundhvahe*	रुन्धाथे *rundhâthe*	रुन्धाते *rundhâte*	रुन्ध्महे *rundhmahe*	रुन्द्ध्वे *runddhve*	रुन्धते *rundhate*

Root.	Verbal Base.	ÂTMANEPADA. Imperfect.								
	First Division.	इ *i*	थाः *thâḥ*	त *ta*	आवहि *avahi*	इथां *ithâm*	इतां *itâm*	आमहि *amahi*	ध्वं *dhvam*	न्त *nta*
भू *bhû*	भव *bhava*	अभवे *abhave*	अभवथाः *abhavathâḥ*	अभवत *abhavata*	अभवावहि *abhavâvahi*	अभवेथां *abhavethâm*	अभवेतां *abhavetâm*	अभवामहि *abhavâmahi*	अभवध्वं *abhavadhvam*	अभवंत *abhavanta*
तुद् *tud*	तुद *tuda*	अतुदे *atude*	अतुदथाः *atudathâḥ*	अतुदत *atudata*	अतुदावहि *atudâvahi*	अतुदेथां *atudethâm*	अतुदेतां *atudetâm*	अतुदामहि *atudâmahi*	अतुदध्वं *atudadhvam*	अतुदंत *atudanta*
दिव् *dîv*	दीव्य *dîvya*	अदीव्ये *adîvye*	अदीव्यथाः *adîvyathâḥ*	अदीव्यत *adîvyata*	अदीव्यावहि *adîvyâvahi*	अदीव्येथां *adîvyethâm*	अदीव्येतां *adîvyetâm*	अदीव्यामहि *adîvyâmahi*	अदीव्यध्वं *adîvyadhvam*	अदीव्यंत *adîvyanta*
चुर् *chur*	चोरय *choraya*	अचोरये *achoraye*	अचोरयथाः *achorayathâḥ*	अचोरयत *achorayata*	अचोरयावहि *achorayâvahi*	अचोरयेथां *achorayethâm*	अचोरयेतां *achorayetâm*	अचोरयामहि *achorayâmahi*	अचोरयध्वं *achorayadhvam*	अचोरयंत *achorayanta*
	Second Division.	इ *i*	थाः *thâḥ*	त *ta*	वहि *vahi*	आथां *âthâm*	आतां *âtâm*	महि *mahi*	ध्वं *dhvam*	अत *ata*
सु *su*	सुनु *sunu*	असुन्वि *asunvi*	असुनुथाः *asunuthâḥ*	असुनुत *asunuta*	असुनुवहि *asunuvahi*	असुन्वाथां *asunvâthâm*	असुन्वातां *asunvâtâm*	असुनुमहि *asunumahi*	असुनुध्वं *asunudhvam*	असुन्वत *asunvata*
तन् *tan*	तनु *tanu*	अतन्वि *atanvi*	अतनुथाः *atanuthâḥ*	अतनुत *atanuta*	अतनुवहि *atanuvahi*	अतन्वाथां *atanvâthâm*	अतन्वातां *atanvâtâm*	अतनुमहि *atanumahi*	अतनुध्वं *atanudhvam*	अतन्वत *atanvata*
क्री *krî*	क्रीणी क्रीण् *krîṇî krîṇ*	अक्रीणि *akrîṇi*	अक्रीणीथाः *akrîṇîthâḥ*	अक्रीणीत *akrîṇîta*	अक्रीणीवहि *akrîṇîvahi*	अक्रीणाथां *akrîṇâthâm*	अक्रीणातां *akrîṇâtâm*	अक्रीणीमहि *akrîṇîmahi*	अक्रीणीध्वं *akrîṇîdhvam*	अक्रीणत *akrîṇata*
अद् *ad*	अद् *ad*	आदि *âdi*	आत्थाः *âtthâḥ*	आत्त *âtta*	आद्वहि *âdvahi*	आदाथां *âdâthâm*	आदातां *âdâtâm*	आद्महि *âdmahi*	आद्ध्वं *âddhvam*	आदत *âdata*
हु *hu*	जुहु *juhu*	अजुह्वि *ajuhvi*	अजुहुथाः *ajuhuthâḥ*	अजुहुत *ajuhuta*	अजुहुवहि *ajuhuvahi*	अजुह्वाथां *ajuhvâthâm*	अजुह्वातां *ajuhvâtâm*	अजुहुमहि *ajuhumahi*	अजुहुध्वं *ajuhudhvam*	अजुह्वत *ajuhvata*
रुध् *rudh*	रुंध् *rundh*	अरुंधि *arundhi*	अरुंद्धाः *arunddhâḥ*	अरुंद्ध *arunddha*	अरुंध्वहि *arundhvahi*	अरुंधाथां *arundhâthâm*	अरुंधातां *arundhâtâm*	अरुंध्महि *arundhmahi*	अरुंद्ध्वं *arunddhvam*	अरुंधत *arundhata*

ÂTMANEPADA.

Optative.

Root.	Verbal Base.	इय iya	इथाः ithâḥ	इत ita	इवहि ivahi	इयाथां iyâthâm	इयातां iyâtâm	इमहि imahi	इध्वं idhvam	इरन् iran
	First Division.									
भू bhú	भव bhava	भवेय bhaveya	भवेथाः bhavethâḥ	भवेत bhaveta	भवेवहि bhavevahi	भवेयाथां bhaveyâthâm	भवेयातां bhaveyâtâm	भवेमहि bhavemahi	भवेध्वं bhavedhvam	भवेरन् bhaveran
तुद् tud	तुद tuda	तुदेय tudeya	तुदेथाः tudethâḥ	तुदेत tudeta	तुदेवहि tudevahi	तुदेयाथां tudeyâthâm	तुदेयातां tudeyâtâm	तुदेमहि tudemahi	तुदेध्वं tudedhvam	तुदेरन् tuderan
दिव् div	दीव्य dívya	दीव्येय dívyeya	दीव्येथाः dívyethâḥ	दीव्येत dívyeta	दीव्येवहि dívyevahi	दीव्येयाथां dívyeyâthâm	दीव्येयातां dívyeyâtâm	दीव्येमहि dívyemahi	दीव्येध्वं dívyedhvam	दीव्येरन् dívyeran
चुर् chur	चोरय choraya	चोरयेय chorayeya	चोरयेथाः chorayethâḥ	चोरयेत chorayeta	चोरयेवहि chorayevahi	चोरयेयाथां chorayeyâthâm	चोरयेयातां chorayeyâtâm	चोरयेमहि chorayemahi	चोरयेध्वं chorayedhvam	चोरयेरन् chorayeran
	Second Division.	ईय íya	ईथाः íthâḥ	ईत íta	ईवहि ívahi	ईयाथां íyâthâm	ईयातां íyâtâm	ईमहि ímahi	ईध्वं ídhvam	ईरन् íran
सु su	सुनु sunu	सुन्वीय sunvíya	सुन्वीथाः sunvíthâḥ	सुन्वीत sunvíta	सुन्वीवहि sunvívahi	सुन्वीयाथां sunvíyâthâm	सुन्वीयातां sunvíyâtâm	सुन्वीमहि sunvímahi	सुन्वीध्वं sunvídhvam	सुन्वीरन् sunvíran
तन् tan	तनु tanu	तन्वीय tanvíya	तन्वीथाः tanvíthâḥ	तन्वीत tanvíta	तन्वीवहि tanvívahi	तन्वीयाथां tanvíyâthâm	तन्वीयातां tanvíyâtâm	तन्वीमहि tanvímahi	तन्वीध्वं tanvídhvam	तन्वीरन् tanvíran
क्री krí	क्रीणी क्रीण् kríṇí kríṇ	क्रीणीय kríṇíya	क्रीणीथाः kríṇíthâḥ	क्रीणीत kríṇíta	क्रीणीवहि kríṇívahi	क्रीणीयाथां kríṇíyâthâm	क्रीणीयातां kríṇíyâtâm	क्रीणीमहि kríṇímahi	क्रीणीध्वं kríṇídhvam	क्रीणीरन् kríṇíran
अद् ad	अद् ad	अदीय adíya	अदीथाः adíthâḥ	अदीत adíta	अदीवहि adívahi	अदीयाथां adíyâthâm	अदीयातां adíyâtâm	अदीमहि adímahi	अदीध्वं adídhvam	अदीरन् adíran
हु hu	जुहु juhu	जुह्वीय juhvíya	जुह्वीथाः juhvíthâḥ	जुह्वीत juhvíta	जुह्वीवहि juhvívahi	जुह्वीयाथां juhvíyâthâm	जुह्वीयातां juhvíyâtâm	जुह्वीमहि juhvímahi	जुह्वीध्वं juhvídhvam	जुह्वीरन् juhvíran
रुध् rudh	रुन्ध् rundh	रुन्धीय rundhíya	रुन्धीथाः rundhíthâḥ	रुन्धीत rundhíta	रुन्धीवहि rundhívahi	रुन्धीयाथां rundhíyâthâm	रुन्धीयातां rundhíyâtâm	रुन्धीमहि rundhímahi	रुन्धीध्वं rundhídhvam	रुन्धीरन् rundhíran

Root.	Verbal Base.	ÂTMANEPADA. Imperative.								
	First Division.	ए e	स्व sva	तां tâm	आवहै avahai	इथां ithâm	इतां itâm	आमहै amahai	ध्वं dhvam	न्तां ntâm
भू bhû	भव bhava	भवै bhavai	भवस्व bhavasva	भवतां bhavatâm	भवावहै bhavâvahai	भवेथां bhavethâm	भवेतां bhavetâm	भवामहै bhavâmahai	भवध्वं bhavadhvam	भवन्तां bhavantâm
तुद् tud	तुद tuda	तुदै tudai	तुदस्व tudasva	तुदतां tudatâm	तुदावहै tudâvahai	तुदेथां tudethâm	तुदेतां tudetâm	तुदामहै tudâmahai	तुदध्वं tudadhvam	तुदन्तां tudantâm
दिव् div	दीव्य dîvya	दीव्यै dîvyai	दीव्यस्व dîvyasva	दीव्यतां dîvyatâm	दीव्यावहै dîvyâvahai	दीव्येथां dîvyethâm	दीव्येतां dîvyetâm	दीव्यामहै dîvyâmahai	दीव्यध्वं dîvyadhvam	दीव्यन्तां dîvyantâm
चुर् chur	चोरय choraya	चोरयै chorayai	चोरयस्व chorayasva	चोरयतां chorayatâm	चोरयावहै chorayâvahai	चोरयेथां chorayethâm	चोरयेतां chorayetâm	चोरयामहै chorayâmahai	चोरयध्वं chorayadhvam	चोरयन्तां chorayantâm
	Second Division.	ऐ ai	स्व sva	तां tâm	आवहै âvahai	आथां âthâm	आतां âtâm	आमहै âmahai	ध्वं dhvam	अतां atâm
सु su	सुनु सुनो sunu suno	सुनवै sunavai	सुनुष्व sunushva	सुनुतां sunutâm	सुनवावहै sunavâvahai	सुन्वाथां sunvâthâm	सुन्वातां sunvâtâm	सुनवामहै sunavâmahai	सुनुध्वं sunudhvam	सुन्वतां sunvatâm
तन् tan	तनु तनो tanu tano	तनवै tanavai	तनुष्व tanushva	तनुतां tanutâm	तनवावहै tanavâvahai	तन्वाथां tanvâthâm	तन्वातां tanvâtâm	तनवामहै tanavâmahai	तनुध्वं tanudhvam	तन्वतां tanvatâm
क्री krî	क्रीणी क्रीणा क्रीण् krîṇî krîṇâ krîṇ	क्रीणै krîṇai	क्रीणीष्व krîṇîshva	क्रीणीतां krîṇîtâm	क्रीणावहै krîṇâvahai	क्रीणाथां krîṇâthâm	क्रीणातां krîṇâtâm	क्रीणामहै krîṇâmahai	क्रीणीध्वं krîṇîdhvam	क्रीणतां krîṇatâm
अद् ad	अद् अद् ad ad	अदै adai	अत्स्व atsva	अत्तां attâm	अदावहै adâvahai	अदाथां adâthâm	अदातां adâtâm	अदामहै adâmahai	अद्ध्वं addhvam	अदतां adatâm
हु hu	जुहु जुहो juhu juho	जुहवै juhavai	जुहुष्व juhushva	जुहुतां juhutâm	जुहवावहै juhavâvahai	जुह्वाथां juhvâthâm	जुह्वातां juhvâtâm	जुहवामहै juhavâmahai	जुहुध्वं juhudhvam	जुह्वतां juhvatâm
रुध् rudh	रुन्ध् रुणध् rundh ruṇadh	रुणधै ruṇadhai	रुन्त्स्व runtsva	रुन्द्धां runddhâm	रुणधावहै ruṇadhâvahai	रुन्धाथां rundhâthâm	रुन्धातां rundhâtâm	रुणधामहै ruṇadhâmahai	रुन्द्ध्वं runddhvam	रुन्धतां rundhatâm

CHAPTER X.

GENERAL OR UNMODIFIED TENSES.

§ 323. In the tenses which remain, the Reduplicated Perfect, the Periphrastic Perfect, the First and Second Aorist, the Future, the Conditional, the Periphrastic Future, and Benedictive, the distinction of the ten classes vanishes. All verbs are treated alike, to whatever class they belong in the modified tenses; and the distinguishing features, the inserted नु *nu*, उ *u*, नी *nî*, &c., are removed again from the roots to which they had been attached in the Present, the Imperfect, the Optative, and Imperative. Only the verbs of the Chur class preserve their अय *aya* throughout, except in the Aorist and Benedictive.

Reduplicated Perfect.

§ 324. The root in its primitive state is reduplicated. The rules of reduplication have been given above. (§§ 302–319.)

§ 325. The Reduplicated Perfect can be formed of all verbs, except

1. Monosyllabic roots which begin with any vowel prosodially long but अ *a* or आ *â*: such as ईड् *îḍ*, to praise; एध् *edh*, to grow; इन्ध् *indh*, to light; उन्द् *und*, to wet. ऋच्छ् *ṛichchh* and ऊर्णु *ûrṇu* are excepted.
2. Polysyllabic roots, such as चकास् *chakâs*, to be bright.
3. Verbs of the Chur class and derivative verbs, such as Causatives, Desideratives, Intensives, Denominatives.

§ 326. Verbs which cannot form the Perfect by reduplication, form the Periphrastic Perfect by means of composition. (§ 340.)

So do likewise दय् *day*, to pity, &c., अय् *ay*, to go, आस् *âs*, to sit down (Pâṇ. III. 1, 37), कास् *kâs*, to cough (Pâṇ. III. 1, 35); also काश् *kâś*, to shine (Sâr.); optionally उष् *ush*, to burn, (ओषां *oshâm*), विद् *vid*, to know, (विदां *vidâm*), जागृ *jâgṛi*, to wake, (जागरां *jâgarâm*, Pâṇ. III. 1, 38); and, after taking reduplication, भी *bhî* (बिभयां *bibhayâm*), ह्री *hrî* (जिह्रयां *jihrayâm*), भृ *bhṛi* (बिभरां *bibharâm*), and हु *hu* (जुहवां *juhavâm*, Pâṇ. III. 1, 39).

The verb ऊर्णु *ûrṇu*, to cover, although polysyllabic, allows only of ऊर्णुनाव *ûrṇunâva* as its Perfect.

ऋच्छ् *ṛichchh*, to fail, although ending in two consonants, forms only आनर्च्छ *ânarchchha*.

Terminations of the Reduplicated Perfect.

SINGULAR.

1.	अ *a*	ए *e*
2.	इथ *itha*	इषे *ishe*
3.	अ *a*	ए *e*

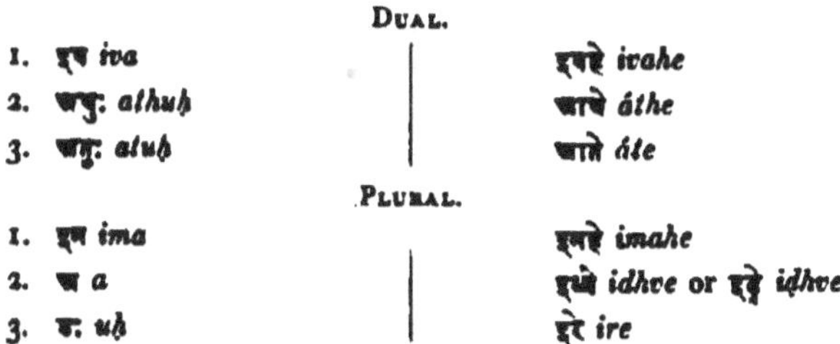

	Dual.	
1.	इव *iva*	इवहे *ivahe*
2.	अथुः *athuḥ*	आथे *âthe*
3.	अतुः *atuḥ*	आते *âte*
	Plural.	
1.	इम *ima*	इमहे *imahe*
2.	अ *a*	इध्वे *idhve* or इढ्वे *iḍhve*
3.	उः *uḥ*	इरे *ire*

These terminations are here given, without any regard to the systems of native or comparative grammarians, in that form in which they may be mechanically added to the reduplicated roots. The rules on the omission of the initial इ *i* of certain terminations will be given below.

§ 327. The accent falls on the terminations in the Parasmaipada and Âtmanepada, except in the *three persons singular Parasmaipada*. In these the accent falls on the root, which therefore is strengthened according to the following rules:

1. Vowels capable of Guṇa, take Guṇa throughout the singular, if followed by a consonant.

   भिद् *bhid*, बिभेद *bibhed-a*, बिभेदिथ *bibhed-itha*, बिभेद *bibhed-a*.

   बुध् *budh*, बुबोध *bubodh-a*, बुबोधिथ *bubodh-itha*, बुबोध *bubodh-a*.

   But जीव् *jîv*, a long medial vowel not being liable to Guṇa, forms जिजीव *jijîv-a*, जिजीविथ *jijîv-itha*, जिजीव *jijîv-a*.

2. Final vowels take Vṛiddhi or Guṇa in the first, Guṇa in the second, Vṛiddhi only in the third person singular.

   नी *nî*, निनाय *ninây-a* or निनय *ninay-a*, निनयिथ *ninay-itha*, निनाय *ninây-a*.

3. अ *a* if followed by a single consonant, takes Vṛiddhi or Guṇa in the first, Guṇa in the second, Vṛiddhi only in the third person singular.

   हन् *han*, जघान *jaghân-a* or जघन *jaghan-a*, जघनिथ *jaghan-itha*, जघान *jaghân-a*.

Note—If the second person singular Parasmaipada is formed by थ *tha*, the accent falls on the root; if with इथ *itha*, the accent may fall on any syllable, but generally it is on the termination. In this case the radical vowel may, in certain verbs, be without Guṇa, विज् *vij*, विवेज *viveja*, but विविजिथ *vivijitha*. (Pâṇ. 1. 2, 2; 3.)

§ 328. As there is a tendency to strengthen the base in the three persons singular Parasmaipada, so there is a tendency to weaken the base, under certain circumstances, before the other terminations of the Perfect, Parasmai and Âtmanepada. Here the following rules must be observed:

1. Roots like पत् *pat*, i. e. roots in which अ *a* is preceded and followed by a single consonant, and which in their reduplicated syllable repeat the initial consonant without any change (this excludes roots beginning with aspirates and with gutturals; roots beginning with व् *v*, and

शस् *śas*[*] and दद् *dad* are likewise excepted), contract such forms as पपत् *papat* into पेत् *pet*, before the accented terminations, (including इथ *itha*, Pâṇ. vi. 4, 120, 121.)

पच् *pach*, पपक्थ *papaktha*, but पेचिथ *pechitha*, पेचिम *pechima*, पेचुः *pechuḥ*.

तन् *tan*, तेनिथ *tenitha*, तेनिम *tenima*, तेनुः *tenuḥ*.

2. Roots mentioned in § 311 take their weak form.

वह् *vah*, उवाह *uvâha*, ऊहिम *ûhima*.

वच् *vach*, उवाच *uvâcha*, ऊचुः *ûchuḥ*.

Note—The roots तॄ *tṛî*, फल् *phal*, भज् *bhaj*, त्रप् *trap*, श्रथ् *śrath* (Pâṇ. vi. 4, 122), and राध् *râdh*, in the sense 'of killing' (123), from their Reduplicated Perfect like पत् *pat*. The roots जॄ *jṛî*, भ्रम् *bhram*, and त्रस् *tras* (124), may do so optionally; and likewise फण् *phaṇ*, राज् *râj*, भ्राज् *bhrâj*, भ्राश् *bhrâś*, भ्लाश् *bhlâś*, स्यम् *syam*, स्वन् *svan*.

3. The roots गम् *gam*, हन् *han*, जन् *jan*, खन् *khan*, घस् *ghas* drop their radical vowel. (Pâṇ. vi. 4, 98.)

गम् *gam*, जग्मतुः *jagmatuḥ*.
हन् *han*, जघ्नतुः *jaghnatuḥ*.
खन् *khan*, चख्नतुः *chakhnatuḥ*.
घस् *ghas*, जक्षतुः *jakshatuḥ*.

4. Roots ending in consonants preceded by a nasal (Pâṇ. i. 2, 5), such as मंथ् *manth*, स्रंस् *sraṁs*, &c., do not drop their nasal in the weakening forms. Ex. 3rd pers. dual: ममंथतुः *mamanthatuḥ*; सस्रंसे *sasraṁse*.

5. The verbs श्रंथ् *śranth*, ग्रंथ् *granth*, दंभ् *dambh*, and स्वंज् *svañj*, however, may be weakened, and form श्रेथतुः *śrethatuḥ*, ग्रेथतुः *grethatuḥ*, देभतुः *debhatuḥ*, सस्वजे *sasvaje* (loss of nasal and *e*, cf. Pâṇ. i. 2, 6, v.). But according to some grammarians the forms शश्रंथतुः *śaśranthatuḥ* &c. are more correct.

§ 329. Roots ending in आ *â*, and many roots ending in diphthongs, drop their final vowel before all terminations beginning with a vowel (Pâṇ. vi. 4, 64). In the general tenses, verbs ending in diphthongs are treated like verbs ending in आ *â*.

The same roots take औ *au* for the termination of the first and third persons singular Parasmai.

दा *dâ*, ददौ *dad-au*, ददिव *dad-iva*, ददथुः *dad-athuḥ*, ददिरे *dad-ire*.

म्लै *mlai*, मम्लौ *maml-au*, मम्लिव *maml-iva*, मम्लथुः *maml-athuḥ*, मम्लिरे *maml-ire*.

Except व्ये *vye*, ह्वे *hve*, &c.; see § 311.

§ 330. Roots ending in इ *i*, ई *î*, ऋ *ṛi*, if preceded by one consonant, change their vowels, before terminations beginning with vowels, into य् *y*, र् *r*.

---

[*] शसु हिंसायामिति केचित् केचित्तु शश प्लुतगतावित्यपि । Prasâda, p. 13 a. In a later passage the Prasâda (p. 17 b) decides for both, शस् *śas* and शश् *śaś*.

If preceded by more than one consonant, they change their vowels into इय् *iy*, अर् *ar* *.

Roots ending in उ *u*, ऊ *ú*, change these vowels always into उव् *uv*.

Most roots ending in ॠ *ṛí*, change the vowel to अर् *ar* (Pâṇ. VII. 4, 11). गॄ *gṛí*, जागरतुः *jagaratuḥ* †.

नी *ní*, निन्यिव *niny-iva*, we two have led.

श्रि *śri*, शिश्रियिव *śiśriy-iva*, we two have gone.

कृ *kṛi*, चक्रथुः *chakr-athuḥ*, you two have done.

स्तृ *stṛi*, तस्तरथुः *tastar-athuḥ*, you two have spread.

यु *yu*, युयुवथुः *yuyuv-athuḥ*, you two have joined.

स्तु *stu*, तुष्टुवथुः *tushṭuv-athuḥ*, you two have praised.

कॄ *kṛí*, चकरथुः *chakar-athuḥ*, you two have scattered.

CHAPTER XI.

THE INTERMEDIATE इ *i*.

§ 331. Before we can proceed to form the paradigms of the Reduplicated Perfect by means of joining the terminations with the root, it is necessary to consider the intermediate इ *i*, which in the Reduplicated Perfect and in the other unmodified tenses has to be inserted between the verbal base and the terminations, originally beginning with consonants. The rules which *require*, *allow*, or *prohibit* the insertion of this इ *i* form one of the most difficult chapters of Sanskrit grammar, and it is the object of the following paragraphs to simplify these rules as much as possible.

The general tendency, and so far the general rule, is that the terminations of the unmodified or general tenses, originally beginning with consonants, insert the vowel इ *i* between base and termination; and from an historical point of view it would no doubt be more correct to speak of the rules which require the addition of an intermediate इ *i* than (as has been done in § 326) to represent the इ *i* as an integral part of the terminations, and to give the rules which require its omission. But as the intermediate इ *i* has prevailed in the vast majority of verbs, it will be easier, for practical purposes, to state the exceptions, i. e. the cases in which the इ *i* is not employed, instead of defining the cases in which it *must* or *may* be inserted.

---

* ऋ *ṛi* forms the perf. आर *âra*, 3rd pers. dual आरतुः *âratuḥ*. ऋच्छ *ṛichchh* forms आनर्च्छ *ânarchchha*, 3rd pers. dual आनर्च्छतुः *ânarchchhatuḥ*. (Pâṇ. VII. 4, 11.)

† In शॄ *śṛí*, दॄ *dṛí*, and पॄ *pṛí* a further shortening may take place; शशरतुः *śaśaratuḥ* being shortened to शश्रतुः *śaśratuḥ*, &c. (Pâṇ. VII. 4, 12.)

One termination only, that of the 3rd pers. plur. Perf. Âtm., इरे *ire*, keeps the intermediate इ *i* under all circumstances. In the Veda, however, this इ *i*, too, has not yet become fixed, and is occasionally omitted; e.g. दुदुह्रे *duduh-re*.

Let it be remembered then, that there are three points to be considered:

1. When is it *necessary* to omit the इ *i*?
2. When is it *optional* to insert or to omit the इ *i*?
3. When is it *necessary* to insert the इ *i*?

For the purposes of reading Sanskrit, all that a student is obliged to know is, When it is *necessary* to omit the इ *i*? Even for writing Sanskrit this knowledge would be sufficient, for in all cases except those in which the omission is necessary, the इ *i* may safely be inserted, although, according to views of native grammarians, it may be equally right to omit it. A student therefore, and particularly a beginner, is safe if he only knows the cases in which इ *i* is necessarily omitted, nor will anything but extensive reading enable him to know the verbs in which the insertion is either optional or necessary. Native grammarians have indeed laid down a number of rules, but both before and after Pâṇini the language of India has changed, and even native grammarians are obliged to admit that on the optional insertion of इ *i* authorities differ; that is to say, that the literary language of India differed so much in different parts of that enormous country, and at different periods of its long history, that no rules, however minute, would suffice to register all its freaks and fancies.

Taking as the starting-point the general axiom (Pâṇ. VII. 2, 35) that every termination beginning originally with a consonant (except य् *y*) takes the इ *i*, which we represent as a portion of the termination, we proceed to state the exceptions, i.e. the cases in which the इ *i* must on no account be inserted, or, as we should say, must be cut off from the beginning of the termination.

§ 332. The following verbs, which have been carefully collected by native grammarians (Pâṇ. VII. 2, 10), are not allowed to take the intermediate इ *i* in the so-called general or unmodified tenses, before terminations or affixes beginning originally with a consonant (except य् *y*). (Note—The reduplicated perfect and its participle in वस् *vas* are not affected by these rules; see § 334.)

1. All monosyllabic roots ending in आ *â*.
2. All monosyllabic roots ending in इ *i*, except श्रि *śri*, to attend (21, 31)*; श्वि *śvi*, to grow (23, 41). (Note—स्मि *smi*, to laugh, must take इ *i* in the Desiderative. Pâṇ. VII. 2, 74.)
3. All monosyllabic roots ending in ई *î*, except डी *ḍî*, to fly (22, 72; 26, 26. *anudâtta*), and शी *śî*, to rest (24, 22).

* These figures refer to the Dhâtupâṭha in Westergaard's Radices Linguæ Sanscritæ, 1841.

4. All monosyllabic roots ending in उ *u*, except यु *yu*, to mix (24, 23; not 31, 9); रु *ru*, to sound (24, 24); नु *nu*, to praise (24, 26; 28, 104?); क्षु *kshu*, to sound (24, 27); क्ष्णु *kshṇu*, to sharpen (24, 28). स्नु *snu*, to flow (24, 29), takes इ *i* in Parasmaipada (Pâṇ. VII. 2, 36). (Note—स्तु *stu*, to praise, and सु *su*, to pour, take इ *i* in the I. Aorist Parasmaipada. Pâṇ. VII. 2, 72.)
5. All monosyllabic roots ending in ऋ *ṛi*, except वृ *vṛi*, to choose (31, 38). Important exception: in the Fut. and Cond. in स्य *sya*, all verbs in ऋ *ṛi* take इ *i* (Pâṇ. VII. 2, 70).
   स्वृ *svṛi*, to sound, *may* take इ *i* (Pâṇ. VII. 2, 44). भृ *bhṛi*, to carry, may take इ *i* in the Desider. (Pâṇ. VII. 2, 49). दृ *dṛi*, to regard, धृ *dhṛi*, to hold, and ऋ *ṛi*, to go, take इ *i* in the Desider. (Pâṇ. VII. 2, 74, 75).
   In the Benedictive and I. Aorist verbs ending in ऋ *ṛi* and beginning with a conjunct consonant may take इ *i* (Pâṇ. VII. 2, 43).
6. All monosyllabic roots ending in ए *e*, ऐ *ai*, ओ *o*.
   Therefore, with few exceptions, as mentioned above, all monosyllabic roots ending in vowels, except the vowels ॠ *ṝ* and ॠ *ṛî*, must not take इ *i*.
7. Of roots ending in क् *k*, शक् *śak*, to be able (26, 78; 27, 15).
8. Of roots ending in च् *ch*, पच् *pach*, to cook (23, 27); वच् *vach*, to speak (24, 55); मुच् *much*, to loose (28, 136); सिच् *sich*, to sprinkle (28, 140); रिच् *rich*, to leave (29, 4); विच् *vich*, to separate (29, 5).
9. Of roots ending in छ् *chh*, प्रछ् *prachh*, to ask (28, 120). It must take इ *i* in the Desider. (Pâṇ. VII. 2, 75).
10. Of roots ending in ज् *j*, स्वंज् *svañj*, to embrace (23, 7); त्यज् *tyaj*, to leave (23, 17); संज् *sañj*, to adhere (23, 18); भज् *bhaj*, to worship (23, 29); रंज् *rañj*, to colour (23, 30; 26, 58); यज् *yaj*, to sacrifice (23, 33); निज् *nij*, to clean (25, 11); विज् *vij*, to separate (25, 12; not 28, 9, or 29, 23); [Kâś. मृज् *mṛij*]; युज् *yuj*, to meditate (26, 68), to join (29, 7); सृज् *sṛij*, to let off (26, 69; 29, 121); भ्रस्ज् *bhrajj*, to bake (28, 4, except Desider.); मस्ज् *majj*, to dip (28, 122); रुज् *ruj*, to break (28, 123); भुज् *bhuj*, to bend (28, 124), to protect (29, 17); भंज् *bhañj*, to break (29, 16).
11. Of roots ending in द् *d*, हद् *had*, to evacuate (23, 8); स्कंद् *skand*, to step (23, 10); अद् *ad*, to eat (24, 1); पद् *pad*, to go (26, 60); खिद् *khid*, to be distressed (26, 61; 28, 142; 29, 12); विद् *vid*, to be (26, 62); स्विद् *svid*, to sweat (26, 79); तुद् *tud*, to strike (28, 1); नुद् *nud*, to push (28, 2; 28, 132); सद् *sad*, to droop (28, 133); शद् *śad*, to perish (28, 134); विद् *vid*, to find (28, 138? 29, 13; not 24, 56); भिद् *bhid*, to cut (29, 2); छिद् *chhid*, to divide (29, 3); क्षुद् *kshud*, to pound (29, 6).

12. Of roots ending in ध् *dh*, बुध् *budh*, to know (26, 63); युध् *yudh*, to fight (26, 64); रुध् *rudh*, with अनु *anu*, to love (26, 65), to keep off (29, 6); राध् *rádh*, to grow (26, 71; 27, 16); व्यध् *vyadh*, to strike (26, 72); क्रुध् *krudh*, to be angry (26, 80); क्षुध् *kshudh*, to be hungry (26, 81), except Part. क्षुधित *kshudhita* and Ger. क्षुधित्वा *kshudhitvá* (Pâṇ. VII. 2, 52); शुध् *śudh*, to clean (26, 82); सिध् *sidh*, to succeed (26, 83); साध् *sádh*, to achieve (27, 16); बंध् *bandh*, to bind (31, 37).

13. Of roots ending in न् *n*, हन् *han*, to kill (24, 2), except the Fut. and Cond. (Pâṇ. VII. 2, 70); likewise its substitute वध् *badh*; मन् *man*, to think (26, 67).

14. Of roots ending in प् *p*, तिप् *tip*, to pour (10, 1?); सृप् *sṛip*, to go (23, 14); तप् *tap*, to heat (23, 16; 26, 50); शप् *śap*, to swear (23, 31; 26, 59); वप् *vap*, to sow (23, 34); स्वप् *svap*, to sleep (24, 60); आप् *áp*, to reach (27, 14); क्षिप् *kship*, to throw (28, 5); लुप् *lup*, to cut (28, 137); लिप् *lip*, to anoint (28, 139); छुप् *chhup*, to touch (28, 125). (Note— तृप् *tṛip* and दृप् *dṛip*, which are generally included, may take इ *i*, according to Pâṇ. VII. 2, 45.)

15. Of roots ending in भ् *bh*, रभ् *rabh*, to desire (23, 5); लभ् *labh*, to take (23, 6); यभ् *yabh*, coire (23, 11).

16. Of roots ending in म् *m*, रम् *ram*, to play (20, 23); नम् *nam*, to incline (23, 12); यम् *yam*, to cease (23, 15). But these three take इ *i* in Aor. Par. (Pâṇ. VII. 2, 73). गम् *gam*, to go (23, 13), but it takes इ *i* before स् *s* of Fut., Cond., and Desider. Par. (Pâṇ. VII. 2, 58). Also क्रम् *kram*, to step (13, 31), in Âtm. (Pâṇ. VII. 2, 36).

17. Of roots ending in श् *ś*, क्रुश् *kruś*, to shout (20, 26); दृश् *dṛiś*, to see (23, 19); दंश् *daṁś*, to bite (23, 20); लिश् *liś*, to be small (26, 70; 28, 127); दिश् *diś*, to show (28, 3); रुश् *ruś*, to hurt (28, 126); रिश् *riś*, to hurt (28, 127); स्पृश् *spṛiś*, to touch (28, 128); विश् *viś*, to enter (28, 130); मृश् *mṛiś*, to rub (28, 131).

18. Of roots ending in ष् *sh*, कृष् *kṛish*, to draw (23, 21; 28, 6); त्विष् *tvish*, to shine (23, 32); द्विष् *dvish*, to hate (24, 3); विष् *vish*, to pervade (25, 13), to separate (31, 54; not 17, 47); पुष् *push*, to nourish (26, 73; not 17, 50); शुष् *śush*, to dry (26, 74); तुष् *tush*, to please (26, 75); दुष् *dush*, to spoil (26, 76); श्लिष् *ślish*, to embrace (26, 77); शिष् *śish*, to distinguish (29, 14); पिष् *pish*, to pound (29, 15).

19. Of roots ending in स् *s*, वस् *vas*, to dwell (23, 36), except Part. उषितः *ushitaḥ* and Ger. उषित्वा *ushitvá* (Pâṇ. VII. 2, 52); घस् *ghas*, to eat (17, 65, as substitute for अद् *ad*).

20. Of roots ending in ह् *h*, रुह् *ruh*, to grow (20, 29); दह् *dah*, to burn (23, 22); मिह् *mih*, to sprinkle (23, 23); वह् *vah*, to carry (23, 35);

दुह् *duh*, to milk (24, 4; not 17, 87); दिह् *dih*, to smear (24, 5); लिह् *lih*, to lick (24, 6); नह् *nah*, to bind (26, 57).

§ 333. Other roots there are, which must not take इ *i* in certain only of the general tenses.

A. In the future (formed by ता *tâ*), the future and conditional (formed by स्य *sya*), the desiderative, and the participle in त *ta* (Pâṇ. VII. 2, 15; 44), the verb कृप् *kḷip* must not take इ *i*, if used in the Parasmaipada. (Pâṇ. VII. 2, 60.)

कृप् *kḷip*, to shape, Fut. कल्प्ता *kalptâ*, Fut. कल्प्स्यति *kalpsyati*, Cond. अकल्प्स्यत् *akalpsyat*; Desid. चिक्लृप्सति *chikḷipsati*; Part. क्लृप्तः *kḷiptaḥ*.

B. In the future and conditional (formed by स्य *sya*), the desiderative base, and the participle in त *ta*, the following four verbs must not take इ *i*, if used in the Parasmaipada. (Pâṇ. VII. 2, 59.)

वृत् *vṛit*, to exist, Fut. वर्त्स्यति *vartsyati*, Cond. अवर्त्स्यत् *avartsyat*; Desid. विवृत्सति *vivṛitsati*; Part. वृत्तः *vṛittaḥ*. (Pâṇ. VII. 2, 15; 56.)

वृध् *vṛidh*, to grow, Fut. वर्त्स्यति *vartsyati*, Cond. अवर्त्स्यत् *avartsyat*; Desid. विवृत्सति *vivṛitsati*; Part. वृद्धः *vṛiddhaḥ*.

स्यंद् *syand*, to drop, Fut. स्यंत्स्यति *syantsyati*, Cond. अस्यंत्स्यत् *asyantsyat*; Desid. सिस्यंत्सति *sisyantsati*; Part. स्यन्नः *syannaḥ*.

शृध् *śṛidh*, to hurt, Fut. शर्त्स्यति *śartsyati*, Cond. अशर्त्स्यत् *aśartsyat*; Desid. शिशृत्सति *śiśṛitsati*; Part. शृद्धः *śṛiddhaḥ*.

C. In the desiderative bases, and in the participle in त *ta*, monosyllabic roots ending in उ *u*, ऊ *û*, ऋ *ṛi*, ॠ *ṛî*, and ग्रह् *grah*, to take, and गुह् *guh*, to hide, do not take इ *i*. (Pâṇ. VII. 2, 12.)

भू *bhû*, to be, बुभूषति *bubhûshati*; Part. भूतः *bhûtaḥ*.

ग्रह् *grah*, जिघृक्षति *jighṛikshati*; Part. गृहीतः *gṛihîtaḥ* (long *î* by special rule, cf. Pâṇ. VII. 2, 37).

गुह् *guh*, जुघुक्षति *jughukshati*; Part. गूढः *gûḍhaḥ* (cf. Pâṇ. VII. 2, 44).

(Verbs ending in ॠ *ṛî*, and वृ *vṛi* are liable to exceptions. See § 337. Pâṇ. VII. 2, 38–41.)

D. Participial formations.

1. Roots which *may* be without the इ *i* in any one of the general tenses, *must* be without it in the participle in त *ta*.

(Remark that the participle in त *ta* is most opposed, as the reduplicated perfect is most disposed to the admission of इ *i*.)

Monosyllabic roots ending in उ *u*, ऊ *û*, ऋ *ṛi*, ॠ *ṛî*, do not take इ *i* before the participle in त *ta*, nor before other terminations which tend to weaken a verbal base. (Pâṇ. VII. 2, 11.)

यु *yu*, to join, युतः *yu-taḥ*, युतवान् *yu-tavân*, युत्वा *yu-tvâ*. (Pâṇ. VII. 2, 11.)

लू *lû*, to cut, लूनः *lû-naḥ*, लूनवान् *lû-navân*, लूत्वा *lû-tvâ*. (Except पू *pû*, § 335, II. 6.)

वृ *vṛi*, to cover, वृतः *vṛi-taḥ*, वृतवान् *vṛi-tavân*, वृत्वा *vṛi-tvâ*.

गाह् *gâh*, to enter, may form (Pâṇ. VII. 2, 44) the future as गाहिता *gâh-i-tâ* or गाढा *gâḍhâ*; hence its participle गाढः *gâḍhaḥ* only.

गुप् *gup*, to protect, may form (Pâṇ. VII. 2, 44) the future गोपिता *gop-i-tâ* or गोप्ता *gop-tâ*; hence its participle गुप्तः *guptaḥ* only.

2. Roots which by native grammarians are marked with technical आ *â* or ई *î* do not take इ *i* in the participle in त *ta*. (Pâṇ. VII. 2, 14, 16.) *

स्विद् *svid*, to sweat (marked as ञिष्विदा *ñishvidâ*); स्विन्नः *svinnaḥ*.

लज् *laj*, to be ashamed (marked as ओलजी *olajî*); लग्नः *lagnaḥ*.

List of Participles in त ta *or* न na *which for special reasons and in special senses do not take* इ i.

श्रि *śri*, to go; श्रितः *śritaḥ*, श्रित्वा *śritvâ*. (Pâṇ. VII. 2, 11.) See § 332, 2.

श्वि *śvi*, to swell; शूनः *śûnaḥ*. (Pâṇ. VII. 2, 14.) See § 332, 2.

क्षुभ् *kshubh*, to shake; क्षुब्धः *kshubdhaḥ*, if it means the churning-stick. (Pâṇ. VII. 2, 18.) See § 332, 15.

स्वन् *svan*, to sound; स्वान्तः *svântaḥ*, if it means the mind.

ध्वन् *dhvan*, to sound; ध्वान्तः *dhvântaḥ*, if it means darkness.

लग् *lag*, to be near; लग्नः *lagnaḥ*, if it means attached.

म्लेच्छ् *mlechchh*, to speak indistinctly; म्लिष्टः *mlishṭaḥ*, if it means indistinct.

विरेभ् *virebh*, to sound; विरिब्धः *viribdhaḥ*, if it refers to a note.

फण् *phaṇ*, to prepare; फाण्टः *phâṇṭaḥ*, if it means without an effort.

वाह् *vâh*, to labour; वाढः *vâḍhaḥ*, if it means excessive.

धृष् *dhṛish*, to be confident; धृष्टः *dhṛishṭaḥ*, if it means bold. (Pâṇ. VII. 2, 19.)

विशस् *viśas*, to praise; विशस्तः *viśastaḥ*, if it means arrogant.

दृह् *dṛih*, to grow; दृढः *dṛiḍhaḥ*, if it means strong. (Pâṇ. VII. 2, 20.)

परिवृह् *parivṛih*, to grow; परिवृढः *parivṛiḍhaḥ*, if it means lord. (Pâṇ. VII. 2, 21.)

कष् *kash*, to try; कष्टः *kashṭaḥ*, if it means difficult or impervious. (Pâṇ. VII. 2, 22.)

घुष् *ghush*, to manifest; घुष्टः *ghushṭaḥ*, if it does not mean proclaimed. (Pâṇ. VII. 2, 23.)

अर्द् *ard*, with the prepos. सं *sam*, नि *ni*, वि *vi*, अर्णः *arṇṇaḥ*; समर्णः *samarṇṇaḥ*, plagued. (Pâṇ. VII. 2, 24.)

अर्द् *ard*, with the prepos. अभि *abhi*; अभ्यर्णः *abhyarṇṇaḥ*, if it means near. (Pâṇ. VII. 2, 25.)

वृत् *vṛit* (as causative), वृत्तः *vṛittaḥ*, if it means read.

---

* मिद् *mid*, to be soft, though having a technical आ *â*, may, in certain senses, form its participle as मेदितः *meditaḥ* or मिन्नः *minnaḥ* (Pâṇ. VII. 2, 17). The same applies to all verbs marked by technical आ *â*.

Intermediate इ i *in the Reduplicated Perfect.*

§ 334. The preceding rules, prohibiting in a number of roots the इ *i* for all or most general tenses, do not affect the reduplicated perfect. Most of the verbs just enumerated which must omit इ *i* in all other general tenses, do not omit it in the perfect. So general, in fact, has the use of the इ *i* become in the perfect, that eight roots only are absolutely prohibited from taking it. These are (Pâṇ. VII. 2, 13),

1. कृ *kṛi*, to do, (unless it is changed to स्कृ *skṛi*), 1st pers. dual चकृव *chakṛi-va*; but संचस्करिव *saṁchaskariva*; 2nd pers. sing. संचस्करिथ *saṁchaskaritha*.
2. सृ *sṛi* to go, ससृव *sasṛi-va*.
3. भृ *bhṛi*, to bear, बभृव *babhṛi-va*.
4. वृ *vṛi* (वृञ् *vṛiñ* and वृङ् *vṛiṅ* *), to choose, Par. ववृव *vavṛi-va*†, ववर्थ *vavar-tha*; Âtm. ववृवहे *vavṛi-vahe*, ववृषे *vavṛi-she*.
5. स्तु *stu*, to praise, तुष्टुव *tushṭu-va*. तुष्टोथ *tushṭo-tha*.
6. द्रु *dru*, to run, दुद्रुव *dudru-va*. दुद्रोथ *dudro-tha*.
7. स्रु *sru*, to flow, सुस्रुव *susru-va*. सुस्रोथ *susro-tha*.
8. श्रु *śru*, to hear, शुश्रुव *śuśru-va*. शुश्रोथ *śuśro-tha*.

§ 335. In the second person singular of the reduplicated perfect Par. the इ *i* before थ *tha* must necessarily be left out,

1. In the eight roots, enumerated before. (The form ववर्थ *vavar-tha*, however, being restricted to the Veda, ववरिथ *vavaritha* is considered the right form.)
2. In roots ending in vowels, which are necessarily without इ *i* in the future (ता *tâ*), Pâṇ. VII. 2, 61. See § 332, where these roots are given.

   या *yâ*, to go; Fut. याता *yâtâ*; ययाथ *yayâ-tha*.

   चि *chi*, to gather; Fut. चेता *chetâ*; चिचेथ *chiche-tha*.
3. In roots ending in consonants and having an अ *ă* for their radical vowel, which are necessarily without इ *i* in the future (ता *tâ*), Pâṇ. VII. 2, 62. See § 332, where these roots are given.

   पच् *pach*, to cook; Fut. पक्ता *paktâ*; पपक्थ *papak-tha*.

But कृषति *kṛishati*, he drags; Fut. कर्ष्टा *karshṭâ*; चकर्षिथ *chakarsh-i-tha*. (Bharadvâja requires the omission of इ *i* after roots with ऋ *ṛi* only, which are necessarily without इ *i* in the future (Pâṇ. VII. 2, 63), except root ऋ *ṛi* itself. Hence he allows पेचिथ *pechitha*, besides पपक्थ *papaktha*; इयजिथ *iyajitha*, besides इयष्ठ *iyashṭha*.)

---

* वृञ् *vṛiñ*, (27, 8) वरणे *varaṇe*, Su. वृञ् *vṛiñ*, (34, 8) आवरणे *âvaraṇe*, Chur. वृङ् *vṛiṅ*, (31, 38) संभक्तौ *sambhaktau*, Krî.

† The form ववरिव *vavariva*, which Westergaard mentions, may be derived from another root वॄ *vṝi*, the rule of Pâṇini being restricted by the commentator to वृञ् *vṛiñ* and वृङ् *vṛiṅ*.

4. All other verbs ending in consonants with any other radical vowel but अ *a*, require इ *i*, and so do all verbs with which इ *i* is either optional or indispensable in the future (ता *tá*).

Exceptions:

1. In सृज् *srij* and दृश् *driś*, the omission is optional.

   सृज् *srij*, ससष्ठ *sasrashṭha*, or ससृजिथ *sasrijitha*.

2. The verbs अत्ति *atti*, अर्ति *arti*, व्ययति *vyayati* must take इ *i*.

   अद् *ad*, आदिथ *ád-i-tha*, (exception to No. 3.)

   ऋ *ri*, आरिथ *ár-i-tha*, (exception to No. 2.)

   व्ये *vye*, विव्ययिथ *vivyay-i-tha*, (exception to No. 2.)

Tables showing the cases in which the intermediate इ i *must be omitted between the Unmodified Root and the Terminations of the so-called General Tenses, originally beginning with a Consonant, except* य् y.

§ 336. In these tables त *ta* stands for the Past Participle; सन् *san* stands for the Desiderative; स्य *sya* for the Future and Conditional; ता *tá* for the Periphrastic Future; सिच् *sich* for the First Aorist; लिङ् *liń* for the Benedictive.

I. *For all General Tenses, except the Reduplicated Perfect,*

Omit इ i,

1. Before त *ta*, सन् *san*, स्य *sya*, ता *tá*, सिच् *sich*, लिङ् *liń*:

   In the verbs enumerated § 332.

2. Before त *ta*, सन् *san*, स्य *sya*, ता *tá*:

   In कृप् *klip*, if Parasmaipada. § 333, A.

3. Before त *ta*, सन् *san*, स्य *sya*:

   In वृत् *vrit*, वृध् *vridh*, स्यंद् *syand*, शृध् *śridh*, if Parasmaipada. § 333, B.

4. Before त *ta*, सन् *san*:

   In monosyllabic verbs ending in उ, ऊ *ú*, ऋ, ॠ *rí*, ग्रह् *grah*, and गुह् *guh*. § 333, C.

5. Before त *ta*:

   a. All verbs which by native grammarians are marked with आ *á*, ई *í*, or ऊ *ú**.

   b. The verb श्वि *śvi* and others enumerated in a general list, § 333, D.

II. *For the Reduplicated Perfect,*

Omit इ i,

1. Before all terminations, except इरे *ire*:

   In eight verbs, mentioned § 334.

2. Before थ *tha*, 2nd pers. sing.:

   All verbs of § 332 ending in vowels.

   All verbs of § 332 ending in consonants with अ *a* as radical vowel.

* The technical ऊ *ú* shows that in the other general tenses the इ *i* is optional. § 335, 1.

Optional Insertion of इ i.

§ 337. For practical purposes, as was stated before, it is sufficient to know when it would be wrong to use the intermediate इ *i*; for in all other cases, whatever the views of different grammarians, or the usage of different writers, it is safe to insert the इ *i*.

As native grammarians, however, have been at much pains to collect the cases in which इ *i* must or may be inserted, a short abstract of their rules may here follow, which the early student may safely pass by.

इ i *may or may not* be inserted:

I. Before any *ârdhadhâtuka* (i. e. an affix of the general tenses not requiring the modified verbal base) beginning with consonants, except य् *y*:

1. In the verbs स्वृ *svṛi*; Per. Fut. स्वरिता *svar-i-tâ*, or स्वर्ता *svartâ*, &c. (Pâṇ. VII. 2, 44.) (Except future in स्य *sya*, स्वरिष्यति *svarishyati* only. Pâṇ. VII. 2, 70.)

   षू *sû* (as Ad and Div, not as Tud), सविता *sav-i-tâ*, or सोता *sotâ*, &c.

   धू *dhû* (not as Tud), धविता *dhav-i-tâ*, or धोता *dhotâ*, &c. (Except aorist Parasmaipada, which must take इ *i*. Pâṇ. VII. 2, 72.)

2. In all verbs having a technical ऊ *û*. (Pâṇ. VII. 2, 44.) गाह् *gâh*, Per. Fut. गाहिता *gâh-i-tâ*, or गाढा *gâḍhâ*. (See § 333, D. 1.)

   But अञ्ज् *añj* (though marked अञ्जू *añjû*) *must* take इ *i* in the I. aorist. (Pâṇ. VII. 2, 71.) आञ्जिषुः *âñjishuḥ*.

3. In the eight verbs beginning with रध् *radh*. (Pâṇ. VII. 2, 45.)

(26, 84) रध् *radh*, to perish, रधिता *radh-i-tâ*, or रद्धा *raddhâ*.
(26, 85) नश् *naś*, to vanish, नशिता *naś-i-tâ*, or नंष्टा *naṁshṭâ*.
(26, 86) तृप् *tṛip*, to delight, तर्पिता *tarp-i-tâ*, or तर्प्ता *tarptâ*, or त्रप्ता *traptâ*.
(26, 87) दृप् *dṛip*, to be proud, दर्पिता *darp-i-tâ*, or दर्प्ता *darptâ*, or द्रप्ता *draptâ*.
(26, 88) द्रुह् *druh*, to hate, द्रोहिता *droh-i-tâ*, or द्रोग्धा *drogdhâ*, or द्रोढा *droḍhâ*.
(26, 89) मुह् *muh*, to be bewildered, मोहिता *moh-i-tâ*, or मोग्धा *mogdhâ*, or मोढा *moḍhâ*.
(26, 90) स्नुह् *snuh*, to vomit, स्नोहिता *snoh-i-tâ*, or स्नोग्धा *snogdhâ*, or स्नोढा *snoḍhâ*.
(26, 91) स्निह् *snih*, to love, स्नेहिता *sneh-i-tâ*, or स्नेग्धा *snegdhâ*, or स्नेढा *sneḍhâ*.

   According to some this option extends to the reduplicated perfect: but this is properly denied by others.

4. In the verb कुष् *kush* (Chur class), preceded by निर् *nir*; but here इ *i* is necessary in the participle with त *ta*. (Pâṇ. VII. 2, 46; 47.)

इ i *may or may not* be inserted:

II. Before certain *ârdhadhâtukas* only:

1. Before *ârdhadhâtukas* beginning with त् *t*:

   In the verbs इष् *ish* (Tud only), सह् *sah*, लुभ् *lubh*, रुष् *rush*, रिष् *rish*. (Pâṇ. VII. 2, 48.)

2. Before *ârdhadhâtukas* beginning with स् *s*, but not in the aorist:

In the verbs कृत् *kṛit*, to cut; चृत् *chṛit*, to kill; छृद् *chhṛid*, to play; तृद् *tṛid*, to strike; नृत् *nṛit*, to dance. (Pâṇ. VII. 2, 57.)

3. Before the termination of the desiderative base (सन् *san*):

In the verb वृ *vṛi*, and all verbs ending in ॠ *ṛî*. (Pâṇ. VII. 2, 41.)

In the verbs ending in इव् *iv*, and in ऋध् *ṛidh*, भ्रस्ज् *bhrasj*, दम्भ् *dambh*, श्रि *śri*, स्वृ *svṛi*, यु *yu*, ऊर्णु *ûrṇu*, भृ *bhṛi* (Bhû class), ज्ञप् *jñap*, सन् *san*; also तन् *tan*, पत् *pat*, दरिद्रा *daridrâ*. (Pâṇ. VII. 2, 49.)

4. Before the terminations of the benedictive (लिङ् *liṅ*) and I. aorist (सिच् *sich*) in the Âtmanepada:

In the verb वृ *vṛi*, and all verbs ending in ॠ *ṛî* (Pâṇ. VII. 2, 42). The ॠ *ṛî* is changed into ईर् *îr* or ऊर् *ûr*.

In verbs ending in ऋ *ṛi* and beginning with a conjunct consonant. (Pâṇ. VII. 2, 43.)

5. Before the gerundial termination त्वा *tvâ*:

In verbs having a technical उ *u*. (Pâṇ. VII. 2, 56.)

शम् *śam* (शमु *śamu*), शमित्वा *śamitvâ* or शान्त्वा *śântvâ*.

6. Before the gerundial termination त्वा *tvâ* and the participle in त *ta*:

In the verb क्लिश् *kliś*. (Pâṇ. VII. 2, 50.)

क्लिशित्वा *kliśitvâ* or क्लिष्ट्वा *klishṭvâ*, क्लिशितः *kliśitaḥ* or क्लिष्टः *klishṭaḥ*.

In the verb पू *pû*. (Pâṇ. VII. 2, 51.)

पवित्वा *pavitvâ* or पूत्वा *pûtvâ*, पवितः *pavitaḥ* or पूतः *pûtaḥ*. It must take इ *i* in the desiderative (Pâṇ. VII. 2, 74).

7. Before the participial terminations त *ta* or न *na**:

In the verbs दम् *dam*, to tame, दान्तः *dântaḥ* or दमितः *damitaḥ*. (Pâṇ. VII. 2, 27.)

शम् *śam*, to quiet, शान्तः *śântaḥ* or शमितः *śamitaḥ*.

पूर् *pûr*, to fill, पूर्णः *pûrṇaḥ* or पूरितः *pûritaḥ*.

दस् *das*, to perish, दस्तः *dastaḥ* or दासितः *dâsitaḥ*.

स्पश् *spaś*, to touch, स्पष्टः *spashṭaḥ* or स्पाशितः *spâśitaḥ*.

छद् *chhad*, to cover, छन्नः *chhannaḥ* or छादितः *chhâditaḥ*.

ज्ञप् *jñap*, to inform, ज्ञप्तः *jñaptaḥ* or ज्ञपितः *jñapitaḥ*.

रुष् *rush*, to hurt, रुष्टः *rushṭaḥ* or रुषितः *rushitaḥ*. (Pâṇ. VII. 2, 28.)

अम् *am*, to go, आन्तः *ântaḥ* or अमितः *amitaḥ*.

त्वर् *tvar*, to hasten, तूर्णः *tûrṇaḥ* or त्वरितः *tvaritaḥ*.

संघुष् *saṅ-ghush*, to shout, संघुष्टः *saṅghushṭaḥ* or संघुषितः *saṅghushitaḥ*. (See § 333, D. 2.)

आस्वन् *âsvan*, to sound, आस्वान्तः *âsvântaḥ* or आस्वनितः *âsvanitaḥ*. (See § 333, D. 2.)

---

* See also § 333, D. 2, note.

हृष् *hṛish*, to rejoice, हृष्टः *hṛishṭaḥ* or हृषितः *hṛishitaḥ*, if applied to horripilation. (Pâṇ. VII. 2, 29.)

अपचि *apa-chi*, to honour, अपचितः *apachitaḥ* or अपचायितः *apachâyitaḥ* *.

8. Before the participle of the reduplicated perfect in वस् *vas*:

In the verbs गम् *gam*, to go, जग्मिवान् *jagmivân* or जगन्वान् *jaganvân* †.

हन् *han*, to kill, जघ्निवान् *jaghnivân* or जघन्वान् *jaghanvân*.

विद् *vid*, to know, विविदिवान् *vividivân* or विविद्वान् *vividvân*.

विश् *viś*, to enter, विविशिवान् *viviśivân* or विविश्वान् *viviśvân*.

दृश् *dṛiś*, to see, ददृशिवान् *dadṛiśivân* or ददृश्वान् *dadṛiśvân*.

Necessary Insertion of इ i.

§ 338. इ *i* must be inserted in all verbs in which, as stated before, it is neither prohibited, nor only optionally allowed (Pâṇ. VII. 2, 35). Besides these, the following special cases may be mentioned:

1. Before वस् *vas*, participle of reduplicated perfect:

In the verbs ending in आ *â* (Pâṇ. VII. 2, 67). पा *pâ*, पपिवान् *papivân*.

In the verbs reduced to a single syllable in the reduplicated perfect (Pâṇ. VII. 2, 67). अश् *aś*, to eat, आशिवान् *âśivân*.

In the verb घस् *ghas*, to eat, जक्षिवान् *jakshivân*.

Other verbs reject it.

2. Before स्य *sya* of the future and conditional:

In all verbs ending in ऋ *ṛi*, and in हन् *han* (Pâṇ. VII. 2, 70). In गम् *gam*, if used in the Parasmaipada (Pâṇ. VII. 2, 58).

3. Before the terminations of the I. aorist (सिच् *sich*):

In the verbs ष्टु *stu*, षु *su*, धू *dhû* in the Parasmaipada (Pâṇ. VII. 2, 72). Thus from ष्टु *stu*, to praise, First Aorist (First Form), अस्ताविषम् *astâvisham*; but in the Âtmanepada, अस्तोषि *astoshi*.

4. Before the terminations of the desiderative (सन् *san*):

In the verbs कॄ *kṛî*, गॄ *gṛî*, दृ *dṛi*, धृ *dhṛi*, and प्रछ् *prachh* (Pâṇ. VII. 2, 75); and in गम् *gam*, if used in the Parasmaipada (Pâṇ. VII. 2, 58).

In the verbs स्मि *smi*, पू *pû*, ऋ *ṛi*, अञ्ज् *añj*, and अश् *aś*. (Pâṇ. VII. 2, 74.)

5. Before the gerundial क्त्वा *tvâ* and the participial termination त *ta*. (Pâṇ. VII. 2, 52–54.)

In the verbs वस् *vas*, to dwell; क्षुध् *kshudh*, to hunger; अञ्च् *añch*, to worship; लुभ् *lubh*, to confound (Dh. P. 28, 22).

6. Before क्त्वा *tvâ* only:

In जॄ *jṛî*, to grow old; व्रश्च् *vraśch*, to cut. (Pâṇ. VII. 2, 55.)

7. Before थ *tha*, 2nd pers. sing. reduplicated perfect:

In अद् *ad*, to eat; ऋ *ṛi*, to go; व्ये *vye*, to cover. आदिथ *âditha*, against § 335, 3; आरिथ *âritha*, § 335, 3, note; विव्ययिथ *vivyayitha*.

* Pâṇ. VII. 2, 30. † Pâṇ. VII. 2, 68.

§ 339. The vowel इ *i* thus inserted is never liable to Guṇa or Vṛiddhi.

Insertion of the long ई î.

§ 340. Long ई î *may* be substituted for the short when subjoined to a verb ending in ॠ *ṛî*, also to वृ *vṛi*, except in the reduplicated perfect, the aorist Parasmaipada, and the benedictive. (Pâṇ. VII. 2, 38–40.)

तॄ *tṛî*; Per. Fut. तरीता *tarîtâ* or तरिता *taritâ*, &c.; but Perf. 2nd pers. sing. तेरिथ *teritha*; I. Aor. Par. 3rd pers. plur. अतारिषुः *atârishuḥ*; Bened. 3rd pers. sing. तरिषीष्ट *tarishîshṭa**.

वृ *vṛi*; Per. Fut. वरीता *varîtâ* or वरिता *varitâ*; but Perf. ववरिथ *vavaritha*; Aor. Par. अवारिषुः *avârishuḥ*; Bened. वरिषीष्ट *varishîshṭa*.

§ 341. In the desiderative and in the aorist Âtm. and benedictive Âtm. these verbs may or may not have इ *i* (Pâṇ. VII. 2, 41–42), which, if used, is liable in the aorist Âtm. to be changed to ई *î*.

तॄ *tṛî*; Des. तितरिषति *titarishati*; तितरीषति *titarîshati*; तितीर्षति *titîrshati*; Aor. Âtm. अतरिष्ट *atarishṭa*, अतरीष्ट *atarîshṭa*, and अतीर्ष्ट *atîrshṭa*; Bened. तरिषीष्ट *tarishîshṭa*, तीर्षीष्ट *tîrshîshṭa*.

वृ *vṛi*; Des. विवरिषते *vivarishate*; विवरीषते *vivarîshate*; वुवूर्षते *vuvûrshate*; Aor. Âtm. अवरिष्ट *avarishṭa*, अवरीष्ट *avarîshṭa*, and अवृत *avṛita*; Bened. वरिषीष्ट *varishîshṭa*, वृषीष्ट *vṛishîshṭa*.

The verb ग्रह् *grah*, too, takes the long ई *î*, except in the reduplicated perfect, the desiderative, and certain tenses of the passive. (Pâṇ. VII. 2, 37.)

ग्रह् *grah*; Per. Fut. ग्रहीता *grahîtâ*; Inf. ग्रहीतुं *grahîtum*; but Perf. जगृहिम *jagṛihima*.

Periphrastic Perfect.

§ 342. Verbs which, according to § 325, cannot form a reduplicated perfect, form their perfect by affixing आम् *âm* (an accusative termination of a feminine abstract noun in आ *â*) to the verbal base, and adding to this the reduplicated perfect of कृ *kṛi*, to do, भू *bhû*, to be, or अस् *as*, to be.

उन्द् *und*, to wet, उन्दां चकार, बभूव, आस, *undâm chakâra, babhûva, âsa*.

चकास् *chakâs*, to shine, चकासां चकार, बभूव, आस, *chakâsâm chakâra, babhûva, âsa*.

बोधय *bodhaya*, to make known, बोधयां चकार, बभूव, आस, *bodhayâm chakâra, babhûva, âsa*.

After verbs which are used in the Âtmanepada, the auxiliary verb कृ *kṛi* is conjugated as Âtmanepada, but अस् *as* and भू *bhû* in the Parasmaipada. Hence from एधते *edhate*, he grows,

एधां चक्रे *edh-âm chakre*; but बभूव *babhûva* and आस *âsa*.

In the passive all three auxiliary verbs follow the Âtmanepada.

* The forms given in the Calcutta edition of Pâṇini VII. 2, 42, वरीषीष्ट *varîshîshṭa*, स्तरीषीष्ट *starîshîshṭa*, are wrong. (See Pâṇ. VII. 2, 39.)

§ 343. Intensive bases which can take Guṇa, take it before आं âm; desiderative bases never admit of Guṇa. (§ 339.)

बोभू bobhû, frequentative base of भू bhû, बोभवां चकार bobhav-âm chakâra. But बुबोधिष् bubodhish, desiderative base of बुध् budh, बुबोधिषां चकार &c. bubodhishâm chakâra &c.

Paradigms of the Reduplicated Perfect.

1. Verbal bases in आ â, requiring intermediate इ i.

धा dhâ, to place.

	PARASMAIPADA.			ÂTMANEPADA.		
	SINGULAR.	DUAL.	PLURAL.	SINGULAR.	DUAL.	PLURAL.
1.	दधौ *dadhau*	दधिव *dadhiva*	दधिम *dadhima*	दधे *dadhe*	दधिवहे *dadhivahe*	दधिमहे *dadhimahe*
2.	दधाथ *dadhâtha* or दधिथ *dadhitha**	दधथुः *dadhathuḥ*	दध *dadha*	दधिषे *dadhishe*	दधाथे *dadhâthe*	दधिध्वे *dadhidhve*
3.	दधौ *dadhau*	दधतुः *dadhatuḥ*	दधुः *dadhuḥ*	दधे *dadhe*	दधाते *dadhâte*	दधिरे *dadhire*

2. Verbal bases in इ i and ई î, preceded by *one* consonant, and requiring intermediate इ i.

नी nî, to lead.

	SINGULAR.	DUAL.	PLURAL.	SINGULAR.	DUAL.	PLURAL.
1.	निनाय *ninâya* or निनय *ninaya*	निन्यिव *ninyiva*	निन्यिम *ninyima*	निन्ये *ninye*	निन्यिवहे *ninyivahe*	निन्यिमहे *ninyimahe*
2.	निनेथ *ninetha* or निनयिथ *ninayitha**	निन्यथुः *ninyathuḥ*	निन्य *ninya*	निन्यिषे *ninyishe*	निन्याथे *ninyâthe*	निन्यिध्वे or °ढ्वे (§ 105) *ninyidhve* or *-ḍhve*
3.	निनाय *ninâya*	निन्यतुः *ninyatuḥ*	निन्युः *ninyuḥ*	निन्ये *ninye*	निन्याते *ninyâte*	निन्यिरे *ninyire*

3. Verbal bases in ऋ ṛi, preceded by *one* consonant, and requiring intermediate इ i.

धृ dhṛi, to hold.

	SINGULAR.	DUAL.	PLURAL.	SINGULAR.	DUAL.	PLURAL.
1.	दधार *dadhâra* or दधर *dadhara*	दध्रिव *dadhriva*	दध्रिम *dadhrima*	दध्रे *dadhre*	दध्रिवहे *dadhrivahe*	दध्रिमहे *dadhrimahe*
2.	दधर्थ *dadhartha**	दध्रथुः *dadhrathuḥ*	दध्र *dadhra*	दध्रिषे *dadhrishe*	दध्राथे *dadhrâthe*	दध्रिध्वे or °ढ्वे *dadhridhve* or *-ḍhve*
3.	दधार *dadhâra*	दध्रतुः *dadhratuḥ*	दध्रुः *dadhruḥ*	दध्रे *dadhre*	दध्राते *dadhrâte*	दध्रिरे *dadhrire*

4. Verbal bases in ऋ ṛi, preceded by *one* consonant, not admitting intermediate इ i.

कृ kṛi, to do.

	SINGULAR.	DUAL.	PLURAL.	SINGULAR.	DUAL.	PLURAL.
1.	चकार *chakâra* or चकर *chakara*	चकृव *chakṛiva*	चकृम *chakṛima*	चक्रे *chakre*	चकृवहे *chakṛivahe*	चकृमहे *chakṛimahe*
2.	चकर्थ *chakartha*	चक्रथुः *chakrathuḥ*	चक्र *chakra*	चकृषे *chakṛishe*	चक्राथे *chakrâthe*	चकृढ्वे *chakṛiḍhve*
3.	चकार *chakâra*	चक्रतुः *chakratuḥ*	चक्रुः *chakruḥ*	चक्रे *chakre*	चक्राते *chakrâte*	चक्रिरे *chakrire*

* § 335, 2, and § 335, 3, note †.

5. Verbal bases in इ *i* or ई *î*, preceded by *two* consonants, and requiring intermediate इ *i*.

क्री *krî*, to buy.

1.	चिक्राय *chikrâya* or चिक्रय *chikraya*	चिक्रियिव *chikriyiva*	चिक्रियिम *chikriyima*	चिक्रिये *chikriye*	चिक्रियिवहे *chikriyivahe*	चिक्रियिमहे *chikriyimahe*
2.	चिक्रेथ *chikretha* or चिक्रयिथ *chikrayitha*	चिक्रियथुः *chikriyathuḥ*	चिक्रिय *chikriya*	चिक्रियिषे *chikriyishe*	चिक्रियाथे *chikriyâthe*	चिक्रियिध्वे or °ढ्वे *chikriyidhve* or *-ḍhve*
3.	चिक्राय *chikrâya*	चिक्रियतुः *chikriyatuḥ*	चिक्रियुः *chikriyuḥ*	चिक्रिये *chikriye*	चिक्रियाते *chikriyâte*	चिक्रियिरे *chikriyire*

6. Verbal bases in उ *u* or ऊ *û*, preceded by *one or two* consonants, and requiring intermediate इ *i*.

यु *yu*, to join.

1.	युयाव *yuyâva* or युयव *yuyava*	युयुविव *yuyuviva*	युयुविम *yuyuvima*	युयुवे *yuyuve*	युयुविवहे *yuyuvivahe*	युयुविमहे *yuyuvimahe*
2.	युयविथ *yuyavitha* *	युयुवथुः *yuyuvathuḥ*	युयुव *yuyuva*	युयुविषे *yuyuvishe*	युयुवाथे *yuyuvâthe*	युयुविध्वे or °ढ्वे *yuyuvidhve* or *-ḍhve*
3.	युयाव *yuyâva*	युयुवतुः *yuyuvatuḥ*	युयुवुः *yuyuvuḥ*	युयुवे *yuyuve*	युयुवाते *yuyuvâte*	युयुविरे *yuyuvire*

7. Verbal bases in उ *u*, preceded by *one or two* consonants, and not admitting the intermediate इ *i*.

स्तु *stu*, to praise.

1.	तुष्टाव *tushṭâva* or तुष्टव *tushṭava*	तुष्टुव *tushṭuva*	तुष्टुम *tushṭuma*	तुष्टुवे *tushṭuve*	तुष्टुवहे *tushṭuvahe*	तुष्टुमहे *tushṭumahe*
2.	तुष्टोथ *tushṭotha* †	तुष्टुवथुः *tushṭuvathuḥ*	तुष्टुव *tushṭuva*	तुष्टुषे *tushṭushe*	तुष्टुवाथे *tushṭuvâthe*	तुष्टुढ्वे *tushṭuḍhve*
3.	तुष्टाव *tushṭâva*	तुष्टुवतुः *tushṭuvatuḥ*	तुष्टुवुः *tushṭuvuḥ*	तुष्टुवे *tushṭuve*	तुष्टुवाते *tushṭuvâte*	तुष्टुविरे *tushṭuvire*

8. Verbal bases in ऋ *ṛi*, preceded by *two* consonants, and requiring intermediate इ *i*.

स्तृ *stṛi*, to spread.

1.	तस्तार *tastâra* or तस्तर *tastara*	तस्तरिव *tastariva*	तस्तरिम *tastarima*	तस्तरे *tastare*	तस्तरिवहे *tastarivahe*	तस्तरिमहे *tastarimahe*
2.	तस्तर्थ *tastartha*	तस्तरथुः *tastarathuḥ*	तस्तर *tastara*	तस्तरिषे *tastarishe*	तस्तराथे *tastarâthe*	तस्तरिध्वे or °ढ्वे *tastaridhve* or *-ḍhve*
3.	तस्तार *tastâra*	तस्तरतुः *tastaratuḥ*	तस्तरुः *tastaruḥ*	तस्तरे *tastare*	तस्तराते *tastarâte*	तस्तरिरे *tastarire*

9. Verbal bases in ॠ *ṛî*, requiring intermediate इ *i*.

कॄ *kṛî*, to scatter.

1.	चकार *chakâra* or चकर *chakara*	चकरिव *chakariva*	चकरिम *chakarima*	चकरे *chakare*	चकरिवहे *chakarivahe*	चकरिमहे *chakarimahe*
2.	चकरिथ *chakaritha*	चकरथुः *chakarathuḥ*	चकर *chakara*	चकरिषे *chakarishe*	चकराथे *chakarâthe*	चकरिध्वे or °ढ्वे *chakaridhve* or *-ḍhve*
3.	चकार *chakâra*	चकरतुः *chakaratuḥ*	चकरुः *chakaruḥ*	चकरे *chakare*	चकराते *chakarâte*	चकरिरे *chakarire*

* If यु *yu* is taken from Dhâtupâṭha 31, 9, it may form युयोथ *yuyotha*. (See § 335, 2, and Westergaard, Radices, p. 46, note.)

† Bharadvâja might allow तुष्टविथ *tushṭavitha* even against Pâṇ. VII. 2, 13.

10. Verbal bases in consonants, requiring intermediate इ *i*.

तुद् *tud*, to strike.

1. तुतोद *tutoda*	तुतुदिव *tutudiva*	तुतुदिम *tutudima*	तुतुदे *tutude*	तुतुदिवहे *tutudivahe*	तुतुदिमहे *tutudimahe*
2. तुतोदिथ *tutoditha*	तुतुदथुः *tutudathuḥ*	तुतुद *tutuda*	तुतुदिषे *tutudishe*	तुतुदाथे *tutudáthe*	तुतुदिध्वे *tutudidhve*
3. तुतोद *tutoda*	तुतुदतुः *tutudatuḥ*	तुतुदुः *tutuduḥ*	तुतुदे *tutude*	तुतुदाते *tutudáte*	तुतुदिरे *tutudire*

11. Verbal bases in consonants, having ए *e*, and requiring intermediate इ *i*.

तन् *tan*, to stretch.

1. ततान *tatána* or ततन *tatana*	तेनिव *teniva*	तेनिम *tenima*	तेने *tene*	तेनिवहे *tenivahe*	तेनिमहे *tenimahe*
2. तेनिथ *tenitha*	तेनथुः *tenathuḥ*	तेन *tena*	तेनिषे *tenishe*	तेनाथे *tenáthe*	तेनिध्वे *tenidhve*
3. ततान *tatána*	तेनतुः *tenatuḥ*	तेनुः *tenuḥ*	तेने *tene*	तेनाते *tenáte*	तेनिरे *tenire*

12. Verbal bases in consonants, having *Samprasárańa*, and requiring इ *i*.

यज् *yaj*, to sacrifice.

1. इयाज *iyája* or इयज *iyaja*	ईजिव *íjiva*	ईजिम *íjima*	ईजे *íje*	ईजिवहे *íjivahe*	ईजिमहे *íjimahe*
2. इयष्ठ *iyashṭha* or इयजिथ *iyajitha*	ईजथुः *íjathuḥ*	ईज *íja*	ईजिषे *íjishe*	ईजाथे *íjáthe*	ईजिध्वे *íjidhve*
3. इयाज *iyája*	ईजतुः *íjatuḥ*	ईजुः *íjuḥ*	ईजे *íje*	ईजाते *íjáte*	ईजिरे *íjire*

13. Verbal bases in consonants, requiring contraction, and intermediate इ *i*.

हन् *han*, to kill.

1. जघान *jaghána* or जघन *jaghana*	जघ्निव *jaghniva*	जघ्निम *jaghnima*	जघ्ने *jaghne*	जघ्निवहे *jaghnivahe*	जघ्निमहे *jaghnimahe*
2. जघंथ *jaghantha* or जघनिथ *jaghanitha*	जघ्नथुः *jaghnathuḥ*	जघ्न *jaghna*	जघ्निषे *jaghnishe*	जघ्नाथे *jaghnáthe*	जघ्निध्वे *jaghnidhve*
3. जघान *jaghána*	जघ्नतुः *jaghnatuḥ*	जघ्नुः *jaghnuḥ*	जघ्ने *jaghne*	जघ्नाते *jaghnáte*	जघ्निरे *jaghnire*

14. Verbal base भू *bhú* (irregular).

1. बभूव *babhúva*	बभूविव *babhúviva*	बभूविम *babhúvima*	बभूवे *babhúve*	बभूविवहे *babhúvivahe*	बभूविमहे *babhúvimahe*
2. बभूविथ *babhúvitha*	बभूवथुः *babhúvathuḥ*	बभूव *babhúva*	बभूविषे *babhúvishe*	बभूवाथे *babhúváthe*	बभूविध्वे or °ढ्वे *babhúvidhve* or *-ḍhve*
3. बभूव *babhúva*	बभूवतुः *babhúvatuḥ*	बभूवुः *babhúvuḥ*	बभूवे *babhúve*	बभूवाते *babhúváte*	बभूविरे *babhúvire*

CHAPTER XII.

STRENGTHENING AND WEAKENING OF THE VERBAL BASES IN THE SIX REMAINING GENERAL TENSES.

§ 344. It may be useful, without entering into minute details, to distinguish between two sets of general tenses, moods, and verbal derivatives, which differ from each other by a tendency either to strengthen or to weaken their base. The strengthening takes place chiefly by Guṇa, but, under special circumstances, likewise by Vṛiddhi, by lengthening of the vowel, or by nasalization. The weakening takes place by shortening, by changing ॠ ṛî to ईर् îr, by Samprasâraṇa, or by dropping of a nasal. There are many roots, however, which either cannot be strengthened or cannot be weakened, and which therefore are liable to change in one only of these sets. Some resist both strengthening and weakening, as, for instance, all derivative bases, causatives, desideratives, and intensives (in the Âtm.), which generally have been strengthened, as far as their bases will allow, previously to their taking the conjugational terminations.

The first set comprises:

1. The Future.
2. The Conditional.
3. The Periphrastic Future.
4. The Benedictive Âtmanepada.
   (Except bases ending in conson. or ऋ ṛi, and not taking interm. इ i. Pâṇ. I. 2, 11; 12. VII. 2, 42.)
5. The First Aorist, I. II.
   (Except First Aor. II. Âtm. of verbs ending in conson., ऋ ṛi, or आ â.)

The second set comprises:

1. The Participle in त ta (unless it takes intermediate इ i).
2. The Gerund in त्वा tvâ (unless it takes intermediate इ i).
3. The Passive.
4. The Benedictive Parasmaipada.
5. The First Aorist, IV.
6. The Second Aorist.
   (Except verbs in ऋ ṛi, &c.)

Note—Among derivative verbs, causatives strengthen their base, intensives do not strengthen it, and desideratives admit of both, according to general rules to be stated hereafter.

I. Root.	Base strengthened.	Future.	Conditional.	Per. Fut.	Ben. Âtm. (Except bases ending in cons. not taking interm. इ i.)	First Aor. I. II.
भू	भो	भविष्यति	अभविष्यत्	भविता	भविषीष्ट	अभविष्ट Âtm.
bhû	*bho*	*bhavishyati*	*abhavishyat*	*bhavitâ*	*bhavishîshṭa*	*abhavishṭa*
तुद्	तोद्	तोत्स्यति	अतोत्स्यत्	तोत्ता	(तुत्सीष्ट)	अतौत्सीत्
tud	*tod*	*totsyati*	*atotsyat*	*tottâ*	(*tutsîshṭa*)	*atautsît*
दिव्	देव्	देविष्यति	अदेविष्यत्	देविता	देविषीष्ट	अदेवीत्
div	*dev*	*devishyati*	*adevishyat*	*devitâ*	*devishîshṭa*	*adevît*
चुर्	चोरय्	चोरयिष्यति	अचोरयिष्यत्	चोरयिता	चोरयिषीष्ट	
chur	*choray*	*chorayishyati*	*achorayishyat*	*chorayitâ*	*chorayishîshṭa*	
कृ	कर्	करिष्यति	अकरिष्यत्	करिता	करिषीष्ट	अकारीत्
kṛi	*kar*	*karishyati*	*akarishyat*	*karitâ*	*karishîshṭa*	*akârît*

सु	सो	सोष्यति	असोष्यत्	सोता	सोषीष्ट	असावीत्
su	*so*	*soshyati*	*asoshyat*	*sotá*	*soshíshṭa*	*asávít*
तन्	तन्	तनिष्यति	अतनिष्यत्	तनिता	तनिषीष्ट	अतनीत् or अतानीत्
tan	*tan*	*tanishyati*	*atanishyat*	*tanitá*	*tanishíshṭa*	*atanít* or *atánít*
क्री	क्रे	क्रेष्यति	अक्रेष्यत्	क्रेता	क्रेषीष्ट	अक्रैषीत्
krí	*kre*	*kreshyati*	*akreshyat*	*kretá*	*kreshíshṭa*	*akraishít*
द्विष्	द्वेष्	द्वेक्ष्यति	अद्वेक्ष्यत्	द्वेष्टा	(द्विक्षीष्ट)	
dvish	*dvesh*	*dvekshyati*	*advekshyat*	*dveshṭá*	(*dvikshíshṭa*)	
हु	हो	होष्यति	अहोष्यत्	होता	होषीष्ट	अहौषीत्
hu	*ho*	*hoshyati*	*ahoshyat*	*hotá*	*hoshíshṭa*	*ahaushít*
रुध्	रोध्	रोत्स्यति	अरोत्स्यत्	रोद्धा	(रुत्सीष्ट)	अरौत्सीत्
rudh	*rodh*	*rotsyati*	*arotsyat*	*roddhá*	(*rutsíshṭa*)	*arautsít*
कृ	Caus. कारय्	कारयिष्यति	अकारयिष्यत्	कारयिता	कारयिषीष्ट	
kṛi	*káray*	*kárayishyati*	*akárayishyat*	*kárayitá*	*kárayishíshṭa*	
कृ	Des. चिकीर्ष्	चिकीर्षिष्यति	अचिकीर्षिष्यत्	चिकीर्षिता	चिकीर्षिषीष्ट	अचिकीर्षीत्
kṛi	*chikírsh*	*chikírshishyati*	*achikírshishyat*	*chikírshitá*	*chikírshishíshṭa*	*achikírshít*
कृ	Int. चेक्रीय्	चेक्रीयिष्यते	अचेक्रीयिष्यत	चेक्रीयिता	चेक्रीयिषीष्ट	अचेक्रीयिष्ट
kṛi	*chekríy*	*chekríyishyate*	*achekríyishyata*	*chekríyitá*	*chekríyishíshṭa*	*achekríyishṭa*

II. Root.	Base not strengthened.	Part. त *ta*, without इ *i*.	Ger. त्वा *tvá*, without इ *i*.	Passive.	Ben. Par.	Second Aor.	First Aor. IV. and II. Âtm.
भू	भू	भूतः	भूत्वा	भूयते	भूयात्	अभूत्	
bhú	*bhú*	*bhútaḥ*	*bhútvá*	*bhúyate*	*bhúyát*	*abhút*	
तुद्	तुद्	तुन्नः	तुत्त्वा	तुद्यते	तुद्यात्		अतुत्त
tud	*tud*	*tunnaḥ*	*tuttvá*	*tudyate*	*tudyát*		*atutta*
कॄ	कीर्	कीर्णः	कीर्त्वा	कीर्यते	कीर्यात्		अकीर्ष्ट
kṝ	*kír*	*kírṇaḥ*	*kírtvá*	*kíryate*	*kíryát*		*akírshṭa*
{ दिव् *div*	दिव् *div*[1]	द्यूतः *dyútaḥ*	द्यूत्वा *dyútvá*	दीव्यते *dívyate*[2]	दीव्यात् *dívyát*		
{ पुष् *push*	पुष् *push*	पुष्टः *pushṭaḥ*	पुष्ट्वा *pushṭvá*	पुष्यते *pushyate*	पुष्यात् *pushyát*	अपुषत् *apushat*	
चुर्	(चोरय्)	(चोरितः)	(चोरयित्वा)	(चोर्यते)	(चोर्यात्)	अचूचुरत्	
chur	(*choray*)	(*choritaḥ*)	(*chorayitvá*)	(*choryate*)	(*choryát*)	*achúchurat*	
सु	सु	सुतः	सुत्वा	सूयते[3]	सूयात्		
su	*su*	*sutaḥ*	*sutvá*	*súyate*	*súyát*		
तन्	तन् & त	ततः	तत्वा[4]	तन्यते[5]	तन्यात्		अतत
tan	*tan* & *ta*	*tataḥ*	*tatvá*	*tanyate*	*tanyát*		*atata*
क्री	क्री	क्रीतः	क्रीत्वा	क्रीयते	क्रीयात्		
krí	*krí*	*krítaḥ*	*krítvá*	*kríyate*	*kríyát*		
द्विष्	द्विष्	द्विष्टः	द्विष्ट्वा	द्विष्यते	द्विष्यात्		अद्विक्षत्
dvish	*dvish*	*dvishṭaḥ*	*dvishṭvá*	*dvishyate*	*dvishyát*		*advikshat*
हु	हु	हुतः	हुत्वा	हूयते	हूयात्		
hu	*hu*	*hutaḥ*	*hutvá*	*húyate*	*húyát*		

[1] Or द्यू *dyú*. [2] § 143. [3] See rules on the formation of the passive base.
[4] Or तनित्वा *tanitvá*. [5] Or तायते *táyate*.

रुध्		रुध्	रुद्धः	रुद्ध्वा	रुध्यते	रुध्यात्	अरुधत्	अरुद्ध
rudh		*rudh*	*ruddhaḥ*	*ruddhvá*	*rudhyate*	*rudhyát*	*arudhat*	*aruddha*
कृ	Caus.	कारय्	कारितः	कारयित्वा	कार्यते	कार्यात्	अचीकरत्	
kṛi		*káray*	*káritaḥ*	*kárayitvá*	*káryate*	*káryát*	*achíkarat*	
कृ	Des.	चिकीर्ष्	चिकीर्षितः	चिकीर्षित्वा	चिकीर्ष्यते	चिकीर्ष्यात्		
kṛi		*chikírsh*	*chikírshitaḥ*	*chikírshitvá*	*chikírshyate*	*chikírshyát*		
कृ	Int.	चेक्रीय्	चेक्रीयितः	चेक्रीयित्वा				
kṛi		*chekríy*	*chekríyitaḥ*	*chekríyitvá*				

§ 345. Certain roots which strengthen their base in a peculiar manner, by Vṛiddhi, like मृज् *mṛij*, by lengthening, like गुह् *guh*, by transposition, like सृज् *sṛij*, by changing इ *i* into आ *á*, like मि *mi*, by nasalization, like नश् *naś*, drop all these marks of strengthening, in the weak forms.

I. Root.	Base strengthened.		Future.	Conditional.	Per. Fut.	Ben. Âtm.	First Aorist.
मृज्	मार्ज्[1]		मार्क्ष्यति	अमार्क्ष्यत्	मार्ष्टा	मार्जिषीष्ट	अमार्क्षीत्
mṛij	*márj*		*márkshyati*	*amárkshyat*	*márshṭá*	*márjishíshṭa*	*amárkshít*
		or	मार्जिष्यति	अमार्जिष्यत्	मार्जिता	(मृक्षीष्ट)	अमार्जीत्
			márjishyati	*amárjishyat*	*márjitá*	(*mṛikshíshṭa*)	*amárjít*
गुह्	गूह्[2]		घोक्ष्यति	अघोक्ष्यत्	गोढा	(घुक्षीष्ट)	
guh	*gúh*		*ghokshyati*	*aghokshyat*	*goḍhá*	(*ghukshíshṭa*)	
		or	गूहिष्यति	अगूहिष्यत्	गूहिता	गूहिषीष्ट	अगूहीत्
			gúhishyati	*agúhishyat*	*gúhitá*	*gúhishíshṭa*	*agúhít*
सृज्	स्रज्[3]		स्रक्ष्यति	अस्रक्ष्यत्	स्रष्टा		अस्राक्षीत्
sṛij	*sraj*		*srakshyati*	*asrakshyat*	*srashṭá*		*asrákshít*
मि	मा[4]		मास्यति	अमास्यत्	माता	मासीष्ट	अमासीत्
mi	*má*		*másyati*	*amásyat*	*mátá*	*másíshṭa*	*amásít*
नश्	नंश्[5]		नंक्ष्यति	अनंक्ष्यत्	नंष्टा		
naś	*naṁś*		*naṅkshyati*	*anaṅkshyat*	*naṁshṭá*		
स्रंस्	स्रंस्[6]		स्रंसिष्यते	अस्रंसिष्यत	स्रंसिता	स्रंसिषीष्ट	अस्रंसिष्ट
sraṁs	*sraṁs*		*sraṁsishyate*	*asraṁsishyata*	*sraṁsitá*	*sraṁsishíshṭa*	*asraṁsishṭa*
बंध्	बंध्		भंत्स्यति	अभंत्स्यत्	बंद्धा		अभांत्सीत्
bandh	*bandh*		*bhantsyati*	*abhantsyat*	*banddhá*		*abhántsít*

II. Root.	Base not strengthened.	Part. त *ta*, without इ *i*.	Ger. त्वा *tvá*, without इ *i*.	Passive.	Ben. Par.	Sec. Aor.	First Aor. IV. and II. Âtm.
मृज्	मृज्	मृष्टः	मृष्ट्वा[7]	मृज्यते	मृज्यात्		
mṛij	*mṛij*	*mṛishṭaḥ*	*mṛishṭvá*	*mṛijyate*	*mṛijyát*		
गुह्	गुह्	गूढः[8]	गूढ्वा	गुह्यते	गुह्यात्		अघुक्षत्
guh	*guh*	*gúḍhaḥ*	*gúḍhvá*	*guhyate*	*guhyát*		*aghukshat*

[1] Pâṇ. VII. 2, 114. [2] Pâṇ. VI. 4, 89. [3] Pâṇ. VI. 1, 58.
[4] Pâṇ. VI. 1, 50. [5] Pâṇ. VII. 1, 60. [6] Pâṇ. VI. 4, 24.
[7] But with इ *i*, मार्जित्वा *márjitvá*, not मर्जित्वा *marjitvá*.
[8] As to the long ऊ *ú*, see § 128.

सृज् *sṛij*	सृज् *sṛij*	सृष्टः *sṛishṭaḥ*	सृष्टा *sṛishṭā*	सृज्यते *sṛijyate*	सृज्यात् *sṛijyāt*	
मि *mi*	मि *mi*	मितः *mitaḥ*	मिता *mitā*	मीयते *mīyate*	मेयात् *meyāt*	
नश् *naś*	नश् *naś*	नष्टः *nashṭaḥ*	नष्टा* *nashṭā*	नश्यते *naśyate*	नश्यात् *naśyāt*	अनशत् *anaśat*
स्रंस् *sraṁs*	स्रस् *sras*	स्रस्तः† *srastaḥ*	स्रस्ता‡ *srastā*	स्रस्यते *srasyate*	स्रस्यात् *srasyāt*	अस्रसत् *asrasat*
बंध् *bandh*	बध् *badh*	बद्धः *baddhaḥ*	बद्धा *baddhā*	बध्यते *badhyate*	बध्यात् *badhyāt*	

Note—The verbs beginning with कुट् *kuṭ* (Dhâtupâṭha 28, 73—108) do not strengthen their base; कुट् *kuṭ*, to be bent, Fut. कुटिष्यति *kuṭishyati*, Per. Fut. कुटिता *kuṭitā*, First Aor. अकुटीत् *akuṭīt* (Pāṇ. I. 2, 1). विज् *vij*, to fear, never takes Guṇa before intermediate इ *i*; Per. Fut. विजिता *vijitā* (Pāṇ. I. 2, 2). ऊर्णु *ūrṇu*, to cover, may do so optionally; ऊर्णुविता *ūrṇuvitā* or ऊर्णविता *ūrṇavitā* (Pāṇ. I. 2, 3).

CHAPTER XIII.

AORIST.

§ 346. We can distinguish in Sanskrit, as in Greek, between two kinds of Aorists, one formed by means of a sibilant inserted between root and termination,—this we call the First,—another, formed by adding the terminations to the base, this we call the Second Aorist.

Both Aorists take the Augment, and, with some modifications, the terminations of the Imperfect.

§ 347. The First Aorist is formed in four different ways.

---

* Or नंष्टा *naṁshṭā*.

† Roots which thus may drop their nasal, are written in the Dhâtupâṭha with their nasal, स्रंस् or स्रन्स् *sraṁs*: while others which retain their nasal throughout, are written without the nasal, but with an indicatory इ *i*; नदि *nad*, &c. (Pāṇ. VI. 4, 24; VII. 1, 58). Two verbs thus marked by इ *i*, लगि *lag* and कपि *kap*, may, however, drop their nasal, the general rule notwithstanding, if used in certain meanings, विलगितं *vilagitam*, burnt; विकपितं *vikapitam*, deformed (Pāṇ. VI. 4, 24, v.). वृहि *vṛih*, वृंहति *vṛiṁhati*, drops its nasal before terminations beginning with a vowel, but not before the intermediate इ *i*; वर्हयति *varhayati*, but वृंहिता *vṛiṁhitā*. रंज् *rañj*, to tinge, may drop its nasal, even in the causative (i. e. before a vowel), if it means to sport; रजयति *rajayati* (Pāṇ. VI. 4, 24, v.). The same root, like some others, drops its nasal before *sārvadhātuka* affixes; रजति *rajati*, &c. (Pāṇ. VI. 4, 26). अंच् *añch*, if it means to worship, must retain its nasal (Pāṇ. VI. 4, 30) and take the intermediate इ *i* (Pāṇ. VII. 2, 53): अंचितः *añchitaḥ*, worshipped; otherwise अक्तः *aktaḥ* or अंचितः *añchitaḥ*, bent.

‡ Or स्रंसित्वा *sraṁsitvā*.

Terminations of the First Aorist.

1. First Form.

Parasmaipada.			Âtmanepada.		
इषं *isham*	इष्व *ishva*	इष्म *ishma*	इषि *ishi*	इष्वहि *ishvahi*	इष्महि *ishmahi*
ईः *îḥ* *	इष्टं *ishṭam*	इष्ट *ishṭa*	इष्ठाः *ishṭhâḥ*	इषाथां *ishâthâm*	इध्वं or इढ्वं *idhvam* or *iḍhvam*
ईत् *ît* *	इष्टां *ishṭâm*	इषुः *ishuḥ*	इष्ट *ishṭa*	इषातां *ishâtâm*	इषत *ishata*

In this first set of terminations the intermediate इ *i* stands as part of the terminations, because all the verbs that take this form are verbs liable to take the intermediate इ *i*. The first and second forms of the First Aorist differ, in fact, by this only, that the former is peculiar to verbs which take, the latter to verbs which reject intermediate इ *i*. (See § 332, 4, note.)

2. Second Form.

Parasmaipada.			Âtmanepada.		
सं *sam*	स्व *sva*	स्म *sma*	सि *si*	स्वहि *svahi*	स्महि *smahi*
सीः *sîḥ*	स्तं *stam* or तं *tam*	स्त *sta* or त *ta*	स्थाः *sthâḥ* or थाः *thâḥ*	साथां *sâthâm*	ध्वं *dhvam* or ढ्वं *ḍhvam*
सीत् *sît*	स्तां *stâm* or तां *tâm*	सुः *suḥ*	स्त *sta* or त *ta*	सातां *sâtâm*	सत *sata*

3. Third Form.

There are some verbs which add स् *s* to the end of the root before taking the terminations of the Aorist, and which after this स् *s*, employ the usual terminations with इ *i*, viz. इषं *isham*, &c. They are conjugated in the Parasmaipada only.

Parasmaipada.		
सिषं *s-i-sham*	सिष्व *s-ishva*	सिष्म *s-ishma*
सीः *s-îḥ* (originally for सिषीः *s-i-shîḥ*)	सिष्टं *s-ishṭam*	सिष्ट *s-ishṭa*
सीत् *s-ît* (originally for सिषीत् *s-i-shît*)	सिष्टां *s-ishṭâm*	सिषुः *s-ishuḥ*

4. Fourth Form.

Lastly, there are some few verbs, ending in श् *ś*, ष् *sh*, ह् *h*, preceded by इ *i*, उ *u*, ऋ *ṛi*, which take the following terminations, without an intermediate इ *i* (*ksa*).

Parasmaipada.			Âtmanepada.		
सं *sam*	साव *sâva*	साम *sâma*	सि *si*	सावहि *sâvahi* or वहि *vahi*	सामहि *sâmahi*
सः *saḥ*	सतं *satam*	सत *sata*	सथाः *sathâḥ* or थाः *thâḥ*	साथां *sâthâm*	सध्वं *sadhvam* or ध्वं *dhvam*
सत् *sat*	सतां *satâm*	सन् *san*	सत *sata* or त *ta*	सातां *sâtâm*	सन्त *santa*

Special Rules for the First Form of the First Aorist.

§ 348. For final vowel, Vṛiddhi in Parasmaipada†. लू *lû*, to cut, अलाविषं *alâvisham* (Pâṇ. VII. 2, 1).

* For इषीः *ishîḥ* and इषीत् *ishît*.

† Except श्वि *śvi*, to swell, अश्वयीत् *aśvayît*; जागृ *jâgṛi*, to wake, अजागरीत् *ajâgarît* (Pâṇ. VII. 2, 5). ऊर्णु *ûrṇu*, to cover, may or may not take Vṛiddhi; और्णुवीत् *aurṇuvît*, or और्णावीत् *aurṇâvît*, or और्णवीत् *aurṇavît* (Pâṇ. VII. 2, 6).

For final vowel, Guṇa in Âtmanepada. लू lû, अलविषि alavishi.

For medial or initial vowel, Guṇa (if possible) both in Par. and Âtm. बुध् budh, to know; Par. अबोधिषं abodhisham; Âtm. अबोधिषि abodhishi.

The vowel अ a, followed by a single final consonant, may or may not take Vṛiddhi in Par. if the verb begins with a consonant*. कण् kaṇ, to sound, अकाणिषं akâṇisham or अकणिषं akaṇisham (Pâṇ. vii. 2, 7); Âtm. अकणिषि akaṇishi.

§ 349. No Guṇa takes place in desiderative bases. बुध् budh; Desid. बुबोधिष् bubodhish; Aor. अबुबोधिषिषं abubodhishisham.

Intensives in य् y, if preceded by a consonant, *must*, certain denominatives in य् y *may*, drop their final य् y. If the intensive य् y is preceded by a vowel, य् y is left between the final vowel and the intermediate इ i. भिद् bhid, to cut; Int. base बेभिद्य् bebhidy; Aor. Âtm. अबेभिदिषि abebhidishi. भू bhû, to be; Int. base बोभूय् bobhûy; Aor. Âtm. अबोभूयिषि abobhûyishi. Denom. base नमस्य् namasy, to worship; Aor. अनमस्यिषं anamasy-isham or अनमसिषं anamas-isham.

Special Rules for the Second Form of the First Aorist.

§ 350. Vṛiddhi in Parasmaipada. क्षिप् kship, अक्षैप्सं akshaipsam; शि śi, अशैषं aśaisham (Pâṇ. vii. 2, 1); पच् pach, अपाक्षीत् apâkshît (Pâṇ. vii. 2, 3).

Guṇa in Âtmanepada, if the verb ends in इ, ई î, उ, ऊ û (not in ऋ ṛi, Pâṇ. i. 2, 12); otherwise no change of vowel. शि śi, अशेषि aśeshi; but क्षिप् kship, अक्षिप्सि akshipsi; कृ kṛi, अकृषि akṛishi. Final ॠ ṛî becomes ईर् îr.

§ 351. Terminations beginning with स्त् st or स्थ् sth drop their स् s if the base ends in a short vowel or in a consonant, except nasals. Ex. 2. p. dual अक्षैप्तं akshaip-tam, 3. p. dual अक्षैप्तां akshaip-tâm, 2. p. plur. अक्षैप्त akshaip-ta, of क्षिप् kship; 2. p. sing. Âtm. अकृथाः akṛithâḥ, 3. p. sing. अकृत akṛita, of कृ kṛi, Âtm. But from मन्यते manyate, अमंस्त amaṁsta.

§ 352. The roots स्था sthâ, to stand, दा dâ, to give, धा dhâ, to place, दे de, to pity, धे dhe, to feed, दो do, to cut, change their final vowels into इ i before the terminations of the Âtmanepada (Pâṇ. i. 2, 17). स्था sthâ, उपास्थित upâsthi-ta; उपास्थिषातां upâsthi-shâtâm. In the Parasmaipada they take the second aorist. (§ 368.)

* Roots ending in अल् al or अर् ar always take Vṛiddhi in the Parasmaipada; ज्वल् jval, to burn, अज्वालीत् ajvâlît (Pâṇ. vii. 2, 2). Likewise वद् vad, to speak, and व्रज् vraj, to go (Pâṇ. vii. 2, 3). Roots ending in ह् h, म् m, य् y, the roots क्षण् kshaṇ, to hurt, श्वस् śvas, to breathe, and verbs of the Chur class, roots with technical ए e, do not take Vṛiddhi (Pâṇ. vii. 2, 5). ग्रह् grah, to take, अग्रहीत् agrahît; स्यम् syam, to sound, अस्यमीत् asyamît; व्यय् vyay, to throw, अव्ययीत् avyayît; क्षण् kshaṇ, to hurt, अक्षणीत् akshaṇît; श्वस् śvas, to breathe, अश्वसीत् aśvasît; ऊनय् ûnay, to minish, औनयीत् aunayît; रग् rag, to suspect, अरगीत् aragît. दीधी dîdhî, to shine, वेवी vevî, to desire, and दरिद्रा daridrâ, to be poor, drop their final vowels, according to the rules on intermediate इ i: दरिद्रा daridrâ, अदरिद्रीत् adaridrît.

§ 353. The roots मी *mî* (*minâti*), to destroy, मि *mi* (*minoti*), to throw, and दी *dî*, to destroy, change their final vowels into आ *â* in the Âtmanepada; and ली *lî*, to stick, does so optionally. ली *lî*, अलासीत् *alâsît* (§ 358) or अलैषीत् *alaishît*.

§ 354. हन् *han*, to kill, drops its nasal in the Âtmanepada (Pâṇ. I. 2, 14); अहत *ahata*, अहसातां *ahasâtâm*.

§ 355. गम् *gam*, to go, drops its nasal in the Âtmanepada optionally (Pâṇ. I. 2, 13); अगत *agata* or अगंस्त *agaṁsta*. The same rule applies to the benedictive Âtmanepada; गसीष्ट *gasîshṭa* or गंसीष्ट *gaṁsîshṭa*.

§ 356. यम् *yam* drops its nasal, necessarily or optionally, according to its various meanings; उदयत *udayata*, he divulged (Pâṇ. I. 2, 15); उपायत *upâyata*, he espoused, or उपायंस्त *upâyaṁsta* (Pâṇ. I. 2, 16).

Special Rules for the Third Form of the First Aorist.

§ 357. Most verbs taking this form of the Aorist end in आ *â*, or in diphthongs which take आ *â* as their substitute. This आ *â* remains unchanged. In the Âtmanepada these verbs take the Second Form.

§ 358. The verbs मि *mi*, to throw, मी *mî*, to destroy, and ली *lî*, to stick, if taking this form, change likewise their final vowels into आ *â*. Ex. अमासिषं *amâsisham*, I threw, and I destroyed; अलासिषं *alâsisham* (or अलैषं *alaisham*).

§ 359. Three roots ending in म् *m* take this form; यम् *yam*, to hold, रम् *ram*, to rejoice, नम् *nam*, to bend, Aor. अयंसिषं *ayaṁsisham*, &c. (Pâṇ. VII. 2, 73).

Special Rules for the Fourth Form of the First Aorist.

§ 360. The roots which take this form must end in श् *ś* (except दृश् *dṛiś*, to see, Pâṇ. III. 1, 47), ष् *sh*, स् *s*, ह् *h*, preceded by any vowel but अ, आ *â*. They must be verbs which reject the intermediate इ *i*; § 332, 17–20; (Pâṇ. III. 1, 45.) Their radical vowel remains unchanged.

§ 361. The root श्लिष् *ślish* takes this form only if it means to embrace (Pâṇ. III. 1, 46); अश्लिक्षत् *aślikshat*. Other verbs, such as पुष् *push* and शुष् *śush*, are specially excepted. (§ 366.)

§ 362. The roots दुह् *duh*, to milk, दिह् *dih*, to anoint, लिह् *lih*, to lick, गुह् *guh*, to hide (Pâṇ. VII. 3, 73), may take in the Âtmanepada

थाः *thâḥ* instead of सथाः *sathâḥ*. वहि *vahi* instead of सावहि *sâvahi*.
त *ta* — सत *sata*. ध्वं *dhvam* — सध्वं *sadhvam*.

They thus approach to the Second Form of the first aorist in most, yet not in all persons.

Ex. दुह् *duh*; 2. p. sing. Âtm. अदुग्धाः *adugdhâḥ* or अधुक्षथाः *adhukshathâḥ*.
3. p. sing. Âtm. अदुग्ध *adugdha* or अधुक्षत *adhukshata*.
1. p. dual Âtm. अदुह्वहि *aduhvahi* or अधुक्षावहि *adhukshâvahi*.
2. p. plur. Âtm. अधुग्ध्वं *adhugdhvam* or अधुक्षध्वं *adhukshadhvam*.

First Aorist.

First Form,

with intermediate इ *i.*

a. Verbs ending in a vowel; लू *lû*, to cut.

Vṛiddhi in Parasmaipada, Guṇa in Âtmanepada.

PARASMAIPADA.

1.	अलाविषम् *alâv-isham*	अलाविष्व *alâv-ishva*	अलाविष्म *alâv-ishma*
2.	अलावीः *alâv-îḥ*	अलाविष्टम् *alâv-ishṭam*	अलाविष्ट *alâvi-shṭa*
3.	अलावीत् *alâv-ît*	अलाविष्टाम् *alâv-ishṭâm*	अलाविषुः *alâvi-shuḥ*

ÂTMANEPADA.

1.	अलविषि *alav-ishi*	अलविष्वहि *alav-ishvahi*	अलविष्महि *alav-ishmahi*
2.	अलविष्ठाः *alav-ishṭhâḥ*	अलविषाथाम् *alav-ishâthâm*	अलविध्वम् *alav-idhvam* or °ढ्वम् *-ḍhvam*
3.	अलविष्ट *alav-ishṭa*	अलविषाताम् *alav-ishâtâm*	अलविषत *alav-ishata*

b. Verbs ending in consonants; बुध् *budh*, to know.

Guṇa in Parasmaipada and Âtmanepada.

PARASMAIPADA.

1.	अबोधिषम् *abodh-isham*	अबोधिष्व *abodh-ishva*	अबोधिष्म *abodh-ishma*
2.	अबोधीः *abodh-îḥ*	अबोधिष्टम् *abodh-ishṭam*	अबोधिष्ट *abodh-ishṭa*
3.	अबोधीत् *abodh-ît*	अबोधिष्टाम् *abodh-ishṭâm*	अबोधिषुः *abodh-ishuḥ*

ÂTMANEPADA.

1.	अबोधिषि *abodh-ishi*	अबोधिष्वहि *abodh-ishvahi*	अबोधिष्महि *abodh-ishmahi*
2.	अबोधिष्ठाः *abodh-ishṭhâḥ*	अबोधिषाथाम् *abodh-ishâthâm*	अबोधिध्वम् *abodh-idhvam*
3.	अबोधिष्ट *abodh-ishṭa*	अबोधिषाताम् *abodh-ishâtâm*	अबोधिषत *abodh-ishata*

Second Form,

without intermediate इ *i.*

a. Verbs ending in consonants; क्षिप् *kship*, to throw.

Vṛiddhi in Parasmaipada, no change in Âtmanepada.

PARASMAIPADA.

1.	अक्षैप्सम् *akshaip-sam*	अक्षैप्स्व *akshaip-sva*	अक्षैप्स्म *akshaip-sma*
2.	अक्षैप्सीः *akshaip-sîḥ*	अक्षैप्तम् *akshaip-tam* (§ 351)	अक्षैप्त *akshaip-ta*
3.	अक्षैप्सीत् *akshaip-sît*	अक्षैप्ताम् *akshaip-tâm*	अक्षैप्सुः *akshaip-suḥ*

ÂTMANEPADA.

1.	अक्षिप्सि *akship-si*	अक्षिप्स्वहि *akship-svahi*	अक्षिप्स्महि *akship-smahi*
2.	अक्षिप्थाः *akship-thâḥ*	अक्षिप्साथाम् *akship-sâthâm*	अक्षिब्ध्वम् *akshib-dhvam*
3.	अक्षिप्त *akship-ta*	अक्षिप्साताम् *akship-sâtâm*	अक्षिप्सत *akship-sata*

b. Verbs ending in vowels (इ, ई *î*, उ, ऊ *û*); नी *nî*, to lead.

Vṛiddhi in Parasmaipada, Guṇa in Âtmanepada.

PARASMAIPADA.

1.	अनैषम् *anaisham*	अनैष्व *anaishva*	अनैष्म *anaishma*
2.	अनैषीः *anaishîḥ*	अनैष्टम् *anaishṭam*	अनैष्ट *anaishṭa*
3.	अनैषीत् *anaishît*	अनैष्टाम् *anaishṭâm*	अनैषुः *anaishuḥ*

Âtmanepada.

1. अनेषि *ane-shi*	अनेष्वहि *aneshvahi*	अनेष्महि *aneshmahi*
2. अनेष्ठाः *ane-shṭhâḥ*	अनेषाथां *aneshâthâm*	अनेढ्वं *aneḍhvam*
3. अनेष्ट *ane-shṭa*	अनेषातां *aneshâtâm*	अनेषत *aneshata*

c. Verbs ending in ऋ *ṛi*; कृ *kṛi*, to do.

Vṛiddhi in Parasmaipada, no change in Âtmanepada.

Parasmaipada.

1. अकार्षं *akârsham*	अकार्ष्व *akârshva*	अकार्ष्म *akârshma*
2. अकार्षीः *akârshîḥ*	अकार्ष्टं *akârshṭam*	अकार्ष्ट *akârshṭa*
3. अकार्षीत् *akârshît*	अकार्ष्टां *akârshṭâm*	अकार्षुः *akârshuḥ*

Âtmanepada.

1. अकृषि *akṛishi*	अकृष्वहि *akṛishvahi*	अकृष्महि *akṛishmahi*
2. अकृथाः *akṛithâḥ*	अकृषाथां *akṛishâthâm*	अकृढ्वं *akṛiḍhvam*
3. अकृत *akṛita*	अकृषातां *akṛishâtâm*	अकृषत *akṛishata*

d. Verbs ending in आ *â*; दा *dâ*, to give.

Âtmanepada only; आ *â* changed into इ *i*.

Âtmanepada.

1. अदिषि *adishi*	अदिष्वहि *adishvahi*	अदिष्महि *adishmahi*
2. अदिथाः *adithâḥ*	अदिषाथां *adishâthâm*	अदिढ्वं *adiḍhvam*
3. अदित *adita*	अदिषातां *adishâtâm*	अदिषत *adishata*

e. Verbs ending in ॠ *ṛî*; स्तॄ *stṛî*, to stretch.

Vṛiddhi in Parasmaipada, with intermediate इ *i*.

In Âtmanepada the insertion of इ *i* is optional. (See § 337, II. 4. Pâṇ. VII. 2, 42.)
If इ *i* is inserted, then Guṇa (§ 348) and optionally lengthening of इ *i*. (§ 341.)
If इ *i* is not inserted, then ॠ *ṛî* changed to ईर् *îr*. (§ 350.)

Parasmaipada.

अस्तारिषं *astârisham*, &c., like *First Form.*

First Form, with इ *i.*	Âtmanepada.	*Second Form,* without इ *i.*
	SINGULAR.	
1. अस्तरिषि or अस्तरीषि *astarishi* or *astarîshi*		अस्तीर्षि *astîrshi*
2. अस्तरिष्ठाः or अस्तरीष्ठाः *astarishṭhâḥ* or *astarîshṭhâḥ*		अस्तीर्ष्ठाः *astîrshṭhâḥ*
3. अस्तरिष्ट or अस्तरीष्ट *astarishṭa* or *astarîshṭa*		अस्तीर्ष्ट *astîrshṭa*
	DUAL.	
1. अस्तरिष्वहि or अस्तरीष्वहि *astarishvahi* or *astarîshvahi*		अस्तीर्ष्वहि *astîrshvahi*
2. अस्तरिषाथां or अस्तरीषाथां *astarishâthâm* or *astarîshâthâm*		अस्तीर्षाथां *astîrshâthâm*
3. अस्तरिषातां or अस्तरीषातां *astarishâtâm* or *astarîshâtâm*		अस्तीर्षातां *astîrshâtâm*
	PLURAL.	
1. अस्तरिष्महि or अस्तरीष्महि *astarishmahi* or *astarîshmahi*		अस्तीर्ष्महि *astîrshmahi*
2. अस्तरिध्वं °ढ्वं or अस्तरीध्वं °ढ्वं *astaridhvam -ḍhvam* or *astarîdhvam -ḍhvam*		अस्तीर्ढ्वं *astîrḍhvam*
3. अस्तरिषत or अस्तरीषत *astarishata* or *astarîshata*		अस्तीर्षत *astîrshata*

f. Verbs with penultimate ऋ *ṛi;* सृज् *sṛij*, to let off.

Peculiar Vṛiddhi in Parasmaipada, no change in Âtmanepada.

PARASMAIPADA.

1. अस्राक्षं *asráksham*	अस्राक्ष्व *asrákshva*	अस्राक्ष्म *asrákshma*
2. अस्राक्षीः *asrákshíḥ*	अस्राष्टं *asráshṭam*	अस्राष्ट *asráshṭa*
3. अस्राक्षीत् *asrákshít*	अस्राष्टां *asráshṭám*	अस्राक्षुः *asrákshuḥ*

ÂTMANEPADA.

1. असृक्षि *asṛikshi*	असृक्ष्वहि *asṛikshvahi*	असृक्ष्महि *asṛikshmahi*
2. असृष्ठाः *asṛishṭháḥ*	असृक्षाथां *asṛikshátháṁ*	असृड्ढ्वं *asṛiḍḍhvam*
3. असृष्ट *asṛishṭa*	असृक्षातां *asṛikshátám*	असृक्षत *asṛikshata*

g. Verbs ending in ह् *h;* दह् *dah*, to burn.

PARASMAIPADA.

1. अधाक्षं *adháksham*	अधाक्ष्व *adhákshva*	अधाक्ष्म *adhákshma*
2. अधाक्षीः *adhákshíḥ*	अदाग्धं *adágdham*	अदाग्ध *adágdha*
3. अधाक्षीत् *adhákshít*	अदाग्धां *adágdhám*	अधाक्षुः *adhákshuḥ*

ÂTMANEPADA.

1. अधक्षि *adhakshi*	अधक्ष्वहि *adhakshvahi*	अधक्ष्महि *adhakshmahi*
2. अदग्धाः *adagdháḥ*	अधक्षाथां *adhakshátháṁ*	अधग्ध्वं *adhagdhvam*
3. अदग्ध *adagdha*	अधक्षातां *adhakshátám*	अधक्षत *adhakshata*

FIRST AORIST.

Third Form.

PARASMAIPADA ONLY.

या *yá*, to go.

1. अयासिषं *ayásisham*	अयासिष्व *ayásishva*	अयासिष्म *ayásishma*
2. अयासीः *ayásíḥ*	अयासिष्टं *ayásishṭam*	अयासिष्ट *ayásishṭa*
3. अयासीत् *ayásít*	अयासिष्टां *ayásishṭám*	अयासिषुः *ayásishuḥ*

नम् *nam*, to bend.

1. अनंसिषं *anaṁsisham*	अनंसिष्व *anaṁsishva*	अनंसिष्म *anaṁsishma*
2. अनंसीः *anaṁsíḥ*	अनंसिष्टं *anaṁsishṭam*	अनंसिष्ट *anaṁsishṭa*
3. अनंसीत् *anaṁsít*	अनंसिष्टां *anaṁsishṭám*	अनंसिषुः *anaṁsishuḥ*

FIRST AORIST.

Fourth Form.

दिश् *diś*, to show.

PARASMAIPADA.

1. अदिक्षं *adiksham*	अदिक्षाव *adiksháva*	अदिक्षाम *adikshâma*
2. अदिक्षः *adikshaḥ*	अदिक्षतं *adikshatam*	अदिक्षत *adikshata*
3. अदिक्षत् *adikshat*	अदिक्षतां *adikshatám*	अदिक्षन् *adikshan*

ÂTMANEPADA.

1.	अदिक्षि *adikshi*	अदिक्षावहि *adikshávahi*	अदिक्षामहि *adikshámahi*
2.	अदिक्षथाः *adikshatháḥ*	अदिक्षाथां *adikshátháṃ*	अदिक्षध्वं *adikshadhvam*
3.	अदिक्षत *adikshata*	अदिक्षातां *adikshátám*	अदिक्षंत *adikshanta*

गुह् *guh*, to hide.

PARASMAIPADA.

1.	अघुक्षं *aghuksham*	अघुक्षाव *aghukshâva*	अघुक्षाम *aghukshâma*
2.	अघुक्षः *aghukshaḥ*	अघुक्षतं *aghukshatam*	अघुक्षत *aghukshata*
3.	अघुक्षत् *aghukshat*	अघुक्षतां *aghukshatâm*	अघुक्षन् *aghukshan*

ÂTMANEPADA.

1.	अघुक्षि *aghukshi*	अघुक्षावहि *aghukshâvahi* or अगुह्वहि *aguhvahi*	अघुक्षामहि *aghukshâmahi*
2.	अघुक्षथाः *aghukshathâḥ* or अगूढाः *agûḍhâḥ*	अघुक्षाथां *aghukshâthâm*	अघुक्षध्वं or अघूढ्वं[1]
3.	अघुक्षत *aghukshata* or अगूढ *agûḍha*	अघुक्षातां *aghukshâtâm*	अघुक्षंत *aghukshanta*

It may also follow the First Form, अगूहिषं *agûhisham* and अगूहिषि *agûhishi*. (§ 337, I. 1.)

लिह् *lih*, to smear.

PARASMAIPADA.

1.	अलिक्षं *aliksham*	अलिक्षाव *alikshâva*	अलिक्षाम *alikshâma*
2.	अलिक्षः *alikshaḥ*	अलिक्षतं *alikshatam*	अलिक्षत *alikshata*
3.	अलिक्षत् *alikshat*	अलिक्षतां *alikshatâm*	अलिक्षन् *alikshan*

ÂTMANEPADA.

1.	अलिक्षि *alikshi*	अलिक्षावहि *alikshâvahi* or अलिह्वहि *alihvahi*	अलिक्षामहि *alikshâmahi*
2.	अलिक्षथाः *alikshathâḥ* or अलीढाः *alîḍhâḥ*	अलिक्षाथां *alikshâthâm*	अलिक्षध्वं or अलीढ्वं[2]
3.	अलिक्षत *alikshata* or अलीढ *alîḍha*	अलिक्षातां *alikshâtâm*	अलिक्षंत *alikshanta*

दुह् *duh*, to milk.

PARASMAIPADA.

अधुक्षं *adhuksham*, &c.

ÂTMANEPADA.

1.	अधुक्षि *adhukshi*	अधुक्षावहि *adhukshâvahi* or अदुह्वहि *aduhvahi*	अधुक्षामहि *adhukshâmahi*
2.	अधुक्षथाः *adhukshathâḥ* or अदुग्धाः *adugdhâḥ*	अधुक्षाथां *adhukshâthâm*	अधुक्षध्वं or अधुग्ध्वं[3]
3.	अधुक्षत *adhukshata* or अदुग्ध *adugdha*	अधुक्षातां *adhukshâtâm*	अधुक्षंत *adhukshanta*

दिह् *dih*, to anoint.

PARASMAIPADA.

अधिक्षं *adhiksham*, &c.

ÂTMANEPADA.

1.	अधिक्षि *adhikshi*	अधिक्षावहि or अदिह्वहि[4]	अधिक्षामहि *adhikshâmahi*
2.	अधिक्षथाः or अदिग्धाः[5]	अधिक्षाथां *adhikshâthâm*	अधिक्षध्वं or अधिग्ध्वं[6]
3.	अधिक्षत or अदिग्ध[7]	अधिक्षातां *adhikshâtâm*	अधिक्षंत *adhikshanta*

[1] *aghukshadhvam* or *aghûḍhvam*.
[2] *alikshadhvam* or *alîḍhvam*.
[3] *adhukshadhvam* or *adhugdhvam*.
[4] *adhikshâvahi* or *adihvahi*.
[5] *adhikshathâḥ* or *adigdhâḥ*.
[6] *adhikshadhvam* or *adhigdhvam*.
[7] *adhikshata* or *adigdha*.

Second Aorist.

First Form.

§ 363. Verbs adopting this form take the augment, and attach the terminations (First Division) of the imperfect to a verbal base ending in अ *a*, like those of the Tud form.

सिच् *sich*, to sprinkle. Pres. सिंचामि *siñchâmi*; Impf. असिंचं *asiñcham*.

Parasmaipada.

1. असिचं *asicham*	असिचाव *asichâva*	असिचाम *asichâma*
2. असिचः *asichaḥ*	असिचतं *asichatam*	असिचत *asichata*
3. असिचत् *asichat*	असिचतां *asichatâm*	असिचन् *asichan*

Âtmanepada.

1. असिचे *asiche*	असिचावहि *asichâvahi*	असिचामहि *asichâmahi*
2. असिचथाः *asichathâḥ*	असिचेथां *asichethâm*	असिचध्वं *asichadhvam*
3. असिचत *asichata*	असिचेतां *asichetâm*	असिचंत *asichanta*

ह्वे *hve*, to call. Pres. ह्वयामि *hvayâmi*; Impf. अह्वयं *ahvayam*; General base हू *hû*.

Parasmaipada.

1. अह्वं *ahvam*	अह्वाव *ahvâva*	अह्वाम *ahvâma*
2. अह्वः *ahvaḥ*	अह्वतं *ahvatam*	अह्वत *ahvata*
3. अह्वत् *ahvat*	अह्वतां *ahvatâm*	अह्वन् *ahvan*

Âtmanepada.

1. अह्वे *ahve*	अह्वावहि *ahvâvahi*	अह्वामहि *ahvâmahi*
2. अह्वथाः *ahvathâḥ*	अह्वेथां *ahvethâm*	अह्वध्वं *ahvadhvam*
3. अह्वत *ahvata*	अह्वेतां *ahvetâm*	अह्वंत *ahvanta*

§ 364. Roots ending in आ *â*, ए *e*, इ *i*, drop these vowels, and substitute a base ending in अ *a*: ह्वे *hve* substitutes ह्व *hva*, Aor. अह्वं *ahvam*; श्वि *śvi* substitutes श्व *śva*, Aor. अश्वं *aśvam*. Roots ending in ऋ *ṛi*, and the root दृश् *dṛiś*, to see, take Guṇa (Pâṇ. VII. 4, 16), and then form a base ending in short अ *a*: सृ *sṛi*, to go, असरत् *asarat*; दृश् *dṛiś*, to see, अदर्शत् *adarśat*.

§ 365. Roots with penultimate nasal, drop it: स्कंद् *skand*, to step, अस्कदं *askadam*.

§ 366. Irregular forms are, अवोचं *avocham*, I spoke, from वच् *vach* (according to Bopp a contracted reduplicated aorist, § 370, for अववचं *avavacham*); अपप्तं *apaptam*, I flew, from पत् *pat* (possibly a contracted reduplicated aorist for अपपतं *apapatam*); अनेशं *aneśam*, I perished (possibly for अननशं *ananaśam*); अशिषं *aśisham*, I ordered, from शास् *śâs*; आस्थं *âstham*, I threw, from अस् *as*.

§ 367. Roots which take this form are,

अस् *as*, to throw (आस्थं *âstham**), वच् *vach*, to speak (अवोचं *avocham*), ख्या *khyâ*, to speak (अख्यं *akhyam*), if the agent is implied. (Pâṇ. III. 1, 52.)

लिप् *lip*, to paint, सिच् *sich*, to sprinkle, ह्वे *hve*, to call (irregularly अह्वं *ahvam*),

* आस्थं *âstham* stands irregularly for आसं *âsam*. (Pâṇ. VII. 4, 17.)

in Par., and optionally in Âtm. (Pâṇ. III. 1, 53, 54). Par. अलिपत् *alipat*, Âtm. अलिपत *alipata* or अलिप्त *alipta*.

The verbs classed as पुषादि *pushâdi*, beginniug with पुष् *push* (Dh. P. 26, 73–136), द्युतादि *dyutâdi*, beginning with द्युत् *dyut* (Dh. P. 18), and tbose marked by a technical ऌ *ḷi*, in the Parasmaipada. (Pâṇ. III. 1, 55.)

The verbs सृ *sṛi*, to go, शास् *śâs*, to order, and ऋ *ṛi*, to go (आरं *âram*), in Par. and Âtm. (Pâṇ. III. 1, 56.)

Optionally, verbs technically marked by इर् *ir*, but in the Parasmaipada only (Pâṇ. III. 1, 57). अभिदत् *abhidat* or अभैत्सीत् *abhaitsît*.

Optionally, जॄ *jṝi*, to fail, स्तम्भ् *stambh*, to stiffen (अस्तभत् *astabhat* or अस्तम्भीत् *astambhît*), म्रुच् *mruch*, to go (अम्रुचत् *amruchat* or अम्रोचीत् *amrochît*), म्लुच् *mluch*, to go, ग्रुच् *gruch*, to steal, ग्लुच् *gluch*, to steal, ग्लुञ्च् *gluñch*, to go (अग्लुचत् *agluchat* or अग्लुञ्चीत् *agluñchît*), श्वि *śvi*, to grow (irregularly अश्वत् *aśvat*), but in the Parasmaipada only. (Pâṇ. III. 1, 58.)

§ 368. There are a few verbs, ending in आ *â*, ए *e*, ओ *o*, which take this form of the second aorist in the Parasmaipada; also भू *bhû*, to be. They retain throughout the long final vowel, except before the उः *uḥ* of the 3rd pers. plur., before which the final आ *â* is rejected. In the Âtmanepada these verbs in आ *â* take the Second Form of the first aorist, and change आ *â* to इ *i*.

दा *dâ*, to give. Pres. ददामि *dadâmi*; Impf. अददां *adadâm*.

Parasmaipada.

1. अदां *adâm*	अदाव *adâva*	अदाम *adâma*
2. अदाः *adâḥ*	अदातं *adâtam*	अदात *adâta*
3. अदात् *adât*	अदातां *adâtâm*	अदुः *aduḥ*

भू *bhû*, to be. Pres. भवामि *bhavâmi*; Impf. अभवं *abhavam*.

Parasmaipada.

1. अभूवं *abhûvam* *	अभूव *abhûva*	अभूम *abhûma*
2. अभूः *abhûḥ*	अभूतं *abhûtam*	अभूत *abhûta*
3. अभूत् *abhût*	अभूतां *abhûtâm*	अभूवन् *abhûvan*

Verbs which take this form are,

गा *gâ*, to go; दा *dâ*, to give; धा *dhâ*, to place; पा *pâ*, to drink; स्था *sthâ*, to stand; दे *de*, to guard; दो *do*, to cut; भू *bhû*, to be. (Pâṇ. II. 4, 77.)

Optionally, घ्रा *ghrâ*, to smell; धे *dhe*, to drink; शो *śo*, to sharpen; छो *chho*, to cut; सो *so*, to destroy. (Pâṇ. II. 4, 78.)

§ 369. The nine roots of the Tan class ending in न् *n* or ण् *ṇ* may form the 2nd and 3rd pers. sing. Âtm. in थाः *thâḥ* and त *ta*, before which the final nasal is rejected. तन् *tan*, to stretch; Aor. अतनिष्ट *atanishṭa* or अतत *atata*; अतनिष्ठाः *atanishṭhâḥ* or अतथाः *atathâḥ* (Pâṇ. II. 4, 79). These forms might

* Irregular in the 1st pers. sing., dual, and plur., and in the 3rd pers. plur.

be considered as irregular Âtmanepada forms of the second aorist, or of the first aorist II, with loss of initial स् *s*.

Second Aorist.

Second or Reduplicated Form.

§ 370. A few primitive verbs, and the very numerous class of the Chur roots, the denominatives and causatives in अय् *ay*, reduplicate their base in the second aorist, taking the augment as before, and the usual terminations of the imperfect.

§ 371. The primitive verbs which take this form are,

श्रि *śri*, to go, द्रु *dru*, to run, स्रु *sru*, to flow, कम् *kam*, to love (Pâṇ. III. 1, 48), if expressing the agent; अशिश्रियत् *aśiśriyat*.

Optionally, श्वि *śvi*, to grow, धे *dhe*, to suck (Pâṇ. III. 1, 49), if expressing the agent; अदधत् *adadhat*, § 364, (or अधात् *adhât* or अधासीत् *adhâsît*).

Their reduplicative syllable, as far as consonants are concerned, is formed like that of the reduplicated perfect.

अशिश्रियत् *aśiśriyat*, he went. अदुद्रुवत् *adudruvat*, he ran. असुस्रुवत् *asusruvat*, he flowed. अचकमत् *achakamat*, he loved. अदधत् *adadhat*, he sucked. अशिश्वियत् *aśiśviyat*, he grew; also Sec. Aor. अश्वत् *aśvat* and First Aor. अश्वयीत् *aśvayît* (Pâṇ. III. 1, 49). ह्वे *hve*, to call, forms its Aor. Caus. अजूहवत् *ajûhavat* (Pâṇ. VI. 1, 32).

§ 372. The verbs in अय् *ay* drop अय् *ay*, and (with certain exceptions*) reduce their Guṇa and Vṛiddhi vowels to the simple base vowels: आ *á* to अ *ă*; ए *e* to इ *i*; ओ *o* to उ *u*; अर्, आर् *ăr*, to ऋ *ṛi*; ईर् *îr* to ऋ *ṛi*.

Thus मादयति *mádayati* would become मद् *mad*, (Aor. अमीमदं *amîmadam*.)

भेदयति *bhedayati* — — भिद् *bhid*, (Aor. अबीभिदं *abîbhidam*.)

मोदयति *modayati* — — मुद् *mud*, (Aor. अमूमुदं *amûmudam*.)

§ 373. In the exceptional roots, which do not admit this shortening process, आ *á*, ई *í*, ए *e*, ऐ *ai*, ऊ *ú*, ओ *o*, औ *au* are represented in the reduplicative syllable by अ *ă*, इ *ĭ*, इ *ĭ*, इ *ĭ*, उ *ŭ*, उ *ŭ*, उ *ŭ*†.

---

* These exceptional verbs are (Pâṇ. VII. 4, 2),

Certain denominatives: From माला *mâlâ*, a garland, is formed the denominative मालयति *mâlayati*, Red. Aor. अममालत् *amamâlat*; शास् *śâs*, Caus. शासयति *śâsayati*, he punishes, Red. Aor. अशशासत् *aśaśâsat*.

Those with technical ऋ *ṛi*: बाध् *bâdh*, to hurt; Caus. बाधयति *bâdhayati*; Aor. अबबाधत् *ababâdhat*.

भ्राज् *bhrâj*, to shine, भास् *bhâs*, to shine, भाष् *bhâsh*, to speak, दीप् *dîp*, to lighten, जीव् *jîv*, to live, मील् *mîl*, to meet, पीड् *pîḍ*, to vex, shorten their vowel optionally. Ex. भ्राज् *bhrâj*: अबभ्राजत् *ababhrâjat* or अबिभ्रजत् *abibhrajat* (§ 374).

† वेष्टय् *veshṭay*, to surround, चेष्टय् *cheshṭay*, to move, take either इ *i* or अ *a* in the reduplicative syllable; अववेष्टत् *avaveshṭat* or अविवेष्टत् *aviveshṭat*. द्योतय् *dyotay*, to lighten, takes इ *i*; अदिद्युतत् *adidyutat*.

मालयति *mâlayati*, अममालं *amamâlam*. टीकयति *ṭîkayati*, अटिटीकं *aṭiṭîkam*.
लोकयति *lokayati*, अलुलोकं *alulokam*.

§ 374. In the vast majority of roots, however, the shortening takes place, thus leaving bases with short अ *a*, इ *i*, उ *u*, ऋ *ṛi*. Here the tendency is to make the reduplicated base, with the augment, either ⏑ – ⏑ or ⏑ ⏑ –. Hence all roots in which the shortened vowel is not long by position, lengthen the vowel of the reduplicative syllable (*amûmudat*). Those in which the vowel is long by position, leave the vowel of the reduplicative syllable short (*ararakshat*).

Where, as in roots beginning with double consonants, the vowel of the reduplicative syllable is necessarily long by position, it is not changed into the long vowel (*achuchyutat*, not *achûchyutat*). In roots beginning and ending in two consonants, this metrical rhythm is necessarily broken (*achaskandat*).

§ 375. In the roots which do not resist the shortening process,

अ *a*, इ *i*, उ *u*, ऋ *ṛi* are represented in the reduplicative syllable by
अ *a* or इ *i*, इ *i*, उ *u*, इ *i*; and all lengthened, where necessary.

Second Aorist.

Second or Reduplicated Form.

1. ⏑ – ⏑.

पच् *pach*, to cook, पाचयति *pâchayati*; अपीपचत् *apîpachat* *.
भिद् *bhid*, to cut, भेदयति *bhedayati*; अबीभिदत् *abîbhidat*.
मुद् *mud*, to rejoice, मोदयति *modayati*; अमूमुदत् *amûmudat*.
वृत् *vṛit*, to exist, वर्तयति *vartayati*; अवीवृतत् *avîvṛitat*.
मृज् *mṛij*, to cleanse, मार्जयति *mârjayati*; अमीमृजत् *amîmṛijat*.
कृत् *kṛit*, to praise, कीर्तयति *kîrtayati*; अचीकृतत् *achîkṛitat* †.

The lengthening becomes superfluous before roots beginning with two consonants, because the two consonants make the short vowel heavy (*guru*).

त्यज् *tyaj*, to leave, त्याजयति *tyâjayati*; अतित्यजत् *atityajat*.
भ्राज् *bhrâj*, to shine, भ्राजयति *bhrâjayati*; अबिभ्रजत् *abibhrajat*.
क्षिप् *kship*, to throw, क्षेपयति *kshepayati*; अचिक्षिपत् *achikshipat*.
च्युत् *chyut*, to fall, च्योतयति *chyotayati*; अचुच्युतत् *achuchyutat*.
स्वृ *svṛi*, to sound, स्वारयति *svârayati*; असिस्वरत् *asisvarat*.

---

* गणय् *gaṇay* and कथय् *kathay* take ई *î* or अ *a* optionally; अजीगणत् *ajîgaṇat* or अजगणत् *ajagaṇat*.

† The following verbs take अ *a* instead of इ *i* or ई *î* in the reduplicative syllable of the aorist in the causative:

स्मृ *smṛi*, दृ *dṛî*, त्वर् *tvar*, प्रथ् *prath*, म्रद् *mrad*, स्तॄ *stṛî*, स्पश् *spaś*.

स्मृ *smṛi*; Caus. स्मारयति *smârayati*; Aor. असस्मरत् *asasmarat*.

The same verbs which, as will be shown hereafter, reduplicate अव् *av*, (the Guṇa of उ, ऊ *û*,) in the desiderative by उ *u*, take उ *u* instead of इ *i* in the reduplicated aorist:

नु *nu*; Caus. नावयति *nâvayati*; Des. नुनावयिषति *nunâvayishati*; Aor. of Caus. अनूनवं *anûnavam*.

2. ⏑ ⏑ –.

रक्ष् *raksh*, to protect, रक्षयति *rakshayati*; अररक्षत् *ararakshat* *.

भिक्ष् *bhiksh*, to beg, भिक्षयति *bhikshayati*; अबिभिक्षत् *abibhikshat*.

§ 376. If the root begins and ends with double consonants, this rhythmical law is broken.

प्रछ् *prachh*, to ask, प्रच्छयति *prachchhayati*; अपप्रच्छत् *apaprachchhat*.

स्कंद् *skand*, to step, स्कंदयति *skandayati*; अचस्कंदत् *achaskandat*.

§ 377. Roots with radical ऋ *ṛi*, followed by a consonant, may optionally take the ⏑ – ⏑ or ⏑ ⏑ – forms.

वृत् *vṛit*, to be, वर्तयति *vartayati*; अवीवृतत् *avîvṛitat* or अववर्तत् *avavartat*. (Pâṇ. VII. 4, 7.)

मृज् *mṛij*, to cleanse, मार्जयति *mârjayati*; अमीमृजत् *amîmṛijat* or अममार्जत् *amamârjat*.

कृत् *kṛît*, to praise, कीर्तयति *kîrtayati*; अचीकृतत् *achîkṛitat* or अचिकीर्तत् *achikîrtat*.

§ 378. Roots beginning with a vowel have the same internal reduplication, which will be described hereafter in the desiderative bases.

Thus अश् *aś* forms the Caus. आशय् *âśay*. This after throwing off अय् *ay*, and shortening the vowel, becomes अश् *aś*; this reduplicated, अशिश् *aś-iś*; and lastly, with augment and termination, आशिशं *âś-iś-am*.

In the same manner, आर्चिचं *ârchicham*, औब्जिजं *aubjijam*, &c.

§ 379. Are slightly irregular:

पा *pâ*, to drink, which forms its causal aorist as अपीप्यत् *apîpyat* (instead of अपीपयत् *apîpayat*).

स्था *sthâ*, to stand, which forms its causal aorist as अतिष्ठिपत् *atishṭhipat* (instead of अतिष्ठपत् *atishṭhapat*).

घ्रा *ghrâ*, to smell, which forms its causal aorist as अजिघ्रिपत् *ajighripat* or अजिघ्रपत् *ajighrapat*.

Reduplicated Aorist.

Parasmaipada.

1.	अशिश्रयं *aśiśrayam*	अशिश्रयाव *aśiśrayâva*	अशिश्रयाम *aśiśrayâma*
2.	अशिश्रयः *aśiśrayaḥ*	अशिश्रयतं *aśiśrayatam*	अशिश्रयत *aśiśrayata*
3.	अशिश्रयत् *aśiśrayat*	अशिश्रयतां *aśiśrayatâm*	अशिश्रयन् *aśiśrayan*

Âtmanepada.

1.	अशिश्रये *aśiśraye*	अशिश्रयावहि *aśiśrayâvahi*	अशिश्रयामहि *aśiśrayâmahi*
2.	अशिश्रयथाः *aśiśrayathâḥ*	अशिश्रयेथां *aśiśrayethâm*	अशिश्रयध्वं *aśiśrayadhvam*
3.	अशिश्रयत *aśiśrayata*	अशिश्रयेतां *aśiśrayetâm*	अशिश्रयंत *aśiśrayanta*

§ 380. In the preceding §§ occasional rules have been given as to the particular forms of the aorist which certain verbs or classes of verbs adopt. As in Greek, so in Sanskrit, too, practice only can effectually teach which forms do actually occur of each verb; and the rules of grammarians,

* Radical अ *a* is reduplicated by अ *a* if the root ends in a double consonant.

however minute and complicated, are not unfrequently contradicted by the usage of Sanskrit authors.

However, the general rule is that verbs follow the first aorist, unless this is specially prohibited, and that they take the first form of the first aorist, unless they are barred by general rules from the employment of the intermediate इ *i*. Verbs, thus barred, take the second form of the first aorist.

The number of verbs which take the third form of the first aorist is very limited, three roots ending in म् *m*, and roots ending in आ *â*.

The fourth form of the first aorist is likewise of very limited use; see § 360.

As to the second aorist, the roots which must or may follow it are indicated in § 367, and so are the roots which take the reduplicated form of the second aorist in § 371.

Roots which follow the second aorist optionally, or in the Parasmaipada only, are allowed to be conjugated in the first aorist, subject to the general rules.

CHAPTER XIV.

FUTURE, CONDITIONAL, PERIPHRASTIC FUTURE, AND BENEDICTIVE.

Future.

§ 381. Terminations.

Parasmaipada.

	SINGULAR.	DUAL.	PLURAL.
1.	इष्यामि *ishyâmi*	इष्यावः *ishyâvaḥ*	इष्यामः *ishyâmaḥ*
2.	इष्यसि *ishyasi*	इष्यथः *ishyathaḥ*	इष्यथ *ishyatha*
3.	इष्यति *ishyati*	इष्यतः *ishyataḥ*	इष्यन्ति *ishyanti*

Âtmanepada.

	SINGULAR.	DUAL.	PLURAL.
1.	इष्ये *ishye*	इष्यावहे *ishyâvahe*	इष्यामहे *ishyâmahe*
2.	इष्यसे *ishyase*	इष्येथे *ishyethe*	इष्यध्वे *ishyadhve*
3.	इष्यते *ishyate*	इष्येते *ishyete*	इष्यन्ते *ishyante*

The cases in which the इ *i* of इष्यामि *ishyâmi* &c. must be or may be omitted have been stated in chapter XI, §§ 331 seq. For the cases in which इ *i* is changed to ई *î*, see § 340. On the change of ष *sha* and स *sa*, see §§ 100 seq. On the strengthening of the radical vowel, see chapter XII, §§ 344 seq.

§ 382. The changes which the base undergoes before the terminations of the strengthening tenses, the two futures, the conditional, and the benedictive Âtm. are regulated by one general principle, that of giving weight to the base, though their application varies according to the peculiarities of certain verbs. See illustrations in § 344 (*bhavishyâmi*) and § 345 (*mirkshyâmi*). These peculiarities must be learnt by practice, but a few general rules may here be repeated:

1. Final ए *e*, ऐ *ai*, ओ *o* are changed to आ *â*; गै *gai*, to sing, गास्यामि *gâsyâmi*, &c.
2. Final इ *i* and ई *î*, उ *u*, ऊ *û*, ऋ *ṛi* and ॠ *ṛî*, take Guṇa; जि *ji*, to conquer, जेष्यामि *jeshyâmi*; भू *bhû*, भविष्यामि *bhavishyâmi*; कृ *kṛi*, करिष्यामि *karishyâmi*; दॄ *dṛî*, to tear, दरिष्यामि *darishyâmi* or दरीष्यामि *darîshyâmi*. There are the usual exceptions, कू *kû*, to sound, कुविष्यामि *kuvishyâmi*. (§ 345, note.)
3. Penultimate इ *i*, उ *u*, ऋ *ṛi*, prosodially short, take Guṇa; ॠ *ṛî* becomes ईर् *îr*; बुध् *budh*, बोधिष्यामि *bodhishyâmi*; भिद् *bhid*, भेत्स्यति *bhetsyati*.

बुध् *budh*, to know,
with intermediate इ *i*.
PARASMAIPADA.

	SINGULAR.	DUAL.	PLURAL.
1.	बोधिष्यामि *bodhishyâmi*	बोधिष्यावः *bodhishyâvaḥ*	बोधिष्यामः *bodhishyâmaḥ*
2.	बोधिष्यसि *bodhishyasi*	बोधिष्यथः *bodhishyathaḥ*	बोधिष्यथ *bodhishyatha*
3.	बोधिष्यति *bodhishyati*	बोधिष्यतः *bodhishyataḥ*	बोधिष्यन्ति *bodhishyanti*

ÂTMANEPADA.

1.	बोधिष्ये *bodhishye*	बोधिष्यावहे *bodhishyâvahe*	बोधिष्यामहे *bodhishyâmahe*
2.	बोधिष्यसे *bodhishyase*	बोधिष्येथे *bodhishyethe*	बोधिष्यध्वे *bodhishyadhve*
3.	बोधिष्यते *bodhishyate*	बोधिष्येते *bodhishyete*	बोधिष्यन्ते *bodhishyante*

इ *i*, to go,
without intermediate इ *i*.
PARASMAIPADA.

1.	एष्यामि *eshyâmi*	एष्यावः *eshyâvaḥ*	एष्यामः *eshyâmaḥ*
2.	एष्यसि *eshyasi*	एष्यथः *eshyathaḥ*	एष्यथ *eshyatha*
3.	एष्यति *eshyati*	एष्यतः *eshyataḥ*	एष्यन्ति *eshyanti*

ÂTMANEPADA.

1.	एष्ये *eshye*	एष्यावहे *eshyâvahe*	एष्यामहे *eshyâmahe*
2.	एष्यसे *eshyase*	एष्येथे *eshyethe*	एष्यध्वे *eshyadhve*
3.	एष्यते *eshyate*	एष्येते *eshyete*	एष्यन्ते *eshyante*

Conditional.

§ 383. The future is changed into the conditional by the same process by which a present of the Tud class is changed into an imperfect.

बुध् *budh*, to know,
with intermediate इ *i*.
PARASMAIPADA.

	SINGULAR.	DUAL.	PLURAL.
1.	अबोधिष्यम् *abodhishyam*	अबोधिष्याव *abodhishyâva*	अबोधिष्याम *abodhishyâma*
2.	अबोधिष्यः *abodhishyaḥ*	अबोधिष्यतम् *abodhishyatam*	अबोधिष्यत *abodhishyata*
3.	अबोधिष्यत् *abodhishyat*	अबोधिष्यताम् *abodhishyatâm*	अबोधिष्यन् *abodhishyan*

Âtmanepada.

1.	अबोधिष्ये *abodhishye*	अबोधिष्यावहि *abodhishyâvahi*	अबोधिष्यामहि *abodhishyâmahi*
2.	अबोधिष्यथाः *abodhishyathâḥ*	अबोधिष्येथां *abodhishyethâm*	अबोधिष्यध्वं *abodhishyadhvam*
3.	अबोधिष्यत *abodhishyata*	अबोधिष्येतां *abodhishyetâm*	अबोधिष्यन्त *abodhishyanta*

इ *i*,
without intermediate इ *i*.

Parasmaipada.

1.	ऐष्यं *aishyam*	ऐष्याव *aishyâva*	ऐष्याम *aishyâma*
2.	ऐष्यः *aishyaḥ*	ऐष्यतं *aishyatam*	ऐष्यत *aishyata*
3.	ऐष्यत् *aishyat*	ऐष्यतां *aishyatâm*	ऐष्यन् *aishyan*

Âtmanepada.

1.	ऐष्ये *aishye*	ऐष्यावहि *aishyâvahi*	ऐष्यामहि *aishyâmahi*
2.	ऐष्यथाः *aishyathâḥ*	ऐष्येथां *aishyethâm*	ऐष्यध्वं *aishyadhvam*
3.	ऐष्यत *aishyata*	ऐष्येतां *aishyetâm*	ऐष्यन्त *aishyanta*

Periphrastic Future.

§ 384. The terminations are,

Parasmaipada.

1.	इतास्मि *itâsmi*	इतास्वः *itâsvaḥ*	इतास्मः *itâsmaḥ*
2.	इतासि *itâsi*	इतास्थः *itâsthaḥ*	इतास्थ *itâstha*
3.	इता *itâ*	इतारौ *itârau*	इतारः *itâraḥ*

Âtmanepada.

1.	इताहे *itâhe*	इतास्वहे *itâsvahe*	इतास्महे *itâsmahe*
2.	इतासे *itâse*	इतासाथे *itâsâthe*	इताध्वे *itâdhve*
3.	इता *itâ*	इतारौ *itârau*	इतारः *itâraḥ*

These terminations are clearly compounded of ता *tâ* (base तृ *tṛi*), the common suffix for forming *nomina agentis*, and the auxiliary verb अस् *as*, to be. There is, however, with regard to ता *tâ*, no distinction of number and gender in the 1st and 2nd persons, and no distinction of gender in the 3rd person.

On the retention or omission of intermediate इ *i* or ई *î*, see §§ 331 seq. On the strengthening of the radical vowel, see § 382.

बुध् *budh*, to know,
with intermediate इ *i*.

Parasmaipada.

	Singular.	Dual.	Plural.
1.	बोधितास्मि *bodhitâsmi*	बोधितास्वः *bodhitâsvaḥ*	बोधितास्मः *bodhitâsmaḥ*
2.	बोधितासि *bodhitâsi*	बोधितास्थः *bodhitâsthaḥ*	बोधितास्थ *bodhitâstha*
3.	बोधिता *bodhitâ*	बोधितारौ *bodhitârau*	बोधितारः *bodhitâraḥ*

Âtmanepada.

1.	बोधिताहे *bodhitâhe*	बोधितास्वहे *bodhitâsvahe*	बोधितास्महे *bodhitâsmahe*
2.	बोधितासे *bodhitâse*	बोधितासाथे *bodhitâsâthe*	बोधिताध्वे *bodhitâdhve*
3.	बोधिता *bodhitâ*	बोधितारौ *bodhitârau*	बोधितारः *bodhitâraḥ*

इ i,
without intermediate इ i.

PARASMAIPADA.

1. एतास्मि etâsmi	एतास्वः etâsvaḥ	एतास्मः etâsmaḥ
2. एतासि etâsi	एतास्थः etâsthaḥ	एतास्थ etâstha
3. एता etâ	एतारौ etârau	एतारः etâraḥ

ÂTMANEPADA.

1. एताहे etâhe	एतास्वहे etâsvahe	एतास्महे etâsmahe
2. एतासे etâse	एतासाथे etâsâthe	एताध्वे etâdhve
3. एता etâ	एतारौ etârau	एतारः etâraḥ

Benedictive.

§ 385. The so-called benedictive is formed in close analogy to the optative. It differs from the optative by not admitting the full modified verbal base, and, secondly, by the insertion of an स् *s* before the personal terminations. In the Parasmaipada this स् *s* stands between the या *yâ* of the optative and the actual signs of the persons, being lost, however, in the 2nd and 3rd pers. sing. Thus, instead of

Opt. यां, याः, यात्, याव, यातं, याताम्, याम, यात, युः,
yâm, yâḥ, yât, yâva, yâtam, yâtâm, yâma, yâta, yuḥ, we have

Ben. यासं, याः, यात्, यास्व, यास्तं, यास्ताम्, यास्म, यास्त, यासुः.
yâsam, yâḥ, yât, yâsva, yâstam, yâstâm, yâsma, yâsta, yâsuḥ.

These two sets of terminations stand to each other in the same relation as the terminations of the imperfect and those of the first aorist II. यासः *yâsaḥ* and यासत् *yâsat* are contracted to याः *yâḥ* and यात् *yât*, like the 2nd and 3rd pers. sing. of the first aorist I: इषीः *ishîḥ* to ईः *îḥ*, इषीत् *ishît* to ईत् *ît*, or like the सीः *sîḥ* and सीत् *sît* of the first aorist II, which really stand for स् + स् *s* + *s*, and स् + त् *s* + *t*.

In the Âtmanepada the स् *s* stands *before* the terminations of the optative, e.g. सीय *sîya* instead of ईय *îya*. Besides this, the personal terminations originally beginning with त् *t* or थ् *th* take an additional स् *s*. (Remark, that the स् *s* before these terminations is liable to be dropt after a short vowel in the first aorist, § 351.) Thus, instead of

Opt. ईय, ईथाः, ईत, ईवहि, ईयाथां, ईयातां, ईमहि, ईध्वं, ईरन्,
îya, îthâḥ, îta, îvahi, îyâthâm, îyâtâm, îmahi, îdhvam, îran, we have

Ben. सीय, सीष्ठाः, सीष्ट, सीवहि, सीयास्थां, सीयास्तां, सीमहि, सीध्वं, सीरन्.
sîya, sîshṭhâḥ, sîshṭa, sîvahi, sîyâsthâm, sîyâstâm, sîmahi, sîdhvam, sîran.

§ 386. Verbal bases ending in अय् *ay* (Chur, Caus. Denom. &c.) drop अय् *ay* before the terminations of the benedictive Par.: चोरय् *choray*, Ben. चोर्यासं *choryâsam*; but in Âtm. चोरयिषीय *chorayishîya*. Denominative bases in य् *y* drop य् *y* in the Ben. Par.: पुत्रीय् *putrîy*, Ben. पुत्रीयासं *putrî-yâsam*; but in Âtm. पुत्रीयिषीय *putrîyishîya*.

§ 387. The benedictive Parasmaipada belongs to the weakening, the benedictive Âtmanepada to the strengthening forms (§ 344). Hence from चित् *chit*, Par. चित्यासं *chityâsam*, Âtm. चेतिषीय *chetishîya*.

§ 388. The benedictive Parasmaipada never takes intermediate इ *i*. The benedictive Âtmanepada generally takes intermediate इ *i*. Exceptions are provided for by the rules §§ 331 seq.

Weakening of the Base before Terminations beginning with य् *y*.

§ 389. Some of the rules regulating the weakening of the base, which is required in the benedictive Parasmaipada, may here be stated together with the rules that apply to the weakening of the base in the passive and intensive.

§ 390. While, generally speaking, the terminations of the benedictive, passive, and intensive exercise a weakening influence on the verbal base, there is one important, though only apparent, exception to this rule with regard to verbs ending in इ *i*, उ *u*, ऋ *ṛi*. Final इ *i* and उ *u*, before the य् *y* of the terminations of benedictive, passive, and intensive, are lengthened (Pâṇ. VII. 4, 25), but not strengthened by Guṇa.

चि *chi*, to gather; Ben. चीयात् *chîyât*; Pass. चीयते *chîyate*; Int. चेचीयते *chechîyate*.

Final ऋ *ṛi* is changed to रि *ri*. (Pâṇ. VII. 4, 28.)

कृ *kṛi*, to do; Ben. क्रियात् *kriyât*; Pass. क्रियते *kriyate*. (The Intensive has चेक्रीयते *chekrîyate*, Pâṇ. VII. 4, 27.)

In roots, however, beginning with conjunct consonants, final ऋ *ṛi* is actually strengthened by Guṇa, and appears as अर् *ar*. (Pâṇ. VII. 4, 29.)

स्मृ *smṛi*, to remember; Ben. स्मर्यात् *smaryât*; Pass. स्मर्यते *smaryate*; Int. सास्मर्यते *sâsmaryate*.

Also in ऋ *ṛi*, to go; Ben. अर्यात् *aryât*; Pass. अर्यते *aryate*; Int. अरार्यते *arâryate*.

Final ॠ *ṛî* is changed to ईर् *îr*, and, after labials, to ऊर् *ûr*.

स्तॄ *stṛî*, to stretch; Ben. स्तीर्यात् *stîryât*; Pass. स्तीर्यते *stîryate*; Int. तेस्तीर्यते *testîryate*.

पॄ *pṛî*, to fill; Ben. पूर्यात् *pûryât*; Pass. पूर्यते *pûryate*; Int. पोपूर्यते *popûryate*.

Exceptions: शी *śî* is changed to शय् *śay*.

शी *śî*, to lie down; (Ben. शय्यात् *śayyât* does not occur, because the verb is Âtmanepadin); Pass. शय्यते *śayyate*; Int. शाशय्यते *śâśayyate*. (Pâṇ. VII. 4, 22.)

इ *i*, after prepositions, does not lengthen the final इ *i* in the benedictive.

इ *i*, to go; Ben. ईयात् *îyât*; but समियात् *samiyât*. (Pâṇ. VII. 4, 24.)

ऊह् *ûh*, to understand, after prepositions, is shortened to उह् *uh*. (Pâṇ. VII. 4, 23.)

Ben. ऊह्यात् *ûhyât*; Pass. ऊह्यते *ûhyate*.

Ben. समुह्यात् *samuhyât*; Pass. समुह्यते *samuhyate*.

§ 391. The following roots may or may not drop their final न् *n*, and then lengthen the preceding vowel. (Pâṇ. VI. 4, 43.)

जन् *jan*, to beget; Ben. जायात् *jâyât* or जन्यात् *janyât*; Pass. जायते *jâyate* or जन्यते *janyate*; Int. जाजायते *jâjâyate* or जंजन्यते *jañjanyate*.

सन् *san*, to obtain; Ben. सायात् *sáyát* or सन्यात् *sanyát*; Pass. सायते *sáyate* or सन्यते *sanyate*; Int. सासायते *sásáyate* or संसन्यते *saṁsanyate*.

खन् *khan*, to dig; Ben. खायात् *kháyát* or खन्यात् *khanyát*; Pass. खायते *kháyate* or खन्यते *khanyate*; Int. चाखायते *chákháyate* or चंखन्यते *chaṅkhanyate*.

In the passive only, तन् *tan*, to stretch; Ben. तन्यात् *tanyát*; Pass. तायते *táyate* or तन्यते *tanyate*; Int. तंतन्यते *tantanyate*.

§ 392. According to a general rule, roots ending in ऐ *ai* and ओ *o* change their final diphthong in the general tenses into आ *á*: ध्यै *dhyai*, ध्यायते *dhyáyate*. Roots ending in आ *á* retain it: पा *pá*, पायते *páyate*, he is protected. But the following roots change their final vowel into ई *í* in the passive and intensive; into ए *e* in the benedictive Par.; and keep it unchanged before gerundial य *ya*. (Pâṇ. VI. 4, 66, 67, 69.)

The six verbs called घु *ghu**, and the following verbs:

	Passive.	Intensive.	Benedictive †.	Gerund.
दा *dá*, to give	दीयते *díyate*	देदीयते *dedíyate*	देयात् *deyát*	प्रदाय *pradáya*
मा *má*, to measure	मीयते *míyate*	मेमीयते *memíyate*	मेयात् *meyát*	प्रमाय *pramáya*
स्था *sthá*, to stand	स्थीयते *sthíyate*	तेष्ठीयते *teshṭhíyate*	स्थेयात् *stheyát*	प्रस्थाय *prastháya*
गै *gai*, to sing	गीयते *gíyate*	जेगीयते *jegíyate*	गेयात् *geyát*	प्रगाय *pragáya*
पा *pá*, to drink	पीयते *píyate*	पेपीयते *pepíyate*	पेयात् *peyát*	प्रपाय *prapáya*
हा *há*, to leave	हीयते *híyate*	जेहीयते *jehíyate*	हेयात् *heyát*	प्रहाय *praháya*
सो *so*, to finish	सीयते *síyate*	सेषीयते *seshíyate*	सेयात् *seyát*	प्रसाय *prasáya*

§ 393. The following verbs take *Samprasáraṇa* in the benedictive (Pâṇ. III. 4, 104), passive, participle, and gerund. (Pâṇ. VI. 1, 15.)

वच् *vach*, to speak; स्वप् *svap* ‡ ||, to sleep; वश् *vaś* (Pâṇ. VI. 1, 20), to wish; and the यजादि *yajádi*, i. e. those following यज् *yaj*.

Ben. उच्यात् *uchyát*; Pass. उच्यते *uchyate*; Part. उक्तः *uktaḥ*; Ger. उक्त्वा *uktvá*.

The यजादि are, (23, 33–41) यज् *yaj*, to sacrifice; वप् *vap*, to sow; वह् *vah*, to carry; वस् *vas*, to dwell; वे *ve*, to weave; व्ये *vye* ||, to cover; ह्वे *hve* ||, to call; वद् *vad*, to speak; श्वि *śvi* ||, to grow.

* This term comprises the six roots डुदाञ्, दाण्, दो, देङ्, डुधाञ्, and धेट्, all varieties of the radicals दा *dá* and धा *dhá*; but not दाप् and दैप्, i.e. दाति *dáti*, he cuts, and दायति *dáyati*, he cleans (Pâṇ. I. 1, 20). Hence दीयते *díyate*, it is given; but दायते *dáyate*, it is cleaned.

† In other roots, ending in आ *á* or diphthongs, and beginning with more than one consonant, the change into ए *e* in the benedictive Par. is optional (Pâṇ. VI. 4, 68). ग्लै *glai*, to wither; ग्लेयात् *gleyát* or ग्लायात् *gláyát*. ख्या *khyá*, to call; ख्यायात् *khyáyát* or ख्येयात् *khyeyát*.

‡ स्वाप् *sváp*, to send to sleep, takes *Samprasáraṇa* in the reduplicated aorist (Pâṇ. VI. 1, 18). असूषुपत् *asúshupat*.

|| स्वप् *svap*, to sleep, स्यम् *syam*, to sound, and व्ये *vye*, take *Samprasáraṇa* in the intensive also (Pâṇ. VI. 1, 19); सोषुप्यते *soshupyate*, सेसिम्यते *sesimyate*, वेवीयते *vevíyate*. श्वि *śvi* takes *Samprasáraṇa* optionally in the intensive (Pâṇ. VI. 1, 30); शोशूयते *śośúyate* or शेश्वीयते *śeśvíyate*. ह्वे *hve* forms Int. जोहूयते *johúyate* (Pâṇ. VI. 1, 33). In the intensive चाय् *cháy* forms चेकीयते *chekíyate* (Pâṇ. VI. 1, 21); प्याय् *pyáy*, पेपीयते *pepíyate* (Pâṇ. VI. 1, 29).

§ 394. The following verbs take *Samprasâraṇa* in the benedictive, passive, participle, gerund, and intensive. (Pâṇ. VI. 1, 16.)

ग्रह् *grah*, to take; ज्या *jyâ*, to fail; व्यध् *vyadh*, to pierce; व्यच् *vyach*, to surround; व्रश्च् *vraśch*, to cut; प्रछ् *prachh*, to ask; भ्रस्ज् *bhrajj*, to fry.

ग्रह् *grah*; Ben. गृह्यात् *gṛihyât*; Pass. गृह्यते *gṛihyate*; Part. गृहीतः *gṛihîtaḥ*; Ger. गृहीत्वा *gṛihîtvâ*; Int. जरीगृह्यते *jarîgṛihyate*.

§ 395. शास् *śâs*, to rule, substitutes शिष् *śish* in the benedictive, passive, participle, gerund, intensive, also in the second aorist. (Pâṇ. VI. 4, 34.)

Ben. शिष्यात् *śishyât*; Pass. शिष्यते *śishyate*; Part. शिष्टः *śishṭaḥ*; Ger. शिष्ट्वा *śishṭvâ*; Aor. अशिषत् *aśishat*.

§ 396. With regard to the benedictive Âtm. see the general rules as to the strengthening of the base, § 344. Remember, that if the benedictive Âtm. does not take intermediate इ *i*, penultimate इ *i*, उ *u*, ऋ *ṛi* are left unchanged, whereas in other strengthening tenses they take Guṇa (§ 344). Final ऋ *ṛi*, too, remains unchanged, and ॠ *ṛî* becomes ईर् *îr*, or, after labials, ऊर् *ûr*. क्षिप् *kship*, to throw, क्षिप्सीय *kshipsîya*; पॄ *pṛî*, to fill, पूर्षीय *pûrshîya*.

Benedictive.

PARASMAIPADA.

1.	बुध्यासं *budhyâsam*	बुध्यास्व *budhyâsva*	बुध्यास्म *budhyâsma*
2.	बुध्याः *budhyâḥ*	बुध्यास्तं *budhyâstam*	बुध्यास्त *budhyâsta*
3.	बुध्यात् *budhyât*	बुध्यास्तां *budhyâstâm*	बुध्यासुः *budhyâsuḥ*

ÂTMANEPADA.

1.	बोधिषीय *bodhishîya*	बोधिषीवहि *bodhishîvahi*	बोधिषीमहि *bodhishîmahi*
2.	बोधिषीष्ठाः *bodhishîshṭhâḥ*	बोधिषीयास्थां *bodhishîyâsthâm*	बोधिषीढ्वं *bodhishîḍhvam*
3.	बोधिषीष्ट *bodhishîshṭa*	बोधिषीयास्तां *bodhishîyâstâm*	बोधिषीरन् *bodhishîran*

CHAPTER XV.

PASSIVE.

§ 397. The passive takes the terminations of the Âtmanepada.

Special Tenses of the Passive.

§ 398. The present, imperfect, optative, and imperative of the passive are formed by adding य *ya* to the root. This य *ya* is added in the same manner as it is in the Div verbs, so that the Âtmanepada of Div verbs is in all respects (except in the accent) identical with the passive.

Âtm. नह्यते *náhyate*, he binds; Pass. नह्यते *nahyáte*, he is bound.

§ 399. Bases in अय् *ay* (Chur, Caus. Denom. &c.) drop अय् *ay* before य *ya* of the passive.

बोधय् *bodhay*, to make one know; बोध्यते *bodh-yate*, he is made to know.
चोरय् *choray*, to steal; चोर्यते *chor-yate*, he is stolen.

Intensive bases ending in य् *y* retain their य् *y*, to which the य *ya* of the passive is added without any intermediate vowel.

लोलूय् *lolûy*, to cut much; लोलूय्यते *lolûyyate*, he is cut much.

Intensive bases ending in य् *y*, preceded by a consonant, drop their य् *y*.

बेभिद्य् *bebhidy*, to sever; बेभिद्यते *bebhidyate*, it is severed.

दीधी *dîdhî*, to shine, वेवी *vevî*, to yearn, दरिद्रा *daridrâ*, to be poor, drop their final vowel, as usual.

दीधी *dîdhî*, दीध्यते *dîdhyate*, it is lightened, i. e. it lightens.

§ 400. As to the weakening of the base, see the rules given for the benedictive, §§ 389 seq.

Passive.

SINGULAR.

	1.	2.	3.
Pres.	भूये *bhûye*	भूयसे *bhûyase*	भूयते *bhûyate*
Impf.	अभूये *abhûye*	अभूयथाः *abhûyathâḥ*	अभूयत *abhûyata*
Opt.	भूयेय *bhûyeya*	भूयेथाः *bhûyethâḥ*	भूयेत *bhûyeta*
Imp.	भूयै *bhûyai*	भूयस्व *bhûyasva*	भूयतां *bhûyatâm*
		DUAL.	
Pres.	भूयावहे *bhûyâvahe*	भूयेथे *bhûyethe*	भूयेते *bhûyete*
Impf.	अभूयावहि *abhûyâvahi*	अभूयेथां *abhûyethâm*	अभूयेतां *abhûyetâm*
Opt.	भूयेवहि *bhûyevahi*	भूयेयाथां *bhûyeyâthâm*	भूयेयातां *bhûyeyâtâm*
Imp.	भूयावहै *bhûyâvahai*	भूयेथां *bhûyethâm*	भूयेतां *bhûyetâm*
		PLURAL.	
Pres.	भूयामहे *bhûyâmahe*	भूयध्वे *bhûyadhve*	भूयन्ते *bhûyante*
Impf.	अभूयामहि *abhûyâmahi*	अभूयध्वं *abhûyadhvam*	अभूयन्त *abhûyanta*
Opt.	भूयेमहि *bhûyemahi*	भूयेध्वं *bhûyedhvam*	भूयेरन् *bhûyeran*
Imp.	भूयामहै *bhûyâmahai*	भूयध्वं *bhûyadhvam*	भूयन्तां *bhûyantâm*

General Tenses of the Passive.

§ 401. In the general tenses of the passive, य *ya* is dropt, so that, with certain exceptions to be mentioned hereafter, there is no distinction between the general tenses of the passive and those of the Âtmanepada. The य *ya* of the passive is treated, in fact, like one of the conjugational class-marks (*vikaraṇas*), which are retained in the special tenses only, and it differs thereby from the derivative syllables of causative, desiderative, and intensive verbs, which, with certain exceptions, remain throughout both in the special and in the general tenses.

Reduplicated Perfect.

The reduplicated perfect is the same as in the Âtmanepada.

Periphrastic Perfect.

The periphrastic perfect is the same as in the Âtmanepada, but the auxiliary verbs अस् *as* and भू *bhû* must be conjugated in the Âtmanepada, as well as कृ *kṛi*. (§ 342.)

Aorist.

§ 402. Verbs may be conjugated in the three forms of the first aorist which admit of Âtmanepada, and without differing from the paradigms given above, except in the third person singular.

The second aorist Âtmanepada is not to be used in a purely passive sense *.

§ 403. In the third person singular a peculiar form has been fixed in the passive, ending in इ *i*, and requiring Vṛiddhi of final, and Guṇa of medial vowels (but अ *a* is lengthened), followed by *one* consonant.

Thus, instead of अलविष्ट *alavishṭa*, we find अलावि *alâv-i*. } First Form.
अबोधिष्ट *abodhishṭa*, — अबोधि *abodh-i*.

अक्षिप्त *akshipta*, — अक्षेपि *akshep-i*. }
अनेष्ट *aneshṭa*, — अनायि *anây-i*.
अकृत *akṛita*, — अकारि *akâr-i*.
अदित *adita*, — अदायि *adây-i*. } Second Form.
अस्तीर्ष्ट *astîrshṭa*, — अस्तारि *astâr-i*.
असृष्ट *asṛishṭa*, — असर्जि *asarj-i*.
अदग्ध *adagdha*, — अदाहि *adâh-i*.

अदिक्षत *adikshata*, — अदेशि *adeś-i*. }
अघुक्षत *aghukshata*, — अगूहि *agûh-i*.
अलिक्षत *alikshata*, — अलेहि *aleh-i*. } Fourth Form.
अधुक्षत *adhukshata*, — अदोहि *adoh-i*.
अधिक्षत *adhikshata*, — अदेहि *adeh-i*.

§ 404. Verbs ending in आ *â* or diphthongs, take य् *y* before the passive इ *i*.

दा *dâ*, अदायि *adâyi*, instead of अदित *adita*.

§ 405. Verbs ending in अय् *ay* (Chur, Caus. Denom. &c.) drop अय् *ay* before the passive इ *i*, though in the general tenses, after the dropping of the passive य *ya*, the original अय् *ay* may reappear, i.e. the Âtm. may be used as passive.

बोधय् *bodhay*, अबोधि *abodhi*; चोरय् *choray*, अचोरि *achori*; राजय् *râjay*, अराजि *arâji*.

In the other persons these verbs may either drop अय् *ay* or retain it, being conjugated in either case after the first form of the first aorist.

भावय् *bhâvay*; अभाविषि *abhâvishi*, अभाविष्ठाः *abhâvishṭhâḥ*, अभावि *abhâvi*; or अभावयिषि *abhâvayishi*, अभावयिष्ठाः *abhâvayishṭhâḥ*, अभावि *abhâvi*.

§ 406. Intensive bases in य् *y* add the passive इ *i*, without Guṇa.

Int. बोभूय् *bobhûy*, अबोभूयि *abobhûyi*.

Intensive bases ending in य् *y*, preceded by a consonant, drop य् *y*, and refuse Guṇa.

Int. बेभिद्य् *bebhidy*; Aor. अबेभिदि *abebhidi*.

Desiderative bases, likewise, refuse Guṇa.

Des. बुबोधिष् *bubodhish*; Aor. अबुबोधिषि *abubodhishi*.

---

* This would follow if *kartari* extends to Pâṇ. III. 1, 54, 56.

§ 407. The following are a few irregular formations of the 3rd pers. sing. aorist passive:

रभ् *rabh*, to desire, forms अरम्भि *arambhi*. (Pâṇ. vii. 1, 63.) See § 345, †.
रध् *radh*, to kill, — अरन्धि *arandhi*. (Pâṇ. vii. 1, 61.)
जभ् *jabh*, to yawn, — अजम्भि *ajambhi*. (Pâṇ. vii. 1, 61.)
भञ्ज् *bhañj*, to break, — अभञ्जि *abhañji* or अभाजि *abhâji*. (Pâṇ. vi. 4, 33.)
लभ् *labh*, to take, — अलम्भि *alambhi* or अलाभि *alâbhi*. (Pâṇ. vii. 1, 69.)
With prepositions लभ् *labh* always forms अलम्भि *alambhi*.
जन् *jan*, to beget, — अजनि *ajani*. (Pâṇ. vii. 3, 35.)
वध् *badh*, to strike, — अवधि *abadhi*. (Pâṇ. vii. 3, 35.)

§ 408. Roots ending in अम् *am*, which admit of intermediate इ *i*, do not lengthen their radical vowel. (Pâṇ. vii. 3, 34.)

शम् *śam*, अशमि *aśami*; तम् *tam*, अतमि *atami*; but यम् *yam*, अयामि *ayâmi*. Pâṇini excepts आचम् *âcham*, to rinse, which forms आचामि *âchâmi*. Others add कम् *kam*, वम् *vam*, नम् *nam* (Pâṇ. vii. 3, 34, v.).

§ 409. Thus the paradigms given in the Âtmanepada may be used in the passive of the aorist, with the exception of the 3rd pers. sing. (See p. 183.)

अलविषि *alavishi*	अलविष्वहि *alavishvahi*	अलविष्महि *alavishmahi*
अलविष्ठाः *alavishṭhâḥ*	अलविषाथाम् *alavishâthâm*	अलविढ्वम् or °ध्वम् *alavidhvam* or *-ḍhvam*
अलावि *alâvi*	अलविषाताम् *alavishâtâm*	अलविषत *alavishata*

The Two Futures, the Conditional, and the Benedictive Passive.

§ 410. These formations are identically the same in the passive as in the Âtmanepada. Hence

Fut. बोधिष्ये *bodhishye*, I shall be known.
Cond. अबोधिष्ये *abodhishye*, I should be known.
Periphr. Fut. बोधिताहे *bodhitâhe*, I shall be known.
Bened. बोधिषीय *bodhishîya*, May I be known!

Secondary Form of the Aorist, the Two Futures, the Conditional, and Benedictive of Verbs ending in Vowels.

§ 411. All verbs ending in vowels, in अय् *ay*, and likewise हन् *han*, to strike, दृश् *dṛiś*, to see, ग्रह् *grah*, to take, may form a secondary base (really denominative), being identical with the peculiar third person singular of the aorist passive, described before. Thus from लू *lû* we have अलावि *alâvi*, and from this, by treating the final इ *i* as the intermediate इ *i*, we form,

Sing. 1. pers. अलाविषि *alâvi-shi*, by the side of अलविषि *alăvi-shi*.
2. अलाविष्ठाः *alâvi-shṭhâḥ*, — — अलविष्ठाः *alăvi-shṭhâḥ*.
3. अलावि *alâvi*, — — अलावि *alâvi*.

Dual 1. pers. अलाविष्वहि *alâvi-shvahi*, by the side of अलविष्वहि *alăvi-shvahi*.
2. अलाविषाथाम् *alâvi-shâthâm*, — — अलविषाथाम् *alăvi-shâthâm*.
3. अलाविषाताम् *alâvi-shâtâm*, — — अलविषाताम् *alăvi-shâtâm*.
Plur. 1. pers. अलाविष्महि *alâvi-shmahi*, by the side of अलविष्महि *alăvi-shmahi*.
2. अलाविढ्वं *alâvi-dhvam* or °ढ्वं *-ḍhvam* — अलविढ्वं *alăvi-dhvam* or °ढ्वं.
3. अलाविषत *alâvi-shata*, — — अलविषत *alăvi-shata*.
Fut. लाविष्ये *lâvi-shye*, by the side of लविष्ये *lăvi-shye*.
Cond. अलाविष्ये *alâvi-shye*, — — अलविष्ये *alăvi-shye*.
Per. Fut. लाविताहे *lâvi-tâhe*, — — लविताहे *lăvi-tâhe*.
Ben. लाविषीय *lâvi-shîya*, — — लविषीय *lăvi-shîya*.

From चि *chi*, to gather, 3rd pers. sing. Aor. Pass. अचायि *achâyi*; hence
Aor. अचायिषि *achâyishi*, besides अचेषि *acheshi*, &c.
Fut. चायिष्ये *châyishye*, — चेष्ये *cheshye*.
Cond. अचायिष्ये *achâyishye*, — अचेष्ये *acheshye*.
Per. Fut. चायिताहे *châyitâhe*, — चेताहे *chetâhe*.
Ben. चायिषीय *châyishîya*, — चेषीय *cheshîya*.

From घ्रा *ghrâ*, to smell, 3rd pers. sing. Aor. Pass. अघ्रायि *aghrâyi*; hence
Aor. अघ्रायिषि *aghrâyishi*, besides अघ्रासि *aghrâsi*.
Fut. घ्रायिष्ये *ghrâyishye*, — घ्रास्ये *ghrâsye*.
Cond. अघ्रायिष्ये *aghrâyishye*, — अघ्रास्ये *aghrâsye*.
Per. Fut. घ्रायिताहे *ghrâyitâhe*, — घ्राताहे *ghrâtâhe*.
Ben. घ्रायिषीय *ghrâyishîya*, — घ्रासीय *ghrâsîya*.

From ध्वृ *dhvṛi*, to hurt, 3rd pers. sing. Aor. Pass. अध्वारि *adhvâri*; hence
Aor. अध्वारिषि *adhvârishi*, besides अध्वृषि *adhvṛishi* or अध्वरिषि *adhvărishi*.
Fut. ध्वारिष्ये *dhvârishye*, — ध्वरिष्ये *dhvărishye*.
Per. Fut. ध्वारिताहे *dhvâritâhe*, — ध्वर्ताहे *dhvărtâhe*.
Ben. ध्वारिषीय *dhvârishîya*, — ध्वृषीय *dhvṛishîya* or ध्वरिषीय *dhvărishîya**.

From हन् *han*, to kill, 3rd pers. sing. Aor. Pass. अघानि *aghâni*; hence
Aor. अघानिषि *aghânishi*, besides (अवधिषि *avadhishi*). Pâṇ. VI. 4, 62†.
Fut. घानिष्ये *ghânishye*, — हनिष्ये *hanishye*.
Per. Fut. घानिताहे *ghânitâhe*, — हंताहे *hantâhe*.
Ben. घानिषीय *ghânishîya*, — (वधिषीय *vadhishîya*).

From दृश् *dṛiś*, to see, 3rd pers. sing. Aor. Pass. अदर्शि *adarśi*; hence
Aor. अदर्शिषि *adarśishi*, besides अदृक्षि *adṛikshi*.
Fut. दर्शिष्ये *darśishye*, — द्रक्ष्ये *drakshye*.
Per. Fut. दर्शिताहे *darśitâhe*, — द्रष्टाहे *drashṭâhe*.
Ben. दर्शिषीय *darśishîya*, — दृक्षीय *dṛikshîya*.

* See § 332, 5.
† Siddh.-Kaum. vol. II, p. 270, seems to allow अहनि *ahani*.

From ग्रह् *grah*, to take, 3rd pers. sing. Aor. Pass. अग्राहि *agrâhi*; hence

Aor.	अग्राहिषि *agrâhishi*,	besides	अग्रहीषि *agrahîshi*.
Fut.	ग्राहिष्ये *grâhishye*,	—	ग्रहीष्ये *grahîshye*.
Per. Fut.	ग्राहिताहे *grâhitâhe*,	—	ग्रहीताहे *grahîtâhe*.
Ben.	ग्राहिषीय *grâhishîya*,	—	ग्रहीषीय *grahîshîya*.

From रमय् *ramay*, to delight, Caus. of रम् *ram*, 3rd pers. sing. Aor. Pass. अरमि *arami* or अरामि *arâmi*; hence

Aor. अरमिषि *aramishi* or अरामिषि *arâmishi*, besides अरमयिषि *aramayishi*.

§ 412. Certain verbs of an intransitive meaning take the passive इ *i* in the 3rd pers. sing. Aor. Thus उत्पद्यते *utpadyate* (3rd pers. sing. present of the Âtmanepada of a Div verb), he arises, becomes उदपादि *udapâdi*, he arose, he sprang up; but it is regular in the other persons, उदपत्सातां *udapatsâtâm*, they two arose, &c. (Pâṇ. III. 1, 60.)

§ 413. Other verbs of an intransitive character take the same form optionally (Pâṇ. III. 1, 61):

दीप् *dîp* (दीप्यते *dîpyate*, he burns, Div, Âtm.), अदीपि *adîpi* or अदीपिष्ट *adîpishṭa*.

जन् *jan* (जायते *jâyate*, he is born, he is, Div, Âtm.; it cannot be formed from जन् *jan* (Hu, Par.), to beget), अजनि *ajani* or अजनिष्ट *ajanishṭa*.

बुध् *budh* (बुध्यते *budhyate*, he is conscious, Div, Âtm.), अबोधि *abodhi* or अबुद्ध *abuddha*.

पूर् *pûr* (पूरयति *pûrayati*, he fills, Chur.), अपूरि *apûri* or अपूरिष्ट *apûrishṭa*.

ताय् *tây* (तायते *tâyate*, he spreads, Bhû, Âtm.; really Div form of Tan), अतायि *atâyi* or अतायिष्ट *atâyishṭa*.

प्याय् *pyây* (प्यायते *pyâyate*, he grows), अप्यायि *apyâyi* or अप्यायिष्ट *apyâyishṭa*.

CHAPTER XVI.

PARTICIPLES, GERUNDS, AND INFINITIVE.

§ 414. The participle of the present Parasmaipada retains the Vikaraṇas of the ten classes. It is most easily formed by taking the 3rd pers. plur. of the present, and dropping the final इ *i*. This gives us the Aṅga base, from which the Pada and Bha base can be easily deduced according to general rules (§ 182). Thus

भवंति	भवंत्	Nom. S. भवन्	Acc. भवंतं	Instr. भवता &c.
bhavanti	*bhavant*	*bhavan*	*bhavantam*	*bhavatâ*
तुदंति	तुदंत्	तुदन्	तुदंतं	तुदता &c.
tudanti	*tudant*	*tudan*	*tudantam*	*tudatâ*
दीव्यंति	दीव्यंत्	दीव्यन्	दीव्यंतं	दीव्यता &c.
dîvyanti	*dîvyant*	*dîvyan*	*dîvyantam*	*dîvyatâ*

		Nom. S.	Acc.	Instr.
चोरयन्ति *chorayanti*	चोरयन्त् *charayant*	चोरयन् *chorayan*	चोरयन्तं *chorayantam*	चोरयता &c. *chorayatá*
सुन्वन्ति *sunvanti*	सुन्वन्त् *sunvant*	सुन्वन् *sunvan*	सुन्वन्तं *sunvantam*	सुन्वता &c. *sunvatá*
तन्वन्ति *tanvanti*	तन्वन्त् *tanvant*	तन्वन् *tanvan*	तन्वन्तं *tanvantam*	तन्वता &c. *tanvatá*
क्रीणन्ति *kríṇanti*	क्रीणन्त् *kríṇant*	क्रीणन् *kríṇan*	क्रीणन्तं *kríṇantam*	क्रीणता &c. *kríṇatá*
अदन्ति *adanti*	अदन्त् *adant*	अदन् *adan*	अदन्तं *adantam*	अदता &c. *adatá*
जुह्वति *juhvati*	जुह्वत् *juhvat*	जुह्वत् *juhcat*	जुह्वतं *juhvatam*	जुह्वता (§ 184) *juhvatá*
रुन्धन्ति *rundhanti*	रुन्धन्त् *rundhant*	रुन्धन् *rundhan*	रुन्धन्तं *rundhantam*	रुन्धता &c. *rundhatá*
बोभुवति Intens. *babhuvati*	बोभुवत् *bobhuvat*	बोभुवत् *bobhuvat*	बोभुवतं *babhuvatam*	बोभुवता (§ 184) *bobhuvatá*

§ 415. The participle of the future is formed on the same principle.

		Nom. S.	Acc.	Instr.
भविष्यन्ति *bhavishyanti*	भविष्यन्त् *bhavishyant*	भविष्यन् *bhavishyan*	भविष्यन्तं *bhavishyantam*	भविष्यता *bhavishyatá*

§ 416. The participle of the reduplicated perfect may best be formed by taking the 3rd pers. plur. of that tense. This corresponds with the Bha base of the participle, only that the स् *s*, as it is always followed by a vowel, is changed to ष् *sh*. Having the Bha base, it is easy to form the Aṅga and Pada bases, according to § 204. In forming the Aṅga and Pada bases, it must be remembered,

1. That roots ending in a vowel, restore that vowel, which, before उः *uḥ*, had been naturally changed into a semivowel.
2. That, according to the rules on intermediate इ *i*, all verbs which, without counting the उः *uḥ*, are monosyllabic in the 3rd pers. plur., insert इ *i*. (See Necessary इ *i*, § 338, 1; Optional इ *i*, § 337, 8.)

3rd P. Plur.	Instr. Sing.	Nom. Sing.	Acc. Sing.	Instr. Plur.
बभूवुः *babhúvuḥ*	बभूवुषा *babhúvushá*	बभूवान् *babhúván*	बभूवांसं *babhúvámsam*	बभूवद्भिः *babhúvadbhiḥ*
निन्युः *ninyuḥ*	निन्युषा *ninyushá*	निनीवान् *niníván*	निनीवांसं *ninívámsam*	निनीवद्भिः *ninívadbhiḥ*
तुतुदुः *tutuduḥ*	तुतुदुषा *tutudushá*	तुतुद्वान् *tutudván*	तुतुद्वांसं *tutudvámsam*	तुतुद्वद्भिः *tutudvadbhiḥ*
दिदिवुः *didivuḥ*	दिदिवुषा *didivushá*	दिदिवान् (§ 143) *didiván*	दिदिवांसं *didivámsam*	दिदिवद्भिः *didivadbhiḥ*
चोरयामासुः *chorayámásuḥ*	चोरयामासुषा *chorayámásushá*	चोरयामासिवान् *chorayámásiván*	चोरयामासिवांसं *chorayámásivámsam*	चोरयामासिवद्भिः *chorayámásivadbhiḥ*

3rd P. Plur.	Instr. Sing.	Nom. Sing.	Acc. Sing.	Instr. Plur.
शुशुवुः *sushuvuḥ*	शुशुवुषा *sushuvushá*	शुशुवान् *sushuván*	शुशुवांसं *sushuváṁsam*	शुशुवद्भिः *sushuvadbhiḥ*
तेनुः *tenuḥ*	तेनुषा *tenushá*	तेनिवान् *teniván*	तेनिवांसं *teniváṁsam*	तेनिवद्भिः *tenivadbhiḥ*
चिक्रियुः *chikriyuḥ*	चिक्रियुषा *chikriyushá*	चिक्रीवान् *chikríván*	चिक्रीवांसं *chikríváṁsam*	चिक्रीवद्भिः *chikrívadbhiḥ*
आदुः *áduḥ*	आदुषा *ádushá*	आदिवान् *ádiván*	आदिवांसं *ádiváṁsam*	आदिवद्भिः *ádivadbhiḥ*
जुहुवुः *juhuvuḥ*	जुहुवुषा *juhuvushá*	जुहुवान् *juhuván*	जुहुवांसं *juhuváṁsam*	जुहुवद्भिः *juhuvadbhiḥ*
रुरुधुः *rurudhuḥ*	रुरुधुषा *rurudhushá*	रुरुध्वान् *rurudhván*	रुरुध्वांसं *rurudhváṁsam*	रुरुध्वद्भिः *rurudhvadbhiḥ*

§ 417. In five verbs, where the insertion of इ *i* before वस् *vas* is optional (§ 337, 8), we get the following forms:

	3rd P. Plur.	Instr. Sing.	Nom. Sing.	Acc. Sing.	Instr. Plur.
गम् *gam*	जग्मुः *jagmuḥ*	जग्मुषा *jagmushá*	जग्मिवान् or जगन्वान्* *jagmiván* or *jaganván*	जग्मिवांसं *jagmiváṁsam*	जग्मिवद्भिः *jagmivadbhiḥ*
हन् *han*	जघ्नुः *jaghnuḥ*	जघ्नुषा *jaghnushá*	जघ्निवान् or जघन्वान् *jaghniván* or *jaghanván*	जघ्निवांसं *jaghniváṁsam*	जघ्निवद्भिः *jaghnivadbhiḥ*
विद् *vid*	विविदुः *vividuḥ*	विविदुषा *vividushá*	विविद्वान् or विविदिवान् *vividván* or *vividiván*	विविद्वांसं *vividváṁsam*	विविद्वद्भिः *vividvadbhiḥ*
विश् *viś*	विविशुः *viviśuḥ*	विविशुषा *viviśushá*	विविश्वान् or विविशिवान् *viviśván* or *viviśiván*	विविश्वांसं *viviśváṁsam*	विविश्वद्भिः *viviśvadbhiḥ*
दृश् *dṛiś*	ददृशुः *dadṛiśuḥ*	ददृशुषा *dadṛiśushá*	ददृश्वान् or ददृशिवान् *dadṛiśván* or *dadṛiśiván*	ददृश्वांसं *dadṛiśváṁsam*	ददृश्वद्भिः *dadṛiśvadbhiḥ*

§ 418. The participle of the reduplicated perfect Âtmanepada is formed by dropping इरे *ire*, the termination of the 3rd pers. plur. Âtm., and substituting आन *âna*.

बभूविरे *babhûvire*—बभूवानः *babhûvânaḥ*
चक्रिरे *chakrire*—चक्राणः *chakrâṇaḥ*
ददिरे *dadire*—ददानः *dadânaḥ*

§ 419. The participle present Âtmanepada has two terminations,—मान *mâna* for verbs of the First Division (§ 295), आन *âna* for verbs of the Second Division.

In the First Division we may again take the 3rd pers. plur. present Âtm., drop the termination न्ते *nte*, and replace it by मानः *mânaḥ*.

In the Second Division we may likewise take the 3rd pers. plur. present Âtm., drop the termination अते *ate*, and replace it by आनः *ânaḥ*.

* The same optional forms run through all the Pada and Bha cases.

First Division.	Second Division.
भवन्ते *bhava-nte*—भवमानः *bhava-mânaḥ*	सुन्वते *sunv-ate*—सुन्वानः *sunv-ânaḥ*
तुदन्ते *tuda-nte*—तुदमानः *tuda-mânaḥ*	तन्वते *tanv-ate*—तन्वानः *tanv-ânaḥ*
दीव्यन्ते *dîvya-nte*—दीव्यमानः *dîvya-mânaḥ*	क्रीणते *krîṇ-ate*—क्रीणानः *krîṇ-ânaḥ*
चोरयन्ते *choraya-nte*—चोरयमाणः *choraya-mâṇaḥ*	अदते *ad-ate*—अदानः *ad-ânaḥ*
Caus. भावयन्ते *bhâvaya-nte*—भावयमानः *bhâvaya-mânaḥ*	जुह्वते *juhv-ate*—जुह्वानः *juhv-ânaḥ*
Des. बुभूषन्ते *bubhûsha-nte*—बुभूषमाणः *bubhûsha-mâṇaḥ*	रुन्धते *rundh-ate*—रुन्धानः *rundh-ânaḥ*
Int. बोभूयन्ते *bobhûya-nte*—बोभूयमानः *bobhûya-mânaḥ*	

§ 420. The participle of the future Âtmanepada is formed by adding मानः *mânaḥ* in the same manner.

भविष्यन्ते *bhavishya-nte*—भविष्यमाणः *bhavishya-mâṇaḥ*
नेष्यन्ते *neshya-nte*—नेष्यमाणः *neshya-mâṇaḥ*
तोत्स्यन्ते *totsya-nte*—तोत्स्यमानः *totsya-mânaḥ*
एधिष्यन्ते *edhishya-nte*—एधिष्यमाणः *edhishya-mâṇaḥ*

§ 421. The participles of the present and future passive are formed by adding मानः *mânaḥ* in the same manner.

भूयन्ते *bhûya-nte*—भूयमानः *bhûya-mânaḥ*	भाविष्यन्ते—भाविष्यमाणः:
बुध्यन्ते *budhya-nte*—बुध्यमानः *budhya-mânaḥ*	*bhâvishya-nte*—*bhâvishya-mâṇaḥ*
स्तूयन्ते *stûya-nte*—स्तूयमानः *stûya-mânaḥ*	नायिष्यन्ते—नायिष्यमाणः:
क्रियन्ते *kriya-nte*—क्रियमाणः *kriya-mâṇaḥ*	*nâyishya-nte*—*nâyishya-mâṇaḥ*
भाव्यन्ते *bhâvya-nte*—भाव्यमानः *bhâvya-mânaḥ*	Or like the Part. Fut. Âtm.

The Past Participle Passive in तः taḥ *and the Gerund in* त्वा tvâ.

§ 422. The past participle passive is formed by adding तः *taḥ* or नः *naḥ* to the root. कृ *kṛi*, कृतः *kṛitaḥ*, done, masc.; कृता *kṛitâ*, fem.; कृतं *kṛitam*, neut. लू *lû*, लूनः *lûnaḥ*, cut.

This termination त *ta* is, as we saw, most opposed to the insertion of intermediate इ *i*, so much so that verbs which may form any one general tense with or without इ *i*, always form their past participle without it. The number of verbs which must insert इ *i* before त *ta* is very small. (§ 332, D.)

Besides being averse to the insertion of intermediate इ *i*, the participial termination त *ta* is one of those which have a tendency to weaken verbal bases. (See § 344.)

§ 423. The gerund of simple verbs is formed by adding त्वा *tvâ* to the root. कृ *kṛi*, कृत्वा *kṛitvâ*, having done. पू *pû*, पूत्वा *pûtvâ* or पवित्वा *pavitvâ*, having purified.

The rules as to the insertion of the intermediate इ *i* before त्वा *tvâ* have been given before. With regard to the strengthening or weakening of the base, the general rule is that त्वा *tvâ* without intermediate इ *i* weakens, with intermediate इ *i* strengthens the root. In giving a few more special rules on this point, it will be convenient to take the terminations त *ta* and त्वा *tvâ* together, as they agree to a great extent, though not altogether.

I. तः taḥ *and* त्वा tvâ, *with intermediate* इ i.

§ 424. If तः *taḥ* takes intermediate इ *i*, it may in certain verbs produce Guṇa. In this case the Guṇa before त्वा *tvâ* is regular.

शी *śî*, to lie down, शयितः *śayitaḥ* (Pâṇ. 1. 2, 19); शयित्वा *śayitvâ*.
स्विद् *svid*, to sweat, स्वेदितः *sveditaḥ* or स्विन्नः *svinnaḥ*; स्वेदित्वा *sveditvâ*.
मिद् *mid*, to be soft, मेदितः *meditaḥ*; मेदित्वा *meditvâ*.
क्ष्विद् *kshvid*, to drip, क्ष्वेदितः *kshveditaḥ*; क्ष्वेदित्वा *kshveditvâ*.
धृष् *dhṛish*, to dare, धर्षितः *dharshitaḥ*; धर्षित्वा *dharshitvâ*.
मृष् *mṛish*, to bear, मर्षितः *marshitaḥ* (patient), (Pâṇ. 1. 2, 20); मर्षित्वा *marshitvâ*.
पू *pû*, to purify, पवितः *pavitaḥ* (Pâṇ. 1. 2, 22); पवित्वा *pavitvâ*.

§ 425. Verbs with penultimate उ *u* may or may not take Guṇa before त *ta* with intermediate इ *i*, if they are used impersonally.

द्युत् *dyut*, to shine, द्युतितं *dyutitam* or द्योतितं *dyotitam*, it has been shining. (Pâṇ. 1. 2, 21.)

§ 426. If त्वा *tvâ* takes intermediate इ *i*, it requires, as a general rule, Guṇa (Pâṇ. 1. 2, 18), or at all events does not produce any weakening of the base. वृत् *vṛit*, to exist, वर्तित्वा *vartitvâ*. स्रंस् *sraṁs*, to fall, स्रंसित्वा *sraṁsitvâ* (Pâṇ. 1. 2, 23). पू *pû*, to purify, पवित्वा *pavitvâ* (Pâṇ. 1. 2, 22).

Verbs, however, beginning with consonants, and ending in any single consonant except य् *y* or व् *v*, preceded by इ, ई *î* or उ, ऊ *û*, take Guṇa optionally (Pâṇ. 1. 2, 26): द्युत् *dyut*, to shine, द्योतित्वा *dyotitvâ* or द्युतित्वा *dyutitvâ*. The same option applies to तृष् *tṛish*, to thirst; मृष् *mṛish*, to bear; कृश् *kṛiś*, to attenuate (Pâṇ. 1. 2, 25); तृषित्वा *tṛishitvâ* or तर्षित्वा *tarshitvâ*.

§ 427. Though taking intermediate इ *i*, त्वा *tvâ* does not produce Guṇa, but, if possible, weakens the base, in रुद् *rud*, to cry, रुदित्वा *ruditvâ* (Pâṇ. 1. 2, 8); विद् *vid*, to know, विदित्वा *viditvâ*; मुष् *mush*, to steal, मुषित्वा *mushitvâ*; ग्रह् *grah*, to take, गृहीत्वा *gṛihîtvâ*; मृड् *mṛiḍ*, to delight, मृडित्वा *mṛiḍitvâ* (Pâṇ. 1. 2, 7); मृद् *mṛid*, to rub, मृदित्वा *mṛiditvâ*; गुध् *gudh*, to draw, गुधित्वा *gudhitvâ*; क्लिश् *kliś*, to hurt, क्लिशित्वा *kliśitvâ*; वद् *vad*, to speak, उदित्वा *uditvâ*; वस् *vas*, to dwell, उषित्वा *ushitvâ*.

§ 428. Roots ending in थ् *th* or फ् *ph*, preceded by a nasal, may or may not drop the nasal before त्वा *tvâ* (Pâṇ. 1. 2, 23); ग्रन्थित्वा *granthitvâ* or ग्रथित्वा *grathitvâ*, having twisted. The same applies to the roots वञ्च् *vañch*, to cheat, and लुञ्च् *luñch*, to pluck (Pâṇ. 1. 2, 24); वञ्चित्वा *vañchitvâ* or वचित्वा *vachitvâ*.

II. तः taḥ *and* त्वा tvâ, *without intermediate* इ i.

§ 429. Roots ending in nasals lengthen their vowel before तः *taḥ* and त्वा *tvâ* (Pâṇ. VI. 4, 15). शम् *śam*, to rest, शान्तः *śântaḥ*, शान्त्वा *śântvâ*.

क्रम् *kram*, to step, may or may not lengthen its vowel before त्वा *tvâ* (Pâṇ. VI. 4, 18). क्रम् *kram*, क्रान्तः *krântaḥ*, क्रान्त्वा *krântvâ* or क्रन्त्वा *krantvâ*; also क्रमित्वा *kramitvâ*.

§ 430. The following roots, ending in nasals, drop them before तः *taḥ* and त्वा *tvâ*. (Pâṇ. VI. 4, 37.)

यम् *yam*, to check, यतः *yataḥ*, यत्वा *yatvâ**; रम् *ram*, to sport, रतः *rataḥ*, रत्वा *ratvâ*; नम् *nam*, to bend, नतः *nataḥ*, नत्वा *natvâ*; हन् *han*, to kill, हतः *hataḥ*, हत्वा *hatvâ*; गम् *gam*, to go, गतः *gataḥ*, गत्वा *gatvâ*; मन् *man*, to think, मतः *mataḥ*, मत्वा *matvâ*; वन् *van*, to ask; तन् *tan*, to stretch, ततः *tataḥ*, तत्वा *tatvâ*; and the other verbs of the Tan class, ending in न् *n*.

Note—Of the same verbs those ending in न् *n* drop the nasal before the gerundial य *ya* and insert त् *t*; प्रमत्य *pramatya* (Pâṇ. VI. 4, 38): those ending in म् *m* may or may not drop the nasal before the gerundial य *ya*; प्रगत्य *pragatya* or प्रगम्य *pragamya*.

§ 431. The following verbs drop final न् *n*, and lengthen the vowel.

जन् *jan*, to bear, जातः *jâtaḥ*, जात्वा *jâtvâ*; सन् *san*, to obtain, सातः *sâtaḥ*, सात्वा *sâtvâ*; खन् *khan*, to dig, खातः *khâtaḥ*, खात्वा *khâtvâ*.

1. Roots ending in छ् *chh*, or व् *v*, substitute श् *ś* and ऊ *û*. (Pâṇ. VI. 4, 19.)

प्रछ् *prachh*, to ask, पृष्टः *prishṭaḥ* (§ 125), पृष्ट्वा *prishṭvâ*; दिव् *div*, to play, द्यूनः *dyûnaḥ*, द्यूत्वा *dyûtvâ*.

2. Roots ending in र्छ् *rchh*, or र्व् *rv*, drop both their final consonants. (Pâṇ. VI. 4, 21.)

मुर्छ् *murchh*, to faint, मूर्तः *mûrtaḥ*; तुर्व् *turv*, to strike, तूर्णः *tûrṇaḥ*.

§ 432. The following verbs change their व् *v* with the preceding or following vowel into ऊ *û*. (Pâṇ. VI. 4, 20.)

ज्वर् *jvar*, to ail, जूर्णः *jûrṇaḥ*, जूर्त्वा *jûrtvâ*; त्वर् *tvar*, to hasten, तूर्णः *tûrṇaḥ*, तूर्त्वा *tûrtvâ*; स्रिव् *sriv*, to dry, स्रूतः *srûtaḥ*, स्रूत्वा *srûtvâ*; अव् *av*, to protect, ऊतः *ûtaḥ*, ऊत्वा *ûtvâ*; मव् *mav*, to bind, मूतः *mûtaḥ*, मूत्वा *mûtvâ*.

§ 433. Roots ending in ऐ *ai* substitute आ *â*; ध्यै *dhyai*, to meditate, ध्यातः *dhyâtaḥ*, ध्यात्वा *dhyâtvâ*: or ई *î*; गै *gai*, to sing, गीतः *gîtaḥ*, गीत्वा *gîtvâ*. Final ए *e* and आ *â*, too, are changed to ई *î*; पा *pâ*, to drink, पीतः *pîtaḥ*, पीत्वा *pîtvâ*; धे *dhe*, to suck, धीतः *dhîtaḥ*, धीत्वा *dhîtvâ*.

§ 434. The following roots change their final vowel into इ *i*.

दो *do*, to cut, दितः *ditaḥ*, दित्वा *ditvâ* (Pâṇ. VII. 4, 40); सो *so*, to finish, सितः *sitaḥ*, सित्वा *sitvâ*; मा *mâ*, to measure, मितः *mitaḥ*, मित्वा *mitvâ*; स्था *sthâ*, to stand, स्थितः *sthitaḥ*, स्थित्वा *sthitvâ*; धा *dhâ*, to place, हितः *hitaḥ*, हित्वा *hitvâ* (Pâṇ. VII. 4, 42); हा *hâ*, to leave (हीनः *hînaḥ*), हित्वा *hitvâ* (Pâṇ. VII. 4, 43).

* See verbs without intermediate इ *i*. (§ 332, 13, and 16.)

§ 435. शो *śo*, to sharpen, and छो *chho*, to cut, substitute इ *i*, or take the regular आ *á*.

शो *śo*, शितः *śitaḥ* or शातः *śátaḥ*, शित्वा *śitvá* or शात्वा *śátvá* (Pâṇ. VII. 4, 41).

§ 436. Exceptional forms:

दा *dá*, to give, forms दत्तः *dattaḥ**, दत्त्वा *dattvá* (Pâṇ. VII. 4, 46).

स्फाय् *sphây*, to grow, forms स्फीतः *sphítaḥ* (Pâṇ. VI. 1, 22).

स्त्यै *styai*, to call (with प्र *pra*), forms प्रस्तीतः *prastítaḥ* (Pâṇ. VI. 1, 23) and प्रस्तीमः *prastímaḥ* (Pâṇ. VIII. 2, 54).

श्यै *śyai*, to curdle, forms शीनः *śínaḥ*, and शीतः *śítaḥ*, cold; but संश्यानः *saṁśyánaḥ*, rolled up (Pâṇ. VI. 1, 24, 25).

प्याय् *pyáy*, to grow, forms पीनः *pínaḥ*; but प्यानः *pyánaḥ* after certain prepositions (Pâṇ. VI. 1, 28).

§ 437. The verbs which take *Samprasáraṇa* before तः *taḥ* and त्वा *tvá* have been mentioned in § 393, as undergoing the same change in the benedictive and passive. वच् *vach*, to speak, उक्तः *uktaḥ*, उक्त्वा *uktvá*, &c.

§ 438. Roots which can lose their nasal (§ 345†) lose it before तः *taḥ* and त्वा *tvá*. स्रंस् *sraṁs*, to tear, स्रस्तः *srastaḥ*, स्रस्त्वा *srastvá*.

But स्कन्द् *skand*, to stride, forms its gerund स्कन्त्वा *skantvá*, and स्यन्द् *syand*, to flow, स्यन्त्वा *syantvá* (Pâṇ. VI. 4, 31), although their न् *n* is otherwise liable to be lost. Part. स्कन्नः *skannaḥ*, स्यन्नः *syannaḥ*.

नश् *naś*, to perish, and roots ending in ज् *j*, otherwise liable to nasalization, retain the nasal optionally before त्वा *tvá* (Pâṇ. VI. 4, 32). नंष्ट्वा *naṁshṭvá* or नष्ट्वा *nashṭvá* (but only नष्टः *nashṭaḥ*); रंक्त्वा *raṅktvá* or रक्त्वा *raktvá* (but only रक्तः *raktaḥ*); मस्ज् *majj*, to dive, मंक्त्वा *maṅktvá* or मक्त्वा *maktvá* (Pâṇ. VII. 1, 60).

§ 439. Causal verbs form the participle after rejecting अय *aya*; कारयति *kárayati*, कारितः *káritaḥ*, but कारयित्वा *kárayitvá*.

§ 440. Desiderative verbs form the participle and gerund regularly; चिकीर्षति *chikírshati*, चिकीर्षितः *chikírshitaḥ*, चिकीर्षित्वा *chikírshitvá*.

§ 441. Intensive verbs Âtm. of roots ending in vowels form the participle and gerund regularly; चेक्रीयते *chekríyate*, चेक्रीयितः *chekríyitaḥ*, चेक्रीयित्वा *chekríyitvá*. After roots ending in consonants the intensive य् *y* is dropt; बेभिद्यते *bebhidyate*, बेभिदितः *bebhiditaḥ*, बेभिदित्वा *bebhiditvá*.

Intensive verbs Par. form the participle and gerund regularly; चर्कर्ति *charkarti*, चर्कृतः *charkritaḥ*, चर्कृत्वा *charkritvá*.

नः naḥ *instead of* तः taḥ *in the Past Participle.*

§ 442. Certain verbs take नः *naḥ* instead of तः *taḥ* in the past participle passive, provided they do not take the intermediate इ *i*.

* After prepositions ending in vowels, द *da* may be dropt, and the final इ *i* and उ *u* of a preposition lengthened. प्रदत्तः *pradattaḥ*, प्रत्तः *prattaḥ*; सुदत्तः *sudattaḥ*, सूत्तः *súttaḥ*.

1. Twenty-one verbs of the Krî class, beginning with लू *lû*, to cut, लूनः *lûnaḥ* (Dhâtupâṭha 31, 13; Pâṇ. VIII. 2, 44). The most important are, धूनः *dhûnaḥ*, shaken; जीनः *jînaḥ*, decayed. Some of them come under the next rule.

2. Twelve verbs of the Div class, beginning with षू *sû* (Dhâtupâṭha 26, 23–35; Pâṇ. VIII. 2, 45). The most important are, दूनः *dûnaḥ*, pained; दीनः *dînaḥ*, wasted; प्रीणः *prîṇaḥ*, loved.

3. Verbs ending in ॠ *ṛî*, which is changed into ईर् *îr* or ऊर् *ûr*. स्तॄ *stṛî*, स्तीर्णः *stîrṇaḥ*, spread; शीर्णः *śîrṇaḥ*, injured; पूर्णः *pûrṇaḥ*, filled (also पूर्तः *pûrtaḥ*, Pâṇ. VIII. 2, 57); दीर्णः *dîrṇaḥ*, torn; जीर्णः *jîrṇaḥ*, decayed.

4. Verbs ending in द् *d*; भिद् *bhid*, भिन्नः *bhinnaḥ*, broken; छिद् *chhid*, छिन्नः *chhinnaḥ*, cut. But मद् *mad*, मत्तः *mattaḥ*, intoxicated. In नुद् *nud*, to push, विद् *vid*, to find, and उन्द् *und*, to wet, the substitution is optional (Pâṇ. VIII. 2, 56); नुन्नः *nunnaḥ* or नुत्तः *nuttaḥ*.

5. Verbs which native grammarians have marked in the Dhâtupâṭha with an indicatory ओ *o*; भुज् *bhuj* (भुजो *bhujo*, Dhâtupâṭha 28, 124), to bend, भुग्नः *bhugnaḥ*.

6. Verbs beginning with a double consonant, one of them being a semivowel, and ending in आ *â*, or ए *e*, ऐ *ai*, ओ *o*, changeable to आ *â*; ग्लै *glai*, ग्लानः *glânaḥ*, faded. Except ध्यै *dhyai*, to meditate, ध्यातः *dhîtaḥ*; ख्या *khyâ*, to proclaim, ख्यातः *khyâtaḥ*. In त्रै *trai*, to protect, घ्रा *ghrâ*, to smell, the substitution is optional; त्राणः *trâṇaḥ* or त्रातः *trâtaḥ* (Pâṇ. VIII. 2, 56).

7. Miscellaneous participles in नः *naḥ*: क्षीणः *kshîṇaḥ*, from क्षि *kshi*, to waste, द्यूनः *dyûnaḥ*, from दिव् *div*, to play, (not to gamble, where it is द्यूतः *dyûtaḥ*); लग्नः *lagnaḥ*, from लग् *lag*, to be in contact with (Pâṇ. VII. 2, 18); also from लज् *laj*, to be ashamed; शीनः *śînaḥ* and श्यानः *śyânaḥ*, coagulated, but शीतः *śîtaḥ*, cold.

§ 443. Native grammarians enumerate certain words as participles which, though by their meaning they may take the place of participles, are by their formation to be classed as adjectives or substantives rather than as participles. Thus पक्वः *pakvaḥ*, ripe; शुष्कः *śushkaḥ*, dry; क्षामः *kshâmaḥ*, weak; कृशः *kṛiśaḥ*, thin; प्रस्तीमः *prastîmaḥ*, crowded; फुल्लः *phullaḥ*, expanded; क्षीवः *kshîvaḥ*, drunk, &c.

§ 444. By adding the possessive suffix वत् *vat* (§ 187) to the participles in त *ta* and न *na*, a new participle of very common occurrence is formed, being in fact a participle perfect active. Thus कृतः *kṛitaḥ*, done, becomes कृतवान् *kṛitavân*, one who has done, but generally used as a definite verb. स कटं कृतवान् *sa kaṭam kṛitavân*, he has made the mat; or in the feminine सा

सा कृतवती *sâ kṛitavatî*, and in the neuter तत् कृतवत् *tat kṛitavat*. They are regularly declined throughout like adjectives in वत् *vat*.

Gerund in य ya.

§ 445. Compound verbs, but not verbs preceded by the negative particle अ *a*, take य *ya* instead of त्वा *tvâ*. Thus, instead of भूत्वा *bhûtvâ*, we find संभूय *sambhûya*; but अजित्वा *ajitvâ*, not having conquered.

§ 446. Verbs ending in a short vowel take त्य *tya* instead of य *ya*. जि *ji*, to conquer, जित्वा *jitvâ*, having conquered; but विजित्य *vijitya*. भृ *bhṛi*, to carry, भृत्वा *bhṛitvâ*; but संभृत्य *sambhṛitya*, having collected. Except क्षि *kshi*, which forms प्रक्षीय *prakshîya*, having destroyed (Pâṇ. VI. 4, 59).

§ 447. Causative bases with short penultimate vowel, keep the causative suffix अय् *ay* before य *ya* (Pâṇ. VI. 4, 56): गमयति *gamayati*, गमय्य *gamayya*, having caused to go. Otherwise the causative suffix is, as usual, dropt: तारयति *târayati*, प्रतार्य *pratârya*, having caused to advance. प्रापयति *prâpayati* forms प्राप्य *prâpya* and प्रापय्य *prâpayya*, having caused to reach (Pâṇ. VI. 4, 57).

§ 448. The verbs called घु *ghu* (§ 392*), मा *mâ*, to measure, स्था *sthâ*, to stand, गा *gâ*, to sing or to go, पा *pâ*, to drink or to protect, हा *hâ*, to leave, सो *so*, to finish, take आ *â*, not ई *î* (Pâṇ. VI. 4, 69). दो *do*, to cut, अवदाय *avadâya*; स्था *sthâ*, प्रस्थाय *prasthâya*. But पा *pâ*, to drink, may form प्रपाय *prapâya* or प्रपीय *prapîya* (Sâr.).

§ 449. Verbs ending in म् *m*, which do not admit of intermediate इ *i*, may or may not drop their म् *m*. Ex. नम् *nam*, to bow, प्रणम्य *praṇamya* or प्रणत्य *praṇatya*; गम् *gam*, to go, आगम्य *âgamya* or आगत्य *âgatya*. Other verbs ending in nasals, not admitting of intermediate इ *i*, or belonging to the Tan class, always drop their final nasal. Ex. हन् *han*, प्रहत्य *prahatya*; तन् *tan*, प्रतत्य *pratatya* †. खन् *khan* and जन् *jan* form खन्य *khanya* or खाय *khâya*, जन्य *janya* or जाय *jâya*.

§ 450. Verbs ending in ॠ *ṛî* change it to ईर् *îr*, and, after labials, into ऊर् *ûr*. Ex. वितीर्य *vitîrya*, having crossed; संपूर्य *sampûrya*, having filled.

§ 451. Certain verbs are irregular in not taking *Samprasâraṇa*. Thus वे *ve*, to weave, forms प्रवाय *pravâya*; ज्या *jyâ*, to fail, उपज्याय *upajyâya*; व्ये *vye*, to cover, प्रव्याय *pravyâya*, but after परि *pari* optionally परिव्याय *parivyâya* or परिवीय *parivîya* (Pâṇ. VI. 1, 41–44).

§ 452. Some verbs change final इ *i* and ई *î* into आ *â*. Thus मी *mî*, मीनाति *mînâti*, he destroys, and मि *mi*, मिनोति *minoti*, he throws, form निमाय *nimâya*; दी *dî*, to destroy, उपदाय *upadâya*; ली *lî*, to melt, optionally विलाय *vilâya* or विलीय *vilîya* (Pâṇ. VI. 1, 50–51).

---

† Versus memorialis of these verbs: रमिर्यमिर्नमी हन्तिरनुदात्ता गमिर्मनिः। तनु क्षण् क्षिण् ऋणु तृणु घृणु वनुर्मनुस्तनादयः॥

CHAPTER XVII.

VERBAL ADJECTIVES.

Verbal Adjectives in तव्यः tavyaḥ, अनीयः anîyaḥ, *or* यः yaḥ.

§ 453. These verbal adjectives (called *Kṛitya*) correspond in meaning to the Latin participles in *ndus*, conveying the idea that the action expressed by the verbs ought to be done or will be done. कर्तव्यः *kartavyaḥ*, करणीयः *karaṇîyaḥ*, कार्यः *káryaḥ*[1], faciendus. Ex. धर्मस्त्वया कर्तव्यः *dharmas tvayá kartavyaḥ*, right is to be done by thee.

§ 454. In order to form the adjective in तव्यः *tavyaḥ*, take the periphrastic future, and instead of ता *tá* put तव्यः *tavyaḥ*.

Thus दा *dá*, to give	दाता *dátá*	दातव्यः *dátavyaḥ*	दानीयः *dánîyaḥ*	देयः *deyaḥ*
गै *gai*, to sing	गाता *gátá*	गातव्यः *gátavyaḥ*	गानीयः *gánîyaḥ*	गेयः *geyaḥ*
जि *ji*, to conquer	जेता *jetá*	जेतव्यः *jetavyaḥ*	जयनीयः *jayanîyaḥ*	जेयः *jeyaḥ*
भू *bhú*, to be	भविता *bhavitá*	भवितव्यः *bhavitavyaḥ*	भवनीयः *bhavanîyaḥ*	भव्यः or भाव्यः[2]
कृ *kṛi*, to do	कर्ता *kartá*	कर्तव्यः *kartavyaḥ*	करणीयः *karaṇîyaḥ*	कार्यः *káryaḥ*
जॄ *jṝ*, to grow old	जरिता or जरीता[3]	जरितव्यः or जरीतव्यः[4]	जरणीयः *jaraṇîyaḥ*	जार्यः *járyaḥ*
क्ष्विद् *kshvid*, to sweat	क्ष्वेदिता *kshveditá*	क्ष्वेदितव्यः *kshveditavyaḥ*	क्ष्वेदनीयः *kshvedanîyaḥ*	क्ष्वेद्यः *kshvedyaḥ*
बुध् *budh*, to know	बोधिता *bodhitá*	बोधितव्यः *bodhitavyaḥ*	बोधनीयः *bodhanîyaḥ*	बोध्यः *bodhyaḥ*
कृष् *kṛish*, to draw	कर्ष्टा or क्रष्टा[5]	कर्ष्टव्यः or क्रष्टव्यः[6]	कर्षणीयः *karshaṇîyaḥ*	कृष्यः *kṛishyaḥ*
कुच् *kuch*[7], to squeeze	कुचिता *kuchitá*	कुचितव्यः *kuchitavyaḥ*	कुचनीयः *kuchanîyaḥ*	कुच्यः *kuchyaḥ*
मिह् *mih*, to sprinkle	मेढा *meḍhá*	मेढव्यः *meḍhavyaḥ*	मेहनीयः *mehanîyaḥ*	मेह्यः *mehyaḥ*
गम् *gam*, to go	गन्ता *gantá*	गन्तव्यः *gantavyaḥ*	गमनीयः *gamanîyaḥ*	गम्यः *gamyaḥ*
दृश् *dṛiś*, to see	द्रष्टा *drashṭá*	द्रष्टव्यः *drashṭavyaḥ*	दर्शनीयः *darśanîyaḥ*	दृश्यः *dṛiśyaḥ*
दंश् *daṁś*, to bite	दंष्टा *daṁshṭá*	दंष्टव्यः *daṁshṭavyaḥ*	दंशनीयः *daṁśanîyaḥ*	दंश्यः *daṁśyaḥ*
Caus. भावय् *bhávay*, to cause to be	भावयिता *bhávayitá*	भावयितव्यः *bhávayitavyaḥ*	भावनीयः *bhávanîyaḥ*	भाव्यः *bhávyaḥ*
Des. बुभूष् *bubhúsh*, to wish to be	बुभूषिता *bubhúshitá*	बुभूषितव्यः *bubhúshitavyaḥ*	बुभूषणीयः *bubhúshaṇîyaḥ*	बुभूष्यः *bubhúshyaḥ*
Int. बोभूय् *bobhúy*	बोभूयिता *bobhúyitá*	बोभूयितव्यः *bobhúyitavyaḥ*	बोभूयनीयः *bobhúyanîyaḥ*	बोभूय्यः *bobhúyyaḥ*
Int. बोभू *bobhú*	बोभविता *bobhavitá*	बोभवितव्यः *bobhavitavyaḥ*	बोभवनीयः *bobhavanîyaḥ*	बोभव्यः *bobhavyaḥ*
Int. बेभिद्य् *bebhidy*	बेभिदिता *bebhiditá*	बेभिदितव्यः *bebhiditavyaḥ*	बेभिदनीयः *bebhidanîyaḥ*	बेभिद्यः *bebhidyaḥ*

[1] Another suffix for forming verbal adjectives is एलिमः *elimaḥ*, which is, however, of rare occurrence; पच् *pach*, to cook, पचेलिमा माषाः *pachelimá máshâḥ*, beans fit to cook; भिदेलिमः *bhidelimaḥ*, fragile. (Pâṇ. III, 1, 96, v.)

[2] *bhavyaḥ* or *bhávyaḥ*. [3] *jaritá* or *jarîtá*. [4] *jaritavyaḥ* or *jarîtavyaḥ*.

[5] *karshṭá* or *krashṭá*. [6] *karshṭavyaḥ* or *krashṭavyaḥ*. [7] Never takes Guṇa (§ 345, note).

§ 455. In order to form the adjective in अनीयः *anîyaḥ*, it is generally sufficient to take the root as it appears before तव्यः *tavyaḥ*, omitting, however, intermediate इ *i*, and putting अनीयः *anîyaḥ* instead. Guṇa-vowels before अनीयः *anîyaḥ* have, of course, the semivowel for their final element, and there can be no occasion for the intermediate इ *i*. The अय् *ay* of the causative and the य् *y* after consonants of intensives and other derivative verbs are, as usual, rejected. बुध् *budh*, बोधयति *bodhayati*, बोधनीयः *bodhanîyaḥ*; भिद् *bhid*, बेभिद्यते *bebhidyate*, बेभिदनीयः *bebhidanîyaḥ*.

§ 456. In order to form the adjective in यः *yaḥ*, it is generally sufficient to take the adjective in अनीयः *anîyaḥ* and to cut off अनी *anî*. Thus भवनीयः *bhav-anî-yaḥ* becomes भव्यः *bhavyaḥ*; चेतनीयः *chet-anî-yaḥ*, चेत्यः *chetyaḥ*; वयनीयः *vay-anî-yaḥ*, वेयः *veyaḥ*; बोधनीयः *bodh-anî-yaḥ*, बोध्यः *bodhyaḥ*. A few more special rules, however, have here to be mentioned:

1. Final आ *â*, ए *e*, ऐ *ai*, ओ *o*, become ए *e*. दा *dâ*, to give, देयः *deyaḥ*; गै *gai*, to sing, गेयः *geyaḥ*. (Pâṇ. III. 1, 98; VI. 4, 65.)

2. Final इ *i* and ई *î* take Guṇa, as before अनीय *anîya*; जि *ji*, जेयः *jeyaḥ*, to be conquered, different from जय्यः *jayyaḥ*, conquerable; क्षि *kshi*, to destroy, क्षेयः *ksheyaḥ*, different from क्षय्यः *kshayyaḥ*, destructible (Pâṇ. VI. 1, 81). Final उ *u* and ऊ *û*, under the same circumstances, are changed to अव् *av*, or, after अवश्य *avaśya*, when a high degree of necessity is expressed, to आव् *âv*: भव्यः *bhavyaḥ* or अवश्यभाव्यः *avaśya-bhâvyaḥ*; विप्रेण शुचिना भाव्यं *vipreṇa śuchinâ bhâvyam*, a Brâhman must be pure. Final ऊ *û* if it appears as उव् *uv* before अनीय *anîya*, appears as ऊ *û* before य *ya*; गू *gû*, to sound, गुवनीय *guvanîya*, गूय *gûya*.

3. Final ऋ *ṛi* and ॠ *ṛî* before यः *yaḥ*, but not before अनीयः *anîyaḥ*, take Vṛiddhi instead of Guṇa. कार्यः *kâryaḥ*; पार्यः *pâryaḥ*. (Pâṇ. III. 1, 120, 124.)

4. Penultimate ऋ *ṛi*, which takes Guṇa before अनीयः *anîyaḥ*, does not take Guṇa before यः *yaḥ*, with few exceptions; वृध्यः *vṛidhyaḥ*, दृश्यः *dṛiśyaḥ* (Pâṇ. III. 1, 110). But कृप् *kṛip*, to do, forms कल्प्यः *kalpyaḥ*; वृष् *vṛish*, to sprinkle, वृष्यः *vṛishyaḥ* or वर्ष्यः *varshyaḥ* (Pâṇ. III. 1, 120). Penultimate ॠ *ṛî* becomes ईर् *îr*; कॄत् *kṛît*, कीर्त्यः *kîrtyaḥ*.

5. Penultimate इ *i* and उ *u* take Guṇa before यः *yaḥ*, as before अनीयः *anîyaḥ*; विद् *vid*, वेद्यः *vedyaḥ*; शुष् *śush*, शोष्यः *śoshyaḥ*.

6. Penultimate अ *a*, prosodially short, before यः *yaḥ*, but not before अनीयः *anîyaḥ*, is lengthened, unless the final consonant is a labial (Pâṇ. III. 1, 98; 124); हस् *has*, to laugh, हास्यः *hâsyaḥ*; वह् *vah*, वाह्यः *vâhyaḥ*. But शप् *śap*, to curse, शप्यः *śapyaḥ*; लभ् *labh*, लभ्यः *labhyaḥ*. The अ *a* remains likewise short in शक्यः *śakyaḥ*, from शक् *śak*, to be able; in

सह्यः *sahyaḥ*, from सह् *sah*, to bear (Pâṇ. III. 1, 99), and some other verbs*. खन् *khan* forms खेयः *kheyaḥ* (Pâṇ. III. 1, 111), which, however, may be derived from खै *khai*, to dig; हन् *han*, वध्यः *vadhyaḥ* or घात्यः *ghâtyaḥ*.

§ 457. The following are a few derivatives in यः *yaḥ*, formed against the general rules.

गुप् *gup*, to protect, may form गुप्यः *gupyaḥ*; गुह् *guh*, to hide, गुह्यः *guhyaḥ*; जुष् *jush*, to cherish, जुष्यः *jushyaḥ*; ग्रह् *grah*, to take, गृह्यः *gṛihyaḥ*, after प्रति *prati* and अपि *api*; वद् *vad*, to speak, उद्यः *udyaḥ*, in composition (Pâṇ. III. 1, 106; 114. ब्रह्मोद्या कथा *brahmodyá kathá*, a story told by a Brâhman); भू *bhû*, to be, भूय *bhûya*, in composition (Pâṇ. III. 1, 107. ब्रह्मभूयं गतः *brahmabhûyam gataḥ*, arrived at Brahmahood); शास् *śâs*, to rule, शिष्यः *śishyaḥ*, pupil.

We find त् *t* inserted before यः *yaḥ*, in analogy to the gerunds in य *ya*, in the following verbs:

इ *i*, to go, इत्यः *ityaḥ*; स्तु *stu*, to praise, स्तुत्यः *stutyaḥ*; वृ *vṛi*, to choose, वृत्यः *vṛityaḥ*; दृ *dṛi*, to regard, दृत्यः *dṛityaḥ*; भृ *bhṛi*, to bear, भृत्यः *bhṛityaḥ*; कृ *kṛi*, to do, कृत्यः *kṛityaḥ*. But many of these forms are only used in certain senses, and must not be considered as supplanting the regular verbal adjectives. Thus गुह्यः *guhyaḥ* and गोह्यः *gohyaḥ* both occur; दुह्यः *duhyaḥ* and दोह्यः *dohyaḥ*, &c.

§ 458. Verbs ending in च् *ch* or ज् *j* change their final consonant into क् *k* or ग् *g* if the following य *ya* (*ṇyat*) requires the lengthening of the vowel. पच् *pach*, पाक्यं *pâkyam*; भुज् *bhuj*, to enjoy, भोग्यं *bhogyam*, but भोज्यं *bhojyam*, what is to be eaten (Pâṇ. VII. 3, 69).

There are, however, several exceptions. Verbs beginning with a guttural do not admit the substitution of gutturals. Likewise the following verbs: यज् *yaj*, याच् *yâch*, रुच् *ruch*, प्रवच् *pravach*, ऋच् *ṛich*, त्यज् *tyaj*, पूज् *pûj*, अज् *aj*, व्रज् *vraj*, वंच् *vañch* (to go). Thus याज्यं *yâjyam*, याच्यं *yâchyam*, रोच्यं *rochyam*, प्रवाच्यं *pravâchyam*, अर्च्यं *archyam*, त्याज्यं *tyâjyam*, पूज्यं *pûjyam* (Prakriyâ-Kaumudî, p. 55b).

Infinitive in तुं tum.

§ 459. The infinitive is formed by adding तुं *tum*. The base has the same form as before the ता *tâ* of the periphrastic future, or before the तव्यः *tavyaḥ* of the verbal adjective. बुध् *budh*, बोधितुं *bodhitum*. (See § 454.) Ex. कृष्णं द्रष्टुं व्रजति *krishṇam drashṭum vrajati*, he goes to see Kṛishṇa; भोक्तुं कालः *bhoktum kâlaḥ*, it is time to eat.

* Pâṇini (III. 1, 100) mentions only गद् *gad*, मद् *mad*, चर् *char*, यम् *yam*, if used without preposition. The Sârasvatî (III. 7, 7) includes among the Śakâdi verbs, शक् *śak*, सह् *sah*, गद् *gad*, मद् *mad*, चर् *char*, यम् *yam*, तक् *tak*, शस् *śas*, चत् *chat*, यत् *yat*, पत् *pat*, जन् *jan*, हन् *han*, (रध् *radh*), शल् *śal*, रुच् *ruch*.

Verbal Adverb.

§ 460. By means of the suffix अं *am*, which, as a general rule, is added to that form which the verb assumes before the passive इ *i* (3rd pers. sing. aor. pass., § 403), a verbal adverb is formed. From भुज् *bhuj*, to eat, भोजं *bhojam*; from पा *pâ*, to drink, पायं *pâyam*. Ex. अग्रे भोजं व्रजति *agre bhojam vrajati*, having first eaten, he goes. This verbal adverb is most frequently used twice over. Ex. भोजं भोजं व्रजति *bhojam bhojam vrajati*, having eaten and eaten, he goes (Pâṇ. III. 4, 22). It is likewise used at the end of compounds; द्वैधंकारं *dvaidhaṁkâram*, having divided; उच्चैःकारं *uchchaiḥkâram*, loudly.

CHAPTER XVIII.

CAUSATIVE VERBS.

§ 461. Simple roots are changed into causal bases by Guṇa or Vṛiddhi of their radical vowel, and by the addition of a final इ *i*. The root is then treated as following the Bhû class, so that इ *i* appears in the special tenses as अय *aya*. Thus भू *bhû* becomes भावि *bhâvi* and भावयति *bhâvayati*, he causes to be; बुध् *budh* becomes बोधि *bodhi* and बोधयति *bodhayati*, he causes to know.

§ 462. The rules according to which the vowel takes either Guṇa or Vṛiddhi are as follows:

1. Final इ *i* and ई *î*, उ *u* and ऊ *û*, ऋ *ṛi* and ॠ *ṛî* take Vṛiddhi.

Thus स्मि *smi*, to laugh, स्माययति *smâyayati*, he makes laugh.
नी *nî*, to lead, नाययति *nâyayati*, he causes to lead.
प्लु *plu*, to swim, प्लावयति *plâvayati*, he makes swim.
भू *bhû*, to be, भावयति *bhâvayati*, he causes to be.
कृ *kṛi*, to make, कारयति *kârayati*, he causes to make.
कॄ *kṛî*, to scatter, कारयति *kârayati*, he causes to scatter.

2. Medial इ *i*, उ *u*, ऋ *ṛi*, ऌ *ḷi*, followed by a single consonant, take Guṇa; ॠ *ṛî* becomes ईर् *îr*.

Thus विद् *vid*, to know, वेदयति *vedayati*, he makes know.
बुध् *budh*, to know, बोधयति *bodhayati*, he makes know.
कृत् *kṛit*, to cut, कर्तयति *kartayati*, he causes to cut.
कॢप् *kḷip*, to be able, कल्पयति *kalpayati*, he renders fit.

3. Medial अ *a* followed by a single consonant is lengthened, but there are many exceptions.

सद् *sad*, to sit, सादयति *sâdayati*, he sets.
पत् *pat*, to fall, पातयति *pâtayati*, he fells.

Exceptions:

I. Most verbs ending in अम् *am* do not lengthen their vowel:

गम् *gam*, to go, गमयति *gamayati*, he makes go.
क्रम् *kram*, to stride, क्रमयति *kramayati*, he causes to stride.

Verbs in अम् *am* which do lengthen the vowel are,

कम् *kam*, to desire, कामयते *kâmayate*, he desires; Caus. कामयति *kâmayati*, he makes desire.

अम् *am*, to move, अमति *amati*, he moves; Caus. आमयति *âmayati*, he makes move.

चम् *cham*, to eat, चमति *chamati*, he eats; Caus. चामयति *châmayati*, he makes eat.

शम् *śam*, if it means to see, शाम्यति *śâmyati*, he sees; Caus. शामयति *śâmayati*, he shows; but शमयति *śamayati*, he quiets.

यम् *yam*, unless it means to eat, यच्छति *yachchhati*; Caus. यामयति *yâmayati*, he extends; but यमयति *yamayati*, he feeds.

नम् *nam*, to bend, necessarily lengthens its vowel after a preposition; विनामयति *vinâmayati*, he bends. In the simple verb the lengthening is optional.

वम् *vam*, to vomit, necessarily shortens its vowel after a preposition; उद्वमयति *udvamayati*, he makes vomit. In the single verb the lengthening is optional.

II. A class of verbs collected by native grammarians, and beginning with घट् *ghaṭ* (Dh. P. 19, 1), do not lengthen their vowel. The same verbs may optionally retain their short vowel in the 3rd pers. sing. aorist of the causative passive (§ 405). The following list contains the more important among these verbs:

Root.	Causative. 3rd Pers. Sing. Pres. Par.	3rd Pers. Sing. Aor. Passive.
1. घट् *ghaṭ*, to strive	घटयति *ghaṭayati*	अघटि or अघाटि *aghâṭi*
2. व्यथ् *vyath*, to fear	व्यथयति *vyathayati*	अव्यथि or अव्याथि *avyâthi*
3. प्रथ् *prath*, to be famous	प्रथयति *prathayati*	अप्रथि or अप्राथि *aprâthi*
4. म्रद् *mrad*, to rub	म्रदयति *mradayati*	अम्रदि or अम्रादि *amrâdi*
5. क्रप् *krap*, to pity	क्रपयति *krapayati*	अक्रपि or अक्रापि *akrâpi*
6. त्वर् *tvar*, to hurry	त्वरयति *tvarayati*	अत्वरि or अत्वारि *atvâri*
7. ज्वर् *jvar*, to burn with fever	ज्वरयति *jvarayati*	अज्वरि or अज्वारि *ajvâri*
8. नट् *naṭ*, to dance	नटयति *naṭayati*	अनटि or अनाटि *anâṭi*
9. श्रथ् *śrath*, to kill	श्रथयति *śrathayati*	अश्रथि or अश्राथि *aśrâthi*
10. वन् *van*, to act *	प्रवनयति *pravanayati*	प्रावनि or प्रावानि *prâvâni*
11. ज्वल् *jval*, to shine *	प्रज्वलयति *prajvalayati*	प्राज्वलि or प्राज्वालि *prâjvâli*
12. स्मृ *smṛi*, to regret	स्मरयति *smarayati*	अस्मरि or अस्मारि *asmâri*
13. दॄ *dṝ*, to respect, (not to tear)	दरयति *darayati*	अदरि or अदारि *adâri*
14. श्रा *śrâ*, to boil	श्रपयति *śrapayati*	अश्रपि or अश्रापि *aśrâpi*
15. ज्ञा *jñâ*, to slay, to please, to sharpen (?), to perceive	ज्ञपयति *jñapayati*	अज्ञपि or अज्ञापि *ajñâpi*

* With a preposition, and optionally without a preposition.

16. चल् *chal*, to tremble — चलयति *chalayati* — अचलि or अचालि *achâli*
17. मद् *mad*, to rejoice, &c. — मदयति *madayati* — अमदि or अमादि *amâdi*
18. ध्वन् *dhvan*, to sound, to ring — ध्वनयति *dhvanayati* — अध्वनि or अध्वानि *adhvâni*
19. दल् *dal*, to cut — दलयति *dalayati* (optional) — अदलि or अदालि *adâli*
20. वल् *val*, to cover — वलयति *valayati* (optional) — अवलि or अवालि *avâli*
21. स्खल् *skhal*, to drop — स्खलयति *skhalayati* (optional) — अस्खलि or अस्खालि *askhâli*
22. त्रप् *trap*, to be ashamed — त्रपयति *trapayati* — अत्रपि or अत्रापि *atrâpi*
23. क्षै *kshai*, to wane — क्षपयति *kshapayati* — अक्षपि or अक्षापि *akshâpi*
24. जन् *jan* (Div), nasci — जनयति *janayati* — अजनि *ajani* *
25. जॄ *jṛî* (Div), to grow old — जरयति *jarayati* — अजरि or अजारि *ajâri*
26. रञ्ज् *rañj* (Bhû), to hunt, to dye — रजयति or रञ्ज° *rajayati* or *rañja-* — अरञ्जि or अराञ्जि *arâñji*
27. ग्ला *glâ* † or ग्लै *glai*, to fade — ग्लपयति or ग्लापयति *glâpayati* — अग्लपि or अग्लापि *aglâpi*
28. स्ना *snâ* †, to wash — स्नपयति or स्नापयति *snâpayati* — अस्नपि or अस्नापि *asnâpi*
29. वन् *van* †, to cherish — वनयति or वानयति *vânayati* — अवनि or अवानि *avâni*
30. फण् *phaṇ*, to approach — फणयति or फाणयति (?) *phâṇayati* — अफणि or अफाणि *aphâṇi*

Note—Some of these verbs are to be considered as *mit*, i. e. as having a short vowel in the causative, if employed in the sense given above; while if they occur again in other sections of the Dhâtupâṭha and with different meanings, they may be conjugated likewise as ordinary verbs.

§ 463. Some verbs form their causative base anomalously:

I. Nearly all verbs ending in आ *â*, and most ending in ए *e*, ऐ *ai*, ओ *o*, changeable to आ *â*, insert प् *p* before the causal termination. (Pâṇ. VII. 3, 36.)

Thus दा *dâ*, to give, ददाति *dadâti*, he gives; दापयति *dâpayati*, he causes to give.

दे *de*, to pity, दयते *dayate*, he pities; दापयति *dâpayati*, he causes pity.

दो *do*, to cut, दाति *dâti* or द्यति *dyati*, he cuts; दापयति *dâpayati*, he causes cutting.

दै *dai*, to purify, दायति *dâyati*, he purifies; दापयति *dâpayati*, he causes to purify.

II. Other irregular causatives are given in the following list. Their irregularity consists chiefly in taking प् *p* with Guṇa or Vṛiddhi of the radical vowel; sometimes in lengthening the vowel instead of raising it to Guṇa; and frequently in substituting a new base.

1. इ *i*, to go, in अधीते *adhîte*, he reads; Caus. अध्यापयति *adhyâpayati*, he teaches ‡. (Pâṇ. VI. 1, 48.)

2. ऋ *ṛi*, to go, ऋच्छति *ṛichchhati*; Caus. अर्पयति *arpayati*, he places. (Pâṇ. VII. 3, 36.)

* Pâṇ. VII. 3, 35.

† Optionally as simple verbs; with prepositions, 27 and 28 do not shorten the vowel in the causative; 29 does shorten it.

‡ प्रति + इ *prati* + *i*, to approach, forms its causal regular when it means to make a person understand, प्रत्याययति *pratyâyayati*. Otherwise the causative of इ *i* is formed from गम् *gam*.

3. क्नूय् *knûy*, to sound, क्नूनाति *knûnâti*; Caus. क्नोपयति *knopayati*, he causes to sound.
4. क्री *krî*, to buy, क्रीणाति *krîṇâti*; Caus. क्रापयति *krâpayati*, he causes to buy.
5. क्ष्माय् *kshmây*, to tremble, क्ष्मायते *kshmâyate*; Caus. क्ष्मापयति *kshmâpayati*, he causes to tremble. (Pâṇ. VII. 3, 36.)
6. चि *chi*, to collect, चिनोति *chinoti*; Caus. चापयति *châpayati*, or regularly चाययति *châyayati*, he causes to collect. (Pâṇ. VI. 1, 54.)
7. छो *chho*, to cut, छ्यति *chhyati*; Caus. छाययति *chhâyayati*, he causes to cut.
8. जागृ *jâgṛi*, to be awake, जागर्ति *jâgarti*; Caus. जागरयति *jâgarayati*, he rouses.
9. जि *ji*, to conquer, जयति *jayati*; Caus. जापयति *jâpayati*, he causes to conquer.
10. दरिद्रा *daridrâ*, to be poor, दरिद्राति *daridrâti*; Caus. दरिद्रयति *daridrayati*, he makes poor.
11. दीधी *dîdhî*, to shine, दीधीते *dîdhîte*; Caus. दीधयति *dîdhayati*, he causes to shine.
12. दुष् *dush*, to sin, दुष्यति *dushyati*; Caus. दूषयति *dûshayati*, he causes to sin; also दोषयति *doshayati*, he demoralizes. (Pâṇ. VI. 4, 91.)
13. धू *dhû*, to shake, धूनोति *dhûnoti*; Caus. धूनयति *dhûnayati*, he causes to shake.
14. पा *pâ*, to drink, पिबति *pibati*; Caus. पाययति *pâyayati*, he causes to drink; also पै *pai*, पायति *pâyati*, to be dry.
15. पा *pâ*, to protect, पाति *pâti*; Caus. पालयति *pâlayati*, he protects.
16. प्री *prî*, to love, प्रीणाति *prîṇâti*; Caus. प्रीणयति *prîṇayati*, he delights.
17. भ्रज्ज् *bhrajj*, to roast, भृज्जति *bhṛijjati*; Caus. भ्रज्जयति *bhrajjayati*, he makes roast, or भर्ज्जयति *bharjjayati*, from भृज् *bhṛij*.
18. भी *bhî*, to fear, बिभेति *bibheti*; Caus. भापयते *bhâpayate* or भीषयते *bhîshayate*, he frightens; also regularly भाययति *bhâyayati*. (Pâṇ. VI. 1, 56.)
19. मि *mi*, to throw, मिनोति *minoti*, and मी *mî*, to destroy, मिनाति *minâti*, form their Caus. like मा *mâ*.
20. री *rî*, to flow, or to go, रीयते *rîyate*; Caus. रेपयति *repayati*, he makes flow.
21. रुह् *ruh*, to grow, रोहति *rohati*; Caus. रोहयति *rohayati*, रोपयति *ropayati*, he causes to grow. (Pâṇ. VII. 3, 43.)
22. ली *lî*, to adhere, लिनाति *linâti* and लीयते *lîyate*; Caus. लीनयति *lînayati*, लापयति *lâpayati*, and लाययति *lâyayati*; and, if the root takes the form ला *lâ*, also लालयति *lâlayati* (Pâṇ. VII. 3, 39). The meaning varies; see Pâṇ. VI. 1, 48; 51.
23. वा *vâ*, to blow, वाति *vâti*; Caus. वाजयति *vâjayati*, if it means he shakes.
24. वी *vî*, to obtain, वेति *veti*; Caus. वापयति *vâpayati* or वाययति *vâyayati*, if it means to make conceive. (Pâṇ. VI. 1, 55.)
25. वे *ve*, to weave, वयति *vayati*; Caus. वाययति *vâyayati*, he causes to weave.
26. वेवी *vevî*, to conceive, वेवीते *vevîte*; Caus. वेवयति *vevayati*.
27. व्ये *vye*, to cover, व्ययति *vyayati*; Caus. व्याययति *vyâyayati*, he causes to cover.
28. व्ली *vlî*, to choose, व्लिनाति *vlinâti*; Caus. व्लेपयति *vlepayati*, he causes to choose.
29. शद् *śad*, to fall, शीयते *śîyate*; Caus. शातयति *śâtayati*, he fells; but not, if it means to move. (Pâṇ. VII. 3, 42.)

30. शो *śo*, to sharpen, श्यति *śyati*; Caus. शाययति *śâyayati*, he causes to sharpen.

31. सिध् *sidh*, to succeed, सिध्यति *sidhyati*; Caus. साधयति *sâdhayati*, he performs; but सेधयति *sedhayati*, he performs sacred acts.

32. सो *so*, to destroy, स्यति *syati*; Caus. साययति *sâyayati*, he causes to destroy.

33. स्फुर् *sphur*, to sparkle, स्फुरति *sphurati*; Caus स्फारयति *sphârayati* and स्फोरयति *sphorayati*, he makes sparkle.

34. स्फाय् *sphây*, to grow, स्फायते *sphâyate*; Caus. स्फावयति *sphâvayati*, he causes to grow.

35. स्मि *smi*, to smile, स्मयते *smayate*; Caus. स्मापयते *smâpayate*, he astonishes; also स्माययति *smâyayati*, he causes a smile by something. (Pâṇ. VI. 1, 57.)

36. ह्री *hrî*, to be ashamed, जिह्रेति *jihreti*; Caus. ह्रेपयति *hrepayati*, he makes ashamed. (Pâṇ. VII. 3, 36.)

37. ह्वे *hve*, to call, ह्वयति *hvayati*; Caus. ह्वाययति *hvâyayati*, he causes to call.

38. हन् *han*, to kill, हन्ति *hanti*; Caus. घातयति *ghâtayati*, he causes to kill.

§ 464. As causative verbs are conjugated exactly like verbs of the Chur class, there is no necessity for giving here a complete paradigm. Like Chur verbs they retain अय् *ay* throughout, except in the reduplicated aorist and the benedictive Parasmaipada; and they form the perfect periphrastically. The only difficulty in causative verbs is the formation of their bases, and the formation of the aorist. Thus कृ *kṛi*, as causative, forms Pres. Par. and Âtm. कारयति, °ते, *kârayati*, *-te*; Impf. अकारयत्, °त, *akârayat*, *-ta*; Opt. कारयेत्, °त, *kârayet*, *-ta*; Imp. कारयतु, °तां, *kârayatu*, *-tâm*; Red. Perf. कारयांचकार, °चक्रे, *kârayâñchakâra*, *-chakre* (§ 342); Aor. अचीकरत्, °त, *achîkarat*, *-ta*; Fut. कारयिष्यति, °ते, *kârayishyati*, *-te*; Cond. अकारयिष्यत्, °त, *akârayishyat*, *-ta*; Per. Fut. कारयिता *kârayitâ*; Ben. कार्यात् *kâryât*; कारयिषीष्ट *kârayishîshṭa*.

§ 465. If a causative verb has to be used in the passive, अय् *ay* is dropt (§ 399), but the root remains the same as it would have been with अय् *ay*. Hence Pres. कार्यते *kâryate*, he is made to do; रोप्यते *ropyate*, from रुह् *ruh*, he is made to grow. The imperfect, optative, and imperative are formed regularly. The perfect is periphrastic with the auxiliary verbs in the Âtmanepada.

§ 466. In the general tenses, however, where the य *ya* of the passive disappears (§ 401), the causative अय् *ay* may or may not reappear, and we thus get two forms throughout (see Colebrooke, p. 198, note):

Fut. भावयिष्ये *bhâvayishye* or भाविष्ये *bhâvishye*.
Cond. अभावयिष्ये *abhâvayishye* or अभाविष्ये *abhâvishye*.
Per. Fut. भावयिताहे *bhâvayitâhe* or भाविताहे *bhâvitâhe*.
Ben. भावयिषीय *bhâvayishîya* or भाविषीय *bhâvishîya*.
First Aor. I. 1. p. अभावयिषि *abhâvayishi* or अभाविषि *abhâvishi*.
2. p. अभावयिष्ठाः *abhâvayishṭhâḥ* or अभाविष्ठाः *abhâvishṭhâḥ*.
3. p. अभावि *abhâvi*.

CHAPTER XIX.

DESIDERATIVE VERBS.

§ 467. Desiderative bases are formed by reduplication, the peculiarities of which will have to be treated separately, and by adding स् *s* to the root. Thus from भू *bhû*, to be, बुभूष् *bubhûsh*, to wish to be.

§ 468. These new bases are conjugated like Tud roots. बुभूषामि *bubhûshâmi*, बुभूषसि *bubhûshasi*, बुभूषति *bubhûshati*, बुभूषावः *bubhûshâvaḥ*, &c.

§ 469. The roots which take the intermediate इ *i* have been given before (§§ 331, 340), as well as those which take intermediate ई *î*. Thus from विद् *vid*, to know, विविदिष् *vividish*, to wish to know; from तॄ *tṛî*, to cross, तितरिष् *titarish* or तितरीष् *titarîsh*, to wish to cross.

§ 470. As a general rule, though liable to exceptions, it may be stated that bases ending in one consonant may be strengthened by Guṇa, if they take the intermediate इ *i*. Thus बुध् *budh* forms बुबोधिषति *bubodhishati*; वृध् *vṛidh*, विवर्धिषति *vivardhishati*; दिव् *div*, दिदेविषति *didevishati*: also कॄ *kṛî*, चिकरिषति *chikarishati*; दॄ *dṛi*, दिदरिषति *didarishati*. But भिद् *bhid*, Des. बिभित्सति *bibhitsati* (Pâṇ. I. 2, 10); गुह् *guh*, जुघुक्षति *jughukshati* (Pâṇ. VII. 2, 12). In fact, no Guṇa without intermediate इ *i*.

§ 471. But there are important exceptions. In many cases the base of the desiderative is neither strengthened nor weakened; रुद् *rud*, रुरुदिषति *rurudishati*. Other bases may be strengthened optionally; द्युत् *dyut*, दिद्युतिषते *didyutishate* or दिद्योतिषते *didyotishate*. Certain bases which do not take intermediate इ *i* are actually weakened; स्वप् *svap*, सुषुप्सति *sushupsati*.

1. Verbs which do *not* take Guṇa, though they have intermediate इ *i*.

रुद् *rud*, to cry, रुरुदिषति *rurudishati*; विद् *vid*, to know, विविदिषति *vividishati*; मुष् *mush*, to steal, मुमुषिषति *mumushishati*. (Pâṇ. I. 2, 8.)

2. Verbs which may or may not take Guṇa, though they have intermediate इ *i*.

Verbs beginning with consonants, and ending in any single consonant, except य् *y* or व् *v*, and having इ *i* or उ *u* for their vowel. (Pâṇ. I. 2, 26.)

द्युत् *dyut*, दिद्युतिषति *didyutishati* or दिद्योतिषति *didyotishati*.

But दिव् *div*, दिदेविषति *didevishati* or, without इ *i*, दुद्यूषति *dudyûshati* (Pâṇ. VII. 2, 49); वृत् *vṛit*, विवर्तिषते *vivartishate* or विवृत्सति *vivṛitsati*.

3. Verbs ending in इ *i* or उ *u*, not taking intermediate इ *i*, lengthen their vowel; final ऋ *ṛi* and ॠ *ṛî* become ईर् *îr*, and, after labials, ऊर् *ûr*. (Pâṇ. VI. 4, 16.)

जि *ji*, to conquer, जिगीषति *jigîshati*; यु *yu*, to mix, युयूषति *yuyûshati*.
कृ *kṛi*, to do, चिकीर्षति *chikîrshati*; तॄ *tṛî*, to cross, तितीर्षति *titîrshati*.
मृ *mṛi*, to die, मुमूर्षति *mumûrshati*; पॄ *pṛî*, to fill, पुपूर्षति *pupûrshati*.

If, however, they take intermediate इ *i*, they likewise take Guṇa.

स्मि *smi*, to smile, सिस्मयिषति *sismayishati*; पू *pû*, to purify, पिपविषते *pipavishate*; गॄ *gṛî*, to swallow, जिगरिषति *jigarishati*; दृ *dṛi*, to respect, दिदरिषते *didarishate*.

4. गम् *gam*, to go, as a substitute for इ *i*, to go, and हन् *han*, to kill, lengthen their vowel before the स् *s* of the desiderative. (Pâṇ. vi. 4, 16.)

गम् *gam*, अधिजिगांसते *adhijigâṁsate*, he wishes to read; but जिगमिषति *jigamishati*, he wishes to go.

हन् *han*, जिघांसति *jighâṁsati*, he wishes to kill.

5. तन् *tan*, to stretch, lengthens its vowel optionally. (Pâṇ. v. 4, 17.)

तन् *tan*, तितांसति *titâṁsati* or तितंसति *titaṁsati*; but also तितनिषति *titanishati*. (Pâṇ. vii. 2, 49, v.)

6. सन् *san*, to obtain, drops its न् *n* and lengthens the vowel before the स् *s* of the desiderative. (Pâṇ. vi. 4, 42.)

सन् *san*, सिषासति *sishâsati*; but सिसनिषति *sisanishati*.

7. ग्रह् *grah*, to take, स्वप् *svap*, to sleep, and प्रछ् *prachh*, to ask, shorten their bases by *Samprasâraṇa*. (Pâṇ. i. 2, 8.)

ग्रह् *grah*, जिघृक्षति *jighṛikshati*. स्वप् *svap*, सुषुप्सति *sushupsati*.

प्रछ् *prachh*, पिपृच्छिषति *pipṛichchhishati*.

8. The following verbs shorten their vowel to इ *i* before the स् *s* of the desiderative, insert त् *t* (Pâṇ. vii. 4, 54), and reject the reduplication.

मी *mî* (मीनाति *mînâti*, to destroy, and मिनोति *minoti*, to throw), Des. मित्सति *mitsati*.

मा *mâ* (माति *mâti*, to measure, मिमीते *mimîte*, to measure, मयते *mayate*, to change), Des. मित्सति *mitsati*, मित्सते *mitsate*.

दा *dâ* (ददाति *dadâti*, to give, दाति *dâti*, to cut, द्यति *dyati*, to cut, दयते *dayate*, to pity), Des. दित्सति *ditsati*, दित्सते *ditsate*.

धा *dhâ* (दधाति *dadhâti*, to place, धयति *dhayati*, to drink), Des. धित्सति *dhitsati*.

9. Other desideratives formed without reduplication:

रभ् *rabh*, to begin (रभते *rabhate*), Des. रिप्सते *ripsate*.

लभ् *labh*, to take (लभते *labhate*), Des. लिप्सते *lipsate*.

शक् *śak*, to be able (शक्नोति *śaknoti*, शक्यति *śakyati*), Des. शिक्षति *śikshati*.

पत् *pat*, to fall (पतति *patati*), Des. पित्सति *pitsati*.

पद् *pad*, to go (पद्यते *padyate*), Des. पित्सते *pitsate*.

आप् *âp*, to obtain (आप्नोति *âpnoti*), Des. ईप्सति *îpsati*.

ज्ञप् *jñap*, to command (ज्ञपयति *jñapayati*), Des. ज्ञीप्सति *jñîpsati*.

ऋध् *ṛidh*, to grow (ऋध्नोति *ṛidhnoti*), Des. ईर्त्सति *îrtsati*.

दंभ् *dambh*, to deceive (दभ्नोति *dabhnoti*), Des. धीप्सति *dhîpsati* or धिप्सति *dhipsati*.

मुच् *much*, to free (मुंचति *muñchati*), Des. मोक्षते *mokshate* or मुमुक्षते *mumukshate*, he wishes for spiritual freedom.

राध् *râdh*, to finish (राध्यति *râdhyati*), Des. प्रतिरित्सति *prati-ritsati*, in the sense of injuring, otherwise रिरात्सति *rirâtsati*, also रिरित्सति *riritsati*.

§ 472. Certain verbs which are commonly considered to belong to the Bhû class are really desiderative bases.

कित् *kit*, चिकित्सते *chikitsate*, he cures.
गुप् *gup*, जुगुप्सते *jugupsate*, he despises.
तिज् *tij*, तितिक्षते *titikshate*, he bears.
मान् *mân*, मीमांसते *mîmâṁsate*, he investigates.
बध् *badh*, बीभत्सते *bîbhatsate*, he loathes.
दान् *dân*, दीदांसते *dîdâṁsate*, he straightens.
शान् *śân*, शीशांसते *śîśâṁsate*, he sharpens.

Reduplication in Desideratives.

§ 473. Besides the general rules of reduplication given in §§ 302–319*, the following special rules with regard to the vowel of the reduplicative syllable are to be observed in forming the desiderative base:

Radical अ *a* and आ *â* are represented by इ *i* in the reduplicative syllable (Pâṇ. VII. 4, 79).

पच् *pach*, पिपक्षति *pipakshati*; स्था *sthâ*, तिष्ठासति *tishṭhâsati*.

§ 474. अव् *av* and आव् *âv*, standing as Guṇa or Vṛiddhi of radical उ *u* or ऊ *û*, are represented by इ *i* in the reduplicative syllable, provided they be preceded by प् *p*, फ् *ph*, ब् *b*, भ् *bh*, म् *m*, य् *y*, र् *r*, ल् *l*, व् *v*, ज् *j* (Pâṇ. VII. 4, 80).

पू *pû*, पिपावयिषति *pipâvayishati*, (Red. Aor. अपीपवत् *apîpavat*.) See § 375.
भू *bhû*, बिभावयिषति *bibhâvayishati*; (Red. Aor. अबीभवत् *abîbhavat*.)
यु *yu*, यियविषति *yiyavishati*, and Caus. Desid. यियावयिषति *yiyâvayishati*.
जु *ju*, जिजावयिषति *jijâvayishati*, (Red. Aor. अजीजवत् *ajîjavat*.)

But नु *nu*, नुनावयिषति *nunâvayishati*, (Red. Aor. अनूनवत् *anûnavat*.) See § 375†.

§ 475. Roots स्रु *sru*, to flow, श्रु *śru*, to hear, द्रु *dru*, to run, प्रु *pru*, to approach, प्लु *plu*, to swim, च्यु *chyu*, to fall, may under similar circumstances optionally take इ *i* or उ *u* in the reduplicative syllable.

स्रु *sru*, सिस्रावयिषति *sisrâvayishati* or सुस्रावयिषति *susrâvayishati*; but the simple desiderative सुस्रूषति *susrûshati* only.

स्वापय् *svâpay*, the Caus. of स्वप् *svap*, forms सुष्वापयिषति *sushvâpayishati*.

§ 476. Roots beginning with a vowel have a peculiar kind of internal reduplication, to which allusion was made in § 378. Thus (Pâṇ. VI. 1, 2)

अश् *aś* forms अशिश् + इषति *aśiś + ishati*.
अट् *aṭ* forms अटिट् + इषति *aṭiṭ + ishati*.
अक्ष् *aksh* forms अचिक्ष् + इषति *achiksh + ishati*.
उच्छ् *uchchh* forms उचिच्छ् + इषति *uchichchh + ishati*.

---

* Exceptional reduplication occurs in चिकीषति *chikîshati*, besides चिचीषति *chichîshati*, from चि *chi* (Pâṇ. VII. 3, 58); in जिघीषति *jighîshati* from हि *hi* (Pâṇ. VII. 3, 56), &c.

§ 477. If the root ends in a double consonant, the first letter of which is न् *n*, द् *d*, or र् *r*, then the second letter is reduplicated.

अर्च् *arch*, अर्चिचिषति *archich-ishati*.

उन्द् *und*, उन्दिदिषति *undid-ishati*.

उब्ज् *ubj*, उब्जिजिषति *ubjij-ishati*.

In ईर्ष्य् *îrshy* the last consonant is reduplicated.

ईर्ष्य् *îrshy*, ईर्ष्यियिषति *îrshyiy-ishati*.

In the verbs beginning with कण्डूयति *kaṇḍûyati* (§ 498) the final य् *y* is reduplicated.

कण्डूय् *kaṇḍûy*, कण्डूयियिषति *kaṇḍûyiy-ishati*.

CHAPTER XX.

INTENSIVE VERBS.

§ 478. Intensive, or, as they are sometimes called, frequentative bases are meant to convey an intenseness or frequent repetition of the action expressed by the simple verb. Simple verbs, expressive of motion, sometimes receive the idea of tortuous motion, if used as intensives. Some intensive bases convey the idea of reproach or disgrace, &c.

§ 479. Only bases beginning with a consonant, and consisting of one syllable, are liable to be turned into intensive bases. Verbs of the Chur class cannot be changed into intensive verbs. There are, however, some exceptions. Thus अट् *aṭ*, to go, though beginning with a vowel, forms अटाट्यते *aṭâṭyate*, he wanders about; अश् *aś*, to eat, अशाश्यते *aśâśyate;* ऋ *ṛi*, to go, अरार्यते *arâryate* and अरर्ति *ararti* (Siddh.-Kaum. vol. II. p. 216); ऊर्णु *ûrṇu*, to cover, ऊर्णोनूयते *ûrṇonûyate* (Pâṇ. III. 1, 22).

§ 480. There are two ways of forming intensive verbs:

1. By a peculiar reduplication and adding य *ya* at the end.
2. By the same peculiar reduplication without any modification in the final portion of the base. The latter occurs very seldom.

Bases formed in the former way admit of Âtmanepada only.

Ex. भू *bhû*, बोभूयते *bobhûyate*.

Bases formed in the latter way admit of Parasmaipada only, though, according to some grammarians, the Âtmanepada also may be formed.

Ex. भू *bhû*, बोभवीति *bobhavîti* or बोभोति *bobhoti*.

The Âtmanepada would be बोभूते *bobhûte*.

§ 481. When य *ya* is added, the effect on the base is generally the same as in the passive and benedictive Par. (§ 389). Thus final vowels are lengthened: चि *chi*, to gather, चेचीयते *chechîyate;* श्रु *śru*, to hear, शोश्रूयते *śośrûyate*. आ *â* is changed to ई *î:* धा *dhâ*, to place, देधीयते *dedhîyate*. ऋ *ṛî* becomes ईर् *îr*, or, after labials, ऊर् *ûr :* तॄ *tṛî*, to cross, तेतीर्यते *tetîryate;* पॄ *pṛî*, to fill, पोपूर्यते *popûryate*. Final ॠ *ṛî*, however, when following a simple consonant, is changed to री *rî*, not to रि *ri*: कॄ *kṛî*, to do, चेक्रीयते *chekrîyate*. When following a double consonant it is changed to अर् *ar*: स्मॄ *smṛî*, to remember, सास्मर्यते *sâsmaryate*. These intensive bases are conjugated like bases of the Div class in the Âtmanepada. It should be observed, however, that in the general tenses roots ending in vowels retain य् *y* before the intermediate इ *i*, while roots ending in consonants throw off the य *ya* of the special tenses altogether. Thus from बोभूय *bobhûya*, बोभूयिता *bobhû-y-itâ*; from बेभिद्य *bebhidya*, बेभिदिता *bebhiditâ*.

§ 482. When य *ya* is not added, the intensive bases are treated like bases of the Hu class. The rules of reduplication are the same. Observe, however, that verbs with final or penultimate ऋ *ṛi* have peculiar forms of their own (§§ 489, 490), and verbs in ॠ *ṛî* start from a base in अर् *ar*, and therefore have आ *â* in the reduplicative syllable. तॄ *tṛî*, तर् *tar*, तातर्मि *tâtarmi*; 3rd pers. plur. तातिरति *tâtirati*.

§ 483. According to the rules of the Hu class, the weak terminations require Guṇa (§ 297). Hence from बोबुध् *bobudh*, बोबोध्मि *bobodhmi*; but बोबुध्मः *bobudhmaḥ*. From बोभू *bobhû*, बोभोमि *bobhomi*, बोभवानि *bobhavâni*; but बोभूमः *bobhûmaḥ*. Remark, however, that in 1. 2. 3. p. sing. Pres., 2. 3. p. sing. Impf., 3. p. sing. Imp. ई *î* may be optionally inserted:

बोबोध्मि *bobodhmi* or बोबुधीमि *bobudhîmi*; बोभोमि *bobhomi* or बोभवीमि *bobhavîmi*.

And remark further, that before this intermediate ई *î*, and likewise before weak terminations beginning with a vowel, intensive bases ending in consonants do not take Guṇa (Pâṇ. vii. 3, 87). Hence बोबुधीमि *bobudhîmi*, बोबुधानि *bobudhâni*, अबोबुधम् *abobudham*. From विद् *vid*,

Present.	Imperfect.	Imperative.
वेवेद्मि or वेविदीमि *vevedmi* or *vevidîmi*	अवेविदम् *avevidam*	वेविदानि *vevidâni*
वेवेत्सि or वेविदीषि *vevetsi* or *vevidîshi*	अवेवेत् or अवेविदीः *avevet* or *avevidîḥ*	वेविद्धि *veviddhi*
वेवेत्ति or वेविदीति *vevetti* or *vevidîti*	अवेवेत् or अवेविदीत् *avevet* or *avevidît*	वेवेत्तु or वेविदीतु *vevettu* or *vevidîtu*
वेविद्वः *vevidvaḥ*, &c.	अवेविद्व *avevidva*	वेविदाव *vevidâva*

Rules of Reduplication for Intensives.

§ 484. The simplest way to form the peculiar reduplication of intensives, is to take the base used in the general tenses, to change it into a passive base by adding य *ya*, then to reduplicate, according to the general rules of reduplication, and lastly, to raise, where possible, the vowel of the reduplicative syllable by Guṇa (Pâṇ. vii. 4, 82), and अ *a* to आ *â* (Pâṇ. vii. 4, 83).

चि *chi*, to gather, चीय *chîya*, चेचीयते *chechîyate*; चेचेति *checheti*.

क्रुश् *kruś*, to abuse, क्रुश्य *kruśya*, चोक्रुश्यते *chokruśyate*; चोक्रोष्टि *chokroshṭi*.

त्रौक् *trauk*, to approach, त्रौक्य *traukya*, तोत्रौक्यते *totraukyate*; तोत्रौक्ति *totraukti*.
रेक् *rek*, to suspect, रेक्य *rekya*, रेरेक्यते *rerekyate*; रेरेक्ति *rerekti*.
कृ *kṛi*, to do, क्रीय *krîya*, चेक्रीयते *chekrîyate*; चर्कर्ति *charkarti*.
कॄ *kṛî*, to scatter, कीर्य *kîrya*, चेकीर्यते *chekîryate*; चाकर्ति *châkarti*. (§ 482.)
पॄ *pṛî*, to fill, पूर्य *pûrya*, पोपूर्यते *popûryate*; पापर्ति *pâparti*.
स्मृ *smṛi*, to remember, स्मर्य *smarya*, सास्मर्यते *sâsmaryate*; सर्स्मर्ति *sarsmarti**.
दा *dâ*, to give, दीय *dîya*, देदीयते *dedîyate*; दादाति *dâdâti*.
ह्वे *hve*, to call, हूय *hûya*, जोहूयते *johûyate*; जोहोति *johoti*.

§ 485. The roots वंच् *vañch*, स्रंस् *sraṁs*, ध्वंस् *dhvaṁs*, भ्रंस् *bhraṁs*, कस् *kas*, पत् *pat*, पद् *pad*, स्कंद् *skand*, place नी *nî* between the reduplicative syllable and the root. (Pâṇ. VII. 4, 84.)

वंच् *vañch*, to go round, वनीवच्यते *va nî vachyate*; वनीवंचीति *vanîvañchîti*.
स्रंस् *sraṁs*, to tear, सनीस्रस्यते *sa nî srasyate*; सनीस्रंसीति *sanîsraṁsîti*.
ध्वंस् *dhvaṁs*, to fall, दनीध्वस्यते *da nî dhvasyate*; दनीध्वंसीति *danîdhvaṁsîti*.
भ्रंस् *bhraṁs*, to fall, बनीभ्रस्यते *ba nî bhrasyate*; बनीभ्रंसीति *banîbhraṁsîti*.
कस् *kas*, to go, चनीकस्यते *cha nî kasyate*; चनीकसीति *chanîkasîti*.
पत् *pat*, to fly, पनीपत्यते *pa nî patyate*; पनीपतीति *panîpatîti*.
पद् *pad*, to go, पनीपद्यते *pa nî padyate*; पनीपदीति *panîpadîti*.
स्कंद् *skand*, to step, चनीस्कद्यते *cha nî skadyate*; चनीस्कंदीति *chanîskandîti*.

§ 486. Roots ending in a nasal, preceded by अ *a*, repeat the nasal in the reduplicative syllable (Pâṇ. VII. 4, 85). The repeated nasal is treated like म् *m*, and the vowel, being long by position, is not lengthened.

गम् *gam*, to go, जंगम्यते *jaṅgamyate*; जंगमीति *jaṅgamîti*.
भ्रम् *bhram*, to roam, बंभ्रम्यते *bambhramyate*; बंभ्रमीति *bambhramîti*.
हन् *han*, to kill, जंघन्यते *jaṅghanyate*; जंघनीति *jaṅghanîti*.

§ 487. The roots जप् *jap*, to recite, जभ् *jabh*, to yawn, दह् *dah*, to burn, दंश् *daṁś*, to bite, भंज् *bhañj*, to break, पश् *paś*, to bind, insert a nasal in the reduplicative syllable. (Pâṇ. VII. 4, 86.)

जप् *jap*, जंजप्यते *jañjapyate*; जंजपीति *jañjapîti*.
दंश् *daṁś*, दंदश्यते *daṁdaśyate*; दंदशीति *daṁdaśîti*.

§ 488. The roots चर् *char* and फल् *phal* form their intensives as,
चंचूर्यते *chañchûryate* and चंचुरीति *chañchurîti* or चंचूर्ति *chañchûrti*.
पंफुल्यते *pamphulyate* and पंफुलीति *pamphulîti* or पंफुल्ति *pamphulti*. (Pâṇ. VIII. 4, 87.)

§ 489. Roots with penultimate ऋ *ṛi* insert री *rî* in their reduplicative syllable. (Pâṇ. VII. 4, 90.)

वृत् *vṛit*, वरीवृत्यते *va rî vṛityate*; वरीवृतीति *va rî vṛitîti*.

In the Par. these roots allow of six formations. (Pâṇ. VII. 4, 91.)

वर्वृतीति *va r vṛitîti*. वर्वर्ति *varvarti*.

---

* This form follows from Pâṇ. VII. 4, 92, and is supported by the Mâdhavîya-dhâtuvṛitti. Other grammarians give सास्मर्ति *sâsmarti*.

वरिवृतीति *va ri vṛitíti.* वरिवर्ति *varivarti.*
वरीवृतीति *va rí vṛitíti.* वरीवर्ति *varívarti.*

§ 490. The same applies to roots ending in ऋ *ṛi*, if used in the Parasmaipada. (Pâṇ. vii. 4, 92.)

कृ *kṛi*; चर्करीति *cha r karíti.* चर्कर्ति *charkarti.*
चरिकरीति *cha ri karíti.* चरिकर्ति *charikarti.*
चरीकरीति *cha rí karíti.* चरीकर्ति *charíkarti.*

§ 491. A few frequentative bases are peculiar in the formation of their base*.

स्वप् *svap*, to sleep, सोषुप्यते *soshupyate*; but सास्वप्ति *sâsvapti.* (Pâṇ. vi. 1, 19.)
स्यम् *syam*, to sound, सेसिम्यते *sesimyate*; but संस्यन्ति *saṁsyanti.*
व्ये *vye*, to cover, वेवीयते *vevíyate*; but वाव्याति *vâvyâti*; or (§ 483) वाव्येति *vâvyeti.*
वश् *vaś*, to desire, वावश्यते *vâvaśyate*; वावष्टि *vâvashṭi.* (Pâṇ. vi. 1, 20.)
चाय् *chây*, to regard, चेकीयते *chekíyate*; चेकेति *cheketi.* (Pâṇ. vi. 1, 21.)
प्याय् *pyây*, to grow, पेपीयते *pepíyate*; पाप्याति *pâpyâti.* (Pâṇ. vi. 1, 29.)
श्वि *śvi*, to swell, शोशूयते *śośûyate* or शेश्वीयते *śeśvíyate*; शेश्वेति *śeśveti.* (Pâṇ. vi. 1, 30.)
हन् *han*, to kill, जेघ्नीयते *jeghníyate*; जंघन्ति *jaṅghanti.* (Pâṇ. vii. 4, 30, v.)
घ्रा *ghrâ*, to smell, जेघ्रीयते *jeghríyate*; जाघ्राति *jâghrâti.* (Pâṇ. vii. 4, 31.)
ध्मा *dhmâ*, to blow, देध्मीयते *dedhmíyate*; दाध्माति *dâdhmâti.* (Pâṇ. vii. 4, 31.)
गॄ *grí*, to swallow, जेगिल्यते *jegilyate*; जागर्ति *jâgarti.* (Pâṇ. viii. 2, 20.)
शी *śí*, to lie down, शाशय्यते *śâśayyate*; शेशेति *śeśeti.* (Pâṇ. vii. 4, 22.)

§ 492. From derivative verbs new derivatives may be formed, most of which, however, are rather the creation of grammarians, than the property of the spoken language. Thus from भावयति *bhâvayati*, the causal of भू *bhû*, he causes to be, a new desiderative is derived, बिभावयिषति *bibhâvayishati*, he wishes to cause existence. So from the intensive बोभूयते *bobhûyate*, he exists really, is formed बोभूयिषति *bobhûyishati*, he wishes to exist really;

* The formation and conjugation of the Intensive in the Parasmaipada, or the so-called Charkarita, have given rise to a great deal of discussion among native grammarians. According to their theory यङ् *yaṅ*, the sign of the Intensive Âtmanepada, has to be suppressed by लुक् *luk*. By this suppression the changes produced in the verbal base by यङ् *yaṅ* would cease (Pâṇ. i. 1, 63), except certain changes which are considered as Anaṅgakârya, changes not affecting the base, such as reduplication. Changes of the root that are to take place not only in the Intens. Âtm., but also in the Intens. Par., are distinctly mentioned by Pâṇini, vii. 4, 82—92. About other changes, not directly extended to the Intens. Par., grammarians differ. Thus the Prakriyâ-Kaumudî forms सोषोप्ति *soshopti*, because Pâṇ. vi. 1, 19, prescribes सोषुप्यते *soshupyate*; other authorities form only सास्वप्ति *sâsvapti* or सास्वपीति *sâsvapîti*. Colebrooke allows चेकेति *cheketi* (p. 332), because Pâṇ. vi. 1, 21, prescribes चेकीयते *chekíyate*, and the commentary argues in favour of चेकेति *cheketi*. But Colebrooke (p. 321) declines to form सेसिंते *sesiṅte*, because it is in the Âtm. only that Pâṇ. vi. 1, 19, allows सेसिम्यते *sesimyate*. Whether the Perfect should be periphrastic or reduplicated is likewise a moot-point among grammarians; some forming बोभवांचकार *bobhavâñchakâra*, others बोभूव *bobhûva*, others बोभाव *bobhâva*.

then a new causative may be formed, बोभूयिषयति *bobhûyishayati*, he causes a wish to exist really; and again a new desiderative, बोभूयिषयिषति *bobhûyishayishati*, he wishes to excite the desire of real existence.

CHAPTER XXI.

DENOMINATIVE VERBS.

§ 493. There are many verbs in Sanskrit which are clearly derived from nominal bases*, and which generally have the meaning of behaving like, or treating some one like, or wishing for or doing whatever is expressed by the noun. Thus from श्येन *śyena*, hawk, we have श्येनायते *śyenâyate*, he behaves like a hawk; from पुत्र *putra*, son, पुत्रीयति *putrîyati*, he treats some one like a son, or he wishes for a son. Some denominatives are formed without any derivative syllable. Thus from कृष्ण *kṛishṇa*, कृष्णति *kṛishṇati*, he behaves like Kṛishṇa; from पितृ *pitṛi*, father, पितरति *pitarati*, he behaves like a father.

These denominative verbs, however, cannot be formed at pleasure; and many even of those which would be sanctioned by the rules of native grammarians, are of rare occurrence in the national literature of India. These verbs should therefore be looked for in the dictionary rather than in a grammar. A few rules, however, on their formation and general meaning, may here be given.

Denominatives in य ya, *Parasmaipada.*

§ 494. By adding य *ya* to the base of a noun, denominatives are formed expressing a wish. From गो *go*, cow, गव्यति *gavyati*, he wishes for cows. These verbs might be called nominal desideratives, and they never govern a new accusative.

§ 495. By adding the same य *ya*, denominatives are formed expressing one's looking upon or treating something like the subject expressed by the noun. Thus from पुत्र *putra*, son, पुत्रीयति शिष्यं *putrîyati śishyam*, he treats the pupil like a son. By a similar process प्रासादीयति *prâsâdîyati*, from प्रासाद *prâsâda*, palace, means to behave as if one were in a palace; प्रासादीयति कुट्यां भिक्षुः *prâsâdîyati kuṭyâm bhikshuḥ*, the beggar lives in his hut as if it were a palace.

§ 496. Before this य *ya*,

1. Final अ *a* and आ *â* are changed to ई *î*; सुता *sutâ*, daughter, सुतीयति *sutîyati*, he wishes for a daughter†.

---

* They are called in Sanskrit लिधु *lidhu*, from लिङ्ग *liṅga*, it is said, a crude sound, and धु *dhu*, for धातु *dhâtu*, root. (Carey, Grammar, p. 543.)

† Minute distinctions are made between अशनीयति *aśanîyati*, he wishes to eat at the proper time, and अशनायति *aśanâyati*, he is ravenously hungry; between उदकीयति *udakîyati*, he wishes for water, and उदन्यति *udanyati*, he starves and craves for water; between धनायति *dhanâyati*, he is greedy for wealth, and धनीयति *dhanîyati*, he asks for some money. (Pâṇ. VII. 4, 34.)

2. इ *i* and उ *u* are lengthened; पति *pati*, master, पतीयति *patíyati*, he treats like a master; कवि *kavi*, poet, कवीयति *kavíyati*, he wishes to be a poet.
3. ऋ *ṛi* becomes री *rí*, ओ *o* becomes अव् *av*, औ *au* becomes आव् *âv*; पितृ *pitṛi*, father, पित्रीयति *pitríyati*, he treats like a father; नौ *nau*, ship, नाव्यति *návyati*, he wishes for a ship.
4. Final न् *n* is dropt, and other final consonants remain unchanged; राजन् *rájan*, king, राजीयति *rájíyati*, he treats like a king; पयस् *payas*, milk, पयस्यति *payasyati*, he wishes for milk; वाच् *vách*, speech, वाच्यति *váchyati* (Pâṇ. I. 4, 15); नमस् *namas*, worship, नमस्यति *namasyati*, he worships (Pâṇ. III. 1, 19).

Denominatives in य ya, *Âtmanepada.*

§ 497. A second class of denominatives, formed by adding य *ya*, has the meaning of behaving like, or becoming like, or actually doing what is expressed by the noun. They differ from the preceding class by generally following the Âtmanepada *, and by a difference in the modification of the final letters of the nominal base. Thus

1. Final अ *a* is lengthened; श्येन *śyena*, hawk, श्येनायते *śyenáyate*, he behaves like a hawk; शब्द *śabda*, sound, शब्दायते *śabdáyate*, he makes a sound, he sounds; भृश *bhṛiśa*, much, भृशायते *bhṛiśáyate*, he becomes much; कष्ट *kashṭa*, mischief, कष्टायते *kashṭáyate*, he plots; रोमन्थ *romantha*, ruminating, रोमन्थायते *romantháyate*, he ruminates. The final ई *í* of feminine bases is generally dropt, and the masculine base taken instead; कुमारी *kumárí*, girl, कुमारायते *kumáráyate*, he behaves like a girl. (Pâṇ. VI. 3, 36–41.)
2 and 3. Final इ *i* and उ *u*, ऋ *ṛi*, ओ *o*, औ *au* are treated as in § 496; शुचि *śuchi*, pure, शुचीयते *śuchíyate*, he becomes pure.
4. Final न् *n* is dropt, and the preceding vowel is lengthened; राजन् *rájan*, king, राजायते *rájáyate*, he behaves like a king; उष्मन् *ushman*, heat, उष्मायते *ushmáyate*, it sends out heat.

Some nominal bases in स् *s* and त् *t* may, others must (Pâṇ. III. 1, 11) be treated like nominal bases in अ *a*. Hence from विद्वस् *vidvas*, wise, विद्वस्यते *vidvasyate* or विद्वायते *vidváyate*, he behaves like a wise man; from पयस् *payas*, milk, पयस्यते *payasyate* or पयायते *payáyate*, it becomes milk; from अप्सरस् *apsaras*, अप्सरायते *apsaráyate*, she behaves like an Apsaras; from बृहत् *bṛihat*, great, बृहायते *bṛiháyate*, he becomes great. (Pâṇ. III. 1, 12.)

§ 498. Some verbs are classed together by native grammarians as

---

* Those that may take both Parasmaipada and Âtmanepada are said to be formed by क्यष् *kyash*, the rest by क्यङ् *kyaṅ*. Thus from लोहित *lohita*, red, लोहितायति or °ते *lohitáyati* or -*te*, he becomes red. (Pâṇ. III. 1, 13.)

Kaṇḍvâdi's, i. e. beginning with Kaṇḍû. They take य *ya*, both in Parasmaipada and Âtmanepada, and keep it through the general tenses under the restrictions applying to other denominatives in य *ya* (§ 501). Nouns ending in अ *a* drop it before य *ya*. Thus from अगद *agada*, free from illness, अगद्यति *agadyati*, he is free from illness; from सुख *sukha*, pleasure, सुख्यति *sukhyati*, he gives pleasure; from कंडू *kaṇḍû*, scratching, कंडूयति or °ते *kaṇḍûyati* or *-te*, he scratches.

Denominatives in स्य sya.

§ 499. Certain denominative verbs, which express a wish, take स्य *sya* instead of य *ya*. Thus from क्षीर *kshîra*, milk, क्षीरस्यति *kshîrasyati*, the child longs for milk; from लवण *lavaṇa*, salt, लवणस्यति *lavaṇasyati*, he desires salt. Likewise अश्वस्यति *aśvasyati*, the mare longs for the horse; वृषस्यति *vṛishasyati*, the cow longs for the bull (Pâṇ. vii. 1, 52). Some authorities admit स्य *sya* and अस्य *asya*, in the sense of extreme desire, after all nominal bases. Thus from मधु *madhu*, honey, मधुस्यति *madhusyati* or मध्वस्यति *madhvasyati*, he longs for honey.

Denominatives in काम्य kâmya.

§ 500. It is usual to form desiderative verbs by compounding a nominal base with काम्य *kâmya*, a denominative from काम *kâma*, love. Thus पुत्रकाम्यति *putrakâmyati*, he has the wish for a son; Fut. पुत्रकाम्यिता *putrakâmyitâ*. Here the य् *y*, it is said, is not liable to be dropt. (Siddh.-Kaum. vol. ii. p. 222.)

§ 501. The denominatives in य *ya* are conjugated like verbs of the Bhû class in the Parasmaipada and Âtmanepada. Pres. पुत्रीयामि *putrîyâmi*, Impf. अपुत्रीयम् *aputrîyam*, Imp. पुत्रीयाणि *putrîyâṇi*, Opt. पुत्रीयेयम् *putrîyeyam*. Pres. श्येनाये *śyenâye*, Impf. अश्येनाये *aśyenâye*, Imp. श्येनायै *śyenâyai*, Opt. श्येनायेय *śyenâyeya*. In the general tenses the base is पुत्रीय् *putrîy* or श्येनाय् *śyenây*; but when the denominative य् *y* is preceded by a consonant, य् *y* may or may not be dropt in the general tenses (Pâṇ. vi. 4, 50). Hence, Per. Perf. पुत्रीयामास *putrîyâmâsa* (§ 325, 3), Aor. अपुत्रीयिषम् *aputrîyisham*, Fut. पुत्रीयिष्यामि *putrîyishyâmi*, Per. Fut. पुत्रीयिता *putrîyitâ*, Ben. पुत्रीयासम् *putrîyâsam*.

From श्येनायते *śyenâyate*, Per. Perf. श्येनायामास *śyenâyâmâsa*, Aor. अश्येनायिषि *aśyenâyishi*, Fut. श्येनायिष्ये *śyenâyishye*, &c.

From समिध् *samidh*, fuel, समिध्यति *samidhyati*, he wishes for fuel; Per. Fut. समिध्यिता *samidhyitâ* or समिधिता *samidhitâ*, &c. (Pâṇ. vi. 4, 50).

Denominatives in अय aya.

§ 502. Some denominative verbs are formed by adding अय *aya* to certain nominal bases. They generally express the act implied by the nominal base. They may be looked upon as verbs of the Chur class. They are conjugated in the Parasmaipada and Âtmanepada, some in the Âtmanepada only. They retain अय् *ay* in the general tenses under the limitations that apply to verbs of the Chur class and causatives (viz. benedictive Par., reduplicated aorist, &c.), and their radical vowels are modified according to the rules applying to the verbs of the Chur class (§ 296, 4).

Thus from पाश *pâśa*, fetter, विपाशयति *vipâśayati*, he unties; from वर्मन् *varman*, armour, संवर्मयति *saṁvarmayati*, he arms, (the final न् *n* being dropt); from मुण्ड *muṇḍa*, shaven, मुण्डयति *muṇḍayati*, he shaves; from शब्द *śabda*, sound, शब्दयति *śabdayati*, he makes a sound (Dhâtupâṭha 33, 40); from मिश्र *miśra*, mixed, मिश्रयति *miśrayati*, he mixes (Pâṇ. III. 1, 21; 25).

Some of these verbs are always Âtmanepada. Thus from पुच्छ *puchchha*, tail, उत्पुच्छयते *utpuchchhayate*, he lifts up the tail (Pâṇ. III. 1, 20).

If अय *aya* is to be added to nouns formed by the secondary affixes मत् *mat*, वत् *vat*, मिन् *min*, विन् *vin*, these affixes must be dropt. From स्रग्विन् *sragvin*, having garlands, स्रजयति *srajayati*.

If अय *aya* is added to feminine bases, they are generally replaced by the corresponding masculine base. From श्येनी *śyenî* (§ 247), white, श्येतयति *śyetayati*, he makes her white (Pâṇ. VI. 3, 36).

Certain adjectives which change their base before इष्ठ *ishṭha* of the superlative, do the same before अय *aya*. मृदु *mṛidu*, soft, म्रदयति *mradayati*, he softens; दूर *dûra*, far, दवयति *davayati*, he removes.

Some nominal bases take आपय *âpaya*. Thus from सत्य *satya*, true, सत्यापयति *satyâpayati*, he speaks truly; from अर्थ *artha*, sense, अर्थापयति *arthâpayati*, he explains.

Denominatives without any Affix.

§ 503. According to some authorities every nominal base may be turned into a denominative verb by adding the ordinary verbal terminations of the First Division, and treating the base like a verbal base of the Bhû class. अ *a* is added to the base, except where it exists already as the final of the nominal base; other final and medial vowels take Guṇa, where possible, as in the Bhû class.

Thus from कृष्ण *kṛishṇa*, कृष्णति *kṛishṇati*, he behaves like Kṛishṇa; from माला *mâlâ*, garland, मालाति *mâlâti*, it is like a garland, Impf. अमालात् *amâlât*, Aor. अमालासीत् *amâlâsît*; from कवि *kavi*, poet, कवयति *kavayati*, he behaves like a poet; from वि *vi*, bird, वयति *vayati*, he flies like a bird; from पितृ *pitṛi*, father, पितरति *pitarati*, he is like a father; from राजन् *râjan*, king, राजानति *râjânati*, he is like a king (Pâṇ. VI. 4, 15).

CHAPTER XXII.

PREPOSITIONS AND PARTICLES.

§ 504. The following prepositions may be joined with verbs, and are then called *Upasarga* in Sanskrit (Pâṇ. I. 4, 59).

अति *ati*, beyond. अधि *adhi*, over; (sometimes धि *dhi*.) अनु *anu*, after. अप *apa*, off. अपि *api*, upon; (sometimes पि *pi*.) अभि *abhi*, towards. अव *ava*, down; (sometimes व *va*.) आ *â*, near to. उद् *ud*, up. उप *upa*, next, below. दुः *duḥ*, ill. नि *ni*, into, downwards. निः *niḥ*, without. परा *parâ*, back, away. परि *pari*, around. प्र *pra*, before. प्रति *prati*, back. वि *vi*, apart. सं *sam*, together. सु *su*, well.

§ 505. Certain adverbs, called *Gati* in Sanskrit, a term applicable also to the *Upasargas* (Pâṇ. I. 4, 60), may be prefixed, like prepositions, to certain verbs, particularly to भू *bhû*, to be, अस् *as*, to be, कृ *kṛi*, to do, and गम् *gam*, to go.

अच्छ *achchha*; e. g. अच्छगत्य *achchhagatya*, having approached (§ 445); अच्छोद्य *achchhodya*, having addressed. अदः *adaḥ*; e. g. अदःकृत्य *adaḥkṛitya*, having done it thus. अंतर् *antar*; e. g. अंतरित्य *antaritya*, having passed between. अलं *alam*; e. g. अलंकृत्य *alaṅkṛitya*, having ornamented. अस्तं *astam*; e. g. अस्तंगत्य *astaṅgatya*, having gone to rest, having set. आविः *âviḥ*; e. g. आविर्भूय *âvirbhûya*, having appeared. तिरः *tiraḥ*; e. g. तिरोभूय *tirobhûya*, having disappeared. पुरः *puraḥ*; e. g. पुरस्कृत्य *puraskṛitya*, having placed before (§ 89, II. 1). प्रादुः *prâduḥ*; e. g. प्रादुर्भूय *prâdurbhûya*, having become manifest. सत् *sat* and असत् *asat*, when expressing regard or contempt; e. g. असत्कृत्य *asatkṛitya*, having disregarded. साक्षात् *sâkshât*; e. g. साक्षात्कृत्य *sâkshâtkṛitya*, having made known. Words like शुक्ली *śuklî*, in शुक्लीकृत्य *śuklîkṛitya*, having made white. (Here the final अ *a* of शुक्ल *śukla* is changed to ई *î*. Sometimes, but rarely, final अ *a* or आ *â* is changed to आ *â*. Final इ *i* and उ *u* are lengthened; ऋ *ṛi* is changed to री *rî*; final अन् *an* and अस् *as* are changed to ई *î*; e. g. राजीकृत्य *râjîkṛitya*, having made king.) Words like ऊरी *ûrî*, in ऊरीकृत्य *ûrîkṛitya*, having assented. Words like खाट् *khâṭ*, imitative of sound; e. g. खाट्कृत्य *khâṭkṛitya*, having made *khâṭ*, the sound produced in clearing one's throat.

§ 506. Several of the prepositions mentioned in § 503 are also used with nouns, and are then said to govern certain cases. They are then called *Karmapravachanîya*, and they frequently follow the noun which is governed by them (Pâṇ. I. 4, 83).

The accusative is governed by अति *ati*, beyond; अभि *abhi*, towards; परि *pari*, around; प्रति *prati*, against; अनु *anu*, after; उप *upa*, upon. Ex. गोविंदमति नेश्वरः *govindam ati neśvaraḥ*, Iśvara is not beyond Govinda; हरं प्रति

हरं प्रति हलाहलम् *haram prati halâhalam*, venom was for Hara; विष्णुमन्वर्च्यते *vishṇu-manvarchyate*, he is worshipped after Vishṇu; अनु हरिं सुराः *anu harim surâḥ*, the gods are less than Hari.

The ablative is governed by प्रति *prati*, परि *pari*, अप *apa*, आ *â*. Ex. भक्तेः प्रत्यमृतं *bhakteḥ praty amṛitam*, immortality in return for faith; आ मृत्योः *â mṛityoḥ*, until death; अप त्रिगर्तेभ्यो वृष्टो देवः *apa trigartebhyo vṛishṭo devaḥ*, it has rained away from Trigarta, or परि त्रिगर्तेभ्यः *pari trigartebhyaḥ*, round Trigarta, without touching Trigarta.

The locative is governed by उप *upa* and अधि *adhi*. Ex. उप निष्के कार्षापणं *upa nishke kârshâpaṇam*, a Kârshâpaṇa is more than a Nishka; अधि पंचालेषु ब्रह्मदत्तः *adhi pañchâleshu brahmadattaḥ*, Brahmadatta governs over the Pañchâlas.

§ 507. There are many other adverbs in Sanskrit, some of which may here be mentioned.

1. The accusative of adjectives in the neuter may be used as an adverb. Thus from मंदः *mandaḥ*, slow, मंदं मंदं *mandam mandam*, slowly, slowly; शीघ्रं *śîghram*, quickly; ध्रुवं *dhruvam*, truly.

2. Certain compounds, ending like accusatives of neuters, are used adverbially, such as यथाशक्ति *yathâśakti*, according to one's power. For these see the rules on composition.

3. Adverbs of place:

अंतर् *antar*, within, with loc. and gen.; between, with acc. अंतरा *antarâ*, between, with acc. अंतरेण *antareṇa*, between, with acc.; without, with acc. आरात् *ârât*, far off, with abl. वहिः *vahiḥ*, outside, with abl. समया *samayâ*, near, with acc. निकषा *nikashâ*, near, with acc. उपरि *upari*, above, over, with acc. and gen. उच्चैः *uchchaiḥ*, high, or loud. नीचैः *nîchaiḥ*, low. अधः *adhaḥ*, below, with gen. and abl. अवः *avaḥ*, below, with gen. तिरः *tiraḥ*, across, with acc. or loc. इह *iha*, here. पुरा *purâ*, before. समक्षं *samaksham*, साक्षात् *sâkshât*, in the presence. सकाशात् *sakâśât*, from. पुरः *puraḥ*, before, with gen. अमा *amâ*, सचा *sachâ*, साकं *sâkam*, समा *samâ*, सार्धं *sârdham*, together, with instr. अभितः *abhitaḥ*, on all sides, with acc. उभयतः *ubhayataḥ*, on both sides, with acc. समंतात् *samantât*, from all sides. दूरं *dûram*, far, with acc., abl., and gen. अंतिकं *antikam*, near, with acc., abl., and gen. ऋधक् *ṛidhak*, पृथक् *pṛithak*, apart.

4. Adverbs of time:

प्रातर् *prâtar*, early. सायं *sâyam*, at eve. दिवा *divâ*, by day. अह्नाय *ahnâya*, by day. दोषा *doshâ*, by night. नक्तं *naktam*, by night. उषा *ushâ*, early. युगपद् *yugapad*, at the same time. अद्य *adya*, to-day. ह्यः *hyaḥ*, yesterday. पूर्वेद्युः *pûrvedyuḥ*, yesterday. श्वः *śvaḥ*, to-morrow. परेद्यवि *paredyavi*, to-morrow. ज्योक् *jyok*, long. चिरं *chiram*, चिरेण *chireṇa*, चिराय *chirâya*, चिरात् *chirât*, चिरस्य *chirasya*, long. सना *sanâ*, सनात् *sanât*, सनत् *sanat*, perpetually. अरं *aram*, quickly. शनैः *śanaiḥ*, slowly. सद्यः *sadyaḥ*, at once. संप्रति *samprati*, now. पुनर् *punar*, मुहुः *muhuḥ*, भूयः *bhûyaḥ*, वारं *vâram*, again. सकृत् *sakṛit*, once. पुरा *purâ*, formerly. पूर्वं *pûrvam*, before. ऊर्ध्वं *ûrdhvam*, after. सपदि *sapadi*, immediately. पश्चात् *paśchât*, after, with abl. जातु *jâtu*, once upon a time, ever. अधुना *adhunâ*, now. इदानीं *idânîm*, now. सदा *sadâ*, संततं *santatam*, अनिशं *aniśam*, always. अलं *alam*, enough, with dat. or instr.

5. Adverbs of circumstance:

मृषा *mṛishâ*, मिथ्या *mithyâ*, falsely. मनाक् *manâk*, ईषत् *îshat*, a little. तूष्णीं *tûshṇîm*, quietly. वृथा *vṛithâ*, मुधा *mudhâ*, in vain. सामि *sâmi*, half. अकस्मात् *akasmât*, unexpectedly. उपांशु *upâṁśu*, in a whisper. मिथः *mithaḥ*, together. प्रायः *prâyaḥ*, frequently, almost. अतीव *atîva*, exceedingly. कामं *kâmam*, जोषं *josham*, gladly. अवश्यं *avaśyam*, certainly. किल *kila*, indeed. खलु *khalu*, certainly. विना *vinâ*, without, with acc., instr., or abl. ऋते *ṛite*, without, with acc. or abl. नाना *nânâ*, variously. सुष्ठु *sushṭhu*, well. दुष्ठु *dushṭhu*, badly. दिष्ट्या *dishṭyâ*, luckily. प्रभृति *prabhṛiti*, et cetera, and the rest, with abl. कुवित् *kuvit*, really? कच्चित् *kachchit*, really? कथं *katham*, how? इति *iti*, इत्थं *ittham*, thus. इव *iva*, as; हरिरिव *harir iva*, like Hari. वत् *vat*, enclitic; हरिवत् *harivat*, like Hari.

Conjunctions and other Particles.

§ 508. अथ *atha*, अथो *atho*, now then. इति *iti*, thus. यदि *yadi*, when. यद्यपि *yadyapi*, although. तथापि *tathâpi*, yet. चेत् *chet*, if. न *na*, नो *no*, not. च *cha*, and, always enclitic, like *que*. किंच *kiṁcha*, and. मा *mâ* or मा स्म *mâ sma*, not, prohibitively. वा *vâ*, or. वा—वा *vâ—vâ*, either—or. अथवा *athavâ*, or. एव *eva*, even, very; (स एव *sa eva*, the same.) एवं *evam*, thus. नूनं *nûnam*, doubtlessly. यावत्—तावत् *yâvat—tâvat*, as much as. यथा *yathâ*—तथा *tathâ*, as—so. येन *yena*—तेन *tena*, यद् *yad*—तद् *tad*, and other correlatives, because—therefore. तथाहि *tathâhi*, thus, for. तु *tu*, परं *param*, किंतु *kintu*, but. चित् *chit*, चन *chana*, subjoined to the interrogative pronoun किं *kim*, any, some; as कश्चित् *kaśchit*, some one; कथंचन *kathañchana*, anyhow. हि *hi*, for, because. उत *uta*, उताहो *utâho*, or. नाम *nâma*, namely. प्रत्युत *pratyuta*, on the contrary. नु *nu*, perhaps. ननु *nanu*, Is it not? स्वित् *svit*, किंस्वित् *kiṁsvit*, perhaps. अपि *api*, also, even. अपि च *api cha*, again. नूनं *nûnam*, certainly.

Interjections.

§ 509. हे *he*, भो *bho*, vocative particles. अये *aye*, हये *haye*, Ah! धिक् *dhik*, रे *re*, अरे *are*, Fie!

CHAPTER XXIII.

COMPOUND WORDS.

§ 510. The power of forming two or more words into one, which belongs to all Aryan languages, has been so largely developed in Sanskrit that a few of the more general rules of composition claim a place even in an elementary grammar.

As a general rule, all words which form a compound drop their inflectional terminations, except the last. They appear in that form which is called their base, and when they have more than one, in their Pada base (§ 180). Hence देवदासः *deva-dásaḥ*, a servant of god; राजपुरुषः *rájapurushaḥ*, a king's man; प्रत्यग्मुखः *pratyagmukhaḥ*, facing west.

§ 511. Sometimes the sign of the feminine gender in the prior elements of a compound may be retained. This is chiefly the case when the feminine is treated as an appellative, and would lose its distinctive meaning by losing the feminine suffix: कल्याणीमाता *kalyáṇímátá*, the mother of a beautiful daughter (Pâṇ. VI. 3, 34); कठीभार्यः *kaṭhíbháryaḥ*, having a Kaṭhî for one's wife (Pâṇ. VI. 3, 41). If the feminine forms a mere predicate, it generally loses its feminine suffix; शोभनभार्यः *śobhanabháryaḥ*, having a beautiful wife (Pâṇ. VI. 3, 34; 42).

The phonetic rules to be observed are those of external Sandhi with certain modifications, as explained in §§ 24 seq.*

§ 512. Compound words might have been divided into substantival, adjectival, and adverbial. Thus words like तत्पुरुषः *tatpurushaḥ*, his man, नीलोत्पलं *nílotpalam*, blue lotus, द्विगवं *dvigavam*, two oxen, अग्निधूमौ *agni-dhúmau*, fire and smoke, might have been classed as substantival; बहुव्रीहिः *bahuvríhiḥ*, possessing much rice, as an adjectival; and यथाशक्ति *yathâśakti*, according to one's strength, as an adverbial compound.

Native grammarians, however, have adopted a different principle of division, classing all compounds under six different heads, under the names of *Tatpurusha*, *Karmadháraya*, *Dvigu*, *Dvandva*, *Bahuvríhi*, and *Avyayíbháva*.

---

* Occasionally bases ending in a long vowel shorten it, and bases ending in a short vowel lengthen it in the middle of a compound; उदक *udaka*, water, पाद *páda*, foot, हृदय *hṛidaya*, heart, frequently substitute the bases उदन् *udan* (i. e. उद *uda*), पद् *pad*, and हृद् *hṛid*. हृद्रोगः *hṛidrogaḥ*, heart-disease, or हृदयरोगः *hṛidayarogaḥ*. (Pâṇ. VI. 3, 51—60.)

The particle कु *ku*, which is intended to express contempt, as कुब्राह्मणः *kubráhmaṇaḥ*, a bad Bráhman, substitutes कद् *kad* in a determinative compound before words beginning with consonants: कदुष्ट्रः *kadushṭraḥ*, a bad camel. The same takes place before रथ *ratha*, वद *vada*, and तृण *tṛiṇa*: कद्रथः *kadrathaḥ*, a bad carriage; कत्तृणं *kattṛiṇam*, a bad kind of grass. The same particle is changed to का *ká* before पथिन् *pathin* and अक्ष *aksha*: कापथः *kápathaḥ*, and optionally before पुरुष *purusha*. (Pâṇ. VI. 3, 101—107.)

I. *Tatpurusha* is a compound in which the last word is determined by the preceding words, for instance, तत्पुरुषः *tat-purushaḥ*, his man, or राजपुरुषः *rája-purushaḥ*, king's man.

As a general term the *Tatpurusha* compound comprehends the two subdivisions of *Karmadháraya* (I *b*) and *Dvigu* (I *c*). The Karmadháraya is in fact a Tatpurusha compound, in which the last word is determined by a preceding adjective, e.g. नीलोत्पलं *nîlotpalam*, blue lotus. The component words, if dissolved, would stand in the same case, whereas in other Tatpurushas the preceding word is governed by the last, the man of the king, or fire-wood, i. e. wood for fire.

The *Dvigu* again may be called a subdivision of the Karmadhâraya, being a compound in which the first word is not an adjective in general, but always a numeral: द्विगवं *dvigavam*, two oxen, or द्विगुः *dviguḥ*, bought for two oxen.

These three classes of compounds may be comprehended under the general name of *Determinative Compounds*, while the Karmadhâraya (I *b*) may be distinguished as *appositional* determinatives, the Dvigu (I *c*) as *numeral* determinatives.

II. The next class, called *Dvandva*, consists of compounds in which two words are simply joined together, the compound taking either the terminations of the dual or plural, according to the number of compounded nouns, or the terminations of the singular, being treated as a collective term: अग्निधूमौ *agni-dhûmau*, fire and smoke; शशकुशपलाशाः *śaśa-kuśa-palâśâḥ*, nom. plur. masc. three kinds of plants, or शशकुशपलाशं *śaśa-kuśa-palâśam*, nom. sing. neut. They will be called *Collective Compounds*.

III. The next class, called *Bahuvrîhi* by native grammarians, comprises compounds which are used as adjectives. The notion expressed by the last word, and which may be variously determined, forms the predicate of some other subject. They may be called *Possessive Compounds*. Thus बहुव्रीहिः *bahu-vrîhiḥ*, possessed of much rice, scil. देशः *deśaḥ*, country; रूपवद्भार्यः *rûpavad-bhâryaḥ*, possessing a handsome wife, scil. राजा *rájá*, king.

Determinative compounds may be turned into possessive compounds, sometimes without any change, except that of accent, sometimes by slight changes in the last word.

The gender of possessive compounds, like that of adjectives, conforms to the gender of the substantives to which they belong.

IV. The last class, called *Avyayîbháva*, is formed by joining an indeclinable particle with another word. The resulting compound, in which the indeclinable particle always forms the first element, is again indeclinable, and generally ends, like adverbs, in the ordinary terminations of the nom. or acc. neut.: अधिस्त्रि *adhi-stri*, for woman, as in अधिस्त्रि गृहकार्याणि *adhistri gṛihakâryâṇi*, household duties are for women. They may be called *Adverbial Compounds*.

I. *Determinative Compounds.*

§ 513. This class (Tatpurusha) comprehends compounds in which generally the last word governs the preceding one. The last word may be a substantive or a participle or an adjective, if capable of governing a noun.

1. Compounds in which the first noun would be in the Accusative:

कृष्णश्रितः *kṛishṇa-śritaḥ*, m. f. n. gone to Kṛishṇa, dependent on Kṛishṇa, instead of कृष्णं श्रितः *kṛishṇam śritaḥ*. दुःखातीतः *duḥkha-atîtaḥ*, m. f. n. having overcome pain, instead of दुःखमतीतः *duḥkham atîtaḥ*. वर्षभोग्यः *varsha-bhogyaḥ*, m. f. n. to be enjoyed a year long. ग्रामप्राप्तः *grâma-prâptaḥ*, m. f. n. having reached the village, instead of ग्रामं प्राप्तः *grâmam prâptaḥ*: it is more usual, however, to say प्राप्तग्रामः *prâptagrâmaḥ* (Pâṇ. II. 2, 4). Similarly are formed determinatives by means of adverbs or prepositions, such as अतिगिरि *atigiri*, past the hill, used as an adverb, or as an adjective, अतिगिरिः *atigiriḥ*, ultramontane; अभिमुखं *abhimukham*, facing, &c.

2. Compounds in which the first noun would be in the Instrumental:

धान्यार्थः *dhânya-arthaḥ*, m. wealth (*arthaḥ*) (acquired) by grain (*dhânyena*). शङ्कुलाखण्डः *śaṅkulâ-khaṇḍaḥ*, m. a piece (*khaṇḍaḥ*) (cut) by nippers (*śaṅkulâbhiḥ*). दात्रच्छिन्नः *dâtra-chchhinnaḥ*, m. f. n. cut (*chhinnaḥ*) by a knife (*dâtreṇa*). हरित्रातः *hari-trâtaḥ*, m. f. n. protected (*trâtaḥ*) by Hari. देवदत्तः *deva-dattaḥ*, given (*dattaḥ*) by the gods (*devaiḥ*), or as a proper name with the supposed auspicious sense, may the gods give him (*Dieu-donné*). पितृसमः *pitṛi-samaḥ*, m. f. n. like the father, i. e. *pitrâ samaḥ*. नखनिर्भिन्नः *nakha-nirbhinnaḥ*, m. f. n. cut asunder (*nirbhinnaḥ*) by the nails (*nakhaiḥ*). विश्वोपास्यः *viśva-upâsyaḥ*, m. f. n. to be worshipped by all. स्वयंकृतः *svayam-kṛitaḥ*, m. f. n. done by oneself.

3. Compounds in which the first noun would be in the Dative:

यूपदारु *yûpa-dâru*, n. wood (*dâru*) for a sacrificial stake (*yûpâya*). गोहितः *go-hitaḥ*, m. f. n. good (*hitaḥ*) for cows (*gobhyaḥ*). द्विजार्थः *dvija-arthaḥ*, m. f. n. object (*artha*), i. e. intended for Brâhmans. Determinative compounds, when treated as possessive, take the terminations of the masc., fem., and neut.; e. g. द्विजार्था यवागूः *dvijârthâ yavâgûḥ*, fem. gruel for Brâhmans.

4. Compounds in which the first noun would be in the Ablative:

चोरभयः *chora-bhayaḥ*, m. fear (*bhayaḥ*) arising from thieves (*chorebhyaḥ*). स्वर्गपतितः *svarga-patitaḥ*, m. f. n. fallen from heaven. अपग्रामः *apa-grâmaḥ*, m. f. n. gone from the village.

5. Compounds in which the first noun would be in the Genitive:

- तत्पुरुषः *tat-purushaḥ*, m. his man, instead of *tasya*, of him, *purushaḥ*, the man*. राजपुरुषः *râja-purushaḥ*, m. the king's man, instead of *râjñaḥ*, of the king, *purushaḥ*, the man. राजसखः *râja-sakhaḥ*, m. the king's friend. In these compounds *sakhi*, friend, is changed to *sakhaḥ*. कुम्भकारः *kumbha-káraḥ*, a maker (*kâraḥ*) of pots (*kumbhânâm*). गोशतं *go-śatam*, a hundred of cows.

6. Compounds in which the first noun would be in the Locative:

अक्षशौण्डः *aksha-śauṇḍaḥ*, m. f. n. devoted to dice. उरोजः *uro-jaḥ*, m. f. n. produced on the breast.

§ 514. Certain Tatpurusha compounds retain the case-terminations in the governed noun.

सहसाकृतः *sahasâ-kritaḥ*, done suddenly (Pâṇ. VI. 3, 3). आत्मनाषष्ठः *âtmanâ-shashṭhaḥ*, the sixth with oneself (Pâṇ. VI. 3, 6). अक्ष्णाकाणः *akshṇâ-kâṇaḥ*, blind in the eye. परस्मैपदं *parasmai-padam*, a word for the sake of another, i. e. the transitive form of verbs (Pâṇ. VI. 3, 7, 8). कृच्छ्राल्लब्धं *krichchhrâl-labdham*, obtained with difficulty. स्वसुःपुत्रः *svasuḥ-putraḥ*, sister's son (Pâṇ. VI. 3, 23). दिवस्पतिः *divas-patiḥ*, lord of heaven. वाचस्पतिः *vâchas-patiḥ*, lord of speech. देवानांप्रियः *devânâm-priyaḥ*, beloved of the gods, a goat, an ignorant person. गेहेपण्डितः *gehe-paṇḍitaḥ*, learned at home, i. e. where no one can contradict him. खेचरः *khecharaḥ*, moving in the air. सरसिजः *sarasi-jaḥ*, born in a pond, water-lily. हृदिस्पृश् *hridi-spriś*, touching the heart. युधिष्ठिरः *yudhishṭhiraḥ*, firm in battle, a proper name (Pâṇ. VI. 3, 9).

§ 515. To this class a number of compounds are referred in which the governing element is supposed to take the first place. Ex. पूर्वकायः *pûrva-kâyaḥ*, the fore-part of the body, i. e. the fore-body; पूर्वरात्रः *pûrva-râtraḥ*, the first part of the night, i. e. the fore-night; राजदन्तः *râjadantaḥ*, the king of teeth, lit. the king-teeth, i. e. the fore-teeth. (Pâṇ. II. 2, 1.)

§ 516. If the second part of a determinative compound is a verbal base, no change takes place in bases ending in consonants or long vowels, except that diphthongs, as usual, are changed to आ *â*. Hence जलमुच् *jalamuch*, water-dropping, i. e. a cloud; सोमपा *soma-pâ*, Soma-drinking, nom. sing. सोमपाः *somapâḥ* (§ 239).

Bases ending in short vowels generally take a final त् *t*: विश्वजित् *viśvajit*, all-conquering, from जि *ji*, to conquer. Other suffixes used for the same purpose are अ *a*, इन् *in*, &c.

* Most words ending in तृ *tri* or क *ka* are not allowed to form compounds of this kind. Hence कटस्य कर्ता *kaṭasya kartâ*, maker of a mat, not कटकर्ता *kaṭakartâ*; पुरां भेत्ता *purâm bhettâ*, breaker of towns. There are, however, many exceptions, such as देवपूजकः *deva-pûjakaḥ*, worshipper of the gods, &c.

I b. *Appositional Determinative Compounds.*

§ 517. These compounds (Karmadhâraya) form a subdivision of the determinative compounds (Tatpurusha). In them the first portion stands as the predicate of the second portion, such as in *black-beetle*, *sky-blue*, &c.

The following are some instances of appositional compounds:

नीलोत्पलं *nîla-utpalam*, neut. the blue lotus. परमात्मा *parama-âtmâ*, masc. the supreme spirit. शाकपार्थिवः *śâka-pârthivaḥ*, masc. a Śâka-king, explained as a king such as the Śâkas would like, not as the king of the Śâkas. सर्वरात्रः *sarva-râtraḥ*, masc. the whole night, from *sarva*, whole, and *râtriḥ*, night. *Râtriḥ*, fem., is changed to *râtra*; cf. पूर्वरात्रः *pûrva-râtraḥ*, masc. the fore-night; मध्यरात्रः *madhya-râtraḥ*, masc. midnight; पुण्यरात्रः *puṇya-râtraḥ*, masc. a holy night. द्विरात्रं *dvi-râtram*, neut. a space of two nights, is a numeral compound (Dvigu). महाराजः *mahâ-râjaḥ*, masc. a great king. In these compounds महत् *mahat*, great, always becomes महा *mahâ* (Pâṇ. VI. 3, 46), and राजन् *râjan*, king, राजः *râjaḥ*; as परमराजः *parama-râjaḥ*, a supreme king: but सुराजा *su-râjâ*, a good king, किंराजा *kiṁrâjâ*, a bad king (Pâṇ. V. 4, 69, 70). प्रियसखः *priya-sakhaḥ*, masc. a dear friend. सखि *sakhi* is changed to सखः *sakhaḥ*. परमाहः *parama-ahaḥ*, masc. the highest day. In these compounds अहन् *ahan*, day, becomes अह *aha*; cf. उत्तमाहः *uttamâhaḥ*, the last day. Sometimes अह्न *ahna* is substituted for अहन् *ahan*; पूर्वाह्णः *pûrvâhṇaḥ*, the fore-noon. कुपुरुषः *ku-purushaḥ*, masc. a bad man, or कापुरुषः *kâpurushaḥ*. प्राचार्यः *pra-âchâryaḥ*, masc. a hereditary teacher, i. e. one who has been a teacher (*âchârya*) before or formerly (*pra*). अब्राह्मणः *a-brâhmaṇaḥ*, masc. a non-Brâhman, i.e. not a Brâhman. अनश्वः *an-aśvaḥ*, masc. a non-horse, i.e. not a horse. घनश्यामः *ghana-śyâmaḥ*, m. f. n. cloud-black, from *ghana*, cloud, and *śyâma*, black. ईषत्पिङ्गलः *îshat-piṅgalaḥ*, m. f. n. a little brown, from *îshat*, a little, and *piṅgala*, brown. सामिकृतः *sâmi-kṛitaḥ*, m. f. n. half-done, from *sâmi*, half, and *kṛita*, done.

§ 518. In some appositional compounds, the qualifying word is placed last. विप्रगौरः *vipragauraḥ*, a white Brâhman; राजाधमः *râjâdhamaḥ*, the lowest king; भरतश्रेष्ठः *bharata-śreshṭhaḥ*, the best Bharata; पुरुषव्याघ्रः *purusha-vyâghraḥ*, a tiger-like man, a great man; गोवृन्दारकः *govṛindârakaḥ*, a prime cow.

I c. *Numeral Determinative Compounds.*

§ 519. Determinative compounds, the first portion of which is a numeral, are called *Dvigu*. The numeral is always the predicate of the noun which follows. They are generally neuters, or feminines, and are meant to express aggregates, but they may also form adjectives, thus becoming possessive compounds, with or without secondary suffixes.

If an aggregate compound is formed, final अ *a* is changed to ई *î*, fem., or in some cases to अं *am*, neut. Final अन् *an* and आ *â* are changed to ई *î* or अं *am*.

पंचगवं *pañcha-gavam*, neut. an aggregate of five cows, from *pañchan*, five, and *go*, cow. गो *go* (in an aggregate compound) is changed to गव *gava* (Pâṇ. II. 1, 23), and नौ *nau* to नाव *nâva*. पंचगुः *pañcha-guḥ*, as an adjective, worth five cows (Pâṇ. v. 4, 92). द्विनौः *dvinauḥ*, bought for two ships. द्व्यंगुलं *dvy-aṅgulam*, neut. what has the measure of two fingers, from *dvi*, two, and *aṅguliḥ*, finger; final *i* being changed to *a*. द्व्यहः *dvy-ahaḥ*, masc. a space of two days; *ahan* changed to *ahaḥ* (Pâṇ. II. 1, 23). पंचकपालः *pañcha-kapâlaḥ*, m. f. n. an offering (*puroḍâśaḥ*) made in a dish with five compartments, from *pañchan*, five, and *kapâlam*, neut. (Pâṇ. II. 1, 51, 52; IV. 1, 88). त्रिलोकी *tri-lokî*, fem. the three worlds: here the Dvigu compound takes the fem. termination to express an aggregate (Pâṇ. IV. 1, 21). त्रिभुवनं *tri-bhuvanam*, neut. the three worlds: here the Dvigu compound takes the neut. termination. दशकुमारी *daśa-kumârî*, fem. an assemblage of ten youths. चतुर्युगं *chatur-yugam*, neut. the four ages.

§ 520. The following rules apply to the changes of the final syllables in determinative compounds. Very few of them are general as requiring a change without any regard to the preceding words in the compound. The general rules are given first, afterwards the more special, while rules for the formation of one single compound are left out, such compounds being within the sphere of a dictionary rather than of a grammar.

1. ऋच् *rich*, verse, पुर् *pur*, town, अप् *ap*, water, धुर् *dhur*, charge, पथिन् *pathin*, path, add final अ *a* (Pâṇ. v. 4, 74); अर्धर्चः *ardharchaḥ*, a half-verse. This is optional with पथिन् *pathin* after the negative अ *a*; अपथं *apatham* or अपंथाः *apanthâḥ*.
2. राजन् *râjan*, king, अहन् *ahan*, day, सखि *sakhi*, friend, become राज *râja*, अह *aha*, सख *sakha*; महाराजः *mahârâjaḥ*. (Pâṇ. v. 4, 91.)
3. उरस् *uras*, if it means chief, becomes उरस *urasa*; अश्वोरसं *aśvorasam*, an excellent horse (Pâṇ. v. 4, 93). Likewise after प्रति *prati*, if the locative is expressed; प्रत्युरसं *pratyurasam*, on the chest (Pâṇ. v. 4, 82).
4. अक्षि *akshi*, eye, becomes अक्ष *aksha*, if it ceases to mean eye. गवाक्षः *gavâkshaḥ*, a window; but ब्राह्मणाक्षि *brâhmaṇâkshi*, the eye of a Brâhman. (Pâṇ. v. 4, 76.)
5. अनस् *anas*, cart, अश्मन् *aśman*, stone, अयस् *ayas*, iron, सरस् *saras*, lake, take final अ *a* if the compound expresses a kind or forms a name. कालायसं *kâlâyasam*, black-iron; but सदयः *sadayaḥ*, a piece of good iron. (Pâṇ. v. 4, 94.)
6. ब्रह्मन् *brahman* becomes ब्रह्म *brahma*, if preceded by the name of a country; सुराष्ट्रब्रह्मः *surâshṭrabrahmaḥ*, a Brâhman of Surâshṭra (Pâṇ. v. 4, 104). After कु *ku* and महा *mahâ* that substitution is optional (Pâṇ. v. 4, 105).

7. तक्षन् *takshan* takes final अ *a* after ग्राम *grâma* and कौट *kauṭa*; ग्रामतक्षः *grâmatakshaḥ*, village carpenter. (Pâṇ. v. 4, 95.)

8. श्वन् *śvan*, dog, takes final अ *a* after अति *ati*, and after certain words, not the names of animals, with which it is compared; आकर्षश्वः *âkarshaśvaḥ*, a dog of a die, a bad throw (?). (Pâṇ. v. 4, 97.)

9. अध्वन् *adhvan* becomes अध्व *adhva* after prepositions; प्राध्वः *prâdhvaḥ*. (Pâṇ. v. 4, 85.)

10. सामन् *sâman*, hymn, and लोमन् *loman*, hair, become साम *sâma* and लोम *loma* after प्रति *prati*, अनु *anu*, and अव *ava*; अनुलोमः *anulomaḥ*, regular; अनुलोमं *anulomam*, adv. with the hair or grain, i.e. regularly. (Pâṇ. v. 4, 75.)

11. तमस् *tamas* becomes तमस *tamasa* after अव *ava*, सं *sam*, and अंध *andha*; अंधतमसं *andhatamasam*, blind darkness. (Pâṇ. v. 4, 79.)

12. रहस् *rahas* becomes रहस *rahasa* after अनु *anu*, अव *ava*, and तप्त *tapta*; अनुरहसः *anurahasaḥ*, solitary. (Pâṇ. v. 4, 81.)

13. वर्चस् *varchas* becomes वर्चस *varchasa* after ब्रह्म *brahma* and हस्ति *hasti*; ब्रह्मवर्चसं *brahmavarchasam*, the power of a Brâhman. (Pâṇ. v. 4, 78.)

14. गो *go* becomes गव *gava*, except at the end of an adjectival Dvigu. पंचगवं *pañchagavam*, five cows; but पंचगुः *pañchaguḥ*, bought for five cows. (Pâṇ. v. 4, 92.)

15. नौ *nau*, ship, becomes नाव *nâva*, if it forms a numerical aggregate; पंचनावं *pañchanâvam*, five ships: not when it forms a numerical adjective; पंचनौः *pañchanauḥ*, worth five ships. (Pâṇ. v. 4, 99.)

16. नौ *nau*, ship, after अर्ध *ardha*, becomes नाव *nâva*; अर्धनावं *ardhanâvam*, half a ship. (Pâṇ. v. 4, 100.)

17. खारी *khârî*, a measure of grain, becomes खार *khâra* as an aggregate; द्विखारं *dvikhâram*.

18. खारी *khârî*, a measure of corn, becomes खार *khâra* after अर्ध *ardha*; अर्धखारं *ardhakhâram*. (Pâṇ. v. 4, 101.)

19. अंजलि *añjali*, a handful, after द्वि *dvi* or त्रि *tri*, may, as an aggregate, take final अ *a*; द्व्यंजलं *dvyañjalam* or द्व्यंजलि *dvyañjali*, two handfuls. (Pâṇ. v. 4, 102.)

20. अंगुलि *aṅguli*, finger, after numerals and indeclinables, becomes अंगुल *aṅgula*; द्व्यंगुलं *dvyaṅgulam*, a length of two fingers. (Pâṇ. v. 4, 86.)

21. सक्थि *sakthi*, thigh, becomes सक्थ *saktha* after उत्तर *uttara*, मृग *mṛiga*, and पूर्व *pûrva*; पूर्वसक्थं *pûrvasaktham*. (Pâṇ. v. 4, 98.)

22. रात्रि *râtri*, night, after सर्व *sarva*, after partitive words, after संख्यात *saṅkhyâta*, पुण्य *puṇya*, likewise after numerals and indeclinables, becomes रात्र *râtra*; सर्वरात्रः *sarvarâtraḥ*, the whole night; पूर्वरात्रः *pûrvarâtraḥ*, the fore-night; द्विरात्रं *dvirâtram*, two nights. (Pâṇ. v. 4, 87.)

23. अहन् *ahan*, day, under the same circumstances, becomes अह्न *ahna*; सर्वाह्णः *sarvâhṇaḥ*, the whole day: but not after a numeral when it expresses an

aggregate; द्व्यहः *dvyahaḥ*, two days. Except also पुण्याहं *puṇyâham*, a good day, and एकाहं *ekâham*, n. and m. a single day. (Pâṇ. v. 4, 88–90.)

II. *Collective Compounds.*

§ 521. Collective compounds (Dvandva) are divided into two classes. The first class (called इतरेतर *itaretara*) comprises compounds in which two or more words, that would naturally be connected by *and*, are united, the last taking the terminations either of the dual or the plural, according to the number of words forming the compound. The second class (called समाहार *samâhâra*) comprises the same kind of compounds but formed into neuter nouns in the singular. हस्त्यश्वौ *hasty-aśvau*, an elephant and a horse, is an instance of the former, हस्त्यश्वं *hastyaśvam*, the elephants and horses (in an army), an instance of the latter class. Likewise शुक्लकृष्णौ *śukla-kṛishṇau*, white and black; गवाश्वं *gavâśvam*, a cow and a horse.

If instead of a horse and an elephant, हस्त्यश्वौ *hastyaśvau*, the intention is to express horses and elephants, the compound takes the terminations of the plural, हस्त्यश्वाः *hastyaśvâḥ*.

§ 522. Some rules are given as to which words should stand first in a Dvandva compound. Words with fewer syllables should stand first: शिवकेशवौ *śiva-keśavau*, Śiva and Keśava; not केशवशिवौ *keśavaśivau*. Words beginning with a vowel and ending in अ *a* should stand first: ईशकृष्णौ *îśa-kṛishṇau*, Îśa and Kṛishṇa. Words ending in इ *i* (gen. एः *eḥ*) and उ *u* (gen. ओः *oḥ*) should stand first: हरिहरौ *hari-harau*, Hari and Hara; also भोक्तृभोग्यौ *bhoktṛi-bhogyau*, the enjoyer and the enjoyed. Lastly, words of greater importance should have precedence: देवदैत्यौ *deva-daityau*, the god and the demon; ब्राह्मणक्षत्रियौ *brâhmaṇa-kshatriyau*, a Brâhman and a Kshatriya; मातापितरौ *mâtâ-pitarau*, mother and father, but in earlier Sanskrit पितरामातरा *pitarâ-mâtarâ*, father and mother. (Pâṇ. vi. 3, 33.)

§ 523. Words ending in ऋ *ṛi*, expressive of relationship or sacred titles, forming the first member of a compound, and being followed by another word ending in ऋ *ṛi*, or by पुत्र *putra*, son, change their ऋ *ṛi* into आ *â* (Pâṇ. vi. 3, 25). मातृ *mâtṛi* + पितृ *pitṛi* form मातापितरौ *mâtâpitarau*, father and mother; पितृ *pitṛi* + पुत्र *putra* form पितापुत्रौ *pitâputrau*; होतृ *hotṛi* + पोतृ *potṛi* form होतापोतारौ *hotâpotârau*, the Hotṛi and Potṛi priests.

§ 524. When the names of certain deities are compounded, the first sometimes lengthens its final vowel (Pâṇ. vi. 3, 26). Thus मित्रावरुणौ *mitrâ-varuṇau*, Mitra and Varuṇa; अग्नीषोमौ *agnîshomau*, Agni and Soma. Similar irregularities appear in words like द्यावापृथिव्यौ *dyâvâ-pṛithivyau*, heaven and earth; उषासानक्तं *ushâsâ-naktam*, dawn and night (Pâṇ. vi. 3, 29–31).

§ 525. If the compound takes the termination of the singular, then final

च् *ch*, छ् *chh*, ज् *j*, झ् *jh*, द् *d*, ष् *sh*, and ह् *h* take an additional अ *a*. वाच् *vách* + त्वच् *tvach* form वाक्त्वचं *váktvacham*, speech and skin (Pâṇ. v. 4, 106). अहन् *ahan*, day (see §§ 90, 196), and रात्रि *rátri*, night, form the compound अहोरात्रः *ahorátraḥ*, a day and night, a νυχθήμερον (Pâṇ. v. 4, 87).

§ 526. भ्रातरौ *bhrátarau* may be used in the sense of brother and sister; पुत्रौ *putrau* in the sense of son and daughter; पितरौ *pitarau* in the sense of father and mother; श्वशुरौ *śvaśurau* in the sense of father and mother-in-law. Man and wife may be expressed by जायापती *jáyá-patí*, जंपती *jampatí*, or दंपती *dampatí*.

III. *Possessive Compounds.*

§ 527. Possessive compounds (Bahuvríhi) are always predicates referring to some subject or other. A determinative may be used as a possessive compound by a mere change of termination or accent. Thus नीलोत्पलं *níla-utpalam*, a blue lotus, is a determinative compound (Tatpurusha, subdivision Karmadhâraya); but in नीलोत्पलं सरः *nílotpalam saraḥ*, a blue lotus lake, *nílotpalam* is an adjective and as such a predicative or possessive compound; (see Pâṇ. II. 2, 24, com.) In the same manner अनश्वः *anaśvaḥ*, not-a-horse, is a determinative, अनश्वो रथः *anaśvo rathaḥ*, a cart without a horse, a horseless cart, a possessive compound.

Examples: प्राप्तोदको ग्रामः *prápta-udako grâmaḥ*, a water-reached village, a village reached by water. ऊढरथोऽनड्वान् *úḍha-ratho 'naḍván*, a bull by whom a cart (*rathaḥ*) is drawn (*úḍha*). उपहृतपशू रुद्रः *upahṛita-paśú rudraḥ*, Rudra to whom cattle (*paśuḥ*) is offered (*upahṛita*). पीताम्बरो हरिः *píta-ambaro hariḥ*, Hari possessing yellow garments. प्रपर्णः *pra-parṇaḥ*, leafless, i. e. a tree from which the leaves are fallen off. अपुत्रः *a-putraḥ*, sonless. चित्रगुः *chitra-guḥ*, possessed of a brindled cow. रूपवद्भार्यः *rúpavad-bháryaḥ*, possessed of a beautiful wife. द्विमूर्धः *dvi-múrdhaḥ*, two-headed: here *múrdha* stands for *múrdhan*. द्विपाद् *dvi-pád*, two-legged: here *pád* stands for *páda*. सुहृद् *su-hṛid*, having a good heart, a friend. भक्षितभिक्षुः *bhakshita-bhikshuḥ*, one who has eaten his alms. नीलोज्ज्वलवपुः *níla-ujjvala-vapuḥ*, having a blue resplendent body.

§ 528. Bahuvríhi compounds frequently take suffixes. The following rules apply to the changes of the final syllables in possessive compounds:

1. सक्थि *sakthi*, thigh, and अक्षि *akshi*, eye, if they mean really thigh and eye, take final अ *a*; कमलाक्षः *kamalákshaḥ*, lotus-eyed. (Pâṇ. v. 4, 113.)
2. अङ्गुलि *aṅguli*, finger, substitutes final अ *a* if it refers to wood; द्व्यङ्गुलं दारु *dvyaṅgulam dáru*, a piece of wood with two prongs*. (Pâṇ. v. 4, 114.)
3. मूर्धन् *múrdhan*, head, substitutes final अ *a* after द्वि *dvi* and त्रि *tri*; द्विमूर्धः *dvimúrdhaḥ*, having two heads. (Pâṇ. v. 4, 115.)

* अङ्गुलिसदृशावयवं धान्यादिविक्षेपणकाष्ठं, Prakriyâ-Kaumudî.

4. लोमन् *loman*, hair, substitutes final अ *a* after अन्तर् *antar* and बहिः *vahiḥ*; अन्तर्लोमः *antarlomaḥ*, having the hairy part inside. (Pâṇ. v. 4, 117.)

5. नासिका *nâsikâ*, nose, becomes नस *nasa*, if it stands at the end of a name; गोनसः *gonasaḥ*, cow-nosed, i. e. a snake; but not after स्थूल *sthûla*; स्थूलनासिकः *sthûla-nâsikaḥ*, large-nosed, i. e. a hog. The same change takes place after prepositions; उन्नसः *unnasaḥ*, with a prominent nose*.

6. After अ *a*, दुः *duḥ*, or सु *su*, हलि *hali*, furrow, and सक्थि *sakthi*, thigh, may substitute final अ *a*; अहलः *ahalaḥ* or अहलिः *ahaliḥ*. (Pâṇ. v. 4, 121.)

7. After the same particles, प्रजा *prajâ*, progeny, and मेधा *medhâ*, mind, are treated like nouns ending in अस् *as*; दुर्मेधाः *durmedhâḥ*. (Pâṇ. v. 4, 122.)

8. धर्म *dharma*, law, preceded by one word, is treated like a noun ending in अन् *an*; कल्याणधर्मा *kalyâṇadharmâ*. (Pâṇ. v. 4, 124.)

9. जंभा *jambhâ*, jaw, after certain words, becomes जंभन् *jambhan*; सुजंभा *sujambhâ*.

10. जानु *jânu*, knee, after प्र *pra* and सं *sam*, becomes ज्ञु *jñu*; प्रज्ञुः *prajñuḥ* (Pâṇ. v. 4, 129). This is optional after ऊर्ध्व *ûrdhva* (Pâṇ. v. 4, 130).

11. ऊधस् *ûdhas*, udder, becomes ऊधन् *ûdhan*; कुण्डोध्नी *kuṇḍodhnî*. (Pâṇ. v. 4, 131.)

12. धनुस् *dhanus*, bow, becomes धन्वन् *dhanvan*; पुष्पधन्वा *pushpadhanvâ*, having a bow of flowers (Pâṇ. v. 4, 132). In names this is optional.

13. जाया *jâyâ*, wife, becomes जानि *jâni*; शुभजानिः *śubhajâniḥ*. (Pâṇ. v. 4, 134.)

14. गंध *gandha*, smell, substitutes गंधि *gandhi* after certain words; सुगंधिः *sugandhiḥ*. (Pâṇ. v. 4, 135–137.)

15. पाद *pâda*, foot, becomes पाद् *pâd* after certain words; व्याघ्रपाद् *vyâghrapâd*†.

16. दंत *danta*, tooth, becomes दत् *dat* after many words; द्विदन् *dvidan*, having two teeth, (sign of a certain age); fem. द्विदती *dvidatî*. (Pâṇ. v. 4, 141–145.)

17. ककुद *kakuda*, hump, becomes ककुद् *kakud* after certain words and in certain senses; अजातककुद् *ajâtakakud*, a young bull before his humps have grown‡.

18. उरस् *uras* and other words belonging to the same class add final क *ka*; व्यूढोरस्कः *vyûḍhoraskaḥ*, broad-chested. (Pâṇ. v. 4, 151.)

19. Words in इन् *in* add final क *ka* in the feminine; बहुस्वामिका *bahusvâmikâ*, having many masters, from स्वामिन् *svâmin*, master. (Pâṇ. v. 4, 152.)

20. Feminine words in ई *î*, like नदी *nadî*, and words in ऋ *ṛi*, add final क *ka*; बहुकुमारीकः *bahukumârîkaḥ*, having many maidens; बहुभर्तृकः *bahubhartṛikaḥ*, having many husbands. (Pâṇ. v. 4, 153.)

21. Most other words may or may not add final क *ka*; बहुमालकः *bahumâlakaḥ* or बहुमालः *bahumâlaḥ*. (Pâṇ. v. 4, 154.)

IV. *Adverbial Compounds.*

§ 529. Adverbial or indeclinable compounds (Avyayîbhâva) are formed by joining an indeclinable particle with another word. The resulting com-

* Pâṇ. v. 4, 118, 119. † Pâṇ. v. 4, 138—140. ‡ Pâṇ. v. 4, 146—148.

pounds, in which the indeclinable particle forms always the first element, are again indeclinable, and generally end, like adverbs, in the ordinary terminations of the nom. or acc. neut.

Examples: अधिहरि *adhi-hari*, upon Hari, instead of अधि हरौ *adhi harau*, loc. sing. अनुविष्णु *anu-vishṇu*, after Vishṇu, instead of अनु विष्णुं *anu vishṇum*, acc. sing. उपकृष्णं *upa-kṛishṇam*, near to Kṛishṇa. निर्मक्षिकं *nir-makshikam*, free from flies, flylessly. अतिहिमं *ati-himam*, past the winter, after the winter, instead of अति हिमं *ati himam*, acc. sing. प्रदक्षिणं *pradakshiṇam*, to the right. अनुरूपं *anu-rûpam*, after the form, i. e. accordingly, instead of अनु रूपं *anu rûpam*, acc. sing. यथाशक्ति *yathâ-śakti*, according to one's ability, instead of शक्तिर्यथा *śaktir yathâ*. सतृणं *sa-tṛiṇam*, with the grass; सतृणमत्ति *satṛiṇam atti*, he eats (everything) even the grass, instead of तृणेन सह *tṛiṇena saha*, with the grass. यावच्छ्लोकं *yâvach-chhlokam*, at every verse. आमुक्ति *âmukti*, until final delivery. अनुगंगं *anu-gaṅgam*, near the Gaṅgâ. उपशरदं *upa-śaradam*, near the autumn; from शरद् *śarad*, autumn (Pâṇ. v. 4, 107). उपजरसं *upa-jarasam*, at the approach of old age; from जरस् *jaras*, old age (§ 167). उपसमित् *upa-samit* or उपसमिधं *upa-samidham*, near the fire-wood; from समिध् *samidh*, fire-wood. उपराजं *upa-râjam*, near the king; from राजन् *râjan*, king.

§ 530. There are some Avyayîbhâvas the first element of which is not an indeclinable particle. Ex. तिष्ठद्गु *tishṭhad-gu*, at the time when the cows stand to be milked; पंचगंगं *pañcha-gaṅgam*, at the place where the five Gaṅgâs meet, (near the Mâdhav-râo ghâṭ at Benares); प्रत्यग्ग्रामं *pratyag-grâmam*, west of the village.

§ 531. The following rules apply to the changes of the final syllables in adverbial compounds:

1. Words ending in mutes (*k, kh, g, gh, ch, chh, j, jh, ṭ, ṭh, ḍ, ḍh, t, th, d, dh, p, ph, b, bh*) may or may not take final अ *a*; उपसमिधं *upasamidham* or उपसमित् *upasamit*, near the fire-wood. (Pâṇ. v. 4, 111.)
2. Words ending in अन् *an* substitute final अ *a*; अध्यात्मं *adhyâtmam*, with regard to oneself. (Pâṇ. v. 4, 108.)
3. But neuters in अन् *an* may or may not; उपचर्मं *upacharmam* or उपचर्म *upacharma*, near the skin. (Pâṇ. v. 4, 109.)
4. नदी *nadî*, पौर्णमासी *paurṇamâsî*, आग्रहायणी *âgrahâyaṇî*, and गिरि *giri* may or may not take final अ *a*; उपनदि *upanadi* or उपनदं *upanadam*, near the river. (Pâṇ. v. 4, 110, and 112.)
5. Words belonging to the class beginning with शरद् *śarad* take final अ *a*; उपशरदं *upaśaradam*, about autumn. (Pâṇ. v. 4, 107.)

APPENDIX.

LIST OF VERBS.

Explanation of some of the Verbal Anubandhas or Indicatory Letters.

अ *a* is put at the end of roots ending in a consonant in order to facilitate their pronunciation.

Accent.—The last letter of a root is accented with the acute, the grave, or circumflex accent, in order to show that the verb follows the Parasmaipada, the Âtmanepada, or both forms.

The roots themselves are divided into *udâtta*, acutely accented, and *anudâtta*, gravely accented, the former admitting, the latter rejecting the intermediate इ *i*.

आ *â* prohibits the use of the intermediate इ *i* in the formation of the Nishṭhâs (§ 333, D. 2), Pâṇ. VII. 2, 16. Ex. फुल्लः *phullaḥ* from ञिफला *ñiphalâ*.

इ *i* requires the insertion of a nasal after the last radical vowel, which nasal is not to be omitted where a nasal that is actually written would be omitted (§ 345†), Pâṇ. VII. 1, 58; VI. 4, 24. Ex. नंदति *nandati* from नदि *nadi*, Pass. नंद्यते *nandyate;* but from मंथ् or मन्थ् *manth*, Pres. मंथति *manthati*, Pass. मथ्यते *mathyate*.

इर् *ir* shows that a verb may take the first or second aorist in the Parasmaipada (§ 367), Pâṇ. III. 1, 57. Ex. अच्युतत् *achyutat* or अच्योतीत् *achyotît* from च्युतिर् *chyutir*.

ई *î* prohibits the use of the intermediate इ *i* in the formation of the Nishṭhâs (§ 333, D. 2), Pâṇ. VII. 2, 14. Ex. उन्नः *unnaḥ* from उंदी *undî*.

उ *u* renders the admission of the intermediate इ *i* optional before the gerundial त्वा *tvâ* (§ 337, II. 5), Pâṇ. VII. 2, 56; and therefore inadmissible in the past participle (Pâṇ. VII. 2, 15). Ex. शमित्वा *śamitvâ* or शांत्वा *śântvâ* from शमु *śamu;* but शांतः *śântaḥ*.

ऊ *û* renders the admission of the intermediate इ *i* optional in the general tenses before all consonants but य् *y* (§ 337, I. 2), Pâṇ. VII. 2, 44; and therefore inadmissible in the past participle (Pâṇ. VII. 2, 15). Ex. सेद्धा *seddhâ* or सेधिता *sedhitâ* from षिधू *sidhû;* but सिद्धः *siddhaḥ*.

ऋ *ṛi* prevents the substitution of the short for the long vowel in the reduplicated aorist of causals (§ 372*), Pâṇ. VII. 4, 2. Ex. अलुलोकत् *alulokat* from लोकृ *lokṛi*.

ऌ *ḷi* shows that the verb takes the second aorist in the Parasmaipada (§ 367), Pâṇ. III. 1, 55. Ex. अगमत् *agamat* from गम्ऌ *gamḷi*.

ए *e* forbids Vṛiddhi in the first aorist (§ 348*), Pâṇ. vii. 2, 5. Ex. अमथीत् *amathît* from मथे *mathe*.

ओ *o* indicates that the participle is formed in न *na* instead of त *ta* (§ 442, 5), Pâṇ. viii. 2, 45. Ex. पीनः *pînaḥ* from ओप्यायी *opyâyî*.

ङ् *ṅ* shows that the verb follows the Âtmanepada (Pâṇ. i. 3, 12).

ञ् *ñ* shows that the verb follows both the Âtmanepada and Parasmaipada, the former if the act reverts to the subject (Pâṇ. i. 3, 72).

ञि *ñî* shows that the past participle has the power of the present (Pâṇ. iii. 2, 187). Ex. फुल्लः *phullaḥ*, blown, from ञिफला *ñiphalâ*.

म् *m* shows that the vowel is not lengthened in the causative (§ 462, note), Pâṇ. vi. 4, 92; and that the vowel is optionally lengthened in the aorist of the passive (Pâṇ. vi. 4, 93).

Bhû Class (*Bhvâdi, I Class*).

I. Parasmaipada Verbs.

1. भू *bhû*, to be.

Parasmaipada: P. 1. भवामि *bhavâmi*, 2. भवसि *bhavasi*, 3. भवति *bhavati*, 4. भवावः *bhavâvaḥ*, 5. भवथः *bhavathaḥ*, 6. भवतः *bhavataḥ*, 7. भवामः *bhavâmaḥ*, 8. भवथ *bhavatha*, 9. भवन्ति *bhavanti*, I. 1. अभवं *abhavam*, 2. अभवः *abhavaḥ*, 3. अभवत् *abhavat*, 4. अभवाव *abhavâva*, 5. अभवतं *abhavatam*, 6. अभवतां *abhavatâm*, 7. अभवाम *abhavâma*, 8. अभवत *abhavata*, 9. अभवन् *abhavan*, O. 1. भवेयं *bhaveyam*, 2. भवेः *bhaveḥ*, 3. भवेत् *bhavet*, 4. भवेव *bhaveva*, 5. भवेतं *bhavetam*, 6. भवेतां *bhavetâm*, 7. भवेम *bhavema*, 8. भवेत *bhaveta*, 9. भवेयुः *bhaveyuḥ*, I. 1. भवानि *bhavâni* 2. भव *bhava*, 3. भवतु *bhavatu*, 4. भवाव *bhavâva*, 5. भवतं *bhavatam*, 6. भवतां *bhavatâm*, 7. भवाम *bhavâma*, 8. भवत *bhavata*, 9. भवन्तु *bhavantu* ॥ Pf. 1. बभूव *babhûva*† (see p. 175), 2. बभूविथ *babhûvitha*, 3. बभूव *babhûva*, 4. बभूविव *babhûviva*, 5. बभूवथुः *babhûvathuḥ*, 6. बभूवतुः *babhûvatuḥ*, 7. बभूविम *babhûvima*, 8. बभूव *babhûva*, 9. बभूवुः *babhûvuḥ*, II A. 1. अभूवं *abhûvam* (see p. 188), 2. अभूः *abhûḥ*, 3. अभूत् *abhût*, 4. अभूव *abhûva*, 5. अभूतं *abhûtam*, 6. अभूतां *abhûtâm*, 7. अभूम *abhûma*, 8. अभूत *abhûta*, 9. अभूवन् *abhûvan*, F. 1. भविष्यामि *bhavishyâmi*, 2. भविष्यसि *bhavishyasi*, 3. भविष्यति *bhavishyati*, 4. भविष्यावः *bhavishyâvaḥ*, 5. भविष्यथः *bhavishyathaḥ*, 6. भविष्यतः *bhavishyataḥ*, 7. भविष्यामः *bhavishyâmaḥ*, 8. भविष्यथ *bhavishyatha*, 9. भविष्यन्ति *bhavishyanti*, C. 1. अभविष्यं *abhavishyam*, 2. अभविष्यः *abhavishyaḥ*, 3. अभविष्यत् *abhavishyat*, 4. अभविष्याव *abhavishyâva*, 5. अभविष्यतं *abhavishyatam*, 6. अभविष्यतां *abhavishyatâm*, 7. अभविष्याम *abhavishyâma*, 8. अभविष्यत *abhavishyata*, 9. अभविष्यन् *abhavishyan*, P. F. 1. भवितास्मि *bhavitâsmi*, 2. भवितासि *bhavitâsi*, 3. भविता *bhavitâ*, 4. भवितास्वः *bhavitâsvaḥ*, 5. भवितास्थः *bhavitâsthaḥ*, 6. भवितारौ *bhavitârau*, 7. भवितास्मः *bhavi-*

---

† The reduplicative syllable ब *ba* is irregular, instead of बु *bu*. The base, too, is irregular (Pâṇ. i. 2, 6); the regular form would have been बुभाव *bubhâva*.

tâsmaḥ, 8. भवितास्थ bhavitâstha, 9. भवितारः bhavitâraḥ, B. 1. भूयासं bhûyâsam, 2. भूयाः bhûyâḥ, 3. भूयात् bhûyât, 4. भूयास्व bhûyâsva, 5. भूयास्तं bhûyâstam, 6. भूयास्तां bhûyâstâm, 7. भूयास्म bhûyâsma, 8. भूयास्त bhûyâsta, 9. भूयासुः bhûyâsuḥ ॥ Part. Pres. भवन् bhavan, Perf. बभूवान् babhûvân, Fut. भविष्यन् bhavishyan, Ger. भूत्वा bhûtvâ or °भूय -bhûya, Adj. भवितव्यः bhavitavyaḥ, भवनीयः bhavanîyaḥ, भाव्यः bhâvyaḥ (§ 456).

Âtmanepada*: P. 1. भवे bhave, 2. भवसे bhavase, 3. भवते bhavate, 4. भवावहे bhavâvahe, 5. भवेथे bhavethe, 6. भवेते bhavete, 7. भवामहे bhavâmahe, 8. भवध्वे bhavadhve, 9. भवन्ते bhavante, I. 1. अभवे abhave, 2. अभवथाः abhavathâḥ, 3. अभवत abhavata, 4. अभवावहि abhavâvahi, 5. अभवेथां abhavethâm, 6. अभवेतां abhavetâm, 7. अभवामहि abhavâmahi, 8. अभवध्वं abhavadhvam, 9. अभवन्त abhavanta, O. 1. भवेय bhaveya, 2. भवेथाः bhavethâḥ, 3. भवेत bhaveta, 4. भवेवहि bhavevahi, 5. भवेयाथां bhaveyâthâm, 6. भवेयातां bhaveyâtâm, 7. भवेमहि bhavemahi, 8. भवेध्वं bhavedhvam, 9. भवेरन् bhaveran, I. 1. भवै bhavai, 2. भवस्व bhavasva, 3. भवतां bhavatâm, 4. भवावहै bhavâvahai, 5. भवेथां bhavethâm, 6. भवेतां bhavetâm, 7. भवामहै bhavâmahai, 8. भवध्वं bhavadhvam, 9. भवन्तां bhavantâm ॥ Pf. 1. बभूवे babhûve (see note †, page 246), 2. बभूविषे babhûvishe, 3. बभूवे babhûve, 4. बभूविवहे babhûvivahe, 5. बभूवाथे babhûvâthe, 6. बभूवाते babhûvâte, 7. बभूविमहे babhûvimahe, 8. बभूविध्वे or °ढ्वे babhûvidhve or -ḍhve (see § 105), 9. बभूविरे babhûvire, I A. 1. अभविषि abhavishi, 2. अभविष्ठाः abhavishṭhâḥ, 3. अभविष्ट abhavishṭa, 4. अभविष्वहि abhavishvahi, 5. अभविषाथां abhavishâthâm, 6. अभविषातां abhavishâtâm, 7. अभविष्महि abhavishmahi, 8. अभविध्वं or °ढ्वं abhavidhvam or -ḍhvam, 9. अभविषत abhavishata, F. भविष्ये bhavishye &c., C. अभविष्ये abhavishye &c., P. F. 1. भविताहे bhavitâhe, 2. भवितासे bhavitâse, 3. भविता bhavitâ, 4. भवितास्वहे bhavitâsvahe, 5. भवितासाथे bhavitâsâthe, 6. भवितारौ bhavitârau, 7. भवितास्महे bhavitâsmahe, 8. भविताध्वे bhavitâdhve, 9. भवितारः bhavitâraḥ, B. 1. भविषीय bhavishîya, 2. भविषीष्ठाः bhavishîshṭhâḥ, 3. भविषीष्ट bhavishîshṭa, 4. भविषीवहि bhavishîvahi, 5. भविषीयास्थां bhavishîyâsthâm, 6. भविषीयास्तां bhavishîyâstâm, 7. भविषीमहि bhavishîmahi, 8. भविषीध्वं or °ढ्वं bhavishîdhvam or -ḍhvam, 9. भविषीरन् bhavishîran ॥ Part. Pres. भवमानः bhavamânaḥ, Perf. बभूवानः babhûvânaḥ, Fut. भविष्यमाणः bhavishyamâṇaḥ.

Passive: P. 1. भूये bhûye‡, 2. भूयसे bhûyase, 3. भूयते bhûyate, 4. भूयावहे bhûyâvahe, 5. भूयेथे bhûyethe, 6. भूयेते bhûyete, 7. भूयामहे bhûyâmahe, 8. भूयध्वे bhûyadhve, 9. भूयन्ते bhûyante, I. अभूये abhûye &c., O. भूयेय bhûyeya &c., I. भूयै bhûyai &c. ॥ Pf. बभूवे babhûve &c., like Âtmanepada, I A. 1. अभविषि or अभाविषि abhâ̆vishi, 2. अभविष्ठाः or अभाविष्ठाः abhâ̆vishṭhâḥ, 3. अभावि abhâvi, 4. अभविष्वहि abhâ̆vishvahi &c., like Âtmanepada, F. भविष्ये or भाविष्ये bhâ̆vishye &c., C. अभविष्ये or अभाविष्ये

---

* भू bhû may be used in the Âtmanepada after certain prepositions. Even by itself it is used in the sense of obtaining: स श्रियं भवते sa śriyam bhavate, he obtains happiness. (Sâr. p. 4, l. 3.)

‡ भू bhû with अनु anu means to perceive, and may yield a passive.

abhâvishye &c., P. F. भविताहे or भाविताहे bhâvitâhe &c., B. भविषीय or भाविषीय bhâvishîya &c. ॥ Part. Pres. भूयमानः bhûyamânaḥ, Fut. भविष्यमाणः bhâvishyamâṇaḥ, Past भूतः bhûtaḥ.

Causative, Parasmaipada: P. भावयामि bhâvayâmi, I. अभावयम् abhâvayam, O. भावयेयम् bhâvayeyam, I. भावयानि bhâvayâni ॥ Pf. भावयांचकार bhâvayâñchakâra, II A. अबीभवम् abîbhavam, F. भावयिष्यामि bhâvayishyâmi, C. अभावयिष्यम् abhâvayishyam, P. F. भावयितास्मि bhâvayitâsmi, B. भाव्यासम् bhâvyâsam.

Causative, Âtmanepada: P. भावये bhâvaye, I. अभावये abhâvaye, O. भावयेय bhâvayeya, I. भावयै bhâvayai ॥ Pf. भावयांचक्रे bhâvayâñchakre, II A. अबीभवे abîbhave, F. भावयिष्ये bhâvayishye, C. अभावयिष्ये abhâvayishye, P. F. भावयिताहे bhâvayitâhe, B. भावयिषीय bhâvayishîya.

Causative, Passive: P. भाव्ये bhâvye, I. अभाव्ये abhâvye, O. भाव्येय bhâvyeya, I. भाव्यै bhâvyai ॥ Pf. भावयांचक्रे, °बभूवे, °आसे, bhâvayâñchakre, -babhûve, -âse, I A. अभावयिषि abhâvayishi or अभाविषि abhâvishi, F. भावयिष्ये bhâvayishye or भाविष्ये bhâvishye, C. अभावयिष्ये abhâvayishye or अभाविष्ये abhâvishye, P. F. भावयिताहे bhâvayitâhe or भाविताहे bhâvitâhe, B. भावयिषीय bhâvayishîya or भाविषीय bhâvishîya.

Desiderative, Parasmaipada: P. बुभूषामि bubhûshâmi, I. अबुभूषम् abubhûsham, O. बुभूषेयम् bubhûsheyam, I. बुभूषाणि bubhûshâṇi ॥ Pf. बुभूषांचकार bubhûshâñchakâra, I A. अबुभूषिषम् abubhûshisham, F. बुभूषिष्यामि bubhûshishyâmi, C. अबुभूषिष्यम् abubhûshishyam, P. F. बुभूषितास्मि bubhûshitâsmi, B. बुभूष्यासम् bubhûshyâsam.

Desiderative, Âtmanepada: P. बुभूषे bubhûshe, I. अबुभूषे abubhûshe, O. बुभूषेय bubhûsheya, I. बुभूषै bubhûshai ॥ Pf. बुभूषांचक्रे bubhûshâñchakre, I A. 1. अबुभूषिषि abubhûshishi, 2. अबुभूषिष्ठाः abubhûshishṭhâḥ, 3. अबुभूषिष्ट abubhûshishṭa, F. बुभूषिष्ये bubhûshishye, C. अबुभूषिष्ये abubhûshishye, P. F. बुभूषिताहे bubhûshitâhe, B. बुभूषिषीय bubhûshishîya.

Desiderative, Passive: P. बुभूष्ये bubhûshye, I. अबुभूष्ये abubhûshye, O. बुभूष्येय bubhûshyeya, I. बुभूष्यै bubhûshyai ॥ Pf. बुभूषांचक्रे bubhûshâñchakre, I A. 1. अबुभूषिषि abubhûshishi, 2. अबुभूषिष्ठाः abubhûshishṭhâḥ, 3. अबुभूषि abubhûshi (see § 406), F. बुभूषिष्ये bubhûshishye, C. अबुभूषिष्ये abubhûshishye, P. F. बुभूषिताहे bubhûshitâhe, B. बुभूषिषीय bubhûshishîya.

Intensive, Âtmanepada: P. 1. बोभूये bobhûye, 2. बोभूयसे bobhûyase, 3. बोभूयते bobhûyate, 4. बोभूयावहे bobhûyâvahe, 5. बोभूयेथे bobhûyethe, 6. बोभूयेते bobhûyete, 7. बोभूयामहे bobhûyâmahe, 8. बोभूयध्वे bobhûyadhve, 9. बोभूयन्ते bobhûyante, I. 1. अबोभूये abobhûye, 2. अबोभूयथाः abobhûyathâḥ, 3. अबोभूयत abobhûyata, 4. अबोभूयावहि abobhûyâvahi, 5. अबोभूयेथाम् abobhûyethâm, 6. अबोभूयेताम् abobhûyetâm, 7. अबोभूयामहि abobhûyâmahi, 8. अबोभूयध्वम् abobhûyadhvam, 9. अबोभूयन्त abobhûyanta, O. बोभूयेय bobhûyeya &c., I. 1. बोभूयै bobhûyai, 2. बोभूयस्व bobhûyasva, 3. बोभूयताम् bobhûyatâm, 4. बोभूयावहै bobhûyâvahai, 5. बोभूयेथाम् bobhûyethâm, 6. बोभूयेताम् bobhûyetâm, 7. बोभूयामहै bobhûyâmahai, 8. बोभूयध्वम् bobhûyadhvam, 9. बोभूयन्ताम् bobhûyantâm ॥

Pf. बोभूयांचक्रे *bobhúyáṁchakre*, I A. 1. अबोभूयिषि *abobhúyishi*, 2. अबोभूयिष्ठाः *abobhúyishṭháḥ*, 3. अबोभूयिष्ट *abobhúyishṭa*, 4. अबोभूयिष्वहि *abobhúyishvahi*, 5. अबोभूयिषाथां *abobhúyisháthám*, 6. अबोभूयिषातां *abobhúyishátám*, 7. अबोभूयिष्महि *abobhúyishmahi*, 8. अबोभूयिढ्वं or °ध्वं *abobhúyiḍhvam* or *-dhvam*, 9. अबोभूयिषत *abobhúyishata*, F. बोभूयिष्ये *bobhúyishye*, C. अबोभूयिष्ये *abobhúyishye*, P. F. बोभूयिताहे *bobhúyitáhe*, B. बोभूयिषीय *bobhúyishíya*.

Intensive, Parasmaipada: P. 1. बोभोमि *bobhomi* or बोभवीमि *bobhavími*, 2. बोभोषि *bobhoshi* or बोभवीषि *bobhavíshi*, 3. बोभोति *bobhoti* or बोभवीति *bobhavíti*, 4. बोभूवः *bobhúvaḥ*, 5. बोभूथः *bobhúthaḥ*, 6. बोभूतः *bobhútaḥ*, 7. बोभूमः *bobhúmaḥ*, 8. बोभूथ *bobhútha*, 9. बोभुवति *bobhuvati*, I. 1. अबोभवं *abobhavam*, 2. अबोभोः *abobhoḥ* or अबोभवीः *abobhavíḥ*, 3. अबोभोत् *abobhot* or अबोभवीत् *abobhavít*, 4. अबोभूव *abobhúva*, 5. अबोभूतं *abobhútam*, 6. अबोभूतां *abobhútám*, 7. अबोभूम *abobhúma*, 8. अबोभूत *abobhúta*, 9. अबोभवुः *abobhavuḥ*, O. बोभूयां *bobhúyám*, I. 1. बोभवानि *bobhaváni*, 2. बोभूहि *bobhúhi*, 3. बोभोतु *bobhotu* or बोभवीतु *bobhavítu*, 4. बोभवाव *bobhaváva*, 5. बोभूतं *bobhútam*, 6. बोभूतां *bobhútám*, 7. बोभवाम *bobhaváma*, 8. बोभूत *bobhúta*, 9. बोभुवतु *bobhuvatu* ॥ Pf. 1. बोभवांचकार *bobhaváṁchakára*, 4. बोभवांचकृव *bobhaváṁchakṛiva*, 7. बोभवांचकृम *bobhaváṁchakṛima*; also 1. बोभाव *bobháva* or बोभूव *bobhúva*, 2. बोभूविथ *bobhúvitha*, 3. बोभाव *bobháva* or बोभूव *bobhúva*, 4. बोभुविव *bobhuviva* or बोभूविव *bobhúviva*, 5. बोभुवथुः *bobhuvathuḥ* or बोभूवथुः *bobhúvathuḥ*, 6. बोभुवतुः *bobhuvatuḥ* or बोभूवतुः *bobhúvatuḥ*, 7. बोभुविम *bobhuvima* or बोभूविम *bobhúvima*, 8. बोभुव *bobhuva* or बोभूव *bobhúva*, 9. बोभुवुः *bobhuvuḥ* or बोभूवुः *bobhúvuḥ*, II A. 1. अबोभूवं *abobhúvam*, 2. अबोभूः *abobhúḥ* or अबोभूवीः *abobhúvíḥ*, 3. अबोभूत् *abobhút* or अबोभूवीत् *abobhúvít*, 4. अबोभूव *abobhúva*, 5. अबोभूतं *abobhútam*, 6. अबोभूतां *abobhútám*, 7. अबोभूम *abobhúma*, 8. अबोभूत *abobhúta*, 9. अबोभुवुः *abobhuvuḥ* (not अबोभूवन् *abobhúvan*), I A. 1. अबोभाविषं *abobhávisham*, 4. अबोभाविष्व *abobhávishva*, 7. अबोभाविष्म *abobhávishma**, F. बोभविष्यामि *bobhavishyámi*, C. अबोभविष्यं *abobhavishyam*, P. F. बोभवितास्मि *bobhavitásmi*, B. बोभूयासं *bobhúyásam*.

Note—Grammarians who allow the intensive without य *ya* to form an Âtmanepada, give the following forms: Pres. बोभूते *bobhúte*, Impf. अबोभूत *abobhúta*, Opt. बोभुवीत *bobhuvíta*, Imp. बोभूतां *bobhútám*, Per. Perf. बोभवांचक्रे *bobhaváṁchakre*, Aor. अबोभविष्ट *abobhavishṭa*, Fut. बोभविष्यते *bobhavishyate*, Cond. अबोभविष्यत *abobhavishyata*, Per. Fut. बोभविता *bobhavitá*, Ben. बोभविषीष्ट *bobhavishíshṭa*. (See Colebrooke, p. 194.)

2. चित् *chit*, to think, (चिती.)

The Anubandha ई *í* shows that the participle in तः *taḥ* takes no intermediate इ *i*.

P. चेतति *chetati*, I. अचेतत् *achetat*, O. चेतेत् *chetet*, I. चेततु *chetatu* ॥ Pf. 1. चिचेत *chicheta*, 2. चिचेतिथ *chichetitha*, 3. चिचेत *chicheta*, 4. चिचितिव

* The first aorist is the usual form for intensives, but in भू *bhú* it is superseded by the second aorist, this being enjoined for the simple verb. Some grammarians, however, admit the first aorist optionally for भू *bhú* (Colebr. p. 193). The conflicting opinions of native grammarians on the conjugation of intensives are fully stated by Colebrooke, p. 191 seq.

chichitiva, 5. चिचितथुः *chichitathuḥ*, 6. चिचिततुः *chichitatuḥ*, 7. चिचितिम *chichitima*, 8. चिचित *chichita*, 9. चिचितुः *chichituḥ*, I A. 1. अचेतिषं *achetisham*, 2. अचेतीः *achetîḥ*, 3. अचेतीत् *achetît*, 4. अचेतिष्व *achetishva*, 5. अचेतिष्टं *achetishṭam*, 6. अचेतिष्टां *achetishṭâm*, 7. अचेतिष्म *achetishma*, 8. अचेतिष्ट *achetishṭa*, 9. अचेतिषुः *achetishuḥ*, F. चेतिष्यति *chetishyati*, C. अचेतिष्यत् *achetishyat*, P. F. चेतिता *chetitâ*, B. चित्यात् *chityât* ‖ Pt. चित्तः *chittaḥ*, चिचित्वान् *chichitvân*, Ger. चेतित्वा *chetitvâ* or चितित्वा *chititvâ*, °चित्य *-chitya*, Adj. चेतितव्यः *chetitavyaḥ*, चेतनीयः *chetanîyaḥ*, चेत्यः *chetyaḥ* ‖ Pass. चित्यते *chityate*, Aor. अचेति *acheti*, Caus. चेतयति *chetayati*, Aor. अचीचितत् *achîchitat*, Des. चिचेतिषति *chichetishati* or *chichitishati*, Int. चेचित्यते *chechityate*, चेचेत्ति *chechetti*.

3. च्युत् *chyut*, to sprinkle, (च्युतिर्.)

The Anubandha इर् *ir* shows that the verb may take the first and second aorist.

P. च्योतति *chyotati*, I. अच्योतत् *achyotat*, O. च्योतेत् *chyotet*, I. च्योततु *chyotatu* ‖ Pf. 1. चुच्योत *chuchyota*, 2. चुच्योतिथ *chuchyotitha*, 4. चुच्युतिव *chuchyutiva*, I A. 1. अच्योतिषं *achyotisham*, 2. अच्योतीः *achyotîḥ*, 3. अच्योतीत् *achyotît*, 9. अच्योतिषुः *achyotishuḥ*, or II A. 1. अच्युतं *achyutam*, 2. अच्युतः *achyutaḥ*, 3. अच्युतत् *achyutat*, 9. अच्युतन् *achyutan*, F. च्योतिष्यति *chyotishyati*, C. अच्योतिष्यत् *achyotishyat*, P. F. च्योतिता *chyotitâ*, B. च्युत्यात् *chyutyât* ‖ Pt. च्युतितः *chyutitaḥ* or *chyotitaḥ*, चुच्युत्वान् *chuchyutvân*, Ger. च्योतित्वा *chyotitvâ* or *chyutitvâ*, Adj. च्योतितव्यः *chyotitavyaḥ* ‖ Pass. च्युत्यते *chyutyate*, Caus. च्योतयति *chyotayati*, Aor. अचुच्युतत् *achuchyutat*, Des. चुच्योतिषति *chuchyotishati* or चुच्युतिषति *chuchyutishati*, Int. चोच्युत्यते *chochyutyate*, चोच्योत्ति *chochyotti*.

4. श्च्युत् *śchyut*, to flow, (श्च्युतिर्.)

P. श्च्योतति *śchyotati*, I. अश्च्योतत् *aśchyotat*, O. श्च्योतेत् *śchyotet*, I. श्च्योततु *śchyotatu* ‖ Pf. 1. चुश्च्योत *chuśchyota*, 9. चुश्च्युतुः *chuśchyutuḥ*, I A. 1. अश्च्योतिषं *aśchyotisham*, 2. अश्च्योतीः *aśchyotîḥ*, or II A. 1. अश्च्युतं *aśchyutam*, F. श्च्योतिष्यति *śchyotishyati*, C. अश्च्योतिष्यत् *aśchyotishyat*, P. F. श्च्योतिता *śchyotitâ*, B. श्च्युत्यात् *śchyutyât* &c.

Note—This verb is sometimes written श्चुत् *śchut*.

5. मन्थ् *manth*, to shake.

P. मन्थति *manthati* ‖ Pf. 1. ममन्थ *mamantha*, 2. ममन्थिथ *mamanthitha*, 3. ममन्थ *mamantha*, 7. ममन्थिम *mamanthima*, 8. ममन्थथुः *mamanthathuḥ* (Pâṇ. I. 2, 5) or, less correctly, ममथथुः *mamathathuḥ* (§ 328, 4), I A. अमन्थीत् *amanthît*, F. मन्थिष्यति *manthishyati*, P. F. मन्थिता *manthitâ*, B. मथ्यात् *mathyât* (§ 345 †) ‖ Pt. मथितः *mathitaḥ*, ममन्थ्वान् *mamanthvân*, Ger. मन्थित्वा *manthitvâ* or मथित्वा *mathitvâ* (Pâṇ. I. 2, 23; § 428), °मथ्य *-mathya*, Adj. मन्थितव्यः *manthitavyaḥ*, मन्थनीयः *manthanîyaḥ*, मन्थ्यः *manthyaḥ* ‖ Pass. मथ्यते *mathyate*, Caus. मन्थयति *manthayati*, Des. मिमन्थिषति *mimanthishati*, Int. मामथ्यते *mâmathyate*, मामन्त्ति *mâmantti* or मामन्थीति *mâmanthîti*, Impf. 3. अमामन् *amâman*.

Note—Roots ending in consonants preceded by a nasal, lose the nasal before weakening (*kit*, *ṅit*) terminations (Pâṇ. VI. 4, 24); but not roots written with Anubandha इ *i*. The terminations of the reduplicated perfect in the dual and plural are weakening (*kit*), except after roots ending in double consonants (Pâṇ. I. 2, 5). According to some, however, the weakening is allowed even after double consonants: केचिदिति । श्रथोऽपोदवधुनिमित्तादेवः । यथा च श्रथोऽपोदवधूनामुङ्के । संयोगादिरिह किद्वा । ररन्थुः ररन्थुरिति ॥ Roots, however, which thus drop the penultimate nasal in the perfect, need not take ए *e* instead of reduplication: न्लोपिनो नेति केचित् ममन्थुः । Prakriyâ-Kaumudî, p. 7 b.

Native grammarians admit a verb मथति *mathati* (*mathe*), and another मथ्नाति *mathnâti*, which supply a variety of verbal derivatives.

6. कुंथ् *kunth*, to strike, (कुथि.)

Roots marked in the Dhâtupâṭha by technical final इ *i* keep their penultimate nasal throughout.

This root can take no Guṇa, on account of its final conjunct consonant.

P. कुंथति *kunthati*, I. अकुंथत् *akunthat*, O. कुंथेत् *kunthet*, I. कुंथतु *kunthatu* ॥ Pf. 1. चुकुंथ *chukuntha*, 2. चुकुंथिथ *chukunthitha*, 9. चुकुंथुः *chukunthuḥ*, I A. अकुंथीत् *akunthît*, 9. अकुंथिषुः *akunthishuḥ*, F. कुंथिष्यति *kunthishyati*, P. F. कुंथिता *kunthitâ*, B. कुंथ्यात् *kunthyât*, (प्रणिकुंथ्यात् *pranikunthyât*, § 99, not with lingual ण् *ṇ*, as Carey gives it) ॥ Pt. कुंथितः *kunthitaḥ*, चुकुंथ्वान् *chukunthvân*, Ger. कुंथित्वा *kunthitvâ*, °कुंथ्य *-kunthya*, Adj. कुंथितव्यः *kunthitavyaḥ* ॥ Pass. कुंथ्यते *kunthyate*, Caus. कुंथयति *kunthayati*, Des. चुकुंथिषति *chukunthishati*, Int. चोकुंथ्यते *chokunthyate*, चोकुंत्ति *chokuntti*.

7. सिध् *sidh*, to go (षिध्), and सिध् *sidh*, to command (षिधू).

P. सेधति *sedhati* (निसेधति *nisedhati**), I. असेधत् *asedhat* ॥ Pf. 1. सिषेध *sishedha*, 2. सिषेधिथ *sishedhitha*, 9. सिषिधुः *sishidhuḥ*, I A. असेधीत् *asedhît*, F. सेधिष्यति *sedhishyati*, P. F. सेधिता *sedhitâ*, B. सिध्यात् *sidhyât*.

In the sense of commanding or ordaining, this root is marked by technical ऊ *û* (षिधू *shidhû*), and hence the intermediate इ *i* may be omitted. Thus Pf. 2. सिषेधिथ *sishedhitha* or सिषेद्ध *sisheddha*, 4. सिषिधिव *sishidhiva* or सिषिध्व *sishidhva* &c., F. सेधिष्यति *sedhishyati* or सेत्स्यति *setsyati*, P. F. सेधिता *sedhitâ* or सेद्धा *seddhâ*, I A. असेधीत् *asedhît* (as before), or 1. असैत्सं *asaitsam*, 2. असैत्सीः *asaitsîḥ*, 3. असैत्सीत् *asaitsît*, 4. असैत्स्व *asaitsva*, 5. असैद्धं *asaiddham*, 6. असैद्धां *asaiddhâm*, 7. असैत्स्म *asaitsma*, 8. असैद्ध *asaiddha*, 9. असैत्सुः *asaitsuḥ* ॥ Pt. सिद्धः *siddhaḥ*, Ger. सेधित्वा *sedhitvâ* or सिद्ध्वा *siddhvâ*, °सिध्य *-sidhya*, Adj. सेधितव्यः *sedhitavyaḥ* or सेद्धव्यः *seddhavyaḥ* ॥ Pass. सिध्यते *sidhyate*, Caus. सेधयति *sedhayati*, Des. सिसेधिषति *sisedhishati* or सिषित्सति *sishitsati* (§ 103), Int. सेषिध्यते *seshidhyate*, सेषेद्धि *sesheddhi*.

---

* The change of स् *s* into ष् *sh* is forbidden by Pâṇini VIII. 3, 113, when सिध् *sidh* means to go. It is admitted by the Sâr. The Anubandha उ *u* is sometimes added to सिध् *sidh*, to go, but is explained to be for the sake of pronunciation only. Colebrooke marks it as erroneous. Its proper meaning would be that intermediate इ *i* is optional in the gerund, and forbidden in the past participle (§ 337, II. 5). The forms without intermediate इ *i* belong properly only to सिध् *sidh*, to command. This verb must change its initial स् *s* after prepositions; निषेधति *nishedhati*.

8. खद् *khad*, to be steady, to kill, to eat.

P. खदति *khadati* ‖ Pf. 1. चखाद *chakhâda*, 2. चखदिथ *chakhaditha*, 3. चखाद *chakhâda*, 4. चखदिव *chakhadiva*, 5. चखदथुः *chakhadathuḥ*, 6. चखदतुः *chakhadatuḥ*, 7. चखदिम *chakhadima*, 8. चखद *chakhada*, 9. चखदुः *chakhaduḥ*, I A. अखादीत् or अखदीत् *akhâdît* (Pâṇ. VII. 2, 7; § 348), F. खदिष्यति *khadishyati*, P. F. खदिता *khaditâ*, B. खद्यात् *khadyât* ‖ Pt. खदितः *khaditaḥ*, चखद्वान् *chakhadvân*, Ger. खदित्वा *khaditvâ*, °खद्य -*khadya*, Adj. खदितव्यः *khaditavyaḥ* ‖ Pass. खद्यते *khadyate*, Caus. खादयति *khâdayati*, Des. चिखदिषति *chikhadishati*, Int. चाखद्यते *châkhadyate*, चाखत्ति *châkhatti*.

9. गद् *gad*, to speak.

P. गदति *gadati* (प्रणिगदति *praṇigadati*), I. अगदत् *agadat* (प्राण्यगदत् *praṇyagadat*), O. गदेत् *gadet*, I. गदतु *gadatu* ‖ Pf. 1. जगाद *jagâda*, 2. जगदिथ *jagaditha*, 9. जगदुः *jagaduḥ*, I A. अगादीत् or अगदीत् *agâdît* (Pâṇ. VII. 2, 7; § 348), F. गदिष्यति *gadishyati*, C. अगदिष्यत् *agadishyat*, P. F. गदिता *gaditâ*, B. गद्यात् *gadyât* ‖ Caus. गादयति *gâdayati*, Des. जिगदिषति *jigadishati*, Int. जागद्यते *jâgadyate*, जागत्ति *jâgatti*.

10. रद् *rad*, to trace, to scratch.

P. रदति *radati* ‖ Pf. 1. रराद *rarâda*, 2. रेदिथ *reditha*, 9. रेदुः *reduḥ*, I A. अरादीत् or अरदीत् *arâdît* (§ 348).

11. नद् *nad*, to hum, (णद.)

P. नदति *nadati* (प्रणदति *praṇadati*, प्रणिनदति *praṇinadati*) ‖ Pf. 1. ननाद *nanâda*, 2. नेदिथ *neditha*, 9. नेदुः *neduḥ*, I A. अनादीत् or अनदीत् *anâdît*.

12. अर्द् *ard*, to go, to ask, to pain.

P. अर्दति *ardati*, I. आर्दत् *ârdat* ‖ Pf. 1. आनर्द *ânarda*, 2. आनर्दिथ *ânarditha*, 9. आनर्दुः *ânarduḥ*, I A. आर्दीत् *ârdît*, F. अर्दिष्यति *ardishyati* ‖ Pt. अर्दितः *arditaḥ*, not आर्तः *ârtaḥ*, see also p. 166 ‖ Caus. अर्दयति *ardayati*, आर्दिदत् *ârdidat*, Des. अर्दिदिषति *ardidishati*.

13. इंद् *ind*, to govern, (इदि.)

P. इंदति *indati*, I. ऐंदत् *aindat*, O. इंदेत् *indet*, I. इंदतु *indatu* ‖ Pf. इंदांचकार *indâṁchakâra* (§ 325) or इंदामास *indâmâsa* or इंदांबभूव *indâmbabhûva*, I A. 1. ऐंदिषं *aindisham*, 2. ऐंदीः *aindîḥ*, F. इंदिष्यति *indishyati*, C. ऐंदिष्यत् *aindishyat*, P. F. इंदिता *inditâ*, B. इंद्यात् *indyât* ‖ Pt. इंदितः *inditaḥ*, Perf. इंदांचकृवान् *indâṁchakṛivân* or बभूवान् *babhûvân* or आसिवान् *âsivân*, Perf. Pass. इंदांचक्राणः *indâṁchakrâṇaḥ* or बभूवानः *babhûvânaḥ* or आसानः *âsânaḥ*.

14. निंद् *nind*, to blame, (णिदि.)

P. निंदति *nindati* (प्रनिंदनं *pranindanam* or प्रणिंदनं *praṇindanam*, § 98, 8, 2) ‖ Pf. निनिंद *nininda*, I A. अनिंदीत् *anindît*, F. निंदिष्यति *nindishyati*, P. F. निंदिता *ninditâ*, B. निंद्यात् *nindyât*.

15. निक्ष् *niksh*, to kiss, (णिक्ष.)

P. निक्षति *nikshati* (प्रणिक्षति *praṇikshati*, not प्रनिक्षति *pranikshati*, § 98, 8, 2) ‖ Pf. निनिक्ष *niniksha*, I A. अनिक्षीत् *anikshît*, F. निक्षिष्यति *nikshishyati*, P. F. निक्षिता *nikshitâ*, B. निक्ष्यात् *nikshyât*.

16. उख् *ukh*, to go.

P. ओखति *okhati* (प्रोखति *prokhati*, § 43), I. औखत् *aukhat* ‖ Pf. 1. उवोख *uvokha* (§ 314), 2. उवोखिथ *uvokhitha*, 3. उवोख *uvokha*, 7. ऊखिम *ûkhima*, I A. औखीत् *aukhît*, F. ओखिष्यति *okhishyati*, C. औखिष्यत् *aukhishyat*, P. F. ओखिता *okhitâ*, B. उख्यात् *ukhyât* ‖ Pass. उख्यते *ukhyate*, Caus. ओखयति *okhayati*, Des. ओचिखिषति *ochikhishati*.

17. अंच् *añch*, to go, to worship, (अंचु and अचि.)

The Anubandha उ *u* of अंचु *añchu* allows the option of intermediate इ *i* in the gerund, अंचित्वा *añchitvâ* or अक्त्वा *aktvâ*, and its nasal remains, except before weakening forms (see *manth*, No. 5); but the Anubandha इ *i* of अचि *achi* requires the nasal throughout (Dhâtupâṭha 7, 6).

P. अंचति *añchati* ‖ Pf. 1. आनंच *ânañcha* (§ 313), 9. आनंचुः *ânañchuḥ* (but see No. 5, note), I A. आंचीत् *âñchît*, F. अंचिष्यति *añchishyati*, C. आंचिष्यत् *âñchishyat*, P. F. अंचिता *añchitâ*, B. अंच्यात् *añchyât* (may he worship), अच्यात् *achyât* (may he go), § 345†.

Pass. अच्यते *achyate* and अंच्यते *añchyate*, Caus. अंचयति *añchayati*, Des. अंचिचिषति *añchichishati*.

Distinguish between अंचितः *añchitaḥ*, worshipped, Ger. अंचित्वा *añchitvâ*, having worshipped, and अक्तः *aktaḥ*, moved (Pâṇ. VII. 2, 53; VI. 4, 30); अंच् *añch* never seems to lose its nasal when it means to honour: Pass. अंच्यते *añchyate*, he is honoured, अच्यते *achyate*, he is moved. The two roots, however, are not always kept distinct.

18. आंछ् *âñchh*, to stretch, (आछि.)

P. आंछति *âñchhati* ‖ Pf. आनांछ *ânâñchha* or आंछ *âñchha* (§ 313), I A. आंछीत् *âñchhît*, F. आंछिष्यति *âñchhishyati* ‖ Caus. आंछयति *âñchhayati*, Des. आंचिच्छिषति *âñchichchhishati*.

19. म्रुच् *mruch*, to go, (म्रुचु.)

म्रोचति *mrochati* ‖ This and other verbs enumerated § 367 take optionally the first or second aorist; अम्रोचीत् *amrochît* or अम्रुचत् *amruchat* ‖ Pt. म्रुक्तः *mruktaḥ*, Perf. मुम्रुच्वान् *mumruchvân*, Ger. म्रुचित्वा *mruchitvâ* or म्रुक्त्वा *mruktvâ*.

20. हुर्छ् *hurchh*, to be crooked, (हुर्छा.)

P. हूर्च्छति *hûrchchhati* (§ 143) ‖ Pf. जुहूर्च्छ *juhûrchchha*, I A. अहूर्च्छीत् *ahûrchchhît* ‖ Pt. हूर्च्छितः *hûrchchhitaḥ* or हूर्णः *hûrṇaḥ* (§ 431, 2).

21. वज् *vaj*, to go.

P. वजति *vajati* ‖ Pf. 1. ववाज *vavâja*, 2. ववजिथ *vavajitha* (§ 328), I A. अवाजीत् *avâjît*, F. वजिष्यति *vajishyati*.

22. व्रज् *vraj*, to go.

P. व्रजति *vrajati* ॥ Pf. 1. वव्राज *vavrâja*, 2. वव्रजिथ *vavrajitha*, I A. अव्राजीत् *avrâjît* (§ 348*) ॥ Pt. व्रजितः *vrajitaḥ* ॥ Caus. व्राजयति *vrâjayati*, Des. विव्रजिषति *vivrajishati*, Int. वाव्रज्यते *vâvrajyate*, वाव्रक्ति *vâvrakti*.

23. अज् *aj*, to go, to throw.

P. अजति *ajati*, I. आजत् *âjat* ॥ वी *vî* must be substituted in the general tenses before terminations beginning with vowels. Before all consonants except य् *y* (Pâṇ. II. 4, 56, v.) this substitution is optional, i.e. both अज् *aj* and वी *vî* may be used ॥ Pf. 1. विवाय *vivâya*, 2. विवेथ *vivetha* or विवयिथ *vivayitha* (§ 335, 3), [आजिथ *âjitha*], 3. विवाय *vivâya*, 4. विव्यिव *vivyiva* (§ 334), [आजिव *âjiva*], 5. विव्यथुः *vivyathuḥ*, 6. विव्यतुः *vivyatuḥ*, 7. विव्यिम *vivyima* [आजिम *âjima*], 8. विव्य *vivya*, 9. विव्युः *vivyuḥ*, I A. अवैषीत् *avaishît* [आजीत् *âjît*], 9. अवैषुः *avaishuḥ*, F. वेष्यति *veshyati* (§ 332, 3), C. अवेष्यत् *aveshyat*, P. F. वेता *vetâ*, B. वीयात् *vîyât* [F. अजिष्यति *ajishyati*, C. आजिष्यत् *âjishyat*, P. F. अजिता *ajitâ*] ॥ Pt. वीतः *vîtaḥ* [अजितः *ajitaḥ*], Perf. विवीवान् *vivîvân* [आजिवान् *âjivân*], Ger. वीत्वा *vîtvâ* [अजित्वा *ajitvâ*], °वीय *-vîya*, Adj. वेतव्यः *vetavyaḥ* [अजितव्यः *ajitavyaḥ*], वयनीयः *vayanîyaḥ*, वेयः *veyaḥ* ॥ Pass. वीयते *vîyate*, Caus. वाययति *vâyayati*, Des. विवीषति *vivîshati* [अजिजिषति *ajijishati*], Int. वेवीयते *vevîyate*, वेवेति *veveti*.

24. क्षि *kshi*, to wane.

P. क्षयति *kshayati* ॥ Pf. 1. चिक्षाय *chikshâya*, 2. चिक्षेथ *chikshetha* or चिक्षयिथ *chikshayitha*, 9. चिक्षियुः *chikshiyuḥ*, I A. अक्षैषीत् *akshaishît*, F. क्षेष्यति *ksheshyati*, B. क्षीयात् *kshîyât* (§ 390) ॥ Pt. क्षितः *kshitaḥ* or क्षीणः *kshîṇaḥ*, Caus. क्षययति *kshayayati*, Des. चिक्षीषति *chikshîshati*, Int. चेक्षीयते *chekshîyate*, चेक्षेति *cheksheti*. The Caus. क्षपयति *kshapayati* is better referred to क्षै *kshai* (§ 462, II. 23).

25. कट् *kaṭ*, to rain, to encompass, (कटे.)

The Anubandha ए *e* prevents the lengthening of the vowel in the aorist.

P. कटति *kaṭati* ॥ Pf. चकाट *chakâṭa*, I A. अकटीत् *akaṭît* (no Vṛiddhi, § 348†).

26. गुप् *gup*, to protect, (गुपू.)

The verbs गुप् *gup*, to guard, धूप् *dhûp*, to warm, विच्छ् *vichh*, to go, पण् *paṇ*, to traffic, पन् *pan*, to praise, take आय *âya* in the special tenses, and take it optionally in the rest. (Pâṇ. III. 1, 28; 31.)

P. गोपायति *gopâyati*, I. अगोपायत् *agopâyat*, O. गोपायेत् *gopâyet*, I. गोपायतु *gopâyatu* ॥ Pf. गोपायांचकार *gopâyâṁchakâra* (§ 325, 3) or जुगोप *jugopa*, I A. अगोपायीत् *agopâyît*, अगोपीत् *agopît* or अगौप्सीत् *agaupsît* (§ 337, I. 2), 6. अगौप्ताम् *agauptâm*, F. गोपायिष्यति *gopâyishyati*, गोपिष्यति *gopishyati*, or गोप्स्यति *gopsyati*, P. F. गोपायिता *gopâyitâ*, गोपिता *gopitâ*, or गोप्ता *goptâ*, B. गोपाय्यात् *gopâyyât* or गुप्यात् *gupyât* ॥ Pt. गोपायितः *gopâyitaḥ* or गुप्तः *guptaḥ*, Ger. गोपायित्वा *gopâyitvâ*, गोपित्वा *gopitvâ*, or गुप्त्वा *guptvâ*, Adj. गोपायितव्यः *gopâyitavyaḥ*, गोपितव्यः *gopitavyaḥ*, or गोप्यः gopyaḥ ॥ Caus. गोपयति gopayati or गोपाययति gopâyayati, Des. जुगुप्सति jugupsati, जुगुपिषति jugupishati, जुगोपिषति jugopishati, or जुगोपायिषति jugopâyishati, Int. जोगुप्यते jogupyate, जोगोप्ति jogopti.

27. धूप् dhûp, to warm.

P. धूपायति dhûpâyati ॥ Pf. धूपायांचकार dhûpayâṁchakâra or दुधूप dudhûpa (no Guṇa, because the vowel is long), I A. अधूपायीत् adhûpâyît or अधूपीत् adhûpît.

28. तप् tap, to burn, (§ 332, 14).

P. तपति tapati ॥ Pf. 1. तताप tatâpa, 2. ततप्थ tataptha or तेपिथ tepitha (§ 335, 3), 3. तताप tatâpa, I A. 1. अताप्सम् atâpsam, 2. अताप्सीः atâpsîḥ, 3. अताप्सीत् atâpsît, 6. अताप्ताम् atâptâm (§ 351), F. तप्स्यति tapsyati, P. F. तप्ता taptâ, B. तप्यात् tapyât ॥ Pt. तप्तः taptaḥ, तेपिवान् tepivân, Ger. तप्त्वा taptvâ, Adj. तप्तव्यः taptavyaḥ, तप्यः tapyaḥ (short, because it ends in प् p, § 456, 6) ॥ Pass. तप्यते tapyate, Caus. तापयति tâpayati, Des. तितप्सति titapsati, Int. तातप्यते tâtapyate, तातप्ति tâtapti.

Note—With certain prepositions तप् tap takes the Âtmanepada (Pâṇ. 1. 3, 27); उत्तपते uttapate, वितपते vitapate, it shines. It has an active sense in the passive (i.e. Div Âtm.), if it refers to तपः tapaḥ, austere devotion; तप्यते तपस्तापसः tapyate tapas tâpasaḥ, the devotee performs austere devotion. In the sense of regretting (being burnt) it forms the Aor. अतप्त atapta; अन्ववातप्त पापेन कर्मणा anvavâtapta pâpena karmaṇâ, he was distressed by a sinful act. (Colebr.)

29. चम् cham, to eat, (चमु.)

The following verbs lengthen their vowel in the special tenses (Pâṇ. VII. 3, 75, 76): चम् cham, if preceded by आ â, to rinse, आचामति âchâmati; ष्ठिव् shṭhiv, to spit, ष्ठीवति shṭhîvati (see No. 35); क्रम् kram, to stride, क्रामति krâmati (see No. 30); क्लम् klam, to tire, क्लामति klâmati; गुह् guh, to hide, गूहति gûhati, follows a different rule, lengthening its vowel throughout, instead of taking Guṇa, when a vowel follows. (Pâṇ. VI. 4, 89.)

P. चमति chamati, but after the prep. आ â, आचामति âchâmati ॥ Pf. 1. चचाम chachâma, चचमिथ chachamitha or चेमिथ chemitha &c., I A. अचमीत् achamît (§ 348*) ॥ Pt. चान्तः chântaḥ, Ger. चान्त्वा chântvâ or चमित्वा chamitvâ, Adj. चमितव्यः chamitavyaḥ, चाम्यः châmyaḥ (Pâṇ. III. 1, 126) ॥ Caus. चामयति châmayati (§ 462).

30. क्रम् kram, to stride, (क्रमु.)

क्रमु kram, to stride, भ्राशृ bhrâś, to shine, भ्लाशृ bhlâś, to shine, भ्रमु bhram, to roam, क्लमु klam, to fail, त्रसी tras, to tremble, त्रुटु truṭ, to cut, लष lash, to desire, may take य ya in the special tenses. Hence भ्राम्यति bhrâmyati or भ्रमति bhramati. (Pâṇ. III. 1, 70.)

P. क्रामति krâmati or क्राम्यति krâmyati, I. अक्रामत् akrâmat or अक्राम्यत् akrâmyat ॥ Pf. चक्राम chakrâma, I A. अक्रमीत् akramît (§ 348*), F. क्रमिष्यति kramishyati, P. F. क्रमिता kramitâ, B. क्रम्यात् kramyât ॥

क्रम् kram lengthens its vowel in the general tenses (śit) of the Parasmaipada (Pâṇ. VII. 3, 76). Hence क्रामति krâmati, but क्रमते kramate. It takes no intermediate इ *i* in the Âtm.; Fut. क्रंस्यते *kraṁsyate*, P. F. क्रंता *krantá*, Aor. अक्रंस्त *akraṁsta;* but some grammarians admit intermediate इ *i*.

Pt. क्रांतः *krántaḥ*, Perf. चक्रन्वान् *chakranván*, Ger. क्रांत्वा *krántvá* or क्रमित्वा *kramitvá* (§ 429), Adj. क्रमितव्यः *kramitavyaḥ* ॥ Pass. क्रम्यते *kramyate*, Caus. क्रमयति *kramayati*, § 461, (after prep. also क्रामयति *krámayati*), Des. चिक्रमिषति *chikramishati* or चिक्रंसते *chikraṁsate*, Int. चंक्रम्यते *chaṅkramyate*, चंक्रंति *chaṅkranti*.

Note—It is by no means certain that क्रम् *kram* in the Div class forms क्राम्यति *krámyati*. It is not one of the eight Sam verbs (Pâṇ. VII. 3, 74); and in Pâṇ. VII. 3, 76, *śyan* is no longer valid. The Prasâda gives क्रम्यति *kramyati;* but adds, श्यनि तु इयन्यपि दीर्घः क्राम्यतीति। The Sârasvatî decides for क्राम्यति *krámyati*, giving the general rule (II. 1, 145) क्रमादीनां दीर्घो भवति यकारे परे। and enumerating as क्रमादि, क्लम् दम् चम् भ्रम् श्रम् क्षम् मद्.

31. यम् *yam*, to stop.

The roots गम् *gam*, to go, यम् *yam*, to cease, and इष् *ish*, to wish, substitute छ *chchha* for their final in the special tenses. (Pâṇ. VII. 3, 77.)

P. यच्छति *yachchhati*, I. अयच्छत् *ayachchhat* ॥ Pf. 1. ययाम *yayáma*, 2. ययंथ *yayantha* or येमिथ *yemitha*, 9. येमुः *yemuḥ*, I A. अयंसीत् *ayaṁsît* (§ 359), F. यंस्यति *yaṁsyati*, P. F. यंता *yantá*, B. यम्यात् *yamyát* ॥ Pt. यतः *yataḥ*, येमिवान् *yemiván*, Ger. यत्वा *yatvá*, °यम्य *-yamya* or °यत्य *-yatya*, Adj. यंतव्यः *yantavyaḥ*, यम्यः *yamyaḥ* (नियाम्यः *niyámyaḥ*) ॥ Pass. यम्यते *yamyate*, Caus. यमयति *yámayati*, II A. अयीयमत् *ayîyamat*, Des. यियंसति *yiyaṁsati*, Int. यंयम्यते *yaṁyamyate* or यंयंति *yaṁyanti*.

Note—यम् *yam* may be used in the Âtm. with the prep. आ *á*, if it is either intransitive, आयच्छते तरुः *áyachchhate taruḥ*, the tree spreads, or governs as its object a member of the agent's body; आयच्छते पाणिं *áyachchhate páṇim*, he puts forth his hand. Likewise with the prep. आ *á*, सं *sam*, उद् *ud*, if it is used reflectively; संयच्छते व्रीहीन् *saṁyachchhate vrîhîn*, he heaps together his own rice. Likewise after उप *upa*, when it means to espouse; रामः सीतामुपायंस्त *rámaḥ sîtám upáyaṁsta*, Râma married Sîtâ: here the Aor. may also be उपायत *upáyata;* like उदायत *udáyata*, he divulged another's faults. (§ 356.)

32. नम् *nam*, to bow, (णम्.)

P. नमति *namati* ॥ Pf. 1. ननाम *nanáma*, 2. ननंथ *nanantha* or नेमिथ *nemitha*, 9. नेमुः *nemuḥ*, I A. अनंसीत् *anaṁsît* (§ 359), F. नंस्यति *naṁsyati*, P. F. नंता *nantá*, B. नम्यात् *namyát* &c., like यम् *yam*.

Note—नम् *nam* may be conjugated in the Âtmanepada. (Pâṇ. III. 1, 89.)
The Anubandha ण *ṇ* given to it by some grammarians is declared wrong by others.

33. गम् *gam*, to go, (गम्लृ.)

P. गच्छति *gachchhati* ॥ Pf. 1. जगाम *jagáma*, 2. जगमिथ *jagamitha* or जगंथ *jagantha*, 3. जगाम *jagáma*, 4. जग्मिव *jagmiva* (§ 328, 3), 5. जग्मथुः *jagmathuḥ* &c., II A. अगमत् *agamat* (§ 367), F. गमिष्यति *gamishyati* (§ 338, 2), P. F. गंता *gantá*, B. गम्यात् *gamyát* ॥ Pt. गतः *gataḥ*, Perf. जग्मिवान् *jagmiván* or जगन्वान् *jaganván*, Ger. गत्वा *gatvá*, °गम्य *-gamya* or °गत्य *-gatya*, Adj. गंतव्यः *gantavyaḥ*, गम्यः *gamyaḥ* ॥

Pass. गम्यते *gamyate*, Caus. गमयति *gamayati*, Aor. अजीगमत् *ajîgamat*, Des. जिगमिषति *jigamishati*, Int. जंगम्यते *jaṅgamyate* or जंगन्ति *jaṅganti*.

Note—With prep. सं *sam* it follows the Âtm., if intransitive. The Caus. too, with the prep. आ *â*, may follow the Âtm., if it means to have patience; आगमयस्व तावत् *âgamayasva tâvat*, wait a little. In the Âtm. the final म् *m* may be dropt in the Aor. and Ben.; समगत *samagata* or समगंस्त *samagaṁsta*, संगसीष्ट *saṅgasîshṭa* or संगंसीष्ट *saṅgaṁsîshṭa*. (See § 355.)

34. फल् *phal*, to burst, (ञिफला.)

P. फलति *phalati* ॥ Pf. 1. पफाल *paphâla*, 2. फेलिथ *phelitha* (§ 336, II. 2), 3. पफाल *paphâla*, 4. फेलिव *pheliva*, I A. अफालीत् *aphâlît* (§ 348*), F. फलिष्यति *phalishyati* ॥ Pt. फुल्लः *phullaḥ* (Pâṇ. VIII. 2, 55), Ger. फलित्वा *phalitvâ* ॥ Pass. फल्यते *phalyate*, Caus. फालयति *phâlayati*, Aor. अपीफलत् *apîphalat*, Des. पिफलिषति *piphalishati*, Int. पंफुल्यते *pamphulyate*, पंफुल्ति *pamphulti*. (Pâṇ. VII. 4, 87–89.)

35. ष्ठिव् *shṭhiv*, to spit, (ष्ठिवु.)

P. ष्ठीवति *shṭhîvati* ॥ Pf. तिष्ठेव *tishṭheva* or टिष्ठेव *ṭishṭheva*, I A. अष्ठेवीत् *ashṭhevît*, F. ष्ठेविष्यति *shṭhevishyati* ॥ Pt. ष्ठ्यूतः *shṭhyûtaḥ* ॥ Pass. ष्ठीव्यते *shṭhîvyate* (§ 143), Caus. ष्ठेवयति *shṭhevayati*, Des. तिष्ठीविषति *tishṭhîvishati* or टुष्ठ्यूषति *ṭushṭhyûshati* (Pâṇ. VII. 2, 49), Int. तेष्ठीव्यते *teshṭhîvyate*. No Intensive Parasmaipada.

Vowel lengthened in special tenses (see No. 29). Initial sibilant unchangeable (§ 103).

36. जि *ji*, to excel.

P. जयति *jayati* ॥ Pf. 1. जिगाय *jigâya*, 2. जिगेथ *jigetha* or जिगयिथ *jigayitha*, 3. जिगाय *jigâya*, 4. जिग्यिव *jigyiva*, 5. जिग्यथुः *jigyathuḥ*, 6. जिग्यतुः *jigyatuḥ*, 7. जिग्यिम *jigyima*, 8. जिग्य *jigya*, 9. जिग्युः *jigyuḥ*, I A. अजैषीत् *ajaishît* (§ 350), F. जेष्यति *jeshyati*, P. F. जेता *jetâ*, B. जीयात् *jîyât* ॥ Pt. जितः *jitaḥ*, Perf. जिगीवान् *jigîvân*, Ger. जित्वा *jitvâ*, Adj. जेतव्यः *jetavyaḥ*, जयनीयः *jayanîyaḥ*, जेयः *jeyaḥ*, and जय्यः *jayyaḥ* (§ 456, 2), जित्यः *jityaḥ* only with हलिः *haliḥ* (Pâṇ. III. 1, 117) ॥ Pass. जीयते *jîyate*, Aor. अजायि *ajâyi*, Caus. जापयति *jâpayati*, Aor. अजीजपत् *ajîjapat*, Des. जिगीषति *jigîshati*, Int. जेजीयते *jejîyate*, जेजेति *jejeti*. It follows the Âtmanepada with the prepositions परा *parâ* and वि *vi*.

The change of ज् *j* into ग् *g* in the reduplicated perfect is anomalous (§ 319). It does not take place in ज्या *jyâ*, to wither (जिनाति *jinâti*), although the rule of Pâṇini might seem to comprehend that root after it has taken *Samprasâraṇa*. ज्या *jyâ* forms its reduplicated perfect जिज्यौ *jijyau*.

37. अक्ष् *aksh*, to obtain, (अक्षू.)

अक्ष् *aksh* follows also the Su class, अक्ष्णोति *akshṇoti* &c.

P. अक्षति *akshati* ॥ Pf. 1. आनक्ष *ânaksha*, 2. आनक्षिथ *ânakshitha* or आनष्ठ *ânashṭha*, 3. आनक्ष *ânaksha*, 4. आनक्षिव *ânakshiva* or आनक्ष्व *ânakshva*, 5. आनक्षथुः *ânakshathuḥ*, 6. आनक्षतुः *ânakshatuḥ*, 7. आनक्षिम *ânakshima* or आनक्ष्म *ânakshma*, 8. आनक्ष *ânaksha*, 9. आनक्षुः *ânakshuḥ*, I A. 1. आक्षिषं *âkshisham* or आक्षं *âksham*,

2. आक्षीः *âkshîḥ*, 3. आक्षीत् *âkshît*, 4. आक्षिष्व *âkshishva* or आक्ष्व *âkshva*, 5. आक्षिष्टं *âkshishṭam* or आष्टं *âshṭam*, 6. आक्षिष्टां *âkshishṭâm* or आष्टां *âshṭâm*, 7. आक्षिष्म *âkshishma* or आक्ष्म *âkshma*, 8. आक्षिष्ट *âkshishṭa* or आष्ट *âshṭa*, 9. आक्षिषुः *âkshishuḥ* or आक्षुः *âkshuḥ*, F. अक्षिष्यति *akshishyati* or अक्ष्यति *akshyati*, P. F. अक्षिता *akshitâ* or अष्टा *ashṭâ* ‖ Pt. अष्टः *ashṭaḥ*, Ger. अष्ट्वा *ashṭvâ* or अक्षित्वा *akshitvâ* ‖ Pass. अक्ष्यते *akshyate*, Caus. अक्षयति *akshayati*, Aor. आचिक्षत् *âchikshat*, Des. आचिक्षिषति *âchikshishati* (§ 476).

तक्ष् *taksh*, to hew, follows अक्ष् *aksh* throughout, also in the optional forms of the Su class.

38. कृष् *kṛish*, to drag along, to furrow.

P. कर्षति *karshati* ‖ Pf. 1. चकर्ष *chakarsha*, 2. चकर्षिथ *chakarshitha*, 3. चकर्ष *chakarsha*, 4. चकृषिव *chakṛishiva* (§ 335, 3), I A. 1. अकार्क्षम् *akârksham*, 2. अकार्क्षीः *akârkshîḥ*, 3. अकार्क्षीत् *akârkshît*, 4. अकार्क्ष्व *akârkshva*, 5. अकार्ष्टं *akârshṭam*, 6. अकार्ष्टां *akârshṭâm*, 7. अकार्क्ष्म *akârkshma*, 8. अकार्ष्ट *akârshṭa*, 9. अकार्क्षुः *akârkshuḥ*; or अक्राक्षं *akrâksham* &c., or I A. 4. अकृक्षं *akṛiksham* &c. If used in the Âtmanepada, the two forms would be,

I A. 2. 1. अकृक्षि *akṛikshi*,	2. अकृष्ठाः *akṛishṭhâḥ*,	3. अकृष्ट *akṛishṭa*,
I A. 4. 1. id.	2. अकृक्षथाः *akṛikshathâḥ*,	3. अकृक्षत *akṛikshata*,
I A. 2. 4. अकृक्ष्वहि *akṛikshvahi*,	5. अकृक्षाथां *akṛikshâthâm*,	6. अकृक्षातां *akṛikshâtâm*,
I A. 4. 4. अकृक्षावहि *akṛikshâvahi*,	5. id.	6. id.
I A. 2. 7. अकृक्ष्महि *akṛikshmahi*,	8. अकृढ्वं *akṛiḍhvam*,	9. अकृक्षत *akṛikshata*,
I A. 4. 7. अकृक्षामहि *akṛikshâmahi*,	8. अकृक्षध्वं *akṛikshadhvam*,	9. अकृक्षन्त *akṛikshanta*.

F. क्रक्ष्यति *krakshyati* or कर्क्ष्यति *karkshyati*, P. F. क्रष्टा *krashṭâ* or कर्ष्टा *karshṭâ* ‖ Pt. कृष्टः *kṛishṭaḥ*, Ger. कृष्ट्वा *kṛishṭvâ* ‖ Pass. कृष्यते *kṛishyate*, Caus. कर्षयति *karshayati*, Aor. अचकर्षत् *achakarshat* or अचीकृषत् *achîkṛishat*, Des. चिकृक्षति *chikṛikshati*, Int. चरीकृष्यते *charîkṛishyate*, चरीकर्ष्टि *charîkarshṭi* or चरीक्रष्टि *charîkrashṭi*.

The peculiar Guṇa and Vṛiddhi of ऋ *ṛi*, viz. र *ra* and रा *râ*, instead of अर् *ar* and आर् *âr*, take place necessarily in सृज् *sṛij*, to emit, and दृश् *dṛiś*, to see (Pâṇ. VI. 1, 58); स्रष्टा *srashṭâ*, द्रष्टा *drashṭâ*, अस्राक्षीत् *asrâkshît*, and अद्राक्षीत् *adrâkshît*: optionally in verbs with penultimate ऋ *ṛi*, which reject intermediate इ *i* (Pâṇ. VI. 1, 59); तृप् *tṛip*, to rejoice, त्रप्ता *traptâ* or तर्प्ता *tarptâ*, Aor. अतार्प्सीत् *atârpsît*, अत्राप्सीत् *atrâpsît* or अतृपत् *atṛipat*.

39. रुष् *rush*, to kill.

P. रोषति *roshati* ‖ Pf. 1. रुरोष *rurosha*, 2. रुरोषिथ *ruroshitha*, 9. रुरुषुः *rurushuḥ*, I A. अरोषीत् *aroshît*, F. रोषिष्यति *roshishyati*, P. F. रोष्टा *roshṭâ* or रोषिता *roshitâ* (§ 337, II. 1).

40. उष् *ush*, to burn.

P. ओषति *oshati*, I. औषत् *aushat* ‖ Pf. 1. ओषांचकार *oshâṁchakâra* or उवोष *uvosha* (§ 326), 2. उवोषिथ *uvoshitha*, 3. उवोष *uvosha*, 4. ऊषिव *ûshiva* &c., I A. औषीत् *aushît*, F. ओषिष्यति *oshishyati*, P. F. ओषिता *oshitâ*, B. उष्यात् *ushyât* ‖ Pt. उषितः *ushitaḥ* or ओषितः *oshitaḥ* (§ 425) ‖ Des. ओषिषिषति *oshishishati*.

41. मिह् *mih*, to sprinkle.

P. मेहति *mehati* ॥ Pf. 1. मिमेह *mimeha*, 2. मिमेहिथ *mimehitha*, I A. अमिक्षत् *amikshat* (§ 360), F. मेक्ष्यति *mekshyati*, P. F. मेढा *meḍhâ* ॥ Pt. मीढः *mîḍhaḥ*, Perf. मीढ्वान् *mîḍhvân* (मिमिह्वान् *mimihvân*), Ger. मीढ्वा *mîḍhvâ* ॥ Caus. मेहयति *mehayati*, अमीमिहत् *amîmihat*, Des. मिमिक्षति *mimikshati*, Int. मेमेह्यते *memehyate*, मेमेढि *memeḍhi*, (मेमिढि *memiḍhi*, Westerg.)

42. दह् *dah*, to burn.

P. दहति *dahati* ॥ Pf. 1. ददाह *dadâha*, 2. देहिथ *dehitha* or ददग्ध *dadagdha*, F. धक्ष्यति *dhakshyati* (§ 118), P. F. दग्धा *dagdhâ*, B. दह्यात् *dahyât*, I A. 1. अधाक्षम् *adhâksham*, 2. अधाक्षीः *adhâkshîḥ*, 3. अधाक्षीत् *adhâkshît*, 4. अधाक्ष्व *adhâkshva*, 5. अदाग्धम् *adâgdham*, 6. अदाग्धाम् *adâgdhâm*, 7. अधाक्ष्म *adhâkshma*, 8. अदाग्ध *adâgdha*, 9. अधाक्षुः *adhâkshuḥ* (see p. 185) ॥ Pt. दग्धः *dagdhaḥ* ॥ Caus. दाहयति *dâhayati*, Aor. अदीदहत् *adîdahat*, Des. दिधक्षति *didhakshati*, Int. दंदह्यते *dandahyate*, दंदग्धि *dandagdhi*.

43. ग्लै *glai*, to droop; also म्लै *mlai*, to fade.

P. ग्लायति *glâyati*, O. ग्लायेत् *glâyet* ॥ Pf. 1. जग्लौ *jaglau* (§ 329), 2. जग्लिथ *jaglitha* or जग्लाथ *jaglâtha*, 3. जग्लौ *jaglau*, 4. जग्लिव *jagliva*, 5. जग्लथुः *jaglathuḥ*, 6. जग्लतुः *jaglatuḥ*, 7. जग्लिम *jaglima*, 8. जग्ल *jagla*, 9. जग्लुः *jagluḥ*, I A. 1. अग्लासिषम् *aglâsisham* (§ 357), 2. अग्लासीः *aglâsîḥ*, 3. अग्लासीत् *aglâsît*, 4. अग्लासिष्व *aglâsishva*, 5. अग्लासिष्टम् *aglâsishṭam*, 6. अग्लासिष्टाम् *aglâsishṭâm*, 7. अग्लासिष्म *aglâsishma*, 8. अग्लासिष्ट *aglâsishṭa*, 9. अग्लासिषुः *aglâsishuḥ*, F. ग्लास्यति *glâsyati*, P. F. ग्लाता *glâtâ*, B. ग्लायात् *glâyât* or ग्लेयात् *gleyât* (§ 392†) ॥ Pt. ग्लानः *glânaḥ*, Ger. ग्लात्वा *glâtvâ*, °ग्लाय *-glâya*, Adj. ग्लातव्यः *glâtavyaḥ*, ग्लानीयः *glânîyaḥ*, ग्लेयः *gleyaḥ* ॥ Pass. (impers.) ग्लायते *glâyate*, Caus. ग्लापयति or ग्लपयति *glâpayati*, Des. जिग्लासति *jiglâsati*, Int. जाग्लायते *jâglâyate*, जाग्लाति *jâglâti*.

44. गै *gai*, to sing; also रै *rai*, to bark, कै *kai*, to croak.

P. गायति *gâyati* ॥ Pf. जगौ *jagau*, I A. अगासीत् *agâsît*, F. गास्यति *gâsyati*, P. F. गाता *gâtâ*, B. गेयात् *geyât* (§ 392). Mark the difference between गै *gai* and ग्लै *glai* in the Bened. ॥ Pt. गीतः *gîtaḥ*, Ger. गीत्वा *gîtvâ*, °गाय *-gâya*, Adj. गातव्यः *gâtavyaḥ*, गानीयः *gânîyaḥ*, गेयः *geyaḥ* ॥ Pass. गीयते *gîyate*, Aor. अगायि *agâyi*, Caus. गापयति *gâpayati*, Aor. अजीगपत् *ajîgapat*, Des. जिगासति *jigâsati*, Int. जेगीयते *jegîyate*, जागाति *jâgâti*.

45. ष्ट्यै *shṭyai*, to sound, to gather; also स्त्यै *styai*, the same. (§ 103.)

P. ष्ट्यायति *shṭyâyati* (§ 103), I. अष्ट्यायत् *ashṭyâyat* ॥ Pf. तष्ट्यौ *tashṭyau*, I A. अष्ट्यासीत् *ashṭyâsît*, F. ष्ट्यास्यति *shṭyâsyati*, P. F. ष्ट्याता *shṭyâtâ*, B. ष्ट्यायात् *shṭyâyât* or ष्ट्येयात् *shṭyeyât* ॥ Pt. स्त्यानः *styânaḥ*, प्रस्तीतः *prastîtaḥ*, प्रस्तीमः *prastîmaḥ* (§ 443).

Note—With regard to the initial lingual sibilant, the Prasâda quotes the Vârttika to Pâṇ. vi. 1, 64, as सुब्धातुष्ठिवुष्वष्कतीनां सत्वप्रतिषेधः । A marginal note says, सुब्धातुष्ठिवुष्वष्क- [illegible] ।

46. दै *dai*, to cleanse, (दैप्.)

This verb is distinguished by a mute प् *p* from other verbs, like दा *dá* &c. It is therefore not comprised under the घु *ghu* verbs (§ 392*); it takes the first aorist (3rd form), and does not substitute ई *í* or ए *e* for आ *á*.

P. दायति *dáyati* ‖ Pf. ददौ *dadau*, I A. 1. अदासिषम् *adásisham*, 2. अदासीः *adásíḥ* &c., F. दास्यति *dásyati*, P. F. दाता *dátá*, B. दायात् *dáyát* ‖ Pt. दातः *dátaḥ* ‖ Pass. दायते *dáyate*, Caus. दापयति *dápayati*, Des. दिदासति *didásati*, Int. दादायते *dádáyate*, दादाति *dádáti*.

47. धे *dhe*, to drink, (धेट्.)

This verb is one of the six so-called घु *ghu* roots (§ 392), roots which in the general tenses have for their base दा *dá* or धा *dhá*.

P. धयति *dhayati* ‖ Pf. 1. दधौ *dadhau*, 2. दधिथ *dadhitha* or दधाथ *dadhátha*, 3. दधौ *dadhau*, 4. दधिव *dadhiva*, 5. दधथुः *dadhathuḥ*, 6. दधतुः *dadhatuḥ*, 7. दधिम *dadhima*, 8. दध *dadha*, 9. दधुः *dadhuḥ*. It admits I A. 3. (§ 357), II A. (§ 368), and Red. II A. (§ 371):

1. अधासिषम् *adhásisham*, 2. अधासीः *adhásíḥ*, 9. अधासिषुः *adhásishuḥ*,
1. अधाम् *adhám*, 2. अधाः *adháḥ*, 9. अधुः *adhuḥ*,
1. अदधम् *adadham*, 2. अदधः *adadhaḥ*, 9. अदधन् *adadhan*.

F. धास्यति *dhásyati*, P. F. धाता *dhátá*, B. धेयात् *dheyát* ‖ Pt. धीतः *dhítaḥ*, Ger. धीत्वा *dhítvá*, °धाय *-dháya* ‖ Pass. धीयते *dhíyate*, Caus. धापयति *dhápayati* (Âtm. °ते *-te*, to swallow), Aor. अदीधपत् *adídhapat*, Des. धित्सति *dhitsati*, Int. देधीयते *dedhíyate*, दाधाति *dádháti*, or, with the always optional ई *í*, दाधेति *dádheti*.

48. दृश् *dṛiś*, to see, (दृशिर्.)

This root substitutes पश्य *paśya* in the special tenses.

P. पश्यति *paśyati*, I. अपश्यत् *apaśyat*, O. पश्येत् *paśyet*, I. पश्यतु *paśyatu* ‖ Pf. 1. ददर्श *dadarśa*, 2. ददर्शिथ *dadarśitha* or दद्रष्ठ *dadrashṭha* (§ 335), 3. ददर्श *dadarśa*, 4. ददृशिव *dadṛiśiva*, 5. ददृशथुः *dadṛiśathuḥ*, 6. ददृशतुः *dadṛiśatuḥ*, 7. ददृशिम *dadṛiśima*, 8. ददृश *dadṛiśa*, 9. ददृशुः *dadṛiśuḥ*, I A. 1. अद्राक्षम् *adráksham*, 2. अद्राक्षीः *adrákshíḥ*, 3. अद्राक्षीत् *adrákshít*, 4. अद्राक्ष्व *adrákshva*, 5. अद्राष्टम् *adráshṭam*, 6. अद्राष्टाम् *adráshṭám*, 7. अद्राक्ष्म *adrákshma*, 8. अद्राष्ट *adráshṭa*, 9. अद्राक्षुः *adrákshuḥ* (§§ 360, 364); or II A. 1. अदर्शम् *adarśam*, 9. अदर्शन् *adarśan*, F. द्रक्ष्यति *drakshyati*, P. F. द्रष्टा *drashṭá*, B. दृश्यात् *dṛiśyát* ‖ Pt. दृष्टः *dṛishṭaḥ*, Ger. दृष्ट्वा *dṛishṭvá*, °दृश्य *-dṛiśya*, Adj. द्रष्टव्यः *drashṭavyaḥ*, दर्शनीयः *darśaníyaḥ*, दृश्यः *dṛiśyaḥ* ‖ Pass. दृश्यते *dṛiśyate*, F. दर्शिष्यते *darśishyate* or द्रक्ष्यते *drakshyate* (§ 411), P. F. दर्शिता *darśitá* or द्रष्टा *drashṭá*, B. दर्शिषीष्ट *darśishíshṭa* or दृक्षीष्ट *dṛikshíshṭa*, Aor. अदर्शि *adarśi*, Caus. दर्शयति *darśayati*, Aor. अदीदृशत् *adídṛiśat* or अददर्शत् *adadarśat*, Des. दिदृक्षते *didṛikshate* (Âtm.), Int. दरीदृश्यते *darídṛiśyate*, दर्दर्ष्टि *dardarshṭi*.

दृश् *dṛiś* and सृज् *sṛij* take र *ra* and रा *rá*, instead of अर् *ar* and आर् *ár*, as their Guṇa and Vṛiddhi before consonantal terminations (Pâṇ. vi. 1, 58). See No. 38.

Other verbs which substitute different bases in the special tenses (Pâṇ. VII. 3, 78): ऋ ṛi forms ऋच्छति ṛichchhati; सृ sṛi, धावति dhâvati; शद् śad, शीयते śîyate (Âtm.); सद् sad, सीदति sîdati; पा pâ, पिबति pibati; घ्रा ghrâ, जिघ्रति jighrati; ध्मा dhmâ, धमति dhamati; स्था sthâ, तिष्ठति tishṭhati; म्ना mnâ, मनति manati; दा dâ, यच्छति yachchhati.

49. ऋ ṛi, to go.

P. ऋच्छति *ṛichchhati* (उपार्छति *upârchhati*, § 44), I. आर्छत् *ârchhat* ‖ Pf. 1. आर *âra*, 2. आरिथ *âritha* (§ 338, 7), 3. आर *âra*, 4. आरिव *âriva*, 5. आरथुः *ârathuḥ*, 6. आरतुः *âratuḥ*, 7. आरिम *ârima*, 8. आर *âra*, 9. आरुः *âruḥ*, II A. 1. आरं *âram*, 2. आरः *âraḥ*, 3. आरत् *ârat*, 9. आरन् *âran* (§ 364); or I A. 1. आर्षं *ârsham*, 2. आर्षीः *ârshîḥ*, 3. आर्षीत् *ârshît*, 9. आर्षुः *ârshuḥ*, F. अरिष्यति *arishyati* (§ 338, 2), C. आरिष्यत् *ârishyat*, P. F. अर्ता *artâ*, B. अर्यात् *aryât* (§ 390) ‖ Pt. ऋतः *ṛitaḥ* or ऋणः *ṛiṇaḥ*, Ger. ऋत्वा *ṛitvâ*, °ऋत्य *-ṛitya* ‖ Pass. अर्यते *aryate*, Caus. अर्पयति *arpayati*, Des. अरिरिषति *aririshati*, Int. अरार्यते *arâryate*, अरर्ति *ararti*, अरियर्ति *ariyarti*, अररीति *ararîti*, अरियरीति *ariyarîti* (exceptional intensive, § 479, with the sense of moving tortuously).

50. सृ sṛi, to go.

P. धावति *dhâvati* always means to run, while सरति *sarati* is used likewise in the sense of going ‖ Pf. 1. ससार *sasâra*, 2. ससर्थ *sasartha* (§ 335, 3), 3. ससार *sasâra*, 4. सस्रिव *sasṛiva*, 5. सस्रथुः *sasrathuḥ*, 6. सस्रतुः *sasratuḥ*, 7. सस्रिम *sasṛima*, 8. सस्र *sasra*, 9. सस्रुः *sasruḥ*, II A. 1. असरं *asaram*, 2. असरः *asaraḥ*, 3. असरत् *asarat*; or I A. 1. असार्षं *asârsham*, 2. असार्षीः *asârshîḥ*, 3. असार्षीत् *asârshît*, F. सरिष्यति *sarishyati*, P. F. सर्ता *sartâ*, B. स्रियात् *sriyât* (§ 390) ‖ Pt. सृतः *sṛitaḥ* ‖ Caus. सारयति *sârayati*, Des. सिसीर्षति *sisîrshati*, Int. सेस्रीयते *sesrîyate*, सर्सर्ति *sarsarti* (§ 490).

51. शद् śad, to wither, (शदॢ.)

The special tenses take the Âtmanepada.

P. शीयते *śîyate*, I. अशीयत *aśîyata*, O. शीयेत *śîyeta*, I. शीयतां *śîyatâm* ‖ Pf. 1. शशाद *śaśâda*, 2. शशत्थ *śaśattha* or शेदिथ *śeditha*, 9. शेदुः *śeduḥ*, II A. अशदत् *aśadat*, F. शत्स्यति *śatsyati*, P. F. शत्ता *śattâ*, B. शद्यात् *śadyât* ‖ Caus. शातयति *śâtayati* (शादयति *śâdayati*, he drives), Des. शिशत्सति *śiśatsati*, Int. शाशद्यते *śâśadyate*, शाशत्ति *śâśatti*.

52. सद् sad, to perish, (षदॢ.)

P. सीदति *sîdati* (निषीदति *nishîdati*) ‖ Pf. 1. ससाद *sasâda*, 2. सेदिथ *seditha* or ससत्थ *sasattha*, 9. सेदुः *seduḥ*, II A. असदत् *asadat* (न्यषदत् *nyashadat*), F. सत्स्यति *satsyati*, P. F. सत्ता *sattâ*, B. सद्यात् *sadyât* ‖ Pt. सन्नः *sannaḥ* ‖ Pass. सद्यते *sadyate*, Aor. असादि *asâdi*, Caus. सादयति *sâdayati*, Aor. असीषदत् *asîshadat*, Des. सिषत्सति *sishatsati*, Int. सासद्यते *sâsadyate*, सासत्ति *sâsatti*.

53. पा pâ, to drink.

P. पिबति *pibati* ‖ Pf. 1. पपौ *papau*, 2. पपिथ *papitha* or पपाथ *papâtha*, 9. पपुः

papuḥ, II A. अपात् *apât*, F. पास्यति *pâsyati*, P. F. पाता *pâtá*, B. पेयात् *peyât* (§ 392) ॥ Pt. पीतः *pîtaḥ*, Ger. पीत्वा *pîtvá*, °पाय *-pâya*, Adj. पातव्यः *pâtavyaḥ*, पानीयः *pânîyaḥ*, पेयः *peyaḥ* ॥ Pass. पीयते *pîyate*, Aor. अपायि *apâyi*, Caus. पाययति *pâyayati* (or °ते *-te*, to swallow), Aor. अपीप्यत् *apîpyat* (Pâṇ. VII. 4, 4), Des. पिपासति *pipâsati*, Int. पेपीयते *pepîyate*, पापाति *pâpâti*.

54. घ्रा *ghrâ*, to smell, to perceive odour.

P. जिघ्रति *jighrati*, I. अजिघ्रत् *ajighrat*, O. जिघ्रेत् *jighret*, I. जिघ्रतु *jighratu* ॥ Pf. 1. जघ्रौ *jaghrau*, 2. जघ्रिथ *jaghritha* or जघ्राथ *jaghrâtha*, 9. जघ्रुः *jaghruḥ*, II A. अघ्रात् *aghrât*, or I A. अघ्रासीत् *aghrâsît* (§§ 368, 357), F. घ्रास्यति *ghrâsyati*, P. F. घ्राता *ghrâtâ*, B. घ्रायात् *ghrâyât* or घ्रेयात् *ghreyât* (§ 392 †) ॥ Pt. घ्रातः *ghrâtaḥ* or घ्राणः *ghrâṇaḥ*, Ger. घ्रात्वा *ghrâtvâ* ॥ Pass. घ्रायते *ghrâyate*, Aor. अघ्रायि *aghrâyi*, Caus. घ्रापयति *ghrâpayati*, अजिघ्रपत् *ajighrapat* or अजिघ्रिपत् *ajighripat* (Pâṇ. VII. 4, 6), Des. जिघ्रासति *jighrâsati*, Int. जेघ्रीयते *jeghrîyate*, जाघ्राति *jâghrâti*.

55. ध्मा *dhmâ*, to blow.

P. धमति *dhamati* ॥ Pf. दध्मौ *dadhmau*, I A. अध्मासीत् *adhmâsît*, F. ध्मास्यति *dhmâsyati*, B. ध्मायात् *dhmâyât* or ध्मेयात् *dhmeyât* ॥ Pt. ध्मातः *dhmâtaḥ* ॥ Pass. ध्मायते *dhmâyate*, Aor. अध्मायि *adhmâyi*, Caus. ध्मापयति *dhmâpayati*, Aor. अदिध्मपत् *adidhmapat*, Des. दिध्मासति *didhmâsati*, Int. देध्मीयते *dedhmîyate*, दाध्माति *dâdhmâti*.

56. स्था *sthâ*, to stand, (ष्ठा.)

P. तिष्ठति *tishṭhati* ॥ Pf. तस्थौ *tasthau* (अधितष्ठौ *adhitashṭhau*), II A. अस्थात् *asthât* (न्यष्ठात् *nyashṭhât*), 9. अस्थुः *asthuḥ*, F. स्थास्यति *sthâsyati*, B. स्थेयात् *stheyât* (§ 392) ॥ Pt. स्थितः *sthitaḥ*, स्थित्वा *sthitvâ*, °स्थाय *-sthâya*, Adj. स्थातव्यः *sthâtavyaḥ*, स्थानीयः *sthânîyaḥ*, स्थेयः *stheyaḥ* ॥ Pass. स्थीयते *sthîyate*, Aor. अस्थायि *asthâyi*, Caus. स्थापयति *sthâpayati*, Aor. अतिष्ठिपत् *atishṭhipat*, Des. तिष्ठासति *tishṭhâsati*, Int. तेष्ठीयते *teshṭhîyate*, तास्थाति *tâsthâti*.

Note—After सं *sam*, अव *ava*, प्र *pra*, and वि *vi*, स्था *sthâ* is used in the Âtm.; also after आ *â*, if it means to affirm; with उद् *ud*, if it means to strive, not to rise; or with उप *upa*, if it means to worship, &c.: Pres. तिष्ठते *tishṭhate*, Red. Perf. तस्थे *tasthe*, Aor. अस्थित *asthita*, 9. अस्थिषत *asthishata*, Fut. स्थास्यते *sthâsyate*, Ben. स्थासीष्ट *sthâsîshṭa*.

57. म्ना *mnâ*, to study.

P. मनति *manati* ॥ Pf. 1. मम्नौ *mamnau*, 2. मम्निथ *mamnitha* or मम्नाथ *mamnâtha*, 9. मम्नुः *mamnuḥ*, I A. अम्नासीत् *amnâsît*, B. म्नायात् *mnâyât* or म्नेयात् *mneyât* ॥ Pt. म्नातः *mnâtaḥ* ॥ Pass. म्नायते *mnâyate*, Caus. म्नापयति *mnâpayati*, Aor. अमिम्नपत् *amimnapat*, Des. मिम्नासति *mimnâsati*, Int. माम्नायते *mâmnâyate*, माम्नाति *mâmnâti*.

58. दा *dâ*, to give, (दाण्.)

P. यच्छति *yachchhati** (प्रणियच्छति *praṇiyachchhati*) ॥ Pf. ददौ *dadau*, II A.

* After the preposition सं *sam* it may be used in the Âtmanepada.

अदात् adât, B. देयात् deyât (§ 392) ॥ Pt. दत्तः dattaḥ, Ger. दत्त्वा dattvâ (Pâṇ. vii. 4, 46), °दाय -dâya, Adj. दातव्यः dâtavyaḥ, दानीयः dânîyaḥ, देयः deyaḥ ॥ Pass. दीयते dîyate, Caus. दापयति dâpayati, Des. दित्सति ditsati, Int. देदीयते dedîyate, दादाति dâdâti.

59. ह्वृ hvṛi, to bend.

P. ह्वरति hvarati ॥ Pf. 1. जह्वार jahvâra, 2. जह्वर्थ jahvartha (§ 335), 3. जह्वार jahvâra, 4. जह्वरिव jahvariva (§§ 330, 334), 9. जह्वरुः jahvaruḥ, I A. अह्वार्षीत् ahvârshît, 9. अह्वार्षुः ahvârshuḥ, F. ह्वरिष्यति hvarishyati (§ 338), P. F. ह्वर्ता hvartâ, B. ह्वर्यात् hvaryât (§ 390) ॥ Pt. ह्वृतः hvṛitaḥ, Ger. ह्वृत्वा hvṛitvâ, °ह्वृत्य -hvṛitya, Adj. ह्वर्तव्यः hvartavyaḥ, ह्वरणीयः hvaraṇîyaḥ, ह्वार्यः hvâryaḥ ॥ Pass. ह्वर्यते hvaryate, Caus. ह्वारयति hvârayati, Des. जुह्वूर्षति juhvûrshati, Int. जाह्वर्यते jâhvaryate, जरीह्वर्ति jarîhvarti.

60. स्कन्द् skand, to approach, (स्कन्दिर्.)

P. स्कन्दति skandati (परिस्कन्दति pariskandati or परिष्कन्दति parishkandati, Pâṇ. viii. 3, 73, 74) ॥ Pf. 1. चस्कन्द chaskanda, 2. चस्कन्दिथ chaskanditha or चस्कन्थ chaskanttha, 9. चस्कन्दुः chaskanduḥ or चस्कदुः chaskaduḥ (see manth, No. 5), I A. अस्कान्त्सीत् askântsît, 6. अस्कान्त्ताम् askânttâm, 9. अस्कान्त्सुः askântsuḥ; or II A. अस्कदम् askadam, F. स्कन्त्स्यति skantsyati, P. F. स्कन्त्ता skanttâ, B. स्कद्यात् skadyât (§ 345†) ॥ Pt. स्कन्नः skannaḥ (§ 103, 6), Ger. स्कन्त्वा skantvâ (§ 438) ॥ Pass. स्कद्यते skadyate, Caus. स्कन्दयति skandayati, Aor. अचस्कन्दत् achaskandat (§ 374), Des. चिस्कन्त्सति chiskantsati, Int. चनीस्कद्यते chanîskadyate (§ 485), चनीस्कन्ति chanîskanti.

61. तॄ tṝ, to cross.

P. तरति tarati ॥ Pf. 1. ततार tatâra, 2. तेरिथ teritha, 3. ततार tatâra, 4. तेरिव teriva, I A. अतारीत् atârît, F. तरिष्यति or तरीष्यति tarîshyati (§ 340), P. F. तरिता or तरीता tarîtâ, B. तीर्यात् tîryât. If used in the Âtmanepada, it forms P. तिरते tirate, Pf. तेरे tere, Aor. अतीर्ष्ट atîrshṭa or अतरिष्ट atarishṭa or अतरीष्ट atarîshṭa, F. तरीष्यते tarîshyate, B. तरिषीष्ट tarishîshṭa or तीर्षीष्ट tîrshîshṭa ॥ Pt. तीर्णः tîrṇaḥ, Ger. तीर्त्वा tîrtvâ, °तीर्य -tîrya ॥ Pass. तीर्यते tîryate, Aor. अतारि atâri, Caus. तारयति târayati, Des. तितरिषति titarishati or तितरीषति titarîshati or तितीर्षति titîrshati, Int. तेतीर्यते tetîryate, तातर्ति tâtarti.

62. रञ्ज् rañj, to tinge.

This verb and दंश् daṁś, to bite, संज् sañj, to stick, and स्वंज् svañj, to embrace (Pâṇ. vi. 4, 25, 26), drop the penultimate nasal in the special tenses (§ 345†) and in the weakening forms (§ 344).

P. रजति rajati, I. अरजत् arajat, O. रजेत् rajet, I. रजतु rajatu ॥ Pf. 1. ररञ्ज rarañja, 2. ररञ्जिथ rarañjitha or ररङ्क्थ raraṅktha, 3. ररञ्ज rarañja, 4. ररञ्जिव rarañjiva, 9. ररञ्जुः rarañjuḥ, I A. अराङ्क्षीत् arâṅkshît, F. रङ्क्ष्यति raṅkshyati, P. F. रङ्क्ता raṅktâ, B. रज्यात् rajyât. Also used in the Âtmanepada: P. रजते rajate, Pf. 1. ररञ्जे rarañje, 2. ररञ्जिषे rarañjishe, I A. 3. अरङ्क्त araṅkta, 9. अरङ्क्षत araṅkshata ॥ Pt. रक्तः raktaḥ, Ger. रक्त्वा raktvâ or रङ्क्त्वा raṅktvâ (§ 438) ॥ Pass. रज्यते rajyate (Pâṇ.

III. 1, 90), Caus. रञ्जयति *rañjayati* or रजयति *rajayati*, to hunt (§ 462, 26), Aor. अरीरजत् *arîrajat* or अररञ्जत् *ararañjat*, Des. रिरङ्क्षति *rirankshati*, Int. रारज्यते *râra-jyate*, रारङ्क्ति *râraṅkti*.

63. कित् *kit*, to cure, (कित.)

This and some other verbs which are referred to the Bhû class always take the desiderative terminations, if used in certain senses. कित् *kit*, if it means to dwell, belongs to the Chur class, or, according to Vopadeva, it may be regularly conjugated as a Bhû verb; but if it means to cure, it is चिकित्सति *chikitsati*.

P. चिकित्सति *chikitsati*, I. अचिकित्सत् *achikitsat* &c. ॥ Pf. चिकित्सांचकार *chi-kitsâṁchakâra*, I A. अचिकित्सीत् *achikitsît*, F. चिकित्सिष्यति *chikitsishyati*, P. F. चिकित्सिता *chikitsitâ*.

Thus are conjugated (§ 472):

1. गुप् *gup* (to conceal), जुगुप्सते *jugupsate*, he despises.
2. तिज् *tij* (to sharpen), तितिक्षते *titikshate*, he endures.
3. मान् *mân* (to revere), मीमांसते *mîmâṁsate*, he investigates.
4. बध् *badh* (to bind), बीभत्सते *bîbhatsate*, he loathes.
5. दान् *dân* (to cut), दीदांसति *dîdâṁsati*, he straightens.
6. शान् *śân* (to sharpen), शीशांसति *śîśâṁsati*, he sharpens.

64. पत् *pat*, to fall, (पतॢ.)

P. पतति *patati* (प्रणिपतति *praṇipatati*) ॥ Pf. 1. पपात *papâta*, 9. पेतुः *petuḥ*, II A. अपप्तम् *apaptam* (§ 366), F. पतिष्यति *patishyati* ॥ Pt. पतितः *patitaḥ* ॥ Pass. पत्यते *patyate*, Aor. अपाति *apâti*, Caus. पातयति *pâtayati*, Des. पिपतिषति *pipati-shati* or पित्सति *pitsati* (§ 337, II. 3).

65. वस् *vas*, to dwell.

P. वसति *vasati* ॥ Pf. 1. उवास *uvâsa*, 2. उवसिथ *uvasitha* or उवस्थ *uvastha*, 3. उवास *uvâsa*, 4. ऊषिव *ûshiva*, 5. ऊषथुः *ûshathuḥ*, 6. ऊषतुः *ûshatuḥ*, 7. ऊषिम *ûshima*, 8. ऊष *ûsha*, 9. ऊषुः *ûshuḥ*, I A. 1. अवात्सम् *avâtsam* (§ 132), 2. अवात्सीः *avâtsîḥ*, 3. अवात्सीत् *avâtsît*, 6. अवात्ताम् *avâttâm* (§ 351), F. वत्स्यति *vatsyati*, P. F. वस्ता *vastâ*, B. उष्यात् *ushyât* ॥ Pt. उषितः *ushitaḥ*, Ger. उषित्वा *ushitvâ*, °उष्य *-ushya* ॥ Pass. उष्यते *ushyate*, Aor. अवासि *avâsi*, Caus. वासयति *vâsayati*, Aor. अवीवसत् *avî-vasat*, Des. विवत्सति *vivatsati*, Int. वावस्यते *vâvasyate*, वावस्ति *vâvasti*.

66. वद् *vad*, to speak.

P. वदति *vadati* ॥ Pf. 1. उवाद *uvâda*, 2. उवदिथ *uvaditha*, 9. ऊदुः *ûduḥ*, I A. अवा-दीत् *avâdît*, F. वदिष्यति *vadishyati*, B. उद्यात् *udyât* ॥ Pt. उदितः *uditaḥ*, Ger. उदित्वा *uditvâ* ॥ Pass. उद्यते *udyate*, Aor. अवादि *avâdi*, Caus. वादयति *vâdayati*, Aor. अवी-वदत् *avîvadat*, Des. विवदिषति *vivadishati*, Int. वावद्यते *vâvadyate*, वावत्ति *vâvatti*.

67. श्वि *śvi*, to swell, (टुओश्वि.)

P. श्वयति *śvayati* ॥ Pf. 1. शुशाव *śuśâva* or शिश्वाय *śiśvâya*, 2. शुशविथ *śuśavitha* or शिश्वयिथ *śiśvayitha*, 3. शुशाव *śuśâva* or शिश्वाय *śiśvâya*, 4. शुशुविव *śuśuviva* or

शिश्वियिव *śiśviyiva*, 5. शुशुवथुः *śuśuvathuḥ* or शिश्वियथुः *śiśviyathuḥ*, 9. शुशुवुः *śuśuvuḥ* or शिश्वियुः *śiśviyuḥ*, I A. अश्वयीत् *aśvayît*, II A. अश्वत् *aśvat* or अशिश्वियत् *aśiśviyat*, F. श्वयिष्यति *śvayishyati*, P. F. श्वयिता *śvayitâ*, B. शूयात् *śûyât* ॥ Pt. शूनः *śûnaḥ* ॥ Pass. शूयते *śûyate*, Caus. श्वाययति *śvâyayati*, Aor. अशिश्वयत् *aśiśvayat*, Des. शिश्वयिषति *śiśvayishati*, Int. शेश्वीयते *śeśvîyate* or शोशूयते *śośûyate*.

II. Âtmanepada Verbs.

68. एध् *edh*, to grow.

P. एधते *edhate*, I. ऐधत *aidhata*, O. एधेत *edheta*, I. एधताम् *edhatâm* ॥ Pf. एधामास *edhâmâsa**, F. एधिष्यते *edhishyate*, C. ऐधिष्यत *aidhishyata*, P. F. एधिता *edhitâ*, I A. 1. ऐधिषि *aidhishi*, 2. ऐधिष्ठाः *aidhishṭhâḥ*, 3. ऐधिष्ट *aidhishṭa*, 4. ऐधिष्वहि *aidhishvahi*, 5. ऐधिषाथाम् *aidhishâthâm*, 6. ऐधिषाताम् *aidhishâtâm*, 7. ऐधिष्महि *aidhishmahi*, 8. ऐधिढ्वम् *aidhiḍhvam*, 9. ऐधिषत *aidhishata*, B. एधिषीष्ट *edhishîshṭa* ॥ Pt. एधितः *edhitaḥ* ॥ Pass. एध्यते *edhyate*, Aor. ऐधि *aidhi*, Caus. Pres. एधयति, °ते, *edhayati*, *-te*, Perf. एधयामास *edhayâmâsa*, F. एधयिष्यति, °ते, *edhayishyati*, *-te*, Cond. ऐधयिष्यत्, °त, *aidhayishyat*, *-ta*, P. F. एधयिता *edhayitâ*, II A. ऐदिधत्, °त, *aididhat*, *-ta*, B. एधयिषीष्ट *edhayishîshṭa*, Des. एदिधिषते *edidhishate*.

69. ईक्ष् *îksh*, to see.

P. ईक्षते *îkshate*, I. ऐक्षत *aikshata*, O. ईक्षेत *îksheta*, I. ईक्षताम् *îkshatâm* ॥ Pf. ईक्षांचक्रे *îkshâṁchakre*, I A. ऐक्षिष्ट *aikshishṭa*, F. ईक्षिष्यते *îkshishyate*, C. ऐक्षिष्यत *aikshishyata*, P. F. ईक्षिता *îkshitâ*, B. ईक्षिषीष्ट *îkshishîshṭa* ॥ Pt. ईक्षितः *îkshitaḥ* ॥ Caus. ईक्षयति *îkshayati*, Aor. ऐचिक्षत् *aichikshat*, Des. ईचिक्षिषते *îchikshishate*.

70. दद् *dad*, to give.

P. ददते *dadate*, I. अददत *adadata*, O. ददेत *dadeta*, I. ददताम् *dadatâm* ॥ Pf. 3. ददते *dadade* (§ 328, 1), 6. दददाते *dadadâte*, 9. दददिरे *dadadire* (Pâṇ. vi. 4, 126), I A. अददिष्ट *adadishṭa*, F. ददिष्यते *dadishyate*, P. F. ददिता *daditâ*, B. ददिषीष्ट *dadishîshṭa* ॥ Pt. ददितः *daditaḥ* ॥ Pass. दद्यते *dadyate*, Aor. अदादि *adâdi*, Caus. दादयति *dâdayati*, Aor. अदीददत् *adîdadat*, Des. दिददिषते *didadishate*, Int. दादद्यते *dâdadyate*, दादत्ति *dâdatti*.

71. ष्वष्क् *shvashk*, to go.

P. ष्वष्कते *shvashkate*, I. अष्वष्कत *ashvashkata* ॥ Pf. षष्वष्के *shashvashke*, I A. अष्वष्किष्ट *ashvashkishṭa*, F. ष्वष्किष्यते *shvashkishyate*, P. F. ष्वष्किता *shvashkitâ*, B. ष्वष्किषीष्ट *shvashkishîshṭa*.

Note—The initial ष् *sh* is not liable to become स् *s*. (See No. 45; Pâṇ. vi. 1, 64, 1. Colebrooke, p. 219.)

---

* आस *âsa* and बभूव *babhûva* are used in the Parasmaipada, चक्रे *chakre* in the Âtmanepada. It is only in the passive that आस *âsa* and बभूव *babhûva* take Âtmanepada terminations.

72. ऋज् *ṛij*, to go, to gain, &c.

P. अर्जते *arjate*, I. आर्जत *árjata* ॥ Pf. आनृजे *ánṛije*, I A. आर्जिष्ट *árjishṭa*, F. अर्जिष्यते *arjishyate*, P. F. अर्जिता *arjitá*, B. अर्जिषीष्ट *arjishîshṭa* ॥ Pass. ऋज्यते *ṛijyate* (प्रार्ज्यते *prárjyate*), Caus. अर्जयति *arjayati*, Aor. आर्जिजत् *árjijat*, Des. अर्जिजिषते *arjijishate*.

73. स्वंज् *svañj*, to embrace.

दंश् *daṁś*, संज् *sañj*, स्वंज् *svañj* drop their nasal in the special tenses (Pâṇ. VI. 4, 25). See No. 62.

P. स्वजते *svajate*, I. अस्वजत *asvajata* ॥ Pf. सस्वंजे *sasvañje* or सस्वजे *sasvaje* (Pâṇ. I. 2, 6, v.), I A. 1. अस्वंक्षि *asvaṅkshi*, 2. अस्वंक्थाः *asvaṅkthâḥ*, 3. अस्वंक्त *asvaṅkta*, 4. अस्वंक्ष्वहि *asvaṅkshvahi*, 5. अस्वंक्षाथां *asvaṅkshâthâm*, 6. अस्वंक्षातां *asvaṅkshâtâm*, 7. अस्वंक्ष्महि *asvaṅkshmahi*, 8. अस्वंग्ध्वं *asvaṅgdhvam*, 9. अस्वंक्षत *asvaṅkshata*, F. स्वंक्ष्यते *svaṅkshyate*, B. स्वंक्षीष्ट *svaṅkshîshṭa* ॥ Pass. स्वज्यते *svajyate*, Caus. स्वंजयति *svañjayati*, Des. सिस्वंक्षते *sisvaṅkshate*, Int. सास्वज्यते *sâsvajyate*, सास्वंक्ति *sâsvaṅkti*.

74. त्रप् *trap*, to be ashamed, (त्रपूष्.)

P. त्रपते *trapate*, I. अत्रपत *atrapata* ॥ Pf. 3. त्रेपे *trepe* (Pâṇ. VI. 4, 122), 6. त्रेपाते *trepâte*, 9. त्रेपिरे *trepire*, I A. 1. अत्रपिषि *atrapishi* or अत्रप्सि *atrapsi*, 2. अत्रपिष्ठाः *atrapishṭhâḥ* or अत्रप्थाः *atrapthâḥ*, 3. अत्रपिष्ट *atrapishṭa* or अत्रप्त *atrapta*, F. त्रपिष्यते *trapishyate* or त्रप्स्यते *trapsyate*, B. त्रपिषीष्ट *trapishîshṭa* or त्रप्सीष्ट *trapsîshṭa*.

75. तिज् *tij*, to forbear.

P. तितिक्षते *titikshate* ॥ Pf. तितिक्षांचक्रे *titikshâṁchakre*, I A. अतितिक्षिष्ट *atitikshishṭa*, F. तितिक्षिष्यते *titikshishyate*, B. तितिक्षिषीष्ट *titikshishîshṭa* ॥ Caus. तेजयति *tejayati*.

Note—See No. 63. The simple verb is said to form तेजते *tejate*, he sharpens.

76. पण् *paṇ*, to praise.

P. पणायते *paṇâyate*, I. अपणायत *apaṇâyata* ॥ Pf. पणायांचक्रे *paṇâyâṁchakre* or पेणे *peṇe* (without आय् *ây*). Thus likewise Aor. अपणायिष्ट *apaṇâyishṭa* or अपणिष्ट *apaṇishṭa*, F. पणायिष्यते *paṇâyishyate* or पणिष्यते *paṇishyate*, B. पणायिषीष्ट *paṇâyishîshṭa* or पणिषीष्ट *paṇishîshṭa* ॥ Caus. पाणयति *pâṇayati*, Aor. अपीपणत् *apîpaṇat*, Des. पिपणिषते *pipaṇishate*, Int. पंपण्यते *pampaṇyate*.

Note—This verb (see No. 26) takes आय *âya*, but, as it is mentioned by Pâṇini III. 1, 28, together with पन् *pan*, with which it shares but the meaning of to praise, it is argued that it does not take आय *âya*, unless it means to praise. It is likewise argued that पण् *paṇ*, if it takes आय *âya*, does not follow the Âtmanepada, because the Anubandha, requiring the Âtmanepada, applies only to the simple verb, पण् *paṇ*, पणते *paṇate*, he traffics. Other grammarians, however, allow both the Parasmaipada and Âtmanepada. The suffix आय *âya* may be kept in the general tenses. (Pâṇ. III. 1, 31.)

77. कम् *kam*, to love, (कमु.)

P. कामयते *kâmayate*, I. अकामयत *akâmayata* ‖ Pf. कामयांचक्रे *kâmayâṁchakre* or चकमे *chakame*, I A. अचीकमत *achîkamata* or (without अय् *ay*) अचकमत *achakamata* (Pâṇ. III. 1, 48, v.), F. कमिष्यते *kamishyate* or कामयिष्यते *kâmayishyate*, B. कमिषीष्ट *kamishîshṭa* or कामयिषीष्ट *kâmayishîshṭa* ‖ Pass. कम्यते *kamyate*, Aor. अकामि *akâmi* (Pâṇ. VII. 3, 34, v.), Caus. कामयति *kâmayati*, Des. चिकमिषते *chikamishate* or चिकामयिषते *chikâmayishate*, Int. चंकम्यते *chaṅkamyate*.

Note—This verb in the special tenses takes अय *aya*, like a verb of the Chur class, and Vṛiddhi (Pâṇ. III. 1, 30). In the general tenses अय् *ay* is optional. Or, if we admit two roots, the one कम् *kam* would be defective in the special tenses, while the other कामय् *kâmay* is conjugated all through.

78. अय् *ay*, to go.

P. अयते *ayate*, I. आयत *âyata* ‖ Pf. अयांचक्रे *ayâṁchakre* (Pâṇ. III. 1, 37), I A. 1. आयिषि *âyishi*, 2. आयिष्ठाः *âyishṭhâḥ*, 3. आयिष्ट *âyishṭa*, 4. आयिष्वहि *âyishvahi*, 5. आयिषाथां *âyishâthâm*, 6. आयिषातां *âyishâtâm*, 7. आयिष्महि *âyishmahi*, 8. आयिध्वं *âyidhvam* or °ढ्वं *-ḍhvam*, 9. आयिषत *âyishata*, F. अयिष्यते *ayishyate*, B. अयिषीष्ट *ayishîshṭa* ‖ Caus. आययति *âyayati*, Des. अयियिषते *ayiyishate*.

With परा *parâ* it forms पलायते *palâyate*, he flees (Pâṇ. VIII. 2, 19), Ger. पलाय्य *palâyya*; with प्र *pra*, प्लायते *plâyate*; and with परि *pari*, पल्ययते *palyayate*.

79. ईह् *îh*, to aim.

P. ईहते *îhate*, I. ऐहत *aihata* ‖ Pf. ईहांचक्रे *îhâṁchakre*, I A. ऐहिष्ट *aihishṭa*, F. ईहिष्यते *îhishyate*, B. ईहिषीष्ट *îhishîshṭa* ‖ Caus. ईहयति *îhayati*, Aor. ऐजिहत् *aijihat*, Des. ईजिहिषते *îjihishate*.

80. काश् *kâś*, to shine, (काशृ.)

P. काशते *kâśate* ‖ Pf. चकाशे *chakâśe* or काशांचक्रे *kâśâṁchakre* (§ 326), I A. अकाशिष्ट *akâśishṭa*, F. काशिष्यते *kâśishyate* ‖ Caus. काशयति *kâśayati*, Aor. अचकाशत् *achakâśat*, Des. चिकाशिषते *chikâśishate*, Int. चाकाश्यते *châkâśyate*, चाकाष्टि *châkâshṭi*.

81. कास् *kâs*, to cough, (कासृ.)

P. कासते *kâsate* ‖ Pf. कासांचक्रे *kâsâṁchakre* (§ 326) ‖ Caus. कासयति *kâsayati*, Aor. अचकासत् *achakâsat* (§ 372*).

82. सिव् *siv*, to serve, (षेवृ.)

P. सेवते *sevate* (परिषेवते *parishevate*) ‖ Pf. सिषेवे *sisheve*, I A. असेविष्ट *asevishṭa*, F. सेविष्यते *sevishyate* ‖ Caus. सेवयति *sevayati*, Aor. असिषेवत् *asishevat*, Des. सिसेविषते *sisevishate*, Int. सेषेव्यते *seshevyate*.

83. गा *gâ*, to go, (गाङ्.)

P. 3. गाते *gâte*, 6. गाते *gâte*, 9. गाते *gâte*, 1st pers. sing. गै *gai*, I. गातां *gâtâm*, 1st pers. sing. गै *gai*, O. गेत *geta*, I. अगात *agâta* ‖ Pf. 3. जगे *jage*, 6. जगाते *jagâte*, 9. जगिरे *jagire*, I A. 1. अगासि *agâsi*, 2. अगास्थाः *agâsthâḥ*, 3. अगास्त *agâsta* &c.,

F. गास्यते *gâsyate*, B. गासीष्ट *gâsishṭa* ॥ Pass. गीयते *gîyate*, Aor. अगायि *agâyi*, Caus. गापयति *gâpayati*, Aor. अजीगपत् *ajîgapat*, Des. जिगासते *jigâsate*, Int. जेगीयते *jegîyate*.

84. रु *ru*, to go, to kill (?), to speak, (रुङ्.)

P. रवते *ravate* ॥ Pf. 3. रुरुवे *ruruve*, 6. रुरुवाते *ruruvâte*, 9. रुरुविरे *ruruvire*, I A. अरविष्ट *aravishṭa* or अरोष्ट *aroshṭa* (?) ॥ Caus. रावयति *râvayati*, Aor. अरीरवत् *arîravat* (§ 474 and § 375†).

85. दे *de*, to protect, (देङ्.)

P. दयते *dayate* ॥ Pf. 1. दिग्ये *digye* (Pâṇ. VII. 4, 9), 2. दिग्यिषे *digyishe*, 3. दिग्ये *digye*, I A. 1. अदिषि *adishi*, 2. अदिथाः *adithâḥ*, 3. अदित *adita*, F. दास्यते *dâsyate*, B. दासीष्ट *dâsîshṭa* ॥ Pt. दत्तः *dattaḥ* ॥ Pass. दीयते *dîyate*, Caus. दापयति *dâpayati*, Des. दित्सते *ditsate*, Int. देदीयते *dedîyate*.

Note—It is one of the घु *ghu* verbs; दै *dai*, to protect, forms दायते *dâyate* in the present, but follows दे *de* in the general tenses.

86. द्युत् *dyut*, to shine, (द्युतङ्.)

P. द्योतते *dyotate* ॥ Pf. दिद्युते *didyute* (Pâṇ. VII. 4, 67), I A. अद्योतिष्ट *adyotishṭa* or अद्युतत् *adyutat* (§ 367: Pâṇ. I. 3, 91; III. 1, 55), F. द्योतिष्यते *dyotishyate*, B. द्योतिषीष्ट *dyotishîshṭa* ॥ Caus. द्योतयति *dyotayati*, Aor. अदिद्युतत् *adidyutat*, Des. दिद्युतिषते *didyutishate* or *didyotishate*, Int. देद्युत्यते *dedyutyate*, देद्योत्ति *dedyotti*.

Note—The verbs beginning with द्युत् *dyut* optionally admit the II Aor. Parasmaipada (§ 367).

87. वृत् *vṛit*, to be, (वृतुङ्.)

P. वर्तते *vartate* ॥ Pf. ववृते *vavṛite*, I A. अवर्तिष्ट *avartishṭa* or अवृतत् *avṛitat*, F. वर्तिष्यते *vartishyate* or वर्त्स्यति *vartsyati*, B. वर्तिषीष्ट *vartishîshṭa* ॥ Caus. वर्तयति *vartayati*, Aor. अवीवृतत् *avîvṛitat* or अववर्तत् *avavartat* (Pâṇ. VII. 4, 7), Des. विवर्तिषते *vivartishate* or विवृत्सति *vivṛitsati*, Int. वरीवृत्यते *varîvṛityate*.

Note—The verbs beginning with वृत् *vṛit*, i.e. वृत् *vṛit*, वृध् *vṛidh*, शृध् *śṛidh*, स्यंद् *syand*, कृप् *kṛip*, are optionally Parasmaipada in the aorist, future, conditional, desiderative (Pâṇ. I. 3, 91—93). The same verbs do not take इ *i* in their Parasmaipada tenses (Pâṇ. VII. 2, 59); as to कॢप् *klip*, see Pâṇ. VII. 2, 60, and I. 3, 93.

88. स्यंद् *syand*, to sprinkle or drop, (स्यंदू.)

P. स्यंदते *syandate* ॥ Pf. 1. सस्यंदे *sasyande*, 2. सस्यंदिषे *sasyandishe* or सस्यंत्से *sasyantse*, 4. सस्यंदिवहे *sasyandivahe* or सस्यंद्वहे *sasyandvahe*, I A. 3. अस्यंदिष्ट *asyandishṭa*, 6. अस्यंदिषातां *asyandishâtâm*; or अस्यंत्त *asyantta* (6. अस्यंत्सातां *asyantsâtâm*), or II A. अस्यदत् *asyadat* (not अस्यंदत् *asyandat*), F. स्यंदिष्यते *syandishyate* or स्यंत्स्यते *syantsyate* or स्यंत्स्यति *syantsyati* (Pâṇ. VII. 2, 59; see No. 87), B. स्यंदिषीष्ट *syandishîshṭa* or स्यंत्सीष्ट *syantsîshṭa* ॥ Pt. स्यन्नः *syannaḥ*, Ger. स्यंदित्वा *syanditvâ* or स्यंत्वा *syantvâ* (Pâṇ. VI. 4, 31) ॥ Caus. स्यंदयति *syandayati*, Des. सिस्यंदिषते *sisyandishate* or सिस्यंत्सते *sisyantsate* or सिस्यंत्सति *sisyantsati*.

89. कृप् *krip*, to be able, (कृपू.)

P. कल्पते *kalpate* ॥ Pf. चक्लृपे *chakḷipe*, I A. 3. अकल्पिष्ट *akalpishṭa* or अक्लृप्त *akḷipta*, 6. अक्लृप्साताम् *akḷipsâtâm*, 9. अक्लृप्सत *akḷipsata*, or II Aor. Par. अक्लृपत् *akḷipat*, F. कल्पिष्यते *kalpishyate* or कल्प्स्यते *kalpsyate* or कल्प्स्यति *kalpsyati*, P. F. 2. कल्पितासे *kalpitâse* or कल्प्तासे *kalptâse* or कल्प्तासि *kalptâsi*, B. कल्पिषीष्ट *kalpishîshṭa* or क्लृप्सीष्ट *kḷipsîshṭa* ॥ Pt. क्लृप्तः *kḷiptaḥ* ॥ Caus. कल्पयति *kalpayati*, Des. चिकल्पिषते *chikalpishate* or चिक्लृप्सति *chikḷipsati*, Int. चलीकल्प्यते *chalîkalpyate* or चलिकल्प्यते *chalikalpyate* or चल्कल्प्यते *chalkalpyate*.

90. व्यथ् *vyath*, to fear, to suffer pain.

P. व्यथते *vyathate* ॥ Pf. विव्यथे *vivyathe* (Pâṇ. VII. 4, 68), I A. अव्यथिष्ट *avyathishṭa*, F. व्यथिष्यते *vyathishyate* ॥ Pass. व्यथ्यते *vyathyate*, Aor. अव्याथि *avyâthi* (§ 461). Caus. व्यथयति *vyathayati*, Des. विव्यथिषते *vivyathishate*, Int. वाव्यथ्यते *vâvyathyate*, वाव्यत्ति *vâvyatti*.

91. रम् *ram*, to sport, (रमु.)

P. रमते *ramate*; with वि *vi*, आ *â*, परि *pari*, उप *upa*, optionally Parasmaipada; विरमति *viramati* (Pâṇ. I. 3, 83) ॥ Pf. रेमे *reme*, I A. अरंस्त *araṁsta*, after prepositions व्यरंसीत् *vyaraṁsît*, F. रंस्यते *raṁsyate* ॥ Pt. रतः *rataḥ*, Ger. रत्वा *ratvâ*, °रम्य *-ramya* or °रत्य *-ratya* ॥ Caus. रमयति *ramayati*, Aor. अरीरमत् *arîramat*, Des. रिरंसते *riraṁsate*, Int. रंरम्यते *raṁramyate*, रंरमीति *raṁramîti*.

92. त्वर् *tvar*, to hurry, (ञित्वरा.)

The verbs ज्वर् *jvar*, त्वर् *tvar*, स्रिव् *sriv*, अव् *av*, मव् *mav*, substitute जुर् *jur*, तुर् *tur*, स्रुव् *sruv*, उव् *uv*, मुव् *muv* (Pâṇ. VI. 4, 20) before weakening terminations beginning with consonants, except semivowels, and if used as monosyllabic nominal bases. The vowels are lengthened according to § 143. Hence जूर्णः *jûrṇaḥ*, तूर्णः *tûrṇaḥ*, स्रूतः *srûtaḥ*, ऊतः *ûtaḥ*, मूतः *mûtaḥ*.

P. त्वरते *tvarate* ॥ Pf. तत्वरे *tatvare*, I A. 3. अत्वरिष्ट *atvarishṭa*, 8. अत्वरिध्वम् *atvaridhvam* or अत्वरिढ्वम् *atvariḍhvam*, F. त्वरिष्यते *tvarishyate* ॥ Pt. तूर्णः *tûrṇaḥ* (§ 432) or त्वरितः *tvaritaḥ* ॥ Caus. त्वरयति *tvarayati* (§ 462, II. 6), Aor. अतत्वरत् *atatvarat* (§ 375†), Des. तित्वरिषति *titvarishati*, Int. तात्वर्यते *tâtvaryate*, तोतूर्ति *totûrti*.

93. सह् *sah*, to bear, (षह.)

P. सहते *sahate* ॥ Pf. सेहे *sehe*, I A. असहिष्ट *asahishṭa*, F. सहिष्यते *sahishyate*, P. F. सहिता *sahitâ* or सोढा *soḍhâ* (§ 337, II. 2) ॥ Pt. सोढः *soḍhaḥ*, Adj. सह्यः *sahyaḥ* (§ 456, 6) ॥ Pass. सह्यते *sahyate*, Caus. साहयति *sâhayati*, Aor. असीषहत् *asîshahat*, Caus. Des. सिसाहयिषति *sisâhayishati*, Des. सिसहिषते *sisahishate*, Int. सासह्यते *sâsahyate*, सासोढि *sâsoḍhi*.

Note—सह् *sah* and वह् *vah* change अ *a* into ओ *o* when अ *a* would be followed by ढ् *ḍh*, the result of the amalgamation of ह् *h* with a following dental (§ 128). Pâṇ. VI. 3, 112.

III. Parasmaipada and Âtmanepada Verbs.

94. राज् *râj*, to shine, (राजृ.)

P. राजति *râjati*, °ते *-te* ‖ Pf. रराज *rarája*, रराजे *raráje* or रेजे *reje* (Pâṇ. VI. 4, 125), I A. अराजीत् *arâjît*, अराजिष्ट *arâjishṭa*, F. राजिष्यति *râjishyati*, °ते *-te*, B. राज्यात् *râjyât*, राजिषीष्ट *rajishîshṭa* ‖ Caus. राजयति *râjayati*, Aor. अरराजत् *ararâjat*, Des. रिराजिषति *rirâjishati*, °ते *-te*, Int. राराज्यते *rârâjyate*, राराष्टि *rârâshṭi*.

95. खन् *khan*, to dig.

P. खनति *khanati** ‖ Pf. 3. चखान *chakhâna*, 6. चख्नतुः *chakhnatuḥ*, 9. चख्नुः *chakhnuḥ* (§ 328, 3), I A. अखानीत् *akhânît* (§ 348), but Âtm. अखनिष्ट *akhanishṭa* only, F. खनिष्यति *khanishyati*, B. खन्यात् *khanyât* or खायात् *khâyât* (§ 391) ‖ Pt. खातः *khâtaḥ*, Ger. खात्वा *khâtvâ* or खनित्वा *khanitvâ*, Adj. खेयः *kheyaḥ* (§ 456, 6) ‖ Pass. खन्यते *khanyate* or खायते *khâyate* (§ 391), Caus. खानयति *khânayati*, Aor. अचीखनत् *achîkhanat*, Des. चिखनिषति *chikhanishati*, °ते *-te*, Int. चंखन्यते *chaṅkhanyate* or चाखायते *châkhâyate* (§ 391), चंखन्ति *chaṅkhanti*.

96. हृ *hṛi*, to take, (हृञ्.)

P. हरति *harati* ‖ Pf. 1. जहार *jahâra*, 2. जहर्थ *jahartha*, 9. जह्रुः *jahruḥ*, I A. अहार्षीत् *ahârshît*, Âtm. अहृत *ahṛita* (§ 351), F. हरिष्यति *harishyati*, P. F. हर्ता *hartâ*, B. ह्रियात् *hriyât* ‖ Pt. हृतः *hṛitaḥ*, Ger. हृत्वा *hṛitvâ*, Adj. हार्यः *hâryaḥ* ‖ Pass. ह्रियते *hriyate*, Aor. अहारि *ahâri*, Caus. हारयति *hârayati*, Des. जिहीर्षति *jihîrshati*, °ते *-te*, Int. जेह्रीयते *jehrîyate*, जर्हर्ति *jarharti* &c.

97. गुह् *guh*, to hide, (गुहू.)

गुह् *guh* takes ऊ *û* before terminations beginning with vowels that would ordinarily require Guṇa.

P. गूहति *gûhati* ‖ Pf. 1. जुगूह *jugûha*, 2. जुगूहिथ *jugûhitha* or जुगोढ *jugoḍha*, 3. जुगूह *jugûha*, 4. जुगुहिव *juguhiva*, 5. जुगुहथुः *juguhathuḥ* &c., Âtm. 1. जुगुहे *juguhe*, 2. जुघुक्षे *jughukshe* or जुगुहिषे *juguhishe* &c., I Aor. see § 362, F. गूहिष्यति *gûhishyati* or घोक्ष्यति *ghokshyati*, P. F. गूहिता *gûhitâ* or गोढा *goḍhâ*, Ben. Âtm. गूहिषीष्ट *gûhishîshṭa* or घुक्षीष्ट *ghukshîshṭa* (§ 345) ‖ Pt. गूढः *gûḍhaḥ*, Adj. गुह्यः *guhyaḥ* or गोह्यः *gohyaḥ* (§ 457) ‖ Pass. गुह्यते *guhyate*, Aor. अगूहि *agûhi*, Caus. गूहयति *gûhayati*, Aor. अजूगुहत् *ajûguhat*, Des. जुघुक्षति *jughukshati* (§ 470), Int. जोगुह्यते *joguhyate*, जोगोढि *jogoḍhi*.

98. श्रि *śri*, to go, to serve, (श्रिञ्.)

P. श्रयति *śrayati* ‖ Pf. 1. शिश्राय *śiśrâya*, 2. शिश्रयिथ *śiśrayitha*, 3. शिश्राय *śiśrâya*, 4. शिश्रियिव *śiśriyiva*, 5. शिश्रियथुः *śiśriyathuḥ*, II A. अशिश्रियत् *aśiśriyat* (§ 371),

---

* The Âtmanepada forms will in future only be given when they have peculiarities of their own, or are otherwise difficult.

F. श्रयिष्यति *śrayishyati*, B. श्रीयात् *śrîyât* ॥ Pass. श्रीयते *śrîyate*, Aor. अश्रायि *aśrâyi*, Caus. श्राययति *śrâyayati*, Aor. अशिश्रयत् *aśiśrayat*, Des. शिश्रयिषति *śiśrayishati* or शिश्रीषति *śiśrîshati* (§ 471, 3; § 337, II. 3), Int. शेश्रीयते *śeśrîyate*.

99. यज् *yaj*, to worship.

P. यजति *yajati* ॥ Pf. 1. इयाज *iyâja* (§ 311), 2. इयजिथ *iyajitha* or इयष्ठ *iyashṭha* (§ 335, 3), 4. ईजिव *îjiva*, 5. ईजथुः *îjathuḥ*, 6. ईजतुः *îjatuḥ*, 7. ईजिम *îjima*, 8. ईज *îja*, 9. ईजुः *îjuḥ*, I A. 1. अयाक्षं *ayâksham*, 2. अयाक्षीः *ayâkshîḥ*, 3. अयाक्षीत् *ayâkshît*, 4. अयाक्ष्व *ayâkshva*, 5. अयाष्टं *ayâshṭam*, 6. अयाष्टां *ayâshṭâm*, 7. अयाक्ष्म *ayâkshma*, 8. अयाष्ट *ayâshṭa*, 9. अयाक्षुः *ayâkshuḥ*, I Aor. Âtm. 1. अयक्षि *ayakshi*, 2. अयष्ठाः *ayashṭhâḥ*, 3. अयष्ट *ayashṭa*, 4. अयक्ष्वहि *ayakshvahi*, 5. अयक्षाथां *ayakshâthâm*, 6. अयक्षातां *ayakshâtâm*, 7. अयक्ष्महि *ayakshmahi*, 8. अयड्ढ्वं *ayaḍḍhvam* (not अयग्ध्वं *ayagdhvam*), 9. अयक्षत *ayakshata*, F. यक्ष्यति *yakshyati*, P. F. यष्टा *yashṭâ* (§ 124), B. इज्यात् *ijyât* (§ 393) ॥ Pt. इष्टः *ishṭaḥ*, Ger. इष्ट्वा *ishṭvâ*, °इज्य *-ijya* ॥ Pass. इज्यते *ijyate*, Caus. याजयति *yâjayati*, Aor. अयीयजत् *ayîyajat*, Des. यियक्षति *yiyakshati*, Int. यायज्यते *yâyajyate*, यायष्टि *yâyashṭi*.

100. वप् *vap*, to sow, to weave, (डुवप्.)

P. वपति *vapati* ॥ Pf. 1. उवाप *uvâpa*, 2. उवपिथ *uvapitha* or उवप्थ *uvaptha*, 9. ऊपुः *ûpuḥ*, I A. अवाप्सीत् *avâpsît*, Âtm. अवप्त *avapta*, F. वप्स्यति *vapsyati*, P. F. वप्ता *vaptâ*, B. उप्यात् *upyât* ॥ Pt. उप्तः *uptaḥ* ॥ Pass. उप्यते *upyate*.

101. वह् *vah*, to carry.

P. वहति *vahati* ॥ Pf. 1. उवाह *uvâha*, 2. उवहिथ *uvahitha* or उवोढ *uvoḍha*, 3. उवाह *uvâha*, 4. ऊहिव *ûhiva*, 5. ऊहथुः *ûhathuḥ*, 6. ऊहतुः *ûhatuḥ*, 7. ऊहिम *ûhima*, 8. ऊह *ûha*, 9. ऊहुः *ûhuḥ*, I A. 1. अवाक्षं *avâksham*, 2. अवाक्षीः *avâkshîḥ*, 3. अवाक्षीत् *avâkshît*, 4. अवाक्ष्व *avâkshva*, 5. अवोढं *avoḍham*, 6. अवोढां *avoḍhâm*, 7. अवाक्ष्म *avâkshma*, 8. अवोढ *avoḍha*, 9. अवाक्षुः *avâkshuḥ*, I Aor. Âtm. 1. अवक्षि *avakshi*, 2. अवोढाः *avoḍhâḥ*, 3. अवोढ *avoḍha*, 4. अवक्ष्वहि *avakshvahi*, 5. अवक्षाथां *avakshâthâm*, 6. अवक्षातां *avakshâtâm*, 7. अवक्ष्महि *avakshmahi*, 8. अवोढ्वं *avoḍhvam*, 9. अवक्षत *avakshata*, F. वक्ष्यति *vakshyati*, P. F. वोढा *voḍhâ*, B. उह्यात् *uhyât* ॥ Pt. ऊढः *ûḍhaḥ*, Adj. वाह्यः *vâhyaḥ* ॥ Pass. उह्यते *uhyate*, Caus. वाहयति *vâhayati*, Aor. अवीवहत् *avîvahat*, Des. विवक्षति *vivakshati*, Int. वावह्यते *vâvahyate*, वावोढि *vâvoḍhi*.

102. वे *ve*, to weave, (वेञ्.)

P. वयति *vayati* ॥ Pf. 3. ववौ *vavau*, 6. ववतुः *vavatuḥ* (or ऊवतुः *ûvatuḥ*), 9. ववुः *vavuḥ* (or ऊवुः *ûvuḥ*); or 3. उवाय *uvâya*, 6. ऊयतुः *ûyatuḥ*, 9. ऊयुः *ûyuḥ* (§ 311), I A. 1. अवासिषं *avâsisham*, 2. अवासीः *avâsîḥ*, 3. अवासीत् *avâsît*, Âtm. अवास्त *avâsta*, F. वास्यति *vâsyati*, P. F. वाता *vâtâ*, B. ऊयात् *ûyât*, Âtm. वासीष्ट *vâsîshṭa* ॥ Pt. उतः *utaḥ* (Pâṇ. VI. 4, 2) ॥ Pass. ऊयते *ûyate*, Caus. वाययति *vâyayati*, Des. विवासति *vivâsati*, Int. वावायते *vâvâyate*, वावाति *vâvâti*.

103. ह्वे *hve*, to emulate, to call, (ह्वेञ्.)

P. ह्वयति *hvayati* ॥ Pf. 1. जुहाव *juhâva*, 2. जुहविथ *juhavitha* or जुहोथ *juhotha*, 3. जुहाव *juhâva*, 4. जुहुविव *juhuviva*, II A. अह्वत् *ahvat* (§ 363), Âtm. अह्वत *ahvata*, or I A. अह्वास्त *ahvâsta*, F. ह्वास्यति *hvâsyati*, B. हूयात् *hûyât* ॥ Pt. हूतः *hûtaḥ*, Ger. °हूय *-hûya* ॥ Pass. हूयते *hûyate*, Aor. अह्वायि *ahvâyi*, Caus. ह्वाययति *hvâyayati*, Aor. अजूहवत् *ajûhavat* (§ 371), Des. जुहूषति *juhûshati*, Int. जोहूयते *johûyate*, जोहोति *johoti*.

Tud Class (*Tudâdi*, *VI Class*).

I. Parasmaipada and Âtmanepada Verbs.

104. तुद् *tud*, to strike.

P. तुदति *tudati* ॥ Pf. तुतोद *tutoda*, F. तोत्स्यति *totsyati*, P. F. तोत्ता *tottâ*, I A. अतौत्सीत् *atautsît*, Âtm. अतुत्त *atutta* ॥ Pt. तुन्नः *tunnaḥ*, Ger. तुत्त्वा *tuttvâ* ॥ Pass. तुद्यते *tudyate*, Caus. तोदयति *todayati*, Aor. अतूतुदत् *atûtudat*, Des. तुतुत्सति *tututsati*, Int. तोतुद्यते *totudyate*, तोतोत्ति *tototti*.

105. भ्रस्ज् *bhrajj*, to fry, (भ्रस्जो.)

भ्रस्ज् *bhrajj* takes *Samprasâraṇa* before weakening terminations, the same as ग्रह् *grah*, ज्या *jyâ*, वय् *vay*, व्यध् *vyadh*, वश् *vaś*, व्यच् *vyach*, व्रश्च् *vraśch*, प्रछ् *prachh* (Pâṇ. vi. 1, 16). The terminations of the special tenses of Tud verbs are never strengthening, but weakening, if possible.

P. भृज्जति *bhṛijjati* ॥ Pf. 1. बभ्रज्ज *babhrajja*, 2. बभ्रज्जिथ *babhrajjitha* or बभ्रष्ठ *babhrashṭha*, 9. बभ्रज्जुः *babhrajjuḥ* (Pâṇ. 1. 2, 5), or बभर्ज्ज *babharjja* &c. (Pâṇ. vi. 4, 47), I A. अभ्राक्षीत् *abhrâkshît* or अभार्क्षीत् *abhârkshît*, Âtm. अभ्रष्ट *abhrashṭa* or अभर्ष्ट *abharshṭa*, F. भ्रक्ष्यति *bhrakshyati* or भर्क्ष्यति *bharkshyati*, P. F. भ्रष्टा *bhrashṭâ* or भर्ष्टा *bharshṭâ*, B. भृज्ज्यात् *bhṛijjyât*, Âtm. भ्रक्षीष्ट *bhrakshîshṭa* or भर्क्षीष्ट *bharkshîshṭa* ॥ Pt. भृष्टः *bhṛishṭaḥ* ॥ Pass. भृज्ज्यते *bhṛijjyate*, Caus. भ्रज्जयति *bhrajjayati*, Aor. अबभ्रज्जत् *ababhrajjat* or अबभर्ज्जत् *ababharjjat*, Des. बिभ्रक्षति *bibhrakshati* or बिभर्क्षति *bibharkshati*, Int. बरीभृज्ज्यते *barîbhṛijjyate*.

106. कृष् *kṛish*, to draw a line. (See No. 38.)

P. कृषति *kṛishati* ॥ Pf. चकर्ष *chakarsha*, I A. अकार्क्षीत् *akârkshît* or अक्राक्षीत् *akrâkshît*, Âtm. अकृक्षत *akṛikshata* or अकृष्ट *akṛishṭa*, F. कर्क्ष्यति *karkshyati* or क्रक्ष्यति *krakshyati*, P. F. कर्ष्टा *karshṭâ* or क्रष्टा *krashṭâ*, B. कृष्यात् *kṛishyât*, Âtm. कृक्षीष्ट *kṛikshîshṭa* ॥ Pt. कृष्टः *kṛishṭaḥ* ॥ Pass. कृष्यते *kṛishyate*, Caus. कर्षयति *karshayati*, Aor. अचकर्षत् *achakarshat* or अचीकृषत् *achîkṛishat*, Des. चिकृक्षति *chikṛikshati*, Int. चरीकृष्यते *charîkṛishyate*.

107. मुच् *much*, to loosen, (मुच्लृ.)

Certain verbs beginning with मुच् *much* take a nasal in the special tenses. They are, मुच् *much*, लुप् *lup*, to cut, विद् *vid*, to find, लिप् *lip*, to paint, सिच् *sich*, to sprinkle, कृत् *krit*, to cut, खिद् *khid*, to pain, पिश् *piś*, to form. (Pâṇ. vii. 1, 59.)

P. मुञ्चति *muñchati* ॥ Pf. मुमोच *mumocha*, I A. अमुचत् *amuchat*, Âtm. अमुक्त *amukta* (§ 367), Des. मुमुक्षति *mumukshati* or मोक्षते *mokshate* (§ 471, 9).

108. विद् *vid*, to find, (विदॢ.)

P. विन्दति *vindati* ‖ Pf. विवेद *viveda*, II A. अविदत् *avidat*, Âtm. अवित्त *avitta*, F. वेत्स्यति *vetsyati* or वेदिष्यति *vedishyati* (§ 332, 11) ‖ Pt. वित्तः *vittaḥ*.

109. लिप् *lip*, to paint.

P. लिम्पति *limpati* ‖ Pf. लिलेप *lilepa*, II A. अलिपत् *alipat* (§ 367), Âtm. II A. अलिपत *alipata* or I A. अलिप्त *alipta* (§ 367).

II. Parasmaipada Verbs.

110. कृत् *kṛit*, to cut, (कृती.)

P. कृन्तति *kṛintati* (see No. 107) ‖ Pf. चकर्त *chakarta*, I A. अकर्तीत् *akartît*, F. कर्तिष्यति *kartishyati* or कर्त्स्यति *kartsyati* (§ 337, II. 2), P. F. कर्तिता *kartitâ*, B. कृत्यात् *kṛityât* ‖ Pt. कृत्तः *kṛittaḥ* ‖ Pass. कृत्यते *kṛityate*, Caus. कर्तयति *kartayati*, Aor. अचकर्तत् *achakartat* or अचीकृतत् *achîkṛitat*, Des. चिकर्तिषति *chikartishati* or चिकृत्सति *chikṛitsati* (§ 337, II. 2), Int. चरीकृत्यते *charîkṛityate*.

111. कुट् *kuṭ*, to be crooked, to bend.

Certain verbs beginning with कुट् *kuṭ* (Dhâtupâṭha 28, 73—108) do not admit of Guṇa or Vṛiddhi, except in the reduplicated perfect, the causative, and the intensive Parasmaipada. (Pâṇ. 1. 2, 1; § 345, note.)

P. कुटति *kuṭati* ‖ Pf. 1. चुकोट *chukoṭa*, 2. चुकुटिथ *chukuṭitha*, I A. अकुटीत् *akuṭît*, F. कुटिष्यति *kuṭishyati*, P. F. कुटिता *kuṭitâ* ‖ Caus. कोटयति *koṭayati*, Int. चोकुट्यते *chokuṭyate*, चोकोट्टि *chokoṭṭi*.

112. व्रश्च् *vraśch*, to cut, (ओव्रश्चू.)

P. वृश्चति *vṛiśchati* (see No. 105) ‖ Pf. 1. वव्रश्च *vavraścha*, 2. वव्रश्चिथ *vavraśchitha* or वव्रष्ठ *vavrashṭha*, I A. अव्रश्चीत् *avraśchît* or अव्राक्षीत् *avrâkshît* (§ 337, I. 2), F. व्रश्चिष्यति *vraśchishyati* or व्रक्ष्यति *vrakshyati*, B. वृश्च्यात् *vṛiśchyât* ‖ Pt. वृक्णः *vṛikṇaḥ*.

113. कॄ *kṛî*, to scatter.

P. किरति *kirati* ‖ Pf. 3. चकार *chakâra*, 6. चकरतुः *chakaratuḥ*, 9. चकरुः *chakaruḥ* (Pâṇ. vii. 4, 11), I A. अकारीत् *akârît*, F. करिष्यति or करीष्यति *karîshyati* (§ 340), B. कीर्यात् *kîryât* ‖ Pt. कीर्णः *kîrṇaḥ* ‖ Pass. कीर्यते *kîryate*, Caus. कारयति *kârayati*, Des. चिकरिषति *chikarishati*.

Note—After उप *upa* and प्रति *prati*, कॄ *kṛî* takes an initial स् *s* if it means to cut or to strike: उपस्किरति *upaskirati*, he cuts, उपस्कार *upaskâra*; प्रतिस्किरति *pratiskirati*, he cuts or he strikes (Pâṇ. vi. 1, 140, 141). Also अपस्किरते *apaskirate*, he drops (Pâṇ. vi. 1, 142).

114. स्पृश् *spṛiś*, to touch.

P. स्पृशति *spṛiśati* ‖ Pf. पस्पर्श *pasparśa*, I A. अस्प्राक्षीत् *asprâkshît* or अस्पार्क्षीत् *aspârkshît* or अस्पृक्षत् *aspṛikshat*, F. स्प्रक्ष्यति *sprakshyati* or स्पर्क्ष्यति *sparkshyati*, B. स्पृश्यात् *spṛiśyât* ‖ Pt. स्पृष्टः *spṛishṭaḥ* ‖ Des. पिस्पृक्षति *pispṛikshati*, Int. परीस्पृश्यते *parîspṛiśyate*, परीस्पर्ष्टि *parîsparshṭi*.

115. प्रछ् *prachh*, to ask.

P. पृच्छति *pṛichchhati* (see No. 105) ‖ Pf. 1. पप्रच्छ *paprachchha*, 2. पप्रच्छिथ *paprachchhitha* or पप्रष्ठ *paprashṭha*, 9. पप्रच्छुः *paprachchhuḥ*, I A. अप्राक्षीत् *aprâkshît*, F. प्रक्ष्यति *prakshyati*, B. पृच्छ्यात् *pṛichchhyât* ‖ Pt. पृष्टः *pṛishṭaḥ* ‖ Pass. पृच्छ्यते *pṛichchhyate*, Caus. प्रच्छयति *prachchhayati*, Des. पिपृच्छिषति *pipṛichchhishati*, Int. परीपृच्छ्यते *parîpṛichchhyate*.

116. सृज् *sṛij*, to let off.

P. सृजति *sṛijati* ‖ Pf. 1. ससर्ज *sasarja*, 2. ससर्जिथ *sasarjitha* or सस्रष्ठ *sasrashṭha* (see No. 48), I A. अस्राक्षीत् *asrâkshît*, F. स्रक्ष्यति *srakshyati* ‖ Pt. सृष्टः *sṛishṭaḥ*.

117. मस्ज् *majj*, to sink, (मस्जो.)

मस्ज् *majj* and नश् *naś* (Div) insert a nasal before strengthening terminations beginning with consonants, except nasals and semivowels. (Pâṇ. VII. 1, 60.)

P. मज्जति *majjati* ‖ Pf. 1. ममज्ज *mamajja*, 2. ममज्जिथ *mamajjitha* or ममंक्थ *mamaṅktha*, I A. 3. अमांक्षीत् *amâṅkshît* (§ 345), 6. अमांक्ताम् *amâṅktâm*, 9. अमांक्षुः *amâṅkshuḥ*, F. मंक्ष्यति *maṅkshyati*, P. F. मंक्ता *maṅktâ* ‖ Pt. मग्नः *magnaḥ*, Ger. मंक्त्वा *maṅktvâ* or मक्त्वा *maktvâ* (§ 438) ‖ Caus. मज्जयति *majjayati*, Aor. अममज्जत् *amamajjat*, Des. मिमंक्षति *mimaṅkshati*, Int. मामज्ज्यते *mâmajjyate*, मामंक्ति *mâmaṅkti*.

118. इष् *ish*, to wish, (इषु.)

P. इच्छति *ichchhati* (see No. 31), I. ऐच्छत् *aichchhat* ‖ Pf. 1. इयेष *iyesha*, 2. इयेषिथ *iyeshitha*, 3. इयेष *iyesha*, 4. ईषिव *îshiva*, 5. ईषथुः *îshathuḥ*, 6. ईषतुः *îshatuḥ*, 7. ईषिम *îshima*, 8. ईष *îsha*, 9. ईषुः *îshuḥ*, I A. ऐषीत् *aishît*, F. एषिष्यति *eshishyati*, P. F. एष्टा *eshṭâ* or एषिता *eshitâ* (§ 337, II. 1) ‖ Pt. इष्टः *ishṭaḥ*, Ger. इष्ट्वा *ishṭvâ* or इषित्वा *ishitvâ* ‖ Pass. इष्यते *ishyate*, Aor. ऐषि *aishi*, Caus. एषयति *eshayati*, Aor. ऐषिषत् *aishishat*, Des. एषिषिषति *eshishishati*.

III. Âtmanepada Verbs.

119. मृ *mṛi*, to die, (मृङ्.)

मृ *mṛi*, to die, though an Âtmanepada verb, takes Âtmanepada forms only in the special tenses, the aorist, and benedictive. (Pâṇ. I. 3, 61.)

P. म्रियते *mriyate* *, I. अम्रियत *amriyata*, O. म्रियेत *mriyeta*, I. म्रियै *mriyai* ‖ Pf. 1. ममार *mamâra*, 2. ममर्थ *mamartha*, 3. ममार *mamâra*, 4. मम्रिव *mamriva*, 5. मम्रथुः *mamrathuḥ*, I A. 1. अमृषि *amṛishi*, 2. अमृथाः *amṛithâḥ*, 3. अमृत *amṛita*, F. मरिष्यति *marishyati*, P. F. मर्तास्मि *martâsmi*, B. मृषीष्ट *mṛishîshṭa* ‖ Pt. मृतः *mṛitaḥ* ‖ Pass. म्रियते *mriyate*, Caus. मारयति *mârayati*, Des. मुमूर्षति *mumûrshati*, Int. मेम्रीयते *memrîyate*.

---

* Final ऋ *ṛi* is changed to रि *ri* (§ 110) in the special tenses of Tud verbs, likewise before the य *ya* of the passive and benedictive (Pâṇ. VII. 4, 28). Afterwards रि *ri* again becomes रिय् *riy*, according to Pâṇ. VI. 4, 77.

120. दृ dṛi, to observe, (दृङ्.)

P. द्रियते driyate ॥ Pf. दद्रे dadre, I A. अदृत adṛita, F. दरिष्यते darishyate, P. F. दर्ता dartá, B. दृषीष्ट dṛishíshṭa ॥ Pass. द्रियते driyate, Caus. दारयति dárayati, Des. दिदरिषते didarishate (§ 332, 5). It is chiefly used with the preposition आ á, to regard, to consider.

Div Class (Divâdi, IV Class).

I. Parasmaipada Verbs.

121. दिव् div, to play, (दिवु.)

P. दीव्यति dívyati (§ 143) ॥ Pf. दिदेव dideva, I A. अदेवीत् adevít, F. देविष्यति devishyati, P. F. देविता devitá, B. दीव्यात् dívyát ॥ Pt. द्यूनः dyúnaḥ (§ 442, 7), Ger. द्यूत्वा dyútvá (§ 431, 1) or देवित्वा devitvá ॥ Caus. देवयति devayati, Des. दिदेविषति didevishati or दुद्यूषति dudyúshati (§ 474), Int. देदीव्यते dedívyate.

122. नृत् nṛit, to dance, (नृती.)

P. नृत्यति nṛityati ॥ Pf. 3. ननर्त nanarta, 9. ननृतुः nanṛituḥ, I A. अनर्तीत् anartít, F. नर्तिष्यति nartishyati or नर्त्स्यति nartsyati (§ 337, II. 2) ॥ Pt. नृत्तः nṛittaḥ ॥ Caus. नर्तयति nartayati, Aor. अननर्तत् ananartat or अनीनृतत् anínṛitat, Des. निनर्तिषति ninartishati or निनृत्सति ninṛitsati.

123. जॄ jṛí, to grow old, (जॄष्.)

P. जीर्यति jíryati* ॥ Pf. 3. जजार jajára, 9. जजरुः jajaruḥ (Guṇa, § 330) or जेरुः jeruḥ (§ 328, 2), I A. अजारीत् ajárít or II A. अजरत् ajarat (§ 367), F. जरिष्यति jarishyati or जरीष्यति jaríshyati (§ 340), B. जीर्यात् jíryát ॥ Pt. जीर्णः jírṇaḥ ॥ Caus. जरयति jarayati (§ 462, 25), Des. जिजरिषति jijarishati or जिजीर्षति jijírshati (§ 337, II. 3).

124. शो śo, to sharpen.

Verbs ending in ओ o drop ओ o before the य ya of the Div class (Pâṇ. vii. 3, 71); e.g. छो chho, to cut, सो so, to finish, दो do, to cut.

P. श्यति śyati, I. अश्यत् aśyat, O. श्येत् śyet, I. श्यतु śyatu ॥ Pf. शशौ śaśau (§ 329), I A. अशासीत् aśásít or II A. अशात् aśát, F. शास्यति śásyati, P. F. शाता śátá, B. शायात् śáyát (§ 392) ॥ Pt. शातः śátaḥ or शितः śitaḥ (§ 435) ॥ Pass. शायते śáyate, Caus. शाययति śáyayati, Des. शिशासति śiśásati, Int. शाशायते śáśáyate.

125. सो so, to finish.

P. स्यति syati ॥ Pf. ससौ sasau, I A. असासीत् asásít, II A. असात् asát, F. सास्यति sásyati, P. F. साता sátá, B. सेयात् seyát (§ 392) ॥ Pt. सितः sitaḥ, Ger. °साय -sáya ॥ Pass. सीयते síyate (§ 392), Caus. साययति sáyayati, Des. सिषासति sisásati, Int. सेषीयते seshíyate.

---

* Final ॠ ṛí, changed to ईर् ír, and lengthened before य् y.

126. व्यध् *vyadh*, to strike.

P. विध्यति *vidhyati* (see No. 105) ‖ Pf. 3. विव्याध *vivyâdha* (§ 311), 9. विविधुः *vividhuḥ*, I A. 1. अव्यात्सम् *avyâtsam*, 2. अव्यात्सीः *avyâtsîḥ*, 3. अव्यात्सीत् *avyâtsît*, 4. अव्यात्स्व *avyâtsva*, 5. अव्याद्धं *avyâddham*, 6. अव्याद्धां *avyâddhâm*, 7. अव्यात्स्म *avyâtsma*, 8. अव्याद्ध *avyâddha*, 9. अव्यात्सुः *avyâtsuḥ*, F. व्यत्स्यति *vyatsyati*, P. F. व्यद्धा *vyaddhâ*, B. विध्यात् *vidhyât* ‖ Pt. विद्धः *viddhaḥ* ‖ Pass. विध्यते *vidhyate*, Caus. व्याधयति *vyâdhayati*, Des. विव्यत्सति *vivyatsati*, Int. वेविध्यते *vevidhyate*.

127. तृप् *tṛip*, to delight.

P. तृप्यति *tṛipyati* ‖ Pf. 1. ततर्प *tatarpa*, 2. ततर्पिथ *tatarpitha* or ततर्प्थ *tatarptha* or तत्रप्थ *tatraptha*, 3. ततर्प *tatarpa*, 4. ततृपिव *tatṛipiva* or ततृप्व *tatṛipva*, I A. अतर्पीत् *atarpît* or अतार्प्सीत् *atârpsît* (§ 337, I. 3) or अत्राप्सीत् *atrâpsît* (see No. 38) or II A. अतृपत् *atṛipat*, F. तर्पिष्यति *tarpishyati* or तर्प्स्यति *tarpsyati* or त्रप्स्यति *trapsyati*, P. F. तर्पिता *tarpitâ*, तर्प्ता *tarptâ* or त्रप्ता *traptâ*, B. तृप्यात् *tṛipyât* ‖ Pt. तृप्तः *tṛiptaḥ* ‖ Pass. तृप्यते *tṛipyate*, Caus. तर्पयति *tarpayati*, Aor. अतीतृपत् *atîtṛipat* or अततर्पत् *atatarpat*, Des. तितृप्सति *titṛipsati* or तितर्पिषति *titarpishati*, Int. तरीतृप्यते *tarîtṛipyate*.

128. मुह् *muh*, to be foolish.

P. मुह्यति *muhyati* ‖ Pf. 1. मुमोह *mumoha*, 2. मुमोहिथ *mumohitha* or मुमोग्ध *mumogdha* or मुमोढ *mumoḍha*, II A. अमुहत् *amuhat* (§ 367, *pushâdi*)*, F. मोक्ष्यति *mokshyati* or मोहिष्यति *mohishyati*, P. F. मोग्धा *mogdhâ* or मोढा *moḍhâ* (§ 129) or मोहिता *mohitâ* ‖ Pt. मुग्धः *mugdhaḥ* or मूढः *mûḍhaḥ* ‖ Pass. मुह्यते *muhyate*, Caus. मोहयति *mohayati*, Des. मुमुक्षति *mumukshati* or मुमोहिषति *mumohishati*, Int. मोमुह्यते *momuhyate*, मोमोग्धि *momogdhi* or मोमोढि *momoḍhi*.

129. नश् *naś*, to perish, (णश्.)

P. नश्यति *naśyati* ‖ Pf. 3. ननाश *nanâśa*, 9. नेशुः *neśuḥ*, II A. अनशत् *anaśat* (*pushâdi*) or अनेशत् *aneśat* (§ 366), F. नशिष्यति *naśishyati* or नंक्ष्यति *naṅkshyati* (see No. 117) ‖ Pt. नष्टः *nashṭaḥ*, Ger. नष्ट्वा *nashṭvâ* or नंष्ट्वा *naṁshṭvâ* (§ 438).

130. शम् *śam*, to cease, (शमु.)

Eight Div verbs, शम् *śam*, तम् *tam*, दम् *dam*, श्रम् *śram*, भ्रम् *bhram*, क्षम् *ksham*, क्लम् *klam*, मद् *mad*, lengthen their vowel in the special tenses. (Pâṇ. VII. 3, 74.)

P. शाम्यति *śâmyati* ‖ Pf. 3. शशाम *śaśâma*, 9. शेमुः *śemuḥ*, II A. अशमत् *aśamat*,

* The Sârasvatî gives besides the second aorist the optional forms of the first aorist अमोहीत् *amohît* or अमौक्षीत् *amaukshît* (§ 337, I. 3, *radhâdi*) or अमुक्षत् *amukshat* (§ 360). According to Pâṇ. III. 1, 55 (§ 367), the forms of the first aorist are allowed in the Âtmanepada only; but later grammarians frequently admit forms as optional which are opposed to the grammatical system of Pâṇini. Sometimes the evasion of the strict rules of Pâṇini may be explained by the admission of different roots, as, for instance, in No. 130, where the first aorist Parasmaipada अशमीत् *aśamît*, given in the Sârasvatî, which is wrong in the Div class, might be referred to the Krî class.

F. शमिष्यति *śamishyati*, P. F. शमिता *śamitâ* ‖ Pt. शान्तः *śântaḥ* (§ 429), Ger. शान्त्वा *śântvâ* or शमित्वा *śamitvâ* ‖ Pass. शम्यते *śamyate*, Caus. शमयति *śamayati* (§ 462), he quiets, but शामयते *śâmayate* or °ति *-ti*, he sees. (Dhâtupâṭha 19, 70.)

131. मिद् *mid*, to be wet, (ञिमिदा.)

मिद् *mid* takes Guṇa in the special tenses. (Pâṇ. VII. 3, 82.)

P. मेद्यति *medyati* ‖ Pt. मिन्नः *minnaḥ*, wet, or मेदितः *meditaḥ* (§ 333, D. 2*).

II. Âtmanepada Verbs.

132. जन् *jan*, to spring up, (जनी.)

जन् *jan* substitutes जा *jâ* in the special tenses. (Pâṇ. VII. 3, 79.)

P. जायते *jâyate* ‖ Pf. जज्ञे *jajñe* (§ 328, 3), I A. अजनिष्ट *ajanishṭa* or अजनि *ajani* (§ 413), F. जनिष्यते *janishyate*, P. F. जनिता *janitâ*, B. जनिषीष्ट *janishîshṭa* ‖ Pt. जातः *jâtaḥ*, Caus. जनयति *janayati*, Des. जिजनिषते *jijanishate*, Int. जाजायते *jâjâyate* or जञ्जन्यते *jañjanyate*.

133. पद् *pad*, to go.

P. पद्यते *padyate* ‖ Pf. पेदे *pede*, I A. 3. अपादि *apâdi* (§ 412), 6. अपत्साताम् *apatsâtâm*, 9. अपत्सत *apatsata*, F. पत्स्यते *patsyate*, P. F. पत्ता *pattâ*, B. पत्सीष्ट *patsîshṭa* ‖ Pt. पन्नः *pannaḥ* ‖ Caus. पादयति *pâdayati*, Aor. अपीपदत् *apîpadat*, Des. पित्सते *pitsate* (§ 471, 9), Int. पनीपद्यते *panîpadyate* (§ 485).

134. बुध् *budh*, to perceive.

P. बुध्यते *budhyate* ‖ Pf. बुबुधे *bubudhe*, I A. 1. अभुत्सि *abhutsi*, 2. अबुद्धाः *abuddhâḥ*, 3. अबुद्ध *abuddha* or अबोधि *abodhi*, 4. अभुत्स्वहि *abhutsvahi*, 5. अभुत्साथाम् *abhutsâthâm*, 6. अभुत्साताम् *abhutsâtâm*, 7. अभुत्स्महि *abhutsmahi*, 8. अभुद्ध्वम् *abhuddhvam*, 9. अभुत्सत *abhutsata*, F. भोत्स्यते *bhotsyate*, P. F. बोद्धा *boddhâ*, B. भुत्सीष्ट *bhutsîshṭa* ‖ Pt. बुद्धः *buddhaḥ* ‖ Caus. बोधयति *bodhayati*, Aor. अबूबुधत् *abûbudhat*, Des. बुबोधिषते *bubodhishate* or बुभुत्सते *bubhutsate*, Int. बोबुध्यते *bobudhyate*.

III. Parasmaipada and Âtmanepada Verbs.

135. नह् *nah*, to bind, (णह्.)

P. नह्यति *nahyati* or °ते *-te* ‖ Pf. 1. ननाह *nanâha*, 2. ननद्ध *nanaddha* (§ 130) or नेहिथ *nehitha*, Âtm. नेहे *nehe*, I A. 1. अनात्सम् *anâtsam*, 2. अनात्सीः *anâtsîḥ*, 3. अनात्सीत् *anâtsît*, 4. अनात्स्व *anâtsva*, 5. अनाद्धम् *anâddham*, 6. अनाद्धाम् *anâddhâm*, 7. अनात्स्म *anâtsma*, 8. अनाद्ध *anâddha*, 9. अनात्सुः *anâtsuḥ*, Âtm. 1. अनत्सि *anatsi*, 2. अनद्धाः *anaddhâḥ*, 3. अनद्ध *anaddha*, 4. अनत्स्वहि *anatsvahi*, 5. अनत्साथाम् *anatsâthâm*, 6. अनत्साताम् *anatsâtâm*, 7. अनत्स्महि *anatsmahi*, 8. अनद्ध्वम् *anaddhvam*, 9. अनत्सत *anatsata*, F. नत्स्यति *natsyati*, P. F. नद्धा *naddhâ* ‖ Pt. नद्धः *naddhaḥ*, Ger. नद्ध्वा *naddhvâ*, °नह्य *-nahya* ‖ Pass. नह्यते *nahyate*, Aor. अनाहि *anâhi*, Caus. नाहयति *nâhayati*, Des. निनत्सते *ninatsate*, Int. नानह्यते *nânahyate*.

Chur Class (*Churâdi, X Class*).

Parasmaipada Verbs only.

136. चुर् *chur*, to steal.

P. चोरयति *chorayati* ॥ Pf. चोरयांचकार *chorayâṁchakâra*, I A. अचूचुरत् *achúchurat*, F. चोरयिष्यति *chorayishyati*, P. F. चोरयिता *chorayitâ*, B. चोर्यात् *choryât* (§ 386) ॥ Pt. चोरितः *choritaḥ*, Ger. चोरयित्वा *chorayitvâ* ॥ Pass. चोर्यते *choryate*, Caus. चोरयति *chorayati*, Des. चुचोरयिषति *chuchorayishati*. No Intensive (§ 479).

137. चि *chi*, to gather, (चिञ्.)

The changes which roots undergo as causatives, take likewise place if the same roots are treated as Chur verbs. Hence according to § 463, II. 6, चि *chi*, as a Chur verb, may form P. चपयति *chapayati* or चययति *chayayati*, the vowel, however, remaining short because, as a Chur verb, चि *chi* is said to be मित् *mit* (§ 462, note) ॥ I A. अचीचपत् *achíchapat* or अचीचयत् *achíchayat*, B. चप्यात् *chapyât* or चय्यात् *chayyât*.

Note—Several Chur verbs are marked as मित् *mit*, i. e. as not lengthening their vowel, some of which were mentioned in § 462, among the causatives. Such are ज्ञप् *jñap*, to know, to make known; चप् *chap*, to pound; चह् *chah*, to pound; यम् *yam*, if it means to feed; वल् *val*, to live.

138. कृत् *krit*, to praise.

P. कीर्तयति *kírtayati* (§ 462, 2) ॥ I A. अचीकृतत् *achíkritat* or अचिकीर्तत् *achikírtat* (§ 377).

Su Class (*Svâdi, V Class*).

I. Parasmaipada and Âtmanepada Verbs.

139. सु *su*, to distil, (षुञ्.)

P. सुनोति *sunoti*, I. 2. सुनु *sunu* (§ 321*) ॥ Pf. सुषाव *sushâva*, Âtm. सुषुवे *sushuve*, I A. असावीत् *asâvít* (§ 332, 4); the Sârasvatî allows also असौषीत् *asaushít*, Âtm. असोष्ट *asoshṭa*; the Sâr. allows also असविष्ट *asavishṭa* (but see Pâṇ. VII. 2, 72); F. सोष्यति *soshyati*, P. F. सोता *sotâ*, B. सूयात् *súyât* ॥ Pass. सूयते *súyate*, Aor. असावि *asâvi*, Caus. सावयति *sâvayati*, Aor. असूषवत् *asúshavat*, Des. सुसूषति *susúshati*, Int. सोषूयते *soshúyate*.

Note—The उ *u* of नु *nu* may be dropt before terminations beginning with व् *v* or म् *m*, and not requiring Guṇa; but this is not the case if नु *nu* is preceded by a consonant. This explains the double forms सुनुवः *sunuvaḥ* and सुन्वः *sunvaḥ*, सुनुमः *sunumaḥ* and सुन्मः *sunmaḥ*, असुनुव *asunuva* and असुन्व *asunva*, असुनुम *asunuma* and असुन्म *asunma*; and Âtm. सुनुवहे *sunuvahe* or सुन्वहे *sunvahe*, सुनुमहे *sunumahe* or सुन्महे *sunmahe*, असुनुवहि *asunuvahi* or असुन्वहि *asunvahi*, असुनुमहि *asunumahi* or असुन्महि *asunmahi*. The same rule applies to the Tan verbs.

140. चि *chi*, to collect, (चिञ्.)

P. चिनोति *chinoti* ॥ Pf. 3. चिचाय *chichâya* or चिकाय *chikâya*, 9. चिच्युः *chichyuḥ* or चिक्युः *chikyuḥ*, Âtm. चिच्ये *chichye* or चिक्ये *chikye* (Pâṇ. VII. 3, 58), I A. अचैषीत् *achaishít*, Âtm. अचेष्ट *acheshṭa*, F. चेष्यति *cheshyati*, P. F. चेता *chetâ*,

B. चीयात् *chîyât* ॥ Pass. चीयते *chîyate*, Caus. चाययति *châyayati* or चापयति *châpayati* (§ 463, II. 6, and No. 137), Des. चिचीषति *chichîshati* or चिकीषति *chikîshati* (Pâṇ. VII. 3, 58), Int. चेचीयते *chechîyate*.

141. स्तृ *stṛi*, to cover, (स्तृञ्.)

P. स्तृणोति *stṛiṇoti* ॥ Pf. तस्तार *tastâra*, Âtm. तस्तरे *tastare*, I A. अस्तार्षीत् *astârshît*, Âtm. अस्तरिष्ट *astarishṭa* (not अस्तरीष्ट *astarîshṭa*, if *svâdi*) or अस्तृत *astṛita* (§ 332, 5, a rule which applies to the Âtmanepada only), F. स्तरिष्यति *starishyati* (§ 332, 5), P. F. स्तर्ता *startâ*, B. स्तर्यात् *staryât*, Âtm. स्तृषीष्ट *stṛishîshṭa* or स्तरिषीष्ट *starishîshṭa* (§ 332, 5) ॥ Pass. स्तर्यते *staryate*, Caus. स्तारयति *stârayati*, Des. तिस्तीर्षति *tistîrshati*, Int. तास्तर्यते *tâstaryate*.

142. वृ *vṛi*, to choose, (वृञ्.)

P. वृणोति *vṛiṇoti* ॥ Pf. 1. ववार *vavâra*, 2. ववरिथ *vavaritha* *, 3. ववार *vavâra*, 4. ववृव *vavṛiva*, 5. वव्रथुः *vavrathuḥ*, 6. वव्रतुः *vavratuḥ*, 7. ववृम *vavṛima*, 8. वव्र *vavra*, 9. वव्रुः *vavruḥ*, I A. अवारीत् *avârît* (§ 332, 5), Âtm. अवरिष्ट *avarishṭa* or अवरीष्ट *avarîshṭa* (§ 340) or अवृत *avṛita* (§ 337, II. 4), F. वरिष्यति *varishyati* or वरीष्यति *varîshyati*, P. F. वरिता *varitâ* or वरीता *varîtâ*, B. व्रियात् *vriyât*, Âtm. वरिषीष्ट *varishîshṭa* (not वरीषीष्ट *varîshîshṭa*, Pâṇ. VII. 2, 39) ॥ Pass. व्रियते *vriyate*, Aor. अवारि *avâri*, Caus. वारयति *vârayati*, Des. विवरिषति *vivarishati* or विवरीषति *vivarîshati*, Int. वेव्रीयते *vevrîyate*.

II. Parasmaipada Verbs.

143. हि *hi*, to go, to grow.

P. हिनोति *hinoti* ॥ Pf. जिघाय *jighâya* (Pâṇ. VII. 3, 56), I A. अहैषीत् *ahaishît*, F. हेष्यति *heshyati*, P. F. हेता *hetâ*, B. हीयात् *hîyât* ॥ Caus. हाययति *hâyayati*, Aor. अजीहयत् *ajîhayat* (Pâṇ. VII. 3, 56), Des. जिघीषति *jighîshati*, Int. जेघीयते *jeghîyate*.

144. शक् *śak*, to be able, (शकॢ.)

P. शक्नोति *śaknoti* ॥ Pf. 3. शशाक *śaśâka*, 9. शेकुः *śekuḥ*, I A. अशकत् *aśakat*, F. शक्ष्यति *śakshyati*, P. F. शक्ता *śaktâ* ॥ Pt. शक्तः *śaktaḥ* ॥ Pass. शक्यते *śakyate* (कर्तुं शक्यते *kartum śakyate*, it can be done), Caus. शाकयति *śâkayati*, Aor. अशीशकत् *aśîśakat*, Des. शिक्षति *śikshati*, Int. शाशक्यते *śâśakyate*.

145. श्रु *śru*, to hear.

This verb is by native grammarians classed with the Bhû verbs, though as irregular. It substitutes शृ *śṛi* for श्रु *śru* in the special tenses.

P. 3. शृणोति *śṛiṇoti*, 6. शृणुतः *śṛiṇutaḥ*, 9. शृण्वन्ति *śṛiṇvanti*; 4. शृणुवः *śṛiṇuvaḥ* or शृण्वः *śṛiṇvaḥ* ॥ Pf. 1. शुश्राव *śuśrâva*, 2. शुश्रोथ *śuśrotha* (§ 334, 8), 3. शुश्राव

* According to Pâṇ. VII. 2, 13, we might form ववर्थ *vavartha*; but Pâṇ. VII. 2, 63, would sanction ववरिथ *vavaritha*. The special restriction, however, of ववर्थ *vavartha* to the Veda in Pâṇ. VII. 2, 64, is sufficient to fix ववरिथ *vavaritha* as the proper form in ordinary Sanskrit.

śuśrâva, 4. शुश्रुव *śuśruva*, 5. शुश्रुवथुः *śuśruvathuḥ*, 6. शुश्रुवतुः *śuśruvatuḥ*, 7. शुश्रुम *śuśruma*, 8. शुश्रुव *śuśruva*, 9. शुश्रुवुः *śuśruvuḥ*, I A. अश्रौषीत् *aśraushît*, F. श्रोष्यति *śroshyati*, P. F. श्रोता *śrotâ*, B. श्रूयात् *śrûyât* ‖ Pass. श्रूयते *śrûyate*, Aor. अश्रावि *aśrâvi*, Caus. श्रावयति *śrâvayati*, Aor. अशुश्रवत् *aśuśravat* or अशिश्रवत् *aśiśravat* (§ 475), Des. शुश्रूषते *śuśrûshate* (Pâṇ. 1. 3, 57), Int. शोश्रूयते *śośrûyate*.

146. आप् *âp*, to obtain, (आप्नु.)

P. 3. आप्नोति *âpnoti*, 4. आप्नुवः *âpnuvaḥ*, 9. आप्नुवन्ति *âpnuvanti*, I. आप्नोत् *âpnot*; O. आप्नुयात् *âpnuyât*, I. 3. आप्नोतु *âpnotu*, 2. आप्नुहि *âpnuhi* ‖ Pf. आप *âpa*, Aor. आपत् *âpat*, F. आप्स्यति *âpsyati*, P. F. आप्ता *âptâ* ‖ Pt. आप्तः *âptaḥ* ‖ Pass. आप्यते *âpyate*, Caus. आपयति *âpayati*, Aor. आपिपत् *âpipat*, Des. ईप्सति *îpsati*.

III. Âtmanepada Verbs.

147. अश् *aś*, to pervade, (अश्नु.)

P. 3. अश्नुते *aśnute*, 6. अश्नुवाते *aśnuvâte*, 9. अश्नुवते *aśnuvate*, 4. अश्नुवहे *aśnuvahe*, I. 1. आश्नुवि *âśnuvi*, 2. आश्नुथाः *âśnuthâḥ*, 3. आश्नुत *âśnuta*, 4. आश्नुवहि *âśnuvahi*, 5. आश्नुवाथां *âśnuvâthâm*, 6. आश्नुवातां *âśnuvâtâm*, 7. आश्नुमहि *âśnumahi*, 8. आश्नुध्वं *âśnudhvam*, 9. आश्नुवत *âśnuvata*, O. अश्नुवीत *aśnuvîta*, I. 1. अश्नवै *aśnavai*, 2. अश्नुष्व *aśnushva*, 3. अश्नुतां *aśnutâm*, 4. अश्नवावहै *aśnavâvahai*, 5. अश्नुवाथां *aśnuvâthâm*, 6. अश्नुवातां *aśnuvâtâm*, 7. अश्नवामहै *aśnavâmahai*, 8. अश्नुध्वं *aśnudhvam*, 9. अश्नुवतां *aśnuvatâm* ‖ Pf. 1. आनशे *ânaśe*, 2. आनशिषे *ânaśishe* or आनक्षे *ânakshe*, I A. 1. आक्षि *âkshi*, 2. आष्ठाः *âshṭhâḥ*, 3. आष्ट *âshṭa*, 4. आक्ष्वहि *âkshvahi*, 5. आक्षाथां *âkshâthâm*, 6. आक्षातां *âkshâtâm*, 7. आक्ष्महि *âkshmahi*, 8. आग्ध्वं *âgdhvam*, 9. आक्षत *âkshata*; or 1. आशिषि *âśishi*, 2. आशिष्ठाः *âśishṭhâḥ*, 3. आशिष्ट *âśishṭa*, P. F. अष्टा *ashṭâ* or अशिता *aśitâ*, F. अक्ष्यते *akshyate* or अशिष्यते *aśishyate*, B. अक्षीष्ट *akshîshṭa* or अशिषीष्ट *aśishîshṭa* ‖ Pt. अष्टः *ashṭaḥ* ‖ Pass. अश्यते *aśyate*, Aor. आशि *âśi*, Caus. आशयति *âśayati*, Aor. आशिशत् *âśiśat*, Des. अशिशिषते *aśiśishate*, Int. अशाश्यते *aśâśyate*.

Tan Class (*Tanvâdi, VIII Class*).

All verbs belonging to this class are Parasmaipada and Âtmanepada Verbs.

148. तन् *tan*, to stretch, (तनु.)

P. तनोति *tanoti*, I. अतनोत् *atanot*, O. तनुयात् *tanuyât*, I. तनोतु *tanotu*; Âtm. P. तनुते *tanute*, I. अतनुत *atanuta*, O. तन्वीत *tanvîta*, I. तनुतां *tanutâm* ‖ Pf. 3. ततान *tatâna*, 9. तेनुः *tenuḥ*, I A. अतानीत् *atânît* or अतनीत् *atanît* (§ 348), Âtm. 3. अतनिष्ट *atanishṭa* or अतत *atata* (§ 369), 2. अतनिष्ठाः *atanishṭhâḥ* or अतथाः *atathâḥ*, F. तनिष्यति *tanishyati*, P. F. तनिता *tanitâ*, B. तन्यात् *tanyât*, Âtm. तनिषीष्ट *tanishîshṭa* ‖ Pt. ततः *tataḥ*, Ger. तत्वा *tatvâ* or तनित्वा *tanitvâ* ‖ Pass. तायते *tâyate* or तन्यते *tanyate* (§ 391), Caus. तानयति *tânayati*, Aor. अतीतनत् *atîtanat*, Des. तितनिषति *titanishati* or तितांसति *titâṁsati*, Int. तंतन्यते *tantanyate*.

Note—Verbs of the Tan class may raise their penultimate short vowel by Guṇa; ऋण् *ṛiṇ*, to go, अर्णोति *arṇoti* or ऋणोति *ṛiṇoti*. तनादेरुपधाया गुणो वा विधि, Sâr. II. II, 3.

149. क्षण् *kshaṇ*, to kill, (क्षणु.)

P. क्षणोति *kshaṇoti* ‖ Pf. चक्षाण *chakshâṇa*, I A. अक्षणीत् *akshaṇît* (§ 348*), Âtm. 3. अक्षणिष्ट *akshaṇishṭa* or अक्षत *akshata*, 2. अक्षणिष्ठाः *akshaṇishṭhâḥ* or अक्षथाः *akshathâḥ*.

150. क्षिण् *kshiṇ*, to kill.

P. क्षिणोति *kshiṇoti* or क्षेणोति *ksheṇoti* ‖ I A. अक्षेणीत् *aksheṇît*, Âtm. अक्षेणिष्ट *aksheṇishṭa* or अक्षित *akshita*.

151. सन् *san*, to obtain, (षणु.)

P. सनोति *sanoti* ‖ Pf. ससान *sasâna*, Âtm. सेने *sene*, I A. असानीत् *asânît*, Âtm. असनिष्ट *asanishṭa* or असात *asâta* (Pâṇ. II. 4, 79; VI. 4, 42).

152. कृ *kṛi*, to do, (डुकृञ्.)

कृ *kṛi* before weak terminations becomes कर् *kar*, but before strong terminations कुर् *kur*. Before व् *v* and म् *m*, and the य् *y* of the optative, the Vikaraṇa उ *u* is rejected, but the radical उ *u* is not lengthened.

P. 1. करोमि *karomi*, 2. करोषि *karoshi*, 3. करोति *karoti*, 4. कुर्वः *kurvaḥ*, 5. कुरुथः *kuruthaḥ*, 6. कुरुतः *kurutaḥ*, 7. कुर्मः *kurmaḥ*, 8. कुरुथ *kurutha*, 9. कुर्वन्ति *kurvanti*, I. 1. अकरवम् *akaravam*, 2. अकरोः *akaroḥ*, 3. अकरोत् *akarot*, 4. अकुर्व *akurva*, 5. अकुरुतम् *akurutam*, 6. अकुरुताम् *akurutâm*, 7. अकुर्म *akurma*, 8. अकुरुत *akuruta*, 9. अकुर्वन् *akurvan*, O. 1. कुर्याम् *kuryâm*, 9. कुर्युः *kuryuḥ*, I. 1. करवाणि *karavâṇi*, 2. कुरु *kuru*, 3. करोतु *karotu*, 4. करवाव *karavâva*, 5. कुरुतम् *kurutam*, 6. कुरुताम् *kurutâm*, 7. करवाम *karavâma*, 8. कुरुत *kuruta*, 9. कुर्वन्तु *kurvantu* ‖ Pf. 1. चकार *chakâra*, 2. चकर्थ *chakartha*, 3. चकार *chakâra*, 4. चकृव *chakṛiva*, 5. चक्रथुः *chakrathuḥ*, 6. चक्रतुः *chakratuḥ*, 7. चकृम *chakṛima*, 8. चक्र *chakra*, 9. चक्रुः *chakruḥ*, I A. 1. अकार्षम् *akârsham*, 2. अकार्षीः *akârshîḥ*, 3. अकार्षीत् *akârshît*, 4. अकार्ष्व *akârshva*, 5. अकार्ष्टम् *akârshṭam*, 6. अकार्ष्टाम् *akârshṭâm*, 7. अकार्ष्म *akârshma*, 8. अकार्ष्ट *akârshṭa*, 9. अकार्षुः *akârshuḥ*, F. करिष्यति *karishyati*, P. F. कर्ता *kartâ*, B. 1. क्रियासम् *kriyâsam*, 2. क्रियाः *kriyâḥ*, 3. क्रियात् *kriyât*, 4. क्रियास्व *kriyâsva*, 5. क्रियास्तम् *kriyâstam*, 6. क्रियास्ताम् *kriyâstâm*, 7. क्रियास्म *kriyâsma*, 8. क्रियास्त *kriyâsta*, 9. क्रियासुः *kriyâsuḥ*.

Âtmanepada: P. 1. कुर्वे *kurve*, 2. कुरुषे *kurushe*, 3. कुरुते *kurute*, 4. कुर्वहे *kurvahe*, 5. कुर्वाथे *kurvâthe*, 6. कुर्वाते *kurvâte*, 7. कुर्महे *kurmahe*, 8. कुरुध्वे *kurudhve*, 9. कुर्वते *kurvate*, I. 1. अकुर्वि *akurvi*, 2. अकुरुथाः *akuruthâḥ*, 3. अकुरुत *akuruta*, 4. अकुर्वहि *akurvahi*, 5. अकुर्वाथाम् *akurvâthâm*, 6. अकुर्वाताम् *akurvâtâm*, 7. अकुर्महि *akurmahi*, 8. अकुरुध्वम् *akurudhvam*, 9. अकुर्वत *akurvata*, O. 1. कुर्वीय *kurvîya* &c., I. 1. करवै *karavai*, 2. कुरुष्व *kurushva*, 3. कुरुताम् *kurutâm*, 4. करवावहै *karavâvahai*, 5. कुर्वाथाम् *kurvâthâm*, 6. कुर्वाताम् *kurvâtâm*, 7. करवामहै *karavâmahai*, 8. कुरुध्वम् *kurudhvam*, 9. कुर्वताम् *kurvatâm* ‖ Pf. 1. चक्रे *chakre*, 2. चकृषे *chakṛishe*, 3. चक्रे

chakre, 4. चकृवहे *chakṛivahe*, 5. चक्राथे *chakrâthe*, 6. चक्राते *chakrâte*, 7. चकृमहे *chakṛimahe*, 8. चकृढ्वे *chakṛiḍhve*, 9. चक्रिरे *chakrire*, I A. 1. अकृषि *akṛishi*, 2. अकृथाः *akṛithâḥ*, 3. अकृत *akṛita*, 4. अकृष्वहि *akṛishvahi*, 5. अकृषाथां *akṛishâthâm*, 6. अकृषातां *akṛishâtâm*, 7. अकृष्महि *akṛishmahi*, 8. अकृढ्वं *akṛiḍhvam*, 9. अकृषत *akṛishata*, F. करिष्यते *karishyate*, B. 3. कृषीष्ट *kṛishîshṭa*, 8. कृषीढ्वं *kṛishîḍhvam* ‖

Pt. कृतः *kṛitaḥ*, Ger. कृत्वा *kṛitvâ* ‖ Pass. क्रियते *kriyate*, Aor. अकारि *akâri*, Caus. कारयति *kârayati*, Aor. अचीकरत् *achîkarat*, Des. चिकीर्षति *chikîrshati*, Int. चेक्रीयते *chekrîyate*, चर्कर्ति *charkarti* &c., or चर्करीति *charkarîti* &c. (§ 490).

Krî Class (*Kryâdi, IX Class*).

I. Parasmaipada and Âtmanepada Verbs.

153. क्री *krî*, to buy, (डुक्रीञ्.)

P. क्रीणाति *krîṇâti* ‖ Pf. 1. चिक्राय *chikrâya*, 2. चिक्रयिथ *chikrayitha* or चिक्रेथ *chikretha*, 3. चिक्राय *chikrâya*, 4. चिक्रियिव *chikriyiva*, 5. चिक्रियथुः *chikriyathuḥ*, 6. चिक्रियतुः *chikriyatuḥ*, 7. चिक्रियिम *chikriyima*, 8. चिक्रिय *chikriya*, 9. चिक्रियुः *chikriyuḥ*, I A. अक्रैषीत् *akraishît*, Âtm. अक्रेष्ट *akreshṭa*, F. क्रेष्यति *kreshyati*, P. F. क्रेता *kretâ*, B. क्रीयात् *krîyât*, Âtm. क्रेषीष्ट *kreshîshṭa* ‖ Pt. क्रीतः *krîtaḥ* ‖ Pass. क्रीयते *krîyate*, Caus. क्रापयति *krâpayati*, Des. चिक्रीषति *chikrîshati*, Int. चेक्रीयते *chekrîyate*.

154. मी *mî*, to kill, (मीञ्.)

The roots मी *mî*, मि *mi* (Su), and दी *dî* (Div) take final आ *â* whenever their ई *î* or इ *i* would be liable to Guṇa or Vṛiddhi, and in the gerund in य *ya* (§ 432). Pâṇ. VI. 1, 50.

P. मीनाति *mînâti* ‖ Pf. 1. ममौ *mamau*, 2. ममाथ *mamâtha* or ममिथ *mamitha*, 3. ममौ *mamau*, 4. मिम्यिव *mimyiva*, 5. मिम्यथुः *mimyathuḥ*, 6. मिम्यतुः *mimyatuḥ*, 7. मिम्यिम *mimyima*, 8. मिम्य *mimya*, 9. मिम्युः *mimyuḥ*, I A. अमासीत् *amâsît* (§ 353), Âtm. अमास्त *amâsta* (§ 353), F. मास्यति *mâsyati*, P. F. माता *mâtâ*, B. मीयात् *mîyât*, Âtm. मासीष्ट *mâsîshṭa* ‖ Pt. मीतः *mîtaḥ*, Ger. मीत्वा *mîtvâ*, °माय *-mâya* ‖ Pass. मीयते *mîyate*, Caus. मापयति *mâpayati* (§ 463, II. 19), Des. मित्सति *mitsati* (§ 471, 8), Int. मेमीयते *memîyate*.

155. स्तम्भ् *stambh*, to support, (स्तम्भु.)

The verbs स्तम्भ् *stambh*, स्तुम्भ् *stumbh*, स्कम्भ् *skambh*, स्कुम्भ् *skumbh*, and स्कु *sku* may be conjugated as Krî or as Su verbs.

P. स्तभ्नाति *stabhnâti* or स्तभ्नोति *stabhnoti* &c., I. अस्तभ्नात् *astabhnât*, O. स्तभ्नीयात् *stabhnîyât*, I. 1. स्तभ्नानि *stabhnâni*, 2. स्तभान *stabhâna**, 3. स्तभ्नातु *stabhnâtu*, 4. स्तभ्नाव *stabhnâva*, 5. स्तभ्नीतं *stabhnîtam*, 6. स्तभ्नीतां *stabhnîtâm*, 7. स्तभ्नाम *stabhnâma*, 8. स्तभ्नीत *stabhnîta*, 9. स्तभ्नन्तु *stabhnantu* ‖ Pf. तस्तम्भ *tastambha*, I A. अस्तम्भीत् *astambhît* or II A. अस्तभत् *astabhat* (§ 367), F. स्तम्भिष्यति *stambhishyati*, P. F. स्तम्भिता *stambhitâ*, B. स्तभ्यात् *stabhyât* ‖ Pt. स्तब्धः *stabdhaḥ*, Ger. स्तम्भित्वा *stambhitvâ* or

---

* Krî verbs ending in consonants form the 2nd pers. sing. imperative in आन *âna*.

स्तब्ध्वा *stabdhvá* ॥ Pass. स्तभ्यते *stabhyate*, Caus. स्तम्भयति *stambhayati*, Des. तिस्तम्भिषति *tistambhishati*, Int. तास्तभ्यते *tástabhyate*.

156. पू *pú*, to purify, (पूञ्.)

The Krî verbs beginning with पू *pú* shorten their vowel in the special tenses (Pâṇ. VII. 3, 80). They stand Dhâtupâṭha 31, 12—32. The more important are, लू *lú*, to cut, स्तॄ *strí*, to cover, वॄ *vrí*, to choose, धू *dhú*, to shake, पॄ *prí*, to fill, दॄ *drí*, to tear, जॄ *jrí*, to wither.

P. पुनाति *punáti*, Âtm. पुनीते *punîte* ॥ Pf. पुपाव *pupáva*, Âtm. पुपुवे *pupuve*, I A. अपावीत् *apávît*, Âtm. अपविष्ट *apavishṭa*, F. पविष्यति *pavishyati*, P. F. पविता *pavitá* ॥ Pt. पूतः *pútaḥ*, Ger. पूत्वा *pútvá* (पवितः *pavitaḥ* and पवित्वा *pavitvá* (§ 424) belong to पूङ् *púṅ*, पवते *pavate* (Bhû class), see § 333. D) ॥ Pass. पूयते *púyate*, Caus. पावयति *pávayati*, Aor. अपीपवत् *apîpavat*, Des. पुपूषति *pupúshati* (पिपविषते *pipavishate* belongs to पूङ् *púṅ*, पवते *pavate*, Bhû class, Pâṇ. VII. 2, 74), Int. पोपूयते *popúyate*.

157. ग्रह् *grah*, to take.

This root takes *Samprasâraṇa* in the special tenses and before other weakening terminations. (Pâṇ. VI. 1, 16.)

P. गृह्णाति *gṛihṇáti*, Âtm. गृह्णीते *gṛihṇîte*, I. अगृह्णात् *agṛihṇát*, Âtm. अगृह्णीत *agṛihṇîta*, O. गृह्णीयात् *gṛihṇîyát*, Âtm. गृह्णीत *gṛihṇîta*, I. गृह्णातु *gṛihṇátu* (2. गृहाण *gṛiháṇa*), Âtm. गृह्णीतां *gṛihṇîtám* ॥ Pf. 1. जग्राह *jagráha*, 2. जग्रहिथ *jagrahitha*, 3. जग्राह *jagráha*, 4. जगृहिव *jagṛihiva*, 5. जगृहथुः *jagṛihathuḥ*, 6. जगृहतुः *jagṛihatuḥ*, 7. जगृहिम *jagṛihima*, 8. जगृह *jagṛiha*, 9. जगृहुः *jagṛihuḥ*, I A. 1. अग्रहीषं *agrahîsham* (§ 341 and § 348*), 2. अग्रहीः *agrahîḥ*, 3. अग्रहीत् *agrahît*, Âtm. 1. अग्रहीषि *agrahîshi*, 2. अग्रहीष्ठाः *agrahîshṭháḥ*, 3. अग्रहीष्ट *agrahîshṭa*, F. ग्रहीष्यति *grahîshyati*, P. F. ग्रहीता *grahîtá*, B. गृह्यात् *gṛihyát*, Âtm. ग्रहीषीष्ट *grahîshîshṭa* ॥ Pt. गृहीतः *gṛihîtaḥ*, Ger. गृहीत्वा *gṛihîtvá* ॥ Pass. गृह्यते *gṛihyate*, Aor. अग्राहि *agráhi*, Fut. ग्रहीष्यते *grahîshyate* or ग्राहिष्यते *gráhishyate* &c., Caus. ग्राहयति *gráhayati*, Des. जिघृक्षति *jighṛikshati*, Int. जरीगृह्यते *jarîgṛihyate*, जाग्राढि *jágráḍhi* (not जाग्रढि *jágraḍhi*).

II. Parasmaipada Verbs.

158. ज्या *jyá*, to grow weak.

This root takes *Samprasâraṇa* in the special tenses and before other weakening terminations. (See No. 157.)

P. जिनाति *jináti*, I. अजिनात् *ajinát*, O. जिनीयात् *jinîyát*, I. जिनातु *jinátu* ॥ Pf. 1. जिज्यौ *jijyau*, 2. जिज्यिथ *jijyitha* or जिज्याथ *jijyátha*, 3. जिज्यौ *jijyau*, 4. जिज्यिव *jijyiva*, I A. अज्यासीत् *ajyásît*, F. ज्यास्यति *jyásyati*, B. जीयात् *jîyát* ॥ Pt. जीनः *jînaḥ*, Ger. जीत्वा *jîtvá*, °ज्याय *-jyáya* ॥ Caus. ज्यापयति *jyápayati*, Des. जिज्यासति *jijyásati*, Int. जेजीयते *jejîyate*.

159. ज्ञा *jñá*, to know.

This verb substitutes जा *já* in the special tenses. (Pâṇ. vii. 3, 79.)

P. जानाति *jánáti*, I. अजानात् *ajánát*, O. जानीयात् *jáníyát*, I. जानातु *jánátu* ॥ Pf. जज्ञौ *jajñau*, I A. अज्ञासीत् *ajñásít*, F. ज्ञास्यति *jñásyati*, P. F. ज्ञाता *jñátá*, B. ज्ञायात् *jñáyát* or ज्ञेयात् *jñeyát* ॥ Pt. ज्ञातः *jñátaḥ* ॥ Pass. ज्ञायते *jñáyate*, Aor. अज्ञायि *ajñáyi*, Caus. ज्ञपयति *jñápayati* (see § 462, II. 15), Aor. अजिज्ञपत् *ajijñapat*, Des. जिज्ञासते *jijñásate*, Int. जाज्ञायते *jâjñáyate*.

160. बन्ध् *bandh*, to bind.

P. बध्नाति *badhnáti*, I. अबध्नात् *abadhnát*, O. बध्नीयात् *badhníyát*, I. बध्नातु *badhnátu* ॥ Pf. 1. बबन्ध *babandha*, 2. बबन्धिथ *babandhitha* or बबन्द्ध *babanddha* or बबन्ध *babandha*, I A. 1. अभान्त्सम् *abhántsam*, 2. अभान्त्सीः *abhántsíḥ*, 3. अभान्त्सीत् *abhántsít*, 4. अभान्त्स्व *abhántsva*, 5. अबान्द्धम् *abânddham*, 6. अबान्द्धाम् *abânddhám*, 7. अभान्त्स्म *abhántsma*, 8. अबान्द्ध *abânddha*, 9. अभान्त्सुः *abhántsuḥ*, F. भन्त्स्यति *bhantsyati*, P. F. बन्द्धा *banddhá*, B. बध्यात् *badhyát* ॥ Pt. बद्धः *baddhaḥ*, Ger. बद्ध्वा *baddhvá* ॥ Pass. बध्यते *badhyate*, Caus. बन्धयति *bandhayati*, Aor. अबबन्धत् *ababandhat*, Des. बिभन्त्सति *bibhantsati*, Int. बाबध्यते *bábadhyate*, बाबन्द्धि *bábanddhi*.

III. Âtmanepada Verbs.

161. वृ *vṛi*, to cherish, (वृङ्.)

P. वृणीते *vṛiṇíte*, I. अवृणीत *avṛiṇíta*, O. वृणीत *vṛiṇíta*, I. वृणीतां *vṛiṇítám* ॥ Pf. वव्रे *vavre*, I A. अवरिष्ट *avarishṭa* or अवरीष्ट *avaríshṭa* or अवृत *avṛita*, F. वरिष्यते or वरीष्यते *varíshyate*, P. F. वरिता or वरीता *varítá*, B. वरिषीष्ट *varishíshṭa* or वृषीष्ट *vṛishíshṭa* ॥ Pt. वृतः *vṛitaḥ* ॥ Pass. व्रियते *vriyate*, Caus. वारयति *várayati*, Des. विवरिषते or विवरीषते *vivaríshate*, Int. वेव्रीयते *vevríyate*, वर्वर्ति *varvarti* &c. Contracted forms of the Des. and Int., वुवूर्षति *vuvúrshati* and वोवूर्यते *vovúryate*.

Ad Class (Adâdi, II Class).

I. Parasmaipada Verbs.

162. अद् *ad*, to eat.

P. 1. अद्मि *admi*, 2. अत्सि *atsi*, 3. अत्ति *atti*, 4. अद्वः *advaḥ*, 5. अत्थः *atthaḥ*, 6. अत्तः *attaḥ*, 7. अद्मः *admaḥ*, 8. अत्थ *attha*, 9. अदन्ति *adanti*, I. 1. आदम् *ádam*, 2. आदः *ádaḥ* (Pâṇ. vii. 3, 100)*, 3. आदत् *ádat*, 4. आद्व *ádva*, 5. आत्तम् *áttam*, 6. आत्तां *áttám*, 7. आद्म *ádma*, 8. आत्त *átta*, 9. आदन् *ádan*, O. अद्यात् *adyát*, I. 1. अदानि *adáni*, 2. अद्धि *addhi* †, 3. अत्तु *attu*, 4. अदाव *adáva*, 5. अत्तं *attam*, 6. अत्तां *attám*, 7. अदाम *adáma*, 8. अत्त *atta*, 9. अदन्तु *adantu* ॥ Pf. 1. आद *áda*,

* अद् *ad* inserts अ *a* before terminations consisting of one consonant.

† When हि *hi* is added immediately to the final consonant of a root, it is changed to धि *dhi*. (Pâṇ. vi. 4, 101.)

2. आदिथ *ádítha* &c., or substituting घस् *ghas**, 1. जघास *jaghása*, 2. जघसिथ *jaghasitha*, 3. जघास *jaghása*, 4. जक्षिव *jakshiva*, 5. जक्षथुः *jakshathuḥ*, 6. जक्षतुः *jakshatuḥ*, 7. जक्षिम *jakshima*, 8. जक्ष *jaksha*, 9. जक्षुः *jakshuḥ*, II A. 1. अघसं *aghasam*, 2. अघसः *aghasaḥ*, 3. अघसत् *aghasat*, F. अत्स्यति *atsyati*, P. F. अत्ता *attá*, B. अद्यात् *adyát* ‖ Pt. जग्धः *jagdhaḥ*†, Ger. जग्ध्वा *jagdhvá*, °जग्ध्य *-jagdhya* (Páṇ. II. 4, 36) ‖ Pass. अद्यते *adyate*, Caus. आदयति *ádayati*, Aor. आदिदत् *ádidat*, Des. जिघत्सति *jighatsati*.

163. प्सा *psá*, to eat.

P. प्साति *psáti*, I. 3. अप्सात् *apsát*, 9. अप्सान् *apsán* or अप्सुः *apsuḥ* (§ 322 ‡), O. प्सायात् *psáyát*, I. प्सातु *psátu* ‖ Pf. पप्सौ *papsau*, I A. अप्सासीत् *apsásít*, F. प्सास्यति *psásyati*, P. F. प्साता *psátá*, B. प्सायात् *psáyát* or प्सेयात् *pseyát* ‖ Pass. प्सायते *psáyate*, Caus. प्सापयति *psápayati*, Des. पिप्सासति *pipsásati*, Int. पाप्सायते *pápsáyate*.

164. मा *má*, to measure.

P. माति *máti*, I. 3. अमात् *amát*, 9. अमान् *amán* or अमुः *amuḥ*, O. मायात् *máyát*, I. मातु *mátu* ‖ Pf. ममौ *mamau*, I A. अमासीत् *amásít*, F. मास्यति *másyati*, P. F. माता *mátá*, B. मेयात् *meyát* ‖ Pt. मितः *mitaḥ*, Ger. मित्वा *mitvá*, °माय *-máya* ‖ Pass. मीयते *míyate*, Aor. अमायि *amáyi*, Caus. मापयति *mápayati*, Aor. अमीमपत् *amímapat*, Des. मित्सति *mitsati*, Int. मेमीयते *memíyate*, मामाति *mámáti* or मामेति *mámeti*.

165. या *yá*, to go.

P. याति *yáti*, I. 3. अयात् *ayát*, 9. अयान् *ayán* or अयुः *ayuḥ*, O. यायात् *yáyát*, I. यातु *yátu* ‖ Pf. ययौ *yayau*, I A. अयासीत् *ayásít*, F. यास्यति *yásyati*, P. F. याता *yátá*, B. यायात् *yáyát* ‖ Pt. यातः *yátaḥ* ‖ Pass. याये *yáye*, Caus. यापयति *yápayati*, Aor. अयीयपत् *ayíyapat*, Des. यियासति *yiyásati*, Int. यायायते *yáyáyate*.

166. ख्या *khyá*, to proclaim.

P. ख्याति *khyáti*, I. अख्यात् *akhyát*, O. ख्यायात् *khyáyát*, I. ख्यातु *khyátu* ‖ Pf. चख्यौ *chakhyau*, II A. अख्यत् *akhyat*, F. ख्यास्यति *khyásyati*, P. F. ख्याता *khyátá*, B. ख्यायात् *khyáyát* or ख्येयात् *khyeyát* ‖ Pt. ख्यातः *khyátaḥ* ‖ Pass. ख्यायते *khyáyate*, Aor. अख्यायि *akhyáyi*, Caus. ख्यापयति *khyápayati*, Aor. अचिख्यपत् *achikhyapat*, Des. चिख्यासति *chikhyásati*, Int. चाख्यायते *chákhyáyate*.

167. वश् *vaś*, to desire.

This root takes *Samprasáraṇa* before the strong terminations of the special tenses, and in the weakening forms generally.

P. 1. वश्मि *vaśmi*, 2. वक्षि *vakshi* (§§ 125, 120), 3. वष्टि *vashṭi*, 4. उश्वः *uśvaḥ*, 5. उष्ठः *ushṭhaḥ*, 6. उष्टः *ushṭaḥ*, 7. उश्मः *uśmaḥ*, 8. उष्ठ *ushṭha*, 9. उशन्ति *uśanti*,

---

* In the tenses where अद् *ad* is deficient, घस् *ghas* is used instead.

† This is formed from जक्ष् *jaksh*, to eat, a reduplicated form of घस् *ghas*. (Páṇ. II. 4, 36.)

I. 1. अवशम् *avaśam*, 2. अवट् *avaṭ*, 3. अवट् *avaṭ*, 4. औश्व *auśva*, 5. औष्टम् *aushṭam*, 6. औष्टाम् *aushṭâm*, 7. औश्म *auśma*, 8. औष्ट *aushṭa*, 9. औशन् *auśan*, O. उश्यात् *uśyât*, I. 1. वशानि *vaśâni*, 2. उड्ढि *uḍḍhi*, 3. वष्टु *vashṭu*, 4. वशाव *vaśâva*, 5. उष्टम् *ushṭam*, 6. उष्टाम् *ushṭâm*, 7. वशाम *vaśâma*, 8. उष्ट *ushṭa*, 9. उशन्तु *uśantu* ॥ Pf. 3. उवाश *uvâśa*, 9. ऊशुः *ûśuḥ*, I A. अवाशीत् *avâśît*, F. वशिष्यति *vaśishyati*, P. F. वशिता *vaśitâ*, B. उश्यात् *uśyât* ॥ Pass. उश्यते *uśyate*, Caus. वाशयति *vâśayati*, Des. विवशिषति *vivaśishati*, Int. वावश्यते *vâvaśyate*, वावष्टि *vâvashṭi*.

168. हन् *han*, to kill.

This verb drops its final न् *n* before the strong terminations of the special tenses, and in the weakening forms generally, if the terminations begin with any consonants except nasals or semivowels (Pâṇ. VI. 4, 37). Before strong terminations beginning with vowels, हन् *han* becomes घ्न् *ghn* (Pâṇ. VII. 3, 54). In the aorist and benedictive वध् *vadh* is substituted. The desiderative, intensive, and the aorist passive are derived from घन् *ghan*, the causative from घत् *ghat*.

P. 1. हन्मि *hanmi*, 2. हंसि *haṁsi*, 3. हन्ति *hanti*, 4. हन्वः *hanvaḥ*, 5. हथः *hathaḥ*, 6. हतः *hataḥ*, 7. हन्मः *hanmaḥ*, 8. हथ *hatha*, 9. घ्नन्ति *ghnanti*, I. 1. अहनम् *ahanam*, 2. अहन् *ahan*, 3. अहन् *ahan*, 4. अहन्व *ahanva*, 5. अहतम् *ahatam*, 6. अहताम् *ahatâm*, 7. अहन्म *ahanma*, 8. अहत *ahata*, 9. अघ्नन् *aghnan*, O. हन्यात् *hanyât*, I. 1. हनानि *hanâni*, 2. जहि *jahi* (Pâṇ. VI. 4, 36), 3. हन्तु *hantu*, 4. हनाव *hanâva*, 5. हतम् *hatam*, 6. हताम् *hatâm*, 7. हनाम *hanâma*, 8. हत *hata*, 9. घ्नन्तु *ghnantu* ॥ Pf. 1. जघान *jaghâna* (Pâṇ. VII. 3, 55), 2. जघनिथ *jaghanitha* or जघन्थ *jaghantha*, 3. जघान *jaghâna*, 4. जघ्निव *jaghniva*, 5. जघ्नथुः *jaghnathuḥ*, 6. जघ्नतुः *jaghnatuḥ*, 7. जघ्निम *jaghnima*, 8. जघ्न *jaghna*, 9. जघ्नुः *jaghnuḥ*, I A. अवधीत् *avadhît*, F. हनिष्यति *hanishyati*, P. F. हन्ता *hantâ*, B. वध्यात् *vadhyât* ॥ Pt. हतः *hataḥ*, Ger. हत्वा *hatvâ*, °हत्य *-hatya* (§ 449) ॥ Pass. हन्यते *hanyate*, Aor. अघानि *aghâni* or अवधि *avadhi* (§ 407), Caus. घातयति *ghâtayati*, Aor. अजीघतत् *ajîghatat*, Des. जिघांसति *jighâṁsati*, Int. जंघन्यते *jaṅghanyate* or जेघ्नीयते *jeghnîyate* (Pâṇ. VII. 4, 30, v., he kills), जंघन्ति *jaṅghanti*.

169. यु *yu*, to mix.

Verbs of this class ending in उ *u* take, in the special tenses, Vṛiddhi instead of Guṇa before weak terminations beginning with consonants. (Pâṇ. VII. 3, 89.)

P. 1. यौमि *yaumi*, 2. यौषि *yaushi*, 3. यौति *yauti*, 4. युवः *yuvaḥ*, 5. युथः *yuthaḥ*, 6. युतः *yutaḥ*, 7. युमः *yumaḥ*, 8. युथ *yutha*, 9. युवन्ति *yuvanti*, I. 1. अयवम् *ayavam*, 2. अयौः *ayauḥ*, 3. अयौत् *ayaut*, 4. अयुव *ayuva*, 5. अयुतम् *ayutam*, 6. अयुताम् *ayutâm*, 7. अयुम *ayuma*, 8. अयुत *ayuta*, 9. अयुवन् *ayuvan*, O. युयात् *yuyât*, I. 1. यवानि *yavâni*, 2. युहि *yuhi*, 3. यौतु *yautu*, 4. यवाव *yavâva*, 5. युतम् *yutam*, 6. युताम् *yutâm*, 7. यवाम *yavâma*, 8. युतं *yutam*, 9. युवन्तु *yuvantu* ॥ Pf. 3. युयाव *yuyâva*, 9. युयुवुः *yuyuvuḥ*, I A. अयावीत् *ayâvît*, F. यविष्यति *yavishyati*, P. F. यविता *yavitâ*, B. यूयात् *yûyât* ॥ Pt. युतः *yutaḥ* ॥ Pass. यूयते *yûyate*, Aor. अयावि *ayâvi*, Caus. यावयति *yâvayati*, Des. युयूषति *yuyûshati*, Int. योयूयते *yoyûyate*, योयोति *yoyoti*.

170. रु *ru*, to shout.

The verbs तु *tu*, रु *ru*, ष्टु *stu* may take ई *î* before *all* terminations of the special tenses beginning with consonants. (Pâṇ. vii. 3, 95.)

P. 1. रौमि *raumi* or रवीमि *ravîmi*, 2. रौषि *raushi* or रवीषि *ravîshi*, 3. रौति *rauti* or रवीति *ravîti*, 4. रुवः *ruvaḥ* or रुवीवः *ruvîvaḥ*, 5. रुथः *ruthaḥ* or रुवीथः *ruvîthaḥ*, 6. रुतः *rutaḥ* or रुवीतः *ruvîtaḥ*, 7. रुमः *rumaḥ* or रुवीमः *ruvîmaḥ*, 8. रुथ *rutha* or रुवीथ *ruvîtha*, 9. रुवंति *ruvanti*, I. 1. अरवं *aravam*, 2. अरौः *arauḥ* or अरवीः *aravîḥ*, 3. अरौत् *araut* or अरवीत् *aravît*, 4. अरुव *aruva* or अरुवीव *aruvîva*, 5. अरुतं *arutam* or अरुवीतं *aruvîtam*, 6. अरुतां *arutâm* or अरुवीतां *aruvîtâm*, 7. अरुम *aruma* or अरुवीम *aruvîma*, 8. अरुत *aruta* or अरुवीत *aruvîta*, 9. अरुवन् *aruvan*, O. रुयात् *ruyât* or रुवीयात् *ruvîyât*, I. 1. रवाणि *ravâṇi*, 2. रुहि *ruhi* or रुवीहि *ruvîhi*, 3. रौतु *rautu* or रवीतु *ravîtu*, 4. रवाव *ravâva*, 5. रुतं *rutam* or रुवीतं *ruvîtam*, 6. रुतां *rutâm* or रुवीतां *ruvîtâm*, 7. रवाम *ravâma*, 8. रुत *ruta* or रुवीत *ruvîta*, 9. रुवंतु *ruvantu* ‖ Pf. 3. रुराव *rurâva*, 9. रुरुवुः *ruruvuḥ*, I A. अरावीत् *arâvît*, F. रविष्यति *ravishyati*, P. F. रविता *ravitâ*, B. रूयात् *rûyât* ‖ Pt. रुतः *rutaḥ* ‖ Pass. रूयते *rûyate*, Caus. रावयति *râvayati*, Des. रुरूषति *rurûshati*, Int. रोरूयते *rorûyate*.

Note—The Sârasvatî gives अरौषीत् *araushît*, रोष्यति *roshyati*, and रोता *rotâ*; but see § 332, 4. It likewise extends the use of ई *î* to नु *nu*, to praise.

171. इ *i*, to go.

P. 1. एमि *emi*, 2. एषि *eshi*, 3. एति *eti*, 4. इवः *ivaḥ*, 5. इथः *ithaḥ*, 6. इतः *itaḥ*, 7. इमः *imaḥ*, 8. इथ *itha*, 9. यंति *yanti*, I. 1. आयं *âyam*, 2. ऐः *aiḥ*, 3. ऐत् *ait*, 4. ऐव *aiva*, 5. ऐतं *aitam*, 6. ऐतां *aitâm*, 7. ऐम *aima*, 8. ऐत *aita*, 9. आयन् *âyan*, O. इयात् *iyât*, I. 1. अयानि *ayâni*, 2. इहि *ihi*, 3. एतु *etu*, 4. अयाव *ayâva*, 5. इतं *itam*, 6. इतां *itâm*, 7. अयाम *ayâma*, 8. इत *ita*, 9. यंतु *yantu* ‖ Pf. 1. इयाय *iyâya*, 2. इययिथ *iyayitha* or इयेथ *iyetha*, 3. इयाय *iyâya*, 4. ईयिव *îyiva*, 5. ईयथुः *îyathuḥ*, 6. ईयतुः *îyatuḥ*, 7. ईयिम *îyima*, 8. ईय *îya*, 9. ईयुः *îyuḥ*, I A. 1. अगां *agâm* (Pâṇ. ii. 4, 45), 2. अगाः *agâḥ*, 3. अगात् *agât*, 4. अगाव *agâva*, 5. अगातं *agâtam*, 6. अगातां *agâtâm*, 7. अगाम *agâma*, 8. अगात *agâta*, 9. अगुः *aguḥ* (§ 368), F. एष्यति *eshyati*, P. F. एता *etâ*, B. ईयात् *îyât* ‖ Pt. इतः *itaḥ*, Ger. इत्वा *itvâ*, °इत्य *-itya* ‖ Pass. ईयते *îyate*, Aor. अगायि *agâyi* (§ 404), Caus. गमयति *gamayati* (Pâṇ. ii. 4, 46), Des. जिगमिषति *jigamishati* (Pâṇ. ii. 4, 47). But see § 463, II. 1, and § 471, 4, with regard to this and cognate verbs if preceded by prepositions.

172. विद् *vid*, to know.

P. 1. वेद्मि *vedmi*, 2. वेत्सि *vetsi*, 3. वेत्ति *vetti*, 4. विद्वः *vidvaḥ*, 5. वित्थः *vitthaḥ*, 6. वित्तः *vittaḥ*, 7. विद्मः *vidmaḥ*, 8. वित्थ *vittha*, 9. विदंति *vidanti*, I. 1. अवेदं *avedam*, 2. अवेः *aveḥ* or अवेत् *avet* (Pâṇ. viii. 2, 75), 3. अवेत् *avet* (§ 132*), 4. अविद्व *avidva*, 5. अवित्तं *avittam*, 6. अवित्तां *avittâm*, 7. अविद्म *avidma*, 8. अवित्त *avitta*, 9. अविदन् *avidan* or अविदुः *aviduḥ*, O. विद्यात् *vidyât*, I. 1. वेदानि *vedâni* (or

विदांकरवाणि *vidâṁkaravâṇi* &c., Pâṇ. III. 1, 41), 2. विद्धि *viddhi*, 3. वेत्तु *vettu*, 4. वेदाव *vedâva*, 5. वित्तं *vittam*, 6. वित्तां *vittâm*, 7. वेदाम *vedâma*, 8. वित्त *vitta*, 9. विदन्तु *vidantu* ॥ Pf. विवेद *viveda* or विदांचकार *vidâṁchakâra* (§ 326), I A. अवेदीत् *avedît*, F. वेदिष्यति *vedishyati*, P. F. वेदिता *veditâ*, B. विद्यात् *vidyât* ॥

Another form of the Present is, 1. वेद *veda*, 2. वेत्थ *vettha*, 3. वेद *veda*, 4. विद्व *vidva*, 5. विदथुः *vidathuḥ*, 6. विदतुः *vidatuḥ*, 7. विद्म *vidma*, 8. विद *vida*, 9. विदुः *viduḥ* ॥ Pt. विदितः *viditaḥ*, Ger. विदित्वा *viditvâ* ॥ Pass. विद्यते *vidyate*, Aor. अवेदि *avedi*, Caus. वेदयति *vedayati*, Aor. अवीविदत् *avîvidat*, Des. विविदिषति *vividishati* (Pâṇ. I. 2, 8), Int. वेविद्यते *vevidyate*, वेवेत्ति *vevetti*.

173. अस् *as*, to be.

P. 1. अस्मि *asmi*, 2. असि *asi*, 3. अस्ति *asti*, 4. स्वः *svaḥ*, 5. स्थः *sthaḥ*, 6. स्तः *staḥ*, 7. स्मः *smaḥ*, 8. स्थ *stha*, 9. सन्ति *santi*, I. 1. आसं *âsam*, 2. आसीः *âsîḥ*, 3. आसीत् *âsît*, 4. आस्व *âsva*, 5. आस्तं *âstam*, 6. आस्तां *âstâm*, 7. आस्म *âsma*, 8. आस्त *âsta*, 9. आसन् *âsan*, O. 1. स्यां *syâm*, 2. स्याः *syâḥ*, 3. स्यात् *syât*, 4. स्याव *syâva*, 5. स्यातं *syâtam*, 6. स्यातां *syâtâm*, 7. स्याम *syâma*, 8. स्यात *syâta*, 9. स्युः *syuḥ*, I. 1. असानि *asâni*, 2. एधि *edhi*, 3. अस्तु *astu*, 4. असाव *asâva*, 5. स्तं *stam*, 6. स्तां *stâm*, 7. असाम *asâma*, 8. स्त *sta*, 9. सन्तु *santu* ॥ Pf. 1. आस *âsa*, 2. आसिथ *âsitha*, 3. आस *âsa*, 4. आसिव *âsiva*, 5. आसथुः *âsathuḥ*, 6. आसतुः *âsatuḥ*, 7. आसिम *âsima*, 8. आस *âsa*, 9. आसुः *âsuḥ*; Âtm. 1. आसे *âse*, 2. आसिषे *âsishe*, 3. आसे *âse*, 4. आसिवहे *âsivahe*, 5. आसाथे *âsâthe*, 6. आसाते *âsâte*, 7. आसिमहे *âsimahe*, 8. आसिध्वे *âsidhve*, 9. आसिरे *âsire* *.

174. मृज् *mṛij*, to cleanse, (मृजू.)

This verb takes Vṛiddhi instead of Guṇa (Pâṇ. VII. 2, 114); it may take Vṛiddhi likewise before terminations that would not require Guṇa, if the terminations begin with a vowel (Siddh.-Kaum. vol. II. p. 122).

P. 1. मार्ज्मि *mârjmi*, 2. मार्क्षि *mârkshi*, 3. मार्ष्टि *mârshṭi* (§ 124), 4. मृज्वः *mṛijvaḥ*, 5. मृष्ठः *mṛishṭhaḥ*, 6. मृष्टः *mṛishṭaḥ*, 7. मृज्मः *mṛijmaḥ*, 8. मृष्ठ *mṛishṭha*, 9. मृजन्ति *mṛijanti* or मार्जन्ति *mârjanti*, I. 1. अमार्जं *amârjam*, 2. अमार्ट् *amârṭ*, 3. अमार्ट् *amârṭ*, 4. अमृज्व *amṛijva*, 5. अमृष्टं *amṛishṭam*, 6. अमृष्टां *amṛishṭâm*, 7. अमृज्म *amṛijma*, 8. अमृष्ट *amṛishṭa*, 9. अमृजन् *amṛijan* or अमार्जन् *amârjan*, O. मृज्यात् *mṛijyât*, I. 1. मार्जानि *mârjâni*, 2. मृड्ढि *mṛiḍḍhi*, 3. मार्ष्टु *mârshṭu*, 4. मार्जाव *mârjâva*, 5. मृष्टं *mṛishṭam*, 6. मृष्टां *mṛishṭâm*, 7. मार्जाम *mârjâma*, 8. मृष्ट *mṛishṭa*, 9. मृजन्तु *mṛijantu* or मार्जन्तु *mârjantu* ॥ Pf. 1. ममार्ज *mamârja*, 2. ममार्जिथ *mamârjitha* or ममार्ष्ठ *mamârshṭha*, 3. ममार्ज *mamârja*, 4. ममृजिव *mamṛijiva* or ममार्जिव *mamârjiva*, 5. ममृजथुः *mamṛijathuḥ* or ममार्जथुः *mamârjathuḥ*, 6. ममृजतुः *mamṛijatuḥ* or ममार्जतुः *mamârjatuḥ*, 7. ममृजिम *mamṛijima* or ममार्जिम *mamârjima*, 8. ममृज *mamṛija* or ममार्ज *mamârja*, 9. ममृजुः *mamṛijuḥ* or ममार्जुः *mamârjuḥ*, I A. अमार्जीत्

* The perfect both in the Parasmaipada and Âtmanepada is chiefly used at the end of the periphrastic perfect.

amârjît or अमार्क्षीत् *amârkshît*, F. मार्जिष्यति *mârjishyati* or मार्क्ष्यति *mârkshyati*, P. F. मार्जिता *mârjitâ* or मार्ष्टा *mârshṭâ*, B. मृज्यात् *mṛijyât* ‖ Pt. मृष्टः *mṛishṭaḥ*, Ger. मार्जित्वा *mârjitvâ*, °मृज्य *-mṛijya*, Adj. मार्जितव्यः *mârjitavyaḥ* or मार्ष्टव्यः *mârshṭavyaḥ*, मृज्यः *mṛijyaḥ* or मार्ग्यः *mârgyaḥ* (Pâṇ. III. 1, 113) ‖ Pass. मृज्यते *mṛijyate*, Aor. अमार्जि *amârji*, Caus. मार्जयति *mârjayati*, Des. मिमृक्षति *mimṛikshati* or मिमार्जिषति *mimârjishati*, Int. मरीमृज्यते *marîmṛijyate*, मर्मार्ष्टि *marmârshṭi*.

175. वच् *vach*, to speak.

P. 1. वच्मि *vachmi*, 2. वक्षि *vakshi*, 3. वक्ति *vakti*, 4. वच्वः *vachvaḥ*, 5. वक्थः *vakthaḥ*, 6. वक्तः *vaktaḥ*, 7. वच्मः *vachmaḥ*, 8. वक्थ *vaktha*, 9. वदन्ति *vadanti* or ब्रुवन्ति *bruvanti**, I. 1. अवचम् *avacham*, 2. अवक् *avak*, 3. अवक् *avak*, 4. अवच्व *avachva*, 5. अवक्तम् *avaktam*, 6. अवक्ताम् *avaktâm*, 7. अवच्म *avachma*, 8. अवक्त *avakta*, 9. अवदन् *avadan**, O. वच्यात् *vachyât*, I. 1. वचानि *vachâni*, 2. वग्धि *vagdhi*, 3. वक्तु *vaktu*, 4. वचाव *vachâva*, 5. वक्तम् *vaktam*, 6. वक्ताम् *vaktâm*, 7. वचाम *vachâma*, 8. वक्त *vakta*, 9. वदन्तु *vadantu** ‖ Pf. 3. उवाच *uvâcha*, 9. ऊचुः *ûchuḥ*, II A. अवोचत् *avochat* (§ 366), F. वक्ष्यति *vakshyati*, P. F. वक्ता *vaktâ*, B. उच्यात् *uchyât* ‖ Pt. उक्तः *uktaḥ* ‖ Pass. उच्यते *uchyate*, Aor. अवाचि *avâchi*, Caus. वाचयति *vâchayati*, Aor. अवीवचत् *avîvachat*, Des. विवक्षति *vivakshati*, Int. वावच्यते *vâvachyate*.

176. रुद् *rud*, to cry, (रुदिर्.)

The verbs रुद् *rud*, स्वप् *svap*, श्वस् *śvas*, अन् *an*, जक्ष् *jaksh* take इ *i* before the terminations of the special tenses beginning with consonants, except य् *y* (Pâṇ. VII. 2, 76). Before weak terminations consisting of one consonant, ई *î* is inserted (Pâṇ. VII. 3, 98); or, according to others, अ *a* (Pâṇ. VII. 3, 99).

P. 1. रोदिमि *rodimi*, 2. रोदिषि *rodishi*, 3. रोदिति *roditi*, 4. रुदिवः *rudivaḥ*, 9. रुदन्ति *rudanti*, I. 1. अरोदम् *arodam*, 2. अरोदीः *arodîḥ* or अरोदः *arodaḥ*, 3. अरोदीत् *arodît* or अरोदत् *arodat*, 4. अरुदिव *arudiva*, 9. अरुदन् *arudan*, O. रुद्याम् *rudyâm*, I. 1. रोदानि *rodâni*, 2. रुदिहि *rudihi*, 3. रोदितु *roditu*, 4. रोदाव *rodâva*, 5. रुदितम् *ruditam*, 6. रुदिताम् *ruditâm*, 7. रोदाम *rodâma*, 8. रुदित *rudita*, 9. रुदन्तु *rudantu* ‖ Pf. रुरोद *ruroda*, I A. अरोदीत् *arodît* or अरुदत् *arudat*, F. रोदिष्यति *rodishyati*, P. F. रोदिता *roditâ*, B. रुद्यात् *rudyât* ‖ Pt. रुदितः *ruditaḥ* ‖ Pass. रुद्यते *rudyate*, Aor. अरोदि *arodi*, Caus. रोदयति *rodayati*, Aor. अरूरुदत् *arûrudat*, Des. रुरुदिषति *rurudishati*, Int. रोरुद्यते *rorudyate*.

177. जक्ष् *jaksh*, to eat, to laugh‡.

Seven verbs, जक्ष् *jaksh*, जागृ *jâgṛi*, to wake, दरिद्रा *daridrâ*, to be poor, चकास् *chakâs*, to shine, शास् *śâs*, to rule, दीधी *dîdhî*, to shine, वेवी *vevî*, to obtain, are called अभ्यस्त *abhyasta* (reduplicated). They take अति *ati* and अतु *atu* in the 3rd pers. plur. present and imperative, and उः *uḥ* instead of अन् *an* in the 3rd pers. plur. imperfect (§ 321†).

P. 3. जक्षिति *jakshiti*, 9. जक्षति *jakshati*, I. अजक्षीत् *ajakshît* or अजक्षत् *ajakshat*,

* The 3rd pers. plur. present of वच् *vach* does not occur (Siddh.-Kaum. vol. II. p. 120); according to others the whole plural is wanting; according to some no 3rd pers. plur. is formed from वच् *vach*.

‡ जक्ष् *jaksh*, to eat, from घस् *ghas*; जक्ष् *jaksh*, to laugh, from हस् *has*.

O. जक्ष्यात् *jakshyât*, I. 3. अजक्षीत् *ajakshît* or अजक्षत् *ajakshat*, 9. अजक्षुः *ajakshuḥ* (§ 321 ‡) ॥ Pf. जजक्ष *jajaksha*, I A. अजक्षीत् *ajakshît*, F. जक्षिष्यति *jakshishyati*.

178. जागृ *jâgṛi*, to wake.

P. 1. जागर्मि *jâgarmi*, 2. जागर्षि *jâgarshi*, 3. जागर्ति *jâgarti*, 4. जागृवः *jâgṛivaḥ*, 5. जागृथः *jâgṛithaḥ*, 6. जागृतः *jâgṛitaḥ*, 7. जागृमः *jâgṛimaḥ*, 8. जागृथ *jâgṛitha*, 9. जाग्रति *jâgrati*, I. 1. अजागरम् *ajâgaram*, 2. अजागः *ajâgaḥ*, 3. अजागः *ajâgaḥ*, 4. अजागृव *ajâgṛiva*, 5. अजागृतम् *ajâgṛitam*, 6. अजागृताम् *ajâgṛitâm*, 7. अजागृम *ajâgṛima*, 8. अजागृत *ajâgṛita*, 9. अजागरुः *ajâgaruḥ*, O. जागृयात् *jâgṛiyât*, I. 1. जागराणि *jâgarâṇi*, 2. जागृहि *jâgṛihi*, 3. जागर्तु *jâgartu*, 4. जागराव *jâgarâva*, 5. जागृतम् *jâgṛitam*, 6. जागृताम् *jâgṛitâm*, 7. जागराम *jâgarâma*, 8. जागृत *jâgṛita*, 9. जाग्रतु *jâgratu* ॥ Pf. 3. जजागार *jajâgâra* or जागरांचकार *jâgarâṁchakâra* (Pâṇ. III. 1, 38), 9. जजागरुः *jajâgaruḥ*, I A. अजागरीत् *ajâgarît* (see preface, p. xi), F. जागरिष्यति *jâgarishyati*, P. F. जागरिता *jâgaritâ*, B. जागर्यात् *jâgaryât* ॥ Pt. जागरितः *jâgaritaḥ* ॥ Pass. जागर्यते *jâgaryate*, Aor. अजागारि *ajâgâri*, Caus. जागरयति *jâgarayati*, Des. जिजागरिषति *jijâgarishati*. No Intensive.

179. दरिद्रा *daridrâ*, to be poor.

In दरिद्रा *daridrâ* the final आ *â* is replaced by इ *i* in the special tenses before strong terminations beginning with a consonant (Pâṇ. VI. 4, 114). Before strong terminations beginning with vowels the आ *â* is lost (Pâṇ. VI. 4, 112).

P. 1. दरिद्रामि *daridrâmi*, 2. दरिद्रासि *daridrâsi*, 3. दरिद्राति *daridrâti*, 4. दरिद्रिवः *daridrivaḥ*, 9. दरिद्रति *daridrati*, I. 3. अदरिद्रात् *adaridrât*, 6. अदरिद्रिताम् *adaridritâm*, 9. अदरिद्रुः *adaridruḥ*, O. दरिद्रियात् *daridriyât*, I. 1. दरिद्राणि *daridrâṇi*, 2. दरिद्रिहि *daridrihi*, 3. दरिद्रातु *daridrâtu*, 4. दरिद्राव *daridrâva*, 5. दरिद्रितम् *daridritam*, 6. दरिद्रिताम् *daridritâm*, 7. दरिद्राम *daridrâma*, 8. दरिद्रित *daridrita*, 9. दरिद्रतु *daridratu* ॥ Pf. ददरिद्रौ *dadaridrau* or दरिद्रांचकार *daridrâṁchakâra* (Siddh.-Kaum. vol. II. p. 125), I A. अदरिद्रीत् *adaridrît* or अदरिद्रासीत् *adaridrâsît* (Siddh.-Kaum. vol. II. p. 126), F. दरिद्रिष्यति *daridrishyati* (Pâṇ. VI. 4, 114, v.), P. F. दरिद्रिता *daridritâ* (not दरिद्राता *daridrâtâ*).

180. शास् *śâs*, to command.

शास् *śâs* is changed to शिस् *śis* before weakening terminations beginning with consonants, and in the second aorist. (Pâṇ. VI. 4, 34.)

P. 1. शास्मि *śâsmi*, 2. शास्सि *śâssi*, 3. शास्ति *śâsti*, 4. शिष्वः *śishvaḥ*, 9. शासति *śâsati*, I. 1. अशासम् *aśâsam*, 2. अशाः *aśâḥ* or अशात् *aśât*, 3. अशात् *aśât* (§ 132), 4. अशिष्व *aśishva*, 5. अशिष्टम् *aśishṭam*, 6. अशिष्टाम् *aśishṭâm*, 7. अशिष्म *aśishma*, 8. अशिष्ट *aśishṭa*, 9. अशासुः *aśâsuḥ*, O. शिष्यात् *śishyât*, I. 1. शासानि *śâsâni*, 2. शाधि *śâdhi* (§ 132), 3. शास्तु *śâstu*, 4. शासाव *śâsâva*, 5. शिष्टम् *śishṭam*, 6. शिष्टाम् *śishṭâm*, 7. शासाम *śâsâma*, 8. शिष्ट *śishṭa*, 9. शासतु *śâsatu* ॥ Pf. शशास *śaśâsa*, II A. अशिषत् *aśishat*, F. शासिष्यति *śâsishyati*, B. शिष्यात् *śishyât* ॥ Pt. शिष्टः *śishṭaḥ* ॥ Pass. शिष्यते *śishyate*, Caus. शासयति *śâsayati*, Des. शिशासिषति *śiśâsishati*, Int. शेशिष्यते *śeśishyate*.

II. Âtmanepada Verbs.

181. चक्ष् *chaksh*, to speak, (चक्षिङ्.)

P. 1. चक्षे *chakshe*, 2. चक्षे *chakshe*, 3. चष्टे *chashṭe*, 4. चक्ष्वहे *chakshvahe*, 5. चक्षाथे *chakshâthe*, 6. चक्षाते *chakshâte*, 7. चक्ष्महे *chakshmahe*, 8. चड्ढ्वे *chaḍḍhve*, 9. चक्षते *chakshate*, I. 3. अचष्ट *achashṭa*, 9. अचक्षत *achakshata*, O. चक्षीत *chakshîta*, I. चष्टां *chashṭâm* ‖ Pf. चचक्षे *chachakshe*.

The other forms are supplied from ख्या *khyâ* or क्शा *kśâ*, the Red. Perf. optionally, (Pâṇ. II. 4, 54, 55): Pf. चख्यौ *chakhyau* ‖ II A. अख्यत् or °त *akhyat* or *-ta*, F. ख्यास्यति or °ते *khyâsyati* or *-te*, B. ख्यायात् *khyâyât* or ख्येयात् *khyeyât*, or Âtm. ख्यासीष्ट *khyâsîshṭa*.

182. ईश् *îś*, to rule.

The root ईश् *îś* takes इ *i* before the 2nd pers. sing. present and imperative (Pâṇ. VII. 2, 77). ईड् *îḍ* and जन् *jan* do the same, and likewise insert इ *i* before the 2nd pers. plur. present, imperfect, and imperative (Pâṇ. VII. 2, 78). The commentators, however, extend the latter rule to ईश् *îś*.

P. 1. ईशे *îśe*, 2. ईशिषे *îśishe*, 3. ईष्टे *îshṭe*, 8. ईशिध्वे *îśidhve*, I. 3. ऐष्ट *aishṭa*, 8. ऐशिध्वं *aiśidhvam*, O. ईशीत *îśîta*, I. 1. ईशै *îśai*, 2. ईशिष्व *îśishva*, 3. ईष्टां *îshṭâm*, 8. ईशिध्वं *îśidhvam* ‖ Pf. ईशांचक्रे *îśâṁchakre*, I A. ऐशिष्ट *aiśishṭa*.

183. आस् *âs*, to sit.

P. आस्ते *âste*, I. आस्त *âsta*, O. आसीत *âsîta*, I. आस्तां *âstâm* ‖ Pf. आसांचक्रे *âsâṁchakre* (part. आसीनः *âsînaḥ*, Pâṇ. VII. 2, 83), I A. आसिष्ट *âsishṭa*, F. आसिष्यते *âsishyate*.

184. सू *sû*, to bear, (षूङ्.)

P. सूते *sûte*, I. असूत *asûta*, O. सुवीत *suvîta*, I. 1. सुवै *suvai* (Pâṇ. VII. 3, 88), 2. सूष्व *sûshva*, 3. सूतां *sûtâm*, 4. सुवावहै *suvâvahai*, 5. सुवाथां *suvâthâm*, 6. सुवातां *suvâtâm*, 7. सुवामहै *suvâmahai*, 8. सूध्वं *sûdhvam*, 9. सुवतां *suvatâm* ‖ Pf. सुषुवे *sushuve*, I A. असविष्ट *asavishṭa* or असोष्ट *asoshṭa* (§ 337, I. 1), F. सविष्यते *savishyate* or सोष्यते *soshyate*, B. सविषीष्ट *savishîshṭa* or सोषीष्ट *soshîshṭa* ‖ Pt. सूनः *sûnaḥ* (Pâṇ. VIII. 2, 45) ‖ Pass. सूयते *sûyate*, Aor. असावि *asâvi*, Caus. सावयति *sâvayati*, Aor. असूषवत् *asûshavat*, Des. सुसूषते *susûshate* (Pâṇ. VIII. 3, 61), Int. सोषूयते *soshûyate*.

185. शी *śî*, to lie down, to sleep, (शीङ्.)

The verb शी *śî* takes Guṇa in the special tenses (Pâṇ. VII. 4, 21), and inserts र् *r* in the 3rd pers. plur. present, imperfect, and imperative.

P. 1. शये *śaye*, 2. शेषे *śeshe*, 3. शेते *śete*, 4. शेवहे *śevahe*, 5. शयाथे *śayâthe*, 6. शयाते *śayâte*, 7. शेमहे *śemahe*, 8. शेध्वे *śedhve*, 9. शेरते *śerate* (Pâṇ. VII. 1, 6), I. 1. अशयि *aśayi*, 2. अशेथाः *aśethâḥ*, 3. अशेत *aśeta*, 4. अशेवहि *aśevahi*, 5. अशयाथां *aśayâthâm*, 6. अशयातां *aśayâtâm*, 7. अशेमहि *aśemahi*, 8. अशेध्वं *aśedhvam*, 9. अशेरत *aśerata*, O. शयीत *śayîta*, I. 1. शयै *śayai*, 2. शेष्व *śeshva*, 3. शेतां

śetâm, 4. शयावहै śayâvahai, 5. शयाथां śayâthâm, 6. शयातां śayâtâm, 7. शयामहै śayâmahai, 8. शेध्वं śedhvam, 9. शेरतां śeratâm ‖ Pf. शिश्ये śiśye, I A. अशयिष्ट aśayishṭa, F. शयिष्यते śayishyate, B. शयीत śayîta ‖ Pt. शयितः śayitaḥ ‖ Pass. शय्यते śayyate (Pâṇ. VII. 4, 22), Aor. अशायि aśâyi, Caus. शाययति śâyayati, Des. शिशयिषते śiśayishate, Int. शाशय्यते śâśayyate, शेशेति śeśeti.

186. इ i, to go, (इङ्.)

This verb is always used with अधि adhi, in the sense of reading. (Siddh.-Kaum. vol. II. p. 118.)

P. अधीते adhîte, I. 3. अध्यैत adhyaita, 6. अध्यैयातां adhyaiyâtâm (Sâr. II. 5, 8), 9. अध्यैयत adhyaiyata, O. अधीयीत adhîyîta, I. 1. अध्ययै adhyayai, 2. अधीष्व adhîshva, 3. अधीतां adhîtâm, 4. अध्ययावहै adhyayâvahai, 5. अधीयाथां adhîyâthâm, 6. अधीयातां adhîyâtâm, 7. अध्ययामहै adhyayâmahai, 8. अधीध्वं adhîdhvam, 9. अधीयतां adhîyatâm ‖ Pf. अधिजगे adhijage (Pâṇ. II. 4, 49), I A. 3. अध्यैष्ट adhyaishṭa, 6. अध्यैषातां adhyaishâtâm, 9. अध्यैषत adhaishata, or 3. अध्यगीष्ट adhyagîshṭa (Siddh.-Kaum. vol. II. p. 119), 6. अध्यगीषातां adhyagîshâtâm, 9. अध्यगीषत adhyagîshata, F. अध्येष्यते adhyeshyate, Cond. अध्यैष्यत adhyaishyata or अध्यगीष्यत adhyagîshyata, P. F. अध्येता adhyetâ, B. अध्येषीष्ट adhyeshîshṭa ‖ Pt. अधीतः adhîtaḥ ‖ Pass. अधीयते adhîyate, Aor. अध्यगायि adhyagâyi, Caus. अध्यापयति adhyâpayati, Aor. अध्यापिपत् adhyâpipat or अध्यजीगपत् adhyajîgapat, Des. अधीषिषति adhîshishati or अधिजिगांसते adhijigâṁsate.

III. Parasmaipada and Âtmanepada Verbs.

187. द्विष् dvish, to hate.

P. 1. द्वेष्मि dveshmi, 2. द्वेक्षि dvekshi, 3. द्वेष्टि dveshṭi, 4. द्विष्वः dvishvaḥ, 9. द्विषन्ति dvishanti, I. 1. अद्वेषं advesham, 2. अद्वेट् adveṭ, 3. अद्वेट् adveṭ, 4. अद्विष्व advishva, 9. अद्विषन् advishan or अद्विषुः advishuḥ (§ 321 ‡), O. द्विष्यात् dvishyât, I. 1. द्वेषाणि dveshâṇi, 2. द्विड्ढि dviḍḍhi, 3. द्वेष्टु dveshṭu, 4. द्वेषाव dveshâva, 5. द्विष्टं dvishṭam, 6. द्विष्टां dvishṭâm, 7. द्वेषाम dveshâma, 8. द्विष्ट dvishṭa, 9. द्विषन्तु dvishantu ‖ Pf. दिद्वेष didvesha, I A. अद्विक्षत् advikshat, F. द्वेक्ष्यति dvekshyati, P.F. द्वेष्टा dveshṭâ, B. द्विष्यात् dvishyât, Âtm. द्विक्षीष्ट dvikshîshṭa ‖ Pt. द्विष्टः dvishṭaḥ ‖ Pass. द्विष्यते dvishyate, Aor. अद्वेषि adveshi, Caus. द्वेषयति dveshayati, Aor. अदिद्विषत् adidvishat, Des. दिद्विक्षति didvikshati, Int. देद्विष्यते dedvishyate, देद्वेष्टि dedveshṭi.

188. दुह् duh, to milk.

P. 1. दोह्मि dohmi, 2. धोक्षि dhokshi, 3. दोग्धि dogdhi, 4. दुह्वः duhvaḥ, 5. दुग्धः dugdhaḥ, 6. दुग्धः dugdhaḥ, 7. दुह्मः duhmaḥ, 8. दुग्ध dugdha, 9. दुहन्ति duhanti, I. 1. अदोहं adoham, 2. अधोक् adhok, 3. अधोक् adhok, 4. अदुह्व aduhva, O. दुह्यात् duhyât, I. 1. दोहानि dohâni, 2. दुग्धि dugdhi, 3. दोग्धु dogdhu, 4. दोहाव dohâva, 5. दुग्धं dugdham, 6. दुग्धां dugdhâm, 7. दोहाम dohâma, 8. दुग्ध dugdha, 9. दुहन्तु duhantu ‖ Pf. दुदोह dudoha, I A. अधुक्षत् adhukshat &c. (see § 362), F. धोक्ष्यति dhokshyati.

189. स्तु *stu*, to praise, (ष्टुञ्.)

P. 1. स्तौमि *staumi* or स्तवीमि *stavîmi* (see No. 170), 2. स्तौषि *staushi* or स्तवीषि *stavîshi*, 3. स्तौति *stauti* or स्तवीति *stavîti*, 4. स्तुवः *stuvaḥ* or स्तुवीवः *stuvîvaḥ*, 9. स्तुवन्ति *stuvanti*, I. 1. अस्तवम् *astavam*, 2. अस्तौः *astauḥ* or अस्तवीः *astavîḥ*, 3. अस्तौत् *astaut* or अस्तवीत् *astavît*, 4. अस्तुव *astuva* or अस्तुवीव *astuvîva*, 9. अस्तुवन् *astuvan*, O. स्तुयात् *stuyât*, Âtm. स्तुवीत *stuvîta*, I. 1. स्तवानि *stavâni*, 2. स्तुहि *stuhi* or स्तुवीहि *stuvîhi*, 9. स्तौतु *stautu* or स्तवीतु *stavîtu* ॥ Pf. 3. तुष्टाव *tushṭâva*, 2. तुष्टोथ *tushṭotha*, 6. तुष्टुवतुः *tushṭuvatuḥ*, 9. तुष्टुवुः *tushṭuvuḥ*, I A. अस्तावीत् *astâvît* (§ 338, 3), Âtm. अस्तोष्ट *astoshṭa*, F. स्तोष्यति *stoshyati*, P. F. स्तोता *stotâ*, B. स्तूयात् *stûyât*, Âtm. स्तोषीष्ट *stoshîshṭa* ॥ Pt. स्तुतः *stutaḥ* ॥ Pass. स्तूयते *stûyate*, Aor. अस्तावि *astâvi*, Caus. स्तावयति *stâvayati*, Aor. अतुष्टवत् *atushṭavat*, Des. तुष्टूषति *tushṭûshati*, Int. तोष्टूयते *toshṭûyate*, तोष्टोति *toshṭoti*.

190. ब्रू *brû*, to speak, (ब्रूञ्.)

This verb takes ई *î* before weak terminations beginning with consonants in the special tenses (Pâṇ. VII. 3, 93). The perfect आह *âha* may be substituted for five of the persons of the present (Pâṇ. III. 4, 84). It is defective in the general tenses, where वच् *vach* (No. 175) is used instead.

P. 1. ब्रवीमि *bravîmi*, 2. ब्रवीषि *bravîshi* or आत्थ *âttha*, 3. ब्रवीति *bravîti* or आह *âha*, 4. ब्रूवः *brûvaḥ*, 5. ब्रूथः *brûthaḥ* or आहथुः *âhathuḥ*, 6. ब्रूतः *brûtaḥ* or आहतुः *âhatuḥ*, 7. ब्रूमः *brûmaḥ*, 8. ब्रूथ *brûtha*, 9. ब्रुवन्ति *bruvanti* or आहुः *âhuḥ*, I. 1. अब्रवम् *abravam*, 2. अब्रवीः *abravîḥ*, 3. अब्रवीत् *abravît*, 4. अब्रूव *abrûva*, 5. अब्रूतम् *abrûtam*, 6. अब्रूताम् *abrûtâm*, 7. अब्रूम *abrûma*, 8. अब्रूत *abrûta*, 9. अब्रुवन् *abruvan*, O. ब्रूयात् *brûyât*, I. 1. ब्रवाणि *bravâṇi*, 2. ब्रूहि *brûhi*, 3. ब्रवीतु *bravîtu*, 4. ब्रवाव *bravâva*, 5. ब्रूतम् *brûtam*, 6. ब्रूताम् *brûtâm*, 7. ब्रवाम *bravâma*, 8. ब्रूत *brûta*, 9. ब्रुवन्तु *bruvantu*.

191. ऊर्णु *ûrṇu*, to cover, (ऊर्णुञ्.)

This verb may take Vṛiddhi instead of Guṇa before weak terminations beginning with consonants (Pâṇ. VII. 3, 90, 91), except before those that consist of one consonant only. It takes the reduplicated perfect against § 325, and reduplicates the last syllable (Pâṇ. VI. 1, 8). In the general tenses the final उ *u*, before intermediate इ *i*, may or may not take Guṇa (Pâṇ. I. 2, 3).

P. 3. ऊर्णौति *ûrṇauti* or ऊर्णोति *ûrṇoti*, 9. ऊर्णुवन्ति *ûrṇuvanti*, I. और्णोत् *aurṇot*, O. ऊर्णुयात् *ûrṇuyât*, I. ऊर्णौतु *ûrṇautu* or ऊर्णोतु *ûrṇotu* ॥ Pf. 1. ऊर्णुनाव *ûrṇunâva*, 2. ऊर्णुनविथ *ûrṇunavitha* or ऊर्णुनुविथ *ûrṇunuvitha*, 3. ऊर्णुनाव *ûrṇunâva*, 4. ऊर्णुनुविव *ûrṇunuviva*, 5. ऊर्णुनुवथुः *ûrṇunuvathuḥ*, 6. ऊर्णुनुवतुः *ûrṇunuvatuḥ*, 7. ऊर्णुनुविम *ûrṇunuvima*, 8. ऊर्णुनुव *ûrṇunuva*, 9. ऊर्णुनुवुः *ûrṇunuvuḥ*, I A. और्णवीत् *aurṇavît* or और्णुवीत् *aurṇuvît* or और्णावीत् *aurṇâvît* (Pâṇ. VII. 2, 6), F. ऊर्णविष्यति *ûrṇavishyati* or ऊर्णुविष्यति *ûrṇuvishyati*, B. ऊर्णूयात् *ûrṇûyât* ॥ Pass. ऊर्णूयते *ûrṇûyate*, Caus. ऊर्णावयति *ûrṇâvayati*, Aor. और्णूनवत् *aurṇûnavat*, Des. ऊर्णुनूषति *ûrṇunûshati* or ऊर्णुनविषति *ûrṇunavishati* or ऊर्णुनुविषति *ûrṇunuvishati*, Int. ऊर्णोनूयते *ûrṇonûyate*, ऊर्णोनौति *ûrṇonauti*.

Hu Class (*Juhotyâdi*, *III Class*).

I. Parasmaipada Verbs.

192. हु *hu*, to sacrifice.

P. जुहोति *juhoti*, I. अजुहोत् *ajuhot*, O. जुहुयात् *juhuyât*, I. जुहोतु *juhotu* ॥ Pf. जुहाव *juhâva* or जुहवांचकार *juhavâṁchakâra* (§ 326), I A. अहौषीत् *ahaushît*, F. होष्यति *hoshyati*, P. F. होता *hotâ*, B. हूयात् *hûyât* ॥ Pt. हुतः *hutaḥ* ॥ Pass. हूयते *hûyate*, Caus. हावयति *hâvayati*, Aor. अजूहवत् *ajûhavat*, Des. जुहूषति *juhûshati*, Int. जोहूयते *johûyate*, जोहोति *johoti*.

193. भी *bhî*, to fear, (बिभी.)

This verb may shorten the final ई *î* before strong terminations beginning with consonants in the special tenses. (Pâṇ. vi. 4, 115.)

P. 3. बिभेति *bibheti*, 6. बिभीतः or बिभितः *bibhîtaḥ*, 9. बिभ्यति *bibhyati*, I. 3. अबिभेत् *abibhet*, 6. अबिभीतां or अबिभितां *abibhîtam*, 9. अबिभयुः *abibhayuḥ*, O. बिभीयात् or बिभियात् *bibhîyât*, I. बिभेतु *bibhetu* ॥ Pf. बिभाय *bibhâya* or बिभयांचकार *bibhayâṁchakâra* (§ 326), I A. अभैषीत् *abhaishît*, F. भेष्यति *bheshyati*, P. F. भेता *bhetâ*, B. भीयात् *bhîyât* ॥ Pt. भीतः *bhîtaḥ* ॥ Pass. भीयते *bhîyate*, Aor. अभायि *abhâyi*, Caus. भाययति *bhâyayati* or भापयते *bhâpayate* or भीषयते *bhîshayate* (see § 463, II. 18), Des. बिभीषति *bibhîshati*, Int. बेभीयते *bebhîyate*, बेभेति *bebheti*.

194. ह्री *hrî*, to be ashamed.

P. 3. जिह्रेति *jihreti*, 6. जिह्रीतः *jihrîtaḥ*, 9. जिह्रियति *jihriyati* (§ 110), I. अजिह्रेत् *ajihret*, O. जिह्रीयात् *jihrîyât*, I. जिह्रेतु *jihretu* ॥ Pf. 3. जिह्राय *jihrâya*, 6. जिह्रियतुः *jihriyatuḥ*, 9. जिह्रियुः *jihriyuḥ* or जिह्रयांचकार *jihrayâṁchakâra*, I A. अह्रैषीत् *ahraishît*, F. ह्रेष्यति *hreshyati*, P. F. ह्रेता *hretâ*, B. ह्रीयात् *hrîyât* ॥ Pt. ह्रीणः *hrîṇaḥ* or ह्रीतः *hrîtaḥ* (Pâṇ. viii. 2, 56) ॥ Pass. ह्रीयते *hrîyate*, Caus. ह्रेपयति *hrepayati*, Aor. अजिह्रिपत् *ajihripat*, Des. जिह्रीषति *jihrîshati*, Int. जेह्रीयते *jehrîyate*.

195. पॄ *pṛî*, to fill, to guard.

This verb, and others in which final ॠ *ṛî* is preceded by a labial, changes the vowel into उर् *ur*, unless where the vowel requires Guṇa or Vṛiddhi. (Pâṇ. vii. 1, 102.)

P. 1. पिपर्मि *piparmi*, 2. पिपर्षि *piparshi*, 3. पिपर्ति *piparti*, 4. पिपूर्वः *pipûrvaḥ*, 5. पिपूर्थः *pipûrthaḥ*, 6. पिपूर्तः *pipûrtaḥ*, 7. पिपूर्मः *pipûrmaḥ*, 8. पिपूर्थ *pipûrtha*, 9. पिपुरति *pipurati*, I. 1. अपिपरं *apiparam*, 2. अपिपः *apipaḥ* (or अपिपरः *apiparaḥ*, Sâr.), 3. अपिपः *apipaḥ* (or अपिपरत् *apiparat*), 4. अपिपूर्व *apipûrva*, 5. अपिपूर्तं *apipûrtam*, 6. अपिपूर्तां *apipûrtâm*, 7. अपिपूर्म *apipûrma*, 8. अपिपूर्त *apipûrta*, 9. अपिपरुः *apiparuḥ*, O. पिपूर्यात् *pipûryât*, I. 1. पिपराणि *piparâṇi*, 2. पिपूर्हि *pipûrhi*, 3. पिपर्तु *pipartu*, 4. पिपराव *piparâva*, 5. पिपूर्तं *pipûrtam*, 6. पिपूर्तां *pipûrtâm*, 7. पिपराम *piparâma*, 8. पिपूर्त *pipûrta*, 9. पिपुरतु *pipuratu* ॥ Pf. 1. पपार *papâra*, 2. पपरिथ *paparitha*, 3. पपार *papâra*, 4. पपरिव *papariva*, 5. पपरथुः *paparathuḥ* or पप्रथुः *paprathuḥ*, 6. पपरतुः *paparatuḥ* or पप्रतुः *papratuḥ*, 7. पपरिम *paparima*, 8. पपर *papara*,

9. पपरुः *paparuḥ* or पप्रुः *papruḥ* (Pâṇ. VII. 4, 11, 12), I A. अपारीत् *apârît*, F. परीष्यति *parîshyati*, P. F. परिता or परीता *parîtâ*, B. पूर्यात् *pûryât* ‖ Pt. पूर्णः *pûrṇaḥ* or पूरितः *pûritaḥ* (Pâṇ. VII. 2, 27), Ger. पूर्त्वा *pûrtvâ*, °पूर्य *-pûrya* ‖ Pass. पूर्यते *pûryate*, Caus. पारयति *pârayati*, Aor. अपीपरत् *apîparat*, Des. पुपूर्षति *pupûrshati* or पिपरीषति *piparîshati*, Int. पोपूर्यते *popûryate*, पापर्ति *pâparti*.

Several optional forms are derived from another root पृ *pṛi*, with short ऋ *ṛi*. Thus, P. 3. पिपर्ति *piparti*, 6. पिपृतः *pipṛitaḥ*, 9. पिप्रति *piprati*, I. 3. अपिपः *apipaḥ*, 6. अपिपृतां *apipṛitâm*, 9. अपिपरुः *apiparuḥ*, O. पिपृयात् *pipṛiyât* ‖ I A. अपार्षीत् *apârshît*, B. प्रियात् *priyât* ‖ Pass. प्रियते *priyate* (§ 390), Int. पेप्रीयते *peprîyate* (§ 481).

196. हा *hâ*, to leave, (ओहाक्.)

Reduplicated verbs ending in आ *â* (except the घु *ghu* verbs, see § 392*) substitute ई *î* for आ *â* before strong terminations beginning with consonants (Pâṇ. VI. 4, 113). The verb हा *hâ*, however, may also substitute इ *i* (Pâṇ. VI. 4, 116).

P. 1. जहामि *jahâmi*, 2. जहासि *jahâsi*, 3. जहाति *jahâti*, 4. जहीवः *jahîvaḥ*, 5. जहीथः *jahîthaḥ*, 6. जहीतः *jahîtaḥ*, 7. जहीमः *jahîmaḥ*, 8. जहीथ *jahîta*, 9. जहति *jahati*, I. 1. अजहां *ajahâm*, 2. अजहाः *ajahâḥ*, 3. अजहात् *ajahât*, 4. अजहीव *ajahîva*, 9. अजहुः *ajahuḥ*, O. जह्यात् *jahyât* (Pâṇ. VI. 4, 118), I. 1. जहानि *jahâni*, 2. जहीहि *jahîhi* or जहाहि *jahâhi* (Pâṇ. VI. 4, 117), 3. जहातु *jahâtu*, 4. जहाव *jahâva*, 5. जहीतं *jahîtam*, 6. जहीतां *jahîtâm*, 7. जहाम *jahâma*, 8. जहीत *jahîta*, 9. जहतु *jahatu* ‖ Pf. 1. जहौ *jahau*, 2. जहिथ *jahitha* or जहाथ *jahâtha*, 3. जहौ *jahau*, 4. जहिव *jahiva*, 5. जहथुः *jahathuḥ*, 6. जहतुः *jahatuḥ*, 7. जहिम *jahima*, 8. जह *jaha*, 9. जहुः *jahuḥ*, I A. अहासीत् *ahâsît*, F. हास्यति *hâsyati*, P. F. हाता *hâtâ*, B. हेयात् *heyât* ‖ Pt. हीनः *hînaḥ*, Ger. हित्वा *hitvâ* (Pâṇ. VII. 4, 43), °हाय *-hâya* ‖ Pass. हीयते *hîyate*, Caus. हापयति *hâpayati*, Aor. अजीहपत् *ajîhapat*, Des. जिहासति *jihâsati*, Int. जेहीयते *jehîyate*.

197. ऋ *ṛi*, to go.

P. 3. इयर्ति *iyarti*, 6. इयृतः *iyṛitaḥ*, 9. इय्रति *iyrati*, I. 3. ऐयः *aiyaḥ* (or ऐयरत् *aiyarat*), 6. ऐयृतां *aiyṛitâm*, 9. ऐयरुः *aiyaruḥ*, O. इयृयात् *iyṛiyât*, I. 1. इयराणि *iyarâṇi*, 2. इयृहि *iyṛihi*, 3. इयर्तु *iyartu*, 4. इयराव *iyarâva*, 5. इयृतं *iyṛitam*, 6. इयृतां *iyṛitâm*, 7. इयराम *iyarâma*, 8. इयृत *iyṛita*, 9. इय्रतु *iyratu* ‖ Pf. 1. आर *âra*, 2. आरिथ *âritha*, I A. आरत् *ârat*, F. अरिष्यति *arishyati*, P. F. अर्ता *artâ*, B. अर्यात् *aryât*.

II. Âtmanepada Verbs.

198. मा *mâ*, to measure, (माङ्.)

P. 1. मिमे *mime*, 2. मिमीषे *mimîshe*, 3. मिमीते *mimîte*, 4. मिमीवहे *mimîvahe*, 5. मिमाथे *mimâthe*, 6. मिमाते *mimâte*, 7. मिमीमहे *mimîmahe*, 8. मिमीध्वे *mimîdhve*, 9. मिमते *mimate*, I. 1. अमिमि *amimi*, 2. अमिमीथाः *amimîthâḥ*, 3. अमिमीत *amimîta*, 4. अमिमीवहि *amimîvahi*, 5. अमिमाथां *amimâthâm*, 6. अमिमातां *amimâtâm*, 7. अमिमीमहि *amimîmahi*, 8. अमिमीध्वं *amimîdhvam*, 9. अमिमत *amimata*, O. मिमीत *mimîta*, I. 1. मिमै *mimai*, 2. मिमीष्व *mimîshva*, 3. मिमीतां *mimîtâm*, 4. मिमावहै *mimâvahai*,

5. मिमाथां *mimâthâm*, 6. मिमातां *mimâtâm*, 7. मिमामहै *mimâmahai*, 8. मिमीध्वं *mimî-dhvam*, 9. मिमतां *mimatâm* ‖ Pf. 1. ममे *mame*, 2. ममिषे *mamishe*, 3. ममे *mame*, 4. ममिवहे *mamivahe*, 5. ममाथे *mamâthe*, 6. ममाते *mamâte*, 7. ममिमहे *mamimahe*, 8. ममिध्वे *mamidhve*, 9. ममिरे *mamire*, I A. 1. अमासि *amâsi*, 2. अमास्थाः *amâsthâḥ*, 3. अमास्त *amâsta*, 4. अमास्वहि *amâsvahi*, 5. अमासाथां *amâsâthâm*, 6. अमासातां *amâsâtâm*, 7. अमास्महि *amâsmahi*, 8. अमाध्वं *amâdhvam*, 9. अमासत *amâsata*, F. मास्यते *mâsyate*, P. F. माता *mâtâ*, B. मासीष्ट *mâsîshṭa* ‖ Pt. मितः *mitaḥ*, Ger. मित्वा *mitvâ*, °माय *-mâya* (not मीय *mîya*, Pâṇ. VI. 4, 69) ‖ Pass. मीयते *mîyate*, Aor. अमायि *amâyi*, Caus. मापयति *mâpayati*, Des. मित्सते *mitsate*, Int. मेमीयते *memîyate*.

III. Parasmaipada and Âtmanepada Verbs.

199. भृ *bhṛi*, to carry, (डुभृञ्.)

P. 1. बिभर्मि *bibharmi*, 2. बिभर्षि *bibharshi*, 3. बिभर्ति *bibharti*, 4. बिभृवः *bibhṛivaḥ*, 5. बिभृथः *bibhṛithaḥ*, 6. बिभृतः *bibhṛitaḥ*, 7. बिभृमः *bibhṛimaḥ*, 8. बिभृथ *bibhṛitha*, 9. बिभ्रति *bibhrati*, Âtm. 1. बिभ्रे *bibhre*, 2. बिभृषे *bibhṛishe*, 3. बिभृते *bibhṛite*, I. 3. अबिभः *abibhaḥ*, 6. अबिभृतां *abibhṛitâm*, 9. अबिभरुः *abibharuḥ*, Âtm. 3. अबिभृत *abibhṛita*, 6. अबिभ्राते *abibhrâte*, 9. अबिभ्रत *abibhrata*, O. बिभृयात् *bibhṛiyât*, Âtm. बिभ्रीत *bibhrîta*, I. 1. बिभराणि *bibharâṇi*, 2. बिभृहि *bibhṛihi*, 3. बिभर्तु *bibhartu* ‖ Pf. 1. बभार *babhâra*, 2. बभर्थ *babhartha*, 3. बभार *babhâra*, 4. बभृव *babhṛiva* (§ 334; Pâṇ. VII. 2, 13) or बिभरांचकार *bibharâṁchakâra*, I A. अभार्षीत् *abhârshît*, Âtm. अभृत *abhṛita*, F. भरिष्यति *bharishyati*, P. F. भर्ता *bhartâ*, B. भ्रियात् *bhriyât*, Âtm. भृषीष्ट *bhṛishîshṭa* ‖ Pt. भृतः *bhṛitaḥ* ‖ Pass. भ्रियते *bhriyate*, Caus. भारयति *bhârayati*, Des. बुभूर्षति *bubhûrshati* or बिभरिषति *bibharishati* (Pâṇ. VII. 2, 49), Int. बेभ्रीयते *bebhrîyate*, बर्भर्ति *barbharti*.

200. दा *dâ*, to give, (डुदाञ्.)

The घु *ghu* verbs (§ 392 *) drop आ *â* before strong terminations, where other reduplicated verbs (see No. 196) change आ *â* to ई *î*. (Pâṇ. VI. 4, 112, 113.)

P. 1. ददामि *dadâmi*, 2. ददासि *dadâsi*, 3. ददाति *dadâti*, 4. दद्वः *dadvaḥ*, 5. दत्थः *datthaḥ*, 6. दत्तः *dattaḥ*, 7. दद्मः *dadmaḥ*, 8. दत्थ *dattha*, 9. ददति *dadati*, Âtm. 1. ददे *dade*, 2. दत्से *datse*, 3. दत्ते *datte*, 4. दद्वहे *dadvahe*, 5. ददाथे *dadâthe*, 6. ददाते *dadâte*, 7. दद्महे *dadmahe*, 8. दद्ध्वे *daddhve*, 9. ददते *dadate*, I. 1. अददां *adadâm*, 2. अददाः *adadâḥ*, 3. अददात् *adadât*, 4. अदद्व *adadva*, 5. अदत्तं *adattam*, 6. अदत्तां *adattâm*, 7. अदद्म *adadma*, 8. अदत्त *adatta*, 9. अददुः *adaduḥ*, Âtm. 1. अददि *adadi*, 2. अदत्थाः *adatthâḥ*, 3. अदत्त *adatta*, 4. अदद्वहि *adadvahi*, 5. अददाथां *adadâthâm*, 6. अददातां *adadâtâm*, 7. अदद्महि *adadmahi*, 8. अदद्ध्वं *adaddhvam*, 9. अददत *adadata*, O. दद्यात् *dadyât*, Âtm. ददीत *dadîta*, I. 1. ददानि *dadâni*, 2. देहि *dehi* (Pâṇ. VI. 4, 119), 3. दत्तु *dattu*, 4. ददाव *dadâva*, 5. दत्तं *dattam*, 6. दत्तां *dattâm*, 7. ददाम *dadâma*, 8. दत्त *datta*, 9. ददतु *dadatu*, Âtm. 1. ददै *dadai*, 2. दत्स्व *datsva*, 3. दत्तां *dattâm*, 4. ददावहै *dadâvahai*, 5. ददाथां *dadâthâm*, 6. ददातां *dadâtâm*, 7. ददामहै *dadâmahai*, 8. दद्ध्वं

daddhvam, 9. ददतां *dadatâm* ‖ Pf. 1. ददौ *dadau*, 2. ददिथ *daditha* or ददाथ *dadâtha*, 3. ददौ *dadau*, 4. ददिव *dadiva*, 5. ददथुः *dadathuḥ*, 6. ददतुः *dadatuḥ*, 7. ददिम *dadima*, 8. दद *dada*, 9. ददुः *daduḥ*, Âtm. 1. ददे *dade*, 2. ददिषे *dadishe*, 3. ददे *dade*, 4. ददिवहे *dadivahe*, 5. ददाथे *dadâthe*, 6. ददाते *dadâte*, 7. ददिमहे *dadimahe*, 8. ददिध्वे *dadidhve*, 9. ददिरे *dadire*, II A. 1. अदां *adâm*, 9. अदुः *aduḥ*, Âtm. अदिषि *adishi* (see p. 184), F. दास्यति, °ते, *dâsyati*, *-te*, P. F. दाता *dâtâ*, B. देयात् *deyât*, Âtm. दासीष्ट *dâsîshṭa* ‖ Pt. दत्तः *dattaḥ* (§ 436), Ger. दत्त्वा *dattvâ*, °दाय *-dâya* ‖ Pass. दीयते *dîyate*, Aor. अदायि *adâyi*, Caus. दापयति *dâpayati*, Aor. अदीदपत् *adîdapat*, Des. दित्सति *ditsati*, Int. देदीयते *dedîyate*, दादाति *dâdâti*.

201. धा *dhâ*, to place, (डुधाञ्.)

This verb is conjugated like दा *dâ*. It should be remembered, however, that the aspiration of the final ध् *dh*, if lost, must be thrown forward on the initial द् *d;* hence 2nd pers. dual Pres. धत्थः *dhatthaḥ* &c. (§ 118, note). The Pt. is हितः *hitaḥ*, Ger. हित्वा *hitvâ*, °धाय *-dhâya*.

202. निज् *nij*, to cleanse, (णिजिर्.)

The verbs निज् *nij*, विज् *vij*, to separate, and विष् *vish*, to embrace, take Guṇa in their reduplicative syllable. (Pâṇ. VII. 4, 75.)

Reduplicated verbs (*abhyasta*, § 321 †) having a short medial vowel do not take Guṇa before weak terminations beginning with vowels in the special tenses. (Pâṇ. VII. 3, 87.)

P. 1. नेनेज्मि *nenejmi*, 2. नेनेक्षि *nenekshi*, 3. नेनेक्ति *nenekti*, 9. नेनिजति *nenijati*, I. 1. अनेनिजं *anenijam*, 2. अनेनेक् *anenek*, 3. अनेनेक् *anenek*, 7. अनेनिज्म *anenijma*, 9. अनेनिजुः *anenijuḥ*, O. नेनिज्यात् *nenijyât*, I. 1. नेनिजानि *nenijâni*, 2. नेनिग्धि *nenigdhi*, 3. नेनेक्तु *nenektu* ‖ Pf. निनेज *nineja*, I A. अनैक्षीत् *anaikshît* or II A. अनिजत् *anijat*, F. नेक्ष्यति *nekshyati*, P. F. नेक्ता *nektâ*, B. निज्यात् *nijyât*, Âtm. निक्षीष्ट *nikshîshṭa* ‖ Caus. नेजयति *nejayati*, Aor. अनीनिजत् *anînijat*, Des. निनिक्षति *ninikshati*, Int. नेनिज्यते *nenijyate*, नेनेक्ति *nenekti*.

Rudh Class (*Rudhâdi, VII Class*).

I. Parasmaipada and Âtmanepada Verbs.

203. रुध् *rudh*, to shut out, (रुधिर्.)

P. रुणद्धि *ruṇaddhi*, I. अरुणत् *aruṇat*, O. रुन्ध्यात् *rundhyât*, I. रुणद्धु *ruṇaddhu* ‖ Pf. 1. रुरोध *rurodha*, 2. रुरोधिथ *rurodhitha*, 3. रुरोध *rurodha*, 7. रुरुधिम *rurudhima*, 9. रुरुधुः *rurudhuḥ*, I A. अरौत्सीत् *arautsît* or II A. अरुधत् *arudhat*, Âtm. अरुद्ध *aruddha*, F. रोत्स्यति *rotsyati*, P. F. रोद्धा *roddhâ*, B. रुध्यात् *rudhyât*, Âtm. रुत्सीष्ट *rutsîshṭa* ‖ Pt. रुद्धः *ruddhaḥ*, Ger. रुद्ध्वा *ruddhvâ*, °रुध्य *-rudhya* ‖ Pass. रुध्यते *rudhyate*, Aor. अरोधि *arodhi*, Caus. रोधयति *rodhayati*, Des. रुरुत्सति *rurutsati*, Int. रोरुध्यते *rorudhyate*, रोरोद्धि *roroddhi*.

II. Parasmaipada Verbs.

204. शिष् *śish*, to distinguish, (शिषॢ.)

P. 1. शिनष्मि *śinashmi*, 2. शिनक्षि *śinakshi*, 3. शिनक्ति *śinakti*, 4. शिंष्वः *śiṁshvaḥ*, 5. शिंष्ठः *śiṁshṭhaḥ*, 6. शिंष्टः *śiṁshṭaḥ*, 7. शिंष्मः *śiṁshmaḥ*, 8. शिंष्ट *śiṁshṭa*, 9. शिंषन्ति *śiṁshanti*, I. 1. अशिनषं *aśinasham*, 2. अशिनट् *aśinaṭ*, 3. अशिनट् *aśinaṭ*, 4. अशिंष्व *aśiṁshva*, 5. अशिंष्टं *aśiṁshṭam*, 6. अशिंष्टां *aśiṁshṭâm*, 7. अशिंष्म *aśiṁshma*, 8. अशिंष्ट *aśiṁshṭa*, 9. अशिंषन् *aśiṁshan*, O. शिंष्यात् *śiṁshyât*, I. 1. शिनषाणि *śinashâṇi*, 2. शिंड्ढि *śiṇḍḍhi* (or शिण्ढि *śiṇḍhi*), 3. शिनष्टु *śinashṭu* ‖ Pf. शिशेष *śiśesha*, II A. अशिषत् *aśishat*, F. शेक्ष्यति *śekshyati*, P. F. शेष्टा *śeshṭâ*, B. शिष्यात् *śishyât* ‖ Pt. शिष्टः *śishṭaḥ* ‖ Pass. शिष्यते *śishyate*, Caus. शेषयति *śeshayati*, Des. शिशिक्षति *śiśikshati*, Int. शेशिष्यते *śeśishyate*, शेशेष्टि *śeśeshṭi*.

205. हिंस् *hiṁs*, to strike, (हिसि.)

P. हिनस्ति *hinasti*, I. 1. अहिनसं *ahinasam*, 2. अहिनः *ahinaḥ* or अहिनत् *ahinat*, 3. अहिनत् *ahinat* (§ 132), 4. अहिंस्व *ahiṁsva*, 5. अहिंस्तं *ahiṁstam*, 6. अहिंस्तां *ahiṁstâm*, 7. अहिंस्म *ahiṁsma*, 8. अहिंस्त *ahiṁsta*, 9. अहिंसन् *ahiṁsan*, O. हिंस्यात् *hiṁsyât*, I. 1. हिनसानि *hinasâni*, 2. हिन्धि *hindhi*, 3. हिनस्तु *hinastu* ‖ Pf. जिहिंस *jihiṁsa*, I A. अहिंसीत् *ahiṁsît*, F. हिंसिष्यति *hiṁsishyati*, P. F. हिंसिता *hiṁsitâ*, B. हिंस्यात् *hiṁsyât* ‖ Pt. हिंसितः *hiṁsitaḥ* ‖ Pass. हिंस्यते *hiṁsyate*, Caus. हिंसयति *hiṁsayati*, Aor. अजिहिंसत् *ajihiṁsat*, Des. जिहिंसिषति *jihiṁsishati*, Int. जेहिंस्यते *jehiṁsyate*, जेहिंस्ति *jehiṁsti*.

206. भंज् *bhañj*, to break, (भञ्जो.)

P. भनक्ति *bhanakti*, I. अभनक् *abhanak*, O. भंज्यात् *bhañjyât*, I. भनक्तु *bhanaktu* ‖ Pf. बभंज *babhañja*, I A. अभांक्षीत् *abhâṅkshît*, F. भंक्ष्यति *bhaṅkshyati*, P. F. भंक्ता *bhaṅktâ*, B. भज्यात् *bhajyât* ‖ Pt. भग्नः *bhagnaḥ* ‖ Pass. भज्यते *bhajyate*, Aor. अभंजि *abhañji* or अभाजि *abhâji* (§ 407), Caus. भंजयति *bhañjayati*, Des. बिभंक्षति *bibhaṅkshati*, Int. बंभज्यते *bambhajyate*, बंभंक्ति *bambhaṅkti*.

207. अंज् *añj*, to anoint, (अञ्जू.)

P. अनक्ति *anakti*, I. आनक् *ânak*, O. अंज्यात् *añjyât*, I. अनक्तु *anaktu* ‖ Pf. आनंज *ânañja*, I A. आंजीत् *âñjît*, F. अंजिष्यति *añjishyati* or अंक्ष्यति *aṅkshyati*, B. अज्यात् *ajyât* ‖ Pt. अक्तः *aktaḥ*, Ger. अंजित्वा *añjitvâ* or अंक्त्वा *aṅktvâ* or अक्त्वा *aktvâ* (Pâṇ. VI. 4, 32; § 438), °अज्य -*ajya* ‖ Pass. अज्यते *ajyate*, Aor. आंजि *âñji*, Caus. अंजयति *añjayati*, Aor. आंजिजत् *âñjijat*, Des. अंजिजिषति *añjijishati*.

208. तृह् *tṛih*, to kill, (तृह.)

This verb inserts ने *ne* instead of न *na* before weak terminations beginning with consonants. (Pâṇ. VII. 3, 92.)

P. 1. तृणेह्मि *tṛiṇehmi*, 2. तृणेक्षि *tṛiṇekshi*, 3. तृणेढि *tṛiṇeḍhi*, 4. तृंह्वः *tṛiṁhvaḥ*, 5. तृंढः *tṛiṇḍhaḥ*, 6. तृंढः *tṛiṇḍhaḥ*, 7. तृंह्मः *tṛiṁhmaḥ*, 8. तृंढ *tṛiṇḍha*, 9. तृंहन्ति *tṛiṁhati*,

I. 1. अतृणहं *atṛiṇaham*, 2. अतृणेट् *atṛiṇeṭ*, 3. अतृणेट् *atṛiṇeṭ*, 4. अतृंह्व *atṛiṁhva*, 5. अतृंढं *atṛiṇḍham*, 6. अतृंढां *atṛiṇḍhâm*, 7. अतृंह्म *atṛiṁhma*, 8. अतृंढ *atṛiṇḍha*, 9. अतृंहन् *atṛiṁhan*, O. तृंह्यात् *tṛiṁhyât*, I. 1. तृणहानि *tṛiṇahâni*, 2. तृंढि *tṛiṇḍhi*, 3. तृणेढु *tṛiṇeḍhu* ॥ Pf. ततर्ह *tatarha*, I A. अतर्हीत् *atarhît* or अतृक्षत् *atṛikshat*, F. तर्हिष्यति *tarhishyati* or तर्क्ष्यति *tarkshyati*, P. F. तर्हिता *tarhitâ* or तर्ढा *tarḍhâ*, B. तृह्यात् *tṛihyât* ॥ Pt. तृढः *tṛiḍhaḥ* ॥ Pass. तृह्यते *tṛihyate*, Aor. अतर्हि *atarhi*, Caus. तर्हयति *tarhayati*, Aor. अततर्हत् *atatarhat* or अतीतृहत् *atîtṛihat*, Des. तितर्हिषति *titarhishati* or तितृक्षति *titṛikshati*, Int. तरीतृह्यते *tarîtṛihyate*, तरीतर्ढि *tarîtarḍhi*.

III. Âtmanepada Verbs.

209. इन्ध् *indh*, to kindle, (ञिइन्धी.)

P. इन्द्धे *inddhe* or इन्धे *indhe*, I. ऐन्द्ध *ainddha* or ऐन्ध *aindha*, O. इन्धीत *indhîta*, I. 1. इनधै *inadhai*, 2. इन्त्स्व *intsva*, 3. इन्द्धां *inddhâm* or इन्धां *indhâm* ॥ Pf. इन्धांचक्रे *indhâṁchakre* (or ईधे *îdhe*, Pâṇ. 1. 2, 6), I A. ऐन्धिष्ट *aindhishṭa*, F. इन्धिष्यते *indhishyate*, P. F. इन्धिता *indhitâ*, B. इन्धिषीष्ट *indhishîshṭa* ॥ Pt. इद्धः *iddhaḥ* ॥ Pass. इध्यते *idhyate*, Caus. इन्धयति *indhayati*, Des. इन्दिधिषते *indidhishate*.

INDEX OF NOUNS.

NOTE.—The figures refer to the §, not to the page.

अक्का *akkâ*, mother, 238.

अक्षि *akshi*, eye, 234.

अग्निमथ् *agnimath*, fire-kindling, 157.

अतिचमू *atichamû*, better than an army, 227.

अतिलक्ष्मी *atilakshmî*, better than Lakshmî, 227.

अतिस्त्रि *atistri*, better than a woman, m.f., 229.

अदत् *adat*, eating, 182.

°अन् *-an*, 191.

अनडुह् *anaḍuh*, ox, 210.

अनर्वन् *anarvan*, without a foe, 189.

अनेहस् *anehas*, time, 168.

अन्वच् *anvach*, following, 181.

अप् *ap*, water, 211.

अंबिका *ambikâ*, mother, 238.

अयास् *ayâs*, fire, 149.

अर्यमन् *aryaman*, name of a deity, 201.

अर्वत् *arvat*, horse, 189.

अर्वन् *arvan*, hurting, foe, 189.

अवयाज् *avayâj*, priest, 163.

अवाच् *avâch*, south, 180.

अवी *avî*, f. not desiring, 225.

असन् *asan*, blood, 214.

असृज् *asṛij*, blood, 161, 214.

अस्थि *asthi*, bone, 234.

अहन् *ahan*, n. day, 196.

अहन् *ahan*, day, at the end of a compound, 197, 198.

अहर्गण *ahargaṇa*, month, 196.

आत्मन् *âtman*, soul, self, 191, 192.

आपः *âpaḥ*, water, 149, 211.

आशिस् *âśis*, blessing, 172.

आसन् *âsan*, face, 214.

आस्य *âsya*, face, 214.

°इन् *-in*, 203.

ईदृश् *îdṛiś*, such, 174.

°ईयस् *îyas*, 206.

उक्थशास् *ukthaśâs*, reciter of hymns, 177.

उदक *udaka*, water, 214.

उदच् *udach*, upward, northern, 181.

उदन् *udan*, water, 214.

उन्नी *unnî*, leading out, 221.

उपानह् *upânah*, shoe, 174.

उशनस् *uśanas*, nom. prop., 169.

उष्णिह् *ushṇih*, a metre, 174.

ऊर्ज् *ûrj*, strength, 161.

ऋत्विज् *ṛitvij*, priest, 161.

ऋभुक्षिन् *ṛibhukshin*, Indra, 195.

ककुभ् *kakubh*, region, 157.

कति *kati*, how many, 231.

करभू *karabhû*, nail, 221.

कवि *kavi*, poet, 230.

कांत *kânta*, beloved, 238.

कांता *kântâ*, fem. beloved, 238.

कियत् *kiyat*, how much, 190.

किर् *kir*, scattering, 164.

कुधी *kudhî*, m. f. a bad thinker, 221.

कुमारी *kumârî*, m. girlish, 227.

क्री *krî*, m. f. buying, 220.

क्रुंच् *kruñch*, curlew, 159.

क्रोष्टु *kroshṭu*, jackal, 236.
खंज् *khañj*, lame, 163.
गरीयस् *garíyas*, heavier, 206.
गिर् *gir*, voice, 164.
गुप् *gup*, guardian, 157.
गुह् *guh*, covering, 174.
गो *go*, ox, 218.
गोरक्ष् *goraksh*, cowherd, 174.
ग्रामणी *grámaṇí*, leader of a village, 221.
चकास् *chakás*, splendid, 172.
चकासत् *chakásat*, shining, 184.
चिकीर्ष् *chikírsh*, desirous of acting, 172.
चित्रलिख् *chitralikh*, painter, 156.
जक्षत् *jakshat*, eating, 184.
जगत् *jagat*, world, 184.
जगन्वस् *jaganvas*, having gone, 205.
जग्मिवस् *jagmivas*, having gone, 205.
जघन्वस् *jaghanvas*, having killed, 205.
जघ्निवस् *jaghnivas*, having killed, 205.
जरा *jará*, old age, 166.
जलक्री *jalakrí*, m. f. a buyer of water, 221.
जलमुच् *jalamuch*, cloud, 158.
जाग्रत् *jágrat*, waking, 184.
तक्ष् *taksh*, paring, 174.
तक्षन् *takshan*, carpenter, 191.
तति *tati*, so many, 231.
तंत्री *tantrí*, f. lute, 225.
तरी *tarí*, f. boat, 225.
तिर्यंच् *tiryach*, tortuous, 181.
तुराषाह् *turásáh*, Indra, 175.
त्वच् *tvach*, skin, 158.
त्विष् *tvish*, splendour, 174.
दत् *dat*, tooth, 214.
ददत् *dadat*, giving, 184.
दधि *dadhi*, curds, 234.
दधृष् *dadhṛish*, bold, 174.
दंत *danta*, tooth, 214.
दरिद्रत् *daridrat*, poor, 184.
दातृ *dátṛi*, giver, 235.
दामन् *dáman*, rope, fem., 179, 193.
दाराः *dáráḥ*, wife, 149.
दिधक्ष् *didhaksh*, desirous of burning, 174.
दिव् *div* and द्यु *dyu*, sky, 213.
दिश् *diś*, showing, 174.
दिश् *diś*, country, 174.
दुह् *duh*, milking, 174.
दुहितृ *duhitṛi*, daughter, 235.
दृन्भू *dṛinbhú*, thunderbolt, 221.
दृश् *dṛiś*, seeing, 174.
देवेज् *devej*, worshipper, 162.
दोषन् *doshan*, arm, 214.
दोस् *dos*, arm, 172, 214.
द्यु *dyu* and दिव् *div*, sky, 213.
द्यो *dyo*, sky, 219.
द्रुह् *druh*, hating, 174.
द्वार् *dvár*, door, 164.
द्विदाम्नी *dvidámní*, having two ropes, 194.
द्विष् *dvish*, hating, 174.
धनिन् *dhanin*, rich, 203.
धातृ *dhátṛi*, n. providence, 235.
धी *dhí*, m. f. thinking, 220.
धी *dhí*, f. intellect, 224.
धीवरी *dhívarí*, wife of a fisherman, 193.
ध्वस् *dhvas*, falling, 173.
नदी *nadí*, f. river, 225.
नप्तृ *naptṛi*, grandson, 235.
नश् *naś*, destroying, 174.
नस् *nas*, nose, 214.
नह् *nah*, binding, 174.
नामन् *náman*, name, 191.
नासिका *násiká*, nose, 214.
निनीवस् *ninívas*, having led, 205.
निर्जर *nirjara*, ageless, 167.
नृ *nṛi*, man, 237.
नृतू *nṛitú*, m. f. dancer, 222.
नौ *nau*, ship, 217.
न्यच् *nyach*, low, 181.
पंगु *paṅgu*, m., पंगू *paṅgú*, fem. lame, 230.
पति *pati*, lord, 233.
पथिन् *pathin*, m. path, 195.

राज्ञी *rájñí*, queen, 193.
रुच् *ruch*, light, 158.
रुज् *ruj*, disease, 161.
रुरुद्वस् *rurudvas*, crying, 204.
रुष् *rush*, anger, 174.
रै *rai*, wealth, 217.
लक्ष्मी *lakshmí*, f. goddess of prosperity, 225.
लघु *laghu*, m. f. n. light, 230.
लिह् *lih*, licking, 174.
लू *lú*, m. f. cutting, 220.
वणिज् *vaṇij*, merchant, 161.
°वत् *-vat*, 187.
वधू *vadhú*, f. wife, 225.
°वन् *-van*, 191.
वर्षाः *varsháḥ*, rainy season, 149.
वर्षाभू *varshábhú*, frog, 221.
°वस् *-vas*, part. perfect, 204.
वाच् *vách*, speech, 158.
वातप्रमी *vátapramí*, antelope, 222.
वार् *vár*, water, 164.
वारि *vári*, water, 230.
°वाह् *-váh*, carrying, 208.
विद्वस् *vidvas*, knowing, 205.
विपाश् *vipáś*, a river, 174.
विप्रुष् *viprush*, drop of water, 174.
विभ्राज् *vibhráj*, resplendent, 162.
विवक्ष् *vivaksh*, desirous of saying, 174.
विविक्ष् *viviksh*, wishing to enter, 174.
विश् *viś*, entering, 174.
विश्वपा *viśvapá*, all-preserving, 239.
विश्वराज् *viśvaráj*, universal monarch, 162.
विश्वसृज् *viśvasṛij*, creator, 162.
विष् *vish*, ordure, 174.
विष्वच् *vishvach*, all-pervading, 181.
वृक्षलू *vṛikshalú*, tree-hewer, 222.
वृश्च् *vṛiśch*, cutting, 159.
शकन् *śakan*, ordure, 214.
शकृत् *śakṛit*, ordure, 214.
शंखध्मा *śaṅkhadhmá*, shell-blower, 239.
शासत् *śásat*, commanding, 184.
शुचि *śuchi*, m. f. n. bright, 230.
शुद्धधी *śuddhadhí*, thinking pure things, 221.
शुद्धधी *śuddhadhí*, a pure thinker, 221.
शुश्रुवस् *śuśruvas*, having heard, 205.
शुष्की *śushkí*, 222.
श्री *śrí*, f. happiness, 224.
श्वन् *śvan*, dog, 199.
श्वेतवाह् *śvetaváh* and श्वेतवस् *śvetavas*, 209.
संवत् *saṁvat*, year, 149.
सक्थि *sakthi*, thigh, 234.
सखि *sakhi*, friend, 232.
सजुस् *sajus*, friend, 172.
सध्र्यच् *sadhryach*, accompanying, 181.
सम्यच् *samyach*, right, 181.
सम्राज् *samráj*, sovereign, 162.
सर्वशक् *sarvaśak*, omnipotent, 155.
सानु *sánu*, ridge, 214.
सामि *sámi*, half, 149.
सिकताः *sikatáḥ*, sand, 149.
सुखी *sukhí*, wishing for pleasure, 222.
सुगण् *sugaṇ*, ready reckoner, 154.
सुचक्षुस् *suchakshus*, having good eyes, 165.
सुज्योतिस् *sujyotis*, well-lighted, 165.
सुती *sutí*, wishing for a son, 222.
सुतुस् *sutus*, well-sounding, 170.
सुधी *sudhí*, m. f. having a good mind, 226.
सुपिस् *supis*, well-walking, 170.
सुभ्रू *subhrú*, m. f. having good brows, 226.
सुमनस् *sumanas*, well-minded, 165.
सुश्री *suśrí*, well-faring, 221.
सुसखि *susakhi*, a good friend, 232.
सुहिंस् *suhiṁs*, well-striking, 172.
सुहृद् *suhṛid*, friendly, 157.
सृज् *sṛij*, creating, 162.
सोमपा *somapá*, Soma drinker, 239.
स्त्री *strí*, woman, 228.
स्निह् *snih*, loving, 174.
स्नु *snu*, ridge, 214.
स्नुह् *snuh*, spuing, 174.
स्पृश् *spṛiś*, touching, 174.

स्रज् *sraj*, a garland, 161.
स्रस् *sras*, falling, 173.
स्रुच् *sruch*, ladle, 158.
स्वयं *svayam*, self, 149.
स्वयंभू *svayambhú*, self-existing, 221.
स्वर् *svar*, heaven, 149.
स्वसृ *svasṛi*, sister, 235.
स्वाप् *sváp*, having good water, 211.
हन् *han*, killing, 202.
हरित् *harit*, green, 157.
हाहा *háhá*, 240.
हृद् *hṛid*, heart, 214.
हृदय *hṛidaya*, heart, 214.
ह्री *hrí*, f. shame, 224.

INDEX OF VERBS.

NOTE—The number refers to the number of each verb in the Appendix.

अक्ष् *aksh*, to pervade, 37.
अज् *aj*, to go, to throw, (वी *ví*), 23.
अंच् *añch*, to go, to worship, 17.
अंज् *añj*, to anoint, 207.
अद् *ad*, to eat, 162.
अन् *an*, to breathe, 176.
अय् *ay*, to go, 78.
अर्द् *ard*, to go, to pain, 11.
अव् *av*, to help, 92.
अश् *aś*, to pervade, 147.
अस् *as*, to be, 173.
आंछ् *áñchh*, to stretch, 18.
आप् *áp*, to obtain, 146.
आस् *ás*, to sit, 183.
आह् *áha*, to speak, 190.
इ *i*, to go, 171.
इ *i*, to go; अधी *adhí*, to read, 186.
इंद् *ind*, to govern, 13.
इंध् *indh*, to kindle, 209.
इष् *ish*, to wish, 118, 31.
ईक्ष् *íksh*, to see, 69.
ईश् *íś*, to rule, 182.
ईह् *íh*, to aim, 79.
उख् *ukh*, to go, 16.
उष् *ush*, to burn, 40.
ऊर्णु *úrṇu*, to cover, 191.
ऋ *ṛi*, to go, (ऋच्छति *ṛichchhati*), 49.
ॠ *ṝi*, to go, 197.
ऋज् *ṛij*, to gain, 72.
एध् *edh*, to grow, 68.
कट् *kaṭ*, to rain, to encompass, 25.
कम् *kam*, to love, 77.
काश् *káś*, to shine, 80.
कास् *kás*, to cough, 81.
कित् *kit*, to cure, (चिकित्सति *chikitsati*), 63.
कुट् *kuṭ*, to bend, 111.
कुंथ् *kunth*, to strike, 6.
कृ *kṛi*, to do, 152.
कृत् *kṛit*, to cut, 110, 107.
कृप् *kṛip*, to be able, 89, 87.
कृष् *kṛish*, to furrow, 38.
कृष् *kṛish*, to trace, 106.

कॄ *kṛí*, to scatter, 113.
कृत् *kṛít*, to praise, 138.
क्रम् *kram*, to stride, 30, 29.
क्री *krí*, to buy, 153.
क्लम् *klam*, to tire, 29, 30, 130.
क्षण् *kshaṇ*, to kill, 149.
क्षम् *ksham*, to bear, 130.
क्षि *kshi*, to wane, to diminish, 24.
क्षिण् *kshiṇ*, to kill, 150.
खद् *khad*, to eat, 8.
खन् *khan*, to dig, 95.
खिद् *khid*, to vex, 107.
ख्या *khyá*, to proclaim, 166.
गद् *gad*, to speak, 9.
गम् *gam*, to go, 33, 31.
गा *gá*, to go, 83.
गुप् *gup*, to protect, 26, 63.
गुह् *guh*, to hide, 97, 29.
गै *gai*, to sing, 44.
ग्रह् *grah*, to take, 157, 105.
ग्लै *glai*, to droop, 43.
घु *ghu*-class, 46, 47, 200.
घ्रा *ghrá*, to smell, 54.
चकास् *chakás*, to shine, 177.
चक्ष् *chaksh*, to speak, 181.
चप् *chap*, to pound, 137.
चम् *cham*, to eat, 29.
चह् *chah*, to pound, 137.
चि *chi*, to collect, 137, 140.
चित् *chit*, to think, 2.
चुर् *chur*, to steal, 136.
च्युत् *chyut*, to sprinkle, 3.
छो *chho*, to cut, 124.
जक्ष् *jaksh*, to eat, 177, 176.
जन् *jan*, to spring up, 132.
जागृ *jágṛi*, to wake, 178, 177.
जि *ji*, to excel, 36.
जॄ *jṛí*, to grow old, 123, 156.
ज्ञप् *jñap*, to know, to make known, 137.
ज्ञा *jñá*, to know, 159.
ज्या *jyá*, to grow weak, 158, 36, 105.
ज्वर् *jvar*, to suffer, 92.
तक्ष् *taksh*, to hew, 37.
तन् *tan*, to stretch, 148.
तप् *tap*, to burn, 28.
तम् *tam*, to languish, 130.
तिज् *tij*, to forbear, (तितिक्षते *titikshate*), 75, 63.
तु *tu*, to grow, 170.
तुद् *tud*, to strike, 104.
तृप् *tṛip*, to delight, 127, 38.
तृह् *tṛih*, to kill, 208.
तॄ *tṛí*, to cross, 61.
त्रप् *trap*, to be ashamed, 74.
त्रस् *tras*, to tremble, 30.
त्रुट् *truṭ*, to cut, 30.
त्वर् *tvar*, to hurry, 92.
दंश् *daṁś*, to bite, 62, 73.
दद् *dad*, to give, 70.
दम् *dam*, to tame, 130.
दरिद्रा *daridrá*, to be poor, 179, 177.
दह् *dah*, to burn, 42.
दा *dá*, to give, 58.
दा *dá*, to give, 200.
दान् *dán*, दीदांसति *dídáṁsati*, to straighten, 63.
दिव् *div*, to play, 121.
दी *dí*, to decay, 154.
दीधी *dídhí*, to shine, 177.
दुह् *duh*, to milk, 188.
दृ *dṛi*, to observe, 120.
दृश् *dṛiś*, to see, (पश् *paś*), 48, 38.
दॄ *dṛí*, to tear, 156.
दे *de*, to protect, 85.
दै *dai*, to cleanse, 46.
दै *dai*, to protect, 85.
दो *do*, to cut, 124.
द्युत् *dyut*, to shine, 86.
द्विष् *dvish*, to hate, 187.
धा *dhá*, to place, 201.
धू *dhú*, to shake, 156.
धूप् *dhúp*, to warm, 27.

धे *dhe*, to drink, 47.
ध्मा *dhmá*, to blow, 55.
नद् *nad*, to hum, 11.
नम् *nam*, to bow, 32.
नश् *naś*, to perish, 129, 117.
नह् *nah*, to bind, 135.
निक्ष् *niksh*, to kiss, 15.
निज् *nij*, to cleanse, 202.
निंद् *nind*, to blame, 14.
नृत् *nṛit*, to dance, 122.
पण् *paṇ*, to traffic, 26.
पण् *paṇ*, to praise, 76.
पत् *pat*, to fall, 64.
पद् *pad*, to go, 133.
पन् *pan*, to praise, 26, 76.
पश्य *paśya*, to see, 48.
पा *pá*, to drink, 53.
पिश् *piś*, to form, 107.
पू *pú*, to purify, 156.
पृ *prí*, to fill, 195, 156.
प्रछ् *prachh*, to ask, 115, 105.
प्सा *psá*, to eat, 163.
फल् *phal*, to burst, 34.
बध् *badh*, बीभत्सते *bíbhatsate*, to loathe, 63.
बंध् *bandh*, to bind, 160.
बुध् *budh*, to perceive, 134.
ब्रू *brú*, to speak, 190.
भंज् *bhañj*, to break, 206.
भी *bhí*, to fear, 193.
भू *bhú*, to be, 1.
भृ *bhṛi*, to carry, 199.
भ्रज्ज् *bhrajj*, to fry, 105.
भ्रम् *bhram*, to roam, 30, 130.
भ्राश् *bhráś*, to shine, 30.
भ्लाश् *bhláś*, to shine, 30.
मज्ज् *majj*, to sink, 117.
मद् *mad*, to rejoice, 130.
मंथ् *manth*, to shake, to churn, 5.
मव् *mav*, to bind, 92.
मा *má*, to measure, 164.
मा *má*, to measure, 198.
मान् *mán*, मीमांसते *mímáṁsate*, to search, 63.
मि *mi*, to throw, 154.
मिद् *mid*, to be wet, 131.
मिह् *mih*, to sprinkle, 41.
मी *mí*, to kill, 154.
मुच् *much*, to loosen, 107.
मुह् *muh*, to be foolish, 128.
मृ *mṛi*, to die, 119.
मृज् *mṛij*, to clean, 174.
म्ना *mná*, to study, 57.
म्रुच् *mruch*, to go, 19.
यज् *yaj*, to sacrifice, 99.
यम् *yam*, to stop, 31, 58.
यम् *yam*, to feed, 137.
या *yá*, to go, 165.
यु *yu*, to mix, 169.
रंज् *rañj*, to tinge, 62.
रद् *rad*, to trace, 10.
रम् *ram*, to sport, 91.
राज् *ráj*, to shine, 94.
रु *ru*, to go, to kill, 84.
रु *ru*, to shout, 170.
रुद् *rud*, to cry, 176.
रुध् *rudh*, to shut out, 203.
रुष् *rush*, to kill, 39.
लष् *lash*, to desire, 30.
लिप् *lip*, to paint, 109, 107.
लुप् *lup*, to break, 107.
लू *lú*, to cut, 156.
वच् *vach*, to speak, 175.
वज् *vaj*, to go, 21.
वद् *vad*, to speak, 66.
वप् *vap*, to sow, to weave, 100.
वय् *vay*, to go, 105.
वल् *val*, to live, 137.
वश् *vaś*, to desire, 167, 105.
वस् *vas*, to dwell, 65.
वह् *vah*, to carry, 101, 93.
विछ् *vichh*, to go, 26.

विज् *vij*, to separate, 202.

विद् *vid*, to find, 108, 107.

विद् *vid*, to know, 172.

विष् *vish*, to embrace, 202.

वी *vî*, see अज् *aj*.

वृ *vri*, to choose, 142; Parasmaipada.

वृ *vri*, to cherish, 161; Âtmanepada.

वृत् *vrit*, to be, 87.

वृध् *vridh*, to grow, 87.

वॄ *vrî*, to choose, 156.

वे *ve*, to weave, 102.

वेवी *vevî*, to obtain, 177.

व्यच् *vyach*, to surround, 105.

व्यथ् *vyath*, to fear, to suffer pain, 90.

व्यध् *vyadh*, to pierce, 126, 105.

व्रज् *vraj*, to go, 22.

व्रश्च् *vraśch* to cut, 112, 105.

शक् *śak*, to be able, 144.

शद् *śad*, to wither, 51.

शम् *śam*, to cease, 130.

शान् *śân*, शीशांसति *śîśâṁsati*, to sharpen, 63.

शास् *śâs*, to command, 180, 177.

शिष् *śish*, to distinguish, 204.

शी *śî*, to lie down, 185.

शृध् *śridh*, to hurt, 87.

शो *śo*, to sharpen, 124.

श्चुत् *śchut*, to flow, 4.

श्च्युत् *śchyut*, to flow, 4.

श्रम् *śram*, to tire, 130.

श्रि *śri*, to go, to serve, 98.

श्रु *śru*, to hear, 145.

श्वस् *śvas*, to breathe, 176.

श्वि *śvi*, to swell, 67.

ष्ट्यै *shṭyai*, to sound, 45.

ष्ठिव् *shṭhiv*, to spit, 35, 29.

ष्वष्क् *shvashk*, to go, 71.

संज् *sañj*, to stick, 62, 73.

सद् *sad*, to perish, 52.

सन् *san*, to obtain, 151.

सह् *sah*, to bear, 93.

सिच् *sich*, to sprinkle, 107.

सिध् *sidh*, to go, and सिध् *sidh*, to command, 7.

सिव् *siv*, to serve, 82.

सु *su*, to distil, 139.

सू *sû*, to bear, to bring forth, 184.

सृ *sri*, to go, 50.

सृज् *srij*, to let off, 116, 38, 48.

सो *so*, to finish, 125, 124.

स्कंद् *skand*, to approach, 60.

स्कंभ् *skambh*, to support, 155.

स्कु *sku*, 155.

स्कुंभ् *skumbh*, to hold, 155.

स्तंभ् *stambh*, to support, 155.

स्तु *stu*, to praise, 189.

स्तु *stu*, to praise, 170.

स्तुंभ् *stumbh*, to stop, 155.

स्तृ *stri*, to cover, 141.

स्तॄ *strî*, to cover, 156.

स्त्यै *styai*, to sound, 45.

स्था *sthâ*, to stand, 56.

स्पृश् *spriś*, to touch, 114.

स्यंद् *syand*, to sprinkle, to drop, 88, 87.

स्रिव् *sriv*, to go, to dry, 92.

स्वंज् *svañj*, to embrace, 73, 62.

स्वप् *svap*, to sleep, 176.

हन् *han*, to kill, 168.

हा *hâ*, to leave, 196.

हि *hi*, to go, to grow, 143.

हिंस् *hiṁs*, to kill, 205.

हु *hu*, to sacrifice, 192.

हुर्छ् *hurchh*, to be crooked, 20.

हृ *hri*, to take, 96.

ह्री *hrî*, to be ashamed, 194.

ह्वृ *hvri*, to bend, 59.

ह्वे *hve*, to call, 103.

ADDENDA ET CORRIGENDA.

Page 2, line 28, read *ai* instead of *âi*.—P. 8, l. 27, read गवर्णमेण्ट् *Gavarṇmeṇṭ*.—P. 10, l. 30, add, '*ḍ, ṭ, ḍ, ṛṭ*.'—P. 16, l. 32, read उष्णं *ushṇam*.—P. 19, l. 1, dele 'or Visarga.'—P. 30, l. 38, add अहः *ahaḥ*.—P. 39, l. 34, add, 'The change of *n* into *ṇ* in proper names, like *Trinayanaḥ*, is said to be optional (Sâr. I. 16, 23).'—P. 43, l. 11, read 'to shout' instead of 'to be happy.'—P. 43, l. 14, add, 'to sow or' before 'to weave.'—P. 43, l. 33, read परि *pari* instead of प्रति *prati*.—P. 44, note, add, पुंसु *puṁsu* is in reality पुम्सु *pumsu*, but the म् *m* of the base पुम् *pum* being *padânta*, native grammarians are much perplexed as to whether म् *m* should be changed into Anusvâra (§§ 8, 133) or into न् *n* (§ 136).—P. 54, l. ult., read भ्रज्ज् *bhraṭj*.—P. 55, l. 9, read 'he will enter.'—P. 56, l. 14, add, 'The vowel of सह् *sah* and वह् *vah* is changed into ओ o (Pâṇ. VI. 3, 112), unless *Samprasâraṇa* is required, as in Pt. ऊढः *ûḍhaḥ* (Pâṇ. VI. 1, 15).'—P. 56, l. 24, read, 'Certain nominal bases, and see § 173.'—P. 57, l. 5, add, 'Final त् *t*, द् *d*, ध् *dh*, before the स् *s* of the 2nd pers. sing. Impf. Par., may be regularly represented by त् *t*, or by स् *s*; अवेत् *avet* or अवेः *aveḥ*, thou knewest; अरुणत् *aruṇat* or अरुणः *aruṇaḥ*, thou preventedst.'—P. 66, l. ult., read ऊर्जि *ûrji*; in compounds बहूर्जि *bahûrji*, (this form is supported by Colebrooke, the Siddhânta-Kaumudî, and likewise by the Prakriyâ-Kaumudî, which says, ऊर्जि । इमौ नुमोऽन्त केचित् ऊर्जि । बहूर्जि नुम्प्रतिषेधः । बहूर्जि कुलानि । अन्त्यात्पूर्वं नुममिच्छन्त्येके । बहूर्ञ्जि ।).—P. 75, l. 14, dele भ्रस् *bhras*.—P. 77, l. 25, read उक्थशास् *ukthaśâs*.—P. 90, l. 8, read अर्यमा instead of अर्यमणा; l. 9, *aryamâ* instead of *aryamaṇâ*.—P. 99, l. 11, read 'Thus' instead of 'This.'—P. 107, l. 14, read 'four' instead of 'three.'—P. 123, l. 2 from below, read 'Pâṇ. VII. 4, 4.'—P. 132, l. 22, read अधर *adhara*.—P. 133, l. 23, read आः *âḥ*.—P. 141, l. 33, add, 'and the Reduplicated Aorist.'—P. 150, note 1, The rule is applied on page 278, No. 139.—P. 153, note 3, add, 'Hu class, and see the rule on page 284, No. 162 †.'—P. 160, l. 19, read 'ending in more than one consonant.'—P. 163, l. 13, read 'I. Aorist Âtmanepada, see § 337, II. 4.'—P. 167, l. 12, read ववरिथ *vavaritha*, and see § 335, 1, and No. 142.—P. 167, l. 33, read 'in the periphrastic future.'—P. 168, ll. 36 and 37, add, 'if without *i* in the periphrastic future.'—P. 168, note, read '§ 337, I. 2.'—P. 172, ll. 30 seq., As the periphrastic perfect has but one accent it would be better to write it as one word.—P. 176, l. 10, add, 'to इर् *ir*, or before consonants to ईर् *îr*.'—P. 182, l. 3, add, 'Thus from मी *mî* or मि *mi*, अमास्त *amâsta*; from दी *dî*, अदास्त *adâsta*; from ली *lî*, अलास्त *alâsta* or अलेष्ट *aleshṭa*. In the Parasmaipada *mî*, *mi*, and *lî* (optionally) take the third form.'—P. 182, l. 23, read '(as to दृश् *dṛiś*, see Pâṇ. III. 1, 47).'—P. 195, l. 29, The words placed between brackets were meant to be deleted.—P. 203, l. 10, read 'Aorist Âtmanepada.'